50% OFF

Online GED Prep Course!

By Mometrix

Dear Customer,

We consider it an honor and a privilege that you chose our GED Study Guide. As a way of showing our appreciation and to help us better serve you, we are offering **50% off our online GED Prep Course.** Many GED courses cost hundreds of dollars and don't deliver enough value. With our course, you get access to the best GED prep material, and **you only pay half price**.

We have structured our online course to perfectly complement your printed study guide. Our GED Prep Course contains **in-depth lessons** that cover all the most important topics, **330+ video reviews** that explain difficult concepts, over **1,250+ practice questions** to ensure you feel prepared, and more than **300+ digital flashcards**, so you can fit in some studying while you're on the go.

Online GED Prep Course

Topics Covered:

- Reasoning Through Language Arts
    - Reading Comprehension
    - Critical Thinking
    - Writing
- Mathematical Reasoning
    - Number Operations
    - Algebra, Functions, and Patterns
    - Measurement and Geometry
- Science
    - Physical Science
    - Earth and Space Science
- Social Studies
    - History and Government
    - Economics

Course Features:

- GED Study Guide
    - Get content that complements our best-selling study guide.
- 6 Full-Length Practice Tests
    - With over 1,250 practice questions, you can test yourself again and again.
- Mobile Friendly
    - If you need to study on the go, the course is easily accessible from your mobile device.
- GED Flashcards
    - Our course includes a flashcard mode consisting of over 300 content cards to help you study.

To receive this discount, visit our website at mometrix.com/university/ged/ or simply scan this QR code with your smartphone. Enter code **ged50off** at checkout.

If you have any questions or concerns, please contact us at support@mometrix.com.

FREE Study Skills Videos/DVD Offer

Dear Customer,

Thank you for your purchase from Mometrix! We consider it an honor and a privilege that you have purchased our product and we want to ensure your satisfaction.

As part of our ongoing effort to meet the needs of test takers, we have developed a set of Study Skills Videos that we would like to give you for FREE. These videos cover our *best practices* for getting ready for your exam, from how to use our study materials to how to best prepare for the day of the test.

All that we ask is that you email us with feedback that would describe your experience so far with our product. Good, bad, or indifferent, we want to know what you think!

To get your FREE Study Skills Videos, you can use the **QR code** below, or send us an **email** at studyvideos@mometrix.com with *FREE VIDEOS* in the subject line and the following information in the body of the email:

- The name of the product you purchased.
- Your product rating on a scale of 1-5, with 5 being the highest rating.
- Your feedback. It can be long, short, or anything in between. We just want to know your impressions and experience so far with our product. (Good feedback might include how our study material met your needs and ways we might be able to make it even better. You could highlight features that you found helpful or features that you think we should add.)

If you have any questions or concerns, please don't hesitate to contact me directly.

Thanks again!

Sincerely,

Jay Willis
Vice President
jay.willis@mometrix.com
1-800-673-8175

GED®

Study Guide 2023-2024

3 Full-Length Practice Tests

All Subjects: GED Prep Book Secrets, Step-by-Step Review Video Tutorials

Certified Content Alignment

Written and edited by the Mometrix High School Equivalency Test Team

Printed in the United States of America

This paper meets the requirements of ANSI/NISO Z39.48-1992 (Permanence of Paper).

Paperback
ISBN 13: 978-1-5167-2245-7
ISBN 10: 1-5167-2245-0

Dear Future Exam Success Story

First of all, **THANK YOU** for purchasing Mometrix study materials!

Second, congratulations! You are one of the few determined test-takers who are committed to doing whatever it takes to excel on your exam. **You have come to the right place.** We developed these study materials with one goal in mind: to deliver you the information you need in a format that's concise and easy to use.

In addition to optimizing your guide for the content of the test, we've outlined our recommended steps for breaking down the preparation process into small, attainable goals so you can make sure you stay on track.

We've also analyzed the entire test-taking process, identifying the most common pitfalls and showing how you can overcome them and be ready for any curveball the test throws you.

Standardized testing is one of the biggest obstacles on your road to success, which only increases the importance of doing well in the high-pressure, high-stakes environment of test day. Your results on this test could have a significant impact on your future, and this guide provides the information and practical advice to help you achieve your full potential on test day.

Your success is our success

We would love to hear from you! If you would like to share the story of your exam success or if you have any questions or comments in regard to our products, please contact us at **800-673-8175** or **support@mometrix.com**.

Thanks again for your business and we wish you continued success!

Sincerely,
The Mometrix Test Preparation Team

Need more help? Check out our flashcards at:
http://mometrixflashcards.com/GED

Table of Contents

Introduction

Thank you for purchasing this resource! You have made the choice to prepare yourself for a test that could have a huge impact on your future, and this guide is designed to help you be fully ready for test day. Obviously, it's important to have a solid understanding of the test material, but you also need to be prepared for the unique environment and stressors of the test, so that you can perform to the best of your abilities.

For this purpose, the first section that appears in this guide is the **Secret Keys**. We've devoted countless hours to meticulously researching what works and what doesn't, and we've boiled down our findings to the five most impactful steps you can take to improve your performance on the test. We start at the beginning with study planning and move through the preparation process, all the way to the testing strategies that will help you get the most out of what you know when you're finally sitting in front of the test.

We recommend that you start preparing for your test as far in advance as possible. However, if you've bought this guide as a last-minute study resource and only have a few days before your test, we recommend that you skip over the first two Secret Keys since they address a long-term study plan.

If you struggle with **test anxiety**, we strongly encourage you to check out our recommendations for how you can overcome it. Test anxiety is a formidable foe, but it can be beaten, and we want to make sure you have the tools you need to defeat it.

Secret Key #1 – Plan Big, Study Small

There's a lot riding on your performance. If you want to ace this test, you're going to need to keep your skills sharp and the material fresh in your mind. You need a plan that lets you review everything you need to know while still fitting in your schedule. We'll break this strategy down into three categories.

Information Organization

Start with the information you already have: the official test outline. From this, you can make a complete list of all the concepts you need to cover before the test. Organize these concepts into groups that can be studied together, and create a list of any related vocabulary you need to learn so you can brush up on any difficult terms. You'll want to keep this vocabulary list handy once you actually start studying since you may need to add to it along the way.

Time Management

Once you have your set of study concepts, decide how to spread them out over the time you have left before the test. Break your study plan into small, clear goals so you have a manageable task for each day and know exactly what you're doing. Then just focus on one small step at a time. When you manage your time this way, you don't need to spend hours at a time studying. Studying a small block of content for a short period each day helps you retain information better and avoid stressing over how much you have left to do. You can relax knowing that you have a plan to cover everything in time. In order for this strategy to be effective though, you have to start studying early and stick to your schedule. Avoid the exhaustion and futility that comes from last-minute cramming!

Study Environment

The environment you study in has a big impact on your learning. Studying in a coffee shop, while probably more enjoyable, is not likely to be as fruitful as studying in a quiet room. It's important to keep distractions to a minimum. You're only planning to study for a short block of time, so make the most of it. Don't pause to check your phone or get up to find a snack. It's also important to **avoid multitasking**. Research has consistently shown that multitasking will make your studying dramatically less effective. Your study area should also be comfortable and well-lit so you don't have the distraction of straining your eyes or sitting on an uncomfortable chair.

The time of day you study is also important. You want to be rested and alert. Don't wait until just before bedtime. Study when you'll be most likely to comprehend and remember. Even better, if you know what time of day your test will be, set that time aside for study. That way your brain will be used to working on that subject at that specific time and you'll have a better chance of recalling information.

Finally, it can be helpful to team up with others who are studying for the same test. Your actual studying should be done in as isolated an environment as possible, but the work of organizing the information and setting up the study plan can be divided up. In between study sessions, you can discuss with your teammates the concepts that you're all studying and quiz each other on the details. Just be sure that your teammates are as serious about the test as you are. If you find that your study time is being replaced with social time, you might need to find a new team.

Secret Key #2 – Make Your Studying Count

You're devoting a lot of time and effort to preparing for this test, so you want to be absolutely certain it will pay off. This means doing more than just reading the content and hoping you can remember it on test day. It's important to make every minute of study count. There are two main areas you can focus on to make your studying count.

Retention

It doesn't matter how much time you study if you can't remember the material. You need to make sure you are retaining the concepts. To check your retention of the information you're learning, try recalling it at later times with minimal prompting. Try carrying around flashcards and glance at one or two from time to time or ask a friend who's also studying for the test to quiz you.

To enhance your retention, look for ways to put the information into practice so that you can apply it rather than simply recalling it. If you're using the information in practical ways, it will be much easier to remember. Similarly, it helps to solidify a concept in your mind if you're not only reading it to yourself but also explaining it to someone else. Ask a friend to let you teach them about a concept you're a little shaky on (or speak aloud to an imaginary audience if necessary). As you try to summarize, define, give examples, and answer your friend's questions, you'll understand the concepts better and they will stay with you longer. Finally, step back for a big picture view and ask yourself how each piece of information fits with the whole subject. When you link the different concepts together and see them working together as a whole, it's easier to remember the individual components.

Finally, practice showing your work on any multi-step problems, even if you're just studying. Writing out each step you take to solve a problem will help solidify the process in your mind, and you'll be more likely to remember it during the test.

Modality

Modality simply refers to the means or method by which you study. Choosing a study modality that fits your own individual learning style is crucial. No two people learn best in exactly the same way, so it's important to know your strengths and use them to your advantage.

For example, if you learn best by visualization, focus on visualizing a concept in your mind and draw an image or a diagram. Try color-coding your notes, illustrating them, or creating symbols that will trigger your mind to recall a learned concept. If you learn best by hearing or discussing information, find a study partner who learns the same way or read aloud to yourself. Think about how to put the information in your own words. Imagine that you are giving a lecture on the topic and record yourself so you can listen to it later.

For any learning style, flashcards can be helpful. Organize the information so you can take advantage of spare moments to review. Underline key words or phrases. Use different colors for different categories. Mnemonic devices (such as creating a short list in which every item starts with the same letter) can also help with retention. Find what works best for you and use it to store the information in your mind most effectively and easily.

Secret Key #3 – Practice the Right Way

Your success on test day depends not only on how many hours you put into preparing, but also on whether you prepared the right way. It's good to check along the way to see if your studying is paying off. One of the most effective ways to do this is by taking practice tests to evaluate your progress. Practice tests are useful because they show exactly where you need to improve. Every time you take a practice test, pay special attention to these three groups of questions:

- The questions you got wrong
- The questions you had to guess on, even if you guessed right
- The questions you found difficult or slow to work through

This will show you exactly what your weak areas are, and where you need to devote more study time. Ask yourself why each of these questions gave you trouble. Was it because you didn't understand the material? Was it because you didn't remember the vocabulary? Do you need more repetitions on this type of question to build speed and confidence? Dig into those questions and figure out how you can strengthen your weak areas as you go back to review the material.

Additionally, many practice tests have a section explaining the answer choices. It can be tempting to read the explanation and think that you now have a good understanding of the concept. However, an explanation likely only covers part of the question's broader context. Even if the explanation makes perfect sense, **go back and investigate** every concept related to the question until you're positive you have a thorough understanding.

As you go along, keep in mind that the practice test is just that: practice. Memorizing these questions and answers will not be very helpful on the actual test because it is unlikely to have any of the same exact questions. If you only know the right answers to the sample questions, you won't be prepared for the real thing. **Study the concepts** until you understand them fully, and then you'll be able to answer any question that shows up on the test.

It's important to wait on the practice tests until you're ready. If you take a test on your first day of study, you may be overwhelmed by the amount of material covered and how much you need to learn. Work up to it gradually.

On test day, you'll need to be prepared for answering questions, managing your time, and using the test-taking strategies you've learned. It's a lot to balance, like a mental marathon that will have a big impact on your future. Like training for a marathon, you'll need to start slowly and work your way up. When test day arrives, you'll be ready.

Start with the strategies you've read in the first two Secret Keys—plan your course and study in the way that works best for you. If you have time, consider using multiple study resources to get different approaches to the same concepts. It can be helpful to see difficult concepts from more than one angle. Then find a good source for practice tests. Many times, the test website will suggest potential study resources or provide sample tests.

Practice Test Strategy

If you're able to find at least three practice tests, we recommend this strategy:

Untimed and Open-Book Practice

Take the first test with no time constraints and with your notes and study guide handy. Take your time and focus on applying the strategies you've learned.

Timed and Open-Book Practice

Take the second practice test open-book as well, but set a timer and practice pacing yourself to finish in time.

Timed and Closed-Book Practice

Take any other practice tests as if it were test day. Set a timer and put away your study materials. Sit at a table or desk in a quiet room, imagine yourself at the testing center, and answer questions as quickly and accurately as possible.

Keep repeating timed and closed-book tests on a regular basis until you run out of practice tests or it's time for the actual test. Your mind will be ready for the schedule and stress of test day, and you'll be able to focus on recalling the material you've learned.

Secret Key #4 – Pace Yourself

Once you're fully prepared for the material on the test, your biggest challenge on test day will be managing your time. Just knowing that the clock is ticking can make you panic even if you have plenty of time left. Work on pacing yourself so you can build confidence against the time constraints of the exam. Pacing is a difficult skill to master, especially in a high-pressure environment, so **practice is vital**.

Set time expectations for your pace based on how much time is available. For example, if a section has 60 questions and the time limit is 30 minutes, you know you have to average 30 seconds or less per question in order to answer them all. Although 30 seconds is the hard limit, set 25 seconds per question as your goal, so you reserve extra time to spend on harder questions. When you budget extra time for the harder questions, you no longer have any reason to stress when those questions take longer to answer.

Don't let this time expectation distract you from working through the test at a calm, steady pace, but keep it in mind so you don't spend too much time on any one question. Recognize that taking extra time on one question you don't understand may keep you from answering two that you do understand later in the test. If your time limit for a question is up and you're still not sure of the answer, mark it and move on, and come back to it later if the time and the test format allow. If the testing format doesn't allow you to return to earlier questions, just make an educated guess; then put it out of your mind and move on.

On the easier questions, be careful not to rush. It may seem wise to hurry through them so you have more time for the challenging ones, but it's not worth missing one if you know the concept and just didn't take the time to read the question fully. Work efficiently but make sure you understand the question and have looked at all of the answer choices, since more than one may seem right at first.

Even if you're paying attention to the time, you may find yourself a little behind at some point. You should speed up to get back on track, but do so wisely. Don't panic; just take a few seconds less on each question until you're caught up. Don't guess without thinking, but do look through the answer choices and eliminate any you know are wrong. If you can get down to two choices, it is often worthwhile to guess from those. Once you've chosen an answer, move on and don't dwell on any that you skipped or had to hurry through. If a question was taking too long, chances are it was one of the harder ones, so you weren't as likely to get it right anyway.

On the other hand, if you find yourself getting ahead of schedule, it may be beneficial to slow down a little. The more quickly you work, the more likely you are to make a careless mistake that will affect your score. You've budgeted time for each question, so don't be afraid to spend that time. Practice an efficient but careful pace to get the most out of the time you have.

Secret Key #5 – Have a Plan for Guessing

When you're taking the test, you may find yourself stuck on a question. Some of the answer choices seem better than others, but you don't see the one answer choice that is obviously correct. What do you do?

The scenario described above is very common, yet most test takers have not effectively prepared for it. Developing and practicing a plan for guessing may be one of the single most effective uses of your time as you get ready for the exam.

In developing your plan for guessing, there are three questions to address:

- When should you start the guessing process?
- How should you narrow down the choices?
- Which answer should you choose?

When to Start the Guessing Process

Unless your plan for guessing is to select C every time (which, despite its merits, is not what we recommend), you need to leave yourself enough time to apply your answer elimination strategies. Since you have a limited amount of time for each question, that means that if you're going to give yourself the best shot at guessing correctly, you have to decide quickly whether or not you will guess.

Of course, the best-case scenario is that you don't have to guess at all, so first, see if you can answer the question based on your knowledge of the subject and basic reasoning skills. Focus on the key words in the question and try to jog your memory of related topics. Give yourself a chance to bring the knowledge to mind, but once you realize that you don't have (or you can't access) the knowledge you need to answer the question, it's time to start the guessing process.

It's almost always better to start the guessing process too early than too late. It only takes a few seconds to remember something and answer the question from knowledge. Carefully eliminating wrong answer choices takes longer. Plus, going through the process of eliminating answer choices can actually help jog your memory.

Summary: Start the guessing process as soon as you decide that you can't answer the question based on your knowledge.

How to Narrow Down the Choices

The next chapter in this book (**Test-Taking Strategies**) includes a wide range of strategies for how to approach questions and how to look for answer choices to eliminate. You will definitely want to read those carefully, practice them, and figure out which ones work best for you. Here though, we're going to address a mindset rather than a particular strategy.

Your odds of guessing an answer correctly depend on how many options you are choosing from.

Number of options left	5	4	3	2	1
Odds of guessing correctly	20%	25%	33%	50%	100%

You can see from this chart just how valuable it is to be able to eliminate incorrect answers and make an educated guess, but there are two things that many test takers do that cause them to miss out on the benefits of guessing:

- Accidentally eliminating the correct answer
- Selecting an answer based on an impression

We'll look at the first one here, and the second one in the next section.

To avoid accidentally eliminating the correct answer, we recommend a thought exercise called **the $5 challenge**. In this challenge, you only eliminate an answer choice from contention if you are willing to bet $5 on it being wrong. Why $5? Five dollars is a small but not insignificant amount of money. It's an amount you could afford to lose but wouldn't want to throw away. And while losing $5 once might not hurt too much, doing it twenty times will set you back $100. In the same way, each small decision you make—eliminating a choice here, guessing on a question there—won't by itself impact your score very much, but when you put them all together, they can make a big difference. By holding each answer choice elimination decision to a higher standard, you can reduce the risk of accidentally eliminating the correct answer.

The $5 challenge can also be applied in a positive sense: If you are willing to bet $5 that an answer choice *is* correct, go ahead and mark it as correct.

Summary: Only eliminate an answer choice if you are willing to bet $5 that it is wrong.

Which Answer to Choose

You're taking the test. You've run into a hard question and decided you'll have to guess. You've eliminated all the answer choices you're willing to bet $5 on. Now you have to pick an answer. Why do we even need to talk about this? Why can't you just pick whichever one you feel like when the time comes?

The answer to these questions is that if you don't come into the test with a plan, you'll rely on your impression to select an answer choice, and if you do that, you risk falling into a trap. The test writers know that everyone who takes their test will be guessing on some of the questions, so they intentionally write wrong answer choices to seem plausible. You still have to pick an answer though, and if the wrong answer choices are designed to look right, how can you ever be sure that you're not falling for their trap? The best solution we've found to this dilemma is to take the decision out of your hands entirely. Here is the process we recommend:

Once you've eliminated any choices that you are confident (willing to bet $5) are wrong, select the first remaining choice as your answer.

Whether you choose to select the first remaining choice, the second, or the last, the important thing is that you use some preselected standard. Using this approach guarantees that you will not be enticed into selecting an answer choice that looks right, because you are not basing your decision on how the answer choices look.

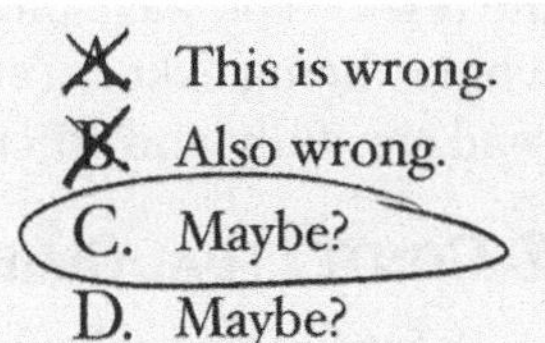

This is not meant to make you question your knowledge. Instead, it is to help you recognize the difference between your knowledge and your impressions. There's a huge difference between thinking an answer is right because of what you know, and thinking an answer is right because it looks or sounds like it should be right.

Summary: To ensure that your selection is appropriately random, make a predetermined selection from among all answer choices you have not eliminated.

Test-Taking Strategies

This section contains a list of test-taking strategies that you may find helpful as you work through the test. By taking what you know and applying logical thought, you can maximize your chances of answering any question correctly!

It is very important to realize that every question is different and every person is different: no single strategy will work on every question, and no single strategy will work for every person. That's why we've included all of them here, so you can try them out and determine which ones work best for different types of questions and which ones work best for you.

Question Strategies

⊘ Read Carefully

Read the question and the answer choices carefully. Don't miss the question because you misread the terms. You have plenty of time to read each question thoroughly and make sure you understand what is being asked. Yet a happy medium must be attained, so don't waste too much time. You must read carefully and efficiently.

⊘ Contextual Clues

Look for contextual clues. If the question includes a word you are not familiar with, look at the immediate context for some indication of what the word might mean. Contextual clues can often give you all the information you need to decipher the meaning of an unfamiliar word. Even if you can't determine the meaning, you may be able to narrow down the possibilities enough to make a solid guess at the answer to the question.

⊘ Prefixes

If you're having trouble with a word in the question or answer choices, try dissecting it. Take advantage of every clue that the word might include. Prefixes can be a huge help. Usually, they allow you to determine a basic meaning. *Pre-* means before, *post-* means after, *pro-* is positive, *de-* is negative. From prefixes, you can get an idea of the general meaning of the word and try to put it into context.

⊘ Hedge Words

Watch out for critical hedge words, such as *likely, may, can, sometimes, often, almost, mostly, usually, generally, rarely*, and *sometimes*. Question writers insert these hedge phrases to cover every possibility. Often an answer choice will be wrong simply because it leaves no room for exception. Be on guard for answer choices that have definitive words such as *exactly* and *always*.

⊘ Switchback Words

Stay alert for *switchbacks*. These are the words and phrases frequently used to alert you to shifts in thought. The most common switchback words are *but, although*, and *however*. Others include *nevertheless, on the other hand, even though, while, in spite of, despite*, and *regardless of*. Switchback words are important to catch because they can change the direction of the question or an answer choice.

☑ Face Value

When in doubt, use common sense. Accept the situation in the problem at face value. Don't read too much into it. These problems will not require you to make wild assumptions. If you have to go beyond creativity and warp time or space in order to have an answer choice fit the question, then you should move on and consider the other answer choices. These are normal problems rooted in reality. The applicable relationship or explanation may not be readily apparent, but it is there for you to figure out. Use your common sense to interpret anything that isn't clear.

Answer Choice Strategies

☑ Answer Selection

The most thorough way to pick an answer choice is to identify and eliminate wrong answers until only one is left, then confirm it is the correct answer. Sometimes an answer choice may immediately seem right, but be careful. The test writers will usually put more than one reasonable answer choice on each question, so take a second to read all of them and make sure that the other choices are not equally obvious. As long as you have time left, it is better to read every answer choice than to pick the first one that looks right without checking the others.

☑ Answer Choice Families

An answer choice family consists of two (in rare cases, three) answer choices that are very similar in construction and cannot all be true at the same time. If you see two answer choices that are direct opposites or parallels, one of them is usually the correct answer. For instance, if one answer choice says that quantity *x* increases and another either says that quantity *x* decreases (opposite) or says that quantity *y* increases (parallel), then those answer choices would fall into the same family. An answer choice that doesn't match the construction of the answer choice family is more likely to be incorrect. Most questions will not have answer choice families, but when they do appear, you should be prepared to recognize them.

☑ Eliminate Answers

Eliminate answer choices as soon as you realize they are wrong, but make sure you consider all possibilities. If you are eliminating answer choices and realize that the last one you are left with is also wrong, don't panic. Start over and consider each choice again. There may be something you missed the first time that you will realize on the second pass.

☑ Avoid Fact Traps

Don't be distracted by an answer choice that is factually true but doesn't answer the question. You are looking for the choice that answers the question. Stay focused on what the question is asking for so you don't accidentally pick an answer that is true but incorrect. Always go back to the question and make sure the answer choice you've selected actually answers the question and is not merely a true statement.

☑ Extreme Statements

In general, you should avoid answers that put forth extreme actions as standard practice or proclaim controversial ideas as established fact. An answer choice that states the "process should be used in certain situations, if…" is much more likely to be correct than one that states the "process should be discontinued completely." The first is a calm rational statement and doesn't even make a definitive, uncompromising stance, using a hedge word *if* to provide wiggle room, whereas the second choice is far more extreme.

☑ Benchmark

As you read through the answer choices and you come across one that seems to answer the question well, mentally select that answer choice. This is not your final answer, but it's the one that will help you evaluate the other answer choices. The one that you selected is your benchmark or standard for judging each of the other answer choices. Every other answer choice must be compared to your benchmark. That choice is correct until proven otherwise by another answer choice beating it. If you find a better answer, then that one becomes your new benchmark. Once you've decided that no other choice answers the question as well as your benchmark, you have your final answer.

☑ Predict the Answer

Before you even start looking at the answer choices, it is often best to try to predict the answer. When you come up with the answer on your own, it is easier to avoid distractions and traps because you will know exactly what to look for. The right answer choice is unlikely to be word-for-word what you came up with, but it should be a close match. Even if you are confident that you have the right answer, you should still take the time to read each option before moving on.

General Strategies

☑ Tough Questions

If you are stumped on a problem or it appears too hard or too difficult, don't waste time. Move on! Remember though, if you can quickly check for obviously incorrect answer choices, your chances of guessing correctly are greatly improved. Before you completely give up, at least try to knock out a couple of possible answers. Eliminate what you can and then guess at the remaining answer choices before moving on.

☑ Check Your Work

Since you will probably not know every term listed and the answer to every question, it is important that you get credit for the ones that you do know. Don't miss any questions through careless mistakes. If at all possible, try to take a second to look back over your answer selection and make sure you've selected the correct answer choice and haven't made a costly careless mistake (such as marking an answer choice that you didn't mean to mark). This quick double check should more than pay for itself in caught mistakes for the time it costs.

☑ Pace Yourself

It's easy to be overwhelmed when you're looking at a page full of questions; your mind is confused and full of random thoughts, and the clock is ticking down faster than you would like. Calm down and maintain the pace that you have set for yourself. Especially as you get down to the last few minutes of the test, don't let the small numbers on the clock make you panic. As long as you are on track by monitoring your pace, you are guaranteed to have time for each question.

☑ Don't Rush

It is very easy to make errors when you are in a hurry. Maintaining a fast pace in answering questions is pointless if it makes you miss questions that you would have gotten right otherwise. Test writers like to include distracting information and wrong answers that seem right. Taking a little extra time to avoid careless mistakes can make all the difference in your test score. Find a pace that allows you to be confident in the answers that you select.

⊘ Keep Moving

Panicking will not help you pass the test, so do your best to stay calm and keep moving. Taking deep breaths and going through the answer elimination steps you practiced can help to break through a stress barrier and keep your pace.

Final Notes

The combination of a solid foundation of content knowledge and the confidence that comes from practicing your plan for applying that knowledge is the key to maximizing your performance on test day. As your foundation of content knowledge is built up and strengthened, you'll find that the strategies included in this chapter become more and more effective in helping you quickly sift through the distractions and traps of the test to isolate the correct answer.

Now that you're preparing to move forward into the test content chapters of this book, be sure to keep your goal in mind. As you read, think about how you will be able to apply this information on the test. If you've already seen sample questions for the test and you have an idea of the question format and style, try to come up with questions of your own that you can answer based on what you're reading. This will give you valuable practice applying your knowledge in the same ways you can expect to on test day.

Good luck and good studying!

Mathematical Reasoning

Basic Math

Numbers

Classifications of Numbers

Numbers are the basic building blocks of mathematics. Specific features of numbers are identified by the following terms:

Integer – any positive or negative whole number, including zero. Integers do not include fractions $\left(\frac{1}{3}\right)$, decimals (0.56), or mixed numbers $\left(7\frac{3}{4}\right)$.

Prime number – any whole number greater than 1 that has only two factors, itself and 1; that is, a number that can be divided evenly only by 1 and itself.

Composite number – any whole number greater than 1 that has more than two different factors; in other words, any whole number that is not a prime number. For example: The composite number 8 has the factors of 1, 2, 4, and 8.

Even number – any integer that can be divided by 2 without leaving a remainder. For example: 2, 4, 6, 8, and so on.

Odd number – any integer that cannot be divided evenly by 2. For example: 3, 5, 7, 9, and so on.

Decimal number – any number that uses a decimal point to show the part of the number that is less than one. Example: 1.234.

Decimal point – a symbol used to separate the ones place from the tenths place in decimals or dollars from cents in currency.

Decimal place – the position of a number to the right of the decimal point. In the decimal 0.123, the 1 is in the first place to the right of the decimal point, indicating tenths; the 2 is in the second place, indicating hundredths; and the 3 is in the third place, indicating thousandths.

The **decimal**, or base 10, system is a number system that uses ten different digits (0, 1, 2, 3, 4, 5, 6, 7, 8, 9). An example of a number system that uses something other than ten digits is the **binary**, or base 2, number system, used by computers, which uses only the numbers 0 and 1. It is thought that the decimal system originated because people had only their 10 fingers for counting.

Rational numbers include all integers, decimals, and fractions. Any terminating or repeating decimal number is a rational number.

Irrational numbers cannot be written as fractions or decimals because the number of decimal places is infinite and there is no recurring pattern of digits within the number. For example, pi (π) begins with 3.141592 and continues without terminating or repeating, so pi is an irrational number.

Real numbers are the set of all rational and irrational numbers.

> **Review Video and Practice: Numbers and Their Classifications**
> Visit mometrix.com/academy and enter code: 461071
>
> **Review Video and Practice: Rational and Irrational Numbers**
> Visit mometrix.com/academy and enter code: 280645
>
> **Review Video and Practice: Prime and Composite Numbers**
> Visit mometrix.com/academy and enter code: 565581

The Number Line

A number line is a graph to see the distance between numbers. Basically, this graph shows the relationship between numbers. So a number line may have a point for zero and may show negative numbers on the left side of the line. Any positive numbers are placed on the right side of the line. For example, consider the points labeled on the following number line:

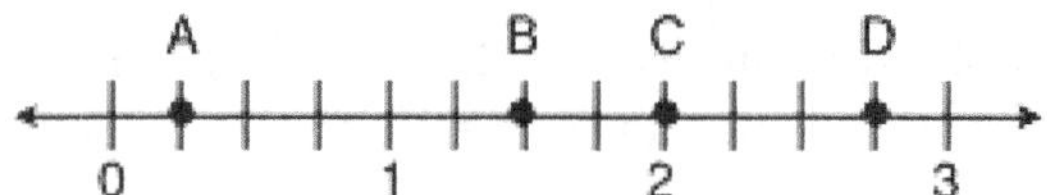

We can use the dashed lines on the number line to identify each point. Each dashed line between two whole numbers is $\frac{1}{4}$. The line halfway between two numbers is $\frac{1}{2}$.

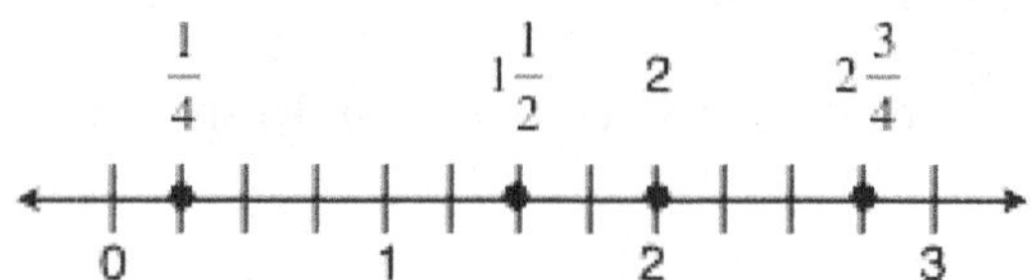

> **Review Video: The Number Line**
> Visit mometrix.com/academy and enter code: 816439

Numbers in Word Form and Place Value

When writing numbers out in word form or translating word form to numbers, it is essential to understand how a place value system works. In the decimal or base-10 system, each digit of a number represents how many of the corresponding place value – a specific factor of 10 – are contained in the number being represented. To make reading numbers easier, every three digits to the left of the decimal place is preceded by a comma. The following table demonstrates some of the place values:

Power of 10	10^3	10^2	10^1	10^0	10^{-1}	10^{-2}	10^{-3}
Value	1,000	100	10	1	0.1	0.01	0.001
Place	thousands	hundreds	tens	ones	tenths	hundredths	thousandths

For example, consider the number 4,546.09, which can be separated into each place value like this:

4: thousands
5: hundreds
4: tens
6: ones
0: tenths
9: hundredths

This number in word form would be *four thousand five hundred forty-six and nine hundredths.*

Review Video: Number Place Value
Visit mometrix.com/academy and enter code: 205433

ABSOLUTE VALUE

A precursor to working with negative numbers is understanding what **absolute values** are. A number's absolute value is simply the distance away from zero a number is on the number line. The absolute value of a number is always positive and is written $|x|$. For example, the absolute value of 3, written as $|3|$, is 3 because the distance between 0 and 3 on a number line is three units. Likewise, the absolute value of -3, written as $|-3|$, is 3 because the distance between 0 and -3 on a number line is three units. So $|3| = |-3|$.

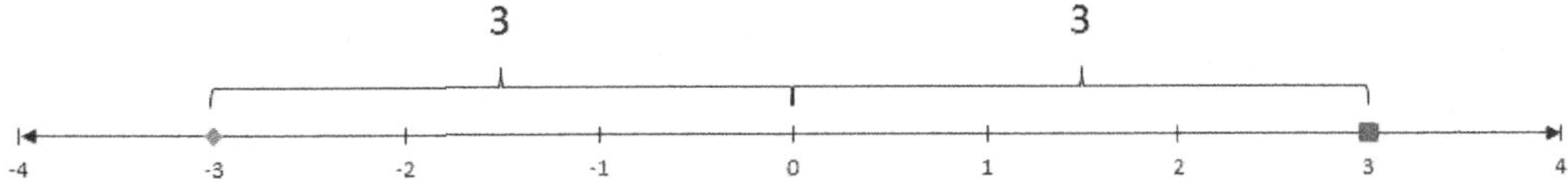

Review Video: Absolute Value
Visit mometrix.com/academy and enter code: 314669

PRACTICE

P1. Write the place value of each digit in 14,059.826

P2. Write out each of the following in words:

(a) 29
(b) 478
(c) 98,542
(d) 0.06
(e) 13.113

P3. Write each of the following in numbers:

(a) nine thousand four hundred thirty-five
(b) three hundred two thousand eight hundred seventy-six
(c) nine hundred one thousandths
(d) nineteen thousandths
(e) seven thousand one hundred forty-two and eighty-five hundredths

Practice Solutions

P1. The place value for each digit would be as follows:

Digit	Place Value
1	ten-thousands
4	thousands
0	hundreds
5	tens
9	ones
8	tenths
2	hundredths
6	thousandths

P2. Each written out in words would be:

(a) twenty-nine
(b) four hundred seventy-eight
(c) ninety-eight thousand five hundred forty-two
(d) six hundredths
(e) thirteen and one hundred thirteen thousandths

P3. Each in numeric form would be:

(a) 9,435
(b) 302, 876
(c) 0.901
(d) 0.019
(e) 7,142.85

Operations

Operations

An **operation** is simply a mathematical process that takes some value(s) as input(s) and produces an output. Elementary operations are often written in the following form: *value operation value*. For instance, in the expression $1 + 2$ the values are 1 and 2 and the operation is addition. Performing the operation gives the output of 3. In this way we can say that $1 + 2$ and 3 are equal, or $1 + 2 = 3$.

Addition

Addition increases the value of one quantity by the value of another quantity (both called **addends**). For example, $2 + 4 = 6; 8 + 9 = 17$. The result is called the **sum**. With addition, the order does not matter, $4 + 2 = 2 + 4$.

When adding signed numbers, if the signs are the same simply add the absolute values of the addends and apply the original sign to the sum. For example, $(+4) + (+8) = +12$ and $(-4) + (-8) = -12$. When the original signs are different, take the absolute values of the addends and subtract the smaller value from the larger value, then apply the original sign of the larger value to the difference. For instance, $(+4) + (-8) = -4$ and $(-4) + (+8) = +4$.

Subtraction

Subtraction is the opposite operation to addition; it decreases the value of one quantity (the **minuend**) by the value of another quantity (the **subtrahend**). For example, $6 - 4 = 2; 17 - 8 = 9$. The result is called the **difference**. Note that with subtraction, the order does matter, $6 - 4 \neq 4 - 6$.

For subtracting signed numbers, change the sign of the subtrahend and then follow the same rules used for addition. For example, $(+4) - (+8) = (+4) + (-8) = -4$.

Multiplication

Multiplication can be thought of as repeated addition. One number (the **multiplier**) indicates how many times to add the other number (the **multiplicand**) to itself. For example, 3×2 (three times two) $= 2 + 2 + 2 = 6$. With multiplication, the order does not matter: $2 \times 3 = 3 \times 2$ or $3 + 3 = 2 + 2 + 2$, either way the result (the **product**) is the same.

If the signs are the same the product is positive when multiplying signed numbers. For example, $(+4) \times (+8) = +32$ and $(-4) \times (-8) = +32$. If the signs are opposite, the product is negative. For example, $(+4) \times (-8) = -32$ and $(-4) \times (+8) = -32$. When more than two factors are multiplied together, the sign of the product is determined by how many negative factors are present. If there are an odd number of negative factors then the product is negative, whereas an even number of negative factors indicates a positive product. For instance, $(+4) \times (-8) \times (-2) = +64$ and $(-4) \times (-8) \times (-2) = -64$.

Division

Division is the opposite operation to multiplication; one number (the **divisor**) tells us how many parts to divide the other number (the **dividend**) into. The result of division is called the **quotient**. For example, $20 \div 4 = 5$; if 20 is split into 4 equal parts, each part is 5. With division, the order of the numbers does matter, $20 \div 4 \neq 4 \div 20$.

The rules for dividing signed numbers are similar to multiplying signed numbers. If the dividend and divisor have the same sign, the quotient is positive. If the dividend and divisor have opposite signs, the quotient is negative. For example, $(-4) \div (+8) = -0.5$.

Review Video: Mathematical Operations
Visit mometrix.com/academy and enter code: 208095

Parentheses

Parentheses are used to designate which operations should be done first when there are multiple operations. Example: $4 - (2 + 1) = 1$; the parentheses tell us that we must add 2 and 1, and then subtract the sum from 4, rather than subtracting 2 from 4 and then adding 1 (this would give us an answer of 3).

Review Video: Mathematical Parentheses
Visit mometrix.com/academy and enter code: 978600

Exponents

An **exponent** is a superscript number placed next to another number at the top right. It indicates how many times the base number is to be multiplied by itself. Exponents provide a shorthand way to write what would be a longer mathematical expression, for example: $2^4 = 2 \times 2 \times 2 \times 2$. A number with an exponent of 2 is said to be "squared," while a number with an exponent of 3 is said to be "cubed." The value of a number raised to an exponent is called its power. So 8^4 is read as "8 to the 4th power," or "8 raised to the power of 4."

The properties of exponents are as follows:

Property	Description
$a^1 = a$	Any number to the power of 1 is equal to itself
$1^n = 1$	The number 1 raised to any power is equal to 1
$a^0 = 1$	Any number raised to the power of 0 is equal to 1
$a^n \times a^m = a^{n+m}$	Add exponents to multiply powers of the same base number
$a^n \div a^m = a^{n-m}$	Subtract exponents to divide powers of the same base number
$(a^n)^m = a^{n \times m}$	When a power is raised to a power, the exponents are multiplied
$(a \times b)^n = a^n \times b^n$ $(a \div b)^n = a^n \div b^n$	Multiplication and division operations inside parentheses can be raised to a power. This is the same as each term being raised to that power.
$a^{-n} = \frac{1}{a^n}$	A negative exponent is the same as the reciprocal of a positive exponent

Note that exponents do not have to be integers. Fractional or decimal exponents follow all the rules above as well. Example: $5^{\frac{1}{4}} \times 5^{\frac{3}{4}} = 5^{\frac{1}{4}+\frac{3}{4}} = 5^1 = 5$.

Review Video: What is an Exponent?
Visit mometrix.com/academy and enter code: 600998

Review Video: Properties of Exponents
Visit mometrix.com/academy and enter code: 532558

Roots

A **root**, such as a square root, is another way of writing a fractional exponent. Instead of using a superscript, roots use the radical symbol ($\sqrt{\ }$) to indicate the operation. A radical will have a number underneath the bar, and may sometimes have a number in the upper left: $\sqrt[n]{a}$, read as "the nth root of a." The relationship between radical notation and exponent notation can be described by this equation: $\sqrt[n]{a} = a^{\frac{1}{n}}$. The two special cases of $n = 2$ and $n = 3$ are called square roots and cube roots. If there is no number to the upper left, it is understood to be a square root ($n = 2$). Nearly all of the roots you encounter will be square roots. A square root is the same as a number raised to the one-half power. When we say that a is the square root of b ($a = \sqrt{b}$), we mean that a multiplied by itself equals b: ($a \times a = b$).

A **perfect square** is a number that has an integer for its square root. There are 10 perfect squares from 1 to 100: 1, 4, 9, 16, 25, 36, 49, 64, 81, 100 (the squares of integers 1 through 10).

Review Video: Roots
Visit mometrix.com/academy and enter code: 795655

Review Video: Square Root and Perfect Squares
Visit mometrix.com/academy and enter code: 648063

Order of Operations

The **order of operations** is a set of rules that dictates the order in which we must perform each operation in an expression so that we will evaluate it accurately. If we have an expression that includes multiple different operations, the order of operations tells us which operations to do first. The most common mnemonic for the order of operations is **PEMDAS**, or "Please Excuse My Dear Aunt Sally." PEMDAS stands for parentheses, exponents, multiplication, division, addition, and subtraction. It is important to understand that multiplication and division have equal precedence, as do addition and subtraction, so those pairs of operations are simply worked from left to right in order.

For example, evaluating the expression $5 + 20 \div 4 \times (2 + 3) - 6$ using the correct order of operations would be done like this:

- **P:** Perform the operations inside the parentheses: $(2 + 3) = 5$
- **E:** Simplify the exponents.
    - The equation now looks like this: $5 + 20 \div 4 \times 5 - 6$
- **MD:** Perform multiplication and division from left to right: $20 \div 4 = 5$; then $5 \times 5 = 25$
    - The equation now looks like this: $5 + 25 - 6$
- **AS:** Perform addition and subtraction from left to right: $5 + 25 = 30$; then $30 - 6 = 24$

Review Video: Order of Operations
Visit mometrix.com/academy and enter code: 259675

Subtraction with Regrouping

A great way to make use of some of the features built into the decimal system would be regrouping when attempting longform subtraction operations. When subtracting within a place value, sometimes the minuend is smaller than the subtrahend, **regrouping** enables you to 'borrow' a unit from a place value to the left in order to get a positive difference. For example, consider subtracting 189 from 525 with regrouping.

First, set up the subtraction problem in vertical form:

$$\begin{array}{r} 525 \\ -\ 189 \\ \hline \end{array}$$

Notice that the numbers in the ones and tens columns of 525 are smaller than the numbers in the ones and tens columns of 189. This means you will need to use regrouping to perform subtraction:

$$\begin{array}{rrrr} & 5 & 2 & 5 \\ - & 1 & 8 & 9 \\ \hline \end{array}$$

To subtract 9 from 5 in the ones column you will need to borrow from the 2 in the tens columns:

$$\begin{array}{rrrr} & 5 & 1 & 15 \\ - & 1 & 8 & 9 \\ \hline & & & 6 \end{array}$$

Next, to subtract 8 from 1 in the tens column you will need to borrow from the 5 in the hundreds column:

$$\begin{array}{rrrr} & 4 & 11 & 15 \\ - & 1 & 8 & 9 \\ \hline & & 3 & 6 \end{array}$$

Last, subtract the 1 from the 4 in the hundreds column:

	4	11	15
-	1	8	9
	3	3	6

PRACTICE

P1. Demonstrate how to subtract 477 from 620 using regrouping.

P2. Simplify the following expressions with exponents:

(a) 37^0
(b) 1^{30}
(c) $2^3 \times 2^4 \times 2^x$
(d) $(3^x)^3$
(e) $(12 \div 3)^2$

PRACTICE SOLUTIONS

P1. First, set up the subtraction problem in vertical form:

	6	2	0
-	4	7	7

To subtract 7 from 0 in the ones column you will need to borrow from the 2 in the tens column:

	6	1	10
-	4	7	7
			3

Next, to subtract 7 from the 1 that's still in the tens column you will need to borrow from the 6 in the hundreds column:

	5	11	10
-	4	7	7
		4	3

Lastly, subtract 4 from the 5 remaining in the hundreds column:

	5	11	10
-	4	7	7
	1	4	3

P2. Using the properties of exponents and the proper order of operations:

(a) Any number raised to the power of 0 is equal to 1: $37^0 = 1$
(b) The number 1 raised to any power is equal to 1: $1^{30} = 1$
(c) Add exponents to multiply powers of the same base: $2^3 \times 2^4 \times 2^x = 2^{(3+4+x)} = 2^{(7+x)}$
(d) When a power is raised to a power, the exponents are multiplied: $(3^x)^3 = 3^{3x}$
(e) Perform the operation inside the parentheses first: $(12 \div 3)^2 = 4^2 = 16$

FACTORING

FACTORS AND GREATEST COMMON FACTOR

Factors are numbers that are multiplied together to obtain a **product**. For example, in the equation $2 \times 3 = 6$, the numbers 2 and 3 are factors. A **prime number** has only two factors (1 and itself), but other numbers can have many factors.

A **common factor** is a number that divides exactly into two or more other numbers. For example, the factors of 12 are 1, 2, 3, 4, 6, and 12, while the factors of 15 are 1, 3, 5, and 15. The common factors of 12 and 15 are 1 and 3.

A **prime factor** is also a prime number. Therefore, the prime factors of 12 are 2 and 3. For 15, the prime factors are 3 and 5.

The **greatest common factor** (**GCF**) is the largest number that is a factor of two or more numbers. For example, the factors of 15 are 1, 3, 5, and 15; the factors of 35 are 1, 5, 7, and 35. Therefore, the greatest common factor of 15 and 35 is 5.

Review Video: Factors
Visit mometrix.com/academy and enter code: 920086

Review Video: GCF and LCM
Visit mometrix.com/academy and enter code: 838699

MULTIPLES AND LEAST COMMON MULTIPLE

Often listed out in multiplication tables, **multiples** are integer increments of a given factor. In other words, dividing a multiple by the factor number will result in an integer. For example, the multiples of 7 include: $1 \times 7 = 7$, $2 \times 7 = 14$, $3 \times 7 = 21$, $4 \times 7 = 28$, $5 \times 7 = 35$. Dividing 7, 14, 21, 28, or 35 by 7 will result in the integers 1, 2, 3, 4, and 5, respectively.

The least common multiple (**LCM**) is the smallest number that is a multiple of two or more numbers. For example, the multiples of 3 include 3, 6, 9, 12, 15, etc.; the multiples of 5 include 5, 10, 15, 20, etc. Therefore, the least common multiple of 3 and 5 is 15.

Review Video: Multiples
Visit mometrix.com/academy and enter code: 626738

RATIONAL NUMBERS

FRACTIONS

A **fraction** is a number that is expressed as one integer written above another integer, with a dividing line between them $\left(\frac{x}{y}\right)$. It represents the **quotient** of the two numbers "x divided by y." It can also be thought of as x out of y equal parts.

The top number of a fraction is called the **numerator**, and it represents the number of parts under consideration. The 1 in $\frac{1}{4}$ means that 1 part out of the whole is being considered in the calculation. The bottom number of a fraction is called the **denominator**, and it represents the total number of equal parts. The 4 in $\frac{1}{4}$ means that the whole consists of 4 equal parts. A fraction cannot have a denominator of zero; this is referred to as "*undefined*."

Fractions can be manipulated, without changing the value of the fraction, by multiplying or dividing (but not adding or subtracting) both the numerator and denominator by the same number. If you divide both numbers by a common factor, you are **reducing** or simplifying the fraction. Two fractions that have the same value but are expressed differently are known as **equivalent fractions**. For example, $\frac{2}{10}, \frac{3}{15}, \frac{4}{20}$, and $\frac{5}{25}$ are all equivalent fractions. They can also all be reduced or simplified to $\frac{1}{5}$.

When two fractions are manipulated so that they have the same denominator, this is known as finding a **common denominator**. The number chosen to be that common denominator should be the least common multiple of the two original denominators. Example: $\frac{3}{4}$ and $\frac{5}{6}$; the least common multiple of 4 and 6 is 12. Manipulating to achieve the common denominator: $\frac{3}{4} = \frac{9}{12}; \frac{5}{6} = \frac{10}{12}$.

Proper Fractions and Mixed Numbers

A fraction whose denominator is greater than its numerator is known as a **proper fraction**, while a fraction whose numerator is greater than its denominator is known as an **improper fraction**. Proper fractions have values *less than one* and improper fractions have values *greater than one.*

A **mixed number** is a number that contains both an integer and a fraction. Any improper fraction can be rewritten as a mixed number. Example: $\frac{8}{3} = \frac{6}{3} + \frac{2}{3} = 2 + \frac{2}{3} = 2\frac{2}{3}$. Similarly, any mixed number can be rewritten as an improper fraction. Example: $1\frac{3}{5} = 1 + \frac{3}{5} = \frac{5}{5} + \frac{3}{5} = \frac{8}{5}$.

Review Video: Fractions and Mixed Numbers
Visit mometrix.com/academy and enter code: 211077

Review Video: Overview of Fractions
Visit mometrix.com/academy and enter code: 262335

Adding and Subtracting Fractions

If two fractions have a common denominator, they can be added or subtracted simply by adding or subtracting the two numerators and retaining the same denominator. If the two fractions do not already have the same denominator, one or both of them must be manipulated to achieve a common denominator before they can be added or subtracted. Example: $\frac{1}{2} + \frac{1}{4} = \frac{2}{4} + \frac{1}{4} = \frac{3}{4}$.

Review Video: Adding and Subtracting Fractions
Visit mometrix.com/academy and enter code: 378080

Multiplying Fractions

Two fractions can be multiplied by multiplying the two numerators to find the new numerator and the two denominators to find the new denominator. Example: $\frac{1}{3} \times \frac{2}{3} = \frac{1 \times 2}{3 \times 3} = \frac{2}{9}$.

Dividing Fractions

Two fractions can be divided by flipping the numerator and denominator of the second fraction and then proceeding as though it were a multiplication. Example: $\frac{2}{3} \div \frac{3}{4} = \frac{2}{3} \times \frac{4}{3} = \frac{8}{9}$.

Review Video: Multiplying and Dividing Fractions
Visit mometrix.com/academy and enter code: 473632

Multiplying a Mixed Number by a Whole Number or a Decimal

When multiplying a mixed number by something, it is usually best to convert it to an improper fraction first. Additionally, if the multiplicand is a decimal, it is most often simplest to convert it to a fraction. For instance, to multiply $4\frac{3}{8}$ by 3.5, begin by rewriting each quantity as a whole number plus a proper fraction. Remember, a mixed number is a fraction added to a whole number and a decimal is a representation of the sum of fractions, specifically tenths, hundredths, thousandths, and so on:

$$4\frac{3}{8} \times 3.5 = \left(4 + \frac{3}{8}\right) \times \left(3 + \frac{1}{2}\right)$$

Next, the quantities being added need to be expressed with the same denominator. This is achieved by multiplying and dividing the whole number by the denominator of the fraction. Recall that a whole number is equivalent to that number divided by 1:

$$= \left(\frac{4}{1} \times \frac{8}{8} + \frac{3}{8}\right) \times \left(\frac{3}{1} \times \frac{2}{2} + \frac{1}{2}\right)$$

When multiplying fractions, remember to multiply the numerators and denominators separately:

$$= \left(\frac{4 \times 8}{1 \times 8} + \frac{3}{8}\right) \times \left(\frac{3 \times 2}{1 \times 2} + \frac{1}{2}\right)$$
$$= \left(\frac{32}{8} + \frac{3}{8}\right) \times \left(\frac{6}{2} + \frac{1}{2}\right)$$

Now that the fractions have the same denominators, they can be added:

$$= \frac{35}{8} \times \frac{7}{2}$$

Finally, perform the last multiplication and then simplify:

$$= \frac{35 \times 7}{8 \times 2} = \frac{245}{16} = \frac{240}{16} + \frac{5}{16} = 15\frac{5}{16}$$

Decimals

Decimals are one way to represent parts of a whole. Using the place value system, each digit to the right of a decimal point denotes the number of units of a corresponding *negative* power of ten. For example, consider the decimal 0.24. We can use a model to represent the decimal. Since a dime is worth one-tenth of a dollar and a penny is worth one-hundredth of a dollar, one possible model to represent this fraction is to have 2 dimes representing the 2 in the tenths place and 4 pennies representing the 4 in the hundredths place:

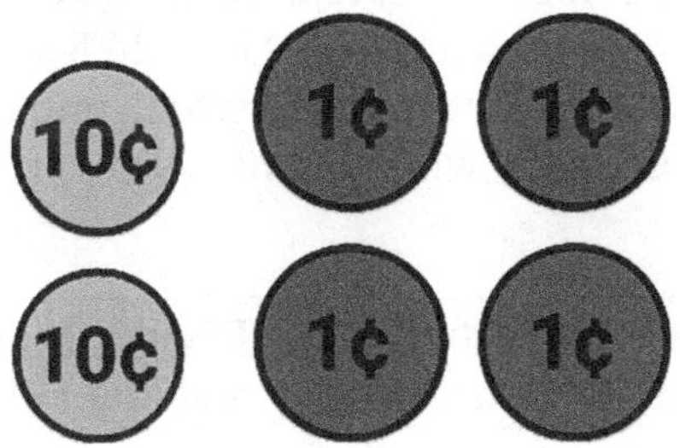

To write the decimal as a fraction, put the decimal in the numerator with 1 in the denominator. Multiply the numerator and denominator by tens until there are no more decimal places. Then simplify the fraction to lowest terms. For example, converting 0.24 to a fraction:

$$0.24 = \frac{0.24}{1} = \frac{0.24 \times 100}{1 \times 100} = \frac{24}{100} = \frac{6}{25}$$

Review Video: Decimals
Visit mometrix.com/academy and enter code: 837268

Adding and Subtracting Decimals

When adding and subtracting decimals, the decimal points must always be aligned. Adding decimals is just like adding regular whole numbers. Example: $4.5 + 2 = 6.5$.

If the problem-solver does not properly align the decimal points, an incorrect answer of 4.7 may result. An easy way to add decimals is to align all of the decimal points in a vertical column visually. This will allow you to see exactly where the decimal should be placed in the final answer. Begin adding from right to left. Add each column in turn, making sure to carry the number to the left if a column adds up to more than 9. The same rules apply to the subtraction of decimals.

Review Video: Adding and Subtracting Decimals
Visit mometrix.com/academy and enter code: 381101

Multiplying Decimals

A simple multiplication problem has two components: a **multiplicand** and a **multiplier**. When multiplying decimals, work as though the numbers were whole rather than decimals. Once the final product is calculated, count the number of places to the right of the decimal in both the multiplicand and the multiplier. Then, count that number of places from the right of the product and place the decimal in that position.

For example, 12.3×2.56 has a total of three places to the right of the respective decimals. Multiply 123×256 to get 31488. Now, beginning on the right, count three places to the left and insert the decimal. The final product will be 31.488.

Review Video: How to Multiply Decimals
Visit mometrix.com/academy and enter code: 731574

Dividing Decimals

Every division problem has a **divisor** and a **dividend**. The dividend is the number that is being divided. In the problem $14 \div 7$, 14 is the dividend and 7 is the divisor. In a division problem with decimals, the divisor must be converted into a whole number. Begin by moving the decimal in the divisor to the right until a whole number is created. Next, move the decimal in the dividend the same number of spaces to the right. For example, 4.9 into 24.5 would become 49 into 245. The decimal was moved one space to the right to create a whole number in the divisor, and then the same was done for the dividend. Once the whole numbers are created, the problem is carried out normally: $245 \div 49 = 5$.

Review Video: How to Divide Decimals
Visit mometrix.com/academy and enter code: 560690

PERCENTAGES

Percentages can be thought of as fractions that are based on a whole of 100; that is, one whole is equal to 100%. The word **percent** means "per hundred." Percentage problems are often presented in three main ways:

- Find what percentage of some number another number is.
  - Example: What percentage of 40 is 8?
- Find what number is some percentage of a given number.
  - Example: What number is 20% of 40?
- Find what number another number is a given percentage of.
  - Example: What number is 8 20% of?

There are three components in each of these cases: a **whole** (W), a **part** (P), and a **percentage** (%). These are related by the equation: $P = W \times \%$. This can easily be rearranged into other forms that may suit different questions better: $\% = \frac{P}{W}$ and $W = \frac{P}{\%}$. Percentage problems are often also word problems. As such, a large part of solving them is figuring out which quantities are what. For example, consider the following word problem:

In a school cafeteria, 7 students choose pizza, 9 choose hamburgers, and 4 choose tacos. What percentage of student choose tacos?

To find the whole, you must first add all of the parts: $7 + 9 + 4 = 20$. The percentage can then be found by dividing the part by the whole ($\% = \frac{P}{W}$): $\frac{4}{20} = \frac{20}{100} = 20\%$.

CONVERTING BETWEEN PERCENTAGES, FRACTIONS, AND DECIMALS

Converting decimals to percentages and percentages to decimals is as simple as moving the decimal point. To *convert from a decimal to a percentage*, move the decimal point **two places to the right**. To *convert from a percentage to a decimal*, move it **two places to the left**. It may be helpful to remember that the percentage number will always be larger than the equivalent decimal number. For example:

$$0.23 = 23\% \qquad 5.34 = 534\% \qquad 0.007 = 0.7\%$$
$$700\% = 7.00 \qquad 86\% = 0.86 \qquad 0.15\% = 0.0015$$

To convert a fraction to a decimal, simply divide the numerator by the denominator in the fraction. To convert a decimal to a fraction, put the decimal in the numerator with 1 in the denominator. Multiply the numerator and denominator by tens until there are no more decimal places. Then simplify the fraction to lowest terms. For example, converting 0.24 to a fraction:

$$0.24 = \frac{0.24}{1} = \frac{0.24 \times 100}{1 \times 100} = \frac{24}{100} = \frac{6}{25}$$

Fractions can be converted to a percentage by finding equivalent fractions with a denominator of 100. Example:

$$\frac{7}{10} = \frac{70}{100} = 70\% \quad \frac{1}{4} = \frac{25}{100} = 25\%$$

To convert a percentage to a fraction, divide the percentage number by 100 and reduce the fraction to its simplest possible terms. Example:

$$60\% = \frac{60}{100} = \frac{3}{5} \quad 96\% = \frac{96}{100} = \frac{24}{25}$$

Review Video: Converting Fractions to Percentages and Decimals
Visit mometrix.com/academy and enter code: 306233

Review Video: Converting Percentages to Decimals and Fractions
Visit mometrix.com/academy and enter code: 287297

Review Video: Converting Decimals to Fractions and Percentages
Visit mometrix.com/academy and enter code: 986765

Review Video: Converting Decimals, Improper Fractions, and Mixed Numbers
Visit mometrix.com/academy and enter code: 696924

Rational Numbers

The term **rational** means that the number can be expressed as a ratio or fraction. That is, a number, r, is rational if and only if it can be represented by a fraction $\frac{a}{b}$ where a and b are integers and b does not equal 0. The set of rational numbers includes integers and decimals. If there is no finite way to represent a value with a fraction of integers, then the number is **irrational**. Common examples of irrational numbers include: $\sqrt{5}$, $(1 + \sqrt{2})$, and π.

Practice

P1. What is 30% of 120?

P2. What is 150% of 20?

P3. What is 14.5% of 96?

P4. Simplify the following expressions:

(a) $\left(\frac{2}{5}\right)/\left(\frac{4}{7}\right)$
(b) $\frac{7}{8} - \frac{8}{16}$
(c) $\frac{1}{2} + \left(3\left(\frac{3}{4}\right) - 2\right) + 4$
(d) $0.22 + 0.5 - (5.5 + 3.3 \div 3)$
(e) $\frac{3}{2} + (4(0.5) - 0.75) + 2$

P5. Convert the following to a fraction and to a decimal: **(a)** 15%; **(b)** 24.36%

P6. Convert the following to a decimal and to a percentage. **(a)** 4/5; **(b)** $3\frac{2}{5}$

P7. A woman's age is thirteen more than half of 60. How old is the woman?

P8. A patient was given pain medicine at a dosage of 0.22 grams. The patient's dosage was then increased to 0.80 grams. By how much was the patient's dosage increased?

P9. At a hotel, $\frac{3}{4}$ of the 100 rooms are occupied today. Yesterday, $\frac{4}{5}$ of the 100 rooms were occupied. On which day were more of the rooms occupied and by how much more?

P10. At a school, 40% of the teachers teach English. If 20 teachers teach English, how many teachers work at the school?

P11. A patient was given blood pressure medicine at a dosage of 2 grams. The patient's dosage was then decreased to 0.45 grams. By how much was the patient's dosage decreased?

P12. Two weeks ago, $\frac{2}{3}$ of the 60 customers at a skate shop were male. Last week, $\frac{3}{6}$ of the 80 customers were male. During which week were there more male customers?

P13. Jane ate lunch at a local restaurant. She ordered a $4.99 appetizer, a $12.50 entrée, and a $1.25 soda. If she wants to tip her server 20%, how much money will she spend in all?

P14. According to a survey, about 82% of engineers were highly satisfied with their job. If 145 engineers were surveyed, how many reported that they were highly satisfied?

P15. A patient was given 40 mg of a certain medicine. Later, the patient's dosage was increased to 45 mg. What was the percent increase in his medication?

P16. Order the following rational numbers from least to greatest: 0.55, 17%, $\sqrt{25}$, $\frac{64}{4}$, $\frac{25}{50}$, 3.

P17. Order the following rational numbers from greatest to least: 0.3, 27%, $\sqrt{100}$, $\frac{72}{9}$, $\frac{1}{9}$, 4.5

P18. Perform the following multiplication. Write each answer as a mixed number.

(a) $\left(1\frac{11}{16}\right) \times 4$
(b) $\left(12\frac{1}{3}\right) \times 1.1$
(c) $3.71 \times \left(6\frac{1}{5}\right)$

P19. Suppose you are making doughnuts and you want to triple the recipe you have. If the following list is the original amounts for the ingredients, what would be the amounts for the tripled recipe?

$1\,^3/_4$	cup	Flour
$1\,^1/_4$	tsp	Baking powder
$^3/_4$	tsp	Salt
$^3/_8$	cup	Sugar
$1\,^1/_2$	Tbsp	Butter
2	large	Eggs
$^3/_4$	tsp	Vanilla extract
$^3/_8$	cup	Sour cream

Practice Solutions

P1. The word *of* indicates multiplication, so 30% of 120 is found by multiplying 120 by 30%. Change 30% to a decimal, then multiply: $120 \times 0.3 = 36$

P2. The word *of* indicates multiplication, so 150% of 20 is found by multiplying 20 by 150%. Change 150% to a decimal, then multiply: $20 \times 1.5 = 30$

P3. Change 14.5% to a decimal before multiplying. $0.145 \times 96 = 13.92$.

P4. Follow the order of operations and utilize properties of fractions to solve each:

(a) Rewrite the problem as a multiplication problem: $\frac{2}{5} \times \frac{7}{4} = \frac{2\times 7}{5\times 4} = \frac{14}{20}$. Make sure the fraction is reduced to lowest terms. Both 14 and 20 can be divided by 2.

$$\frac{14}{20} = \frac{14 \div 2}{20 \div 2} = \frac{7}{10}$$

(b) The denominators of $\frac{7}{8}$ and $\frac{8}{16}$ are 8 and 16, respectively. The lowest common denominator of 8 and 16 is 16 because 16 is the least common multiple of 8 and 16. Convert the first fraction to its equivalent with the newly found common denominator of 16: $\frac{7 \times 2}{8 \times 2} = \frac{14}{16}$. Now that the fractions have the same denominator, you can subtract them.

$$\frac{14}{16} - \frac{8}{16} = \frac{6}{16} = \frac{3}{8}$$

(c) When simplifying expressions, first perform operations within groups. Within the set of parentheses are multiplication and subtraction operations. Perform the multiplication first to get $\frac{1}{2} + \left(\frac{9}{4} - 2\right) + 4$. Then, subtract two to obtain $\frac{1}{2} + \frac{1}{4} + 4$. Finally, perform addition from left to right:

$$\frac{1}{2} + \frac{1}{4} + 4 = \frac{2}{4} + \frac{1}{4} + \frac{16}{4} = \frac{19}{4} = 4\frac{3}{4}$$

(d) First, evaluate the terms in the parentheses $(5.5 + 3.3 \div 3)$ using order of operations. $3.3 \div 3 = 1.1$, and $5.5 + 1.1 = 6.6$. Next, rewrite the problem: $0.22 + 0.5 - 6.6$. Finally, add and subtract from left to right: $0.22 + 0.5 = 0.72$; $0.72 - 6.6 = -5.88$. The answer is -5.88.

(e) First, simplify within the parentheses, then change the fraction to a decimal and perform addition from left to right:

$$\frac{3}{2} + (2 - 0.75) + 2 =$$
$$\frac{3}{2} + 1.25 + 2 =$$
$$1.5 + 1.25 + 2 = 4.75$$

P5. (a) 15% can be written as $\frac{15}{100}$. Both 15 and 100 can be divided by 5: $\frac{15 \div 5}{100 \div 5} = \frac{3}{20}$

When converting from a percentage to a decimal, drop the percent sign and move the decimal point two places to the left: $15\% = 0.15$

(b) 24.36% written as a fraction is $\frac{24.36}{100}$, or $\frac{2436}{10{,}000}$, which reduces to $\frac{609}{2500}$. 24.36% written as a decimal is 0.2436. Recall that dividing by 100 moves the decimal two places to the left.

P6. (a) Recall that in the decimal system the first decimal place is one tenth: $\frac{4\times2}{5\times2}=\frac{8}{10}=0.8$

Percent means "per hundred." $\frac{4\times20}{5\times20}=\frac{80}{100}=80\%$

(b) The mixed number $3\frac{2}{5}$ has a whole number and a fractional part. The fractional part $\frac{2}{5}$ can be written as a decimal by dividing 5 into 2, which gives 0.4. Adding the whole to the part gives 3.4.

To find the equivalent percentage, multiply the decimal by 100. $3.4(100)=340\%$. Notice that this percentage is greater than 100%. This makes sense because the original mixed number $3\frac{2}{5}$ is greater than 1.

P7. "More than" indicates addition, and "of" indicates multiplication. The expression can be written as $\frac{1}{2}(60)+13$. So the woman's age is equal to $\frac{1}{2}(60)+13=30+13=43$. The woman is 43 years old.

P8. The first step is to determine what operation (addition, subtraction, multiplication, or division) the problem requires. Notice the keywords and phrases "by how much" and "increased." "Increased" means that you go from a smaller amount to a larger amount. This change can be found by subtracting the smaller amount from the larger amount: 0.80 grams– 0.22 grams = 0.58 grams.

Remember to line up the decimal when subtracting:

$$\begin{array}{r} 0.80 \\ -\ 0.22 \\ \hline 0.58 \end{array}$$

P9. First, find the number of rooms occupied each day. To do so, multiply the fraction of rooms occupied by the number of rooms available:

$$\text{Number occupied} = \text{Fraction occupied} \times \text{Total number}$$
$$\text{Number of rooms occupied today} = \frac{3}{4}\times 100 = 75$$
$$\text{Number of rooms occupied} = \frac{4}{5}\times 100 = 80$$

The difference in the number of rooms occupied is: $80-75=5$ rooms

P10. To answer this problem, first think about the number of teachers that work at the school. Will it be more or less than the number of teachers who work in a specific department such as English? More teachers work at the school, so the number you find to answer this question will be greater than 20.

40% of the teachers are English teachers. "Of" indicates multiplication, and words like "is" and "are" indicate equivalence. Translating the problem into a mathematical sentence gives $40\%\times t=20$, where t represents the total number of teachers. Solving for t gives $t=\frac{20}{40\%}=\frac{20}{0.40}=50$. Fifty teachers work at the school.

P11. The decrease is represented by the difference between the two amounts:

$$2\text{ grams} - 0.45\text{ grams} = 1.55\text{ grams}.$$

Remember to line up the decimal point before subtracting.

$$\begin{array}{r} 2.00 \\ -\ 0.45 \\ \hline 1.55 \end{array}$$

P12. First, you need to find the number of male customers that were in the skate shop each week. You are given this amount in terms of fractions. To find the actual number of male customers, multiply the fraction of male customers by the number of customers in the store.

$$\begin{aligned} \text{Actual number of male customers} &= \text{fraction of male customers} \times \text{total customers} \\ \text{Number of male customers two weeks ago} &= \frac{2}{3} \times 60 = \frac{120}{3} = 40 \\ \text{Number of male customers last week} &= \frac{3}{6} \times 80 = \frac{1}{2} \times 80 = \frac{80}{2} = 40 \end{aligned}$$

The number of male customers was the same both weeks.

P13. To find total amount, first find the sum of the items she ordered from the menu and then add 20% of this sum to the total.

$$\$4.99 + \$12.50 + \$1.25 = \$18.74$$

$$\$18.74 \times 20\% = (0.20)(\$18.74) = \$3.748 \approx \$3.75$$

$$\text{Total} = \$18.74 + \$3.75 = \$22.49$$

P14. 82% of 145 is $0.82 \times 145 = 118.9$. Because you can't have 0.9 of a person, we must round up to say that 119 engineers reported that they were highly satisfied with their jobs.

P15. To find the percent increase, first compare the original and increased amounts. The original amount was 40 mg, and the increased amount is 45 mg, so the dosage of medication was increased by 5 mg ($45 - 40 = 5$). Note, however, that the question asks not by how much the dosage increased but by what percentage it increased.

$$\begin{aligned} \text{Percent increase} &= \frac{\text{new amount} - \text{original amount}}{\text{original amount}} \times 100\% \\ &= \frac{45\text{ mg} - 40\text{ mg}}{40\text{ mg}} \times 100\% = \frac{5}{40} \times 100\% = 0.125 \times 100\% = 12.5\% \end{aligned}$$

P16. Recall that the term rational simply means that the number can be expressed as a ratio or fraction. Notice that each of the numbers in the problem can be written as a decimal or integer:

$$\begin{aligned} 17\% &= 0.1717 \\ \sqrt{25} &= 5 \\ \frac{64}{4} &= 16 \\ \frac{25}{50} &= \frac{1}{2} = 0.5 \end{aligned}$$

So, the answer is 17%, $\frac{25}{50}$, 0.55, 3, $\sqrt{25}$, $\frac{64}{4}$.

P17. Converting all the numbers to integers and decimals makes it easier to compare the values:

$$27\% = 0.27$$
$$\sqrt{100} = 10$$
$$\frac{72}{9} = 8$$
$$\frac{1}{9} \approx 0.11$$

So, the answer is $\sqrt{100}, \frac{72}{9}, 4.5, 0.3, 27\%, \frac{1}{9}$.

Review Video: Ordering Rational Numbers
Visit mometrix.com/academy and enter code: 419578

P18. For each, convert improper fractions, adjust to a common denominator, perform the operations, and then simplify:

(a) Sometimes, you can skip converting the denominator and just distribute the multiplication.

$$\begin{aligned}\left(1\frac{11}{16}\right) \times 4 &= \left(1 + \frac{11}{16}\right) \times 4 \\ &= 1 \times 4 + \frac{11}{16} \times 4 \\ &= 4 + \frac{11}{16} \times \frac{4}{1} \\ &= 4 + \frac{44}{16} = 4 + \frac{11}{4} = 4 + 2\frac{3}{4} = 6\frac{3}{4}\end{aligned}$$

(b)

$$\begin{aligned}\left(12\frac{1}{3}\right) \times 1.1 &= \left(12 + \frac{1}{3}\right) \times \left(1 + \frac{1}{10}\right) \\ &= \left(\frac{12}{1} \times \frac{3}{3} + \frac{1}{3}\right) \times \left(\frac{10}{10} + \frac{1}{10}\right) \\ &= \left(\frac{36}{3} + \frac{1}{3}\right) \times \frac{11}{10} \\ &= \frac{37}{3} \times \frac{11}{10} \\ &= \frac{407}{30} = \frac{390}{30} + \frac{17}{30} = 13\frac{17}{30}\end{aligned}$$

(c)

$$\begin{aligned}3.71 \times \left(6\frac{1}{5}\right) &= \left(3 + \frac{71}{100}\right) \times \left(6 + \frac{1}{5}\right)\\ &= \left(\frac{300}{100} + \frac{71}{100}\right) \times \left(\frac{6}{1} \times \frac{5}{5} + \frac{1}{5}\right)\\ &= \frac{371}{100} \times \left(\frac{30}{5} + \frac{1}{5}\right)\\ &= \frac{371}{100} \times \frac{31}{5}\\ &= \frac{11501}{500} = \frac{11500}{500} + \frac{1}{500} = 23\frac{1}{500}\end{aligned}$$

P19. Fortunately, some of the amounts are duplicated, so we do not need to figure out every amount.

$$\begin{aligned}1\frac{3}{4} \times 3 &= (1 \times 3) + \left(\frac{3}{4} \times 3\right)\\ &= 3 + \frac{9}{4}\\ &= 3 + 2\frac{1}{4}\\ &= 5\frac{1}{4}\end{aligned}$$

$$\begin{aligned}1\frac{1}{4} \times 3 &= (1 \times 3) + \left(\frac{1}{4} \times 3\right)\\ &= 3 + \frac{3}{4}\\ &= 3\frac{3}{4}\end{aligned}$$

$$\begin{aligned}\frac{3}{4} \times 3 &= \frac{3}{4} \times 3\\ &= \frac{9}{4}\\ &= 2\frac{1}{4}\end{aligned}$$

$$\begin{aligned}\frac{3}{8} \times 3 &= \frac{3}{8} \times 3\\ &= \frac{9}{8}\\ &= 1\frac{1}{8}\end{aligned}$$

$$\begin{aligned}1\frac{1}{2} \times 3 &= 1 \times 3 + \frac{1}{2} \times 3\\ &= 3 + \frac{3}{2}\\ &= 3 + 1\frac{1}{2}\\ &= 4\frac{1}{2}\end{aligned}$$

$$2 \times 3 = 6$$

So, the result for the triple recipe is:

$5\,{}^{1}/_{4}$	cup	Flour
$3\,{}^{3}/_{4}$	tsp	Baking powder
$2\,{}^{1}/_{4}$	tsp	Salt
$1\,{}^{1}/_{8}$	cup	Sugar
$4\,{}^{1}/_{2}$	Tbsp	Butter
6	large	Eggs
$2\,{}^{1}/_{4}$	tsp	Vanilla extract
$1\,{}^{1}/_{8}$	cup	Sour cream

Proportions and Ratios

Proportions

A proportion is a relationship between two quantities that dictates how one changes when the other changes. A **direct proportion** describes a relationship in which a quantity increases by a set amount for every increase in the other quantity, or decreases by that same amount for every decrease in the other quantity. Example: Assuming a constant driving speed, the time required for a car trip increases as the distance of the trip increases. The distance to be traveled and the time required to travel are directly proportional.

An **inverse proportion** is a relationship in which an increase in one quantity is accompanied by a decrease in the other, or vice versa. Example: the time required for a car trip decreases as the speed increases, and increases as the speed decreases, so the time required is inversely proportional to the speed of the car.

Review Video: Proportions
Visit mometrix.com/academy and enter code: 505355

Ratios

A **ratio** is a comparison of two quantities in a particular order. Example: If there are 14 computers in a lab, and the class has 20 students, there is a student to computer ratio of 20 to 14, commonly written as 20:14. Ratios are normally reduced to their smallest whole number representation, so 20:14 would be reduced to 10:7 by dividing both sides by 2.

Review Video: Ratios
Visit mometrix.com/academy and enter code: 996914

Constant of Proportionality

When two quantities have a proportional relationship, there exists a **constant of proportionality** between the quantities. The product of this constant and one of the quantities is equal to the other quantity. For example, if one lemon costs $0.25, two lemons cost $0.50, and three lemons cost $0.75, there is a proportional relationship between the total cost of lemons and the number of lemons purchased. The constant of proportionality is the **unit price**, namely $0.25/lemon. Notice that the total price of lemons, t, can be found by multiplying the unit price of lemons, p, and the number of lemons, n: $t = pn$.

Work/Unit Rate

Unit rate expresses a quantity of one thing in terms of one unit of another. For example, if you travel 30 miles every two hours, a unit rate expresses this comparison in terms of one hour: in one hour you travel 15 miles, so your unit rate is 15 miles per hour. Other examples are how much one ounce of food costs (price per ounce) or figuring out how much one egg costs out of the dozen (price per 1 egg, instead of price per 12 eggs). The denominator of a unit rate is always 1. Unit rates are used to compare different situations to solve problems. For example, to make sure you get the best deal when deciding which kind of soda to buy, you can find the unit rate of each. If soda #1 costs $1.50 for a 1-liter bottle, and soda #2 costs $2.75 for a 2-liter bottle, it would be a better deal to buy soda #2, because its unit rate is only $1.375 per 1-liter, which is cheaper than soda #1. Unit rates can also help determine the length of time a given event will take. For example, if you can paint 2 rooms in 4.5 hours, you can determine how long it will take you to paint 5 rooms by solving for the unit rate per room and then multiplying that by 5.

Review Video: Rates and Unit Rates
Visit mometrix.com/academy and enter code: 185363

SLOPE

On a graph with two points, (x_1, y_1) and (x_2, y_2), the **slope** is found with the formula $m = \frac{y_2 - y_1}{x_2 - x_1}$; where $x_1 \neq x_2$ and m stands for slope. If the value of the slope is **positive**, the line has an *upward direction* from left to right. If the value of the slope is **negative**, the line has a *downward direction* from left to right. Consider the following example:

A new book goes on sale in bookstores and online stores. In the first month, 5,000 copies of the book are sold. Over time, the book continues to grow in popularity. The data for the number of copies sold is in the table below.

# of Months on Sale	1	2	3	4	5
# of Copies Sold (In Thousands)	5	10	15	20	25

So, the number of copies that are sold and the time that the book is on sale is a proportional relationship. In this example, an equation can be used to show the data: $y = 5x$, where x is the number of months that the book is on sale, and y is the number of copies sold. So the slope of the corresponding line is $\frac{\text{rise}}{\text{run}} = \frac{5}{1} = 5$.

Review Video: Finding the Slope of a Line
Visit mometrix.com/academy and enter code: 766664

FINDING AN UNKNOWN IN EQUIVALENT EXPRESSIONS

It is often necessary to apply information given about a rate or proportion to a new scenario. For example, if you know that Jedha can run a marathon (26 miles) in 3 hours, how long would it take her to run 10 miles at the same pace? Start by setting up equivalent expressions:

$$\frac{26 \text{ mi}}{3 \text{ hr}} = \frac{10 \text{ mi}}{x \text{ hr}}$$

Now, cross multiply and, solve for x:

$$26x = 30$$
$$x = \frac{30}{26} = \frac{15}{13}$$
$$x \cong 1.15 \text{ hrs } or \text{ 1 hr 9 min}$$

So, at this pace, Jedha could run 10 miles in about 1.15 hours or about 1 hour and 9 minutes.

PRACTICE

P1. Solve the following for x.

(a) $\frac{45}{12} = \frac{15}{x}$

(b) $\frac{0.50}{2} = \frac{1.50}{x}$

(c) $\frac{40}{8} = \frac{x}{24}$

P2. At a school, for every 20 female students there are 15 male students. This same student ratio happens to exist at another school. If there are 100 female students at the second school, how many male students are there?

P3. In a hospital emergency room, there are 4 nurses for every 12 patients. What is the ratio of nurses to patients? If the nurse-to-patient ratio remains constant, how many nurses must be present to care for 24 patients?

P4. In a bank, the banker-to-customer ratio is 1:2. If seven bankers are on duty, how many customers are currently in the bank?

P5. Janice made $40 during the first 5 hours she spent babysitting. She will continue to earn money at this rate until she finishes babysitting in 3 more hours. Find how much money Janice earns per hour and the total she earned babysitting.

P6. The McDonalds are taking a family road trip, driving 300 miles to their cabin. It took them 2 hours to drive the first 120 miles. They will drive at the same speed all the way to their cabin. Find the speed at which the McDonalds are driving and how much longer it will take them to get to their cabin.

P7. It takes Andy 10 minutes to read 6 pages of his book. He has already read 150 pages in his book that is 210 pages long. Find how long it takes Andy to read 1 page and also find how long it will take him to finish his book if he continues to read at the same speed.

PRACTICE SOLUTIONS

P1. First, cross multiply; then, solve for x:

(a)
$$45x = 12 \times 15$$
$$45x = 180$$
$$x = \frac{180}{45} = 4$$

(b)
$$0.5x = 1.5 \times 2$$
$$0.5x = 3$$
$$x = \frac{3}{0.5} = 6$$

(c)
$$8x = 40 \times 24$$
$$8x = 960$$
$$x = \frac{960}{8} = 120$$

P2. One way to find the number of male students is to set up and solve a proportion.

$$\frac{\text{number of female students}}{\text{number of male students}} = \frac{20}{15} = \frac{100}{\text{number of male students}}$$

Represent the unknown number of male students as the variable x: $\frac{20}{15} = \frac{100}{x}$

Cross multiply and then solve for x:

$$20x = 15 \times 100$$
$$x = \frac{1500}{20}$$
$$x = 75$$

P3. The ratio of nurses to patients can be written as 4 to 12, 4:12, or $\frac{4}{12}$. Because four and twelve have a common factor of four, the ratio should be reduced to 1:3, which means that there is one nurse present for every three patients. If this ratio remains constant, there must be eight nurses present to care for 24 patients.

P4. Use proportional reasoning or set up a proportion to solve. Because there are twice as many customers as bankers, there must be fourteen customers when seven bankers are on duty. Setting up and solving a proportion gives the same result:

$$\frac{\text{number of bankers}}{\text{number of customers}} = \frac{1}{2} = \frac{7}{\text{number of customers}}$$

Represent the unknown number of customers as the variable x: $\frac{1}{2} = \frac{7}{x}$.

To solve for x, cross multiply: $1 \times x = 7 \times 2$, so $x = 14$.

P5. Janice earns \$8 per hour. This can be found by taking her initial amount earned, \$40, and dividing it by the number of hours worked, 5. Since $\frac{40}{5} = 8$, Janice makes \$8 in one hour. This can also be found by finding the unit rate, money earned per hour: $\frac{40}{5} = \frac{x}{1}$. Since cross multiplying yields $5x = 40$, and division by 5 shows that $x = 8$, Janice earns \$8 per hour.

Janice will earn \$64 babysitting in her 8 total hours (adding the first 5 hours to the remaining 3 gives the 8-hour total). Since Janice earns \$8 per hour and she worked 8 hours, $\frac{\$8}{\text{hr}} \times 8 \text{ hrs} = \$64$. This can also be found by setting up a proportion comparing money earned to babysitting hours. Since she earns \$40 for 5 hours and since the rate is constant, she will earn a proportional amount in 8 hours: $\frac{40}{5} = \frac{x}{8}$. Cross multiplying will yield $5x = 320$, and division by 5 shows that $x = 64$.

P6. The McDonalds are driving 60 miles per hour. This can be found by setting up a proportion to find the unit rate, the number of miles they drive per one hour: $\frac{120}{2} = \frac{x}{1}$. Cross multiplying yields $2x = 120$ and division by 2 shows that $x = 60$.

Since the McDonalds will drive this same speed for the remaining miles, it will take them another 3 hours to get to their cabin. This can be found by first finding how many miles the McDonalds have left to drive, which is $300 - 120 = 180$. The McDonalds are driving at 60 miles per hour, so a proportion can be set up to determine how many hours it will take them to drive 180 miles: $\frac{180}{x} =$

$\frac{60}{1}$. Cross multiplying yields $60x = 180$, and division by 60 shows that $x = 3$. This can also be found by using the formula $D = r \times t$ (or distance = rate × time), where $180 = 60 \times t$, and division by 60 shows that $t = 3$.

P7. It takes Andy 10 minutes to read 6 pages, $\frac{10}{6} = 1\frac{2}{3}$ minutes, which is 1 minute and 40 seconds.

Next, determine how many pages Andy has left to read, $210 - 150 = 60$. Since it is now known that it takes him $1\frac{2}{3}$ minutes to read each page, then that rate must be multiplied by however many pages he has left to read (60) to find the time he'll need: $60 \times 1\frac{2}{3} = 100$, so it will take him 100 minutes, or 1 hour and 40 minutes, to read the rest of his book.

Geometry

Lines and Planes

A **point** is a fixed location in space, has no size or dimensions, and is commonly represented by a dot. A **line** is a set of points that extends infinitely in two opposite directions. It has length, but no width or depth. A line can be defined by any two distinct points that it contains. A **line segment** is a portion of a line that has definite endpoints. A **ray** is a portion of a line that extends from a single point on that line in one direction along the line. It has a definite beginning, but no ending.

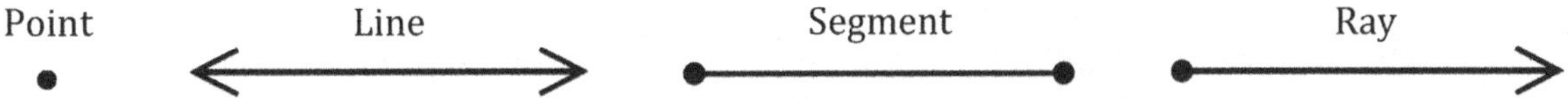

Intersecting lines are lines that have exactly one point in common. **Concurrent lines** are multiple lines that intersect at a single point. **Perpendicular lines** are lines that intersect at right angles. They are represented by the symbol ⊥. The shortest distance from a line to a point not on the line is a perpendicular segment from the point to the line. **Parallel lines** are lines in the same plane that have no points in common and never meet. It is possible for lines to be in different planes, have no points in common, and never meet, but they are not parallel because they are in different planes.

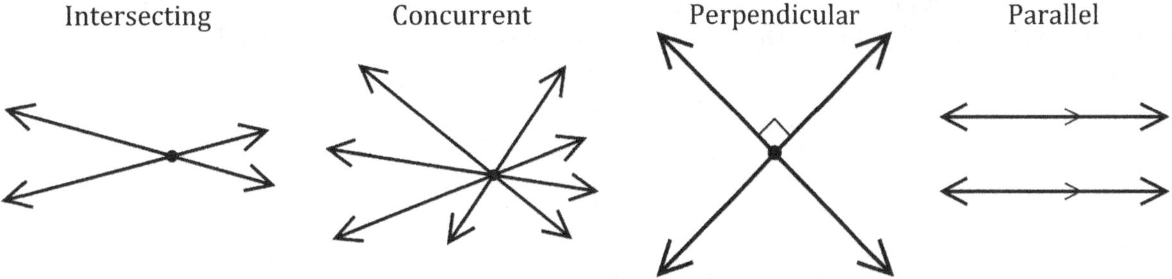

A **transversal** is a line that intersects at least two other lines, which may or may not be parallel to one another. A transversal that intersects parallel lines is a common occurrence in geometry. A **bisector** is a line or line segment that divides another line segment into two equal lengths. A

perpendicular bisector of a line segment is composed of points that are equidistant from the endpoints of the segment it is dividing.

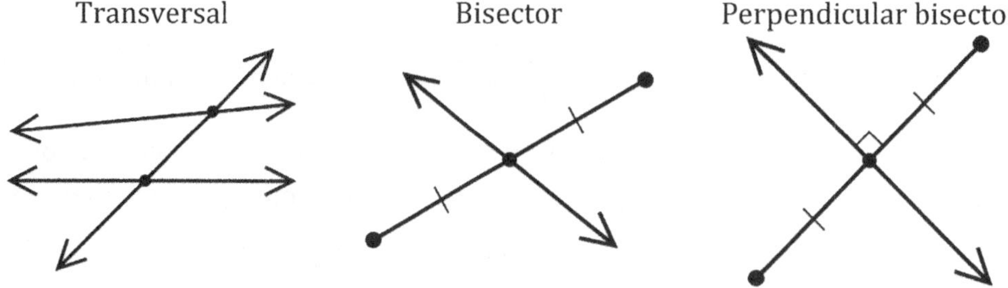

The **projection of a point on a line** is the point at which a perpendicular line drawn from the given point to the given line intersects the line. This is also the shortest distance from the given point to the line. The **projection of a segment on a line** is a segment whose endpoints are the points formed when perpendicular lines are drawn from the endpoints of the given segment to the given line. This is similar to the length a diagonal line appears to be when viewed from above.

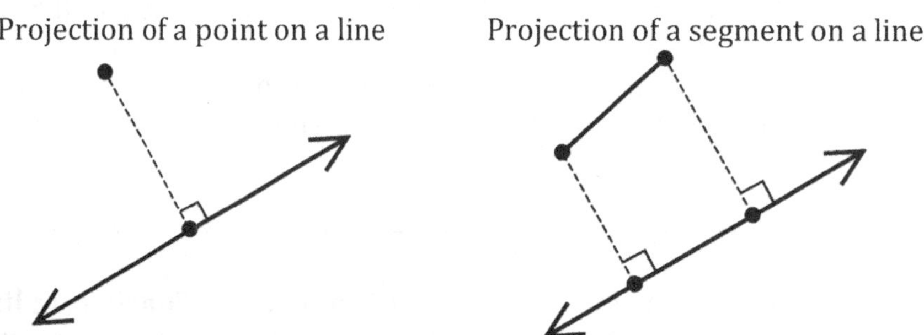

A **plane** is a two-dimensional flat surface defined by three non-collinear points. A plane extends an infinite distance in all directions in those two dimensions. It contains an infinite number of points, parallel lines and segments, intersecting lines and segments, as well as parallel or intersecting rays. A plane will never contain a three-dimensional figure or skew lines, which are lines that don't intersect and are not parallel. Two given planes are either parallel or they intersect at a line. A plane may intersect a circular conic surface to form **conic sections**, such as a parabola, hyperbola, circle or ellipse.

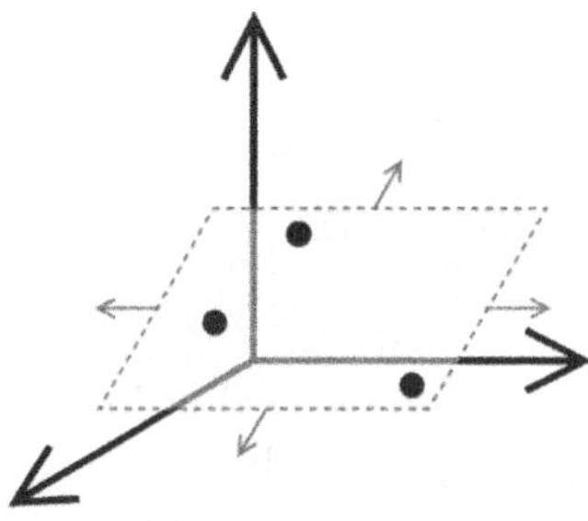

Review Video: Lines and Planes
Visit mometrix.com/academy and enter code: 554267

ANGLES

An **angle** is formed when two lines or line segments meet at a common point. It may be a common starting point for a pair of segments or rays, or it may be the intersection of lines. Angles are represented by the symbol ∠.

The **vertex** is the point at which two segments or rays meet to form an angle. If the angle is formed by intersecting rays, lines, and/or line segments, the vertex is the point at which four angles are formed. The pairs of angles opposite one another are called vertical angles, and their measures are equal.

- An **acute** angle is an angle with a degree measure less than 90°.
- A **right** angle is an angle with a degree measure of exactly 90°.
- An **obtuse** angle is an angle with a degree measure greater than 90° but less than 180°.
- A **straight angle** is an angle with a degree measure of exactly 180°. This is also a semicircle.
- A **reflex angle** is an angle with a degree measure greater than 180° but less than 360°.

A **full angle** is an angle with a degree measure of exactly 360°. This is also a circle.

Review Video: Angles
Visit mometrix.com/academy and enter code: 264624

Two angles whose sum is exactly 90° are said to be **complementary**. The two angles may or may not be adjacent. In a right triangle, the two acute angles are complementary.

Two angles whose sum is exactly 180° are said to be **supplementary**. The two angles may or may not be adjacent. Two intersecting lines always form two pairs of supplementary angles. Adjacent supplementary angles will always form a straight line.

Two angles that have the same vertex and share a side are said to be **adjacent**. Vertical angles are not adjacent because they share a vertex but no common side.

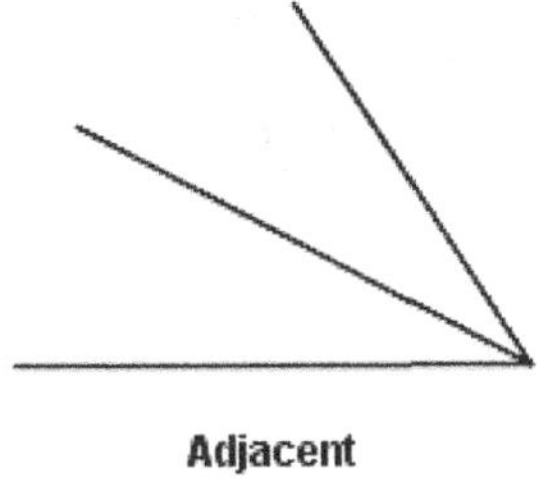

Adjacent
Share vertex and side

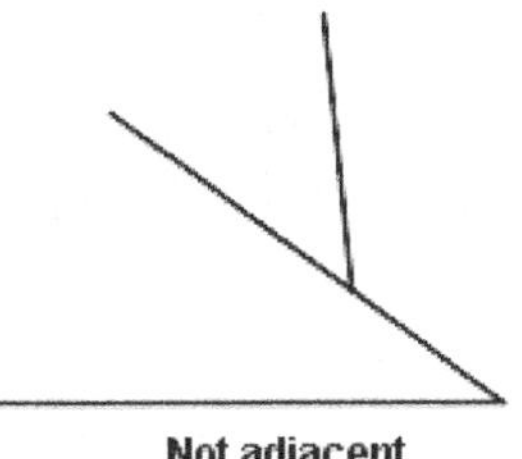

Not adjacent
Share part of side, but not vertex

When two parallel lines are cut by a transversal, the angles that are between the two parallel lines are **interior angles**. In the diagram below, angles 3, 4, 5, and 6 are interior angles.

When two parallel lines are cut by a transversal, the angles that are outside the parallel lines are **exterior angles**. In the diagram below, angles 1, 2, 7, and 8 are exterior angles.

When two parallel lines are cut by a transversal, the angles that are in the same position relative to the transversal and a parallel line are **corresponding angles**. The diagram below has four pairs of corresponding angles: angles 1 and 5; angles 2 and 6; angles 3 and 7; and angles 4 and 8. Corresponding angles formed by parallel lines are congruent.

When two parallel lines are cut by a transversal, the two interior angles that are on opposite sides of the transversal are called **alternate interior angles**. In the diagram below, there are two pairs of alternate interior angles: angles 3 and 6, and angles 4 and 5. Alternate interior angles formed by parallel lines are congruent.

When two parallel lines are cut by a transversal, the two exterior angles that are on opposite sides of the transversal are called **alternate exterior angles**.

In the diagram below, there are two pairs of alternate exterior angles: angles 1 and 8, and angles 2 and 7. Alternate exterior angles formed by parallel lines are congruent.

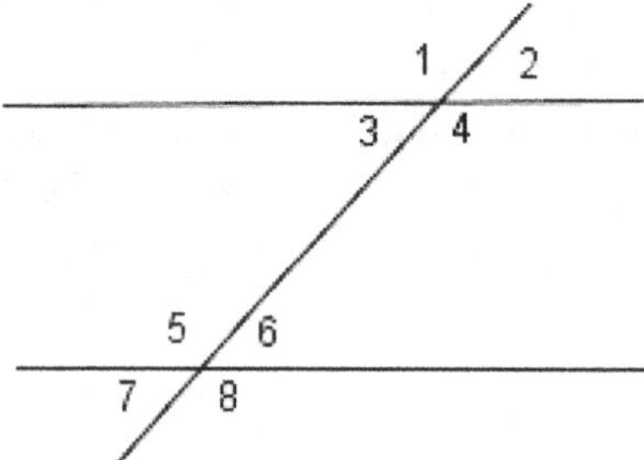

When two lines intersect, four angles are formed. The non-adjacent angles at this vertex are called vertical angles. Vertical angles are congruent. In the diagram, $\angle ABD \cong \angle CBE$ and $\angle ABC \cong \angle DBE$.

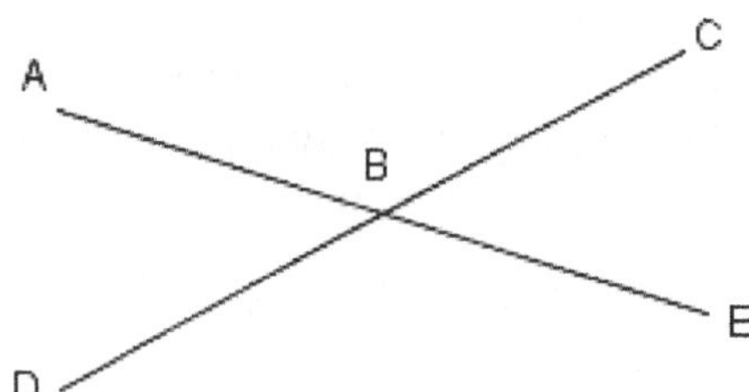

Practice

P1. Find the measure of angles **(a)**, **(b)**, and **(c)** based on the figure with two parallel lines, two perpendicular lines and one transversal:

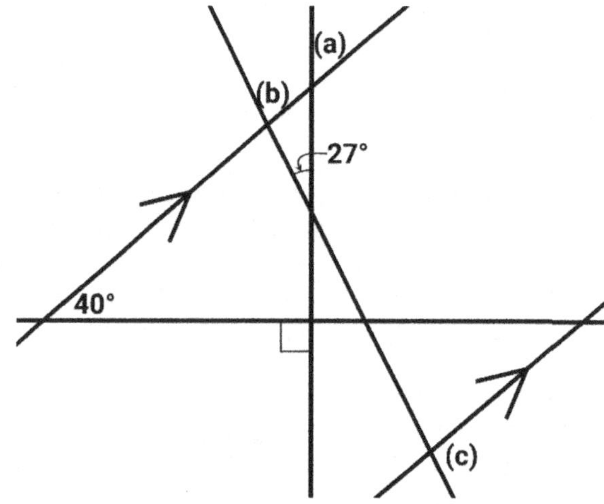

Practice Solutions

P1. (a) The vertical angle paired with (a) is part of a right triangle with the 40° angle. Thus the measure can be found:

$$\begin{aligned} 90^\circ &= 40^\circ + a \\ a &= 50^\circ \end{aligned}$$

(b) The triangle formed by the supplementary angle to (b) is part of a triangle with the vertical angle paired with (a) and the given angle of 27°. Since $a = 50^\circ$:

$$\begin{aligned} 180^\circ &= (180^\circ - b) + 50^\circ + 27^\circ \\ 103^\circ &= 180^\circ - b \\ -77^\circ &= -b \\ 77^\circ &= b \end{aligned}$$

(c) As they are part of a transversal crossing parallel lines, angles (b) and (c) are supplementary. Thus $c = 103^\circ$

$$V = \frac{1}{3}\pi r^2 h = \frac{1}{3}\pi(5\text{ yd})^2(7\text{ yd}) = \frac{35\pi}{3}\text{ yd}^3 \cong 36.65\text{ yd}^3$$

Two-Dimensional Shapes

Polygons

A **polygon** is a closed, two-dimensional figure with three or more straight line segments called **sides**. The point at which two sides of a polygon intersect is called the **vertex**. In a polygon, the number of sides is always equal to the number of vertices. A polygon with all sides congruent and all angles equal is called a **regular polygon**. Common polygons are:

Triangle = 3 sides
Quadrilateral = 4 sides
Pentagon = 5 sides
Hexagon = 6 sides
Heptagon = 7 sides
Octagon = 8 sides
Nonagon = 9 sides
Decagon = 10 sides
Dodecagon = 12 sides

More generally, an n-gon is a polygon that has n angles and n sides.

The sum of the interior angles of an n-sided polygon is $(n - 2) \times 180^\circ$. For example, in a triangle $n = 3$. So the sum of the interior angles is $(3 - 2) \times 180^\circ = 180^\circ$. In a quadrilateral, $n = 4$, and the sum of the angles is $(4 - 2) \times 180^\circ = 360^\circ$.

A line segment from the center of a polygon that is perpendicular to a side of the polygon is called the **apothem**. A line segment from the center of a polygon to a vertex of the polygon is called a

radius. In a regular polygon, the apothem can be used to find the area of the polygon using the formula $A = \frac{1}{2}ap$, where a is the apothem, and p is the perimeter.

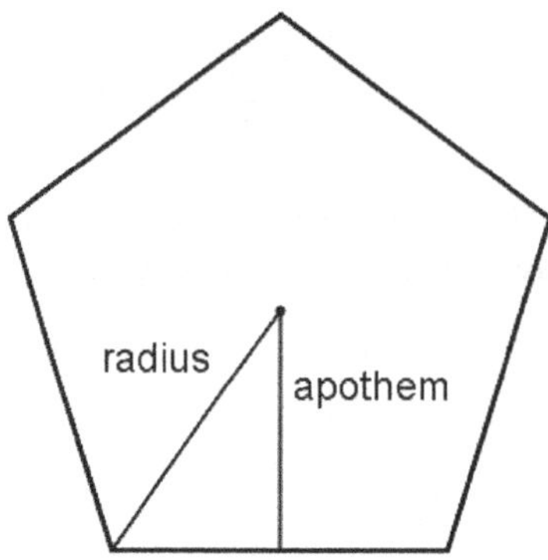

A **diagonal** is a line segment that joins two non-adjacent vertices of a polygon. The number of diagonals a polygon has can be found by using the formula:

$$\text{number of diagonals} = \frac{n(n-3)}{2}$$

Note that n is the number of sides in the polygon. This formula works for all polygons, not just regular polygons.

A **convex polygon** is a polygon whose diagonals all lie within the interior of the polygon. A **concave polygon** is a polygon with a least one diagonal that is outside the polygon. In the diagram below, quadrilateral $ABCD$ is concave because diagonal $\overline{AC}$ lies outside the polygon and quadrilateral $EFGH$ is convex because both diagonals lie inside the polygon

Concave

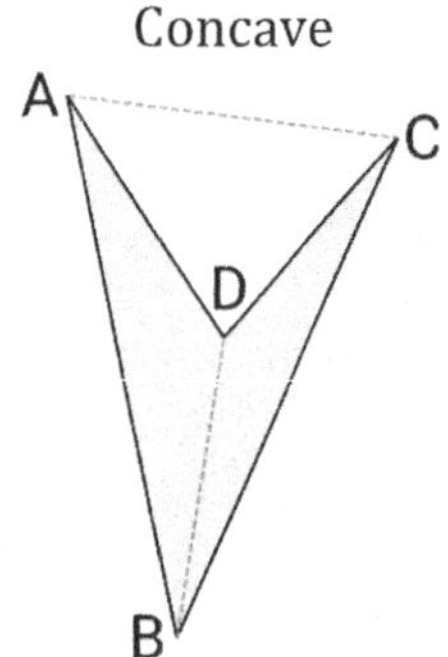

Convex

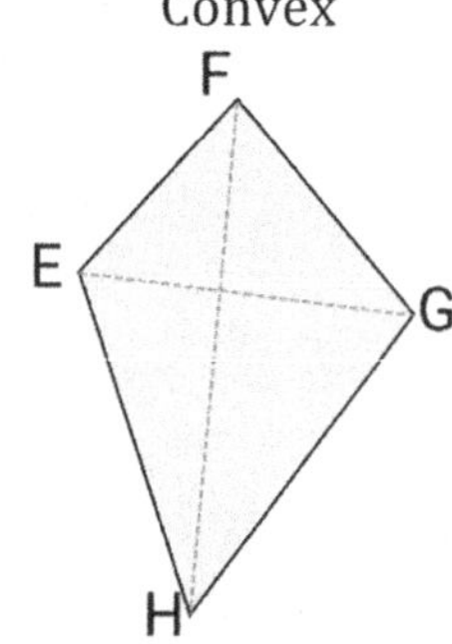

Congruent figures are geometric figures that have the same size and shape. All corresponding angles are equal, and all corresponding sides are equal. Congruence is indicated by the symbol $\cong$.

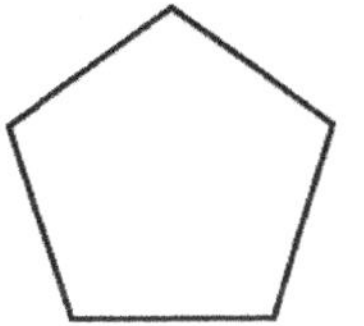
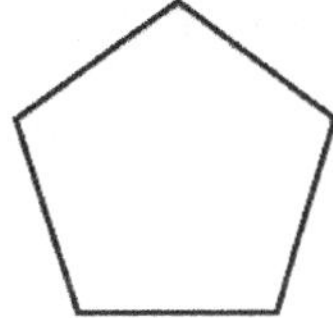

Congruent polygons

Similar figures are geometric figures that have the same shape, but do not necessarily have the same size. All corresponding angles are equal, and all corresponding sides are proportional, but they do not have to be equal. It is indicated by the symbol $\sim$.

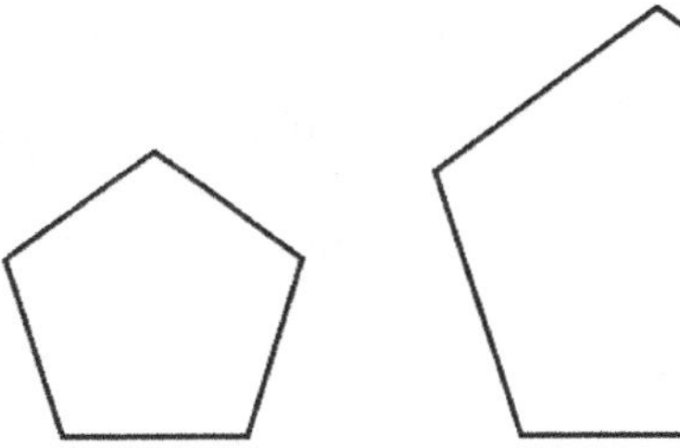

Similar polygons

Note that all congruent figures are also similar, but not all similar figures are congruent.

Review Video: Polygons
Visit mometrix.com/academy and enter code: 271869

Line of Symmetry

A line that divides a figure or object into congruent parts is called a **line of symmetry**. An object may have no lines of symmetry, one line of symmetry, or multiple (i.e., more than one) lines of symmetry.

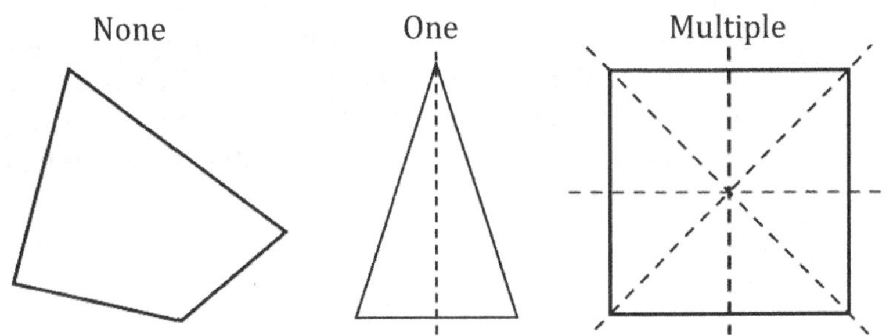

Review Video: Symmetry
Visit mometrix.com/academy and enter code: 528106

Triangles

A triangle is a three-sided figure with the sum of its interior angles being 180° The **perimeter of any triangle** is found by summing the three side lengths; $P = a + b + c$. For an equilateral triangle, this is the same as $P = 3a$, where a is any side length, since all three sides are the same length.

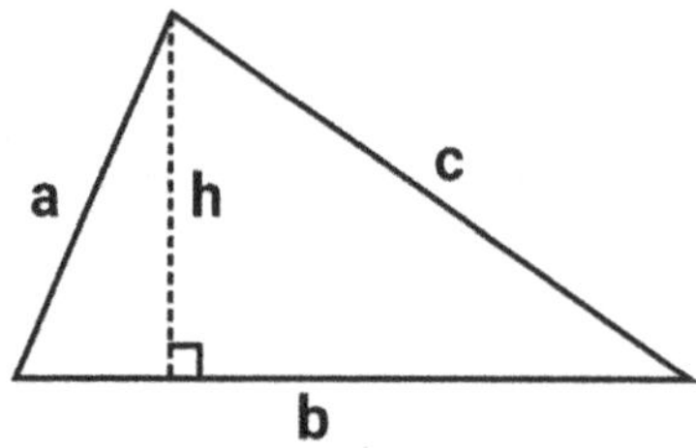

The **area of any triangle** can be found by taking half the product of one side length, referred to as the base and often given the variable b, and the perpendicular distance from that side to the opposite vertex, called the altitude or height and given the variable h. In equation form that is $A = \frac{1}{2}bh$. Another formula that works for any triangle is $A = \sqrt{s(s-a)(s-b)(s-c)}$, where s is the semiperimeter: $\frac{a+b+c}{2}$, and a, b, and c are the lengths of the three sides. Special cases include isosceles triangles: $A = \frac{1}{2}b\sqrt{a^2 - \frac{b^2}{4}}$, where b is the unique side and a is the length of one of the two congruent sides, and equilateral triangles: $A = \frac{\sqrt{3}}{4}a^2$, where a is the length of a side.

Review Video: Area and Perimeter of a Triangle
Visit mometrix.com/academy and enter code: 853779

Parts of a Triangle

An **altitude** of a triangle is a line segment drawn from one vertex perpendicular to the opposite side. In the diagram below, $\overline{BE}$, $\overline{AD}$, and $\overline{CF}$ are altitudes. The length of an altitude is also called the height of the triangle. The three altitudes in a triangle are always concurrent. The point of concurrency of the altitudes of a triangle, O, is called the **orthocenter**. Note that in an obtuse triangle, the orthocenter will be outside the triangle, and in a right triangle, the orthocenter is the vertex of the right angle.

A **median** of a triangle is a line segment drawn from one vertex to the midpoint of the opposite side. In the diagram below, $\overline{BH}$, $\overline{AG}$, and $\overline{CI}$ are medians. This is not the same as the altitude, except the altitude to the base of an isosceles triangle and all three altitudes of an equilateral triangle. The point of concurrency of the medians of a triangle, T, is called the **centroid**. This is the same point as the orthocenter only in an equilateral triangle. Unlike the orthocenter, the centroid is always inside the triangle. The centroid can also be considered the exact center of the triangle. Any shape triangle can be perfectly balanced on a tip placed at the centroid. The centroid is also the point that is two-thirds the distance from the vertex to the opposite side.

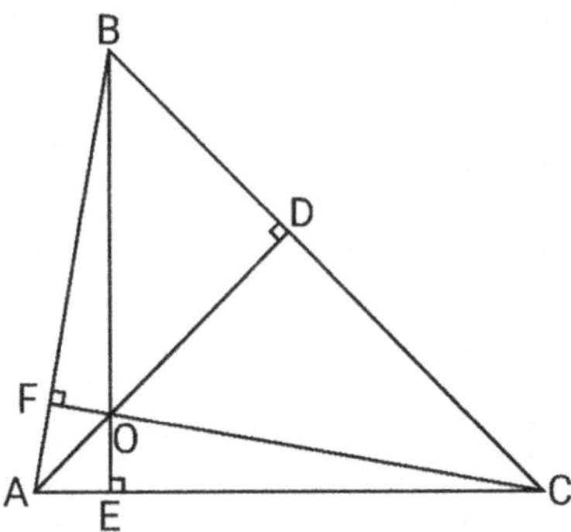

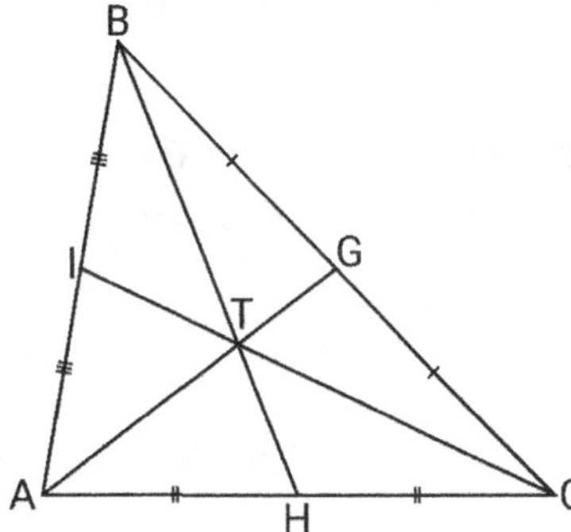

QUADRILATERALS

A **quadrilateral** is a closed two-dimensional geometric figure that has four straight sides. The sum of the interior angles of any quadrilateral is 360°.

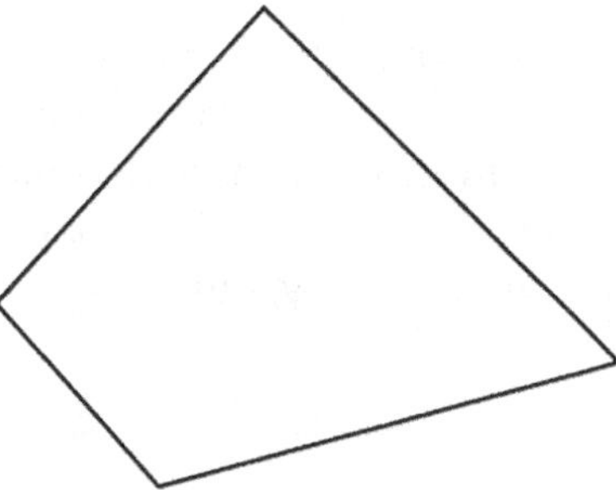

A **kite** is a quadrilateral with two pairs of adjacent sides that are congruent. A result of this is perpendicular diagonals. A kite can be concave or convex and has one line of symmetry.

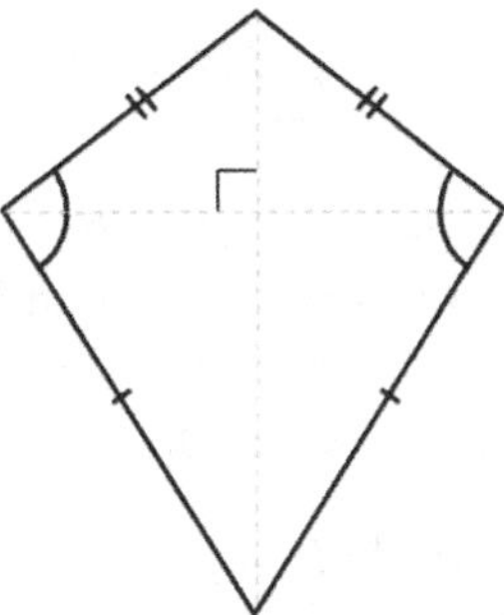

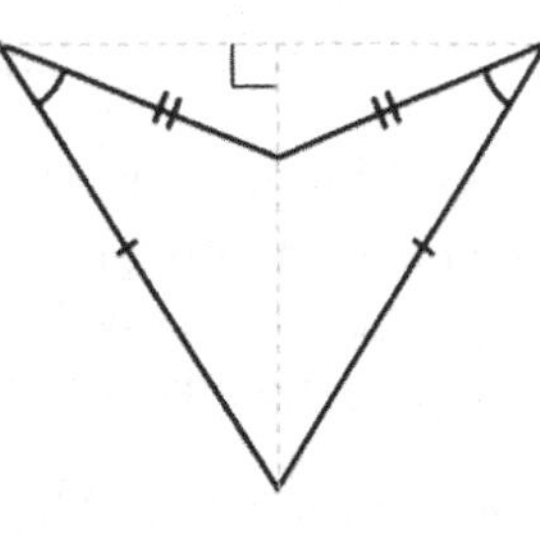

Trapezoid: A trapezoid is defined as a quadrilateral that has at least one pair of parallel sides. There are no rules for the second pair of sides. So there are no rules for the diagonals and no lines of symmetry for a trapezoid.

The **area of a trapezoid** is found by the formula $A = \frac{1}{2}h(b_1 + b_2)$, where h is the height (segment joining and perpendicular to the parallel bases), and b_1 and b_2 are the two parallel sides (bases). Do not use one of the other two sides as the height unless that side is also perpendicular to the parallel bases.

The **perimeter of a trapezoid** is found by the formula $P = a + b_1 + c + b_2$, where a, b_1, c, and b_2 are the four sides of the trapezoid.

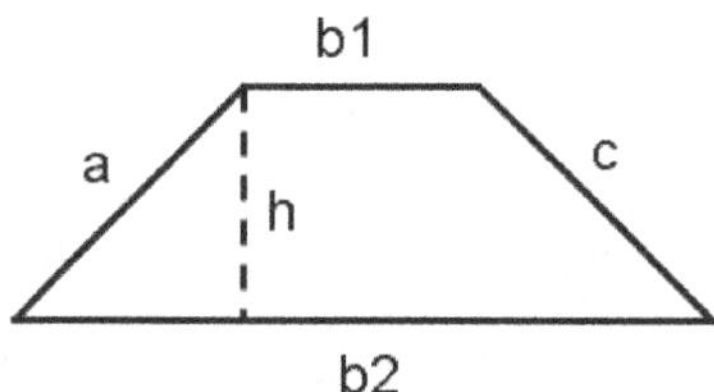

Review Video: Area and Perimeter of a Trapezoid
Visit mometrix.com/academy and enter code: 587523

Parallelogram: A quadrilateral that has two pairs of opposite parallel sides. As such it is a special type of trapezoid. The sides that are parallel are also congruent. The opposite interior angles are always congruent, and the consecutive interior angles are supplementary. The diagonals of a parallelogram divide each other. Each diagonal divides the parallelogram into two congruent triangles. A parallelogram has no line of symmetry, but does have 180-degree rotational symmetry about the midpoint.

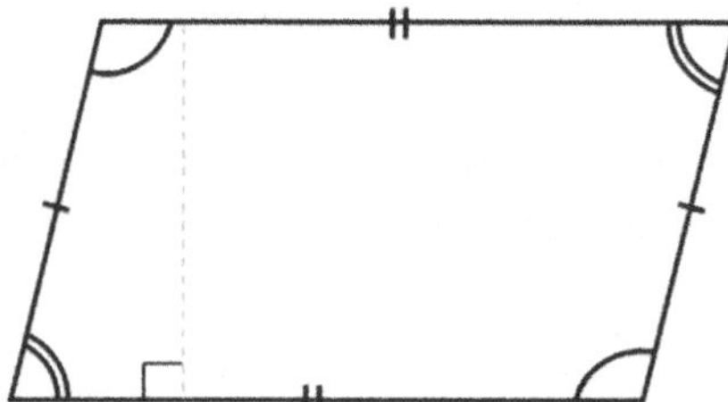

The **area of a parallelogram** is found by the formula $A = bh$, where b is the length of the base, and h is the height. Note that the base and height correspond to the length and width in a rectangle, so this formula would apply to rectangles as well. Do not confuse the height of a parallelogram with the length of the second side. The two are only the same measure in the case of a rectangle.

The **perimeter of a parallelogram** is found by the formula $P = 2a + 2b$ or $P = 2(a + b)$, where a and b are the lengths of the two sides.

Review Video: Area and Perimeter of a Parallelogram
Visit mometrix.com/academy and enter code: 718313

Isosceles trapezoid: A trapezoid with equal base angles. This gives rise to other properties including: the two nonparallel sides have the same length, the two non-base angles are also equal, and there is one line of symmetry through the midpoints of the parallel sides.

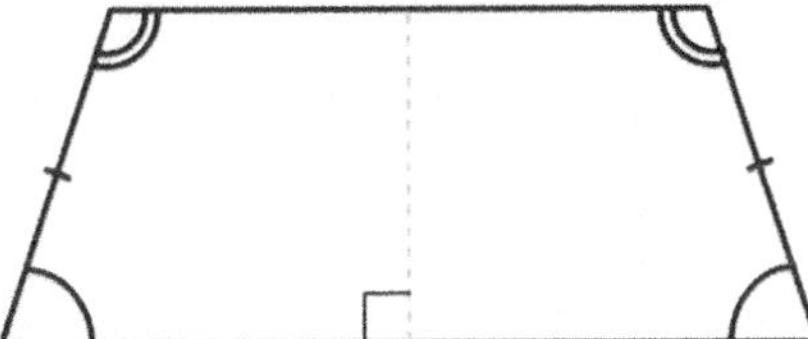

Rectangle: A quadrilateral with four right angles. All rectangles are parallelograms and trapezoids, but not all parallelograms or trapezoids are rectangles. The diagonals of a rectangle are congruent. Rectangles have 2 lines of symmetry (through each pair of opposing midpoints) and 180-degree rotational symmetry about the midpoint.

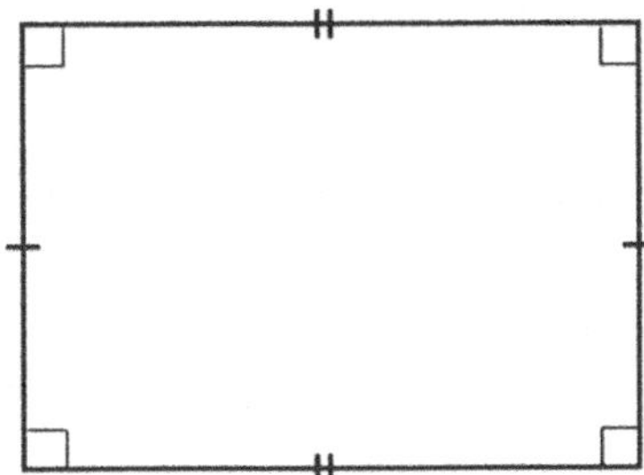

The **area of a rectangle** is found by the formula $A = lw$, where A is the area of the rectangle, l is the length (usually considered to be the longer side) and w is the width (usually considered to be the shorter side). The numbers for l and w are interchangeable.

The **perimeter of a rectangle** is found by the formula $P = 2l + 2w$ or $P = 2(l + w)$, where l is the length, and w is the width. It may be easier to add the length and width first and then double the result, as in the second formula.

Rhombus: A quadrilateral with four congruent sides. All rhombuses are parallelograms and kites; thus, they inherit all the properties of both types of quadrilaterals. The diagonals of a rhombus are perpendicular to each other. Rhombi have 2 lines of symmetry (along each of the diagonals) and 180-degree rotational symmetry. The **area of a rhombus** is half the product of the diagonals: $A = \frac{d_1 d_2}{2}$ and the perimeter of a rhombus is: $P = 2\sqrt{(d_1)^2 + (d_2)^2}$

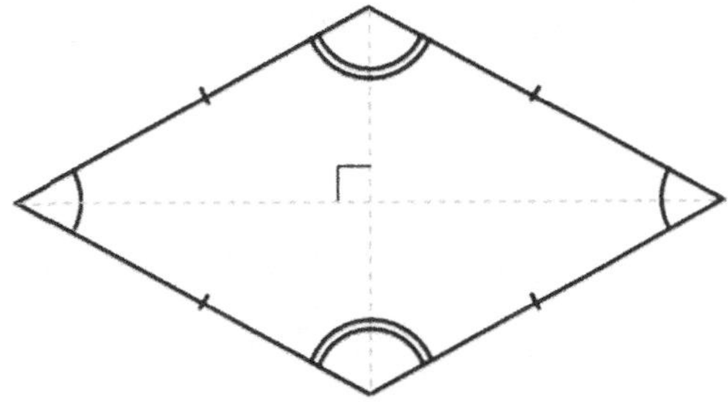

Review Video: Diagonals of Parallelograms, Rectangles, and Rhombi
Visit mometrix.com/academy and enter code: 320040

Square: A quadrilateral with four right angles and four congruent sides. Squares satisfy the criteria of all other types of quadrilaterals. The diagonals of a square are congruent and perpendicular to each other. Squares have 4 lines of symmetry (through each pair of opposing midpoints and along each of the diagonals) as well as 90-degree rotational symmetry about the midpoint.

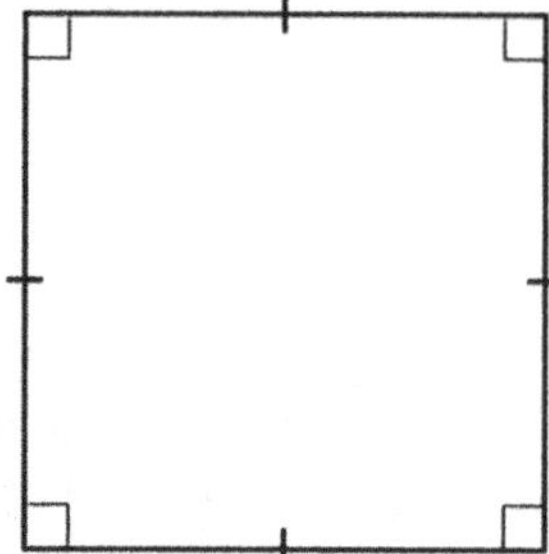

The **area of a square** is found by using the formula $A = s^2$, where s is the length of one side. The **perimeter of a square** is found by using the formula $P = 4s$, where s is the length of one side. Because all four sides are equal in a square, it is faster to multiply the length of one side by 4 than to add the same number four times. You could use the formulas for rectangles and get the same answer.

The hierarchy of quadrilaterals can be shown as follows:

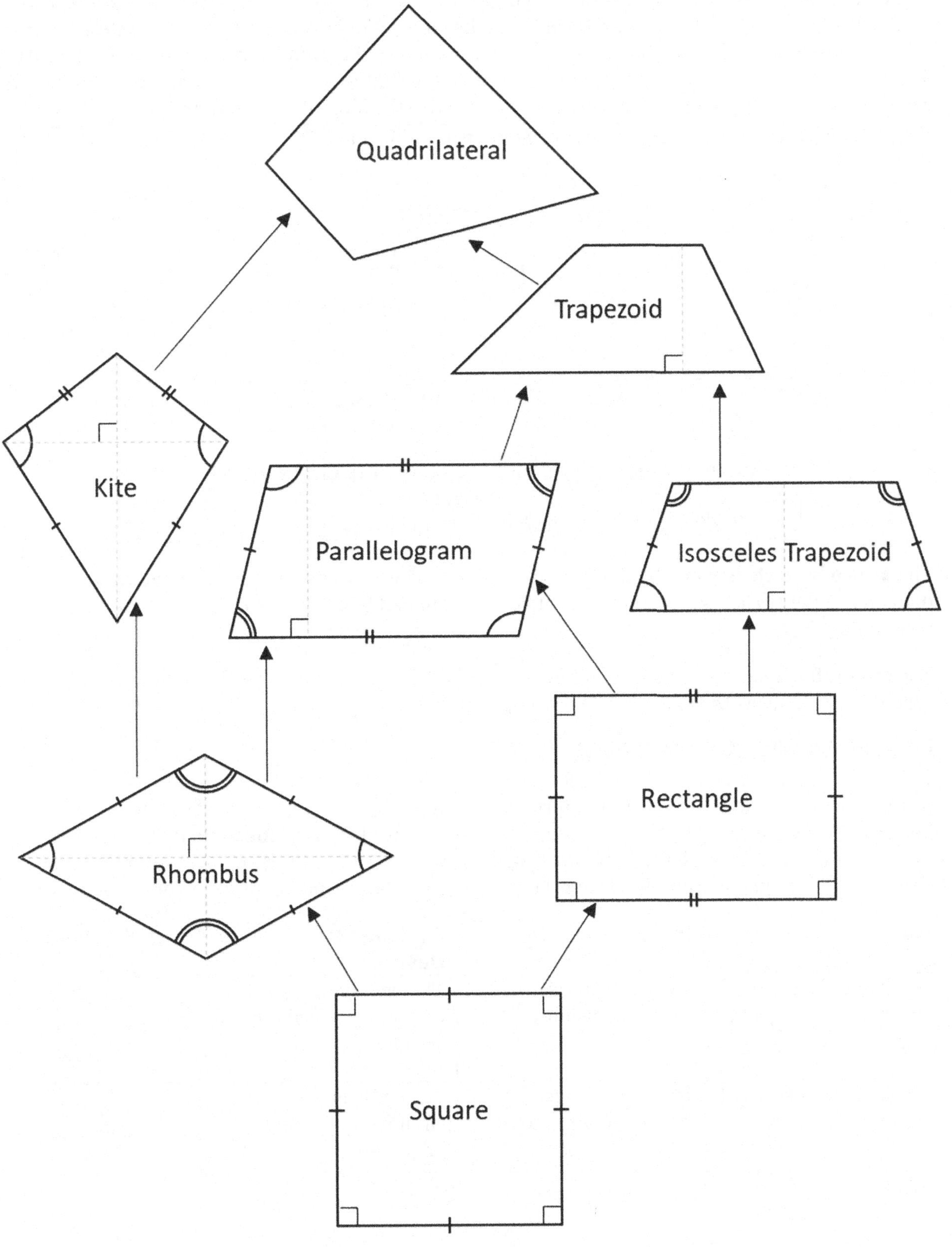

CIRCLES

The **center** of a circle is the single point from which every point on the circle is **equidistant**. The **radius** is a line segment that joins the center of the circle and any one point on the circle. All radii of a circle are equal. Circles that have the same center, but not the same length of radii are **concentric**. The **diameter** is a line segment that passes through the center of the circle and has both endpoints on the circle. The length of the diameter is exactly twice the length of the radius. Point O in the diagram below is the center of the circle, segments $\overline{OX}$, $\overline{OY}$, and $\overline{OZ}$ are radii, and segment $\overline{XZ}$ is a diameter.

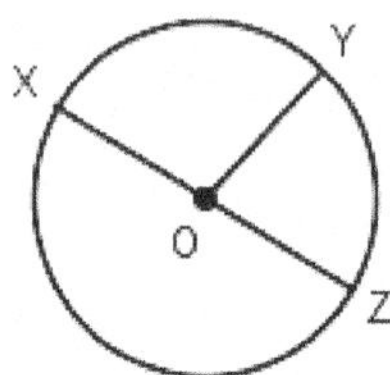

Review Video: Points of a Circle
Visit mometrix.com/academy and enter code: 420746

Review Video: The Diameter, Radius, and Circumference of Circles
Visit mometrix.com/academy and enter code: 448988

The **area of a circle** is found by the formula $A = \pi r^2$, where r is the length of the radius. If the diameter of the circle is given, remember to divide it in half to get the length of the radius before proceeding.

The **circumference** of a circle is found by the formula $C = 2\pi r$, where r is the radius. Again, remember to convert the diameter if you are given that measure rather than the radius.

INSCRIBED AND CIRCUMSCRIBED FIGURES

These terms can both be used to describe a given arrangement of figures, depending on perspective. If each of the vertices of figure A lie on figure B, then it can be said that figure A is **inscribed** in figure B, but it can also be said that figure B is **circumscribed** about figure A. The following table and examples help to illustrate the concept. Note that the figures cannot both be circles, as they would be completely overlapping and neither would be inscribed or circumscribed.

Given	Description	Equivalent Description	Figures
Each of the sides of a pentagon is tangent to a circle	The circle is inscribed in the pentagon	The pentagon is circumscribed about the circle	
Each of the vertices of a pentagon lie on a circle	The pentagon is inscribed in the circle	The circle is circumscribed about the pentagon	

PRACTICE

P1. Find the area and perimeter of the following quadrilaterals:

(a) A square with side length 2.5 cm.

(b) A parallelogram with height 3 m, base 4 m, and other side 6 m.

(c) A rhombus with diagonals 15 in and 20 in.

P2. Calculate the area of a triangle with side lengths of 7 ft, 8 ft, and 9 ft.

P3. Square ABCD is inscribed in a circle with radius 20 m. What is the area of the part of the circle outside of the square?

PRACTICE SOLUTIONS

P1. (a) $A = s^2 = (2.5\text{ cm})^2 = 6.25\text{ cm}^2$; $P = 4s = 4 \times 2.5\text{ cm} = 10\text{ cm}$

(b) $A = bh = (3\text{ m})(4\text{ m}) = 12\text{ m}^2$; $P = 2a + 2b = 2 \times 6\text{ m} + 2 \times 4\text{ m} = 20\text{ m}$

(c) $A = \frac{d_1 d_2}{2} = \frac{(15\text{ in})(20\text{ in})}{2} = 150\text{ in}^2$;
$P = 2\sqrt{(d_1)^2 + (d_2)^2} = 2\sqrt{(15\text{ in})^2 + (20\text{ in})^2} = 2\sqrt{625\text{ in}^2} = 50\text{ in}$

P2. Given only side lengths, we can use the semi perimeter to the find the area based on the formula, $A = \sqrt{s(s-a)(s-b)(s-c)}$, where s is the semiperimeter, $\frac{a+b+c}{2} = \frac{7+8+9}{2} = 12$ ft:

$$\begin{aligned} A &= \sqrt{12(12-7)(12-8)(12-9)} \\ &= \sqrt{(12)(5)(4)(3)} \\ &= 12\sqrt{5}\text{ ft}^2 \end{aligned}$$

P3. Begin by drawing a diagram of the situation, where we want to find the shaded area:

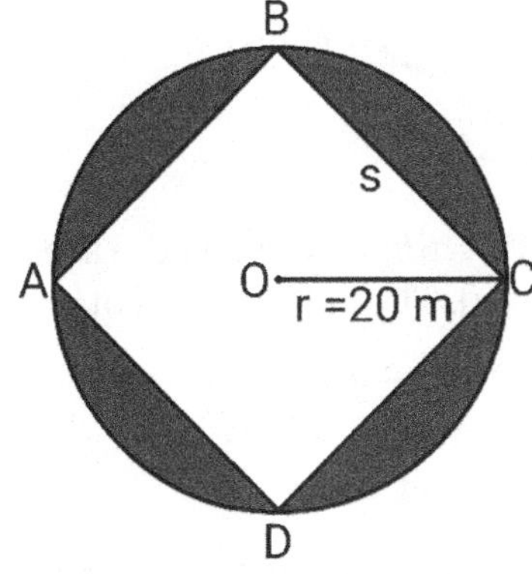

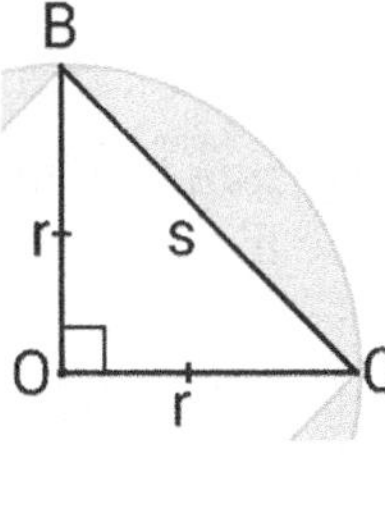

The area of the square is s^2, so the area we want to find is: $\pi r^2 - s^2$. Since the inscribed figure is a square, the triangle BCO is a 45-45-90 right triangle. Now we can find $s^2 = r^2 + r^2 = 2r^2$. So the shaded area is:

$$\begin{aligned} A &= \pi r^2 - s^2 \\ &= \pi r^2 - 2r^2 \\ &= (\pi - 2)r^2 \\ &= (\pi - 2) \times 400 \\ &\cong 456.6 \text{ m}^2 \end{aligned}$$

THREE-DIMENSIONAL SHAPES

SOLIDS

The **surface area of a solid object** is the area of all sides or exterior surfaces. For objects such as prisms and pyramids, a further distinction is made between base surface area (B) and lateral surface area (LA). For a prism, the total surface area (SA) is $SA = LA + 2B$. For a pyramid or cone, the total surface area is $SA = LA + B$.

Review Video: <u>**How to Calculate the Volume of 3D Objects**</u> Visit mometrix.com/academy and enter code: 163343

The **surface area of a sphere** can be found by the formula $A = 4\pi r^2$, where *r* is the radius. The volume is given by the formula $V = \frac{4}{3}\pi r^3$, where *r* is the radius. Both quantities are generally given in terms of π.

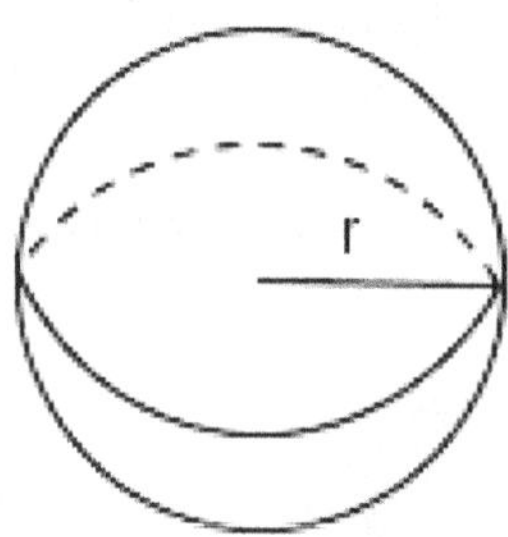

The **volume of any prism** is found by the formula $V = Bh$, where *B* is the area of the base, and *h* is the height (perpendicular distance between the bases). The surface area of any prism is the sum of the areas of both bases and all sides. It can be calculated as $SA = 2B + Ph$, where P is the perimeter of the base.

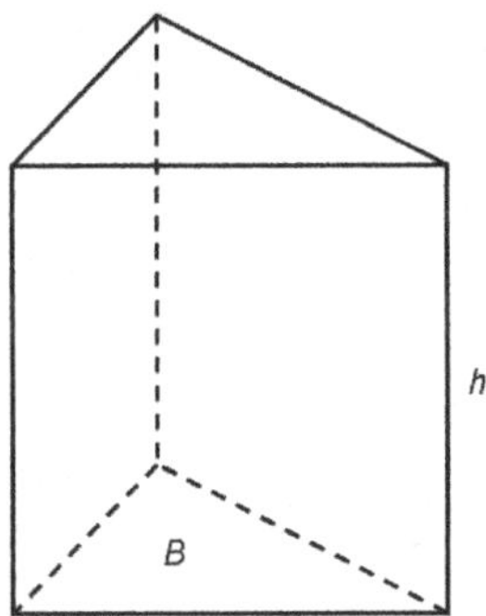

Review Video: Volume and Surface Area of a Prism
Visit mometrix.com/academy and enter code: 420158

For a **rectangular prism**, the volume can be found by the formula $V = lwh$, where V is the volume, l is the length, w is the width, and h is the height. The surface area can be calculated as $SA = 2lw + 2hl + 2wh$ or $SA = 2(lw + hl + wh)$.

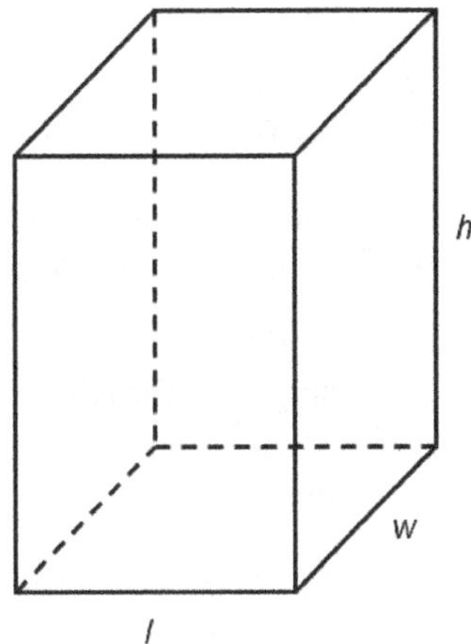

Review Video: Volume and Surface Area of a Rectangular Prism
Visit mometrix.com/academy and enter code: 282814

The **volume of a cube** can be found by the formula $V = s^3$, where s is the length of a side. The surface area of a cube is calculated as $SA = 6s^2$, where SA is the total surface area and s is the length of a side. These formulas are the same as the ones used for the volume and surface area of a rectangular prism, but simplified since all three quantities (length, width, and height) are the same.

Review Video: Volume and Surface Area of a Cube
Visit mometrix.com/academy and enter code: 664455

The **volume of a cylinder** can be calculated by the formula $V = \pi r^2 h$, where r is the radius, and h is the height. The surface area of a cylinder can be found by the formula $SA = 2\pi r^2 + 2\pi rh$. The first term is the base area multiplied by two, and the second term is the perimeter of the base multiplied by the height.

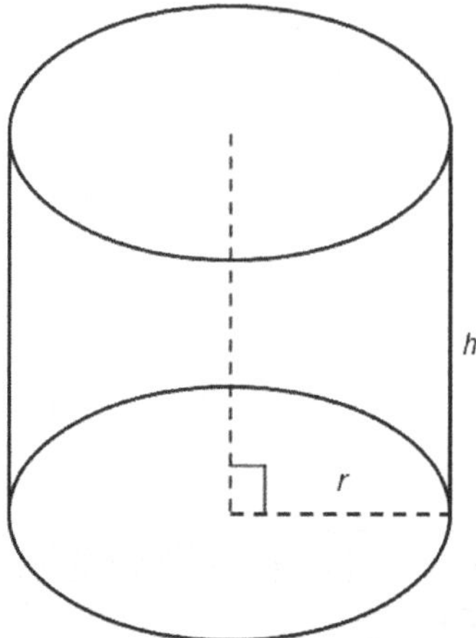

Review Video: Finding the Volume and Surface Area of a Right Circular Cylinder
Visit mometrix.com/academy and enter code: 226463

The **volume of a pyramid** is found by the formula $V = \frac{1}{3}Bh$, where B is the area of the base, and h is the height (perpendicular distance from the vertex to the base). Notice this formula is the same as $\frac{1}{3}$ times the volume of a prism. Like a prism, the base of a pyramid can be any shape.

Finding the **surface area of a pyramid** is not as simple as the other shapes we've looked at thus far. If the pyramid is a right pyramid, meaning the base is a regular polygon and the vertex is directly over the center of that polygon, the surface area can be calculated as $SA = B + \frac{1}{2}Ph_s$, where P is the perimeter of the base, and h_s is the slant height (distance from the vertex to the midpoint of one side of the base). If the pyramid is irregular, the area of each triangle side must be calculated individually and then summed, along with the base.

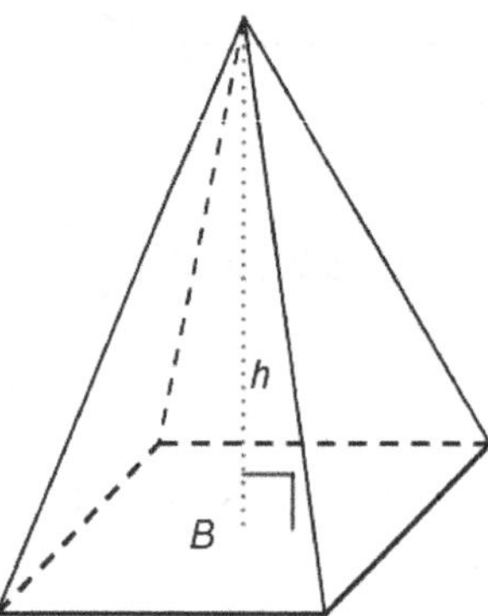

Review Video: Finding the Volume and Surface Area of a Pyramid
Visit mometrix.com/academy and enter code: 621932

The **volume of a cone** is found by the formula $V = \frac{1}{3}\pi r^2 h$, where r is the radius, and h is the height. Notice this is the same as $\frac{1}{3}$ times the volume of a cylinder. The surface area can be calculated as

$SA = \pi r^2 + \pi rs$, where s is the slant height. The slant height can be calculated using the Pythagorean theorem to be $\sqrt{r^2 + h^2}$, so the surface area formula can also be written as $SA = \pi r^2 + \pi r\sqrt{r^2 + h^2}$.

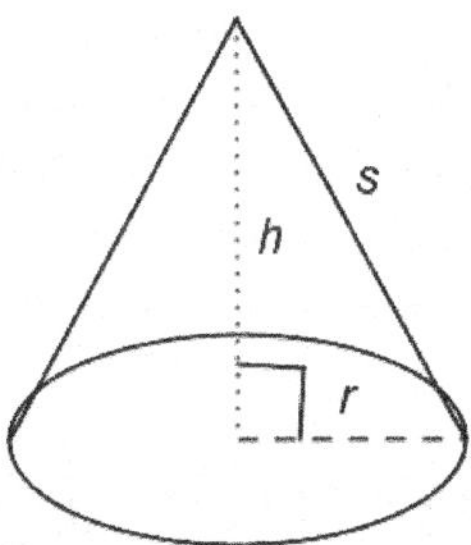

Review Video: Volume and Surface Area of a Right Circular Cone
Visit mometrix.com/academy and enter code: 573574

Practice

P1. Find the surface area and volume of the following solids:

(a) A cylinder with radius 5 m and height 0.5 m.

(b) A trapezoidal prism with base area of 254 mm^2, base perimeter 74 mm, and height 10 mm.

(c) A half sphere (radius 5 yds) on the base of an inverted cone with the same radius and a height of 7 yds.

Practice Solutions

P1. (a) $SA = 2\pi r^2 + 2\pi rh = 2\pi(5\text{ m})^2 + 2\pi(5\text{ m})(0.5\text{ m}) = 55\pi\text{ m}^2 \cong 172.79\text{ m}^2$;
$V = \pi r^2 h = \pi(5\text{ m})^2(0.5\text{ m}) = 12.5\pi\text{ m}^3 \cong 39.27\text{ m}^3$

(b) $SA = 2B + Ph = 2(254\text{ mm}^2) + (74\text{ mm})(10\text{ mm}) = 1248\text{ mm}^2$;
$V = Bh = (254\text{ mm}^2)(10\text{ mm}) = 2540\text{ mm}^3$

(c) We can find s, the slant height using the Pythagorean theorem, and since this solid is made of parts of simple solids, we can combine the formulas to find surface area and volume:

$$s = \sqrt{r^2 + h^2} = \sqrt{(5\text{ yd})^2 + (7\text{ yd})^2} = \sqrt{74}\text{ yd}$$

$$\begin{aligned} SA_{Total} &= (SA_{sphere})/2 + SA_{cone} - SA_{base} \\ &= \frac{4\pi r^2}{2} + (\pi rs + \pi r^2) - \pi r^2 \\ &= 2\pi(5\text{ yd})^2 + \pi(5\text{ yd})(\sqrt{74}\text{ yd}) \\ &= 5\pi(10 + \sqrt{74})\text{ yd}^2 \\ &\cong 292.20\text{ yd}^2 \end{aligned}$$

$$\begin{aligned} V_{Total} &= (V_{sphere})/2 + V_{cone} \\ &= \frac{\frac{4}{3}\pi r^3}{2} + \frac{1}{3}\pi r^2 h \\ &= \frac{2}{3}\pi(5\text{ yd})^3 + \frac{1}{3}\pi(5\text{ yd})^2(7\text{ yd}) \\ &= \frac{5^2 \times \pi}{3}(10 + 7)\text{ yd}^3 \\ &\cong 445.06\text{ yd}^3 \end{aligned}$$

Triangle Classification and Properties

A **scalene triangle** is a triangle with no congruent sides. A scalene triangle will also have three angles of different measures. The angle with the largest measure is opposite the longest side, and the angle with the smallest measure is opposite the shortest side. An **acute triangle** is a triangle whose three angles are all less than 90°. If two of the angles are equal, the acute triangle is also an **isosceles triangle**. An isosceles triangle will also have two congruent angles opposite the two congruent sides. If the three angles are all equal, the acute triangle is also an **equilateral triangle**. An equilateral triangle will also have three congruent angles, each 60°. All equilateral triangles are also acute triangles. An **obtuse triangle** is a triangle with exactly one angle greater than 90°. The other two angles may or may not be equal. If the two remaining angles are equal, the obtuse triangle is also an isosceles triangle. A **right triangle** is a triangle with exactly one angle equal to 90°. All right triangles follow the Pythagorean theorem. A right triangle can never be acute or obtuse.

The table below illustrates how each descriptor places a different restriction on the triangle:

Angles / Sides	**Acute: All angles < 90°**	**Obtuse: One angle > 90°**	**Right: One angle = 90°**
Scalene: No equal side lengths	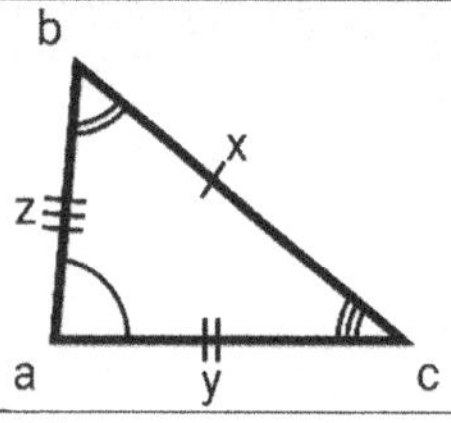 $90° > \angle a > \angle b > \angle c$ $x > y > z$	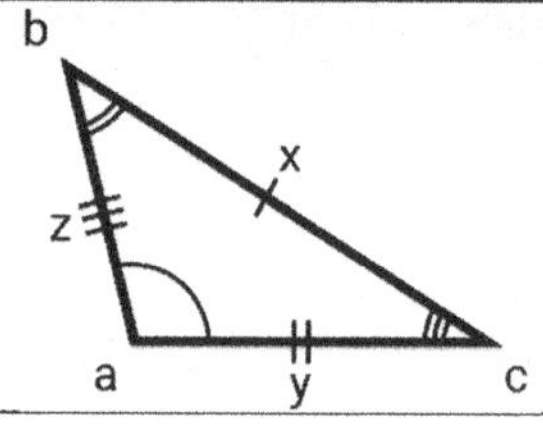 $\angle a > 90° > \angle b > \angle c$ $x > y > z$	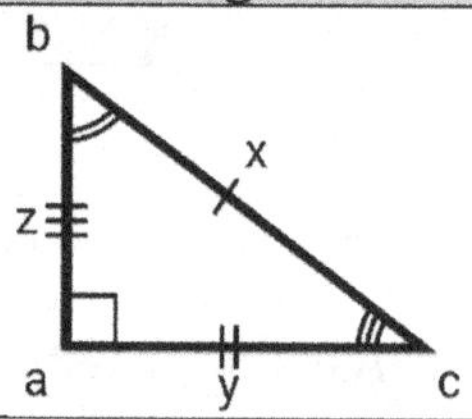 $90° = \angle a > \angle b > \angle c$ $x > y > z$
Isosceles: Two equal side lengths	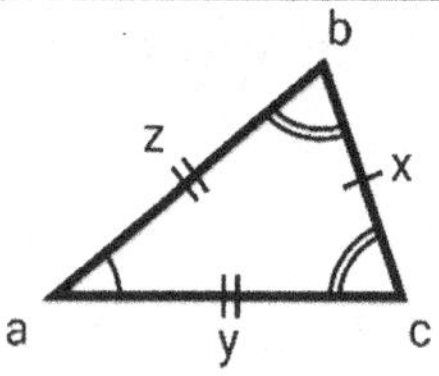 $90° > \angle a, \angle b, or\ \angle c$ $\angle b = \angle c, \quad y = z$	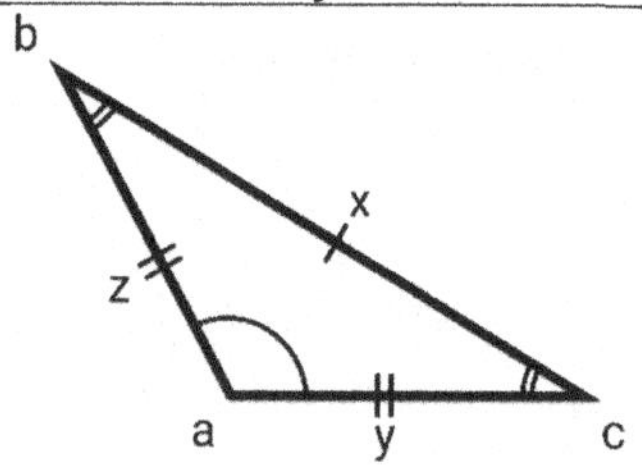 $\angle a > 90° > \angle b = \angle c$ $x > y = z$	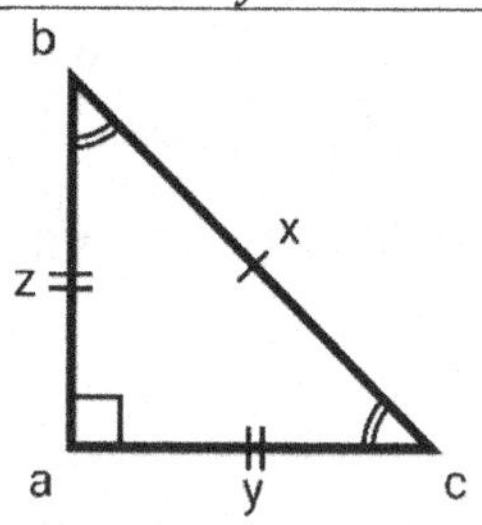 $\angle a = 90°, \angle b = \angle c = 45°$ $x > y = z$
Equilateral: Three equal side lengths	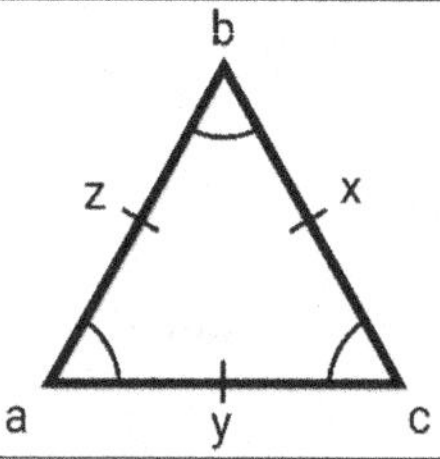 $60° = \angle a = \angle b = \angle c$ $x = y = z$		

Review Video: Introduction to Types of Triangles
Visit mometrix.com/academy and enter code: 511711

Similarity and Congruence Rules

Similar triangles are triangles whose corresponding angles are equal and whose corresponding sides are proportional. Represented by AAA. Similar triangles whose corresponding sides are congruent are also congruent triangles.

Triangles can be shown to be **congruent** in 5 ways:

- **SSS**: Three sides of one triangle are congruent to the three corresponding sides of the second triangle.
- **SAS**: Two sides and the included angle (the angle formed by those two sides) of one triangle are congruent to the corresponding two sides and included angle of the second triangle.
- **ASA**: Two angles and the included side (the side that joins the two angles) of one triangle are congruent to the corresponding two angles and included side of the second triangle.
- **AAS**: Two angles and a non-included side of one triangle are congruent to the corresponding two angles and non-included side of the second triangle.
- **HL**: The hypotenuse and leg of one right triangle are congruent to the corresponding hypotenuse and leg of the second right triangle.

Review Video: Similar Triangles
Visit mometrix.com/academy and enter code: 398538

General Rules for Triangles

The **triangle inequality theorem** states that the sum of the measures of any two sides of a triangle is always greater than the measure of the third side. If the sum of the measures of two sides were equal to the third side, a triangle would be impossible because the two sides would lie flat across the third side and there would be no vertex. If the sum of the measures of two of the sides was less than the third side, a closed figure would be impossible because the two shortest sides would never meet. In other words, for a triangle with sides lengths A, B, and C: $A + B > C$, $B + C > A$, and $A + C > B$

The sum of the measures of the interior angles of a triangle is always 180°. Therefore, a triangle can never have more than one angle greater than or equal to 90°.

In any triangle, the angles opposite congruent sides are congruent, and the sides opposite congruent angles are congruent. The largest angle is always opposite the longest side, and the smallest angle is always opposite the shortest side.

The line segment that joins the midpoints of any two sides of a triangle is always parallel to the third side and exactly half the length of the third side.

Pythagorean Theorem

The side of a triangle opposite the right angle is called the **hypotenuse**. The other two sides are called the legs. The Pythagorean theorem states a relationship among the legs and hypotenuse of a right triangle: $a^2 + b^2 = c^2$, where a and b are the lengths of the legs of a right triangle, and c is the length of the hypotenuse. Note that this formula will only work with right triangles.

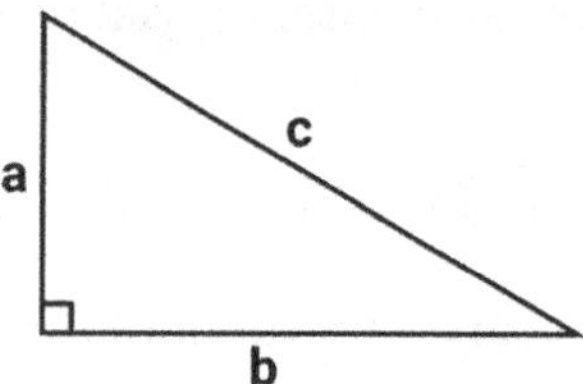

Review Video: Pythagorean Theorem
Visit mometrix.com/academy and enter code: 906576

PRACTICE

P1. Given the following pairs of triangles, determine whether they are similar, congruent, or neither (note that the figures are not drawn to scale):

(a).

(b).

(c).

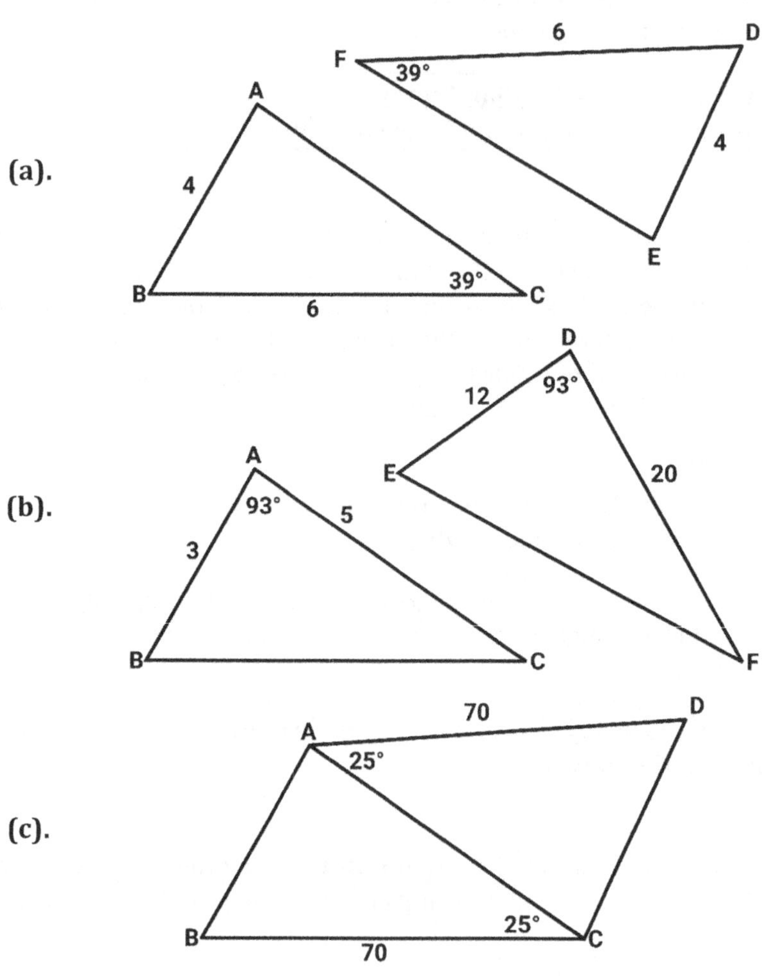

P2. Calculate the following values based on triangle MNO:

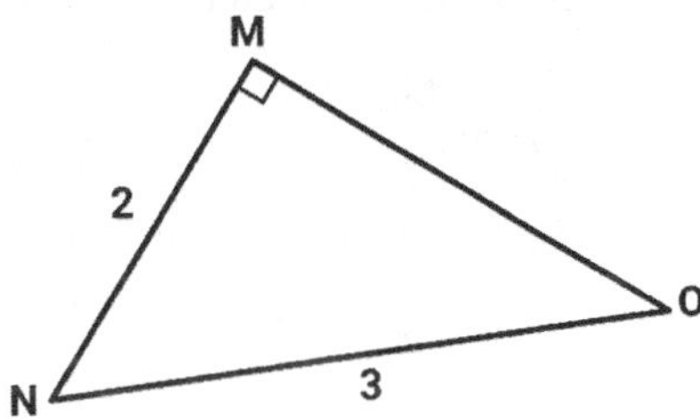

(a) length of $\overline{MO}$

(b) $\sin(\angle NOM)$

(c) area of the triangle, if the units of the measurements are in miles

Practice Solutions

P1. (a). Neither: We are given that two sides lengths and an angle are equal, however, the angle given is not between the given side lengths. That means there are two possible triangles that could satisfy the given measurements. Thus, we cannot be certain of congruence:

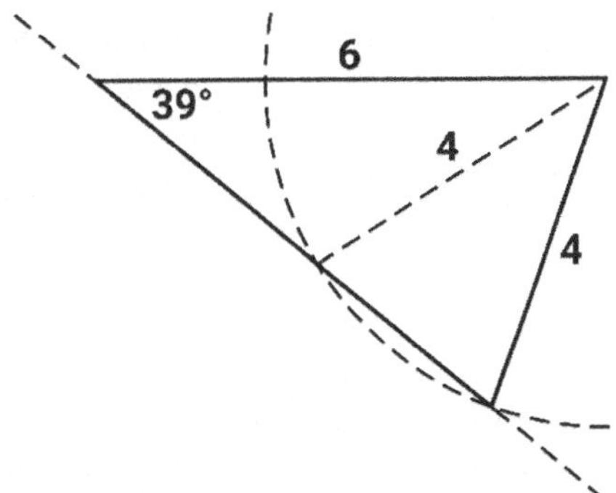

(b) Similar: Since we are given a side-angle-side of each triangle and the side lengths given are scaled evenly $\left(\frac{3}{5} \times \frac{4}{4} = \frac{12}{20}\right)$ and the angles are equal. Thus, $\Delta ABC \sim \Delta DEF$. If the side lengths were equal, then they would be congruent.

(c) Congruent: Even though we aren't given a measurement for the shared side of the figure, since it is shared it is equal. So, this is a case of SAS. Thus, $\Delta ABC \cong \Delta CDA$

P2. (a) Since triangle MNO is a right triangle, we can use the simple form of Pythagoras theorem to find the missing side length:

$$\left(\overline{MO}\right)^2 + 2^2 = 3^2$$
$$\left(\overline{MO}\right)^2 = 9 - 4$$
$$\overline{MO} = \sqrt{5}$$

(b) Recall that sine of an angle in a right triangle is the ratio of the opposite side to the hypotenuse. So, $\sin(\angle NOM) = 2/3$

(c) Since triangle MNO is a right triangle, we can use either of the legs as the height and the other as the base in the simple formula for the area of a triangle:

$$\begin{aligned} A &= \frac{bh}{2} \\ &= \frac{(2\text{ mi})(\sqrt{5}\text{ mi})}{2} \\ &= \sqrt{5}\text{ mi}^2 \end{aligned}$$

Statistics and Probability

DISPLAYING INFORMATION

FREQUENCY TABLES

Frequency tables show how frequently each unique value appears in a set. A **relative frequency table** is one that shows the proportions of each unique value compared to the entire set. Relative frequencies are given as percentages; however, the total percent for a relative frequency table will not necessarily equal 100 percent due to rounding. An example of a frequency table with relative frequencies is below.

Favorite Color	Frequency	Relative Frequency
Blue	4	13%
Red	7	22%
Green	3	9%
Purple	6	19%
Cyan	12	38%

Review Video: Data Interpretation of Graphs
Visit mometrix.com/academy and enter code: 200439

CIRCLE GRAPHS

Circle graphs, also known as *pie charts*, provide a visual depiction of the relationship of each type of data compared to the whole set of data. The circle graph is divided into sections by drawing radii to create central angles whose percentage of the circle is equal to the individual data's percentage of the whole set. Each 1% of data is equal to 3.6° in the circle graph. Therefore, data represented by a 90° section of the circle graph makes up 25% of the whole. When complete, a circle graph often looks like a pie cut into uneven wedges. The pie chart below shows the data from the frequency table referenced earlier where people were asked their favorite color.

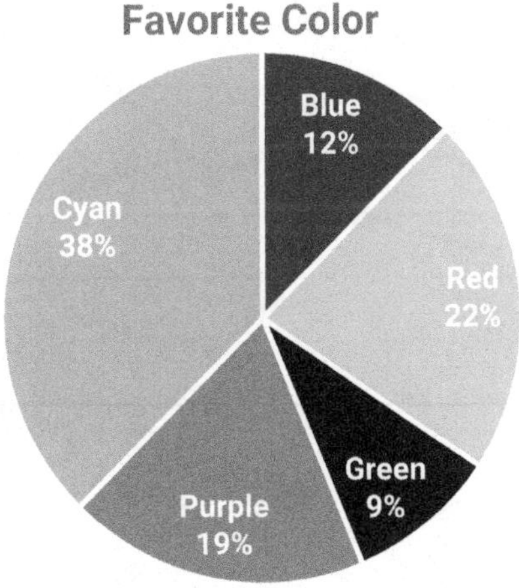

Pictographs

A **pictograph** is a graph, generally in the horizontal orientation, that uses pictures or symbols to represent the data. Each pictograph must have a key that defines the picture or symbol and gives the quantity each picture or symbol represents. Pictures or symbols on a pictograph are not always shown as whole elements. In this case, the fraction of the picture or symbol shown represents the same fraction of the quantity a whole picture or symbol stands for. For example, a row with $3\frac{1}{2}$ ears of corn, where each ear of corn represents 100 stalks of corn in a field, would equal $3\frac{1}{2} \times 100 = 350$ stalks of corn in the field.

Line Graphs

Line graphs have one or more lines of varying styles (solid or broken) to show the different values for a set of data. The individual data are represented as ordered pairs, much like on a Cartesian plane. In this case, the x- and y-axes are defined in terms of their units, such as dollars or time. The individual plotted points are joined by line segments to show whether the value of the data is increasing (line sloping upward), decreasing (line sloping downward) or staying the same (horizontal line). Multiple sets of data can be graphed on the same line graph to give an easy visual comparison. An example of this would be graphing achievement test scores for different groups of students over the same time period to see which group had the greatest increase or decrease in performance from year-to-year (as shown below).

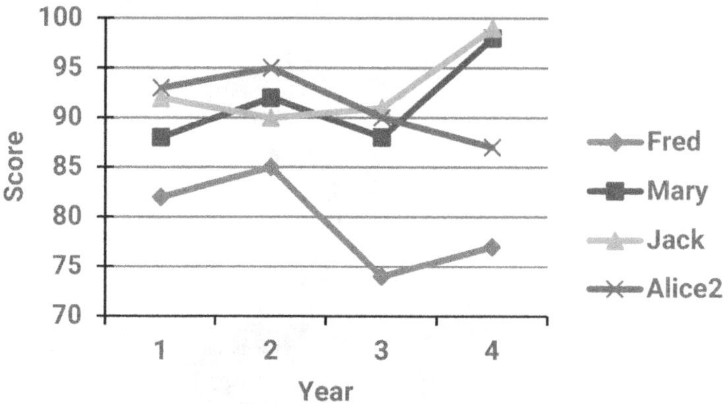

Review Video: How to Create a Line Graph
Visit mometrix.com/academy and enter code: 480147

Line Plots

A **line plot**, also known as a *dot plot*, has plotted points that are not connected by line segments. In this graph, the horizontal axis lists the different possible values for the data, and the vertical axis lists the number of times the individual value occurs. A single dot is graphed for each value to show the number of times it occurs. This graph is more closely related to a bar graph than a line graph. Do not connect the dots in a line plot or it will misrepresent the data.

Review Video: Line Plot
Visit mometrix.com/academy and enter code: 754610

Stem and Leaf Plots

A **stem and leaf plot** is useful for depicting groups of data that fall into a range of values. Each piece of data is separated into two parts: the first, or left, part is called the stem; the second, or right, part is called the leaf. Each stem is listed in a column from smallest to largest. Each leaf that has the common stem is listed in that stem's row from smallest to largest. For example, in a set of two-digit numbers, the digit in the tens place is the stem, and the digit in the ones place is the leaf. With a stem and leaf plot, you can easily see which subset of numbers (10s, 20s, 30s, etc.) is the largest. This information is also readily available by looking at a histogram, but a stem and leaf plot also allows you to look closer and see exactly which values fall in that range. Using all of the test scores from above, we can assemble a stem and leaf plot like the one below.

Test Scores

7	4	8							
8	2	5	7	8	8				
9	0	0	1	2	2	3	5	8	9

Review Video: Stem-and-Leaf Plots
Visit mometrix.com/academy and enter code: 302339

Bar Graphs

A **bar graph** is one of the few graphs that can be drawn correctly in two different configurations – both horizontally and vertically. A bar graph is similar to a line plot in the way the data is organized on the graph. Both axes must have their categories defined for the graph to be useful. Rather than placing a single dot to mark the point of the data's value, a bar, or thick line, is drawn from zero to the exact value of the data, whether it is a number, percentage, or other numerical value. Longer bar lengths correspond to greater data values. To read a bar graph, read the labels for the axes to find the units being reported. Then look where the bars end in relation to the scale given on the corresponding axis and determine the associated value.

The bar chart below represents the responses from our favorite color survey.

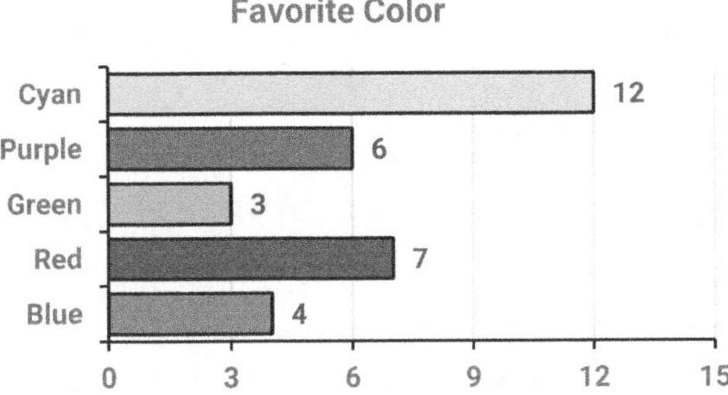

Histograms

At first glance, a **histogram** looks like a vertical bar graph. The difference is that a bar graph has a separate bar for each piece of data and a histogram has one continuous bar for each *range* of data. For example, a histogram may have one bar for the range 0–9, one bar for 10–19, etc. While a bar graph has numerical values on one axis, a histogram has numerical values on both axes. Each range is of equal size, and they are ordered left to right from lowest to highest. The height of each column on a histogram represents the number of data values within that range. Like a stem and leaf plot, a histogram makes it easy to glance at the graph and quickly determine which range has the greatest quantity of values. A simple example of a histogram is below.

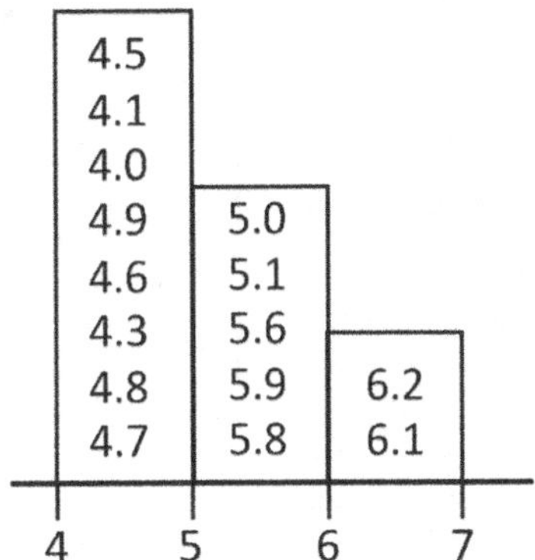

Bivariate Data

Bivariate data is simply data from two different variables. (The prefix *bi-* means *two.*) In a *scatter plot*, each value in the set of data is plotted on a grid similar to a Cartesian plane, where each axis represents one of the two variables. By looking at the pattern formed by the points on the grid, you can often determine whether or not there is a relationship between the two variables, and what that relationship is, if it exists. The variables may be directly proportionate, inversely proportionate, or show no proportion at all. It may also be possible to determine if the data is linear, and if so, to find an equation to relate the two variables. The following scatter plot shows the relationship between preference for brand "A" and the age of the consumers surveyed.

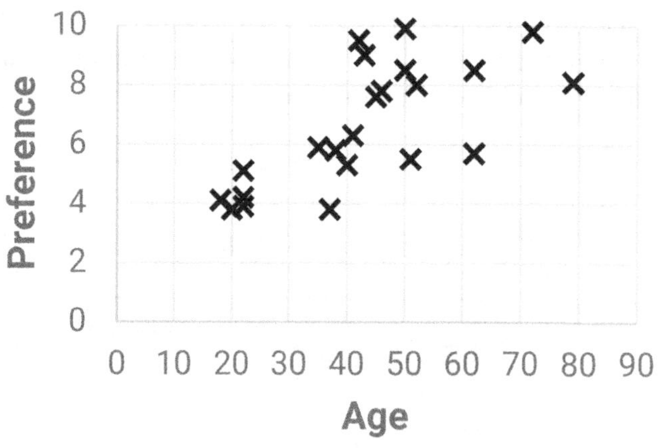

Scatter Plots

Scatter plots are also useful in determining the type of function represented by the data and finding the simple regression. Linear scatter plots may be positive or negative. Nonlinear scatter plots are generally exponential or quadratic. Below are some common types of scatter plots:

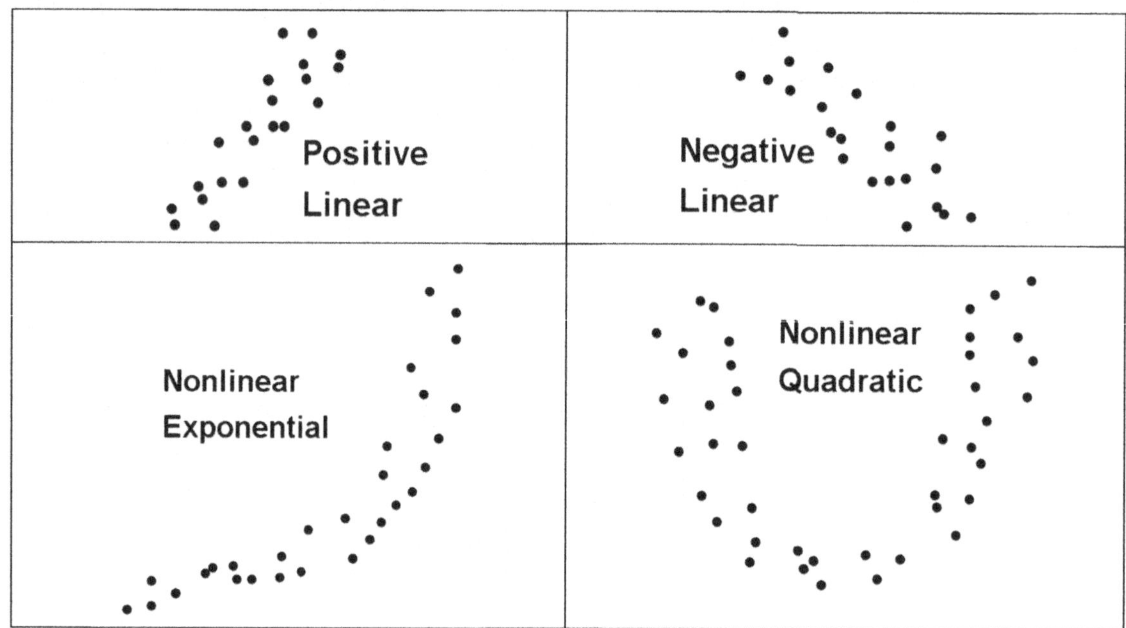

Review Video: What is a Scatter Plot?
Visit mometrix.com/academy and enter code: 596526

5-NUMBER SUMMARY

The **5-number summary** of a set of data gives a very informative picture of the set. The five numbers in the summary include the minimum value, maximum value, and the three quartiles. This information gives the reader the range and median of the set, as well as an indication of how the data is spread about the median.

BOX AND WHISKER PLOTS

A **box-and-whisker plot** is a graphical representation of the 5-number summary. To draw a box-and-whiskers plot, plot the points of the 5-number summary on a number line. Draw a box whose ends are through the points for the first and third quartiles. Draw a vertical line in the box through the median to divide the box in half. Draw a line segment from the first quartile point to the minimum value, and from the third quartile point to the maximum value.

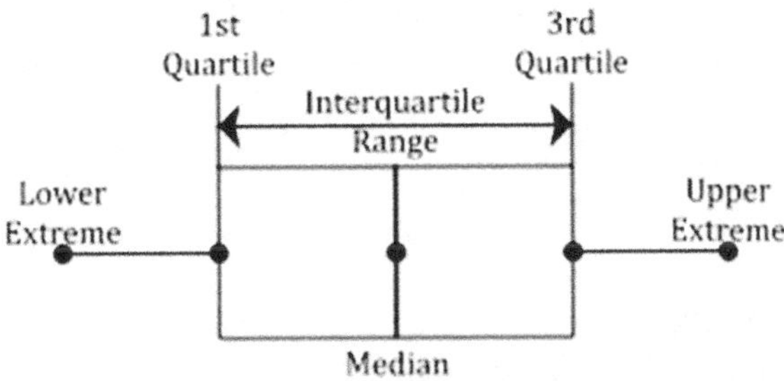

Review Video: Box and Whisker Plots
Visit mometrix.com/academy and enter code: 810817

68-95-99.7 RULE

The **68–95–99.7 rule** describes how a normal distribution of data should appear when compared to the mean. This is also a description of a normal bell curve. According to this rule, 68 percent of the data values in a normally distributed set should fall within one standard deviation of the mean (34 percent above and 34 percent below the mean), 95 percent of the data values should fall within two standard deviations of the mean (47.5 percent above and 47.5 percent below the mean), and 99.7 percent of the data values should fall within three standard deviations of the mean, again, equally distributed on either side of the mean. This means that only 0.3 percent of all data values should fall more than three standard deviations from the mean. On the graph below, the normal curve is centered on the y-axis. The x-axis labels are how many standard deviations away from the center you are. Therefore, it is easy to see how the 68-95-99.7 rule can apply.

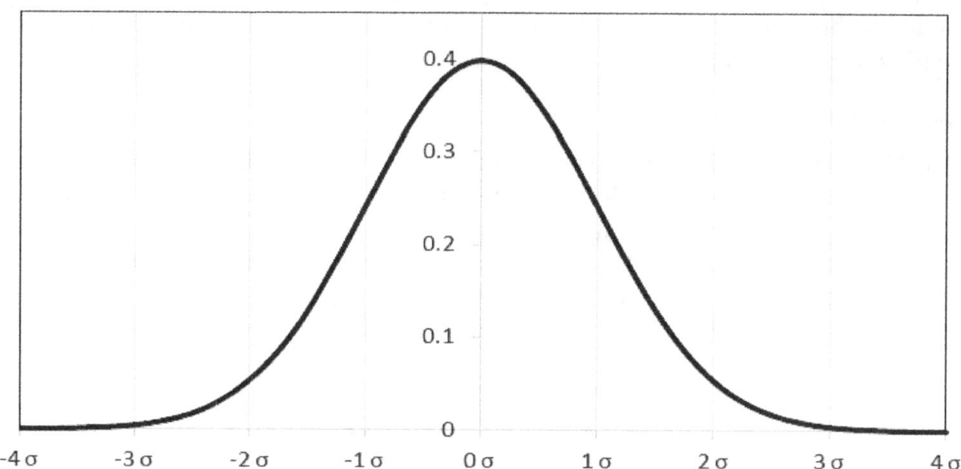

STATISTICAL ANALYSIS

MEASURES OF CENTRAL TENDENCY

A **measure of central tendency** is a statistical value that gives a reasonable estimate for the center of a group of data. There are several different ways of describing the measure of central tendency. Each one has a unique way it is calculated, and each one gives a slightly different perspective on the data set. Whenever you give a measure of central tendency, always make sure the units are the same. If the data has different units, such as hours, minutes, and seconds, convert all the data to the same unit, and use the same unit in the measure of central tendency. If no units are given in the data, do not give units for the measure of central tendency.

MEAN

The **statistical mean** of a group of data is the same as the arithmetic average of that group. To find the mean of a set of data, first convert each value to the same units, if necessary. Then find the sum of all the values, and count the total number of data values, making sure you take into consideration each individual value. If a value appears more than once, count it more than once. Divide the sum of the values by the total number of values and apply the units, if any. Note that the mean does not have to be one of the data values in the set, and may not divide evenly.

$$\text{mean} = \frac{\text{sum of the data values}}{\text{quantity of data values}}$$

For instance, the mean of the data set {88, 72, 61, 90, 97, 68, 88, 79, 86, 93, 97, 71, 80, 84, 89} would be the sum of the fifteen numbers divided by 15:

$$\frac{88 + 72 + 61 + 90 + 97 + 68 + 88 + 79 + 86 + 93 + 97 + 71 + 80 + 84 + 89}{15} = \frac{1242}{15} = 82.8$$

While the mean is relatively easy to calculate and averages are understood by most people, the mean can be very misleading if it is used as the sole measure of central tendency. If the data set has outliers (data values that are unusually high or unusually low compared to the rest of the data values), the mean can be very distorted, especially if the data set has a small number of values. If unusually high values are countered with unusually low values, the mean is not affected as much. For example, if five of twenty students in a class get a 100 on a test, but the other 15 students have an average of 60 on the same test, the class average would appear as 70. Whenever the mean is skewed by outliers, it is always a good idea to include the median as an alternate measure of central tendency.

A **weighted mean**, or weighted average, is a mean that uses "weighted" values. The formula is weighted mean $= \frac{w_1x_1+w_2x_2+w_3x_3...+w_nx_n}{w_1+w_2+w_3+\cdots+w_n}$. Weighted values, such as $w_1, w_2, w_3, ... w_n$ are assigned to each member of the set $x_1, x_2, x_3, ... x_n$. When calculating the weighted mean, make sure a weight value for each member of the set is used.

MEDIAN

The **statistical median** is the value in the middle of the set of data. To find the median, list all data values in order from smallest to largest or from largest to smallest. Any value that is repeated in the set must be listed the number of times it appears. If there are an odd number of data values, the median is the value in the middle of the list. If there is an even number of data values, the median is the arithmetic mean of the two middle values.

For example, the median of the data set {88, 72, 61, 90, 97, 68, 88, 79, 86, 93, 97, 71, 80, 84, 88} is 86 since the ordered set is {61, 68, 71, 72, 79, 80, 84, **86**, 88, 88, 88, 90, 93, 97, 97}.

The big disadvantage of using the median as a measure of central tendency is that is relies solely on a value's relative size as compared to the other values in the set. When the individual values in a set of data are evenly dispersed, the median can be an accurate tool. However, if there is a group of rather large values or a group of rather small values that are not offset by a different group of values, the information that can be inferred from the median may not be accurate because the distribution of values is skewed.

MODE

The **statistical mode** is the data value that occurs the greatest number of times in the data set. It is possible to have exactly one mode, more than one mode, or no mode. To find the mode of a set of data, arrange the data like you do to find the median (all values in order, listing all multiples of data values). Count the number of times each value appears in the data set. If all values appear an equal number of times, there is no mode. If one value appears more than any other value, that value is the mode. If two or more values appear the same number of times, but there are other values that appear fewer times and no values that appear more times, all of those values are the modes.

For example, the mode of the data set {**88**, 72, 61, 90, 97, 68, **88**, 79, 86, 93, 97, 71, 80, 84, **88**} is 88.

The main disadvantage of the mode is that the values of the other data in the set have no bearing on the mode. The mode may be the largest value, the smallest value, or a value anywhere in between in the set. The mode only tells which value or values, if any, occurred the greatest number of times. It does not give any suggestions about the remaining values in the set.

Review Video: Mean, Median, and Mode
Visit mometrix.com/academy and enter code: 286207

DISPERSION

The **measure of dispersion** is a single value that helps to "interpret" the measure of central tendency by providing more information about how the data values in the set are distributed about the measure of central tendency. The measure of dispersion helps to eliminate or reduce the disadvantages of using the mean, median, or mode as a single measure of central tendency, and give a more accurate picture of the dataset as a whole. To have a measure of dispersion, you must know or calculate the range, standard deviation, or variance of the data set.

RANGE

The **range** of a set of data is the difference between the greatest and lowest values of the data in the set. To calculate the range, you must first make sure the units for all data values are the same, and then identify the greatest and lowest values. If there are multiple data values that are equal for the highest or lowest, just use one of the values in the formula. Write the answer with the same units as the data values you used to do the calculations.

Review Video: Statistical Range
Visit mometrix.com/academy and enter code: 778541

PERCENTILE

Percentiles and quartiles are other methods of describing data within a set. **Percentiles** tell what percentage of the data in the set fall below a specific point. For example, achievement test scores are often given in percentiles. A score at the 80th percentile is one which is equal to or higher than 80 percent of the scores in the set. In other words, 80 percent of the scores were lower than that score.

Quartiles are percentile groups that make up quarter sections of the data set. The first quartile is the 25th percentile. The second quartile is the 50th percentile; this is also the median of the dataset. The third quartile is the 75th percentile.

OUTLIER

An outlier is an extremely high or extremely low value in the data set. It may be the result of measurement error, in which case, the outlier is not a valid member of the data set. However, it may also be a valid member of the distribution. Unless a measurement error is identified, the experimenter cannot know for certain if an outlier is or is not a member of the distribution. There are arbitrary methods that can be employed to designate an extreme value as an outlier. One method designates an outlier (or possible outlier) to be any value less than $Q_1 - 1.5(IQR)$ or any value greater than $Q_3 + 1.5(IQR)$.

PRACTICE

P1. Given the following graph, determine the range of patient ages:

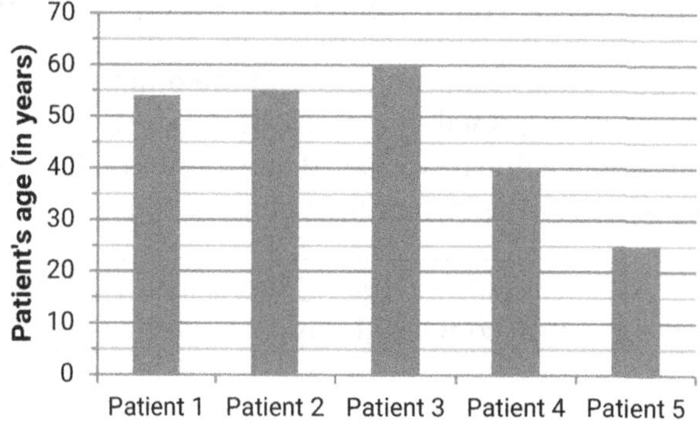

Practice Solutions

P1. Patient 1 is 54 years old; Patient 2 is 55 years old; Patient 3 is 60 years old; Patient 4 is 40 years old; and Patient 5 is 25 years old. The range of patient ages is the age of the oldest patient minus the age of the youngest patient. In other words, $60 - 25 = 35$. The range of ages is 35 years.

Probability

Probability is the likelihood of a certain outcome occurring for a given event. An **event** is a situation that produces a result; that could be something as simple as flipping a coin or as complex as launching a rocket. Determining the probability of an outcome for an event can be equally simple or complex. As such there are specific terms used in the study of probability that need to be understood:

- **Compound event**—an event that involves two or more independent events (rolling a pair of dice and taking the sum)
- **Desired outcome** (or success)—an outcome that meets a particular set of criteria (a roll of 1 or 2 if we are looking for numbers less than 3)
- **Independent events**—two or more events whose outcomes do not affect one another (two coins tossed at the same time)
- **Dependent events**—two or more events whose outcomes affect one another (two cards drawn consecutively from the same deck)
- **Certain outcome**—probability of outcome is 100% or 1
- **Impossible outcome**—probability of outcome is 0% or 0
- **Mutually exclusive outcomes**—two or more outcomes whose criteria cannot all be satisfied in a single event (a coin coming up heads and tails on the same toss)
- **Random variable**—refers to all possible outcomes of a single event which may be discrete or continuous.

Review Video: Intro to Probability
Visit mometrix.com/academy and enter code: 212374

Theoretical and Experimental Probability

Theoretical probability can usually be determined without actually performing the event. The likelihood of an outcome occurring, or the probability of an outcome occurring, is given by the formula:

$$P(A) = \frac{\text{Number of acceptable outcomes}}{\text{Number of possible outcomes}}$$

Note that $P(A)$ is the probability of an outcome A occurring, and each outcome is just as likely to occur as any other outcome. If each outcome has the same probability of occurring as every other possible outcome, the outcomes are said to be equally likely to occur. The total number of acceptable outcomes must be less than or equal to the total number of possible outcomes. If the two are equal, then the outcome is certain to occur and the probability is 1. If the number of acceptable outcomes is zero, then the outcome is impossible and the probability is 0. For example, if there are 20 marbles in a bag and 5 are red, then the theoretical probability of randomly selecting a red marble is 5 out of 20, ($\frac{5}{20} = \frac{1}{4}$, 0.25, or 25%).

If the theoretical probability is unknown or too complicated to calculate, it can be estimated by an experimental probability. **Experimental probability**, also called empirical probability, is an estimate of the likelihood of a certain outcome based on repeated experiments or collected data. In other words, while theoretical probability is based on what *should* happen, experimental probability is based on what *has* happened. Experimental probability is calculated in the same way as theoretical probability, except that actual outcomes are used instead of possible outcomes. The more experiments performed or datapoints gathered, the better the estimate should be.

Theoretical and experimental probability do not always line up with one another. Theoretical probability says that out of 20 coin-tosses, 10 should be heads. However, if we were actually to toss 20 coins, we might record just 5 heads. This doesn't mean that our theoretical probability is incorrect; it just means that this particular experiment had results that were different from what was predicted. A practical application of empirical probability is the insurance industry. There are no set functions that define lifespan, health, or safety. Insurance companies look at factors from hundreds of thousands of individuals to find patterns that they then use to set the formulas for insurance premiums.

Review Video: Empirical Probability
Visit mometrix.com/academy and enter code: 513468

Permutations and Combinations

When trying to calculate the probability of an event using the $\frac{\text{desired outcomes}}{\text{total outcomes}}$ formula, you may frequently find that there are too many outcomes to individually count them. **Permutation** and **combination formulas** offer a shortcut to counting outcomes. A permutation is an arrangement of a specific number of a set of objects in a specific order. The number of **permutations** of r items given a set of n items can be calculated as $_nP_r = \frac{n!}{(n-r)!}$. Combinations are similar to permutations, except there are no restrictions regarding the order of the elements. While ABC is considered a different permutation than BCA, ABC and BCA are considered the same combination. The number of **combinations** of r items given a set of n items can be calculated as $_nC_r = \frac{n!}{r!(n-r)!}$ or $_nC_r = \frac{_nP_r}{r!}$.

Suppose you want to calculate how many different 5-card hands can be drawn from a deck of 52 cards. This is a combination since the order of the cards in a hand does not matter. There are 52 cards available, and 5 to be selected. Thus, the number of different hands is $_{52}C_5 = \frac{52!}{5!\times 47!} =$ 2,598,960.

Review Video: Probability - Permutation and Combination
Visit mometrix.com/academy and enter code: 907664

Complement of an Event

Sometimes it may be easier to calculate the possibility of something not happening, or the **complement of an event**. Represented by the symbol $\bar{A}$, the complement of A is the probability that event A does not happen. When you know the probability of event A occurring, you can use the formula $P(\bar{A}) = 1 - P(A)$, where $P(\bar{A})$ is the probability of event A not occurring, and $P(A)$ is the probability of event A occurring.

Addition Rule

The **addition rule** for probability is used for finding the probability of a compound event. Use the formula $P(A \text{ or } B) = P(A) + P(B) - P(A \text{ and } B)$, where $P(A \text{ and } B)$ is the probability of both events occurring to find the probability of a compound event. The probability of both events occurring at the same time must be subtracted to eliminate any overlap in the first two probabilities.

Conditional Probability

Given two events A and B, the **conditional probability** $P(A|B)$ is the probability that event A will occur, given that event B has occurred. The conditional probability cannot be calculated simply from $P(A)$ and $P(B)$; these probabilities alone do not give sufficient information to determine the conditional probability. It can, however, be determined if you are also given the probability of the intersection of events A and B, $P(A \cap B)$, the probability that events A and B both occur. Specifically, $P(A|B) = \frac{P(A \cap B)}{P(B)}$. For instance, suppose you have a jar containing two red marbles and two blue marbles, and you draw two marbles at random. Consider event A being the event that the first marble drawn is red, and event B being the event that the second marble drawn is blue. $P(A)$ is $\frac{1}{2}$, and $P(A \cap B)$ is $\frac{1}{3}$. (The latter may not be obvious, but may be determined by finding the product of $\frac{1}{2}$ and $\frac{2}{3}$). Therefore $P(A|B) = \frac{1/3}{1/2} = \frac{2}{3}$.

Conditional Probability in Everyday Situations

Conditional probability often arises in everyday situations in, for example, estimating the risk or benefit of certain activities. The conditional probability of having a heart attack given that you exercise daily may be smaller than the overall probability of having a heart attack. The conditional probability of having lung cancer given that you are a smoker is larger than the overall probability of having lung cancer. Note that changing the order of the conditional probability changes the meaning: the conditional probability of having lung cancer given that you are a smoker is a very different thing from the probability of being a smoker given that you have lung cancer. In an extreme case, suppose that a certain rare disease is caused only by eating a certain food, but even then, it is unlikely. Then the conditional probability of having that disease given that you eat the dangerous food is nonzero but low, but the conditional probability of having eaten that food given that you have the disease is 100%!

> **Review Video: Conditional Probability**
> Visit mometrix.com/academy and enter code: 397924

Multiplication Rule

The **multiplication rule** can be used to find the probability of two independent events occurring using the formula $P(A \text{ and } B) = P(A) \times P(B)$, where $P(A \text{ and } B)$ is the probability of two independent events occurring, $P(A)$ is the probability of the first event occurring, and $P(B)$ is the probability of the second event occurring.

The multiplication rule can also be used to find the probability of two dependent events occurring using the formula $P(A \text{ and } B) = P(A) \times P(B|A)$, where $P(A \text{ and } B)$ is the probability of two dependent events occurring and $P(B|A)$ is the probability of the second event occurring after the first event has already occurred. Before using the multiplication rule, you MUST first determine whether the two events are *dependent* or *independent*.

Use a **combination of the multiplication** rule and the rule of complements to find the probability that at least one outcome of the element will occur. This is given by the general formula $P(\text{at least one event occurring}) = 1 - P(\text{no outcomes occurring})$. For example, to find the probability that at least one even number will show when a pair of dice is rolled, find the probability that two odd numbers will be rolled (no even numbers) and subtract from one. You can always use a tree diagram or make a chart to list the possible outcomes when the sample space is small, such as in the dice-rolling example, but in most cases it will be much faster to use the multiplication and complement formulas.

Review Video: Multiplication Rule
Visit mometrix.com/academy and enter code: 782598

Expected Value

Expected value is a method of determining the expected outcome in a random situation. It is a sum of the weighted probabilities of the possible outcomes. Multiply the probability of an event occurring by the weight assigned to that probability (such as the amount of money won or lost). A practical application of the expected value is to determine whether a game of chance is really fair. If the sum of the weighted probabilities is equal to zero, the game is generally considered fair because the player has a fair chance to at least break even. If the expected value is less than zero, then players lose more than they win. For example, a lottery drawing might allow the player to choose any three-digit number, 000–999. The probability of choosing the winning number is 1:1000. If it costs $1 to play, and a winning number receives $500, the expected value is $\left(-\$1 \times \frac{999}{1,000}\right) + \left(\$499 \times \frac{1}{1,000}\right) = -\$0.50$. You can expect to lose on average 50 cents for every dollar you spend.

Review Video: Expected Value
Visit mometrix.com/academy and enter code: 643554

Practice

P1. Determine the theoretical probability of the following events:

(a) Rolling an even number on a regular 6-sided die.

(b) Not getting a red ball when selecting one from a bag of 3 red balls, 4 black balls, and 2 green balls.

(c) Rolling a standard die and then selecting a card from a standard deck that is less than the value rolled.

P2. There is a game of chance involving a standard deck of cards that has been shuffled and then laid on a table. The player wins $10 if they can turn over 2 cards of matching color (black or red), $50 for 2 cards with matching value (A-K), and $100 for 2 cards with both matching color and value. What is the expected value of playing this game?

P3. Today, there were two food options for lunch at a local college cafeteria. Given the following survey data, what is the probability that a junior selected at random from the sample had a sandwich?

	Freshman	Sophomore	Junior	Senior
Salad	15	12	27	36
Sandwich	24	40	43	35
Nothing	42	23	23	30

PRACTICE SOLUTIONS

P1. (a). The values on the faces of a regular die are 1, 2, 3, 4, 5, and 6. Since three of these are even numbers (2, 4, 6), The probability of rolling an even number is $\frac{3}{6} = \frac{1}{2} = 0.5 = 50\%$.

(b) The bag contains a total of 9 balls, 6 of which are not red, so the probability of selecting one non-red ball would be $\frac{6}{9} = \frac{2}{3} \cong 0.667 \cong 66.7\%$.

(c) In this scenario, we need to determine how many cards could satisfy the condition for each possible value of the die roll. If a one is rolled, there is no way to achieve the desired outcome, since no cards in a standard deck are less than 1. If a two is rolled, then any of the four aces would achieve the desired result. If a three is rolled, then either an ace or a two would satisfy the condition, and so on. Note that any value on the die is equally likely to occur, meaning that the probability of each roll is $\frac{1}{6}$. Putting all this in a table can help:

Roll	Cards < Roll	Probability of Card	Probability of Event
1	-	$\frac{0}{52} = 0$	$\frac{1}{6} \times 0 = 0$
2	1	$\frac{4}{52} = \frac{1}{13}$	$\frac{1}{6} \times \frac{1}{13} = \frac{1}{78}$
3	1,2	$\frac{8}{52} = \frac{2}{13}$	$\frac{1}{6} \times \frac{2}{13} = \frac{2}{78}$
4	1,2,3	$\frac{12}{52} = \frac{3}{13}$	$\frac{1}{6} \times \frac{3}{13} = \frac{3}{78}$
5	1,2,3,4	$\frac{16}{52} = \frac{4}{13}$	$\frac{1}{6} \times \frac{4}{13} = \frac{4}{78}$
6	1,2,3,4,5	$\frac{20}{52} = \frac{5}{13}$	$\frac{1}{6} \times \frac{5}{13} = \frac{5}{78}$

Assuming that each value of the die is equally likely, then the probability of selecting a card less than the value of the die is the sum of the probabilities of each way to achieve the desired outcome: $\frac{0+1+2+3+4+5}{78} = \frac{15}{78} = \frac{5}{26} \cong 0.192 \cong 19.2\%$.

P2. First, determine the probability of each way of winning. In each case, the first card simply determines which of the remaining 51 cards in the deck correspond to a win. For the color of the cards to match, there are 25 cards remaining in the deck that match the color of the first, but one of the 25 also matches the value, so only 24 are left in this category. For the value of the cards to match, there are 3 cards remaining in the deck that match the value of the first, but one of the three also matches the color, so only 2 are left in this category. There is only one card in the deck that will match both the color and value. Finally, there are 24 cards left that don't match at all.

Now we can find the expected value of playing the game, where we multiply the value of each event by the probability it will occur and sum over all of them:

$$\$10 \times \frac{24}{51} = \$4.71$$
$$\$50 \times \frac{2}{51} = \$1.96$$
$$\$100 \times \frac{1}{51} = \$1.96$$
$$\$0 \times \frac{24}{51} = \$0$$

$$\$4.71 + \$1.96 + \$1.96 = \$8.63$$

This game therefore has an expected value of $8.63 each time you play, which means if the cost to play is less than $8.63 then you would, on average, *gain* money. However, if the cost to play is more than $8.63, then you would, on average, *lose* money.

P3. With two-way tables it is often most helpful to start by totaling the rows and columns:

	Freshman	Sophomore	Junior	Senior	Total
Salad	15	12	27	36	90
Sandwich	24	40	43	35	142
Nothing	42	23	23	30	118
Total	81	75	93	101	350

Since the question is focused on juniors, we can focus on that column. There was a total of 93 juniors surveyed and 43 of them had a sandwich for lunch. Thus, the probability that a junior selected at random had a sandwich would be $\frac{43}{93} \cong 0.462 \cong 46.2\%$.

Algebra

Units of Measurement

Metric Measurement Prefixes

Giga-: one billion (1 *giga*watt is one billion watts)
Mega-: one million (1 *mega*hertz is one million hertz)
Kilo-: one thousand (1 *kilo*gram is one thousand grams)
Deci-: one tenth (1 *deci*meter is one tenth of a meter)
Centi-: one hundredth (1 *centi*meter is one hundredth of a meter)
Milli-: one thousandth (1 *milli*liter is one thousandth of a liter)
Micro-: one millionth (1 *micro*gram is one millionth of a gram)

Measurement Conversion

When converting between units, the goal is to maintain the same meaning but change the way it is displayed. In order to go from a larger unit to a smaller unit, multiply the number of the known amount by the equivalent amount. When going from a smaller unit to a larger unit, divide the number of the known amount by the equivalent amount.

For complicated conversions, it may be helpful to set up conversion fractions. In these fractions, one fraction is the **conversion factor**. The other fraction has the unknown amount in the numerator.

So, the known value is placed in the denominator. Sometimes the second fraction has the known value from the problem in the numerator, and the unknown in the denominator. Multiply the two fractions to get the converted measurement. Note that since the numerator and the denominator of the factor are equivalent, the value of the fraction is 1. That is why we can say that the result in the new units is equal to the result in the old units even though they have different numbers.

It can often be necessary to chain known conversion factors together. As an example, consider converting 512 square inches to square meters. We know that there are 2.54 centimeters in an inch and 100 centimeters in a meter, and that we will need to square each of these factors to achieve the conversion we are looking for.

$$\frac{512\text{ in}^2}{1} \times \left(\frac{2.54\text{ cm}}{1\text{ in}}\right)^2 \times \left(\frac{1\text{ m}}{100\text{ cm}}\right)^2 = \frac{512\ \cancel{\text{in}^2}}{1} \times \left(\frac{6.4516\ \cancel{\text{cm}^2}}{1\ \cancel{\text{in}^2}}\right) \times \left(\frac{1\text{ m}^2}{10000\ \cancel{\text{cm}^2}}\right) = 0.330\text{ m}^2$$

Review Video: Measurement Conversions
Visit mometrix.com/academy and enter code: 316703

Common Units and Equivalents

Metric Equivalents

1000 µg (microgram)	1 mg
1000 mg (milligram)	1 g
1000 g (gram)	1 kg
1000 kg (kilogram)	1 metric ton
1000 mL (milliliter)	1 L
1000 µm (micrometer)	1 mm
1000 mm (millimeter)	1 m
100 cm (centimeter)	1 m
1000 m (meter)	1 km

Distance and Area Measurement

Unit	Abbreviation	U.S. equivalent	Metric equivalent
Inch	in	1 inch	2.54 centimeters
Foot	ft	12 inches	0.305 meters
Yard	yd	3 feet	0.914 meters
Mile	mi	5280 feet	1.609 kilometers
Acre	ac	4840 square yards	0.405 hectares
Square Mile	mi^2	640 acres	2.590 square kilometers

Capacity Measurements

Unit	Abbreviation	U.S. equivalent	Metric equivalent
Fluid Ounce	fl oz	8 fluid drams	29.573 milliliters
Cup	cp	8 fluid ounces	0.237 liter
Pint	pt	16 fluid ounces	0.473 liter
Quart	qt	2 pints	0.946 liter
Gallon	gal	4 quarts	3.785 liters
Teaspoon	t or tsp	1 fluid dram	5 milliliters
Tablespoon	T or tbsp	4 fluid drams	15 or 16 milliliters
Cubic Centimeter	cc or cm^3	0.271 drams	1 milliliter

Weight Measurements

Unit	Abbreviation	U.S. equivalent	Metric equivalent
Ounce	oz	16 drams	28.35 grams
Pound	lb	16 ounces	453.6 grams
Ton	t	2,000 pounds	907.2 kilograms

Volume and Weight Measurement Clarifications

Always be careful when using ounces and fluid ounces. They are not equivalent.

$$1 \text{ pint} = 16 \text{ fluid ounces} \qquad 1 \text{ fluid ounce} \neq 1 \text{ ounce}$$
$$1 \text{ pound} = 16 \text{ ounces} \qquad 1 \text{ pint} \neq 1 \text{ pound}$$

Having one pint of something does not mean you have one pound of it. In the same way, just because something weighs one pound does not mean that its volume is one pint.

In the United States, the word "ton" by itself refers to a short ton or a net ton. Do not confuse this with a long ton (also called a gross ton) or a metric ton (also spelled *tonne*), which have different measurement equivalents.

$$1 \text{ U.S. ton} = 2000 \text{ pounds} \quad \neq \quad 1 \text{ metric ton} = 1000 \text{ kilograms}$$

Scientific Notation

Scientific notation is a way of writing large numbers in a shorter form. The form $a \times 10^n$ is used in scientific notation, where a is greater than or equal to 1 but less than 10, and n is the number of places the decimal must move to get from the original number to a. Example: The number 230,400,000 is cumbersome to write. To write the value in scientific notation, place a decimal point between the first and second numbers, and include all digits through the last non-zero digit ($a = 2.304$). To find the appropriate power of 10, count the number of places the decimal point had to move ($n = 8$). The number is positive if the decimal moved to the left, and negative if it moved to the right. We can then write 230,400,000 as 2.304×10^8. If we look instead at the number 0.00002304, we have the same value for a, but this time the decimal moved 5 places to the right ($n = -5$). Thus, 0.00002304 can be written as 2.304×10^{-5}. Using this notation makes it simple to compare very large or very small numbers. By comparing exponents, it is easy to see that 3.28×10^4 is smaller than 1.51×10^5, because 4 is less than 5.

Review Video: Scientific Notation
Visit mometrix.com/academy and enter code: 976454

Simple Interest

Simple Interest: Interest that is paid once per year for the principal amount. The principal amount is the original amount that someone borrows from another person or a bank. The formula is $I = Prt$, where I is the amount of interest, P is the principal, r is the annual interest rate, and t is the amount of time in years.

Actual Drawings and Scale Drawings

A map has a key for measurements to compare real distances with a scale distance.

Example: The key on one map says that 2 inches on the map is 12 real miles. Find the distance of a route that is 5 inches long on the map.

A proportion is needed to show the map measurements and real distances. First, write a ratio that has the information in the key. The map measurement can be in the numerator, and the real distance can be in the denominator.

$$\frac{2 \text{ inches}}{12 \text{ miles}}$$

Next, write a ratio with the known map distance and the unknown real distance. The unknown number for miles can be represented with the letter m.

$$\frac{5 \text{ inches}}{m \text{ miles}}$$

Then, write out the ratios in a proportion and solve it for m.

$$\frac{2 \text{ inches}}{12 \text{ miles}} = \frac{5 \text{ inches}}{m \text{ miles}}$$

Now, you have $2m = 60$. So you are left with $m = 30$. Thus, the route is 30 miles long.

PRACTICE

P1. Perform the following conversions:

(a) 1.4 meters to centimeters

(b) 218 centimeters to meters

(c) 42 inches to feet

(d) 15 kilograms to pounds

(e) 80 ounces to pounds

(f) 2 miles to kilometers

(g) 5 feet to centimeters

(h) 15.14 liters to gallons

(i) 8 quarts to liters

(j) 13.2 pounds to grams

PRACTICE SOLUTIONS

P1. (a) $\frac{100 \text{ cm}}{1 \text{ m}} = \frac{x \text{ cm}}{1.4 \text{ m}}$ Cross multiply to get $x = 140$

(b) $\frac{100 \text{ cm}}{1 \text{ m}} = \frac{218 \text{ cm}}{x \text{ m}}$ Cross multiply to get $100x = 218$, or $x = 2.18$

(c) $\frac{12 \text{ in}}{1 \text{ ft}} = \frac{42 \text{ in}}{x \text{ ft}}$ Cross multiply to get $12x = 42$, or $x = 3.5$

(d) $15 \text{ kilograms} \times \frac{2.2 \text{ pounds}}{1 \text{ kilogram}} = 33 \text{ pounds}$

(e) 80 ounces $\times \frac{1 \text{ pound}}{16 \text{ ounces}} = 5$ pounds

(f) 2 miles $\times \frac{1.609 \text{ kilometers}}{1 \text{ mile}} = 3.218$ kilometers

(g) 5 feet $\times \frac{12 \text{ inches}}{1 \text{ foot}} \times \frac{2.54 \text{ centimeters}}{1 \text{ inch}} = 152.4$ centimeters

(h) 15.14 liters $\times \frac{1 \text{ gallon}}{3.785 \text{ liters}} = 4$ gallons

(i) 8 quarts $\times \frac{1 \text{ gallon}}{4 \text{ quarts}} \times \frac{3.785 \text{ liters}}{1 \text{ gallon}} = 7.57$ liters

(j) 13.2 pounds $\times \frac{1 \text{ kilogram}}{2.2 \text{ pounds}} \times \frac{1000 \text{ grams}}{1 \text{ kilogram}} = 6000$ grams

Expressions

Terms and Coefficients

Mathematical expressions consist of a combination of one or more values arranged in terms that are added together. As such, an expression could be just a single number, including zero. A **variable term** is the product of a real number, also called a **coefficient**, and one or more variables, each of which may be raised to an exponent. Expressions may also include numbers without a variable, called **constants** or **constant terms**. The expression $6s^2$, for example, is a single term where the coefficient is the real number 6 and the variable term is s^2. Note that if a term is written as simply a variable to some exponent, like t^2, then the coefficient is 1, because $t^2 = 1t^2$.

Linear Expressions

A **single variable linear expression** is the sum of a single variable term, where the variable has no exponent, and a constant, which may be zero. For instance, the expression $2w + 7$ has $2w$ as the variable term and 7 as the constant term. It is important to realize that terms are separated by addition or subtraction. Since an expression is a sum of terms, expressions such as $5x - 3$ can be written as $5x + (-3)$ to emphasize that the constant term is negative. A real-world example of a single variable linear expression is the perimeter of a square, four times the side length, often expressed: $4s$.

In general, a **linear expression** is the sum of any number of variable terms so long as none of the variables have an exponent. For example, $3m + 8n - \frac{1}{4}p + 5.5q - 1$ is a linear expression, but $3y^3$ is not. In the same way, the expression for the perimeter of a general triangle, the sum of the side lengths $(a + b + c)$ is considered to be linear, but the expression for the area of a square, the side length squared (s^2) is not.

Writing an Expression from Word-to-Symbol

To write an expression, you must first put variables with the unknown values in the problem. Then, translate the words and phrases into expressions that have numbers and symbols.

Inequalities

To write out an inequality, you may need to translate a sentence into an inequality. This translation is putting the words into symbols. When translating, choose a variable to stand for the unknown value. Then, change the words or phrases into symbols. For example, the sum of 2 and a number is at most 12. So, you would write: $2 + b \leq 12$.

Example: A farm sells vegetables and dairy products. One third of the sales from dairy products plus half of the sales from vegetables should be greater than the monthly payment (P) for the farm.

Let d stand for the sales from dairy products. Let v stand for the sales from vegetables. One third of the sales from dairy products is the expression $\frac{d}{3}$. One half of the sales from vegetables is the expression $\frac{v}{2}$. The sum of these expressions should be greater than the monthly payment for the farm. An inequality for this is $\frac{d}{3}+\frac{v}{2}>P$.

Rational Expressions

John and Luke play basketball every week. John can make 5 free throws per minute faster than Luke can make three-point shots. On one day, John made 30 free throws in the same time that it took Luke to make 20 three-point shots. So, how fast are Luke and John scoring points?

First, set up what you know. You know that John made 30 free throws, and he had a rate of 5 free throws per minute faster than Luke's three-point shots: $\frac{30}{x+5}$. The x is for Luke's speed. Also, you know that Luke made 20 three-point shots in the same amount of time that John scored his free throws: $\frac{20}{x}$. So, we can set up proportions because their times are equal.

$$\frac{30}{x+5}=\frac{20}{x}$$

Cross factor the proportion: $30x = 20(x + 5)$

Then distribute the 20 across the values in the parentheses: $30x = 20x + 100$

Now you can subtract 20x from both sides of the equation, and you are left with: $10x = 100$

Divide both sides by 10: $\frac{10x}{10}=\frac{100}{10}$

Now you are left with: $x = 10$. So Luke's speed was 10 three-point shots per minute and John's speed was 15 free throws per minute.

Review Video: Rational Expressions
Visit mometrix.com/academy and enter code: 415183

Polynomial Expressions

Fred buys some CDs for $12 each. He also buys two DVDs. The total that Fred spent is $60. Write an equation that shows the connection between the number of CDs and the average cost of a DVD.

Let c stand for the number of CDs that Fred buys. Also, let d stand for the average cost of one of the DVDs that Fred buys. The expression $12c$ gives the cost of the CDs and the expression $2d$ gives the cost of the DVDs. So the equation $12c + 2d = 60$ states the number of CDs and the average cost of a DVD.

Equations

Linear Equations

Equations that can be written as $ax + b = 0$, where $a \neq 0$, are referred to as **one variable linear equations**. A solution to such an equation is called a **root**. In the case where we have the equation $5x + 10 = 0$, if we solve for x we get a solution of $x = -2$. In other words, the root of the equation is

-2. This is found by first subtracting 10 from both sides, which gives $5x = -10$. Next, simply divide both sides by the coefficient of the variable, in this case 5, to get $x = -2$. This can be checked by plugging -2 back into the original equation $(5)(-2) + 10 = -10 + 10 = 0$.

The **solution set** is the set of all solutions of an equation. In our example, the solution set would simply be -2. If there were more solutions (there usually are in multivariable equations) then they would also be included in the solution set. When an equation has no true solutions, it is referred to as an **empty set**. Equations with identical solution sets are **equivalent equations**. An **identity** is a term whose value or determinant is equal to 1.

Review Video: Linear Equations Basics
Visit mometrix.com/academy and enter code: 793005

Linear equations can be written many ways. Below is a list of some forms linear equations can take:

- **Standard Form**: $Ax + By = C$; the slope is $\frac{-A}{B}$ and the y-intercept is $\frac{C}{B}$
- **Slope Intercept Form**: $y = mx + b$, where m is the slope and b is the y-intercept
- **Point-Slope Form**: $y - y_1 = m(x - x_1)$, where m is the slope and (x_1, y_1) is a point on the line
- **Two-Point Form**: $\frac{y-y_1}{x-x_1} = \frac{y_2-y_1}{x_2-x_1}$, where (x_1, y_1) and (x_2, y_2) are two points on the given line
- **Intercept Form**: $\frac{x}{x_1} + \frac{y}{y_1} = 1$, where $(x_1, 0)$ is the point at which a line intersects the x-axis, and $(0, y_1)$ is the point at which the same line intersects the y-axis

Review Video: Slope-Intercept and Point-Slope Forms
Visit mometrix.com/academy and enter code: 113216

Solving One-Variable Linear Equations

Multiply all terms by the lowest common denominator to eliminate any fractions. Look for addition or subtraction to undo so you can isolate the variable on one side of the equal sign. Divide both sides by the coefficient of the variable. When you have a value for the variable, substitute this value into the original equation to make sure you have a true equation. Consider the following example:

Kim's savings are represented by the table below. Represent her savings using an equation.

X (Months)	Y (Total Savings)
2	$1300
5	$2050
9	$3050
11	$3550
16	$4800

The table shows a function with a constant rate of change, or slope, of 250. Given the points on the table, the slopes can be calculated as $(2050 - 1300)/(5 - 2)$, $(3050 - 2050)/(9 - 5)$, $(3550 - 3050)/(11 - 9)$, and $(4800 - 3550)/(16 - 11)$, each of which equals 250. Thus, the table shows a constant rate of change, indicating a linear function. The slope-intercept form of a linear equation is written as $y = mx + b$, where m represents the slope and b represents the y-intercept. Substituting the slope into this form gives $y = 250x + b$. Substituting corresponding x- and y-values from any point into this equation will give the y-intercept, or b. Using the point, (2, 1300), gives $1300 = 250(2) + b$, which simplifies as b = 800. Thus, her savings may be represented by the equation $y = 250x + 800$.

RULES FOR MANIPULATING EQUATIONS

LIKE TERMS

Like terms are terms in an equation that have the same variable, regardless of whether or not they also have the same coefficient. This includes terms that *lack* a variable; all constants (i.e. numbers without variables) are considered like terms. If the equation involves terms with a variable raised to different powers, the like terms are those that have the variable raised to the same power.

For example, consider the equation $x^2 + 3x + 2 = 2x^2 + x - 7 + 2x$. In this equation, 2 and -7 are like terms; they are both constants. $3x$, x, and $2x$ are like terms; they all include the variable x raised to the first power. x^2 and $2x^2$ are like terms; they both include the variable x, raised to the second power. $2x$ and $2x^2$ are not like terms; although they both involve the variable x, the variable is not raised to the same power in both terms. The fact that they have the same coefficient, 2, is not relevant.

Review Video: Rules for Manipulating Equations
Visit mometrix.com/academy and enter code: 838871

CARRYING OUT THE SAME OPERATION ON BOTH SIDES OF AN EQUATION

When solving an equation, the general procedure is to carry out a series of operations on both sides of an equation, choosing operations that will tend to simplify the equation when doing so. The reason why the same operation must be carried out on both sides of the equation is because that leaves the meaning of the equation unchanged, and yields a result that is equivalent to the original equation. This would not be the case if we carried out an operation on one side of an equation and not the other. Consider what an equation means: it is a statement that two values or expressions are equal. If we carry out the same operation on both sides of the equation—add 3 to both sides, for example—then the two sides of the equation are changed in the same way, and so remain equal. If we do that to only one side of the equation—add 3 to one side but not the other—then that wouldn't be true; if we change one side of the equation but not the other then the two sides are no longer equal.

ADVANTAGE OF COMBINING LIKE TERMS

Combining like terms refers to adding or subtracting like terms—terms with the same variable—and therefore reducing sets of like terms to a single term. The main advantage of doing this is that it simplifies the equation. Often combining like terms can be done as the first step in solving an equation, though it can also be done later, such as after distributing terms in a product.

Review Video: Simplifying Equations by Combining Like Terms
Visit mometrix.com/academy and enter code: 668506

For example, consider the equation $2(x + 3) + 3(2 + x + 3) = -4$. The 2 and the 3 in the second set of parentheses are like terms, and we can combine them, yielding $2(x + 3) + 3(x + 5) = -4$. Now we can carry out the multiplications implied by the parentheses, distributing outer 2 and 3 accordingly: $2x + 6 + 3x + 15 = -4$. The $2x$ and the $3x$ are like terms, and we can add them together: $5x + 6 + 15 = -4$. Now, the constants 6, 15, and -4 are also like terms, and we can combine them as well: subtracting 6 and 15 from both sides of the equation, we get $5x = -4 - 6 - 15$, or $5x = -25$, which simplifies further to $x = -5$.

Canceling Terms on Opposite Sides of an Equation

Two terms on opposite sides of an equation can be canceled if and only if they *exactly* match each other. They must have the same variable raised to the same power and the same coefficient. For example, in the equation $3x + 2x^2 + 6 = 2x^2 - 6$, $2x^2$ appears on both sides of the equation, and can be canceled, leaving $3x + 6 = -6$. The 6 on each side of the equation can*not* be canceled, because it is added on one side of the equation and subtracted on the other. While they cannot be canceled, however, the 6 and -6 are like terms and can be combined, yielding $3x = -12$, which simplifies further to $x = -4$.

It's also important to note that the terms to be canceled must be independent terms and cannot be part of a larger term. For example, consider the equation $2(x + 6) = 3(x + 4) + 1$. We cannot cancel the xs, because even though they match each other they are part of the larger terms $2(x + 6)$ and $3(x + 4)$. We must first distribute the 2 and 3, yielding $2x + 12 = 3x + 12 + 1$. Now we see that the terms with the x's do not match, but the 12s do, and can be canceled, leaving $2x = 3x + 1$, which simplifies to $x = -1$.

Process for Manipulating Equations

Isolating Variables

To **isolate a variable** means to manipulate the equation so that the variable appears by itself on one side of the equation, and does not appear at all on the other side. Generally, an equation or inequality is considered to be solved once the variable is isolated and the other side of the equation or inequality is simplified as much as possible. In the case of a two-variable equation or inequality, only one variable needs to be isolated; it will not usually be possible to simultaneously isolate both variables.

For a linear equation—an equation in which the variable only appears raised to the first power—isolating a variable can be done by first moving all the terms with the variable to one side of the equation and all other terms to the other side. (*Moving* a term really means adding the inverse of the term to both sides; when a term is *moved* to the other side of the equation its sign is flipped.) Then combine like terms on each side. Finally, divide both sides by the coefficient of the variable, if applicable. The steps need not necessarily be done in this order, but this order will always work.

Review Video: Solving Equations with Variables on Both Sides
Visit mometrix.com/academy and enter code: 402497

Equations with More Than One Solution

Some types of non-linear equations, such as equations involving squares of variables, may have more than one solution. For example, the equation $x^2 = 4$ has two solutions: 2 and -2. Equations with absolute values can also have multiple solutions: $|x| = 1$ has the solutions $x = 1$ and $x = -1$.

It is also possible for a linear equation to have more than one solution, but only if the equation is true regardless of the value of the variable. In this case, the equation is considered to have infinitely many solutions, because any possible value of the variable is a solution. We know a linear equation has infinitely many solutions if when we combine like terms the variables cancel, leaving a true statement. For example, consider the equation $2(3x + 5) = x + 5(x + 2)$. Distributing, we get $6x + 10 = x + 5x + 10$; combining like terms gives $6x + 10 = 6x + 10$, and the $6x$ terms cancel to leave $10 = 10$. This is clearly true, so the original equation is true for any value of x. We could also have canceled the 10s leaving $0 = 0$, but again this is clearly true—in general if both sides of the equation match exactly, it has infinitely many solutions.

Equations with No Solution

Some types of non-linear equations, such as equations involving squares of variables, may have no solution. For example, the equation $x^2 = -2$ has no solutions in the real numbers, because the square of any real number must be positive. Similarly, $|x| = -1$ has no solution, because the absolute value of a number is always positive.

It is also possible for an equation to have no solution even if does not involve any powers greater than one or absolute values or other special functions. For example, the equation $2(x + 3) + x = 3x$ has no solution. We can see that if we try to solve it. First, we distribute, leaving $2x + 6 + x = 3x$. But now if we try to combine all the terms with the variable, we find that they cancel: we have $3x$ on the left and $3x$ on the right, canceling to leave us with $6 = 0$. This is clearly false. In general, whenever the variable terms in an equation cancel, leaving different constants on both sides, it means that the equation has no solution. (If we are left with the *same* constant on both sides, the equation has infinitely many solutions instead.)

Features of Equations That Require Special Treatment

Linear Equations

A linear equation is an equation in which variables only appear by themselves; they are not multiplied together, not with exponents other than one, and not inside absolute value signs or any other functions. For example, the equation $x + 1 - 3x = 5 - x$ is a linear equation; while x appears multiple times, it never appears with an exponent other than one, or inside any function. The two-variable equation $2x - 3y = 5 + 2x$ is also a linear equation. In contrast, the equation $x^2 - 5 = 3x$ is *not* a linear equation, because it involves the term x^2. $\sqrt{x} = 5$ is not a linear equation, because it involves a square root. $(x - 1)^2 = 4$ is not a linear equation because even though there's no exponent on the x directly, it appears as part of an expression that is squared. The two-variable equation $x + xy - y = 5$ is not a linear equation because it includes the term xy, where two variables are multiplied together.

Linear equations can always be solved (or shown to have no solution) by combining like terms and performing simple operations on both sides of the equation. Some non-linear equations can be solved by similar methods, but others may require more advanced methods of solution, if they can be solved analytically at all.

Solving Equations Involving Roots

In an equation involving roots, the first step is to isolate the term with the root, if possible, and then raise both sides of the equation to the appropriate power to eliminate it. Consider an example equation, $2\sqrt{x + 1} - 1 = 3$. In this case, begin by adding 1 to both sides, yielding $2\sqrt{x + 1} = 4$, and then dividing both sides by 2, yielding $\sqrt{x + 1} = 2$. Now square both sides, yielding $x + 1 = 4$. Finally, subtracting 1 from both sides yields $x = 3$.

Review Video: Solving Equations Involving Roots
Visit mometrix.com/academy and enter code: 297670

Squaring both sides of an equation may, however, yield a spurious solution—a solution to the squared equation that is *not* a solution of the original equation. It's therefore necessary to plug the solution back into the original equation to make sure it works. In this case, it does: $2\sqrt{3 + 1} - 1 = 2\sqrt{4} - 1 = 2(2) - 1 = 4 - 1 = 3$.

The same procedure applies for other roots as well. For example, given the equation $3 + \sqrt[3]{2x} = 5$, we can first subtract 3 from both sides, yielding $\sqrt[3]{2x} = 2$ and isolating the root. Raising both sides to the third power yields $2x = 2^3$, i.e. $2x = 8$. We can now divide both sides by 2 to get $x = 4$.

SOLVING EQUATIONS WITH EXPONENTS

To solve an equation involving an exponent, the first step is to isolate the variable with the exponent. We can then take the appropriate root of both sides to eliminate the exponent. For instance, for the equation $2x^3 + 17 = 5x^3 - 7$, we can subtract $5x^3$ from both sides to get $-3x^3 + 17 = -7$, and then subtract 17 from both sides to get $-3x^3 = -24$. Finally, we can divide both sides by -3 to get $x^3 = 8$. Finally, we can take the cube root of both sides to get $x = \sqrt[3]{8} = 2$.

Review Video: Solving Equations with Exponents
Visit mometrix.com/academy and enter code: 514557

One important but often overlooked point is that equations with an exponent greater than 1 may have more than one answer. The solution to $x^2 = 9$ isn't simply $x = 3$; it's $x = \pm 3$: that is, $x = 3$ or $x = -3$. For a slightly more complicated example, consider the equation $(x - 1)^2 - 1 = 3$. Adding one to both sides yields $(x - 1)^2 = 4$; taking the square root of both sides yields $x - 1 = 2$. We can then add 1 to both sides to get $x = 3$. However, there's a second solution: we also have the possibility that $x - 1 = -2$, in which case $x = -1$. Both $x = 3$ and $x = -1$ are valid solutions, as can be verified by substituting them both into the original equation.

SOLVING EQUATIONS WITH ABSOLUTE VALUES

When solving an equation with an absolute value, the first step is to isolate the absolute value term. We then consider two possibilities: when the expression inside the absolute value is positive or when it is negative. In the former case, the expression in the absolute value equals the expression on the other side of the equation; in the latter, it equals the additive inverse of that expression—the expression times negative one. We consider each case separately and finally check for spurious solutions.

For instance, consider solving $|2x - 1| + x = 5$ for x. We can first isolate the absolute value by moving the x to the other side: $|2x - 1| = -x + 5$. Now, we have two possibilities. First, that $2x - 1$ is positive, and hence $2x - 1 = -x + 5$. Rearranging and combining like terms yields $3x = 6$, and hence $x = 2$. The other possibility is that $2x - 1$ is negative, and hence $2x - 1 = -(-x + 5) = x - 5$. In this case, rearranging and combining like terms yields $x = -4$. Substituting $x = 2$ and $x = -4$ back into the original equation, we see that they are both valid solutions.

Note that the absolute value of a sum or difference applies to the sum or difference as a whole, not to the individual terms; in general, $|2x - 1|$ is not equal to $|2x + 1|$ or to $|2x| - 1$.

SPURIOUS SOLUTIONS

A **spurious solution** may arise when we square both sides of an equation as a step in solving it, or under certain other operations on the equation. It is a solution to the squared or otherwise modified equation that is *not* a solution of the original equation. To identify a spurious solution, it's useful when you solve an equation involving roots or absolute values to plug the solution back into the original equation to make sure it's valid.

CHOOSING WHICH VARIABLE TO ISOLATE IN TWO-VARIABLE EQUATIONS

Similar to methods for a one-variable equation, solving a two-variable equation involves isolating a variable: manipulating the equation so that a variable appears by itself on one side of the equation, and not at all on the other side. However, in a two-variable equation, you will usually only be able to isolate one of the variables; the other variable may appear on the other side along with constant terms, or with exponents or other functions.

Often one variable will be much more easily isolated than the other, and therefore that's the variable you should choose. If one variable appears with various exponents, and the other only raised it to the first power, the latter variable is the one to isolate. Given the equation $a^2 + 2b = a^3 + b + 3$, the b only appears to the first power, whereas a appears squared and cubed, so b is the variable that can be solved for: combining like terms and isolating the b on the left side of the equation, we get $b = a^3 - a^2 + 3$. If both variables are equally easy to isolate, then it's best to isolate the independent variable, if one is defined. If the two variables are x and y, the convention is that y is the independent variable.

PRACTICE

P1. Seeing the equation $2x + 4 = 4x + 7$, a student divides the first terms on each side by 2, yielding $x + 4 = 2x + 7$, and then combines like terms to get $x = -3$. However, this is incorrect, as can be seen by substituting -3 into the original equation. Explain what is wrong with the student's reasoning.

P2. Describe the steps necessary to solve the equation $2x + 1 - x = 4 + 3x + 7$.

P3. Describe the steps necessary to solve the equation $2(x + 5) = 7(4 - x)$.

P4. Find all real solutions to the equation $1 - \sqrt{x} = 2$.

P5. Find all real solutions to the equation $|x + 1| = 2x + 5$.

P6. Solve for x: $-x + 2\sqrt{x+5} + 1 = 3$.

P7. Ray earns \$10 an hour at his job. Write an equation for his earnings as a function of time spent working. Determine how long Ray has to work in order to earn \$360.

P8. Simplify the following: $3x + 2 + 2y = 5y - 7 + |2x - 1|$

PRACTICE SOLUTIONS

P1. As stated, it's easy to verify that the student's solution is incorrect: $2(-3) + 4 = -2$ and $4(-3) + 7 = -5$; clearly $-2 \neq -5$. The mistake was in the first step, which illustrates a common type of error in solving equations. The student tried to simplify the two variable terms by dividing them by 2. However, it's not valid to multiply or divide only one term on each side of an equation by a number; when multiplying or dividing, the operation must be applied to *every* term in the equation. So, dividing by 2 would yield not $x + 4 = 2x + 7$, but $x + 2 = 2x + \frac{7}{2}$. While this is now valid, that fraction is inconvenient to work with, so this may not be the best first step in solving the equation. Rather, it may have been better to first combine like terms: subtracting $4x$ from both sides yields $-2x + 4 = 7$; subtracting 4 from both sides yields $-2x = 3$; and *now* we can divide both sides by -2 to get $x = -\frac{3}{2}$.

P2. Our ultimate goal is to isolate the variable, x. To that end we first move all the terms containing x to the left side of the equation, and all the constant terms to the right side. Note that when we move a term to the other side of the equation its sign changes. We are therefore now left with $2x - x - 3x = 4 + 7 - 1$.

Next, we combine the like terms on each side of the equation, adding and subtracting the terms as appropriate. This leaves us with $-2x = 10$.

At this point, we're almost done; all that remains is to divide both sides by -2 to leave the x by itself. We now have our solution, $x = -5$. We can verify that this is a correct solution by substituting it back into the original equation.

P3. Generally, in equations that have a sum or difference of terms multiplied by another value or expression, the first step is to multiply those terms, distributing as necessary: $2(x + 5) = 2(x) + 2(5) = 2x + 10$, and $7(4 - x) = 7(4) - 7(x) = 28 - 7x$. So, the equation becomes $2x + 10 = 28 - 7x$. We can now add $7x$ to both sides to eliminate the variable from the right-hand side: $9x + 10 = 28$. Similarly, we can subtract 10 from both sides to move all the constants to the right: $9x = 18$. Finally, we can divide both sides by 9, yielding the final answer, $x = 2$.

P4. It's not hard to isolate the root: subtract one from both sides, yielding $-\sqrt{x} = 1$. Finally, multiply both sides by -1, yielding $\sqrt{x} = -1$. Squaring both sides of the equation yields $x = 1$. However, if we plug this back into the original equation, we get $1 - \sqrt{1} = 2$, which is false. Therefore $x = 1$ is a spurious solution, and the equation has no real solutions.

P5. This equation has two possibilities: $x + 1 = 2x + 5$, which simplifies to $x = -4$; or $x + 1 = -(2x + 5) = -2x - 5$, which simplifies to $x = -2$. However, if we try substituting both values back into the original equation, we see that only $x = -2$ yields a true statement. $x = -4$ is a spurious solution; $x = -2$ is the only valid solution to the equation.

P6. Start by isolating the term with the root. We can do that by moving the $-x$ and the 1 to the other side, yielding $2\sqrt{x+5} = 3 + x - 1$, or $2\sqrt{x+5} = x + 2$. Dividing both sides of the equation by 2 would give us a fractional term that could be messy to deal with, so we won't do that for now. Instead, we square both sides of the equation; note that on the left-hand side the 2 is outside the square root sign, so we have to square it. As a result, we get $4(x + 5) = (x + 2)^2$. Expanding both sides gives us $4x + 20 = x^2 + 4x + 4$. In this case, we see that we have $4x$ on both sides, so we can cancel the $4x$ (which is what allows us to solve this equation despite the different powers of x). We now have $20 = x^2 + 4$, or $x^2 = 16$. Since the variable is raised to an even power, we need to take the positive and negative roots, so $x = \pm 4$: that is, $x = 4$ or $x = -4$. Substituting both values into the original equation, we see that $x = 4$ satisfies the equation but $x = -4$ does not; hence $x = -4$ is a spurious solution, and the only solution to the equation is $x = 4$.

P7. The number of dollars that Ray earns is dependent on the number of hours he works, so earnings will be represented by the dependent variable y and hours worked will be represented by the independent variable x. He earns 10 dollars per hour worked, so his earnings can be calculated as $y = 10x$. To calculate the number of hours Ray must work in order to earn \$360, plug in 360 for y and solve for x:

$$360 = 10x$$
$$x = \frac{360}{10} = 36$$

P8. To simplify this equation, we must isolate one of its variables on one side of the equation. In this case, the x appears under an absolute value sign, which makes it difficult to isolate. The y, on the other hand, only appears without an exponent—the equation is linear in y. We will therefore choose to isolate the y. The first step, then, is to move all the terms with y to the left side of the equation, which we can do by subtracting $5y$ from both sides:

$$3x + 2 - 3y = -7 + |2x - 1|$$

We can then move all the terms that do *not* include y to the right side of the equation, by subtracting $3x$ and 2 from both sides of the equation:

$$-3y = -3x - 9 + |2x - 1|$$

Finally, we can isolate the y by dividing both sides by -3.

$$y = x + 3 - \frac{1}{3}|2x - 1|$$

This is as far as we can simplify the equation; we cannot combine the terms inside and outside the absolute value sign. We can therefore consider the equation to be solved.

INEQUALITIES

WORKING WITH INEQUALITIES

Commonly in algebra and other upper-level fields of math you find yourself working with mathematical expressions that do not equal each other. The statement comparing such expressions with symbols such as < (less than) or > (greater than) is called an *inequality*. An example of an inequality is $7x > 5$. To solve for x, simply divide both sides by 7 and the solution is shown to be $x > \frac{5}{7}$. Graphs of the solution set of inequalities are represented on a number line. Open circles are used to show that an expression approaches a number but is never quite equal to that number.

Review Video: Solving Multi-Step Inequalities
Visit mometrix.com/academy and enter code: 347842

Conditional inequalities are those with certain values for the variable that will make the condition true and other values for the variable where the condition will be false. **Absolute inequalities** can have any real number as the value for the variable to make the condition true, while there is no real number value for the variable that will make the condition false. Solving inequalities is done by following the same rules as for solving equations with the exception that when multiplying or dividing by a negative number the direction of the inequality sign must be flipped or reversed. **Double inequalities** are situations where two inequality statements apply to the same variable expression. An example of this is $-c < ax + b < c$.

Review Video: Conditional and Absolute Inequalities
Visit mometrix.com/academy and enter code: 980164

DETERMINING SOLUTIONS TO INEQUALITIES

To determine whether a coordinate is a solution of an inequality, you can substitute the values of the coordinate into the inequality, simplify, and check whether the resulting statement holds true. For instance, to determine whether $(-2, 4)$ is a solution of the inequality $y \geq -2x + 3$, substitute the values into the inequality, $4 \geq -2(-2) + 3$. Simplify the right side of the inequality and the result is $4 \geq 7$, which is a false statement. Therefore, the coordinate is not a solution of the inequality. You can also use this method to determine which part of the graph of an inequality is shaded. The graph of $y \geq -2x + 3$ includes the solid line $y = -2x + 3$ and, since it excludes the point $(-2, 4)$ to the left of the line, it is shaded to the right of the line.

Flipping Inequality Signs

When given an inequality, we can always turn the entire inequality around, swapping the two sides of the inequality and changing the inequality sign. For instance, $x + 2 > 2x - 3$ is equivalent to $2x - 3 < x + 2$. Aside from that, normally the inequality does not change if we carry out the same operation on both sides of the inequality. There is, however, one principal exception: if we *multiply* or *divide* both sides of the inequality by a *negative number*, the inequality is flipped. For example, if we take the inequality $-2x < 6$ and divide both sides by -2, the inequality flips and we are left with $x > -3$. This *only* applies to multiplication and division, and only with negative numbers. Multiplying or dividing both sides by a positive number, or adding or subtracting any number regardless of sign, does not flip the inequality.

Compound Inequalities

A **compound inequality** is an equality that consists of two inequalities combined with *and* or *or*. The two components of a proper compound inequality must be of opposite type: that is, one must be greater than (or greater than or equal to), the other less than (or less than or equal to). For instance, "$x + 1 < 2$ or $x + 1 > 3$" is a compound inequality, as is "$2x \geq 4$ and $2x \leq 6$." An *and* inequality can be written more compactly by having one inequality on each side of the common part: "$2x \geq 1$ and $2x \leq 6$," can also be written as $1 \leq 2x \leq 6$.

Review Video: Compound Inequalities
Visit mometrix.com/academy and enter code: 786318

In order for the compound inequality to be meaningful, the two parts of an *and* inequality must overlap; otherwise no numbers satisfy the inequality. On the other hand, if the two parts of an *or* inequality overlap, then *all* numbers satisfy the inequality and as such the inequality is usually not meaningful.

Solving a compound inequality requires solving each part separately. For example, given the compound inequality "$x + 1 < 2$ or $x + 1 > 3$," the first inequality, $x + 1 < 2$, reduces to $x < 1$, and the second part, $x + 1 > 3$, reduces to $x > 2$, so the whole compound inequality can be written as "$x < 1$ or $x > 2$." Similarly, $1 \leq 2x \leq 6$ can be solved by dividing each term by 2, yielding $\frac{1}{2} \leq x \leq 3$.

Solving Inequalities Involving Absolute Values

To solve an inequality involving an absolute value, first isolate the term with the absolute value. Then proceed to treat the two cases separately as with an absolute value equation, but flipping the inequality in the case where the expression in the absolute value is negative (since that essentially involves multiplying both sides by -1.) The two cases are then combined into a compound inequality; if the absolute value is on the greater side of the inequality, then it is an *or* compound inequality, if on the lesser side, then it's an *and*.

Consider the inequality $2 + |x - 1| \geq 3$. We can isolate the absolute value term by subtracting 2 from both sides: $|x - 1| \geq 1$. Now, we're left with the two cases $x - 1 \geq 1$ or $x - 1 \leq -1$: note that in the latter, negative case, the inequality is flipped. $x - 1 \geq 1$ reduces to $x \geq 2$, and $x - 1 \leq -1$ reduces to $x \leq 0$. Since in the inequality $|x - 1| \geq 1$ the absolute value is on the greater side, the two cases combine into an *or* compound inequality, so the final, solved inequality is "$x \leq 0$ or $x \geq 2$."

Solving Inequalities Involving Square Roots

Solving an inequality with a square root involves two parts. First, we solve the inequality as if it were an equation, isolating the square root and then squaring both sides of the equation. Second, we restrict the solution to the set of values of x for which the value inside the square root sign is non-negative.

Review Video: Solving Inequalities Involving Square Roots
Visit mometrix.com/academy and enter code: 800288

For example, in the inequality, $\sqrt{x-2}+1<5$, we can isolate the square root by subtracting 1 from both sides, yielding $\sqrt{x-2}<4$. Squaring both sides of the inequality yields $x-2<16$, so $x<18$. Since we can't take the square root of a negative number, we also require the part inside the square root to be non-negative. In this case, that means $x-2\geq 0$. Adding 2 to both sides of the inequality yields $x\geq 2$. Our final answer is a compound inequality combining the two simple inequalities: $x\geq 2$ and $x<18$, or $2\leq x<18$.

Note that we only get a compound inequality if the two simple inequalities are in opposite directions; otherwise we take the one that is more restrictive.

The same technique can be used for other even roots, such as fourth roots. It is *not*, however, used for cube roots or other odd roots—negative numbers *do* have cube roots, so the condition that the quantity inside the root sign cannot be negative does not apply.

SPECIAL CIRCUMSTANCES

Sometimes an inequality involving an absolute value or an even exponent is true for all values of x, and we don't need to do any further work to solve it. This is true if the inequality, once the absolute value or exponent term is isolated, says that term is greater than a negative number (or greater than or equal to zero). Since an absolute value or a number raised to an even exponent is *always* non-negative, this inequality is always true.

GRAPHICAL SOLUTIONS TO EQUATIONS AND INEQUALITIES

When equations are shown graphically, they are usually shown on a **Cartesian coordinate plane**. The Cartesian coordinate plane consists of two number lines placed perpendicular to each other, and intersecting at the zero point, also known as the origin. The horizontal number line is known as the x-axis, with positive values to the right of the origin, and negative values to the left of the origin. The vertical number line is known as the y-axis, with positive values above the origin, and negative values below the origin. Any point on the plane can be identified by an ordered pair in the form (x, y), called coordinates. The x-value of the coordinate is called the abscissa, and the y-value of the coordinate is called the ordinate. The two number lines divide the plane into **four quadrants**: I, II, III, and IV.

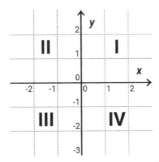

Note that in quadrant I $x>0$ and $y>0$, in quadrant II $x<0$ and $y>0$, in quadrant III $x<0$ and $y<0$, and in quadrant IV $x>0$ and $y<0$.

Recall that if the value of the slope of a line is positive, the line slopes upward from left to right. If the value of the slope is negative, the line slopes downward from left to right. If the y-coordinates are the same for two points on a line, the slope is 0 and the line is a **horizontal line**. If the x-coordinates are the same for two points on a line, there is no slope and the line is a **vertical line**. Two or more lines that have equivalent slopes are **parallel lines. Perpendicular lines** have slopes that are negative reciprocals of each other, such as $\frac{a}{b}$ and $\frac{-b}{a}$.

Graphing Simple Inequalities

To graph a simple inequality, we first mark on the number line the value that signifies the end point of the inequality. If the inequality is strict (involves a less than or greater than), we use a hollow circle; if it is not strict (less than or equal to or greater than or equal to), we use a solid circle. We then fill in the part of the number line that satisfies the inequality: to the left of the marked point for less than (or less than or equal to), to the right for greater than (or greater than or equal to).

For example, we would graph the inequality $x < 5$ by putting a hollow circle at 5 and filling in the part of the line to the left:

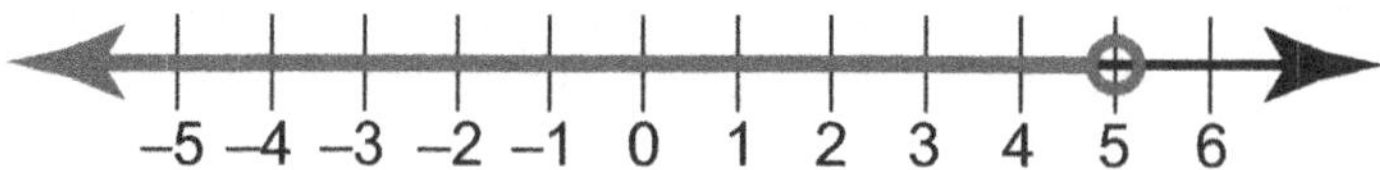

Graphing Compound Inequalities

To graph a compound inequality, we fill in both parts of the inequality for an *or* inequality, or the overlap between them for an *and* inequality. More specifically, we start by plotting the endpoints of each inequality on the number line. For an *or* inequality, we then fill in the appropriate side of the line for each inequality. Typically, the two component inequalities do not overlap, that means the shaded part is *outside* the two points. For an *and* inequality, we instead fill in the part of the line that meets both inequalities.

For the inequality "$x \leq -3$ or $x > 4$," we first put a solid circle at –3 and a hollow circle at 4. We then fill the parts of the line *outside* these circles:

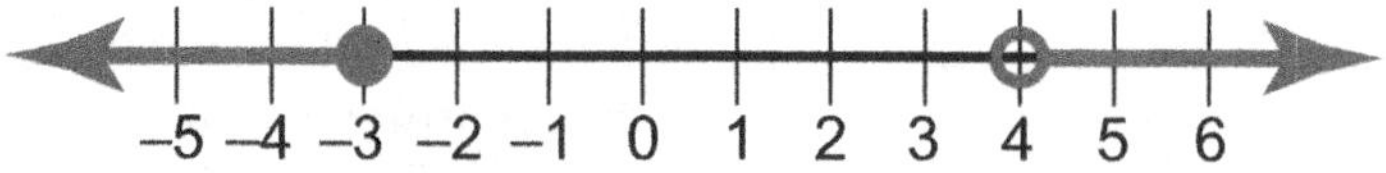

Graphing Inequalities Including Absolute Values

An inequality with an absolute value can be converted to a compound inequality. To graph the inequality, first convert it to a compound inequality, and then graph that normally. If the absolute value is on the greater side of the inequality, we end up with an *or* inequality; we plot the endpoints of the inequality on the number line and fill in the part of the line *outside* those points. If the absolute value is on the smaller side of the inequality, we end up with an *and* inequality; we plot the endpoints of the inequality on the number line and fill in the part of the line *between* those points.

For example, the inequality $|x + 1| \geq 4$ can be rewritten as $x \geq 3$ or $x \leq -5$. We place solid circles at the points 3 and -5 and fill in the part of the line *outside* them:

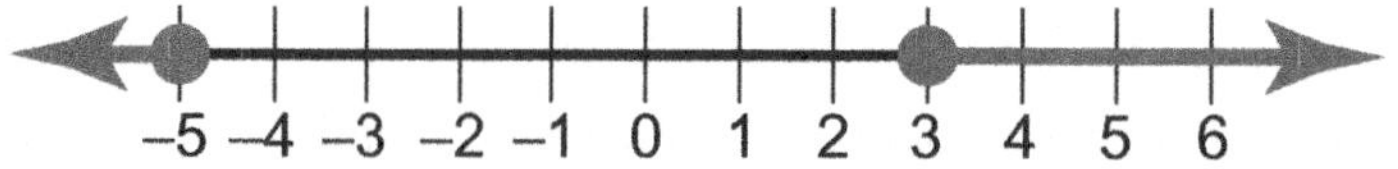

Graphing Equations in Two Variables

One way of graphing an equation in two variables is to plot enough points to get an idea for its shape, and then draw the appropriate curve through those points. A point can be plotted by substituting in a value for one variable and solving for the other. If the equation is linear, we only need two points, and can then draw a straight line between them.

Review Video: Linear Function
Visit mometrix.com/academy and enter code: 699478

For example, consider the equation $y = 2x - 1$. This is a linear equation—both variables only appear raised to the first power—so we only need two points. When $x = 0$, $y = 2(0) - 1 = -1$. When $x = 2$, $y = 2(2) - 1 = 3$. We can therefore choose the points $(0, -1)$ and $(2, 3)$, and draw a line between them:

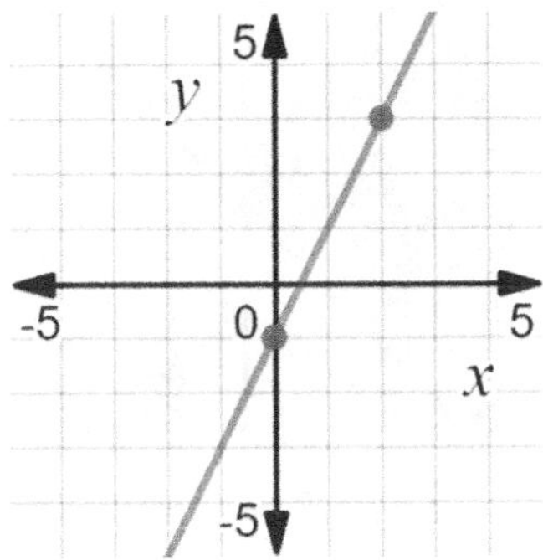

Graphing Inequalities in Two Variables

To graph an inequality in two variables, we first graph the border of the inequality. This means graphing the equation that we get if we replace the inequality sign with an equals sign. If the inequality is strict (> or <), we graph the border with a dashed or dotted line; if it is not strict (≥ or ≤), we use a solid line. We can then test any point not on the border to see if it satisfies the inequality. If it does, we shade in that side of the border; if not, we shade in the other side. As an example, consider $y > 2x + 2$. To graph this inequality, we first graph the border, $y = 2x + 2$. Since it is a strict inequality, we use a dashed line. Then, we choose a test point. This can be any point not on the border; in this case, we will choose the origin, $(0, 0)$. (This makes the calculation easy and is generally a good choice unless the border passes through the origin.) Putting this into the original inequality, we get $0 > 2(0) + 2$, i.e. $0 > 2$. This is *not* true, so we shade in the side of the border that does *not* include the point $(0, 0)$:

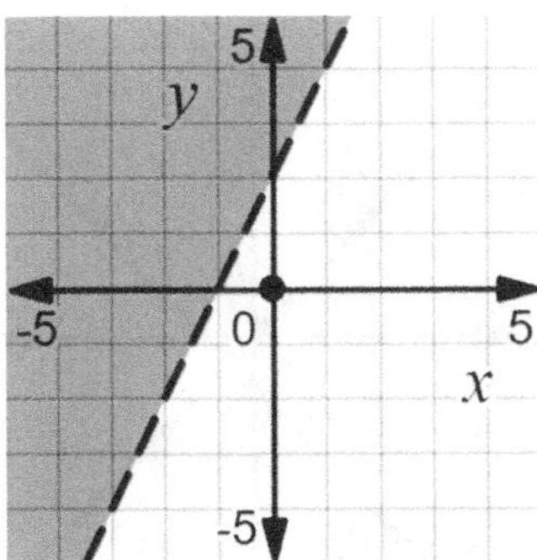

Graphing Compound Inequalities in Two Variables

One way to graph a compound inequality in two variables is to first graph each of the component inequalities. For an *and* inequality, we then shade in only the parts where the two graphs overlap; for an *or* inequality, we shade in any region that pertains to either of the individual inequalities.

> **Review Video: Graphing Solutions to Inequalities**
> Visit mometrix.com/academy and enter code: 391281

Consider the graph of "$y \geq x - 1$ *and* $y \leq -x$":

We first shade in the individual inequalities:

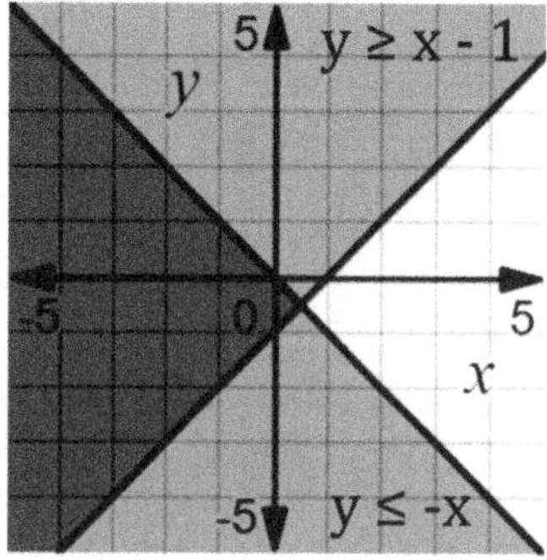

Now, since the compound inequality has an *and*, we only leave shaded the overlap—the part that pertains to *both* inequalities:

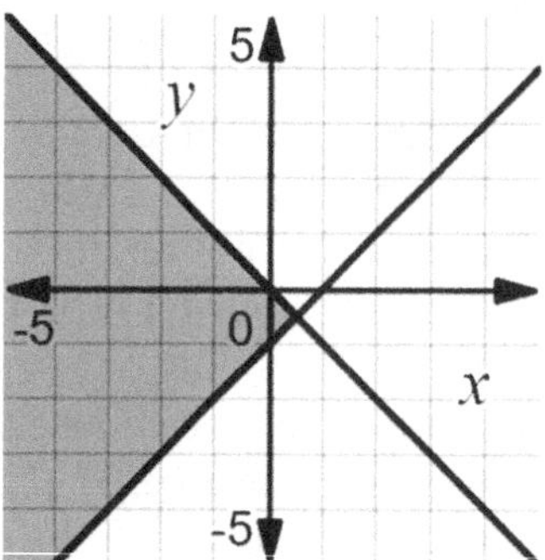

If instead the inequality had been "$y \geq x - 1$ *or* $y \leq -x$," our final graph would involve the *total* shaded area:

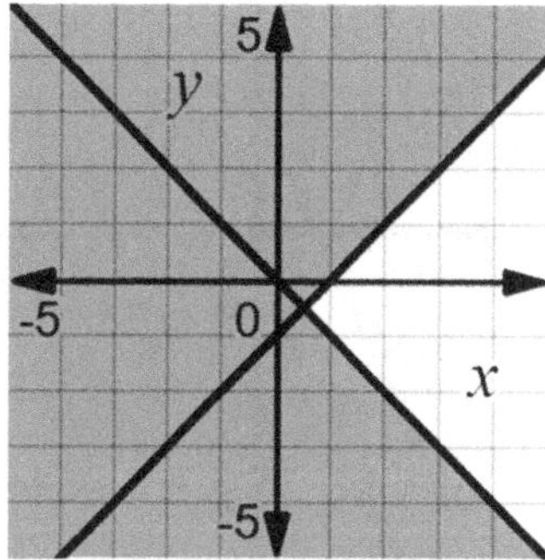

Practice

P1. Analyze the following inequalities:

(a) $2 - |x + 1| < 3$
(b) $2(x - 1)^2 + 7 \leq 1$

P2. Graph the following on a number line:

(a) $x \geq 3$
(b) $-2 \leq x \leq 6$
(c) $|x| < 2$

Practice Solutions

P1. **(a)** Subtracting 2 from both sides yields $-|x + 1| < 1$; multiplying by -1 and flipping the inequality, since we're multiplying by a negative number, yields $|x + 1| > -1$. But since the absolute value cannot be negative, it's *always* greater than -1, so this inequality is true for all values of x.

(b) Subtracting 7 from both sides yields $2(x - 1)^2 \leq -6$; dividing by 2 yields $(x - 1)^2 \leq -3$. But $(x - 1)^2$ must be nonnegative, and hence cannot be less than or equal to -3; this inequality has no solution.

P2. **(a)** We would graph the inequality $x \geq 3$ by putting a solid circle at 3 and filling in the part of the line to the right:

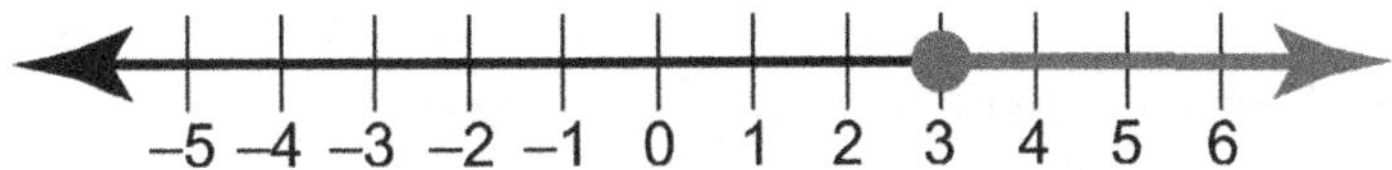

(b) The inequality $-2 \leq x \leq 6$ is equivalent to "$x \geq -2$ and $x \leq 6$." To plot this compound inequality, we first put solid circles at -2 and 6, and then fill in the part of the line *between* these circles:

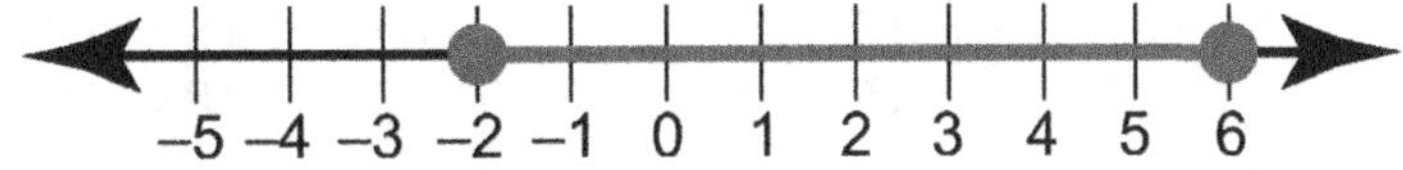

(c) The inequality $|x| < 2$ can be rewritten as "$x > -2$ and $x < 2$." We place hollow circles at the points -2 and 2 and fill in the part of the line between them:

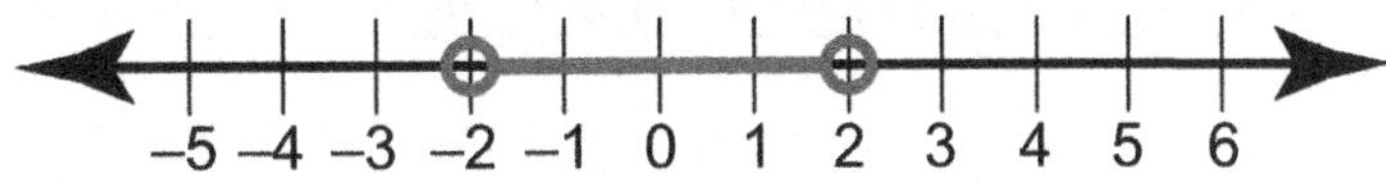

Systems of Equations

Solving Systems of Equations

Systems of equations are sets of simultaneous equations that all use the same variables. A solution to a system of equations must be true for each equation in the system. **Consistent systems** are those with at least one solution. **Inconsistent systems** are systems of equations that have no solution.

Substitution

To solve a system of linear equations by **substitution**, start with the easier equation and solve for one of the variables. Express this variable in terms of the other variable. Substitute this expression in the other equation, and solve for the other variable. The solution should be expressed in the form (x, y). Substitute the values into both of the original equations to check your answer. Consider the following system of equations:

$$x + 6y = 15$$
$$3x - 12y = 18$$

Solving the first equation for x: $x = 15 - 6y$

Substitute this value in place of x in the second equation, and solve for y:

$$3(15 - 6y) - 12y = 18$$
$$45 - 18y - 12y = 18$$
$$30y = 27$$
$$y = \frac{27}{30} = \frac{9}{10} = 0.9$$

Plug this value for y back into the first equation to solve for x:

$$x = 15 - 6(0.9) = 15 - 5.4 = 9.6$$

Check both equations if you have time:

$$9.6 + 6(0.9) = 15 \qquad 3(9.6) - 12(0.9) = 18$$
$$9.6 + 5.4 = 15 \qquad 28.8 - 10.8 = 18$$
$$15 = 15 \qquad 18 = 18$$

Therefore, the solution is $(9.6, 0.9)$.

Review Video: What is the Substitution Method?
Visit mometrix.com/academy and enter code: 565151

Elimination

To solve a system of equations using **elimination**, begin by rewriting both equations in standard form $Ax + By = C$. Check to see if the coefficients of one pair of like variables add to zero. If not, multiply one or both of the equations by a non-zero number to make one set of like variables add to zero. Add the two equations to solve for one of the variables. Substitute this value into one of the original equations to solve for the other variable. Check your work by substituting into the other equation. Now, let's look at solving the following system using the elimination method:

$$5x + 6y = 4$$
$$x + 2y = 4$$

If we multiply the second equation by -3, we can eliminate the y terms:

$$5x + 6y = 4$$
$$-3x - 6y = -12$$

Add the equations together and solve for x:

$$2x = -8$$
$$x = \frac{-8}{2} = -4$$

Plug the value for x back in to either of the original equations and solve for y:

$$-4 + 2y = 4$$
$$y = \frac{4+4}{2} = 4$$

Check both equations if you have time:

$$5(-4) + 6(4) = 4 \qquad -4 + 2(4) = 4$$
$$-20 + 24 = 4 \qquad -4 + 8 = 4$$
$$4 = 4 \qquad 4 = 4$$

Therefore, the solution is (-4, 4).

Review Video: Using Substitution and Elimination to Solve Linear Systems
Visit mometrix.com/academy and enter code: 958611

GRAPHICALLY

To solve a system of linear equations **graphically**, plot both equations on the same graph. The solution of the equations is the point where both lines cross. If the lines do not cross (are parallel), then there is **no solution**.

For example, consider the following system of equations:

$$y = 2x + 7$$
$$y = -x + 1$$

Since these equations are given in slope-intercept form, they are easy to graph; the y intercepts of the lines are $(0, 7)$ and $(0, 1)$. The respective slopes are 2 and –1, thus the graphs look like this:

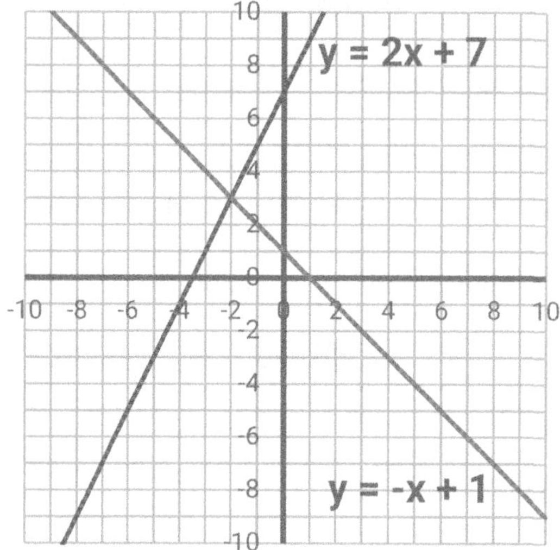

The two lines intersect at the point $(-2, 3)$, thus this is the solution to the system of equations.

Solving a system graphically is generally only practical if both coordinates of the solution are integers; otherwise the intersection will lie between gridlines on the graph and the coordinates will be difficult or impossible to determine exactly. It also helps if, as in this example, the equations are in slope-intercept form or some other form that makes them easy to graph. Otherwise, another method of solution (by substitution or elimination) is likely to be more useful.

Solving Systems of Equations Using the Trace Feature

Using the **trace feature** on a calculator requires that you rewrite each equation, isolating the y-variable on one side of the equal sign. Enter both equations in the graphing calculator and plot the graphs simultaneously. Use the trace cursor to find where the two lines cross. Use the zoom feature if necessary to obtain more accurate results. Always check your answer by substituting into the original equations. The trace method is likely to be less accurate than other methods due to the resolution of graphing calculators, but is a useful tool to provide an approximate answer.

Calculations Using Points

Sometimes you need to perform calculations using only points on a graph as input data. Using points, you can determine what the **midpoint** and **distance** are. If you know the equation for a line you can calculate the distance between the line and the point.

Review Video: Calculations Using Points on a Graph
Visit mometrix.com/academy and enter code: 883228

To find the **midpoint** of two points (x_1, y_1) and (x_2, y_2), average the x-coordinates to get the x-coordinate of the midpoint, and average the y-coordinates to get the y-coordinate of the midpoint. The formula is: $\left(\frac{x_1+x_2}{2}, \frac{y_1+y_2}{2}\right)$.

The **distance** between two points is the same as the length of the hypotenuse of a right triangle with the two given points as endpoints, and the two sides of the right triangle parallel to the x-axis and y-axis, respectively. The length of the segment parallel to the x-axis is the difference between the x-coordinates of the two points. The length of the segment parallel to the y-axis is the difference between the y-coordinates of the two points. Use the Pythagorean theorem $a^2 + b^2 = c^2$ or $c = \sqrt{a^2 + b^2}$ to find the distance. The formula is $d = \sqrt{(x_2 - x_1)^2 + (y_2 - y_1)^2}$.

When a line is in the format $Ax + By + C = 0$, where A, B, and C are coefficients, you can use a point (x_1, y_1) not on the line and apply the formula $d = \frac{|Ax_1 + By_1 + C|}{\sqrt{A^2 + B^2}}$ to find the distance between the line and the point (x_1, y_1).

PRACTICE

P1. Solve the following systems of equations:

(a)
$$\begin{aligned} 3x + 4y &= 9 \\ -12x + 7y &= 10 \end{aligned}$$

(b)
$$\begin{aligned} -3x + 2y &= -1 \\ 4x - 5y &= 6 \end{aligned}$$

P2. Find the distance and midpoint between points (2, 4) and (8,6).

PRACTICE SOLUTIONS

P1. (a) If we multiply the first equation by 4, we can eliminate the x terms:

$$\begin{aligned} 12x + 16y &= 36 \\ -12x + 7y &= 10 \end{aligned}$$

Add the equations together and solve for y:

$$\begin{aligned} 23y &= 46 \\ y &= 2 \end{aligned}$$

Plug the value for y back in to either of the original equations and solve for x:

$$\begin{aligned} 3x + 4(2) &= 9 \\ x &= \frac{9 - 8}{3} = \frac{1}{3} \end{aligned}$$

The solution is $\left(\frac{1}{3}, 2\right)$

(b) Solving the first equation for y:

$$\begin{aligned} -3x + 2y &= -1 \\ 2y &= 3x - 1 \\ y &= \frac{3x - 1}{2} \end{aligned}$$

Substitute this expression in place of y in the second equation, and solve for x:

$$\begin{aligned} 4x - 5\left(\frac{3x-1}{2}\right) &= 6 \\ 4x - \frac{15x}{2} + \frac{5}{2} &= 6 \\ 8x - 15x + 5 &= 12 \\ -7x &= 7 \\ x &= -1 \end{aligned}$$

Plug the value for x back in to either of the original equations and solve for y:

$$\begin{aligned} -3(-1) + 2y &= -1 \\ 3 + 2y &= -1 \\ 2y &= -4 \\ y &= -2 \end{aligned}$$

The solution is $(-1, -2)$

P2. Use the formulas for distance and midpoint:

$$\begin{aligned} \text{Distance} &= \sqrt{(x_2 - x_1)^2 + (y_2 - y_1)^2} \\ &= \sqrt{(8-2)^2 + (6-4)^2} \\ &= \sqrt{(6)^2 + (2)^2} \\ &= \sqrt{36 + 4} \\ &= \sqrt{40} \text{ or } 2\sqrt{10} \end{aligned}$$

$$\begin{aligned} \text{Midpoint} &= \left(\frac{x_1 + x_2}{2}, \frac{y_1 + y_2}{2}\right) \\ &= \left(\frac{2+8}{2}, \frac{4+6}{2}\right) \\ &= \left(\frac{10}{2}, \frac{10}{2}\right) \\ &= (5,5) \end{aligned}$$

POLYNOMIAL ALGEBRA

POLYNOMIALS

Polynomials are made up of monomials and polynomials. A **monomial** is a single constant, variable, or product of constants and variables, such as 7, x, $2x$, or x^3y. There will never be addition or subtraction symbols in a monomial. Like monomials have like variables, but they may have different coefficients. **Polynomials** are algebraic expressions which use addition and subtraction to combine two or more monomials. Two terms make a **binomial**, three terms make a **trinomial**, etc. The **degree of a monomial** is the sum of the exponents of the variables. The **degree of a polynomial** is the highest degree of any individual term.

Review Video: Polynomials
Visit mometrix.com/academy and enter code: 305005

SIMPLIFYING POLYNOMIALS

Simplifying polynomials requires combining like terms. The like terms in a polynomial expression are those that have the same variable raised to the same power. It is often helpful to connect the like terms with arrows or lines in order to separate them from the other monomials. Once you have determined the like terms, you can rearrange the polynomial by placing them together. Remember to include the sign that is in front of each term. Once the like terms are placed together, you can apply each operation and simplify. When adding and subtracting polynomials, only add and subtract the **coefficient**, or the number part; the variable and exponent stay the same.

Review Video: Adding and Subtracting Polynomials
Visit mometrix.com/academy and enter code: 124088

THE FOIL METHOD

In general, multiplying polynomials is done by multiplying each term in one polynomial by each term in the other and adding the results. In the specific case for multiplying binomials, there is useful acronym, FOIL, that can help you make sure to cover each combination of terms. The **FOIL method** for $(Ax + By)(Cx + Dy)$ would be:

F	Multiply the *first* terms of each binomial	$(\overbrace{Ax}^{first} + By)(\overbrace{Cx}^{first} + Dy)$	ACx^2
O	Multiply the *outer* terms	$(\overbrace{Ax}^{outer} + By)(Cx + \overbrace{Dy}^{outer})$	$ADxy$
I	Multiply the *inner* terms	$(Ax + \overbrace{By}^{inner})(\overbrace{Cx}^{inner} + Dy)$	$BCxy$
L	Multiply the *last* terms of each binomial	$(Ax + \overbrace{By}^{last})(Cx + \overbrace{Dy}^{last})$	BDy^2

Then add up the result of each and combine like terms: $ACx^2 + (AD + BC)xy + BDy^2$.

For example, using the FOIL method on binomials $(x + 2)$ and $(x - 3)$:

$$\begin{aligned}
\text{First: } & (\boxed{x} + 2)(\boxed{x} + (-3)) \rightarrow & (x)(x) &= x^2 \\
\text{Outer: } & (\boxed{x} + 2)(x + \boxed{(-3)}) \rightarrow & (x)(-3) &= -3x \\
\text{Inner: } & (x + \boxed{2})(\boxed{x} + (-3)) \rightarrow & (2)(x) &= 2x \\
\text{Last: } & (x + \boxed{2})(x + \boxed{(-3)}) \rightarrow & (2)(-3) &= -6
\end{aligned}$$

This results in: $(x^2) + (-3x) + (2x) + (-6)$

Combine like terms: $x^2 + (-3 + 2)x + (-6) = x^2 - x - 6$

Review Video: Multiplying Terms Using the FOIL Method
Visit mometrix.com/academy and enter code: 854792

DIVIDING POLYNOMIALS

Use long division to divide a polynomial by either a monomial or another polynomial of equal or lesser degree.

When **dividing by a monomial**, divide each term of the polynomial by the monomial.

When **dividing by a polynomial**, begin by arranging the terms of each polynomial in order of one variable. You may arrange in ascending or descending order, but be consistent with both polynomials. To get the first term of the quotient, divide the first term of the dividend by the first term of the divisor. Multiply the first term of the quotient by the entire divisor and subtract that product from the dividend. Repeat for the second and successive terms until you either get a remainder of zero or a remainder whose degree is less than the degree of the divisor. If the quotient has a remainder, write the answer as a mixed expression in the form:

$$\text{quotient} + \frac{\text{remainder}}{\text{divisor}}$$

For example, we can evaluate the following expression in the same way as long division:

$$\frac{x^3 - 3x^2 - 2x + 5}{x - 5}$$

$$\begin{array}{r|llll} & x^2 & +2x & +8 & \\ \hline x-5 & x^3 & -3x^2 & -2x & +5 \\ & x^3 & -5x^2 & & \\ \hline & & 2x^2 & -2x & \\ & & 2x^2 & -10x & \\ \hline & & & 8x & +5 \\ & & & 8x & +40 \\ \hline & & & & 45 \end{array}$$

$$\frac{x^3 - 3x^2 - 2x + 5}{x - 5} = x^2 + 2x + 8 + \frac{45}{x - 5}$$

When **factoring** a polynomial, first check for a common monomial factor, that is look to see if each coefficient has a common factor or if each term has an x in it. If the factor is a trinomial but not a perfect trinomial square, look for a factorable form, such as one of these:

$$x^2 + (a + b)x + ab = (x + a)(x + b)$$
$$(ac)x^2 + (ad + bc)x + bd = (ax + b)(cx + d)$$

For factors with four terms, look for groups to factor. Once you have found the factors, write the original polynomial as the product of all the factors. Make sure all of the polynomial factors are prime. Monomial factors may be *prime* or *composite*. Check your work by multiplying the factors to make sure you get the original polynomial.

Below are patterns of some special products to remember to help make factoring easier:

- Perfect trinomial squares: $x^2 + 2xy + y^2 = (x + y)^2$ or $x^2 - 2xy + y^2 = (x - y)^2$
- Difference between two squares: $x^2 - y^2 = (x + y)(x - y)$
- Sum of two cubes: $x^3 + y^3 = (x + y)(x^2 - xy + y^2)$
  - Note: the second factor is *not* the same as a perfect trinomial square, so do not try to factor it further.
- Difference between two cubes: $x^3 - y^3 = (x - y)(x^2 + xy + y^2)$
  - Again, the second factor is *not* the same as a perfect trinomial square.
- Perfect cubes: $x^3 + 3x^2y + 3xy^2 + y^3 = (x + y)^3$ and $x^3 - 3x^2y + 3xy^2 - y^3 = (x - y)^3$

RATIONAL EXPRESSIONS

Rational expressions are fractions with polynomials in both the numerator and the denominator; the value of the polynomial in the denominator cannot be equal to zero. Be sure to keep track of values that make the denominator of the original expression zero as the final result inherits the same restrictions. For example, a denominator of $x - 3$ indicates that the expression is not defined when $x = 3$ and as such, regardless of any operations done to the expression, it remains undefined there.

To **add or subtract** rational expressions, first find the common denominator, then rewrite each fraction as an equivalent fraction with the common denominator. Finally, add or subtract the numerators to get the numerator of the answer, and keep the common denominator as the denominator of the answer.

When **multiplying** rational expressions factor each polynomial and cancel like factors (a factor which appears in both the numerator and the denominator). Then, multiply all remaining factors in the numerator to get the numerator of the product, and multiply the remaining factors in the denominator to get the denominator of the product. Remember: cancel entire factors, not individual terms.

To **divide** rational expressions, take the reciprocal of the divisor (the rational expression you are dividing by) and multiply by the dividend.

SIMPLIFYING RATIONAL EXPRESSIONS

To simplify a rational expression, factor the numerator and denominator completely. Factors that are the same and appear in the numerator and denominator have a ratio of 1. For example, look at the following expression:

$$\frac{x-1}{1-x^2}$$

The denominator, $(1-x^2)$, is a difference of squares. It can be factored as $(1-x)(1+x)$. The factor $1-x$ and the numerator $x-1$ are opposites and have a ratio of –1. Rewrite the numerator as $-1(1-x)$. So, the rational expression can be simplified as follows:

$$\frac{x-1}{1-x^2} = \frac{-1(1-x)}{(1-x)(1+x)} = \frac{-1}{1+x}$$

Note that since the original expression is only defined for $x \neq \{-1, 1\}$, the simplified expression has the same restrictions.

Review Video: Reducing Rational Expressions
Visit mometrix.com/academy and enter code: 788868

PRACTICE

P1. Expand the following polynomials:

(a) $(x+3)(x-7)(2x)$

(b) $(x+2)^2(x-2)^2$

(c) $(x^2+5x+5)(3x-1)$

P2. Evaluate the following rational expressions:

(a) $\frac{x^3-2x^2-5x+6}{3x+6}$

(b) $\frac{x^2+4x+4}{4-x^2}$

PRACTICE SOLUTIONS

P1. (a) Apply the FOIL method and the distributive property of multiplication:

$$\begin{aligned}(x+3)(x-7)(2x) &= (x^2-7x+3x-21)(2x)\\ &= (x^2-4x-21)(2x)\\ &= 2x^3-8x^2-42x\end{aligned}$$

(b) Note the difference of squares form:

$$\begin{aligned}(x+2)^2(x-2)^2 &= (x+2)(x+2)(x-2)(x-2)\\ &= [(x+2)(x-2)][(x+2)(x-2)]\\ &= (x^2-4)(x^2-4)\\ &= x^4-8x^2+16\end{aligned}$$

(c) Multiply each pair of monomials and combine like terms:

$$\begin{aligned}(x^2+5x+5)(3x-1) &= 3x^3+15x^2+15x-x^2-5x-5\\ &= 3x^3+14x^2+10x-5\end{aligned}$$

P2. (a) Rather than trying to factor the fourth-degree polynomial, we can use long division:

$$\frac{x^3-2x^2-5x+6}{3x+6}=\frac{x^3-2x^2-5x+6}{3(x+2)}$$

$$\begin{array}{r|l} & x^2 \quad -4x \quad +3 \\ x+2 & x^3-2x^2-5x+6 \\ & \underline{x^3+2x^2} \\ & -4x^2-5x \\ & \underline{-4x^2-8x} \\ & 3x+6 \\ & \underline{3x+6} \\ & 0 \end{array}$$

$$\frac{x^3-2x^2-5x+6}{3(x+2)}=\frac{x^2-4x+3}{3}$$

Note that since the original expression is only defined for $x \neq \{-2\}$, the simplified expression has the same restrictions.

(b) The denominator, $(4-x^2)$, is a difference of squares. It can be factored as $(2-x)(2+x)$. The numerator, (x^2+4x+4), is a perfect square. It can be factored as $(x+2)(x+2)$. So, the rational expression can be simplified as follows:

$$\frac{x^2+4x+4}{4-x^2}=\frac{(x+2)(x+2)}{(2-x)(2+x)}=\frac{(x+2)}{(2-x)}$$

Note that since the original expression is only defined for $x \neq \{-2, 2\}$, the simplified expression has the same restrictions.

Quadratics

Solving Quadratic Equations

Quadratic equations are a special set of trinomials of the form $y = ax^2 + bx + c$ that occur commonly in math and real-world applications. The **roots** of a quadratic equation are the solutions that satisfy the equation when $y = 0$; in other words, where the graph touches the x-axis. There are several ways to determine these solutions including using the quadratic formula, factoring, completing the square, and graphing the function.

> **Review Video: Changing Constants in Graphs of Functions: Quadratic Equations**
> Visit mometrix.com/academy and enter code: 476276

Quadratic Formula

The **quadratic formula** is used to solve quadratic equations when other methods are more difficult. To use the quadratic formula to solve a quadratic equation, begin by rewriting the equation in standard form $ax^2 + bx + c = 0$, where a, b, and c are coefficients. Once you have identified the values of the coefficients, substitute those values into the quadratic formula

$$x = \frac{-b \pm \sqrt{b^2 - 4ac}}{2a}$$

Evaluate the equation and simplify the expression. Again, check each root by substituting into the original equation. In the quadratic formula, the portion of the formula under the radical $(b^2 - 4ac)$ is called the **discriminant**. If the discriminant is zero, there is only one root: $-\frac{b}{2a}$. If the discriminant is positive, there are two different real roots. If the discriminant is negative, there are no real roots, you will instead find complex roots. Often these solutions don't make sense in context and are ignored.

> **Review Video: Using the Quadratic Formula**
> Visit mometrix.com/academy and enter code: 163102

Factoring

To solve a quadratic equation by factoring, begin by rewriting the equation in standard form, $x^2 + bx + c = 0$. Remember that the goal of factoring is to find numbers f and g such that $(x + f)(x + g) = x^2 + (f + g)x + fg$, in other words $(f + g) = b$ and $fg = c$. This can be a really useful method when b and c are integers. Determine the factors of c and look for pairs that could sum to b.

For example, consider finding the roots of $x^2 + 6x - 16 = 0$. The factors of -16 include, -4 and 4, -8 and 2, -2 and 8, -1 and 16, and 1 and -16. The factors that sum to 6 are -2 and 8. Write these factors as the product of two binomials, $0 = (x - 2)(x + 8)$. Finally, since these binomials multiply together to equal zero, set them each equal to zero and solve each for x. This results in $x - 2 = 0$, which simplifies to $x = 2$ and $x + 8 = 0$, which simplifies to $x = -8$. Therefore, the roots of the equation are 2 and -8.

> **Review Video: Factoring Quadratic Equations**
> Visit mometrix.com/academy and enter code: 336566

COMPLETING THE SQUARE

One way to find the roots of a quadratic equation is to find a way to manipulate it such that it follows the form of a perfect square $(x^2 + 2px + p^2)$ by adding and subtracting a constant. This process is called **completing the square**. In other words, if you are given a quadratic that is not a perfect square, $x^2 + bx + c = 0$, you can find a constant d that could be added in to make it a perfect square:

$$x^2 + bx + c + (d - d) = 0; \ \{\text{Let } b = 2p \text{ and } c + d = p^2\}$$
$$\text{then: } x^2 + 2px + p^2 - d = 0 \text{ and } d = \frac{b^2}{4} - c$$

Once you have completed the square you can find the roots of the resulting equation:

$$\begin{aligned} x^2 + 2px + p^2 - d &= 0 \\ (x + p)^2 &= d \\ x + p &= \pm\sqrt{d} \\ x &= -p \pm \sqrt{d} \end{aligned}$$

It is worth noting that substituting the original expressions into this solution gives the same result as the quadratic formula where $a = 1$:

$$x = -p \pm \sqrt{d} = -\frac{b}{2} \pm \sqrt{\frac{b^2}{4} - c} = -\frac{b}{2} \pm \frac{\sqrt{b^2 - 4c}}{2} = \frac{-b \pm \sqrt{b^2 - 4c}}{2}$$

Completing the square can be seen as arranging block representations of each of the terms to be as close to a square as possible and then filling in the gaps. For example, consider the quadratic expression $x^2 + 6x + 2$:

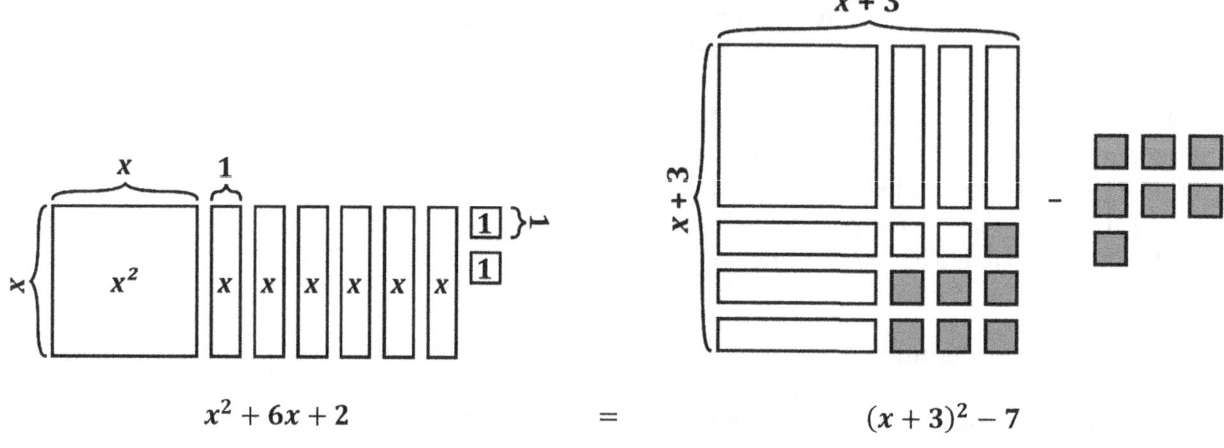

Review Video: Completing the Square
Visit mometrix.com/academy and enter code: 982479

USING GIVEN ROOTS TO FIND QUADRATIC EQUATION

One way to find the roots of a quadratic equation is to factor the equation and use the **zero product property**, setting each factor of the equation equal to zero to find the corresponding root. We can use this technique in reverse to find an equation given its roots. Each root corresponds to a linear equation which in turn corresponds to a factor of the quadratic equation.

For example, we can find a quadratic equation whose roots are $x = 2$ and $x = -1$. The root $x = 2$ corresponds to the equation $x - 2 = 0$, and the root $x = -1$ corresponds to the equation $x + 1 = 0$.

These two equations correspond to the factors $(x - 2)$ and $(x + 1)$, from which we can derive the equation $(x - 2)(x + 1) = 0$, or $x^2 - x - 2 = 0$.

Any integer multiple of this entire equation will also yield the same roots, as the integer will simply cancel out when the equation is factored. For example, $2x^2 - 2x - 4 = 0$ factors as $2(x - 2)(x + 1) = 0$.

Solving a System of Equations Consisting of a Linear Equation and a Quadratic Equation

Algebraically

Generally, the simplest way to solve a system of equations consisting of a linear equation and a quadratic equation algebraically is through the method of substitution. One possible strategy is to solve the linear equation for y and then substitute that expression into the quadratic equation. After expansion and combining like terms, this will result in a new quadratic equation for x which, like all quadratic equations, may have zero, one, or two solutions. Plugging each solution for x back into one of the original equations will then produce the corresponding value of y.

For example, consider the following system of equations:

$$x + y = 1$$
$$y = (x + 3)^2 - 2$$

We can solve the linear equation for y to yield $y = -x + 1$. Substituting this expression into the quadratic equation produces $-x + 1 = (x + 3)^2 - 2$. We can simplify this equation:

$$\begin{aligned} -x + 1 &= (x + 3)^2 - 2 \\ -x + 1 &= x^2 + 6x + 9 - 2 \\ -x + 1 &= x^2 + 6x + 7 \\ 0 &= x^2 + 7x + 6 \end{aligned}$$

This quadratic equation can be factored as $(x + 1)(x + 6) = 0$. It therefore has two solutions: $x_1 = -1$ and $x_2 = -6$. Plugging each of these back into the original linear equation yields $y_1 = -x_1 + 1 = -(-1) + 1 = 2$ and $y_2 = -x_2 + 1 = -(-6) + 1 = 7$. Thus, this system of equations has two solutions, $(-1, 2)$ and $(-6, 7)$.

It may help to check your work by putting each x and y value back into the original equations and verifying that they do provide a solution.

Graphically

To solve a system of equations consisting of a linear equation and a quadratic equation graphically, plot both equations on the same graph. The linear equation will of course produce a straight line, while the quadratic equation will produce a parabola. These two graphs will intersect at zero, one, or two points; each point of intersection is a solution of the system.

For example, consider the following system of equations:

$$y = -2x + 2$$
$$y = -2x^2 + 4x + 2$$

The linear equation describes a line with a y-intercept of $(0, 2)$ and a slope of -2.

To graph the quadratic equation, we can first find the vertex of the parabola: the x-coordinate of the vertex is $h = -\frac{b}{2a} = -\frac{4}{2(-2)} = 1$, and the y coordinate is $k = -2(1)^2 + 4(1) + 2 = 4$. Thus, the vertex lies at $(1, 4)$. To get a feel for the rest of the parabola, we can plug in a few more values of x to find more points; by putting in $x = 2$ and $x = 3$ in the quadratic equation, we find that the points $(2, 2)$ and $(3, -4)$ lie on the parabola; by symmetry thus do $(0, 2)$ and $(-1, -4)$. We can now plot both equations:

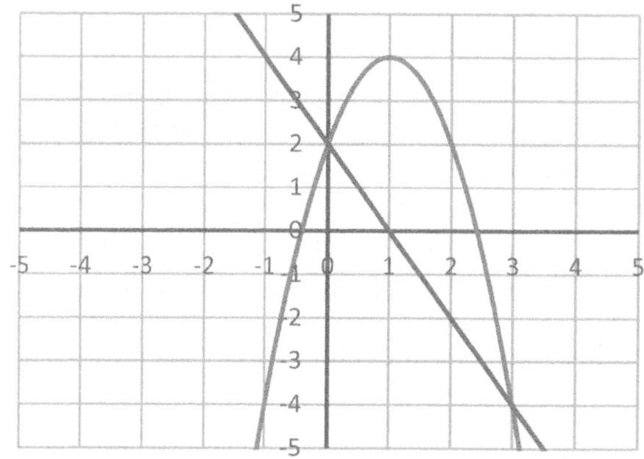

These two curves intersect at the points $(0, 2)$ and $(3, -4)$, thus these are the solutions of the equation.

Review Video: Solving a System of Equations Consisting of a Linear Equation and Quadratic Equations
Visit mometrix.com/academy and enter code: 194870

PRACTICE

P1. Find the roots of $y = 2x^2 + 8x + 4$.

P2. Find a quadratic equation with roots $x = 4$ and $x = -6$.

PRACTICE SOLUTIONS

P1. First, substitute 0 in for y in the quadratic equation: $0 = 2x^2 + 8x + 4$

Next, try to factor the quadratic equation. Since $a \neq 1$, list the factors of ac, or 8:

$$(1, 8), (-1, -8), (2, 4), (-2, -4)$$

Look for the factors of ac that add up to b, or 8. Since none do, the equation cannot be factored with whole numbers. Substitute the values of a, b, and c into the quadratic formula, $x = \frac{-b \pm \sqrt{b^2 - 4ac}}{2a}$:

$$x = \frac{-8 \pm \sqrt{8^2 - 4(2)(4)}}{2(2)}$$

Use the order of operations to simplify:

$$x = \frac{-8 \pm \sqrt{64 - 32}}{4}$$
$$x = \frac{-8 \pm \sqrt{32}}{4}$$

Reduce and simplify:

$$x = \frac{-8 \pm \sqrt{(16)(2)}}{4}$$
$$x = \frac{-8 \pm 4\sqrt{2}}{4}$$
$$x = -2 \pm \sqrt{2}$$
$$x = \left(-2 + \sqrt{2}\right) \text{ and } \left(-2 - \sqrt{2}\right)$$

P2. The root $x = 4$ corresponds to the equation $x - 4 = 0$, and the root $x = -6$ corresponds to the equation $x + 6 = 0$. These two equations correspond to the factors $(x - 4)$ and $(x + 6)$, from which we can derive the equation $(x - 4)(x + 6) = 0$, or $x^2 + 2x - 24 = 0$.

Basic Functions

Function and Relation

When expressing functional relationships, the **variables** x and y are typically used. These values are often written as the **coordinates** (x, y). The x-value is the independent variable and the y-value is the dependent variable. A **relation** is a set of data in which there is not a unique y-value for each x-value in the dataset. This means that there can be two of the same x-values assigned to different y-values. A relation is simply a relationship between the x and y-values in each coordinate but does not apply to the relationship between the values of x and y in the data set. A **function** is a relation where one quantity depends on the other. For example, the amount of money that you make depends on the number of hours that you work. In a function, each x-value in the data set has one unique y-value because the y-value depends on the x-value.

Review Video: Definition of a Function
Visit mometrix.com/academy and enter code: 784611

Functions

A function has exactly one value of **output variable** (dependent variable) for each value of the **input variable** (independent variable). The set of all values for the input variable (here assumed to be x) is the domain of the function, and the set of all corresponding values of output variable (here assumed to be y) is the range of the function. When looking at a graph of an equation, the easiest way to determine if the equation is a function or not is to conduct the vertical line test. If a vertical line drawn through any value of x crosses the graph in more than one place, the equation is not a function.

FINDING THE DOMAIN AND RANGE OF A FUNCTION

The **domain** of a function $f(x)$ is the set of all input values for which the function is defined. The **range** of a function $f(x)$ is the set of all possible output values of the function—that is, of every possible value of $f(x)$, for any value of x in the function's domain. For a function expressed in a table, every input-output pair is given explicitly. To find the domain, we just list all the x values and to find the range, we just list all the values of $f(x)$. Consider the following example:

x	-1	4	2	1	0	3	8	6
$f(x)$	3	0	3	−1	−1	2	4	6

In this case, the domain would be {-1, 4, 2, 1, 0, 3, 8, 6}, or, putting them in ascending order, {-1, 0, 1, 2, 3, 4, 6, 8}. (Putting the values in ascending order isn't strictly necessary, but generally makes the set easier to read.) The range would be {3, 0, 3, −1, −1, 2, 4, 6}. Note that some of these values appear more than once. This is entirely permissible for a function; while each value of x must be matched to a unique value of $f(x)$, the converse is not true. We don't need to list each value more than once, so eliminating duplicates, the range is {3, 0, −1, 2, 4, 6}, or, putting them in ascending order, {−1, 0, 2, 3, 4, 6}.

Note that by definition of a function, no input value can be matched to more than one output value. It is good to double check to make sure that the data given follows this and is therefore actually a function.

Review Video: How to Find Domain and Range
Visit mometrix.com/academy and enter code: 778133

DETERMINING A FUNCTION

You can determine whether an equation is a **function** by substituting different values into the equation for x. These values are called input values. All possible input values are referred to as the **domain**. The result of substituting these values into the equation is called the output, or **range**. You can display and organize these numbers in a data table. A **data table** contains the values for x and y, which you can also list as coordinates. In order for a function to exist, the table cannot contain any repeating x-values that correspond with different y-values. If each x-coordinate has a unique y-coordinate, the table contains a function. However, there can be repeating y-values that correspond with different x-values. An example of this is when the function contains an exponent. For example, if $x^2 = y$, $2^2 = 4$, and $(-2)^2 = 4$.

WRITING A FUNCTION RULE USING A TABLE

If given a set of data, place the corresponding x and y-values into a table and analyze the relationship between them. Consider what you can do to each x-value to obtain the corresponding y-value. Try adding or subtracting different numbers to and from x and then try multiplying or dividing different numbers to and from x. If none of these **operations** give you the y-value, try combining the operations. Once you find a rule that works for one pair, make sure to try it with each additional set of ordered pairs in the table. If the same operation or combination of operations satisfies each set of coordinates, then the table contains a function. The rule is then used to write the equation of the function in "$y =$" form.

DIRECT AND INVERSE VARIATIONS OF VARIABLES

Variables that vary directly are those that either both increase at the same rate or both decrease at the same rate. For example, in the functions $y = kx$ or $y = kx^n$, where k and n are positive, the value of y increases as the value of x increases and decreases as the value of x decreases.

Variables that vary inversely are those where one increases while the other decreases. For example, in the functions $y = \frac{k}{x}$ or $y = \frac{k}{x^n}$ where k and n are positive, the value of y increases as the value of x decreases and decreases as the value of x increases.

In both cases, k is the constant of variation.

PROPERTIES OF FUNCTIONS

There are many different ways to classify functions based on their structure or behavior. Important features of functions include:

- **End behavior**: the behavior of the function at extreme values ($f(x)$ as $x \to \pm\infty$)
- **y-intercept**: the value of the function at $f(0)$
- **Roots**: the values of x where the function equals zero ($f(x) = 0$)
- **Extrema**: minimum or maximum values of the function or where the function changes direction ($f(x) \geq k$ or $f(x) \leq k$)

CLASSIFICATION OF FUNCTIONS

An **invertible function** is defined as a function, $f(x)$, for which there is another function, $f^{-1}(x)$, such that $f^{-1}(f(x)) = x$. For example, if $f(x) = 3x - 2$ the inverse function, $f^{-1}(x)$, can be found:

$$x = 3(f^{-1}(x)) - 2$$
$$\frac{x+2}{3} = f^{-1}(x)$$

$$f^{-1}(f(x)) = \frac{3x - 2 + 2}{3}$$
$$= \frac{3x}{3}$$
$$= x$$

Note that $f^{-1}(x)$ is a valid function over all values of x.

In a **one-to-one function**, each value of x has exactly one value for y on the coordinate plane (this is the definition of a function) and each value of y has exactly one value for x. While the vertical line test will determine if a graph is that of a function, the horizontal line test will determine if a function is a one-to-one function. If a horizontal line drawn at any value of y intersects the graph in more than one place, the graph is not that of a one-to-one function. Do not make the mistake of using the horizontal line test exclusively in determining if a graph is that of a one-to-one function. A one-to-one function must pass both the vertical line test and the horizontal line test. As such, one-to-one functions are invertible functions.

A **many-to-one function** is a function whereby the relation is a function, but the inverse of the function is not a function. In other words, each element in the domain is mapped to one and only one element in the range. However, one or more elements in the range may be mapped to the same element in the domain. A graph of a many-to-one function would pass the vertical line test, but not the horizontal line test. This is why many-to-one functions are not invertible.

A **monotone function** is a function whose graph either constantly increases or constantly decreases. Examples include the functions $f(x) = x$, $f(x) = -x$, or $f(x) = x^3$.

An **even function** has a graph that is symmetric with respect to the y-axis and satisfies the equation $f(x) = f(-x)$. Examples include the functions $f(x) = x^2$ and $f(x) = ax^n$, where a is any real number and n is a positive even integer.

An **odd function** has a graph that is symmetric with respect to the origin and satisfies the equation $f(x) = -f(-x)$. Examples include the functions $f(x) = x^3$ and $f(x) = ax^n$, where a is any real number and n is a positive odd integer.

Constant functions are given by the equation $f(x) = b$, where b is a real number. There is no independent variable present in the equation, so the function has a constant value for all x. The graph of a constant function is a horizontal line of slope 0 that is positioned b units from the x-axis. If b is positive, the line is above the x-axis; if b is negative, the line is below the x-axis.

Identity functions are identified by the equation $f(x) = x$, where every value of the function is equal to its corresponding value of x. The only zero is the point $(0, 0)$. The graph is a line with slope of 1.

In **linear functions**, the value of the function changes in direct proportion to x. The rate of change,represented by the slope on its graph, is constant throughout. The standard form of a linear equation is $ax + cy = d$, where a, c, and d are real numbers. As a function, this equation is commonly in the form $y = mx + b$ or $f(x) = mx + b$ where $m = -\frac{a}{c}$ and $b = \frac{d}{c}$. This is known as the slope-intercept form, because the coefficients give the slope of the graphed function (m) and its y-intercept (b). Solve the equation $mx + b = 0$ for x to get $x = -\frac{b}{m}$, which is the only zero of the function. The domain and range are both the set of all real numbers.

Algebraic functions are those that exclusively use polynomials and roots. These would include polynomial functions, rational functions, square root functions, and all combinations of these functions, such as polynomials as the radicand. These combinations may be joined by addition, subtraction, multiplication, or division, but may not include variables as exponents.

Review Video: Common Functions
Visit mometrix.com/academy and enter code: 629798

Absolute Value Functions

An **absolute value function** is in the format $f(x) = |ax + b|$. Like other functions, the domain is the set of all real numbers. However, because absolute value indicates positive numbers, the range is limited to positive real numbers. To find the zero of an absolute value function, set the portion inside the absolute value sign equal to zero and solve for x. An absolute value function is also known as a piecewise function because it must be solved in pieces—one for if the value inside the absolute value sign is positive, and one for if the value is negative. The function can be expressed as

$$f(x) = \begin{cases} ax + b \text{ if } ax + b \geq 0 \\ -(ax + b) \text{ if } ax + b < 0 \end{cases}$$

This will allow for an accurate statement of the range. The graph of an example absolute value function, $f(x) = |2x - 1|$, is below:

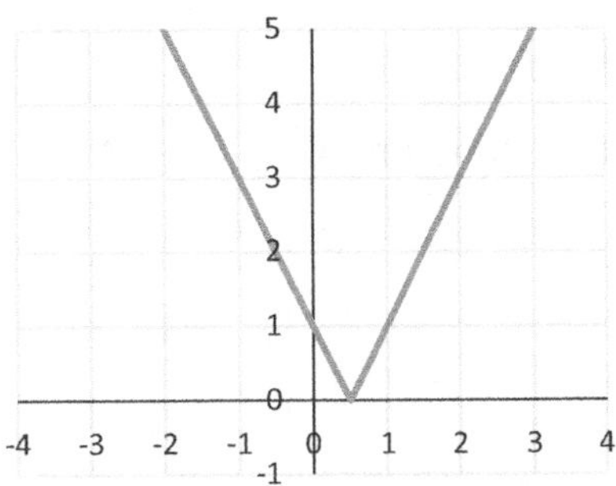

PIECEWISE FUNCTIONS

A **piecewise function** is a function that has different definitions on two or more different intervals. The following, for instance, is one example of a piecewise-defined function:

$$f(x) = \begin{cases} x^2, & x < 0 \\ x, & 0 \le x \le 2 \\ (x-2)^2, & x > 2 \end{cases}$$

To graph this function, we'd simply graph each part separately in the appropriate domain. The final graph would look like this:

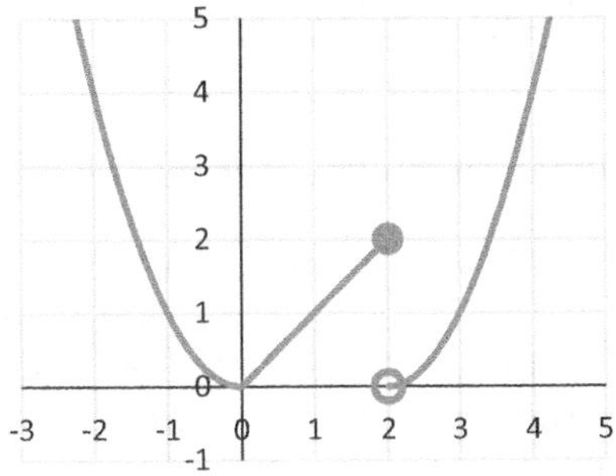

Note the filled and hollow dots at the discontinuity at $x = 2$. This is important to show which side of the graph that point corresponds to. Because $f(x) = x$ on the closed interval $0 \le x \le 2$, $f(2) = 2$. The point $(2, 2)$ is therefore marked with a filled circle, and the point $(2,0)$, which is the endpoint of the rightmost $(x - 2)^2$ part of the graph but *not actually part of the function*, is marked with a hollow dot to indicate this.

Review Video: Piecewise Functions
Visit mometrix.com/academy and enter code: 707921

QUADRATIC FUNCTIONS

A **quadratic function** is a function in the form $y = ax^2 + bx + c$, where a does not equal 0. While a linear function forms a line, a quadratic function forms a **parabola**, which is a u-shaped figure that either opens upward or downward. A parabola that opens upward is said to be a **positive quadratic function** and a parabola that opens downward is said to be a **negative quadratic function**. The shape of a parabola can differ, depending on the values of *a*, *b*, and *c*. All parabolas contain a **vertex**, which is the highest possible point, the **maximum**, or the lowest possible point, the **minimum**. This is the point where the graph begins moving in the opposite direction. A quadratic function can have zero, one, or two solutions, and therefore, zero, one, or two x-intercets. Recall that the x-intercepts are referred to as the zeros, or roots, of a function. A quadratic function will have only one y-intercept. Understanding the basic components of a quadratic function can give you an idea of the shape of its graph.

Example graph of a positive quadratic function, $x^2 + 2x - 3$:

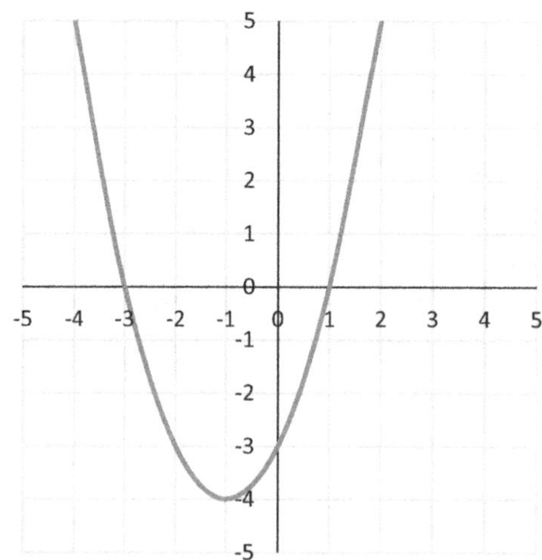

Review Video: Solutions of a Quadratic Equation on a Graph
Visit mometrix.com/academy and enter code: 328231

Polynomial Functions

A **polynomial function** is a function with multiple terms and multiple powers of x, such as:

$$f(x) = a_n x^n + a_{n-1}x^{n-1} + a_{n-2}x^{n-2} + \cdots + a_1 x + a_0$$

where n is a non-negative integer that is the highest exponent in the polynomial and $a_n \neq 0$. The domain of a polynomial function is the set of all real numbers. If the greatest exponent in the polynomial is even, the polynomial is said to be of even degree and the range is the set of real numbers that satisfy the function. If the greatest exponent in the polynomial is odd, the polynomial is said to be odd and the range, like the domain, is the set of all real numbers.

Review Video: Simplifying Rational Polynomial Functions
Visit mometrix.com/academy and enter code: 351038

Rational Functions

A **rational function** is a function that can be constructed as a ratio of two polynomial expressions: $f(x) = \frac{p(x)}{q(x)}$, where $p(x)$ and $q(x)$ are both polynomial expressions and $q(x) \neq 0$. The domain is the set of all real numbers, except any values for which $q(x) = 0$. The range is the set of real numbers that satisfies the function when the domain is applied. When you graph a rational function, you will have vertical asymptotes wherever $q(x) = 0$. If the polynomial in the numerator is of lesser degree than the polynomial in the denominator, the x-axis will also be a horizontal asymptote. If the numerator and denominator have equal degrees, there will be a horizontal asymptote not on the x-axis. If the degree of the numerator is exactly one greater than the degree of the denominator, the graph will have an oblique, or diagonal, asymptote. The asymptote will be along the line $y =$

$\frac{p_n}{q_{n-1}}x + \frac{p_{n-1}}{q_{n-1}}$, where p_n and q_{n-1} are the coefficients of the highest degree terms in their respective polynomials.

SQUARE ROOT FUNCTIONS

A **square root function** is a function that contains a radical and is in the format $f(x) = \sqrt{ax + b}$. The domain is the set of all real numbers that yields a positive radicand or a radicand equal to zero. Because square root values are assumed to be positive unless otherwise identified, the range is all real numbers from zero to infinity. To find the zero of a square root function, set the radicand equal to zero and solve for *x*. The graph of a square root function is always to the right of the zero and always above the *x*-axis.

Example graph of a square root function, $f(x) = \sqrt{2x + 1}$:

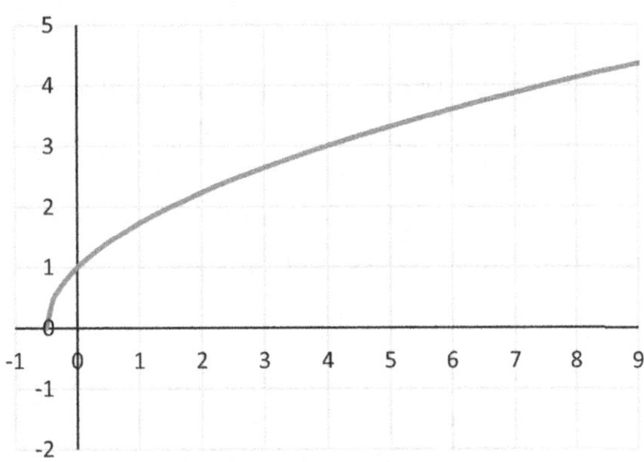

RELATIVE MAXIMUM AND RELATIVE MINIMUM

A **relative maximum** of a function is a point where the function has a higher value than any other point that is near it. In other words, a relative maximum is a point (x, y). Let's say that we choose an acceptable small interval around *x*. Then, $f(x) > f(c)$ for any other point within the interval (c).

A relative minimum is just the opposite. This is a point where the function has a lower value than any other point that is near it. In other words, a point (x, y). Let's say that we choose an acceptable small interval around *x*. Then, $f(x) < f(c)$ for any other point within the interval (c).

A function may have many relative maxima* and relative minima*. However, it may have none. A linear function like $y = x$ has no relative maxima or minima. Now, $y = \sin(x)$ has an unending amount of relative maxima and minima.

*Note that 'maxima' is plural for maximum. Also, 'minima' is plural for minimum.

FINDING A RELATIVE MAXIMUM OR MINIMUM FROM A GRAPH

At a relative maximum, the graph goes from increasing to decreasing. This makes a "peak" on the graph. Also, at a relative minimum, the graph goes from decreasing to increasing. This makes a "trough". On the graph below, the points A and C are relative maxima. The point B is a relative minimum.

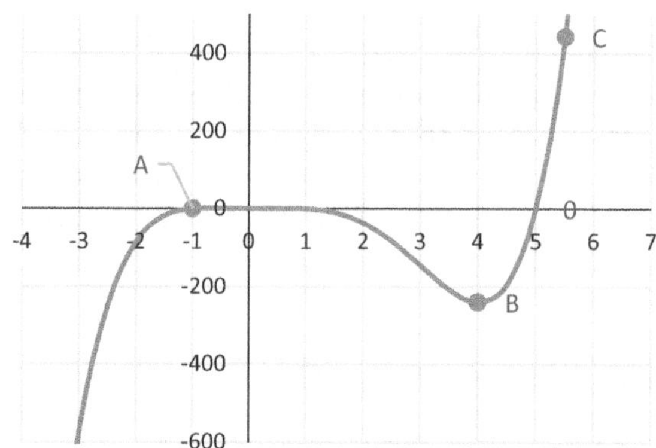

Note that point A is a relative maximum. However, this is not an absolute maximum. Also, this function has a higher value at point C. Now, point B is a relative minimum. However, this is not an absolute minimum. Also, the function has a lower value at the left and right ends of the graph than at point B. Point C is a relative and an absolute maximum. The reason is that at no place on the graph is there a function that has a higher value than at point C.

Periodic Functions

A function is **periodic** if there is a repetition of the same shape. In other words, a periodic function is unchanged if it is moved some distance left or right on the graph. The distance that it has to be moved is called the function's **period** (P). A function $f(x)$ is periodic if $f(x + P) = f(x)$ for all x. Note that if this is true for P, then it's also true for all multiples of P. However, the function's period is known as the smallest possible value of P that the relation holds.

Symmetrical Functions

A function is **symmetrical** if it does not change with certain kinds of transformations. There are many kinds of transformations and symmetries. For functions, the type of transformation that is considered is reflection. Two important pieces are reflections through the y-axis and reflections through the origin on a coordinate plane.

If the mirror image (i.e., reflection) of a function is the same through the y-axis, then the function is symmetrical. This can be written as $f(x) = f(-x)$. This function is known to be **even**. A function can be symmetrical with reflection through the origin. The function needs to stay the same when each point is reflected to the other side of the origin. This can be written as $f(x) = -f(-x)$. This function is known to be **odd**.

A periodic function is also symmetrical. This may not be with reflection. However, this can be done with **translation**. The function is unchanged when translated (i.e., moved) horizontally by a distance that is equal to the function's period.

Function End Behavior

A function's **end behavior** is its tendency or activity at the extreme right and left sides of the graph. In other words, this is what happens to the function as x moves towards positive or negative ∞. There are three main possibilities.

First, $f(x)$ increases without limit (i.e., $f(x)$ goes to infinity). Second, $f(x)$ decreases without limit (i.e., $f(x)$ goes to negative infinity). Third, $f(x)$ tends toward some finite value (i.e., a horizontal asymptote). The behavior may be different at the two sides. For example, while $f(x) = x^2$ goes to ∞ on both sides, $g(x) = x^3$ goes to ∞ on the right side and to $-\infty$ on the left. Also, $h(x) = e^{-x}$ goes to ∞ on the left and approaches the horizontal asymptote $y = 0$ on the right.

PRACTICE

P1. Martin needs a 20% medicine solution. The pharmacy has a 5% solution and a 30% solution. He needs 50 mL of the solution. If the pharmacist must mix the two solutions, how many milliliters of 5% solution and 30% solution should be used?

P2. Describe two different strategies for solving the following problem:

> Kevin can mow the yard in 4 hours. Mandy can mow the same yard in 5 hours. If they work together, how long will it take them to mow the yard?

P3. A car, traveling at 65 miles per hour, leaves Flagstaff and heads east on I-40. Another car, traveling at 75 miles per hour, leaves Flagstaff 2 hours later, from the same starting point and also heads east on I-40. Determine how many hours it will take the second car to catch the first car by:

(a) Using a table.

(b) Using algebra.

PRACTICE SOLUTIONS

P1. To solve this problem, a table may be created to represent the variables, percentages, and total amount of solution. Such a table is shown below:

	mL solution	% medicine	Total mL medicine
5% solution	x	0.05	$0.05x$
30% solution	y	0.30	$0.30y$
Mixture	$x + y = 50$	0.20	$(0.20)(50) = 10$

The variable x may be rewritten as $50 - y$, so the equation $0.05(50 - y) + 0.30y = 10$ may be written and solved for y. Doing so gives $y = 30$. So, 30 mL of 30% solution are needed. Evaluating the expression, $50 - y$ for an x-value of 20, shows that 20 mL of 5% solution are needed.

P2. Two possible strategies both involve the use of rational equations to solve. The first strategy involves representing the fractional part of the yard mowed by each person in one hour and setting this sum equal to the ratio of 1 to the total time needed. The appropriate equation is $1/4 + 1/5 = 1/t$, which simplifies as $9/20 = 1/t$, and finally as $t = 20/9$. So the time it will take them to mow the yard, when working together, is a little more than 2.2 hours.

A second strategy involves representing the time needed for each person as two fractions and setting the sum equal to 1 (representing 1 yard). The appropriate equation is $t/4 + t/5 = 1$, which simplifies as $9t/20 = 1$, and finally as $t = 20/9$. This strategy also shows the total time to be a little more than 2.2 hours.

P3. (a) One strategy might involve creating a table of values for the number of hours and distances for each car. The table may be examined to find the same distance traveled and the corresponding number of hours taken. Such a table is shown below:

Car A		Car B	
x (hours)	y (distance)	x (hours)	y (distance)
0	0	0	
1	65	1	
2	130	2	0
3	195	3	75
4	260	4	150
5	325	5	225
6	390	6	300
7	455	7	375
8	520	8	450
9	585	9	525
10	650	10	600
11	715	11	675
12	780	12	750
13	845	13	825
14	910	14	900
15	975	15	975

The table shows that after 15 hours, the distance traveled is the same. Thus, the second car catches up with the first car after a distance of 975 miles and 15 hours.

(b) A second strategy might involve setting up and solving an algebraic equation. This situation may be modeled as $65x = 75(x - 2)$. This equation sets the distances traveled by each car equal to one another. Solving for x gives $x = 15$. Thus, once again, the second car will catch up with the first car after 15 hours.

Reasoning Through Language Arts

Transform passive reading into active learning! After immersing yourself in this chapter, put your comprehension to the test by taking a quiz. The insights you gained will stay with you longer this way. Scan the QR code to go directly to the chapter quiz interface for this study guide. If you're using a computer, simply visit the bonus page at **mometrix.com/bonus948/ged** and click the Chapter Quizzes link.

Reading for Meaning

This section is organized to introduce you to the passages that you will find on your exam. We cover the different types of passages from narrative to persuasive. Then, we move to the reason that a passage is written. As you may know, some texts are written to persuade. Other passages want to inform.

The devices of writers are important to understand as you practice reading passages. The other parts of a passage we focus on are main ideas, supporting details, and themes. Then, we review making inferences and drawing conclusions. With this step-by-step guide, you will move to a higher score on your test.

Careful reading and thinking about a passage are important in every part of life. Work with this information by reading books, magazines, or newspapers. When you read carefully, you can use this information for other passages. With practice you will strengthen your skills for the future. Truly, with this information, you can show others that you know the *secrets* to your exam.

Literary Genres

A literary genre is used to put different pieces of passages into the basic groups of poetry, drama, fiction, and nonfiction. These basic groups can be broken down further into subgroups. Novels, novellas, and short stories are subgroups of fiction. Drama may also be divided into the main subgroups of comedy and tragedy. Subgroups of nonfiction are journals, textbooks, biographies, and journalism (e.g., newspapers). The differences between genres can be difficult to see. Some examples combine groups like the *nonfiction novel* and *poetic novel.*

Review Video: Types of Literary Genre
Visit mometrix.com/academy and enter code: 587617

Most fiction, nonfiction, and drama are written in prose. Prose is ordinary spoken language compared to poetry (i.e., language with metric patterns). This everyday, normal communication is known as prose. Prose can be found in textbooks, essays, reports, articles, short stories, and novels. Prose is put together with sentences. Also, there should be smooth connections among sentences. The sentences and paragraphs that you are reading right now are written in prose.

Fiction is a general term for any type of narrative that is invented or imagined. Your exam will have a passage that was written for your test. Or, a passage may be taken from a published work. During your exam, you may recognize a passage that you have read. In this case, you still need to follow the rule of reading the passage once. Then, go to the test questions. This rule applies to the other genres as well. Now, let's start with fiction.

Fiction has many subgroups, but the genre can be put into three main subgroups:

- **Short stories**: a fictional passage that has fewer than 20,000 words. Short stories have only a few characters and normally have one important event. The short story began in magazines in the late 1800s.
- **Novels**: longer works of fiction that may have many characters and a far-reaching plot. The attention may be on an event, action, social problem, or an experience. Note: novels may be written like poetry.
- **Novellas**: a work of fiction that is longer than a short story, but shorter than a novel. Novellas may also be called short novels or novelettes. They come from the German tradition and have increased in popularity across the world.

Many elements influence a work of fiction. Some important ones are:

- **Speech and dialogue**: Dialogue is the communication among characters. These characters may speak for themselves. Or, the narrator may share what a character has spoken. This speech or dialogue may seem realistic or obviously imaginary. The choice depends on the author's purpose.
- **External and internal conflict**: External conflict is the action and events that are around the character. Internal conflict is the thoughts and feelings that bother a character. This conflict that happens inside a character is used to develop the plot. Or, the internal conflict can be used to show the growth or lack of growth in a character.
- **Dramatic involvement**: Some narrators want readers to join with the events of the story (e.g., Thornton Wilder's *Our Town*). Other authors try to separate themselves from readers with figurative language.
- **Action**: The events that continue the plot, such as interactions between characters and physical movement and conflict.
- **Duration**: The amount of time that passes in the passage may be long or short. If the author gives an amount of time (e.g., three days later), then that information is important to remember.
- **Setting and description**: Is the setting (i.e., time and place within the passage) important to the plot or characters? How are the action scenes described?
- **Themes**: This is any point of view or topic that is given constant attention.
- **Symbolism**: Authors may share what they mean through imagery and other figurative devices. For example, smoke can be a symbol of danger, and doves are often symbols of peace.

Read slowly and carefully through passages of fiction. The story can become so interesting that the language of the passage (i.e., the author's choice of vocabulary) is forgotten. A reward of careful reading is to see how the author uses different language to describe familiar objects, events, or feelings. Some passages have you focus on an author's unusual use of language. Other passages may make the characters or storyline important. The events of a story are not always the most important parts in a passage. You may find that reading carefully is difficult at first. However, the rewards are greater than the early struggles.

Plot lines are one way to show the information given in a story. Every plot line has the same stages. You can find each of these stages in every story that you read. These stages include the introduction, rising action, conflict, climax, falling action, and resolution. The introduction tells you the point of the story and sets up the plot. The rising action is the events that lead up to the conflict (i.e., an internal or external problem) with the climax at the peak. The falling action is the events that come after the climax of the conflict. The resolution is the conclusion and may have the final solution to the problem in the conflict. A plot line looks like this:

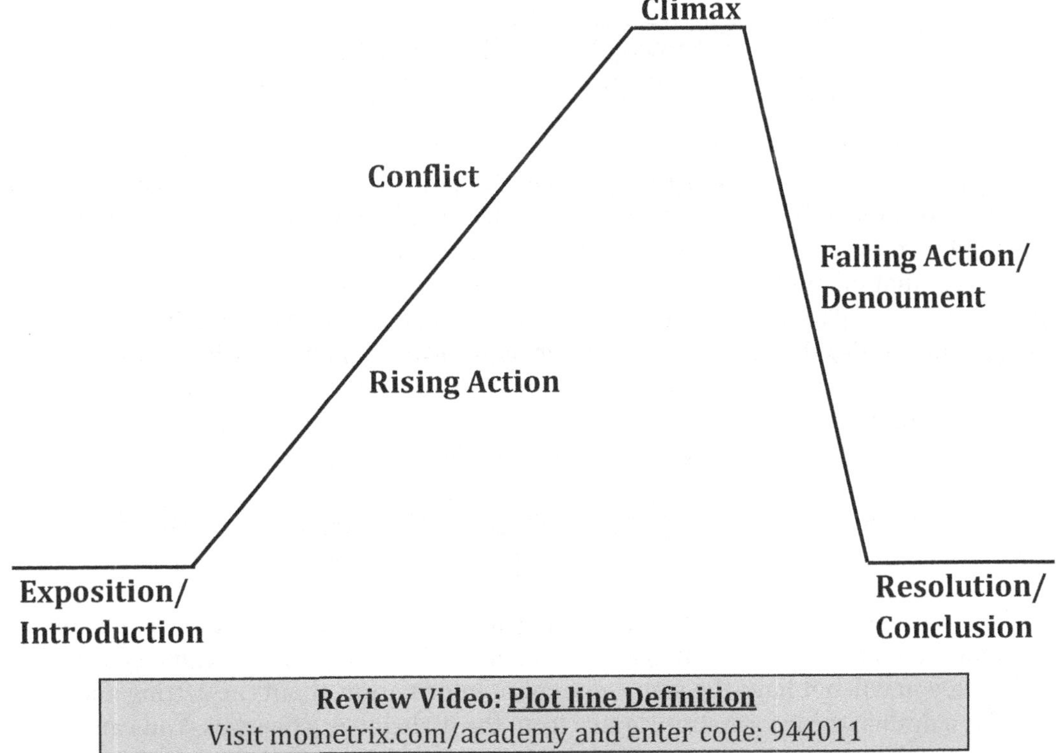

Review Video: Plot line Definition
Visit mometrix.com/academy and enter code: 944011

Most passages put events in chronological order. However, some authors may use an unusual order to have a particular influence on readers. For example, many of the Greek epics begin *in medias res* (i.e., in the middle of things). The passage begins with an introduction to the climax. Then, the author goes to the beginning and shares how events came to that climax. This order is found in many mystery novels. First, a crime is committed. Then, a detective must go back and piece together the events that led to the crime. As you read, try to keep in mind the cause-and-effect relationships that shape the story. A cause must come before an effect. So, use an outline of the different causes and effects in a passage. Be sure that this outline shows the correct chronological order. Remember that the order of events in a story is not always the order that they happened.

The **narrator** can give insight about the purpose of the work and the main themes and ideas. There are important questions to ask about understanding the voice and role of the narrator:

- Who is the narrator of the passage? What is the narrator's perspective: first person or third person? Is the narrator involved in the plot? Are there changes in narrators?
- Does the narrator explain things in the passage? Or, are things explained with the plot and events? Does the narrator give special description to one character or event and not to others? A narrator may express approval or disapproval about a character or events in the work.

- Tone is the attitude of a character through his or her words. If the narrator is involved in the story, how is the narrator addressing others? Is the tone casual or formal? Close or distant? Does the narrator's vocabulary give any information about the narrator?

Review Video: The Narrator
Visit mometrix.com/academy and enter code: 742528

A **character** is someone or something that is connected closely with the plot and growth of the passage. As characters grow in a story, they move along the plot line. Characters can be named as flat or round and static or dynamic. Flat characters are simple individuals that are known for one or two things. Often, they are supporting characters to round characters. Minor flat characters are stock characters that fill out the story without influencing the outcome. Round characters, usually protagonists, are crucial to the story. They are explored widely and explained in much detail. If characters change or develop, they can be known as static or dynamic. Static characters either do not change or change very little in a passage. In other words, who they are at the beginning is who they are at the end. However, dynamic characters change over the course of a passage. In other words, who they are at the beginning is not at all who they are at the end.

Review Video: What is the Definition of a Character in a Story
Visit mometrix.com/academy and enter code: 429493

A **drama** is a play that is meant to be performed by a group. As you read drama, you should use your imagination to re-create the play with characters and settings. Fiction can be read in the same way. However, you will not have the same amount of information about the setting and characters in drama. For a drama, the information comes from the dialogue or speeches. You can help your understanding of the passage with imagination. Many dramas have some dialogue and several scenes of action. In these passages, try to imagine the events taking place. **Action** can be the events that characters do or the things that are done to a character.

There are other devices that authors use in the growth of the plot and characters. Be sure to read carefully to know which characters are speaking to others. **Asides** are moments where no characters or not every character knows that another is speaking. This may be a way of explaining the plot quietly and directly. **Soliloquies** are when the character shares thoughts and opinions out loud when they are alone or with others. So, this device gives insight to a character's motives, feelings, and emotions. Careful review of these devices provides you with many ideas on the major themes and plot of the passage.

Conversations in drama can be difficult to understand. So, your review of speech and dialogue is important as you read the passages. Authors may use speeches to develop their characters. Some characters may have a special way of speaking which highlights aspects of the drama. The placement of stresses in a dramatic dialogue can help you know how to understand a character's lines. Changes in stress are one way to shape a statement in drama. For example, "You *are coming* with me to dinner." The italicized words might mean that the speaker wants a person to come whether the person wants to or not.

You can try to add stress to understand a passage. However, be sure that you are using the surrounding context as a guide. Remember that your attempt may not be the correct one. So, be open to other possibilities. As you begin to understand the characters and situations, you will pick up on the stress of some characters. Other pieces that add to the understanding of dialogue are setting, possible reactions of the characters to a speech, and gestures of the actors.

Review Video: Dramas
Visit mometrix.com/academy and enter code: 216060

Purposes for Writing

To be a careful reader, pay attention to the author's **position** and purpose. Even passages that seem fair and equal--like textbooks--have a position or bias (i.e., the author is unfair or inaccurate with opposing ideas). Readers need to take these positions into account when considering the author's message. Authors who appeal to feelings or like one side of an argument make their position clear. Authors' positions may be found in what they write and in what they don't write. Normally, you would want to review other passages on the same topic to understand the author's position. However, you are in the middle of an exam. So, look for language and arguments that show a position.

Review Video: Author's Position
Visit mometrix.com/academy and enter code: 827954

Sometimes, finding the **purpose** of an author is easier than finding his or her position. In most cases, the author has no interest in hiding his or her purpose. A passage for entertainment will be written to please readers. Most stories are written to entertain. However, they can inform or persuade. Informative texts are easy to recognize. The most difficult purpose of a text to determine is persuasion. In persuasion, the author wants to make the purpose hard to find. When you learn that the author wants to persuade, you should be skeptical of the argument. Persuasive passages may try to establish an entertaining tone and hope to amuse you into agreement. On the other hand, an informative tone may be used to seem fair and equal to all sides.

An author's purpose is clear often in the organization of the text (e.g., section headings in bold font point to an informative passage). However, you may not have this organization in your passages. So, if authors make their main idea clear from the beginning, then their likely purpose is to inform. If the author makes a main argument and gives minor arguments for support, then the purpose is probably to persuade. If the author tells a story, then his or her purpose is most likely to entertain. If the author wants your attention more than to persuade or inform, then his or her purpose is most likely to entertain. You must judge authors on how well they reach their purpose. In other words, think about the type of passage (e.g., technical, persuasive, etc.) that the author has written and if the author has followed the demands of the passage type.

Review Video: Understanding the Author's Intent
Visit mometrix.com/academy and enter code: 511819

The author's purpose will influence his or her writing approach and the reader's reaction. In a **persuasive essay**, the author wants to prove something to readers. There are several important marks of bad persuasive writing. Opinion given as fact is one mark. When some authors try to persuade readers, they give their opinions as if they were facts. Readers must be on guard for statements that sound like facts but cannot be tested. Another mark of persuasive writing is the appeal to feelings. An author will try to play with the feelings of readers by appealing to their ideas of what is right and wrong. When an author uses strong language to excite the reader's feelings, then the author may want to persuade. Many times, a persuasive passage will give an unfair explanation of other sides. Or, the other sides are not shown.

An **informative passage** is written to teach readers. Informative passages are almost always nonfiction. The purpose of an informative passage is to share information in the clearest way. In an informative passage, you may have a thesis statement (i.e., an argument on the topic of a passage that is explained by proof). A thesis statement is a sentence that normally comes at end of the first paragraph. Authors of informative passages are likely to put more importance on being clear. Informative passages do not normally appeal to the feelings. They often contain facts and figures. Informative passages almost never include the opinion of the author. However, you should know that there can be a bias in the facts. Sometimes, a persuasive passage can be like an informative passage. This is true when authors give their ideas as if they were facts.

Entertainment passages describe real or imagined people, places, and events. Entertainment passages are often stories or poems. So, figurative language is a common part of these passages. Often, an entertainment passage appeals to the imagination and feelings. Authors may persuade or inform in an entertainment passage. Or, an entertainment passage may cause readers to think differently about a subject.

When authors want to **share feelings,** they may use strong language. Authors may share feelings about a moment of great pain or happiness. Other times, authors will try to persuade readers by sharing feelings. Some phrases like *I felt* and *I sense* hint that the author is sharing feelings. Authors may share a story of deep pain or great joy. You must not be influenced by these stories. You need to keep some distance to judge the author's argument.

Almost all writing is descriptive. In one way or another, authors try to describe events, ideas, or people. Some texts are concerned only with **description**. A descriptive passage focuses on a single subject and seeks to explain the subject clearly. Descriptive passages contain many adjectives and adverbs (i.e., words that give a complete picture for you to imagine). Normally, a descriptive passage is informative. Yet, the passage may be persuasive or entertaining.

Writing Devices

Style is the manner in which a writer uses language in prose or poetry. Style is affected by:

- Diction or word choices
- Sentence structure and syntax
- Types and extent of use of figurative language
- Patterns of rhythm or sound
- Conventional or creative use of punctuation

Tone is the attitude of the writer or narrator towards the theme of, subject of, or characters in a work. Sometimes the attitude is stated, but it is most often implied through word choices. Examples of tone are serious, humorous, satiric, stoic, cynical, flippant, and surprised.

Authors will use different writing devices to make their message clear for readers. One of those devices is comparison and contrast. As you read already, when authors show how two things are alike, they are **comparing** them. When authors describe how two things are different, they are **contrasting** them. The compare and contrast passage is a common part of nonfiction. Comparisons are known by certain words or phrases: *both, same, like, too*, and *as well*. Yet, contrasts may have words or phrases like *but, however, on the other hand, instead*, and *yet*. Of course, comparisons and contrasts may be understood without using those words or phrases. A single sentence may compare and contrast. Think about the sentence *Brian and Sheila love ice cream, but Brian loves* *vanilla and Sheila loves strawberry*. In one sentence, the author has described both a similarity (e.g., love of ice cream) and a difference (e.g., favorite flavor).

Review Video: Compare and Contrast
Visit mometrix.com/academy and enter code: 171799

Another regular writing device is **cause and effect**. A cause is an act or event that makes something happen. An effect is what results from the cause. A cause and effect relationship is not always easy to find. So, there are some words and phrases that show causes: *since*, *because*, and *due to*. Words and phrases that show effects include *consequently, therefore, this lead(s) to, as a result*. For example, *Because the sky was clear, Ron did not bring an umbrella*. The cause is the clear sky, and the effect is that Ron did not bring an umbrella. Readers may find that the cause and effect relationship is not clear. For example, *He was late and missed the meeting*. This does not have any words that show cause or effect. Yet, the sentence still has a cause (e.g., he was late) and an effect (e.g., he missed the meeting).

Review Video: Rhetorical Strategy of Cause-and-Effect Analysis
Visit mometrix.com/academy and enter code: 725944

Remember the chance for a single cause to have many effects. (e.g., *Single cause*: Because you left your homework on the table, your dog eats the homework. *Many effects*: (1) As a result, you fail your homework. (2) Your parents do not let you see your friends. (3) You miss out on the new movie. (4) You miss holding the hand of an important person.)

Also, there is a chance of a single effect to have many causes. (e.g., *Single effect*: Alan has a fever. *Many causes*: (1) An unexpected cold front came through the area, and (2) Alan forgot to take his multi-vitamin.)

Now, an effect can become the cause of another effect. This is known as a cause and effect chain. (e.g., As a result of her hatred for not doing work, Lynn got ready for her exam. This led to her passing her test with high marks. Hence, her resume was accepted, and her application was accepted.)

Often, authors use analogies to add meaning to their passages. An **analogy** is a comparison of two things. The words in the analogy are connected by a relationship. Look at this analogy: *moo is to cow as quack is to duck*. This analogy compares the sound that a cow makes with the sound that a duck makes. What could you do if the word *quack* was not given? Well, you could finish the analogy if you know the connection between *moo* and *cow*. Relationships for analogies include synonyms, antonyms, part to whole, definition, and actor to action.

Point of view has an important influence on a passage. A passage's point of view is how the author or a character sees or thinks about things. A point of view influences the events of a passage, the meetings among characters, and the ending to the story. For example, two characters watch a child ride a bike. Character one watches outside. Character two watches from inside a house. Both see the same event, yet they are around different noises, sights, and smells. Character one may see different things that happen outside that character two cannot see from inside. Also, point of view can be influenced by past events and beliefs. For example, if character one loves bikes, then she will remember how proud she is of the child. If character two is afraid of riding bikes, then he may not remember the event or fear for the child's safety.

In fiction, the two main points of view are first person and third person. The narrator is the person who tells a story's events. The protagonist is the main character of a story. If the narrator is the protagonist in a story, then the story is written in first-person. In first person, the author writes from the view of *I*. Third-person point of view is the most common among stories. With third person, authors refer to each character by using *he* or *she* and the narrator is not involved in the story. In third-person omniscient, the narrator is not a character in the story and tells the story of all of the characters at the same time.

Review Video: Point of View
Visit mometrix.com/academy and enter code: 383336

Transitional words and phrases are devices that guide readers through a passage. You may know the common transitions. Though you may not have thought about how they are used. Some transitional phrases (*after, before, during, in the middle of*) give information about time. Some hint that an example is about to be given (*for example, in fact, for instance*). Writers use transitions to compare (*also, likewise*) and contrast (*however, but, yet*). Transitional words and phrases can point to addition (*and, also, furthermore, moreover*) and understood relationships (*if, then, therefore, as a result, since*). Finally, transitional words and phrases can separate the chronological steps (*first, second, last*).

Review Video: What are Transition Words?
Visit mometrix.com/academy and enter code: 707563

Types of Passages

A **narrative** passage is a story that can be fiction or nonfiction (i.e., false or true). To be a narrative, the passage must have a few things. First, the text must have a plot (i.e., an order of events). Some narratives are written in a clear order, but this is not necessary. If the narrative is good, then you will find the events interesting, regardless of the order in which they happen. Second, a narrative has characters. These characters can be people, animals, or even lifeless items. As long as they play in the plot, they are a character. Third, a narrative passage often has figurative language. This is a tool that authors use to stir the imagination of readers with comparisons or comments. For example, a metaphor is a comparison between two things without using the words *like* or *as*. *He stood like a king* is not an example of a metaphor. *The moon was a frosty snowball* is an example of a metaphor. In reality, the moon is not a snowball. Yet, the comparison gives a sense of calm to readers.

An **expository** passage aims to inform or teach readers. This type of passage is nonfiction and usually centers around an easily explained topic. Often, an expository passage has helpful organizing words: *first, next, for example*, and *therefore*. These words let readers know where they are in the passage. While expository passages don't need to have difficult vocabulary and fancy writing, they can be better with them. Yet, this can make it difficult to pay attention to an expository passage. Expository passages are not always about things that will interest you. Also, writers focus more on clearness and precision than with keeping the reader's interest. By careful reading, you will establish a good habit of focus when you read an expository passage.

Review Video: What is an Expository Passage?
Visit mometrix.com/academy and enter code: 256515

A **technical** passage is written to describe a complicated thing or action. Technical writing is common in medical and technology fields. In those fields, ideas of mathematics, science, and engineering need to be explained simply and clearly. A technical passage usually proceeds in a step-by-step order to help with understanding the passage. Technical passages often have clear headings and subheadings. These headings act like the organizing words in an expository passage: they let readers know where they are in a passage. Also, you will find that these passages divide sections up with numbers or letters. Many technical passages look more like an outline than the paragraphs that you are reading right now. Depending on the audience, the amount of difficult vocabulary will change in a technical passage. Some technical passages try to stay away from language that readers will have to look up. However, some difficult vocabulary has to be used for writers to share their message.

Review Video: Technical Passages
Visit mometrix.com/academy and enter code: 478923

A **persuasive** passage is written to change the mind of readers so that they agree with the author. The purpose of the passage may be very clear or very difficult to find. A persuasive passage wants to make an acceptable argument and win the trust of the reader. In some cases, a persuasive passage will be similar to an informative passage. Both passages make an argument and offer supporting details. However, a persuasive passage is more likely to appeal to the reader's feelings and make arguments based on opinions. Persuasive passages may not describe other points of view. So, when they do show other points of view, they may show favoritism to one side.

Persuasive passages will focus on one main argument and make many minor arguments (i.e., arguments that help the main argument) along the way. If you are going to accept the main argument, then you need to accept the minor arguments. So, the main argument will only be as strong as the minor arguments. These arguments should be rooted in fact and experience, not opinions. The best persuasive passages give enough supporting detail to back up arguments without confusing readers. Remember that a fact must be open to independent verification (i.e., the fact must be something that can be backed up by someone else). Also, statistics (i.e., data or figures collected for study) are helpful only when they look at other choices. For example, a statistic on the number of bicycles sold would only be useful if it was taken over a limited time period and in a specific area. Good readers are careful with statistics because statistics can show what we want to see. Or, they can hide what we don't want to see. The writers of your test know that their passages will be met by questioning readers. So, your skill at questioning what you read will be a help in your exam.

Review Video: How to Write a Persuasive Essay
Visit mometrix.com/academy and enter code: 621428

Opinions come from how we feel and what we think. Persuasive writers try often to appeal to the emotions (i.e., use or influence someone's feelings) of readers to make their arguments. You should always ask questions about this approach. You should ask questions because an author can pull you into accepting something that you don't want to accept. Sometimes these appeals can be used in a fair way. For example, some subjects cannot be totally addressed without an appeal to a reader's feelings. Think about an article on drunk driving. Some examples in the article will alarm or sadden readers because of the terrible outcome.

On the other hand, appeals to feelings are unacceptable when they try to mislead readers. For example, a presidential candidate (i.e., someone running for president) says that they care about the country. The candidate pushes you to make a connection. You care about the country as well and have positive feelings about the country. The candidate wants you to connect your positive feelings about the country with your thoughts about him or her. If you make more connections with the candidate, then you are likely to vote for him or her. Also, the person running for president hints that other candidates do not care about the country.

Another common and unacceptable appeal to feelings is the use of loaded language. Calling a religious person a 'fanatic' or a person interested in the environment a 'tree hugger' are examples of loaded language.

Comparing Passages

When reading about a single topic that has been the subject of two or more texts, there are several things that must be done to compare them objectively. You need to read each text carefully and take note of the point of view of the author as well as the reason the work was written. For instance, one author may be writing an opinion piece about a person and the person's beliefs, while a second writer may be doing an analysis of what the person has done and the kinds of issues the person is involved in.

These two approaches could work to help you learn more about a subject, from both a subjective and an objective manner. Another author might choose to write a biography about the same subject, which would lend more of an understanding of the person's life and those things that influenced her. When reading multiple texts about a single subject, it is wise to keep notes so that you can refer back and see the various ways in which one topic is presented.

Dual passages, or comparative essays, give two passages from authors with different points of view. The format of the two passages will change with each exam. For example, the author of the first passage may give an idea from his or her point of view. And, the author of the second passage gives an argument against the first passage. Other dual passages will give a topic in the first passage. Then the second passage will help or provide explanation to the topic in the first passage.

You may see that the questions ask about passage one, passage two, and both passages. No matter the length or kind of passages, you should read them in order (i.e., read Passage 1 first, then move on to Passage 2). However, what do you do if you are limited on time? You can read passage 1 first and answer all of the questions for passage 1. Then, read passage 2 and answer the remaining questions.

Organization of the Passage

The way a passage is organized can help readers to understand the author's purpose and his or her conclusions. There are many ways to organize a passage, and each one has an important use.

Some nonfiction texts are organized to **present a problem** followed by a solution. For this type of passage, the problem is explained before the solution is given. When the problem is well known, the solution may be given in a few sentences at the beginning. Other passages may focus on the solution, and the problem will be talked about only a few times. Some passages will outline many solutions to a problem. This will leave you to choose among the possible solutions. If authors have loyalty to one solution, they may not describe some of the other solutions. Be careful with the author's plan when reading a problem-solution passage. When you know the author's point of view, you can make a better judgment of the author's solution.

Sometimes authors will organize information clearly for you to follow and locate the information. However, this is not always the case with passages in an exam. Two common ways to order a passage are cause and effect and chronological order. When using **chronological order** (i.e., a plan that moves in order from the first step to the last), the author gives information in the order that the event happened. For example, biographies are written in chronological order. The person's birth and childhood are first. Their adult life is next. The events leading up to the person's death are last.

In **cause and effect** passages, an author shows one thing that makes something else happen. For example, if one were to go to bed very late and wake up very early, then they would be tired in the morning. The cause is a lack of sleep, with the effect of being tired the next day.

Finding the cause-and-effect relationships in a passage can be tricky. Often, these relationships come with certain words or terms. When authors use words like *because*, *since*, *in order*, and *so*, they are describing a cause and effect relationship. Think about the sentence: *He called her because he needed the homework*. This is a simple causal relationship. The cause was his need for the homework, and the effect was his phone call. Yet, not all cause and effect relationships are marked like this. Think about the sentences: *He called her. He needed the homework.* When the cause-and-effect relationship does not come with a keyword, the relationship can be known by asking why. For example, *He called her*. Why did he call her? The answer is in the next sentence: He needed the homework.

Review Video: Rhetorical Strategy of Cause-and-Effect Analysis
Visit mometrix.com/academy and enter code: 725944

When authors try to change the minds of readers, they may use cause-and-effect relationships. However, these relationships should not always be taken at face value. To read a persuasive essay well, you need to judge the cause-and-effect relationships. For example, imagine an author wrote the following: *The parking deck has not been making money because people want to ride their bikes.* The relationship is clear: the cause is that people want to ride their bikes. The effect is that the parking deck has not been making money. However, you should look at this argument again. Maybe there are other reasons that the parking deck was not a success: a bad economy, too many costs, etc.

Many passages follow the **compare-and-contrast** model. In this model, the similarities and differences between two ideas or things are reviewed. A review of the similarities between ideas is called comparison. In a perfect comparison, the author shows ideas or things in the same way. If authors want to show the similarities between football and baseball, then they can list the equipment and rules for each game. Think about the similarities as they appear in the passage and take note of any differences.

Review Video: Compare and Contrast
Visit mometrix.com/academy and enter code: 798319

Careful thinking about ideas and conclusions can seem like a difficult task. You can make this task easy by understanding the basic parts of ideas and writing skills. Looking at the way that ideas link to others is a good way for you to begin. Sometimes authors will write about two ideas that are against each other. Other times, an author will support a topic, and another author will argue against the topic. The review of these rival ideas is known as **contrast**. In contrast, all ideas should be presented clearly. If the author does favor a side, you need to read carefully to find where the author shows or hides this favoritism. Also, as you read the passage, you should write out how one side views the other.

Understanding a Passage

One of the most important skills in reading comprehension is finding **topics** and **main ideas.** There is a small difference between these two. The topic is the subject of a passage (i.e., what the passage is all about). The main idea is the most important argument being made by the author. The topic is shared in a few words while the main idea needs a full sentence to be understood. As an example, a short passage might have the topic of penguins, and the main idea could be written as *Penguins are different from other birds in many ways.*

In most nonfiction writing, the topic and the main idea will be stated clearly. Sometimes, they will come in a sentence at the very beginning or end of the passage. When you want to know the topic, you may find it in the first sentence of each paragraph. A body paragraph's first sentence is often--but not always--the main topic sentence. The topic sentence gives you a summary of the ideas in the paragraph. You may find that the topic or main idea is not given clearly. So, you must read every sentence of the passage. Then, try to come up with an overall idea from each sentence.

Note: A thesis statement is not the same as the main idea. The main idea gives a brief, general summary of a text. The thesis statement gives a clear idea on an issue that is backed up with evidence.

Review Video: Topics and Main Ideas
Visit mometrix.com/academy and enter code: 407801

Introduction

An introduction has a summary of the passage and the thesis statement. The purpose of the introduction is to grab the reader's attention. To win the reader's attention, authors may use a quote, question, or strong opinion. Some authors choose to use an interesting description or puzzling statement. Also, the introduction is the place that authors use to explain their reason for writing.

Body Paragraphs

Following the introduction, body paragraphs are used to explain the thesis statement. A body paragraph has a topic sentence that may be found in the first sentence. In these paragraphs, there is evidence that helps the argument of the paragraph. Also, the author may have commentary on the evidence. Be careful because this commentary can be filled with bias.

Review Video: How to Write a Body Paragraph
Visit mometrix.com/academy and enter code: 724590

The topic sentence gives the paragraph's subject and the main idea. The rest of the body paragraph should be linked to the topic sentence. Again, the topic sentence should be explained with facts, details, and examples.

The topic sentence is general and covers the ideas in a body paragraph. Sometimes, the topic sentence may be implied (i.e., the sentence is not stated directly by the author). Also, the topic sentence shows the connections among the supporting details.

Conclusion

The conclusion should provide a summary on the passage. New material is not given in the conclusion. The conclusion is the final paragraph that may have a call to action (i.e., something the writer wants readers to do) or a question for the reader to think about.

The main idea is the umbrella argument of a passage. So, **supporting details** back up the main idea. To show that a main idea is correct, authors add details that prove their idea. All passages contain details. However, they are referred to as supporting details when they help an argument in the passage. Supporting details are found in informative and persuasive texts. Sometimes they will come with terms like *for example* or *for instance*. Or, they will be numbered with terms like *first*, *second*, and *last*. You should think about how the author's supporting details back up his or her main idea. Supporting details can be correct, yet they may help the author's main idea. Sometimes supporting details can seem helpful. However, they may be useless when they are based on opinions.

Review Video: Supporting Details
Visit mometrix.com/academy and enter code: 396297

An example of a main idea: *Giraffes live in the Serengeti of Africa*. A supporting detail about giraffes could be: *A giraffe in the Serengeti benefits from a long neck by reaching twigs and leaves on tall trees.* The main idea gives the general idea that the text is about giraffes. The supporting detail gives a clear fact about how the giraffes eat.

A **theme** is an issue, an idea, or a question raised by a passage. For example, a theme of *Cinderella* is determination as Cinderella serves her step-sisters and step-mother. Passages may have many themes, and you must be sure to find only themes that you are asked to find. One common mark of themes is that they give more questions than answers. Authors try to push readers to consider themes in other ways. You can find themes by asking about the general problems that the passage is addressing. A good way to find a theme is to begin reading with a question in mind (e.g., How does this passage use the theme of love?) and to look for answers to that question.

Review Video: Themes in Literature
Visit mometrix.com/academy and enter code: 732074

Figurative Language

When authors want to share their message in a creative way, they use figurative language devices. Learning these devices will help you understand what you read. **Figurative language** is communication that goes beyond the actual meaning of a word or phrase. **Descriptive language** that awakens imagery in the reader's mind is one type of figurative language. Exaggeration is another type of figurative language. Also, when you compare two things, you are using figurative language. Similes and metaphors are the two main ways of comparing things. An example of a simile: *The child howled like a coyote when her mother told her to pick up the toys.* In this example, the child's howling is compared to a coyote. This helps the reader understand the sound being made by the child.

A **figure of speech** is a word or phrase that is not a part of straightforward, everyday language. Figures of speech are used for emphasis, fresh expression, or clearness. However, clearness of a passage may be incomplete with the use of these devices. For example: *I am going to crown you.*

The author may mean:

1. I am going to place a real crown on your head.
2. I am going to make you king or queen of this area.
3. I am going to punch you in the head with my fist.
4. I am going to put a second checker's piece on top of your checker piece to show that it has become a king.

Review Video: Figures of Speech
Visit mometrix.com/academy and enter code: 111295

An **allusion** is a comparison of someone or something to a person or event in history or literature. Allusions that point to people or events that are a part of today's culture are called topical allusions. Those that name a specific person are known as personal allusions. For example, *His desire for power was his Achilles' heel.* This example points to Achilles: a notable hero in Greek mythology who was thought to be invincible (i.e., cannot be hurt) except for his heels. Today, the term *Achilles' heel* points to an individual's weakness.

Review Video: Allusions
Visit mometrix.com/academy and enter code: 294065

Alliteration uses a string of words which begin with the same sound or letter. Alliteration is common in prose, yet the device finds more use in poetry. An example, *We thrashed through the thick forest with our blades.* In this sentence, a *th* sound is an example of alliteration. You may hear how the phrase shows the difficulty of moving through tall grass. Now, think about the description of eyes as *glassy globes of glitter.* This is alliteration since the *gl* sound is used three times. Related to alliteration is **assonance**, the repetition of vowel sounds. For example: *Low and slow, he rolled the coal.* Assonance is used in the same way as alliteration. Remember that vowels are *a, e, i, o, u,* and *y.* **Consonance** is the repetition of consonant sounds.

Review Video: Alliterations Are All Around
Visit mometrix.com/academy and enter code: 462837

A **metaphor** is the comparison of one thing with a different thing. For example: *The bird was an arrow flying across the sky.* In this sentence, the arrow is compared to a bird. The metaphor asks you to think about the bird in another way. Let's continue with this metaphor for a bird. You are asked to view the bird's flight as the flight of an arrow. So, you may imagine the flight to be quick and purposeful. Metaphors allow the author to describe a thing without being direct. Remember that the thing being described will not always be mentioned directly by the author. Think about a forest in winter: *Swaying skeletons reached for the sky and groaned as the wind blew through them.* In this sentence, the author uses *skeletons* as a metaphor for trees without leaves.

Review Video: Metaphors in Writing
Visit mometrix.com/academy and enter code: 133295

Metonymy is naming one thing with words or phrases of a closely related thing. This is similar to metaphor. However, the comparison has a close connection, unlike metaphor. An example of metonymy is to call the news media *the press.* Of course, *the press* is the machine that prints newspapers. Metonymy is a way of naming something without using the same name constantly.

Synecdoche points to the whole by naming one of the parts. An example of synecdoche would be calling a construction worker a *hard hat.* Like metonymy, synecdoche is an easy way of naming something without having to overuse a name. The device allows writers to highlight pieces of the thing being described. For example, referring to businessmen as *suits* suggests professionalism and unity.

Hyperbole is overstatement or exaggeration. For example: *He jumped ten feet in the air when he heard the good news.* Obviously, no person can jump ten feet in the air without help. The author exaggerates because the hyperbole shares a lot of feeling. Let's say that the author shared: *He jumped when he heard the good news.* With this information, you might think that the character is not feeling very excited. Hyperbole can be dangerous if the author does not exaggerate enough. For example: *He jumped two feet in the air when he heard the good news.* You may think that the author is writing a fact. Be careful with confusing hyperboles. Some test questions may have a hyperbole and a fact listed in the answer choices.

Understatement is the opposite of hyperbole. This device discounts or downplays something. Think about someone who climbs Mount Everest. Then, they say that the journey was *a little stroll*. As with other types of figurative language, understatement has a range of uses. The device may show self-defeat or modesty as in the Mount Everest example. However, some may think of understatement as false modesty (i.e., an attempt to bring attention to you or a situation). For example, a woman is praised on her diamond engagement ring. The woman says, *Oh, this little thing?* Her understatement might be heard as stuck-up or unfeeling.

Review Video: Hyperbole and Understatement
Visit mometrix.com/academy and enter code: 308470

A **simile** is a comparison that needs the separation words *like* or *as*. Some examples: *The Sun was like an orange*, *eager as a beaver*, and *quick as a mountain goat*. Because a simile includes *like* or *as*, the comparison uses a different tone than a simple description of something. For example: *the house was like a shoebox*. The tone is different than the author saying that the house *was* a shoebox.

Review Video: Similes
Visit mometrix.com/academy and enter code: 642949

Personification is the explanation of a nonhuman thing with human attributes. The basic purpose of personification is to describe something in a way that readers will understand. An author says that a tree *groans* in the wind. The author does not mean that the tree is giving a low, pained sound from a mouth. However, the author means that the tree is making a noise like a human groan. Of course, this personification creates a tone of sadness or suffering. A different tone would be made if the author said that the tree *sways* or *dances*.

Review Video: Personification
Visit mometrix.com/academy and enter code: 260066

Irony is a statement that hints at the opposite of what you expect. In other words, the device is used when an author or character says one thing but means another. For example, imagine a man who is covered in mud and dressed in tattered clothes. He walks in his front door to meet his wife. Then, his wife asks him, "How was your day?" He says, "Great!" The man's response to his wife is an example of irony. There is a difference between irony and sarcasm. Sarcasm is similar to irony. However, sarcasm is hurtful for the person receiving the sarcastic statement. A sarcastic statement points to the foolishness of a person to believe that a false statement is true.

Review Video: What is the Definition of Irony?
Visit mometrix.com/academy and enter code: 374204

As you read, you will see more words in the context of a sentence. This will strengthen your vocabulary. Be sure to read on a regular basis. This practice will increase the number of ways that you have seen a word in context. Based on experience, a person can remember how a word was used in the past and use that knowledge for a new context. For example, a person may have seen the word *gull* used to mean a bird that is found near the seashore. However, a *gull* can be a person who is tricked easily. If the word in context is used for a person, you will see the insult. After all, gulls are not thought to be very smart. Use your knowledge of a word to find comparisons. This knowledge can be used to learn a new use of a word.

History and Culture in Literature

History has an important influence on passages. The events, information, and thoughts of an author's time impact every part of his or her work. Sometimes, authors use language that would be inappropriate or wrong in a modern setting. However, those ideas were acceptable in the author's time. Think about how an event had an influence on a passage. Then, think about how today's opinions and ideas shape the way that you read passages from the past.

For example: In most societies of the past, women were treated as second-class people. Some authors who wrote in 18th-century England could be considered feminists in their time. However, you may think that they sound hateful toward women. The incorrect assumptions and prejudices of the past should not be excused or forgotten. Instead, they should be thought of as a result of their time and culture.

Studying world literature shows that writers from very different cultures write on similar themes. Dramas like the *Odyssey* and *Hamlet* focus on someone's battle for self-control and independence. In most cultures, authors write about themes of personal growth and the struggle for maturity. Another example is the conflict between the person and society. Works that are as different as *Native Son*, the *Aeneid*, and *1984* show how people try to keep their identity in large (sometimes) abusive groups. Also, many cultures have passages of the hero's or heroine's journey. For this journey, the character must overcome difficulties to gain more knowledge, power, and perspective. Some famous works of this journey are the *Epic of Gilgamesh*, Dante's *Divine Comedy*, and Cervantes' *Don Quixote.*

Authors from different genres and cultures may look at similar themes. Yet, they show these themes in different ways. For example, poets may write on a topic with images and allusions. In a play, the author may show themes with characters that are expressing different points of view. In a passage, the author does not need to write about themes directly. They can be shown with events and actions. Different movements and styles become popular in different regions. For example, in Greece and England, authors tend to use more irony. In the 1950s Latin American authors popularized the use of unusual and surreal events to show themes about real life in the genre of magical realism. Japanese authors use the well-established poetic form of the haiku to organize their treatment of common themes.

Technical Information in Reading Comprehension

Tables show information that has been seen in a field of study and put into a viewable layout. This layout is for easy reading and understanding. At the top of the table, you will see a title. The title says what information is in the table. An example of a title: *Average Income for Different Levels of Education.* Another example: *Price of Milk Compared to Demand.* A table gives information in vertical (i.e., up and down) columns and horizontal (i.e., left to right) rows. Normally, each column will have a label. For example, *Average Income for Different Levels of Education* is the title. Then, the two columns could be labeled *Education Level* and *Average Income.* Each location on the table is called a cell. Cells are named by their column and row (e.g., second column, fifth row). The information for a table is placed in those cells.

Like a table, a **graph** will show information that has been collected. The purpose of the graph is to give information in a layout that keeps track of changes. The graph will have a title that may simply give the names of the two axes (e.g., Income vs. Education). Or, the title may have more description: *A Comparison of Average Income with Level of Education.*

The bar and line graphs are given on two perpendicular lines (i.e., axes). The vertical axis (Note: axes is plural and axis is singular) is called the y-axis, and the horizontal axis is called the x-axis. The

x-axis is the independent variable, and the y-axis is the dependent variable. A variable is an unknown or changing value or quantity. The independent variable is the one being changed or controlled by the person who created the graph. Let's continue with the *Income and Education* example. The independent variable would be *level of education*. The maker of the graph will decide the levels of education (e.g., high school, college, master's degree, etc.). The dependent value is not controlled by the maker of the graph. Instead, the value is a result of the independent variable.

Think about the purpose and the type of graph layout. For example, a bar graph is good for showing specific numbers or amounts and the change among those numbers or amounts. For example, you want to show the amount of money spent on groceries during the months of a year. In that case, a bar graph would be best. The vertical axis would be for values of money. The horizontal axis would give the bar showing each month. On the other hand, let's say that the cost of groceries is put on a line graph, not a bar graph. Then, you would want to know if your amount of spending rose or fell during the year.

A bar graph is good for showing the relationships between the different values placed on a graph. The line graph is good for showing if the values will grow, shrink, or stay the same. Often, the bar graph is chosen over the line graph. There has to be some built-in relationship between the data points because the graph hints at a relationship. The amount of different apples at a store is one example. There is a relationship between the store and the number of apples that the store has for sell. The speed of popular rollercoasters at an amusement park is another example. There is a relationship between the amusement park and the different speeds of roller coasters at the amusement park.

In some examples, the line graph is better (e.g., periods of time or growth). A line graph shows the speed of change between periods of time in a visual layout. Watching a stock on the Dow Jones rise and fall over the course of a month is a good example. Or, keeping track of the height of a child over a period of years is another good use of a line graph.

A **line graph** is used for measuring changes over time. The graph is set up on a vertical and a horizontal axis. The measured variables are listed along the left side and the bottom side of the axes. Points are then placed along the graph. For example, a line graph measures a person's income for each month of the year. If the person earned $1500 in January, there should be a point directly above January and directly to the right of $1500. When all of the amounts are placed on the graph, they are connected with a line from left to right. This line gives a nice picture of the general changes. If the line sloped up, you would see that the person's income had increased over the course of the year.

The **bar graph** is one of the most common pictures of information. The bar graph has two parts: the vertical axis and the horizontal axis. The vertical axis uses numbers or amounts. The horizontal axis uses categories or names. A bar graph that gives the heights of famous basketball players is a good example. The vertical axis would have numbers going from five to eight feet. The horizontal axis would have the names of the players. The length of the bar above the player's name would show his height. In this graph, you would see that Yao Ming is taller than Michael Jordan because Yao's bar would be higher.

A **pie chart** is good for showing how a single thing or group is divided. The standard pie chart is a circle with labeled wedges. Each wedge is proportional in size to a part of the whole. For example, think about a pie chart that shows a student's budget. The whole circle represents all of the money that the student has to spend. Let's say that the student spends half of his or her money on food. So, the pie chart will be divided in half with one half labeled food. The other half is what remains in the student's budget. Now, let's say that he or she spends a quarter of his or her money on movies. Now, the unlabeled half will be divided to show that a quarter of his or her budget is left over. This picture would make it easy to see that the student spends twice the amount of money on food as on movies. So, the wedge of the graph labeled food is proportional to the actual amount of money spent on food. The wedge takes up half of circle, and the amount spent on food is half of the budget.

As you review the information in the graph, ask questions. Has the author chosen the correct format for the information? Did the author remove variables or other information that might upset his or her argument? Be aware of how one variable reacts to a change in another variable. Let's say that someone's education level increases. Does the graph show that there is a rise for income as well? The same can be done with a table.

Be sure that your conclusions come from the information in the graph. In other words, don't infer unknown values from a graph to draw conclusions that have no evidence. Think about a graph that compares the price of eggs to the demand. If the price and demand rise and fall together, you would be right to say that the demand for eggs and the price are connected. However, this simple graph does not say which variable causes the other. So, you cannot say that the price of eggs raises or lowers the demand. With more information, you may find that the demand for eggs could be connected to other things.

Identifying and Creating Arguments

Evaluating a Passage

When you read informational passages, you need to make a conclusion from the author's writing. You can **identify a logical conclusion** (i.e., find a conclusion that makes sense) to know whether you agree or disagree with an author. Coming to this conclusion is like making an inference. You combine the information from the passage with what you already know. From the passage's information and your knowledge, you can come to a conclusion that makes sense. One way to have a conclusion that makes sense is to take notes of all the author's points. When the notes are organized, they may point to the logical conclusion. Another way to reach conclusions is to ask if the author's passage raises any helpful questions. Sometimes you will be able to draw many conclusions from a passage. Yet, some of these may be conclusions that were never imagined by the author. Therefore, find reasons in the passage for the conclusions that you make.

Review Video: How to Support a Conclusion
Visit mometrix.com/academy and enter code: 281653

Text evidence is the information that supports a main argument or minor argument. This evidence, or proof, can lead you to a conclusion. Information used as text evidence is clear, descriptive, and full of facts. Supporting details give evidence to back-up an argument.

For example, a passage may state that winter occurs during opposite months in the Northern hemisphere (i.e., north of the equator) and Southern hemisphere (i.e., south of the equator). Text evidence for this claim may include a list of countries where winter occurs in opposite months. Also, you may be given reasons that winter occurs at different times of the year in these hemispheres (e.g., the tilt of the earth as it rotates around the sun).

Review Video: Textual Evidence
Visit mometrix.com/academy and enter code: 486236

A text is **credible**, or believable, when the author is knowledgeable and fair. The author's motivations for writing the passage have an important part in knowing the credibility of the passage. For example, passages written about a professional soccer game by a sports reporter and one written by an average fan will have different levels of credibility.

Review Video: Author Credibility
Visit mometrix.com/academy and enter code: 827257

A reader should always draw conclusions from passages. Sometimes conclusions are implied (i.e., information that is assumed) from written information. Other times the information is **stated directly** within the passage. You should try to draw conclusions from information stated in a passage. Furthermore, you should always read through the entire passage before drawing conclusions. Many readers expect the author's conclusions at the beginning or the end of the passage. However, many texts do not follow this format.

Implications are things that the author does not say directly. Yet, you can assume from what the author does say. For example, *I stepped outside and opened my umbrella. By the time I got to work, the cuffs of my pants were soaked*. The author never says that it is raining. However, you can conclude that this information is implied. Conclusions from implications must be well supported by the passage. To draw a conclusion, you should have many pieces of proof. Yet, let's say that you have only one piece. Then, you need to be sure that there is no other possible explanation than your conclusion. Practice drawing conclusions from implications in real life events to improve your skills.

Outlining the information in a passage should be a well-known skill to readers. A good outline will show the pattern of the passage and lead to better conclusions. A common outline calls for the main ideas of the passage to be listed in the order that they come. Then, beneath each main idea, you can list the minor ideas and details. An outline does not need to include every detail from the passage. However, the outline should show everything that is important to the argument.

Review Video: Outlining as an Aid to Drawing Conclusions
Visit mometrix.com/academy and enter code: 584445

Another helpful tool is the skill of **summarizing** information. This process is similar to creating an outline. First, a summary should define the main idea of the passage. The summary should have the most important supporting details or arguments. Summaries can be unclear or wrong because they do not stay true to the information in the passage. A helpful summary should have the same message as the passage.

Review Video: Tips on Text Summarization
Visit mometrix.com/academy and enter code: 584445

Ideas from a passage can be organized using **graphic organizers**. A graphic organizer reduces information to a few key points. A graphic organizer like a timeline may have an event listed for each date on the timeline. However, an outline may have an event listed under a key point that happens in the passage.

You need to make a graphic organizer that works best for you. Whatever helps you remember information from a passage is what you need to use. A spider-map is another example. This map takes a main idea from the story and places it in a bubble. From one main idea bubble, you put supporting points that connect to the main idea. A Venn diagram groups information as separate or connected with some overlap.

Review Video: Graphic Organizers
Visit mometrix.com/academy and enter code: 665513

Paraphrasing is another method that you can use to understand a passage. To paraphrase, you put what you have read into your own words. Or, you can *translate* what the author shared into your words by including as many details as you can.

Opinions, Facts, and Fallacies

Critical thinking skills are mastered by understanding the types of writing and the purposes of authors. Every author writes for a purpose. To know the purpose of authors and how they accomplish their purpose has two important steps. First, think carefully about their writing. Then, determine if you agree with their conclusions.

Readers must always be aware of the difference between fact and opinion. A **fact** can be proved or disproved. An **opinion** is the author's personal thoughts or feelings. So, an opinion cannot be proved or disproved.

For example, an author writes that the distance from New York City to Boston is about two hundred miles. The author is giving a fact. We can drive to Boston from New York City and find that it took about 200 miles. However, another author writes that New York City is too crowded. This author is giving an opinion. The reason that this is an opinion is that there is no independent measurement for overpopulation. You may think that where you live is overcrowded. Yet, someone else may say that more people can live in your area.

An opinion may come with words like *believe*, *think*, or *feel*. Know that an opinion can be backed up with facts. For example, someone may give the population density (i.e., the number of people living for each square mile) of New York City as a reason for an overcrowded population. An opinion backed up with facts can seem convincing. However, this does not mean that you should accept the argument.

Use these steps to know the difference between fact and opinion. First, think about the type of source that is presenting information (e.g., Is this information coming from someone or something that is trusted by me and others?). Next, think about the information that backs up a claim (e.g., Are the details for the argument opinions or facts?). Then, think about the author's motivation to have a certain point of view on a topic (e.g., Why does this person care about this issue?).

For example, a group of scientists tests the value of a product. The results are likely to be full of facts. Now, compare the group of scientists to a company. The company sells a product and says that their products are good. The company says this because they want to sell their product. Yet, the scientists use the scientific method (i.e. an independent way of proving ideas and questions) to prove the value of the product. The company's statements about the product may be true. But, the group of scientists *proves* the value of the product.

Review Video: Fact or Opinion
Visit mometrix.com/academy and enter code: 870899

When writers try to persuade, they often make mistakes in their thinking patterns and writing choices. These patterns and choices are important for making an informed decision. Authors show their bias when they ignore fair counterarguments or twist opposing points of view. A **bias** is obvious when the author is unfair or inaccurate with opposing ideas.

A **stereotype** is like a bias. Yet, a stereotype is used only with a group or place. Stereotyping is thought to be wrong because the practice pairs uninformed ideas with people or places. Be very careful with authors who stereotype. These uninformed ideas almost always show the author's ignorance and lack of curiosity.

Review Video: Bias and Stereotype
Visit mometrix.com/academy and enter code: 644829

Inductive and Deductive Reasoning

Logic is the study of good and bad arguments. Inductive reasoning is a path of logic that uses specifics to draw an overall conclusion. This path starts with facts and figures. For example, someone sees for several months that zebras have stripes. The person draws the conclusion that all zebras have stripes. This individual's conclusion (e.g., that all zebras have stripes) is not final. The reason is that every zebra has not been seen.

Inductive reasoning is used to make inferences about the universe. The entire universe has not been seen, but inferences can still be made from what has been studied in the universe. These inferences may be proven false when more facts and figures are ready for use. However, they are considered correct until they are proven to be incorrect.

Deductive reasoning is the use of general facts that leads to a clear conclusion. For example: *Susan is a sophomore in high school, and all sophomores take geometry*. So, you can infer that *Susan takes geometry*. The word *all* does not allow for differences. In other words, all of the sophomores take geometry. So, the statement that Susan is in a geometry class is a valid (i.e., true) conclusion.

Review Video: Inductive and Deductive Reasoning
Visit mometrix.com/academy and enter code: 507014

Logical Fallacies

A logical fallacy is bad reasoning. You want to find logical fallacies because they weaken the author's message. The four most common logical fallacies in writing are the false analogy, circular reasoning, false dichotomy, and overgeneralization.

Review Video: Logical Fallacies
Visit mometrix.com/academy and enter code: 644845

In a **false analogy**, the author argues that two things are similar, yet they are different. Authors use this fallacy when they want to persuade readers that some unknown thing is like some known thing. Authors take advantage of the reader's ignorance to make this incorrect comparison. For example: *People who run a mile everyday are like people who run for president or for mayor. Both want to work hard and do what it takes to reach their goals*. To compare people who exercise with people who run in elections is a false analogy. People who exercise may have no interest in politics. And, people who run for office may have no interest in personal exercise.

Circular reasoning is a logical fallacy that starts at one point and ends on the same point. This reasoning is unhelpful because the conclusion is not explained. The conclusion is simply repeated in the opening arguments. In other words, the argument is repeated simply in different words. A basic example of a circular argument is when a person uses a word to define itself. For example, *Niceness* *is the state of being nice*. If you don't know what *nice* means, then this definition is not useful. Another example, *I know this guy is telling the truth. He just told me so*. There is no evidence that is somehow different in the conclusion.

A common logical fallacy is **false dichotomy**. With this logical fallacy, the author gives the idea that there are only two outcomes for an event. Authors use this fallacy when they want readers to think that their outcome is the one that makes sense. For example, *You need to go to the carnival with me, or you'll just be bored at home*. The writer thinks that there are only two options. Go to the carnival or be bored at home. Of course, this is not a true statement. You can be happy at home, or you can go somewhere else other than the carnival.

Overgeneralization is the use of a broad argument that cannot be proved or disproved. In most cases, authors use this fallacy to create an appearance of authority or confidence. Also, this fallacy can be used when authors want to shape the opinion of the reader. For example, *Everybody knows that she is a terrible teacher*. The author makes an argument that cannot be true. This kind of statement is made when authors want to have the appearance of unity. Most people may think that the teacher is no good. However, you cannot say that *everybody* thinks that the teacher is terrible. That would be an exaggeration. When you spot overgeneralization, you should become doubtful about the author's argument. The author may be hiding a weak argument behind overconfident language.

Review Video: Reading Logical Fallacies
Visit mometrix.com/academy and enter code: 644845

Two other types of logical fallacies are slippery slope arguments and hasty generalizations. In a **slippery slope argument**, the author argues that if something happens, then that means that something else will happen as a result. Yet, this may not be true. For example, *If you study for your exam, then you are going to make a passing grade*. Many people study for their exam, and many people do not pass. Be sure that when you study for your exam that you study all areas well.

Hasty generalization is drawing a conclusion with incomplete evidence. For example, *The boy turned in his work late today. Therefore, the boy is a poor student.* Perhaps the boy is the best student in the class, and he forgot about this one assignment. Or, the boy may have made an agreement with the teacher to turn in the assignment at another time. Be sure that you have all pieces of information before you draw a conclusion.

Another fallacy to watch out for is the **non sequitur fallacy**. Assumptions are claims that are taken to be true without proof. If a claim is controversial, proof should be provided to verify the assumption. When a claim is made that is entirely unrelated to the evidence presented, the writer is guilty of a non sequitur (i.e., "does not follow" in Latin) fallacy. So, any assumption that is not related to the supporting evidence is suspect.

Writers of persuasive passages use these fallacies because they are very powerful. To identify logical fallacies, you need to think carefully and ask questions as you read. Thinking carefully means that you do not take everything at face value. Readers need to think about an author's argument to be sure that their logic is correct.

Responding to a Passage

One part of being a good reader is making predictions. A **prediction** is a guess about what will happen next. Readers make predictions from what they have read and what they already know. For example: *Staring at the computer screen in shock, Kim reached for the glass of water.* The sentence leaves you to think that she is not looking at the glass. So, you may guess that Kim is going to knock over the glass. Yet, in the next sentence, you may read that Kim does not knock over the glass. As you have more information, be ready for your predictions to change.

Review Video: Predictive Reading
Visit mometrix.com/academy and enter code: 437248

Test-taking tip: To respond to questions that ask about predictions, your answer should come from the passage.

You will be asked to understand text that gives ideas without stating them directly. An **inference** is something that is implied but not stated directly by the author. For example: *After the final out of the inning, the fans were filled with joy and rushed the field.* From this sentence, you can infer that the fans were watching baseball and their team won. You should not use information outside of the passage before making inferences. As you practice making inferences, you will find that they need all of your attention.

Review Video: Inference
Visit mometrix.com/academy and enter code: 379203

Test-taking tip: When asked about inferences, look for context clues. Context is what surrounds the words and sentences that add explanation or information to an unknown piece. An answer can be *true* but not *correct*. The context clues will help you find the answer that is best. When asked for the implied meaning of a statement, you should locate the statement first. Then, read the context around the statement. Finally, look for an answer with a similar phrase.

For your exam, you must be able to find a text's **sequence** (i.e., the order that things happen). When the sequence is very important to the author, the passage comes with signal words: *first*, *then*, *next*, and *last*. However, a sequence can be implied. For example, *He walked through the garden and gave water and fertilizer to the plants.* Clearly, the man did not walk through the garden at the beginning. First, he found water. Then, he collected fertilizer. Next, he walked through the garden. Finally, he gave water and fertilizer to the plants. Passages do not always come in a clear sequence. Sometimes they begin at the end. Or, they can start over at the beginning. You can strengthen your understanding of the passage by taking notes to understand the sequence.

Dual passages, or comparative essays, give two passages from authors with different points of view. The format of the two passages will change with each exam. For example, the author of the first passage may give an idea from his or her point of view. The author of the second passage gives an argument against the first passage. Other dual passages will give a topic in the first passage. Then the second passage will help or provide explanation to the topic in the first passage.

You may see that the questions ask about passage one, passage two, and both passages. No matter the length or kind of passages, you should read them in order (i.e., read Passage 1 first, then move on to Passage 2). However, what do you do if you are limited on time? You can read passage 1 first and answer all of the questions for passage 1. Then, read passage 2 and answer the remaining questions.

Foundations of Grammar

The Eight Parts of Speech

Nouns

When you talk about a person, place, thing, or idea, you are talking about **nouns**. The two main types of nouns are **common** and **proper** nouns. Also, nouns can be abstract (i.e., general) or concrete (i.e., specific).

Common nouns are the class or group of people, places, and things (Note: Do not capitalize common nouns). Examples of common nouns:

> *People*: boy, girl, worker, manager
>
> *Places*: school, bank, library, home
>
> *Things*: dog, cat, truck, car

Proper nouns are the names of a specific person, place, or thing (Note: Capitalize all proper nouns). Examples of proper nouns:

> *People*: Abraham Lincoln, George Washington, Martin Luther King, Jr.
>
> *Places*: Los Angeles, California / New York / Asia
>
> *Things*: Statue of Liberty, Earth*, Lincoln Memorial
>
> *Note: When you talk about the planet that we live on, you capitalize *Earth*. When you mean the dirt, rocks, or land, you lowercase *earth*.

General nouns are the names of conditions or ideas. **Specific nouns** name people, places, and things that are understood by using your senses.

General nouns:

> *Condition*: beauty, strength
>
> *Idea*: truth, peace

Specific nouns:

> *People*: baby, friend, father
>
> *Places*: town, park, city hall
>
> *Things*: rainbow, cough, apple, silk, gasoline

Collective nouns are the names for a person, place, or thing that may act as a whole. The following are examples of collective nouns: *class, company, dozen, group, herd, team,* and *public*.

Pronouns

Pronouns are words that are used to stand in for a noun. A pronoun may be classified as personal, intensive, relative, interrogative, demonstrative, indefinite, and reciprocal.

Personal: *Nominative* is the case for nouns and pronouns that are the subject of a sentence. *Objective* is the case for nouns and pronouns that are an object in a sentence. *Possessive* is the case for nouns and pronouns that show possession or ownership.

SINGULAR

	Nominative	Objective	Possessive
First Person	I	me	my, mine
Second Person	you	you	your, yours
Third Person	he, she, it	him, her, it	his, her, hers, its

PLURAL

	Nominative	Objective	Possessive
First Person	we	us	our, ours
Second Person	you	you	your, yours
Third Person	they	them	their, theirs

Intensive: I myself, you yourself, he himself, she herself, the (thing) itself, we ourselves, you yourselves, they themselves

Relative: which, who, whom, whose

Interrogative: what, which, who, whom, whose

Demonstrative: this, that, these, those

Indefinite: all, any, each, everyone, either/neither, one, some, several

Reciprocal: each other, one another

> **Review Video: Nouns and Pronouns**
> Visit mometrix.com/academy and enter code: 312073

VERBS

If you want to write a sentence, then you need a verb in your sentence. Without a verb, you have no sentence. The verb of a sentence explains action or being. In other words, the verb shows the subject's movement or the movement that has been done to the subject.

TRANSITIVE AND INTRANSITIVE VERBS

A transitive verb is a verb whose action (e.g., drive, run, jump) points to a receiver (e.g., car, dog, kangaroo). Intransitive verbs do not point to a receiver of an action. In other words, the action of the verb does not point to a subject or object.

Transitive: He plays the piano. | The piano was played by him.

Intransitive: He plays. | John writes well.

A dictionary will let you know whether a verb is transitive or intransitive. Some verbs can be transitive and intransitive.

ACTION VERBS AND LINKING VERBS

An action verb is a verb that shows what the subject is doing in a sentence. In other words, an action verb shows action. A sentence can be complete with one word: an action verb. Linking verbs are intransitive verbs that show a condition (i.e., the subject is described but does no action).

Linking verbs link the subject of a sentence to a noun or pronoun, or they link a subject with an adjective. You always need a verb if you want a complete sentence. However, linking verbs are not able to complete a sentence.

Common linking verbs include *appear, be, become, feel, grow, look, seem, smell, sound,* and *taste.* However, any verb that shows a condition and has a noun, pronoun, or adjective that describes the subject of a sentence is a linking verb.

Action: He sings. | Run! | Go! | I talk with him every day. | She reads.

Linking:

> Incorrect: I am.
>
> Correct: I am John. | I smell roses. | I feel tired.

Note: Some verbs are followed by words that look like prepositions, but they are a part of the verb and a part of the verb's meaning. These are known as phrasal verbs and examples include *call off, look up*, and *drop off.*

Review Video: Action Verbs and Linking Verbs
Visit mometrix.com/academy and enter code: 743142

VOICE

Transitive verbs come in active or passive voice. If the subject does an action or receives the action of the verb, then you will know whether a verb is active or passive. When the subject of the sentence is doing the action, the verb is **active voice**. When the subject receives the action, the verb is **passive voice**.

> **Active**: Jon drew the picture. (The subject *Jon* is doing the action of *drawing a picture.*)
>
> **Passive**: The picture is drawn by Jon. (The subject *picture* is receiving the action from Jon.)

VERB TENSES

A verb tense shows the different form of a verb to point to the time of an action. The present and past tense are shown by changing the verb's form. An action in the present *I talk* can change form for the past: *I talked.* However, for the other tenses, an auxiliary (i.e., helping) verb is needed to show the change in form. These helping verbs include *am, are, is* | *have, has, had* | *was, were, will* (or *shall*).

Present: I talk	Present perfect: I have talked
Past: I talked	Past perfect: I had talked
Future: I will talk	Future perfect: I will have talked

Present: The action happens at the current time.

Example: He *walks* to the store every morning.

To show that something is happening right now, use the progressive present tense: I *am walking.*

Past: The action happened in the past.

Example: He *walked* to the store an hour ago.

Future: The action is going to happen later.

Example: I *will walk* to the store tomorrow.

Present perfect: The action started in the past and continues into the present.

Example: I *have walked* to the store three times today.

Past perfect: The second action happened in the past. The first action came before the second.

Example: Before I walked to the store (Action 2), I *had walked* to the library (Action 1).

Future perfect: An action that uses the past and the future. In other words, the action is complete before a future moment.

Example: When she comes for the supplies (future moment), I *will have walked* to the store (action completed in the past).

Review Video: Present Perfect, Past Perfect, and Future Perfect Verb Tenses
Visit mometrix.com/academy and enter code: 269472

Conjugating Verbs

When you need to change the form of a verb, you are **conjugating** a verb. The key parts of a verb are first person singular, present tense (dream); first person singular, past tense (dreamed); and the past participle (dreamed). Note: the past participle needs a helping verb to make a verb tense. For example, I *have dreamed* of this day. | I *am dreaming* of this day.

Present Tense: Active Voice

	Singular	Plural
First Person	I dream	We dream
Second Person	You dream	You dream
Third Person	He, she, it dreams	They dream

Mood

There are three moods in English: the indicative, the imperative, and the subjunctive.

The **indicative mood** is used for facts, opinions, and questions.

Fact: You can do this.

Opinion: I think that you can do this.

Question: Do you know that you can do this?

The **imperative** is used for orders or requests.

Order: You are going to do this!

Request: Will you do this for me?

The **subjunctive mood** is for wishes and statements that go against fact.

Wish: I wish that I were going to do this.

Statement against fact: If I were you, I would do this. (This goes against fact because I am not you. You have the chance to do this, and I do not have the chance.)

The mood that causes trouble for most people is the subjunctive mood. If you have trouble with any of the moods, then be sure to practice.

Adjectives

An adjective is a word that is used to modify a noun or pronoun. An adjective answers a question: *Which one? What kind of?* or *How many?* Usually, adjectives come before the words that they modify, but they may also come after a linking verb.

Which one? The *third* suit is my favorite.

What kind? This suit is *navy blue.*

How many? Can I look over the *four* neckties for the suit?

Articles

Articles are adjectives that are used to mark nouns. There are only three: the **definite** (i.e., limited or fixed amount) article *the*, and the **indefinite** (i.e., no limit or fixed amount) articles *a* and *an*. Note: *An* comes before words that start with a vowel sound (i.e., vowels include *a, e, i, o, u*, and *y*). For example, "Are you going to get an **u**mbrella?"

Definite: I lost *the* bottle that belongs to me.

Indefinite: Does anyone have *a* bottle to share?

Comparison with Adjectives

Some adjectives are relative and other adjectives are absolute. Adjectives that are **relative** can show the comparison between things. Adjectives that are **absolute** can show comparison. However, they show comparison in a different way. Let's say that you are reading two books. You think that one book is perfect, and the other book is not exactly perfect. It is not possible for the book to be more perfect than the other. Either you think that the book is perfect, or you think that the book is not perfect.

The adjectives that are relative will show the different **degrees** of something or someone to something else or someone else. The three degrees of adjectives include positive, comparative, and superlative.

The **positive** degree is the normal form of an adjective.

Example: This work is *difficult.* | She is *smart.*

The **comparative** degree compares one person or thing to another person or thing.

Example: This work is *more difficult* than your work. | She is *smarter* than me.

The **superlative** degree compares more than two people or things.

Example: This is the *most difficult* work of my life. | She is the *smartest* lady in school.

Review Video: What is an Adjective?
Visit mometrix.com/academy and enter code: 470154

Adverbs

An adverb is a word that is used to **modify** a verb, adjective, or another adverb. Usually, adverbs answer one of these questions: *When?*, *Where?*, *How?*, and *Why?*. The negatives *not* and *never* are known as adverbs. Adverbs that modify adjectives or other adverbs **strengthen** or **weaken** the words that they modify.

Examples:

He walks quickly through the crowd.

The water flows smoothly on the rocks.

Note: While many adverbs end in *-ly*, you need to remember that not all adverbs end in *-ly*. Also, some words that end in *-ly* are adjectives, not adverbs. Some examples include: *early, friendly, holy, lonely, silly*, and *ugly*. To know if a word that ends in *-ly* is an adjective or adverb, you need to check your dictionary.

Examples:

He is *never* angry.

You talk *too* loudly.

Comparison with Adverbs

The rules for comparing adverbs are the same as the rules for adjectives.

The **positive** degree is the standard form of an adverb.

Example: He arrives soon. | She speaks softly to her friends.

The **comparative** degree compares one person or thing to another person or thing.

Example: He arrives sooner than Sarah. | She speaks more softly than him.

The **superlative** degree compares more than two people or things.

Example: He arrives soonest of the group. | She speaks most softly of any of her friends.

Review Video: What is an Adverb?
Visit mometrix.com/academy and enter code: 713951

Prepositions

A preposition is a word placed before a noun or pronoun that shows the relationship between an object and another word in the sentence.

Common prepositions:

about	before	during	on	under
after	beneath	for	over	until
against	between	from	past	up
among	beyond	in	through	with
around	by	of	to	within
at	down	off	toward	without

Examples:

The napkin is *in* the drawer.

The Earth rotates *around* the Sun.

The needle is *beneath* the haystack.

Can you find me *among* the words?

Review Video: Prepositions
Visit mometrix.com/academy and enter code: 946763

Conjunctions

Conjunctions join words, phrases, or clauses, and they show the connection between the joined pieces. **Coordinating** conjunctions connect equal parts of sentences. **Correlative** conjunctions show the connection between pairs. **Subordinating** conjunctions join subordinate (i.e., dependent) clauses with independent clauses.

Coordinating Conjunctions

The coordinating conjunctions include: *and, but, yet, or, nor, for,* and *so*

Examples:

The rock was small, but it was heavy.

She drove in the night, and he drove in the day.

Correlative Conjunctions

The correlative conjunctions are: *either...or* | *neither...nor* | *not only...but also*

Examples:

Either you are coming *or* you are staying.

He ran *not only* three miles *but also* swam 200 yards.

Review Video: Coordinating and Correlative Conjunctions
Visit mometrix.com/academy and enter code: 390329

Subordinating Conjunctions

Common subordinating conjunctions include:

after	since	whenever
although	so that	where
because	unless	wherever
before	until	whether
in order that	when	while

Examples:

I am hungry *because* I did not eat breakfast.

He went home *when* everyone left.

Review Video: Subordinating Conjunctions
Visit mometrix.com/academy and enter code: 958913

Interjections

An interjection is a word for **exclamation** (i.e., great amount of feeling) that is used alone or as a piece to a sentence. Often, they are used at the beginning of a sentence for an **introduction**. Sometimes, they can be used in the middle of a sentence to show a **change** in thought or attitude.

Common Interjections: Hey! | Oh, | Ouch! | Please! | Wow!

Agreement and Sentence Structure

SUBJECTS AND PREDICATES

SUBJECTS

Every sentence has two things: a subject and a verb. The **subject** of a sentence names who or what the sentence is all about. The subject may be directly stated in a sentence, or the subject may be the implied *you*.

The **complete subject** includes the simple subject and all of its modifiers. To find the complete subject, ask *Who* or *What* and insert the verb to complete the question. The answer is the complete subject. To find the **simple subject**, remove all of the modifiers (adjectives, prepositional phrases, etc.) in the complete subject. Being able to locate the subject of a sentence helps with many problems, such as those involving sentence fragments and subject-verb agreement.

Examples:

The small red car is the one that he wants for Christmas.

(The complete subject is *the small red car.*)

The young artist is coming over for dinner.

(The complete subject is *the young artist.*)

Review Video: Subjects in English
Visit mometrix.com/academy and enter code: 444771

In **imperative** sentences, the verb's subject is understood (e.g., [You] Run to the store) but not actually present in the sentence. Normally, the subject comes before the verb. However, the subject comes after the verb in sentences that begin with *There are* or *There was.*

Direct:

John knows the way to the park.

(Who knows the way to the park? Answer: John)

The cookies need ten more minutes.

(What needs ten minutes? Answer: The cookies)

By five o' clock, Bill will need to leave.

(Who needs to leave? Answer: Bill)

Remember: The subject can come after the verb.

There are five letters on the table for him.

(What is on the table? Answer: Five letters)

There were coffee and doughnuts in the house.

(What was in the house? Answer: Coffee and doughnuts)

Implied:

Go to the post office for me.

(Who is going to the post office? Answer: You are.)

Come and sit with me, please?

(Who needs to come and sit? Answer: You do.)

Predicates

In a sentence, you always have a predicate and a subject. The subject tells what the sentence is about, and the **predicate** explains or describes the subject.

Think about the sentence: *He sings.* In this sentence, we have a subject (He) and a predicate (sings). This is all that is needed for a sentence to be complete. Would we like more information? Of course, we would like to know more. However, if this is all the information that you are given, you have a complete sentence.

Now, let's look at another sentence:

John and Jane sing on Tuesday nights at the dance hall.

What is the subject of this sentence?

Answer: John and Jane.

What is the predicate of this sentence?

Answer: Everything else in the sentence (sing on Tuesday nights at the dance hall).

Subject-Verb Agreement

Verbs **agree** with their subjects in number. In other words, *singular* subjects need *singular* verbs. *Plural* subjects need *plural* verbs. Singular is for one person, place, or thing. Plural is for more than one person, place, or thing. Subjects and verbs must also agree in person: first, second, or third. The present tense ending *-s* is used on a verb if its subject is third person singular; otherwise, the verb takes no ending.

Review Video: Subject-Verb Agreement
Visit mometrix.com/academy and enter code: 479190

Number Agreement Examples:

Single Subject and Verb: *Dan calls home.*

(Dan is one person. So, the singular verb *calls* is needed.)

Plural Subject and Verb: *Dan and Bob call home.*

(More than one person needs the plural verb *call.*)

Person Agreement Examples:

First Person: I *am* walking.

Second Person: You *are* walking.

Third Person: He *is* walking.

Complications with Subject-Verb Agreement

Words Between Subject and Verb

Words that come between the simple subject and the verb may serve as an effective distraction, but they have no bearing on subject-verb agreement.

Examples:

The joy of my life returns home tonight.

(**Singular Subject**: joy. **Singular Verb**: returns)

The phrase *of my life* does not influence the verb *returns*.

The question that still remains unanswered is "Who are you?"

(**Singular Subject**: question. **Singular Verb**: is)

Don't let the phrase "*that still remains...*" trouble you. The subject *question* goes with *is*.

Compound Subjects

A compound subject is formed when two or more nouns joined by *and*, *or*, or *nor* jointly act as the subject of the sentence.

Joined by And

When a compound subject is joined by *and*, it is treated as a plural subject and requires a plural verb.

Examples:

You and Jon are invited to come to my house.

(**Plural Subject**: You and Jon. **Plural Verb**: are)

The pencil and paper belong to me.

(**Plural Subject**: pencil and paper. **Plural Verb**: belong)

Joined by Or/Nor

For a compound subject joined by *or* or *nor*, the verb must agree in number with the part of the subject that is closest to the verb (italicized in the examples below).

Examples:

Today or *tomorrow is* the day.

(**Subject**: Today / tomorrow. **Verb**: is)

Stan or *Phil wants* to read the book.

(**Subject**: Stan / Phil. **Verb**: wants)

Neither the books nor the *pen is* on the desk.

(**Subject**: Books / Pen. **Verb**: is)

Either the blanket or *pillows arrive* this afternoon.

(**Subject**: Blanket / Pillows. **Verb**: arrive)

Indefinite Pronouns as Subject

An indefinite pronoun is a pronoun that does not refer to a specific noun. Indefinite pronouns may be only singular, be only plural, or change depending on how they are used.

Always Singular

Pronouns such as *each*, *either*, *everybody*, *anybody*, *somebody*, and *nobody* are always singular.

Examples:

Each of the runners *has* a different bib number.

(**Singular Subject**: Each. **Singular Verb**: has)

Is either of you ready for the game?

(**Singular Subject**: Either. **Singular Verb**: is)

Note: The words *each* and *either* can also be used as adjectives (e.g., *each* person is unique). When one of these adjectives modifies the subject of a sentence, it is always a singular subject.

Everybody grows a day older every day.

(**Singular Subject**: Everybody. **Singular Verb**: grows)

Anybody is welcome to bring a tent.

(**Singular Subject**: Anybody. **Singular Verb**: is)

Always Plural

Pronouns such as *both*, *several*, and *many* are always plural.

Examples:

Both of the siblings *were* too tired to argue.

(**Plural Subject**: Both. **Plural Verb**: were)

Many have tried, but none have succeeded.

(**Plural Subject**: Many. **Plural Verb**: have tried)

Depend on Context

Pronouns such as *some, any, all, none, more,* and *most* can be either singular or plural depending on what they are representing in the context of the sentence.

Examples:

> *All* of my dog's food *was* still there in his bowl
>
> (**Singular Subject**: All. **Singular Verb**: was)
>
> By the end of the night, *all* of my guests *were* already excited about coming to my next party.
>
> (**Plural Subject**: All. **Plural Verb**: were)

Other Cases Involving Plural or Irregular Form

Some nouns are **singular in meaning but plural in form**: news, mathematics, physics, and economics.

> The *news is* coming on now.
>
> *Mathematics is* my favorite class.

Some nouns are plural in form and meaning, and have **no singular equivalent**: scissors and pants.

> Do these *pants come* with a shirt?
>
> The *scissors are* for my project.

Mathematical operations are **irregular** in their construction, but are normally considered to be **singular in meaning**.

> *One plus one is* two.
>
> *Three times three is* nine.

Note: Look to your **dictionary** for help when you aren't sure whether a noun with a plural form has a singular or plural meaning.

Complements

A complement is a noun, pronoun, or adjective that is used to give more information about the subject or verb in the sentence.

Direct Objects

A direct object is a noun or pronoun that takes or receives the **action** of a verb. (Remember: a complete sentence does not need a direct object, so not all sentences will have them. A sentence needs only a subject and a verb.) When you are looking for a direct object, find the verb and ask *who* or *what*.

Examples:

I took the blanket. (Who or what did I take? *The blanket*)

Jane read books. (Who or what does Jane read? *Books*)

Indirect Objects

An indirect object is a word or group of words that show how an action had an **influence** on someone or something. If there is an indirect object in a sentence, then you always have a direct object in the sentence. When you are looking for the indirect object, find the verb and ask *to/for whom or what.*

Examples:

We taught the old dog a new trick.

(To/For Whom or What was taught? *The old dog*)

I gave them a math lesson.

(To/For Whom or What was given? *Them*)

Review Video: Direct and Indirect Objects
Visit mometrix.com/academy and enter code: 817385

Predicate Nominatives and Predicate Adjectives

As we looked at previously, verbs may be classified as either action verbs or linking verbs. A linking verb is so named because it links the subject to words in the predicate that describe or define the subject. These words are called predicate nominatives (if nouns or pronouns) or predicate adjectives (if adjectives).

Examples:

My father is a *lawyer.*

(Father is the **subject**. Lawyer is the **predicate nominative.**)

Your mother is *patient.*

(Mother is the **subject**. Patient is the **predicate adjective.**)

Pronoun Usage

The **antecedent** is the noun that has been replaced by a pronoun. A pronoun and its antecedent **agree** when they have the same number (singular or plural) and gender (male, female, or neuter).

Examples:

Singular agreement: *John* came into town, and *he* played for us.

(The word *he* replaces *John.*)

Plural agreement: *John and Rick* came into town, and *they* played for us.

(The word *they* replaces *John and Rick.*)

To determine which is the correct pronoun to use in a compound subject or object, try each pronoun **alone** in place of the compound in the sentence. Your knowledge of pronouns will tell you which one is correct.

Example:

> Bob and (I, me) will be going.
>
> Test: (1) *I will be going* or (2) *Me will be going*. The second choice cannot be correct because *me* cannot be used as the subject of a sentence. Instead, *me* is used as an object.
>
> **Answer**: Bob and I will be going.

When a pronoun is used with a noun immediately following (as in "we boys"), try the sentence **without the added noun**.

Example:

> (We/Us) boys played football last year.
>
> Test: (1) *We played football last year* or (2) *Us played football last year*. Again, the second choice cannot be correct because *us* cannot be used as a subject of a sentence. Instead, *us* is used as an object.
>
> **Answer**: We boys played football last year.

Review Video: Pronoun Usage
Visit mometrix.com/academy and enter code: 666500

Review Video: What is Pronoun-Antecedent Agreement?
Visit mometrix.com/academy and enter code: 919704

A pronoun should point clearly to the **antecedent**. Here is how a pronoun reference can be unhelpful if it is not directly stated or puzzling.

> **Unhelpful**: Ron and Jim went to the store, and *he* bought soda.
>
> (Who bought soda? Ron or Jim?)
>
> **Helpful**: Jim went to the store, and *he* bought soda.
>
> (The sentence is clear. Jim bought the soda.)

Some pronouns change their form by their placement in a sentence. A pronoun that is a subject in a sentence comes in the **subjective case**. Pronouns that serve as objects appear in the **objective case**. Finally, the pronouns that are used as possessives appear in the **possessive case**.

Examples:

> **Subjective case**: *He* is coming to the show.
>
> (The pronoun *He* is the subject of the sentence.)

Objective case: Josh drove *him* to the airport.

(The pronoun *him* is the object of the sentence.)

Possessive case: The flowers are *mine*.

(The pronoun *mine* shows ownership of the flowers.)

The word *who* is a subjective-case pronoun that can be used as a **subject**. The word *whom* is an objective-case pronoun that can be used as an **object**. The words *who* and *whom* are common in subordinate clauses or in questions.

Examples:

Subject: He knows who wants to come.

(*Who* is the subject of the verb *wants*.)

Object: He knows the man whom we want at the party.

(*Whom* is the object of *we want*.)

Clauses

A clause is a group of words that contains both a subject and a predicate (verb). There are two types of clauses: independent and dependent. An **independent clause** contains a complete thought, while a **dependent (or subordinate) clause** does not. A dependent clause includes a subject and a verb, and may also contain objects or complements, but it cannot stand as a complete thought without being joined to an independent clause. Dependent clauses function within sentences as adjectives, adverbs, or nouns.

Example:

Independent Clause: I am running

Dependent Clause: because I want to stay in shape

The clause *I am running* is an independent clause: it has a subject and a verb, and it gives a complete thought. The clause *because I want to stay in shape* is a dependent clause: it has a subject and a verb, but it does not express a complete thought. It adds detail to the independent clause to which it is attached.

Combined: I am running because I want to stay in shape.

Review Video: What is a Clause?
Visit mometrix.com/academy and enter code: 940170

Review Video: Independent and Dependent Clause Examples
Visit mometrix.com/academy and enter code: 556903

TYPES OF DEPENDENT CLAUSES

ADJECTIVE CLAUSES

An **adjective clause** is a dependent clause that modifies a noun or a pronoun. Adjective clauses begin with a relative pronoun (*who, whose, whom, which,* and *that*) or a relative adverb (*where, when,* and *why*).

Also, adjective clauses come after the noun that the clause needs to explain or rename. This is done to have a clear connection to the independent clause.

Examples:

> I learned the reason *why I won the award.*
>
> This is the place *where I started my first job.*

An adjective clause can be an essential or nonessential clause. An essential clause is very important to the sentence. **Essential clauses** explain or define a person or thing. **Nonessential clauses** give more information about a person or thing but are not necessary to define them. Nonessential clauses are set off with commas while essential clauses are not.

Examples:

> **Essential**: A person *who works hard at first* can often rest later in life.
>
> **Nonessential**: Neil Armstrong, *who walked on the moon*, is my hero.

Review Video: Adjective Clauses and Phrases
Visit mometrix.com/academy and enter code: 520888

ADVERB CLAUSES

An **adverb clause** is a dependent clause that modifies a verb, adjective, or adverb. In sentences with multiple dependent clauses, adverb clauses are usually placed immediately before or after the independent clause. An adverb clause is introduced with words such as *after, although, as, before, because, if, since, so, unless, when, where*, and *while.*

Examples:

> *When you walked outside*, I called the manager.
>
> I will go with you *unless you want to stay.*

NOUN CLAUSES

A **noun clause** is a dependent clause that can be used as a subject, object, or complement. Noun clauses begin with words such as *how, that, what, whether, which, who,* and *why.* These words can also come with an adjective clause. Unless the noun clause is being used as the subject of the sentence, it should come after the verb of the independent clause.

Examples:

> The real mystery is *how you avoided serious injury.*
>
> *What you learn from each other* depends on your honesty with others.

SUBORDINATION

When two related ideas are not of equal importance, the ideal way to combine them is to make the more important idea an independent clause, and the less important idea a dependent or subordinate clause. This is called **subordination**.

Example:

> **Separate ideas**: The team had a perfect regular season. The team lost the championship.
>
> **Subordinated**: Despite having a perfect regular season, *the team lost the championship.*

PHRASES

A phrase is a group of words that functions as a single part of speech, usually a noun, adjective, or adverb. A phrase is not a complete thought, but it adds **detail** or **explanation** to a sentence, or **renames** something within the sentence.

PREPOSITIONAL PHRASES

One of the most common types of phrases is the prepositional phrase. A **prepositional phrase** begins with a preposition and ends with a noun or pronoun that is the object of the preposition. Normally, the prepositional phrase functions as an **adjective** or an **adverb** within the sentence.

Examples:

> The picnic is *on the blanket.*
>
> I am sick *with a fever* today.
>
> *Among the many flowers*, John found a four-leaf clover.

VERBAL PHRASES

A verbal is a word or phrase that is formed from a verb but does not function as a verb. Depending on its particular form, it may be used as a noun, adjective, or adverb. A verbal does **not** replace a verb in a sentence.

Examples:

> Correct: *Walk* a mile daily.
>
> (*Walk* is the verb of this sentence. The subject is the implied *you.*)
>
> Incorrect: *To walk* a mile.
>
> (*To walk* is a type of verbal. This is not a sentence since there is no functional verb)

There are three types of verbals: **participles**, **gerunds**, and **infinitives**. Each type of verbal has a corresponding **phrase** that consists of the verbal itself along with any complements or modifiers.

PARTICIPLES

A **participle** is a type of verbal that always functions as an adjective. The present participle always ends with *-ing*. Past participles end with *-d, -ed, -n,* or *-t.*

> Examples: Verb: *dance* | Present Participle: *dancing* | Past Participle: *danced*

Participial phrases most often come right before or right after the noun or pronoun that they modify.

Examples:

Shipwrecked on an island, the boys started to fish for food.

Having been seated for five hours, we got out of the car to stretch our legs.

Praised for their work, the group accepted the first-place trophy.

Gerunds

A **gerund** is a type of verbal that always functions as a noun. Like present participles, gerunds always end with *-ing*, but they can be easily distinguished from one another by the part of speech they represent (participles always function as adjectives). Since a gerund or gerund phrase always functions as a noun, it can be used as the subject of a sentence, the predicate nominative, or the object of a verb or preposition.

Examples:

We want to be known for *teaching the poor*. (Object of preposition)

Coaching this team is the best job of my life. (Subject)

We like *practicing our songs* in the basement. (Object of verb)

Infinitives

An **infinitive** is a type of verbal that can function as a noun, an adjective, or an adverb. An infinitive is made of the word *to* + the basic form of the verb. As with all other types of verbal phrases, an infinitive phrase includes the verbal itself and all of its complements or modifiers.

Examples:

To join the team is my goal in life. (Noun)

The animals have enough food *to eat for the night*. (Adjective)

People lift weights *to exercise their muscles*. (Adverb)

Review Video: Gerunds, Participles, and Infinitives
Visit mometrix.com/academy and enter code: 634263

Appositive Phrases

An **appositive** is a word or phrase that is used to explain or rename nouns or pronouns. Noun phrases, gerund phrases, and infinitive phrases can all be used as appositives.

Examples:

> Terriers, *hunters at heart*, have been dressed up to look like lap dogs.
>
> (The noun phrase *hunters at heart* renames the noun *terriers*.)
>
> His plan, *to save and invest his money*, was proven as a safe approach.
>
> (The infinitive phrase explains what the plan is.)

Appositive phrases can be **essential** or **nonessential**. An appositive phrase is essential if the person, place, or thing being described or renamed is too general for its meaning to be understood without the appositive.

Examples:

> **Essential**: Two Founding Fathers George Washington and Thomas Jefferson served as presidents.
>
> **Nonessential**: George Washington and Thomas Jefferson, two Founding Fathers, served as presidents.

ABSOLUTE PHRASES

An absolute phrase is a phrase that consists of **a noun followed by a participle**. An absolute phrase provides **context** to what is being described in the sentence, but it does not modify or explain any particular word; it is essentially independent.

Examples:

> *The alarm ringing*, he pushed the snooze button.
>
> *The music paused*, she continued to dance through the crowd.

Note: Absolute phrases can be confusing, so don't be discouraged if you have a difficult time with them.

PARALLELISM

When multiple items or ideas are presented in a sentence in series, such as in a list, the items or ideas must be stated in grammatically equivalent ways. In other words, if one idea is stated in gerund form, the second cannot be stated in infinitive form. For example, to write, *I enjoy reading and to study* would be incorrect. An infinitive and a gerund are not equivalent. Instead, you should write *I enjoy reading and studying*. In lists of more than two, it can be harder to keep everything straight, but all items in a list must be parallel.

Example:

> **Incorrect**: He stopped at the office, grocery store, and the pharmacy before heading home.
>
> The first and third items in the list of places include the article *the*, so the second item needs it as well.
>
> **Correct**: He stopped at the office, *the* grocery store, and the pharmacy before heading home.

Example:

Incorrect: While vacationing in Europe, she went biking, skiing, and climbed mountains.

The first and second items in the list are gerunds, so the third item must be as well.

Correct: While vacationing in Europe, she went biking, skiing, and *mountain climbing.*

SENTENCE PURPOSE

There are four types of sentences: declarative, imperative, interrogative, and exclamatory.

A **declarative** sentence states a fact and ends with a period.

Example: *The football game starts at seven o'clock.*

An **imperative** sentence tells someone to do something and generally ends with a period. (An urgent command might end with an exclamation point instead.)

Example: *Don't forget to buy your ticket.*

An **interrogative** sentence asks a question and ends with a question mark.

Example: *Are you going to the game on Friday?*

An **exclamatory** sentence shows strong emotion and ends with an exclamation point.

Example: *I can't believe we won the game!*

SENTENCE STRUCTURE

Sentences are classified by structure based on the type and number of clauses present. The four classifications of sentence structure are the following:

Simple: A simple sentence has one independent clause with no dependent clauses. A simple sentence may have **compound elements** (i.e., compound subject or verb).

Examples:

<u>Judy</u> *watered* the lawn. (single <u>subject</u>, single *verb*)

<u>Judy and Alan</u> *watered* the lawn. (compound <u>subject</u>, single *verb*)

<u>Judy</u> *watered* the lawn and *pulled* weeds. (single <u>subject</u>, compound *verb*)

<u>Judy and Alan</u> *watered* the lawn and *pulled* weeds. (compound <u>subject</u>, compound *verb*)

Compound: A compound sentence has two or more <u>independent clauses</u> with no dependent clauses. Usually, the independent clauses are joined with a comma and a coordinating conjunction or with a semicolon.

Examples:

<u>The time has come</u>, and <u>we are ready</u>.

<u>I woke up at dawn</u>; <u>the sun was just coming up</u>.

Complex: A complex sentence has one independent clause and at least one *dependent clause.*

Examples:

Although he had the flu, Harry went to work.

Marcia got married *after she finished college.*

Compound-Complex: A compound-complex sentence has at least two independent clauses and at least one *dependent clause.*

Examples:

John is my friend *who went to India*, and he brought back souvenirs.

You may not realize this, but we heard the music *that you played last night.*

Review Video: Sentence Structure
Visit mometrix.com/academy and enter code: 700478

Sentence Fragments

Usually when the term *sentence fragment* comes up, it is because you have to decide whether or not a group of words is a complete sentence, and if it's not a complete sentence, you're about to have to fix it. Recall that a group of words must contain at least one **independent clause** in order to be considered a sentence. If it doesn't contain even one independent clause, it would be called a **sentence fragment**. (If it contains two or more independent clauses that are not joined correctly, it would be called a run-on sentence.)

Review Video: Fragments and Run-on Sentences
Visit mometrix.com/academy and enter code: 541989

The process to use for **repairing** a sentence fragment depends on what type of fragment it is. If the fragment is a dependent clause, it can sometimes be as simple as removing a subordinating word (e.g., when, because, if) from the beginning of the fragment. Alternatively, a dependent clause can be incorporated into a closely related neighboring sentence. If the fragment is missing some required part, like a subject or a verb, the fix might be as simple as adding it in.

Examples:

Fragment: Because he wanted to sail the Mediterranean.

Removed subordinating word: He wanted to sail the Mediterranean.

Combined with another sentence: Because he wanted to sail the Mediterranean, he booked a Greek island cruise.

Run-on Sentences

Run-on sentences consist of multiple independent clauses that have not been joined together properly. Run-on sentences can be corrected in several different ways:

Join clauses properly: This can be done with a comma and coordinating conjunction, with a semicolon, or with a colon or dash if the second clause is explaining something in the first.

Example:

Incorrect: I went on the trip, we visited lots of castles.

Corrected: I went on the trip, and we visited lots of castles.

Split into separate sentences: This correction is most effective when the independent clauses are very long or when they are not closely related.

Example:

Incorrect: The drive to New York takes ten hours, my uncle lives in Boston.

Corrected: The drive to New York takes ten hours. My uncle lives in Boston.

Make one clause dependent: This is the easiest way to make the sentence correct and more interesting at the same time. It's often as simple as adding a subordinating word between the two clauses

Example:

Incorrect: I finally made it to the store and I bought some eggs.

Corrected: When I finally made it to the store, I bought some eggs.

Reduce to one clause with a compound verb: If both clauses have the same subject, remove the subject from the second clause, and you now have just one clause with a compound verb.

Example:

Incorrect: The drive to New York takes ten hours, it makes me very tired.

Corrected: The drive to New York takes ten hours and makes me very tired.

Note: While these are the simplest ways to correct a run-on sentence, often the best way is to completely reorganize the thoughts in the sentence and rewrite it.

Review Video: Fragments and Run-on Sentences
Visit mometrix.com/academy and enter code: 541989

Dangling and Misplaced Modifiers

Dangling Modifiers

A dangling modifier is a dependent clause or verbal phrase that does not have a **clear logical connection** to a word in the sentence.

Example:

Dangling: *Reading each magazine article*, the stories caught my attention.

The word *stories* cannot be modified by *Reading each magazine article*. People can read, but stories cannot read. Therefore, the subject of the sentence must be a person.

Corrected: Reading each magazine article, *I* was entertained by the stories.

Example:

Dangling: Ever since childhood, my grandparents have visited me for Christmas.

The speaker in this sentence can't have been visited by her grandparents when *they* were children, since she wouldn't have been born yet. Either the modifier should be **clarified** or the sentence should be **rearranged** to specify whose childhood is being referenced.

Clarified: Ever since I was a child, my grandparents have visited for Christmas.

Rearranged: Ever since childhood, I have enjoyed my grandparents visiting for Christmas.

Misplaced Modifiers

Because modifiers are grammatically versatile, they can be put in many different places within the structure of a sentence. The danger of this versatility is that a modifier can accidentally be placed where it is modifying the wrong word or where it is not clear which word it is modifying.

Example:

Misplaced: She read the book to a crowd *that was filled with beautiful pictures.*

The book was filled with beautiful pictures, not the crowd.

Corrected: She read the book *that was filled with beautiful pictures* to a crowd.

Example:

Ambiguous: Derek saw a bus nearly hit a man *on his way to work.*

Was Derek on his way to work? Or was the other man?

Derek: *On his way to work*, Derek saw a bus nearly hit a man.

The other man: Derek saw a bus nearly hit a man *who was on his way to work.*

Split Infinitives

A split infinitive occurs when a modifying word comes between the word *to* and the verb that pairs with *to*.

Example: To *clearly* explain vs. *To explain* clearly | To *softly* sing vs. *To sing* softly

Though considered improper by some, split infinitives may provide better clarity and simplicity in some cases than the alternatives. As such, avoiding them should not be considered a universal rule.

Double Negatives

Standard English allows **two negatives** only when a **positive** meaning is intended. For example, *The team was not displeased with their performance.* Double negatives to emphasize negation are not used in standard English.

Negative modifiers (e.g., never, no, and not) should not be paired with other negative modifiers or negative words (e.g., none, nobody, nothing, or neither). The modifiers *hardly, barely*, and *scarcely* are considered negatives in standard English, so they should not be used with other negatives.

Usage Errors

Commonly Misused Words and Phrases

The phrase *a lot* should always be written as two words; never as *alot.*

Correct: That's a lot of chocolate!

Incorrect: He does that alot.

The word *can* is used to describe things that are possible occurrences; the word *may* is used to described things that are allowed to happen.

Correct: May I have another piece of pie?

Correct: I can lift three of these bags of mulch at a time.

Incorrect: Mom said we can stay up thirty minutes later tonight.

The phrase *could of* is often incorrectly substituted for the phrase *could have.* Similarly, *could of, may of,* and *might of* are sometimes used in place of the correct phrases *could have, may have,* and *might have.*

Correct: If I had known, I would have helped out.

Incorrect: Well, that could of gone much worse than it did.

The word *myself* is a reflexive pronoun, often incorrectly used in place of *I* or *me.*

Correct: He let me do it myself.

Incorrect: The job was given to Dave and myself.

The phrase *off of* is a redundant expression that should be avoided. In most cases, it can be corrected simply by removing *of.*

Correct: My dog chased the squirrel off its perch on the fence.

Incorrect: He finally moved his plate off of the table.

The phrase *suppose to* is sometimes used incorrectly in place of the phrase *supposed to.*

Correct: I was supposed to go to the store this afternoon.

Incorrect: When are we suppose to get our grades?

The phrase *try and* is often used in informal writing and conversation to replace the correct phrase *try to.*

Correct: It's a good policy to try to satisfy every customer who walks in the door.

Incorrect: Don't try and do too much.

Commonly Confused Words

Which, That, and Who

The words *which, that,* and *who* can act as **relative pronouns** to help clarify or describe a noun.

Which is used for things only.

Example: Andrew's car, *which is old and rusty,* broke down last week.

That is used for people or things. *That* is usually informal when used to describe people.

Example: Is this the only book *that Louis L'Amour wrote?*

Example: Is Louis L'Amour the author *that wrote Western novels?*

Who is used for people or for animals that have a name.

Example: Mozart was the composer *who wrote those operas.*

Example: John's dog, *who is called Max,* is large and fierce.

Homophones

Homophones are words that sound alike (or similar), but they have different **spellings** and **definitions**.

To, Too, and Two

To can be an adverb or a preposition for showing direction, purpose, and relationship. See your dictionary for the many other ways to use *to* in a sentence.

Examples: I went to the store. | I want to go with you.

Too is an adverb that means *also, as well, very,* or *more than enough.*

Examples: I can walk a mile too. | You have eaten too much.

Two is the second number in the series of numbers (e.g., one (1), two, (2), three (3)...)

Example: You have two minutes left.

There, Their, and They're

There can be an adjective, adverb, or pronoun. Often, *there* is used to show a place or to start a sentence.

Examples: I went there yesterday. | There is something in his pocket.

Their is a pronoun that is used to show ownership.

Examples: He is their father. | This is their fourth apology this week.

They're is a contraction of *they are.*

Example: Did you know that they're in town?

Knew and New

Knew is the past tense of *know*.

Example: I knew the answer.

New is an adjective that means something is current, has not been used, or is modern.

Example: This is my new phone.

Then and Than

Then is an adverb that indicates sequence or order:

Example: I'm going to run to the library and then come home.

Than is special-purpose word used only for comparisons:

Example: Susie likes chips more than candy.

Its and It's

Its is a pronoun that shows ownership.

Example: The guitar is in its case.

It's is a contraction of *it is*.

Example: It's an honor and a privilege to meet you.

Note: The *h* in honor is silent, so the sound of the vowel *o* must have the article *an*.

Your and You're

Your is a pronoun that shows ownership.

Example: This is your moment to shine.

You're is a contraction of *you are*.

Example: Yes, you're correct.

Affect and Effect

There are two main reasons that *affect* and *effect* are so often confused: 1) both words can be used as either a noun or a verb, and 2) unlike most homophones, their usage and meanings are closely related to each other. Here is a quick rundown of the four usage options:

Affect (n): feeling, emotion, or mood that is displayed

Example: The patient had a flat *affect*. (i.e., his face showed little or no emotion)

Affect (v): to alter, to change, to influence

Example: The sunshine *affects* the plant's growth.

Effect (n): a result, a consequence

Example: What *effect* will this weather have on our schedule?

Effect (v): to bring about, to cause to be

Example: These new rules will *effect* order in the office.

The noun form of *affect* is rarely used outside of technical medical descriptions, so if a noun form is needed on the test, you can safely select *effect*. The verb form of *effect* is not as rare as the noun form of *affect*, but it's still not all that likely to show up on your test. If you need a verb and you can't decide which to use based on the definitions, choosing *affect* is your best bet.

Homographs

Homographs are words that share the same spelling, but have different meanings and sometimes different pronunciations. To figure out which meaning is being used, you should be looking for context clues. The context clues give hints to the meaning of the word. For example, the word *spot* has many meanings. It can mean "a place" or "a stain or blot." In the sentence "After my lunch, I saw a spot on my shirt," the word *spot* means "a stain or blot." The context clues of "After my lunch" and "on my shirt" guide you to this decision.

Bank

(noun): an establishment where money is held for savings or lending

(verb): to collect or pile up

Content

(noun): the topics that will be addressed within a book

(adjective): pleased or satisfied

(verb): to make someone pleased or satisfied

Fine

(noun): an amount of money that acts a penalty for an offense

(adjective): very small or thin

(adverb): in an acceptable way

(verb): to make someone pay money as a punishment

Incense

(noun): a material that is burned in religious settings and makes a pleasant aroma

(verb): to frustrate or anger

Lead

(noun): the first or highest position

(noun): a heavy metallic element

(verb): to direct a person or group of followers

(adjective): containing lead

OBJECT

(noun): a lifeless item that can be held and observed

(verb): to disagree

PRODUCE

(noun): fruits and vegetables

(verb): to make or create something

REFUSE

(noun): garbage or debris that has been thrown away

(verb): to not allow

SUBJECT

(noun): an area of study

(verb): to force or subdue

TEAR

(noun): a fluid secreted by the eyes

(verb): to separate or pull apart

Punctuation

End Punctuation

Periods

Use a period to end all sentences except direct questions, exclamations.

Declarative Sentence

A declarative sentence gives information or makes a statement.

Examples: I can fly a kite. | The plane left two hours ago.

Imperative Sentence

An imperative sentence gives an order or command.

Examples: You are coming with me. | Bring me that note.

Periods for Abbreviations

Examples: 3 P.M. | 2 A.M. | Mr. Jones | Mrs. Stevens | Dr. Smith | Bill Jr. | Pennsylvania Ave.

Note: an abbreviation is a shortened form of a word or phrase.

Question Marks

Question marks should be used following a direct question. A polite request can be followed by a period instead of a question mark.

Direct Question: What is for lunch today? | How are you? | Why is that the answer?

Polite Requests: Can you please send me the item tomorrow. | Will you please walk with me on the track.

> **Review Video: When to Use a Question Mark**
> Visit mometrix.com/academy and enter code: 118471

Exclamation Marks

Exclamation marks are used after a word group or sentence that shows much feeling or has special importance. Exclamation marks should not be overused. They are saved for proper **exclamatory interjections**.

Example: We're going to the finals! | You have a beautiful car! | That's crazy!

> **Review Video: What Does an Exclamation Point Mean?**
> Visit mometrix.com/academy and enter code: 199367

Commas

The comma is a punctuation mark that can help you understand connections in a sentence. Not every sentence needs a comma. However, if a sentence needs a comma, you need to put it in the right place. A comma in the wrong place (or an absent comma) will make a sentence's meaning unclear. These are some of the rules for commas:

1. Use a comma **before a coordinating conjunction** joining independent clauses
   Example: Bob caught three fish, and I caught two fish.

2. Use a comma after an introductory phrase or an adverbial clause

   Examples:

   After the final out, we went to a restaurant to celebrate.
   Studying the stars, I was surprised at the beauty of the sky.

3. Use a comma between items in a series.

   Example: I will bring the turkey, the pie, and the coffee.

4. Use a comma **between coordinate adjectives** not joined with *and*

   Incorrect: The kind, brown dog followed me home.
   Correct: The *kind, loyal* dog followed me home.
   Not all adjectives are **coordinate** (i.e., equal or parallel). There are two simple ways to know if your adjectives are coordinate. One, you can join the adjectives with *and*: *The kind and loyal dog*. Two, you can change the order of the adjectives: *The loyal, kind dog*.

5. Use commas for **interjections** and **after *yes* and *no*** responses

   Examples:

   Interjection: Oh, I had no idea. | Wow, you know how to play this game.
   Yes and No: *Yes,* I heard you. | *No,* I cannot come tomorrow.

6. Use commas to separate nonessential modifiers and nonessential appositives

   Examples:

   Nonessential Modifier: John Frank, who is coaching the team, was promoted today.
   Nonessential Appositive: Thomas Edison, an American inventor, was born in Ohio.

7. Use commas to set off nouns of direct address, interrogative tags, and contrast

   Examples:

   Direct Address: You, *John,* are my only hope in this moment.
   Interrogative Tag: This is the last time, *correct*?
   Contrast: You are my friend, *not my enemy.*

8. Use commas with dates, addresses, geographical names, and titles

   Examples:

   Date: *July 4, 1776,* is an important date to remember.
   Address: He is meeting me at *456 Delaware Avenue, Washington, D.C.,* tomorrow morning.
   Geographical Name: *Paris, France,* is my favorite city.
   Title: John Smith, *Ph. D.,* will be visiting your class today.

9. Use commas to **separate expressions like *he said*** and ***she said*** if they come between a sentence of a quote

   Examples:

   "I want you to know," he began, "that I always wanted the best for you."
   "You can start," Jane said, "with an apology."

Review Video: When To Use a Comma
Visit mometrix.com/academy and enter code: 786797

Semicolons

The semicolon is used to connect major sentence pieces of equal value. Some rules for semicolons include:

1. Use a semicolon **between closely connected independent clauses** that are not connected with a coordinating conjunction.

   Examples:

   She is outside; we are inside.
   You are right; we should go with your plan.

2. Use a semicolon **between independent clauses linked with a transitional word.**

   Examples:

   I think that we can agree on this; *however,* I am not sure about my friends.
   You are looking in the wrong places; *therefore,* you will not find what you need.

3. Use a semicolon **between items in a series that has internal punctuation.**

   Example: I have visited New York, New York; Augusta, Maine; and Baltimore, Maryland.

Review Video: How to Use Semicolons
Visit mometrix.com/academy and enter code: 370605

Colons

The colon is used to call attention to the words that follow it. A colon must come after a **complete independent clause**. The rules for colons are as follows:

1. Use a colon after an independent clause to **make a list**

   Example: I want to learn many languages: Spanish, German, and Italian.

2. Use a colon for **explanations** or to **give a quote**

   Examples:

   Quote: He started with an idea: "We are able to do more than we imagine."
   Explanation: There is one thing that stands out on your resume: responsibility.

3. Use a colon **after the greeting in a formal letter**, to **show hours and minutes**, and to **separate a title and subtitle**

   Examples:

   Greeting in a formal letter: Dear Sir: | To Whom It May Concern:
   Time: It is 3:14 P.M.
   Title: The essay is titled "America: A Short Introduction to a Modern Country"

Review Video: What is a Colon?
Visit mometrix.com/academy and enter code: 868673

Parentheses

Parentheses are used for additional information. Also, they can be used to put labels for letters or numbers in a series. Parentheses should be not be used very often. If they are overused, parentheses can be a distraction instead of a help.

Examples:

Extra Information: The rattlesnake (see Image 2) is a dangerous snake of North and South America.

Series: Include in the email (1) your name, (2) your address, and (3) your question for the author.

Review Video: When to Use Parentheses
Visit mometrix.com/academy and enter code: 947743

Quotation Marks

Use quotation marks to close off **direct quotations** of a person's spoken or written words. Do not use quotation marks around indirect quotations. An indirect quotation gives someone's message without using the person's exact words. Use **single quotation marks** to close off a quotation inside a quotation.

Direct Quote: Nancy said, "I am waiting for Henry to arrive."

Indirect Quote: Henry said that he is going to be late to the meeting.

Quote inside a Quote: The teacher asked, "Has everyone read 'The Gift of the Magi'?"

Quotation marks should be used around the titles of **short works**: newspaper and magazine articles, poems, short stories, songs, television episodes, radio programs, and subdivisions of books or web sites.

Examples:

"Rip van Winkle" (short story by Washington Irving)

"O Captain! My Captain!" (poem by Walt Whitman)

Although it is not standard usage, quotation marks are sometimes used to highlight **irony**, or the use of words to mean something other than their dictionary definition. This type of usage should be employed sparingly, if at all.

Examples:

The boss warned Frank that he was walking on "thin ice."

(Frank is not walking on real ice. Instead, Frank is being warned to avoid mistakes.)

The teacher thanked the young man for his "honesty."

(In this example, the quotation marks around *honesty* show that the teacher does not believe the young man's explanation.)

Review Video: Quotation Marks
Visit mometrix.com/academy and enter code: 884918

Periods and commas are put **inside** quotation marks. Colons and semicolons are put **outside** the quotation marks. Question marks and exclamation points are placed inside quotation marks when they are part of a quote. When the question or exclamation mark goes with the whole sentence, the mark is left outside of the quotation marks.

Examples:

Period and comma: We read "The Gift of the Magi," "The Skylight Room," and "The Cactus."

Semicolon: They watched "The Nutcracker"; then, they went home.

Exclamation mark that is a part of a quote: The crowd cheered, "Victory!"

Question mark that goes with the whole sentence: Is your favorite short story "The Tell-Tale Heart"?

Apostrophes

An apostrophe is used to show **possession** or the **deletion of letters in contractions**. An apostrophe is not needed with the possessive pronouns *his, hers, its, ours, theirs, whose*, and *yours*.

Singular Nouns: David's car | a book's theme | my brother's board game

Plural Nouns with *-s*: the scissors' handle | boys' basketball

Plural Nouns without *-s*: Men's department | the people's adventure

Review Video: When to Use an Apostrophe
Visit mometrix.com/academy and enter code: 213068

Review Video: Punctuation Errors in Possessive Pronouns
Visit mometrix.com/academy and enter code: 221438

Hyphens

Hyphens are used to **separate compound words**. Use hyphens in the following cases:

1. **Compound numbers** between 21 and 99 when written out in words
   Example: This team needs *twenty-five* points to win the game.

2. **Written-out fractions** that are used as **adjectives**
   Correct: The recipe says that we need a *three-fourths* cup of butter.
   Incorrect: *One-fourth* of the road is under construction.

3. Compound words used as **adjectives that come before a noun**
   Correct: The *well-fed* dog took a nap.
   Incorrect: The dog was *well-fed* for his nap.

4. Compound words that would be **hard to read** or **easily confused with other words**
   Examples: Semi-irresponsible | Anti-itch | Re-sort

Note: This is not a complete set of the rules for hyphens. A dictionary is the best tool for knowing if a compound word needs a hyphen.

Review Video: Hyphens
Visit mometrix.com/academy and enter code: 981632

Dashes

Dashes are used to show a **break** or a **change in thought** in a sentence or to act as parentheses in a sentence. When typing, use two hyphens to make a dash. Do not put a space before or after the dash. The following are the rules for dashes:

1. To set off **parenthetical statements** or an **appositive with internal punctuation**
   Example: The three trees—oak, pine, and magnolia—are coming on a truck tomorrow.
2. To show a **break or change in tone or thought**
   Example: The first question—how silly of me—does not have a correct answer.

Ellipsis Marks

The ellipsis mark has three periods (...) to show when **words have been removed** from a quotation. If a full sentence or more is removed from a quoted passage, you need to use four periods to show the removed text and the end punctuation mark. The ellipsis mark should not be used at the beginning of a quotation. The ellipsis mark should also not be used at the end of a quotation unless some words have been deleted from the end of the final sentence.

Example:

> "Then he picked up the groceries...paid for them...later he went home."

Brackets

There are two main reasons to use brackets:

1. When **placing parentheses inside of parentheses**
   Example: The hero of this story, Paul Revere (a silversmith and industrialist [see Ch. 4]), rode through towns of Massachusetts to warn of advancing British troops.
2. When adding **clarification or detail** to a quotation that is **not part of the quotation**
   Example:
   > The father explained, "My children are planning to attend my alma mater [State University]."

Review Video: Using Brackets in Sentences
Visit mometrix.com/academy and enter code: 727546

Building a Vocabulary

Learning the basics of language is helpful to understanding what you read. **Structural analysis** means to break a word into pieces to know the definition of a word. Parts of a word include prefixes, suffixes, and root words. Knowing the meanings of these parts can help you understand the definition of a difficult word.

The main part of a word is known as the root. Prefixes are common letter combinations at the beginning of words. Suffixes are common letter combinations at the end of words. In pieces, a word looks like this: prefix + root word + suffix. First, look at the individual definitions of the root word, prefix, and/or suffix. Then, see how they add to the root. You can use knowledge of a prefix's and/or suffix's definition to determine a close definition of the word. For example, pretend that you don't know the definition of *uninspired*. But you know that *un*- means 'not'. Then, you know that the full word means *not inspired*. Learning the common prefixes and suffixes can help you define difficult words.

Review Video: Determining Word Meanings
Visit mometrix.com/academy and enter code: 894894

Below is a list of common prefixes and their meanings:

Prefixes for Numbers

Prefix	Definition	Examples
bi-	two	bisect, biennial
mono-	one, single	monogamy, monologue
poly-	many	polymorphous, polygamous
semi-	half, partly	semicircle, semicolon
uni-	one	uniform, unity

Prefixes for Time, Direction, and Space

Prefix	Definition	Examples
a-	in, on, of, up, to	abed, afoot
ab-	from, away, off	abdicate, abjure
ad-	to, toward	advance, adventure
ante-	before, previous	antecedent, antedate
anti-	against, opposing	antipathy, antidote
cata-	down, away, thoroughly	catastrophe, cataclysm
circum-	around	circumspect, circumference
com-	with, together, very	commotion, complicate
contra-	against, opposing	contradict, contravene
de-	from	depart
dia-	through, across, apart	diameter, diagnose
dis-	away, off, down, not	dissent, disappear
epi-	upon	epilogue
ex-	out	extract, excerpt
hypo-	under, beneath	hypodermic, hypothesis
inter-	among, between	intercede, interrupt
intra-	within	intramural, intrastate
ob-	against, opposing	objection
per-	through	perceive, permit

Prefix	Definition	Examples
peri-	around	periscope, perimeter
post-	after, following	postpone, postscript
pre-	before, previous	prevent, preclude
pro-	forward, in place of	propel, pronoun
retro-	back, backward	retrospect, retrograde
sub-	under, beneath	subjugate, substitute
super-	above, extra	supersede, supernumerary
trans-	across, beyond, over	transact, transport
ultra-	beyond, excessively	ultramodern, ultrasonic

Negative Prefixes

Prefix	Definition	Examples
a-	without, lacking	atheist, agnostic
in-	not, opposing	incapable, ineligible
non-	not	nonentity, nonsense
un-	not, reverse of	unhappy, unlock

Extra Prefixes

Prefix	Definition	Examples
belli-	war, warlike	bellicose
bene-	well, good	benefit, benefactor
equi-	equal	equivalent, equilibrium
for-	away, off, from	forget, forswear
fore-	previous	foretell, forefathers
homo-	same, equal	homogenized, homonym
hyper-	excessive, over	hypercritical, hypertension
in-	in, into	intrude, invade
magn-	large	magnitude, magnify
mal-	bad, poorly, not	malfunction, malpractice
mis-	bad, poorly, not	misspell, misfire
mor-	death	mortality, mortuary
neo-	new	Neolithic, neoconservative
omni-	all, everywhere	omniscient, omnivore
ortho-	right, straight	orthogonal, orthodox
over-	above	overbearing, oversight
pan-	all, entire	panorama, pandemonium
para-	beside, beyond	parallel, paradox
phil-	love, like	philosophy, philanthropic
prim-	first, early	primitive, primary
re-	backward, again	revoke, recur
sym-	with, together	sympathy, symphony
vis-	to see	visage, visible

Below is a list of common suffixes and their meanings:

Adjective Suffixes

Suffix	Definition	Examples
-able (-ible)	capable of being	toler*able*, ed*ible*
-esque	in the style of, like	picturesque, grotesque
-ful	filled with, marked by	thankful, zestful
-ific	make, cause	terrific, beatific
-ish	suggesting, like	churlish, childish
-less	lacking, without	hopeless, countless
-ous	marked by, given to	religious, riotous

Noun Suffixes

Suffix	Definition	Examples
-acy	state, condition	accuracy, privacy
-ance	act, condition, fact	acceptance, vigilance
-ard	one that does excessively	drunkard, sluggard
-ation	action, state, result	occupation, starvation
-dom	state, rank, condition	serfdom, wisdom
-er (-or)	office, action	teach*er*, elevat*or*, hon*or*
-ess	feminine	waitress, duchess
-hood	state, condition	manhood, statehood
-ion	action, result, state	union, fusion
-ism	act, manner, doctrine	barbarism, socialism
-ist	worker, follower	monopolist, socialist
-ity (-ty)	state, quality, condition	acid*ity*, civil*ity*, twen*ty*
-ment	result, action	Refreshment
-ness	quality, state	greatness, tallness
-ship	position	internship, statesmanship
-sion (-tion)	state, result	revi*sion*, expedi*tion*
-th	act, state, quality	warmth, width
-tude	quality, state, result	magnitude, fortitude

Verb Suffixes

Suffix	Definition	Examples
-ate	having, showing	separate, desolate
-en	cause to be, become	deepen, strengthen
-fy	make, cause to have	glorify, fortify
-ize	cause to be, treat with	sterilize, mechanize

Review Video: Root Words in English
Visit mometrix.com/academy and enter code: 896380

There is more to a word than its dictionary definition. The **denotative** meaning of a word is the actual meaning found in a dictionary. For example, a house and a home are places where people live. The **connotative meaning** is what comes to mind when you think of a word. For example, a house may be a simple, solid building. Yet, a home may be a comfortable, welcoming place where a family lives. Most non-fiction is fact-based with no use of figurative language. So, you can assume that the writer will use denotative meanings. In fiction, drama, and poetry, the author may use the connotative meaning. Use context clues to know if the author is using the denotative or connotative meaning of a word.

Review Video: Connotation and Denotation
Visit mometrix.com/academy and enter code: 310092

Readers of all levels will find new words in passages. The best way to define a word in **context** is to think about the words that are around the unknown word. For example, nouns that you don't know may be followed by examples that give a definition. Think about this example: *Dave arrived at the party in hilarious garb: a leopard-print shirt, buckskin pants, and tennis shoes.* If you didn't know the meaning of garb, you could read the examples (i.e., a leopard-print shirt, buckskin pants, and tennis shoes) and know that *garb* means *clothing*. Examples will not always be this clear. Try another example: *Parsley, lemon, and flowers were just a few of the items he used as garnishes.* The word *garnishes* is explained by parsley, lemon, and flowers. From this one sentence, you may know that the items are used for decoration. Are they decorating a food plate or an ice table with meat? You would need the other sentences in the paragraph to know for sure.

Review Video: Context Clues
Visit mometrix.com/academy and enter code: 613660

Also, you can use contrasts to define an unfamiliar word in context. In many sentences, authors will not describe the unfamiliar word directly. Instead, they will describe the opposite of the unfamiliar word. So, you are given some information that will bring you closer to defining the word. For example: *Despite his intelligence, Hector's bad posture made him look obtuse. Despite* means that Hector's posture is at odds with his intelligence. The author explains that Hector's posture does not prove his intelligence. So, *obtuse* must mean *unintelligent.* Another example: *Even with the horrible weather, we were beatific about our trip to Alaska*. The weather is described as *horrible*. So, *beatific* must mean something positive.

Sometimes, there will be very few context clues to help you define an unknown word. When this happens, **substitution** is a helpful tool. First, try to think of some synonyms for the words. Then, use those synonyms in place of the unknown words. If the passage makes sense, then the substitution has given some information about the unknown word. For example: *Frank's admonition rang in her ears as she climbed the mountain.* Don't know the definition of *admonition*? Then, try some substitutions: *vow*, *promise*, *advice*, *complaint*, or *compliment*. These words hint that an *admonition* is some sort of message. Once in a while substitution can get you a precise definition.

Usually, you can define an unfamiliar word by looking at the descriptive words in context. For example: *Fred dragged the recalcitrant boy kicking and screaming up the stairs.* The words *dragged*, *kicking*, and *screaming* all hint that the boy hates going up the stairs. So, you may think that *recalcitrant* means something like unwilling or protesting. In this example, an unfamiliar adjective was identified.

Description is used more to define an unfamiliar noun than unfamiliar adjectives. For example: *Don's wrinkled frown and constantly shaking fist labeled him as a curmudgeon.* Don is described as having a *wrinkled frown* and *constantly shaking fist*. This hints that a *curmudgeon* must be a grumpy, old man. Contrasts do not always give detailed information about the unknown word. However, they do give you some clues to understand the word.

Many words have more than one definition. So, you may not know how the word is being used in a sentence. For example, the verb *cleave* can mean *join* or *separate*. When you see this word, you need to pick the definition that makes the most sense. For example: *The birds cleaved together as they flew from the oak tree.* The use of the word *together* hints that *cleave* is being used to mean *join*. Another example: *Hermione's knife cleaved the bread cleanly.* A knife cannot join bread together. So, the word must hint at separation. Learning the purpose of a word with many meanings needs the same tricks as defining an unknown word. Look for context clues and think about the substituted words.

To learn more from a passage, you need to understand how words connect to each other. This is done with understanding **synonyms** (e.g., words that mean the same thing) and **antonyms** (e.g., the opposite meaning of a word). For example, *dry* and *arid* are synonyms. However, *dry* and *wet* are antonyms. There are pairs of words in English that can be called synonyms. Yet, they have somewhat different definitions.

For example, *friendly* and *collegial* can be used to describe a warm, close relationship. So, you would be correct to call them synonyms. However, *collegial* (linked to *colleague*) is used for professional or academic relationships. *Friendly* is not linked to professional or academic relationships.

Words should not be called synonyms when their differences are too great. For example, *hot* and *warm* are not synonyms because their meanings are too different. How do you know when two words are synonyms? First, try to replace one word for the other word. Then, be sure that the meaning of the sentence has not changed. Replacing *warm* for *hot* in a sentence gives a different meaning. *Warm* and *hot* may seem close in meaning. Yet, *warm* means that the temperature is normal. And, *hot* means that the temperature is very high.

Antonyms are words with opposite meanings. *Light* and *dark*, *up* and *down*, *right* and *left*, *good* and *bad* are sets of antonyms. However, there is a difference between antonyms and pairs of words that are different. *Black* and *gray* are not antonyms. *Black* is not the opposite of *gray*. On the other hand, *black* and *white* are antonyms. Not every word has an antonym. For example, many nouns do not have an antonym. What would be the antonym of chair?

During your exam, the questions about antonyms are likely to be about adjectives. Remember that adjectives are words that describe a noun. Some common adjectives include *red*, *fast*, *skinny*, and *sweet*. From those four adjectives, *red* is the one that does not have an antonym.

Review Video: What Are Synonyms and Antonyms?
Visit mometrix.com/academy and enter code: 105612

Final Notes on Grammar and Language

Don't Use Your Ear

Read each sentence carefully and put the answer choices into the blanks. Don't stop at the first answer choice if you think that you have the right answer. Read through the choices and think about each choice to know which one is best. At first you may have an answer choice that you think is correct. Then, you may have a different idea after you have read each choice. Don't allow your ear to decide what sounds right. Instead, use your knowledge and think about each answer choice. You may think that some answer choices can be ruled out because they sound incorrect. However, upon closer inspection, you may realize that those are the answer choices that may be correct.

Context Clues

To decide on the best answer, you can use context clues as you read through the answer choices. Key words in the sentence will allow you to decide which answer choice is the best to fill in the blank.

Watch Out for Simplicity

When your answer choices seem simple, you need to be careful with the question. Don't pick an answer choice because one choice is long or complicated. A simple or short sentence can be correct. However, not every simple or short sentence will be correct. An answer that is simple and does not make sense may not be correct.

The phrases *of which [...] are* in the below examples are wordy (i.e., too many words) and unnecessary. They should be removed. You can place a colon after the words *sport* and *following*.

Examples:

1. There are many benefits to running as a sport, *of which the top advantages are*:
2. The necessary school supplies were the following, *of which a few are*:

Strategy for the Extended Response Section

The Reasoning Through Language Arts part of the exam has an extended response or essay section for which you should be sure to prepare. In this portion, a topic will be introduced through one or more reading passages. You may be given two viewpoints or perspectives that have an argument for the reason that they are correct. You will be asked to think about the topic and the arguments. Then, you will need to explain and defend your thoughts on the topic with support from the passages. There is no single *correct* answer for the essay. Instead, you will be graded on your skill to write clearly and to defend your thoughts.

Brainstorm

Spend the first three to five minutes brainstorming for ideas. When you brainstorm, you write down any ideas that you might have on the topic. The purpose is to pull out everything from your memory that will be helpful information. In this stage, anything goes down no matter how good or bad the idea may seem at first glance. Use the scratch paper that you are given to put down your ideas.

Strength Through Different Viewpoints

The best papers will have relevant examples and clear connections between ideas. As you brainstorm, you should think about different viewpoints. There are more than two sides to every topic. On any topic, different groups are impacted and many can come to the same conclusion. Yet, they come to the same conclusion through different paths. Before writing your essay, try to *see* the topic through as many different *eyes* as you can.

Also, you don't have to write about how the topic impacts others. You can draw from your personal experience. The topic may allow you to use a personal narrative. In this case, you can explain your experience and your feelings from that moment. Anything that you've seen in your area can be further explained to round out your ideas on the topic.

Once you are done with brainstorming, you need to stop and review what you wrote on the scratch paper. Which idea allowed you to come up with the most supporting information? Be sure to pick a point of view that will allow you to write as much as necessary on the prompt. Be careful to not write about your personal beliefs. Instead, work on writing a brief (i.e., 1 to 2 pages) and fair answer to the topic.

Every garden of ideas has weeds. The ideas that you brainstormed are going to be odd pieces of information of different values. Go through the pieces carefully and pick out the ones that are the best. The best ideas are strong arguments that will make your writing easier.

Now, you have your main ideas. So, put them in an order that will flow in a smooth, clear path from point to point. Then, your readers will go from one idea to the next in an understandable order. Readers want an essay that has a sense of continuity (i.e., Point 1 to Point 2 to Point 3 and so on). One plan is to save your best idea or argument as the last body paragraph. With this plan, your grader remembers your last and best point. However, some choose to write out their best idea first. With this plan, you have time to write out what you need for your best idea.

Start Your Engines

Now, you have an understandable flow of main ideas for the start of your essay. Begin by developing on the first point, then move to your second point. Pace yourself. Don't spend too much time on any one of the ideas. You want to have time for all of them. Make sure that you watch your time. If you have twenty minutes left to write out your ideas and you have four ideas, then you can only use five minutes for each idea. Writing so much information in so little time can be a difficult task. Yet, if you pace yourself, you can get through all of your ideas. If you find that you are falling behind, then you can remove one of your weaker arguments. This will allow you to give enough support to your remaining ideas.

Once you finish writing on an idea, go back to your brainstorming session where you wrote out your ideas. You can scratch through each idea as you write about them. This will let you see what you need to write about next and what you have left to cover.

Your introduction should have some familiar pieces:

- First, the introduction should have a quick explanation or paraphrase of the topic. Use your own words to explain what the topic is about.
- Second, you should list your ideas. What are the main ideas that you came up with earlier? If someone was to read only your introduction, they should be able to get a good summary of the whole paper.
- Third, you should explain your thoughts on the topic and give an explanation for why you have those thoughts.

Each of your following paragraphs develops one of the ideas listed in your introduction. Use the information from the passage and your knowledge to back up each of your ideas. Examples should back up every main idea.

Once you are done with explaining each of your main ideas, you need a conclusion. In other words, summarize what you wrote in a final paragraph. Explain once more your argument on the topic and review why you feel that way in a few sentences. At this stage, you have already backed up your statements. So, there is no need to do that again. You just need to remind your readers of the main arguments that you made in your essay.

Don't Panic

Whatever you do during the essay, do not panic. When you panic, you will put fewer words on the page and your ideas will be weak. If your mind goes blank when you see the prompt, you need to take a deep breath. Make yourself go through the steps listed above: brainstorm and put anything on scratch paper that comes to mind.

Also, don't get clock fever. You may become afraid when you're looking at a page that is mostly blank. Your mind may be full of thoughts, and the clock is ticking down faster. Once you have brainstormed, you don't have to keep coming up with ideas. If you're running out of time and you have a lot of ideas that you haven't written down, then don't be afraid to make some cuts. Start picking the best ideas that you have left and explain them. Don't feel like you have to write on all of your ideas.

A short paper that is well written and well organized is better than a long paper that is poorly written and poorly organized. Don't keep writing about a subject just to add sentences. Don't repeat a statement or idea that you explained. The goal is 1 to 2 pages of good writing. That is your target but don't mess up your paper by trying to fill up the blank space. Don't worry about your essay being long. A long essay is not a problem when your ideas are clear and flow well from paragraph to paragraph. Remember to explain the ideas that you wrote down in the brainstorming session.

Leave time at the end (at least three minutes) to go back and check over your work. Read over every paragraph and make sure that everything makes sense and flows well. Clean up any spelling or grammar mistakes. Then, clean up any extra information that you might have written that doesn't fit into your paper.

As you read, make sure that you don't have fragments or run-ons. Check for sentences that are too short or too long. If the sentence is too short, look to see if you have a specific subject and an active verb. If it is too long, break up the long sentence into two sentences. Watch out for any "big words" that you may have used. Be sure that you are using those words correctly. Don't be confused; you should try to increase your vocabulary and use educated words in your essay. But, set your goal on explaining your ideas in a clear and precise way.

The Short Overview

The essay may be your hardest or your easiest section. You must write a paper in a limited amount of time which is not always easy. Follow each of the steps listed above. Start with creative flow of brainstorming for ideas. Write down your ideas about the prompt. Organize those ideas into a smooth flow. Pick out the ideas that are the best from your list.

Create a familiar essay pattern in your paper. Start with an introduction that explains what you have decided to argue. Then, choose your main arguments. Use the body paragraphs to touch on those arguments and have a conclusion that wraps up your essay.

Save some time to go back and review what you have written. Clean up any mistakes. Those last important touches can make a huge difference. Finally, be proud of what you have written!

Chapter Quiz

Ready to see how well you retained what you just read? Scan the QR code to go directly to the chapter quiz interface for this study guide. If you're using a computer, simply visit the bonus page at **mometrix.com/bonus948/ged** and click the Chapter Quizzes link.

Science

Transform passive reading into active learning! After immersing yourself in this chapter, put your comprehension to the test by taking a quiz. The insights you gained will stay with you longer this way. Scan the QR code to go directly to the chapter quiz interface for this study guide. If you're using a computer, simply visit the bonus page at **mometrix.com/bonus948/ged** and click the Chapter Quizzes link.

Reading for Meaning in Science

Claims and Evidence in Science

When you carry out a scientific investigation and draw conclusions based on the results, the investigation itself is evidence of the validity of your finding. However, it may not be enough evidence by itself to be fully convincing. There are ways to find more evidence to support your finding. Have other scientists done similar investigations and obtained similar results? You can search through past publications to check (scientists often refer to the body of previously published scientific papers as the literature). Is there some theoretical basis that could explain why you got the results you did? If not, that doesn't necessarily mean you're wrong—maybe you discovered something completely new—but it does set a higher bar for the quality of the evidence that must be gathered.

One of the most important pieces of evidence to support a finding is if you and others can replicate your results. This is why scientific papers include not only the results of a study, but also a detailed explanation of how the study was carried out—so that other scientists can judge its validity and can in principle try to carry out the experiment for themselves.

Scientific Papers

Scientific papers are a specialized form of writing that must be approached differently from other literature. You can't read a scientific paper the way you can a novel or an article in the newspaper and expect to get much out of it. Generally, a scientific paper is not just read once from beginning to end: It requires a different approach.

A scientific paper starts with an **abstract**—a summary of the paper briefly explaining its purpose, its main results, and its conclusion. It's worth reading the abstract first because it gives you the big idea of what the paper is about. After that, it might be useful to *skim* the entire paper, not reading it closely but just looking it over for the main ideas. You may want to pay particular attention to graphs and other visuals that portray the data and the relationships between variables in a comprehensible way. After skimming the paper, you can go back and read in more detail the parts that seem especially relevant to what you're looking for or that you didn't understand from your skimming.

Conflicting Sources

At times, you may run into science sources that may seem to give contradictory information. The most obvious explanation is that one of these sources is incorrect. Do both sources explain the basis for their conclusions, and are the conclusions warranted from their results? Has the information in either of the sources been tested and validated by the greater scientific community? (If one source disagrees with the vast majority of other scientific sources, it could be that the writers of that source are trying to push an idiosyncratic, unsupported point of view.) If one of the sources is a secondary source, check the primary source that it is based on—is it being accurately represented?

However, it could also be that both sources are valid, but they're not as contradictory as they seem. Are they really discussing the same circumstances, or are they discussing phenomena under different conditions? If one source discusses the behavior of a chemical at room temperature and one discusses very different behavior of the same chemical at very cold temperatures, that's not necessarily a contradiction—the chemical may behave differently at different temperatures.

Primary and Secondary Sources

In the sciences and in social science, there is a distinction between primary and secondary sources. A **primary source** is a source that gives information based on direct observation or on the writer's own ideas. In science, the main primary sources are scientific papers. In social science, the primary sources may include journals, letters, and newspaper articles from the time period being studied. A **secondary source** is a source that draws from primary sources, summarizing or restating the information. Articles in popular magazines and on websites are secondary sources as are textbooks and encyclopedias. (Because textbooks and encyclopedias may draw from other secondary sources, they are sometimes considered to be at yet another level, **tertiary sources**, but not everyone makes that distinction.)

Review Video: What are Primary and Secondary Sources?
Visit mometrix.com/academy and enter code: 383328

Because primary sources are where the information ultimately comes from, they are in a sense more reliable; they represent the original source of the information without passing through further layers of bias, rewording, and possible misrepresentation. However, primary sources can be difficult to acquire, and even if you can acquire them, they can be difficult to understand and properly interpret, so secondary (and even tertiary) sources remain useful to comprehend the information.

Science Vocabulary, Terms, and Phrases

Scientific Writing

Scientific writing is different from popular writing in many ways, and to someone not used to reading scientific writing, it may be difficult to understand. One hurdle is the vocabulary: science writing often uses specialist words not used in everyday life, or they are used with different meaning. If there's a word in the passage that you don't understand, skim through the passage to see if it's defined elsewhere in the text. If it's not, it's often possible to guess the meaning from the context.

Even if you understand all the important words in a passage, the dense and technical writing may still be difficult to understand. You can approach a passage of scientific writing similarly to a whole scientific paper. First, skim the passage, not trying yet to understand every detail, but just to grasp the main ideas. Pay particular attention to any figures or diagrams, which may provide crucial information or explanations. Then you can go back and look for specific details you're interested in.

Explaining Scientific Information

When relaying scientific information, it's important to be able to convey that information clearly. In the professional scientific world, information is conveyed primarily through research papers published in scientific journals. These papers have a set formula: first, an **abstract** that summarizes the whole paper; next, an **introduction** that lays out the goals of the study the paper describes and discusses prior work on the subject; then a description of the **methods** used in the study; after that, a relation of the **results** that were obtained; and, finally, a **discussion** of those results and any conclusions drawn from them.

Even outside of the context of formal scientific papers, though, there are still important factors in scientific communication. It's important to choose your words and phrasing carefully to avoid ambiguity; make sure you know what scientific terms mean before you use them. Clarity and explicitness are more important in science communication than brevity or style. Graphs and diagrams are often helpful to convey information.

Variables and Constants in Science

It's often useful in scientific writing to use symbols to represent certain **variables**—i.e., quantities that may change during an investigation or between an investigation—and **constants**—values that are expected to remain the same. As long as these variables are clearly defined, they can make text and formulas much clearer and easier to read than if the quantities had to be spelled out and described every time they were referred to.

Variables and constants are usually symbolized by letters in the Latin or Greek alphabets. Some symbols are standard and widely used: c is an accepted symbol for the speed of light (a constant), and λ, the Greek letter lambda, is often used to represent wavelength (a variable). Other symbols may be defined as the author decides in particular papers. In any case, it is important that any new or nonstandard symbols be explicitly defined in the paper or other passage where they appear. When reading a scientific text, make sure to look for the definitions of any symbols in it.

Scientific Terminology

Like any field of study, science has specialized terminology—i.e., words and phrases that have a particular meaning in that field. This is true not just of science in general, but of particular subfields; chemistry has special terms particular to it, for example, and organic chemistry has further terminology, and so do still more specific fields within organic chemistry.

This specialized terminology aids in comprehension for readers familiar with the field. These scientific terms can concisely but precisely convey concepts that would be difficult or impractically lengthy to express in common language, and they may have unambiguous meanings. However, for nonspecialists who have not encountered these terms before, they can be an obstacle for comprehension; this is one of the factors that makes scientific papers hard for nonscientists to understand. If you run across a scientific term that you don't understand, you can look it up, preferably in a glossary or textbook dedicated to the subject rather than a general dictionary. Sometimes you may be able to determine the gist of the term's meaning from the context, but this may be unreliable or miss important nuances in the meaning that may not be obvious.

There are many words that have specialized meanings in science that may not match their meanings in other contexts. When you're reading a scientific paper, it's important to keep those specialized meanings in mind. Following are just a few of many examples.

Theory: In everyday life, the word "theory" is often used to refer to a guess or a supposition, but in science that's a *hypothesis*—a *theory* is a detailed explanatory framework.

Medium: In biology or chemistry, a *medium* is a substrate in which cell cultures are grown. In physics, it refers to the substance through which a sound wave or other signal travels.

Plant: Often people use the word "plant" to refer to nonmobile organisms including fungi and algae. Biologically, however, fungi and most algae are *not* plants; they belong to different kingdoms (another word with a distinct scientific meaning).

Radiation: To a scientist, radiation is anything that radiates—travels outward from a source. Nuclear radiation is one kind of radiation, but sound and light are also forms of radiation.

Chemical: Though people often think of chemicals as being artificial and potentially harmful, scientifically speaking anything made up of atoms is a chemical. Air and water are chemicals.

Designing and Interpreting Science Experiments

Science Investigations

To design a good scientific investigation, it's useful to define specifically what kinds of effects the investigator is looking for and how they will be measured. Quantitative measurements are more reliable than poorly defined, subjective impressions. For example, if investigating the effect of a chemical on plant growth, deciding that we'll just add the chemical to the plants and see what happens is vague and unhelpful; the height of the plants is a measurable value, and it is a more useful observable quantity.

Generally, in an effective investigation, only one variable is changed at a time. In the plant growth example, all the plants should be kept at the same temperature, given the same amount of water, etc.—the only difference should be the concentration of the chemical. When possible, an experiment should be **controlled**: There should be other samples (called **controls**) that are *not* tampered with, to make sure that the observed effect really is due to the factor being changed. This means that our example investigation should include some plants that have *not* been treated with the chemical.

A good scientific investigation also takes measures to account for and minimize random and systematic error.

Independent and Dependent Variables

In a scientific experiment, generally the investigator is going to change some property of a system and determine what effect this change has on a different property. The property that is changed directly by the experimenter is the **independent variable**; the property having the change that the experimenter is observing is called the **dependent variable**. For instance, if the experimenter wants to test the response time of some insect at different temperatures, the independent variable is the temperature and the dependent variable is the insect's response time.

Review Video: Identifying Independent and Dependent Variables
Visit mometrix.com/academy and enter code: 627181

In some investigations, the investigator may not change anything directly but may still want to observe how some property changes based on another property. In this case, there is still an independent variable and a dependent variable because one variable still depends on the other. Suppose someone wants to investigate how the acidity of a lake changes over time. The investigator is changing neither the acidity of the lake nor the time, but the acidity is the dependent variable and the time is the independent variable because it makes more sense to say that the acidity of the lake depends on the time rather than that the time depends on the acidity of the lake.

Developing a Good Hypothesis for a Scientific Investigation

In a scientific investigation, the **hypothesis** is a prediction of what the investigator expects to happen. The experiment may either **confirm** the hypothesis—i.e., show it to be true—or **falsify** the hypothesis—i.e., show it to be false. Even though it may not turn out to be correct, it's still important to have a hypothesis, because it helps guide the investigation and give the investigator something specific to look for.

A hypothesis should have some reasoning behind it; there should be some rationale why the investigator expects it to happen. It may be an educated guess, but it shouldn't be just a wild guess made at random with no basis whatsoever.

A good hypothesis should be specific and observable. Suppose that an investigator wants to test the effect of a chemical on the growth of a bacterial culture. "The chemical will affect the growth of the bacteria" is not a good hypothesis; it's so vague that it says almost nothing. "The chemical will slow the growth of the bacteria" is a little better, but it is still not very specific. "The bacterial cultures treated with the chemical will grow to only half the normal size" is a good hypothesis because it is specific and measurable.

Minimizing Error and Bias

Random error, also called statistical error, is one of the two main types of error that arise in a scientific investigation. It gets its name from the fact that it is not consistent but may randomly cause the measured value to be either higher or lower than the actual value.

Random error comes about due to unavoidable variability in measurements. For instance, if you're measuring the diameter of a wire with a micrometer (an instrument for measuring very small distances), you may not get exactly the same measurement each time—perhaps because it's hard to tell when the micrometer is firmly in contact with the wire but not so firmly that you're compressing it, or because the wire isn't perfectly round. If your measurements vary from 0.12 mm to 0.14 mm, we may write that as $0.13 \text{ mm} \pm 0.01 \text{ mm}$.

Random error can be minimized by taking many measurements and using the average value. Because random error can make the measurement either larger or smaller than the actual value, on average, for many measurements, it tends to cancel out. Although the random error can't be completely eliminated, the more measurements you take, the smaller it tends to become.

Systematic error is the other main type of error that arises in a scientific investigation. Unlike the first main type of error, random error, systematic error has a consistent effect on all measurements, making all the measurements off in the same direction and by about the same amount.

Systematic error comes about due to often-subtle defects in the measuring instrument or measurement process. For example, suppose you want to measure the amount of liquid in a cup, and you do so by pouring the liquid into a graduated cylinder. It may be, however, that each time you pour the liquid into the cylinder, a few drops are left behind in the cup. All your measurements are then lower than they should be by the volume of those drops.

There is no universal way to avoid systematic error, but it can often be accounted for by careful consideration of the experimental procedure and calibration of measuring instruments. It may also help to try to measure quantities by two or more different methods; if different methods of measuring the same quantity give consistently different results, then at least one of those methods probably has some systematic error.

A scientific investigation is said to have **experimental bias**—or simply to be **biased**—if researchers or experimental subjects influence the recorded observations toward the results they want or expect. This doesn't necessarily mean that they are deliberately and dishonestly fudging the values. Bias is frequently unconscious; the investigators may not be aware that they are letting their preconceptions influence their observations.

Experimental bias is especially likely in investigations with subjective observations. In a medical trial to test whether a drug can alleviate some symptoms, experimental subjects who expect the drug to help them might convince themselves they're feeling better even if the drug actually has no effect. However, even in studies with more objective measurements, investigators have been known to record wrong values due to unconscious bias.

One way to eliminate bias is to make sure, if possible, that the experiment is **blinded**—the investigator doesn't know which of the subjects have been treated and which are untreated controls, so the investigator *can't* change the observations in favor of a particular result. An investigation involving human subjects can be **double-blinded**, so that neither the investigator nor the subjects know which subjects are receiving treatment and which are controls.

Types of Scientific Investigations

In an **experimental investigation**, the investigator changes something about an object or system and observes how that change affects it. For example, if a drug company wishes to know whether a newly developed drug has any side effects, it may arrange for a clinical trial to be carried out in which some of the participants are given the drug and others are given a placebo and the health of the participants is monitored to determine whether those participants who are given the drug experience different symptoms.

Experimental investigations are in many ways the most informative kind of investigation because they can be carefully controlled and directed toward answering specific questions. However, it is not always practical or even possible to carry out an experimental investigation. Astronomers observing distant stars, for example, can't really affect those stars directly, so they cannot carry out an experimental investigation on them. To study how the stars are affected by different factors, they would have to carry out a different kind of investigation, such as a comparative investigation.

In a **descriptive investigation**, the investigator carefully observes an object or system, without necessarily changing it. Descriptive investigations may not include a hypothesis, but they should still include an experimental question. For example, suppose a paleontologist discovers a fossil of a previously unknown animal. The paleontologist is likely to perform a descriptive investigation of the fossil, studying it and trying to draw conclusions from the fossil about what kind of animal it was, what other animals it was related to, what it may have eaten, and other characteristics.

Descriptive investigations are useful for studying little-known phenomena, generating new questions, and laying the groundwork for other investigations later. When limited data sets are available and the scientist cannot directly alter the variables of interest, a descriptive investigation may be the only type of investigation possible. However, it may not be possible to answer specific questions through descriptive investigations, and investigators may be limited in what they can discover.

Comparative investigations involve observations and comparisons of different populations. For example, suppose an investigator wants to study the effects of childhood malnutrition on people's later lives. Obviously, it would not be ethical to select a group of children and intentionally induce malnutrition to carry out an experimental investigation. However, the investigators could locate people who had experienced malnutrition in childhood and study their development and their health as adults, comparing them with those of people who had not experienced such malnutrition and controlling for appropriate variables.

Like descriptive investigations, comparative investigations can be carried out on phenomena that the investigator cannot manipulate directly, and, like experimental investigations, they can include dependent and independent variables and can be used to study specific questions. However, the fact that the investigator is not setting the variables directly may make it difficult to find controls or hold other variables constant.

Using Evidence to Draw Conclusions or Make Predictions

Drawing conclusions from collected data is a central step in scientific investigations, but it's important not to reach too far and draw conclusions that aren't warranted by the data. When reading over the conclusions of an investigation, it's useful to check to make sure there wasn't an error.

This isn't just a matter of verifying that the data show what the conclusion claims—that if the conclusion is that a chemical helps plant growth, for instance, the data don't really show the plants treated with the chemical doing worse. It's possible that such a simple mistake was made, of course, but subtler issues are more likely. Did the investigator take care to eliminate obvious sources of error and bias? If applicable, was the experiment blinded or double-blinded? Reliable conclusions cannot be drawn from biased data.

If the data seem to show a relationship between two variables, is this relationship really statistically significant, or is it likely to be just an artifact of random error? Did the investigator take into account *all* of the data collected, or did the investigator cherry-pick data that led to the desired conclusion, while ignoring other data that might contradict this conclusion?

Statistical Significance

An experimental finding is said to be **statistically significant** if it is significant enough that it is unlikely to be just the result of random error. For example, suppose you wanted to know how temperature affected the rate of a certain chemical change. You timed the change 10 times at each of two different temperatures and took the average time at each temperature, and found that the average was higher at the cold temperature—the change took longer to occur at cold temperatures. Or did it? If the average time was 30 seconds at the high temperature and 90 seconds at the low temperature, then yes; that's a dramatic difference, and it is unlikely to be the result of random error. But if the average time was 30.2 seconds at the high temperature and 30.3 seconds at the low temperature, you can't draw a reliable conclusion; that tiny difference could easily be due to random error in the measurements.

Conclusions from a Graph of Scientific Data

A graph is a useful tool for analyzing data, finding relationships, and drawing conclusions. Sometimes a relationship that is not obvious from looking at the numerical data may become much clearer from looking at a graph. This may be as simple as noticing that one variable tends to increase or decrease as another variable increases—the graph tends to generally slope upward or downward. But it's possible to be more precise. Based on the shape of the graph—whether the data points seem to lie close to a line, to a parabola, or to some other particular kind of curve—it may be possible to infer whether the relationship between the variables is linear, quadratic, etc.

If the relationship is linear, we can draw quantitative conclusions by using a **linear fit**, or a best-fit line. This involves drawing a straight line through the data that come closest to the data points, even if it doesn't exactly pass through all of them. (There are more precise mathematical methods of finding a best-fit line, but drawing it by eye can be a useful approximation.) The equation of this line gives a mathematical formula for the relationship between the variables.

Errors in Conclusions

Although it's important to be able to analyze the results of an investigation and draw conclusions from it, there are a number of possible errors that must be avoided. Some of them have to do with the investigation itself; if the investigation was biased or had systematic errors that are not being taken into account, then no reliable conclusions can be drawn. But even if the investigation was carried out properly, it's easy to leap to unsupported conclusions. It's important to look out for hidden assumptions: Are your conclusions predicated on an assumption that was not tested by the experiment? (One special case of this is assuming that because two variables are correlated, one must have caused the other.) It's also easy to overgeneralize: If your investigation covered a specific case or category, it's not necessarily the case that your results hold more broadly (for example, if you did an investigation using mice, you can't necessarily conclude that your results hold for all mammals). And it's often tempting to introduce new ideas in the conclusion, but that isn't the place for them; you should draw conclusions only based on the investigation that you performed.

Empirical and Theoretical Results

Empirical and theoretical describe two different sources of data, both of which are important for different reasons. **Empirical** results are derived directly from experiment and observation. The researchers obtaining empirical results may not understand *why* they obtain the results they do; they are only recording what they observe. These empirical results may then serve as a basis for later theoretical developments. For example, physicists observed empirically that excited atoms tended to emit light preferentially at certain wavelengths long before quantum theory was developed and explained this phenomenon. **Theoretical** results are predictions as to what one would expect to observe given particular circumstances, based on some established theory. It may not be trivial to obtain these results; theoretical results may come about through detailed calculations and modeling.

Ideally, of course, empirical and theoretical results should match. If they do not, then it indicates that either something was done wrong in the experiment (perhaps, for example, there was some confounding variable that was overlooked) or that the theory used was invalid or had some unrecognized limitations. Either way, this can be an impetus for further research.

Extending Results

In the context of a scientific investigation, a **prediction** is an expression of what you would expect to happen if certain conditions are met. It is not a blanket statement of the future; when you make a scientific prediction, you are not necessarily stating what *will* happen, only what would happen *if* certain conditions hold. For example, we can predict based on what we know about its chemical properties that *if* we place an apple in a solution of concentrated sulfuric acid, it will dissolve.

Predictions are important in science for two reasons: (1) because they permit application of scientific theories—if a theory predicts what will happen under certain circumstances, then we may be able to use that to our benefit—and (2) because they allow hypotheses and theories to be tested—if a theory predicts that something should happen under particular circumstances, and we put that to the test and the event does occur as predicted, that provides further evidence of the validity of the theory. If, on the other hand, the event does *not* match the prediction, the theory may be falsified. A theory that has been validated by numerous successful predictions may come to be widely accepted as valid.

Interpolation is the estimation of the expected value of a dependent variable for a particular value of an independent variable. This estimation is based on the measured value of the dependent variable at values of the independent variable both smaller and larger than the value in question. For example, suppose we know that the height of a tree was 10 meters in 1960 and 20 meters in 1980; by interpolation, we can guess that it may have been 15 meters tall in 1970.

The preceding example assumes a linear relationship and is therefore a case of **linear interpolation**. However, of course not all relationships are linear, and interpolation can take that into account. Interpolation may be done graphically: We can draw a curve through the known data points and use that curve to estimate the value of the dependent variable (y) at some other value of the independent variable (x). If we have many data points, interpolation tends to be fairly reliable, though not completely; it could still be the case that there is some large spike or other change that we don't know about between the measured data points.

Extrapolation is the estimation of the expected value of a dependent variable for a particular value of an independent variable, based on the measured value of the dependent variable at values of the independent variable either smaller or larger than the value in question, but not both. For example, suppose we know that the population of a town was 5,000 in the year 1990, 6,000 in the year 2000, and 7,000 in the year 2010; by extrapolation we can guess that its population may be 8,000 in the year 2020.

Like interpolation, extrapolation does not necessarily assume a linear relationship, and it may be done graphically. However, extrapolation may be less reliable than interpolation. Frequently, a relationship that holds for some range of variables breaks down at higher and lower values. For instance, suppose we note that hanging a 1 kg mass on a spring stretches it by 1 cm, a 2 kg mass by 2 cm, and a 3 kg mass by 3 cm. We extrapolate that a 10 kg mass would stretch the spring by 10 cm. But that isn't necessarily true: There's a limit to the weight a spring can hold before it breaks or is damaged, and 10 kg may exceed that limit.

SCIENCE THEORIES AND PROCESSES

In everyday language, the word "theory" is often used to refer to a guess or speculation. In science, however, a **theory** is a verifiable explanatory framework that accounts for a set of observations. In science, the word "theory" does not imply that an idea is uncertain or unsupported—though it doesn't necessarily imply the opposite, either. Some theories have made many predictions that have been confirmed by observations and are considered strongly supported, such as gravitational theory, the theory of relativity, and evolutionary theory. Other theories remain somewhat speculative and not fully confirmed, such as string theory. Still other theories have been falsified by observations and are today obsolete, such as ether theory, the idea that light was a wave in a pervasive substance called ether.

A **hypothesis** corresponds more to the nonscientific use of the word "theory"—a hypothesis is a speculative proposal that has not yet been fully tested. If further experiment and observation confirm the hypothesis, it may become a basis of a theory. A scientific **law** is a description of some phenomenon that has been repeatedly confirmed by observation. Unlike a theory, a scientific law does not attempt to *explain* the phenomenon in question, only to describe it.

MAIN PROCESSES OF A SCIENTIFIC INVESTIGATION

Scientific investigation involves a number of processes, not all of which are necessarily a part of every investigation. A scientific investigation usually begins with formulating a question—a good investigation is not just a directionless set of observations with no particular goal in mind, but it is designed to answer a specific question. The investigator may also propose a hypothesis, a prediction as to the expected result, to help guide the investigation. The investigator then gathers data, either through observation—i.e., measuring and recording different properties of the system—or through experiment— i.e., making changes to the system and measuring the effects—or a combination of the two.

Once the investigator has collected specific data, another step is to analyze the data. This may involve a qualitative comparison between different sets of data, or it may involve detailed quantitative analysis including graphs and/or statistical methods. Based on the results of the data analysis, the investigator then draws conclusions from the data and uses them to formulate a (perhaps tentative) answer to the initial question and, if applicable, to judge whether the hypothesis is confirmed or falsified.

Process of Observation

In a scientific investigation, **observation** refers to more than simply looking at something. In a preliminary descriptive investigation, the investigator may just be observing the object or phenomenon generally to look for any interesting features that might be worth investigating in more detail, but in most investigations the observation will be guided by an experimental question that the investigator wants to answer and the investigator will be focusing his or her attention on some specific quantity or quality to be observed. The observations should be carefully recorded for later reference and analysis.

If the investigator is observing a measurable quantity, then measurement of that quantity is also part of the observation. An investigator observing the evaporation of the liquid in a beaker over time, for example, will not merely record that the amount of liquid is decreasing. As part of the observation, the investigator will record quantitative measurements of the amount of liquid at different times, such as by weighing the beaker or measuring the depth of the liquid within it.

Process of Inference

Inference is the process of drawing conclusions based on observations. This is an important part of the process of science as well as social studies. It could even be said that the goal of most scientific investigations is to infer an answer to the experimental question.

Often, drawing an inference involves noticing a trend in the data and assuming that the trend continues. For example, if every time an investigator puts a particular chemical in a bacterial culture the bacteria die, it is a reasonable inference that that chemical is deadly to the bacteria. The trend may be more subtle, involving, for example, a relationship between two quantities. An investigator may observe that a certain type of tree tends to be taller at lower altitudes and infer that there is something about higher altitudes that inhibits the trees' growth.

An inference is not necessarily a sure thing, especially if only a few observations have been made; it could be that the relationship on which the inference is based is coincidental, and the inference is not valid. The inference may be used to create a hypothesis that can be tested in further investigations.

Process of Communication

Communication is a frequently overlooked but very important part of a scientific investigation. Investigators must be able to relate the results and conclusions of their investigation to others. If the investigators are unable to effectively communicate their results, then their investigation is ultimately fruitless; even if the investigators themselves are convinced of their results, if no one else knows about them, then they can have no further impact.

Communication in science is more than just telling other investigators what you found. It is also important to relate *how* you found your results. A good scientific report, like those found in published science journals, will describe in detail how the investigation was carried out, include any possible sources of error or uncertainty that the investigators were aware of, and explain precisely how the investigators arrived at their conclusions. Ideally, other investigators should be able to follow every step of the investigators' reasoning and should be provided with enough information in principle to repeat the investigation themselves.

It is also helpful to be able to clearly communicate the gist of the results of an investigation to nonspecialists. This is a separate matter from communication to other knowledgeable investigators but is also important.

Using Numbers and Graphics in Science

Exponential, Linear, and Quadratic Relationships

Exponential, linear, and quadratic relationships are different kinds of possible relationships between two variables. An **exponential relationship** is a relationship in which one variable is proportional to a constant raised to the power of the other variable, as in $y = 2^x$. Although outside of science people may informally refer to any large increase as exponential, the term does have a precise mathematical meaning. A **linear relationship** is a relationship in which one variable increases at a constant rate as the other increases: The two variables obey the equation $y = mx + b$ for some constants m and b. The graph of a linear relationship will be a straight line. A **quadratic relationship** is a relationship in which one variable increases with the *square* of the other variable; the general equation is $y = ax^2 + bx + c$ for some constants a, b, and c. The graph of a quadratic relationship will be a parabola. These three cases do not exhaust all of the possible types of relationship between variables, but they are among the most common.

Scientific Formulas and Statistics

Scientific Formulas

The first step in solving a problem using a scientific formula is to determine which formula to use. Generally, you want to find a formula that includes the unknown that you want to solve for and that otherwise includes only known values. Be careful that you know the context of the formula and that you know what the symbols represent because the same symbol may have multiple meanings. For instance, in the formula for the velocity of a wave in a string, $v = \sqrt{\frac{T}{m/L}}$, T stands for tension, but in the formula for the frequency of a wave, $f = \frac{1}{T}$, T stands for period. Once you have found the appropriate formula, you can put in the known values and solve for your unknown (being careful to convert the units if appropriate).

For example, suppose we're told that the centripetal force on a ball being swung in a circle of 50-cm radius is 16 N, the mass of the ball is 500 g, and we want to know its velocity. An appropriate formula is $F_C = \frac{mv^2}{r}$. For consistency in the units, we should convert the radius to meters and the mass to kilograms; then $16\text{ N} = \frac{(0.500\text{ kg})v^2}{0.50\text{ m}}$, and $v = \sqrt{\frac{(16\text{ N})(0.50\text{ m})}{0.500\text{ kg}}} = 4.0\frac{\text{m}}{\text{s}}$.

Sometimes, no single known formula is sufficient to solve a problem because every formula that includes the unknown quantity that we're trying to solve for also includes another unknown quantity as well. In such a case, it may be necessary to use two or more formulas to solve the problem, using one formula to solve for a variable that we then use in another formula. To determine which formulas to use, it's often useful to work backwards; that is, we figure out what other unknown variables the formula that we want to use includes and then we look for another formula that we can use to solve for those variables.

For example, suppose we are told that an electron is accelerated over a given distance by an electric field of given strength and we are asked for its final velocity. No single equation from a typical textbook will give this quantity. However, there is a well-known equation for velocity given distance and acceleration: $v^2 = v_0^2 + 2a\Delta x$. We don't know the acceleration, but we know it relates to force: $F = ma$. Therefore, if we can find the force on the electron, we can find its acceleration. Finally, there is an equation for the force due to an electric field: $F = qE$.

Descriptive Statistics

When there are large numbers of data points, it's useful to present them in a summarized way that takes all the data into account but is easier to use and understand than just the raw data points themselves. **Statistics** is a method for doing this: The point of statistics is to take many data points and find trends and properties that describe the data set as a whole, or patterns within it. Common statistical properties of a data set include the **mean**, or average, and the **standard deviation**, a measure of the variability of the data set—how much the data points tend to differ. In addition to describing single data sets, statistics can also be used to characterize the relationships between two or more variables. One statistical property that serves this purpose is **correlation**, which describes to what extent the changes in one variable tend to be mirrored by the other.

Conclusions drawn from statistics are generally not absolute, but they are probabilistic: A statistical analysis can only establish that it is *probable* that a particular relationship holds. However, for very large data sets and repeated trials, this probability can be very high.

Precision and Accuracy

Most scientific measurements have some uncertainty or error in them, and the precision and accuracy are some ways of describing the extent: The higher the precision or accuracy, the smaller the error or uncertainty. However, precision and accuracy are not the same thing. **Precision** refers to the *consistency* of the measurements: If multiple measurements all yield values that are close to each other, the measurements are *precise*. **Accuracy** refers to how close the measurements are to the real value of the quantity being measured. Significant random error can lead to low precision; *systematic* error leads to low accuracy.

Review Video: Precision, Accuracy, and Error
Visit mometrix.com/academy and enter code: 520377

It is possible for measurements to be precise but not accurate or vice versa. Suppose an object has a mass of 50.0 g. One investigator tries to measure its mass and obtains measurements of 39.9, 40.0, 39.8, and 40.1 g. These measurements are precise, but not accurate: They are close to each other, but not to the actual value. Another obtains measurements of 40.5, 46.2, 51.8, and 61.1 g. These measurements are accurate, but not precise: There is a wide spread, but their average is close to the actual value.

Probability and Sampling in Science

Experimental Probability

As the name implies, an **experimental probability**, or empirical probability, is the probability of an event as determined by experiment. (This contrasts with the **theoretical probability**, the expected probability that an event should occur based on known principles.) An experimental probability can be found by repeating an experiment multiple times (the more the better) and counting how many times the event occurs. The probability is the number of times the event occurred divided by the number of experiments run. For a simple example, suppose we have a six-sided die, and we want to know the probability that it will come up 6 if we roll it. The theoretical probability, assuming that the die is fair, is 1/6. But suppose we don't know for sure that it's fair, and want to check the probability experimentally. If we roll the die 1,000 times, and it comes up 6 for 230 times, then the experimental probability is 230/1,000, or 0.23—significantly higher than 1/6 (about 0.17), so this is probably not a fair die.

Probabilities—whether experimental or theoretical—are always between 0 and 1. A probability of 0 means that the event has no chance of happening; a probability of 1 means that it always happens.

Joint Probability

The **joint probability** of two events is the probability that *both* events will occur. By definition, the joint probability must be less than or equal to the probability of each event separately, but beyond that it could have any value. There are, however, two important special cases. If the joint probability of two events is zero, then the events are said to be **mutually exclusive**. For example, if you flip a coin, the joint probability of it coming up heads *and* tails is 0—those can't both happen at once.

Another important special case is that in which the joint probability is equal to the products of the probabilities of each event:

$$P(A \text{ and } B) = P(A) \times P(B)$$

This is true when the events are **independent**—whether or not one event happens does not affect whether the other event happens. For instance, if you flip *two* coins, the probability of their both coming up heads is $\left(\frac{1}{2}\right) \times \left(\frac{1}{2}\right) = \frac{1}{4}$.

The joint probability can be used to find the probability that *at least one* event will happen:

$$P(A \text{ or } B) = P(A) + P(B) - P(A \text{ and } B)$$

For mutually exclusive events, this reduces to:

$$P(A \text{ or } B) = P(A) + P(B)$$

Conditional Probability

The **conditional probability** is the probability that one event will occur, given that we know another event has occurred. The conditional probability that event A will occur if event B occurred is written *P(A|B)*, and it can be read as the probability of *A* given *B*. If the two events are independent—if whether one occurs has no effect on whether the other occurs—then $P(A|B) = P(A)$; the conditional probability of event A given B is the same as the probability of event A by itself. Otherwise, *P(A|B)* could have any value from zero (if event A *never* occurs if event B happens) through one (if event A *always* occurs when event B happens). For instance, suppose that event A is the probability that a student will pass the first exam in a class and event B is the probability that a student will pass the second exam. A student who passed the first exam is more likely to also pass the second, so we'd expect that $P(B|A) > P(B)$.

The conditional probability can be used to find the joint probability of the events—the probability that they will both occur:

$$P(A \text{ and } B) = P(B|A) \times P(A)$$

Review Video: Conditional Probability
Visit mometrix.com/academy and enter code: 397924

Sampling

Populations and Samples

In a scientific study, a **sample** is the collection of subjects that are being directly analyzed or measured. This contrasts with the **population**, which is the total collection of all such subjects that exist. The results of the experiment on the sample are extrapolated and assumed to apply to the population as a whole. For example, if a scientist wishes to study the effects of an experimental drug on people with insomnia, it's certainly not possible (or necessarily desirable) to test the drug on everyone in the world who has insomnia. The drug will be tested on a relatively small number of volunteers. These volunteers are the *sample*; the collection of everyone in the world with insomnia is the *population*. In general, the larger the sample, the more reliable the results of the experiment, although the method in which the sample was chosen is also significant.

Sampling is used not only in the natural sciences, but it is used in social studies as well, and even in fields such as politics. Surveys to gauge public opinion, for example, use sampling; the people conducting the survey can't call everyone in the country, so they survey a sample of the population and extrapolate the results.

Random Sample

A **random sample** is a sample chosen from the population completely at random in such a way that no member of the population has any greater chance of being included in the sample than any other member, and the fact that one particular member of the population is chosen for the sample does not affect the chances of any other particular member being chosen.

Because there is no bias in the selection of the sample and there are no assumptions necessary, a random sample is considered to be the kind of sample that is most likely to be representative of the population and most likely to give reliable results. (There is, of course a chance that the sample is unrepresentative just by coincidence—that the random sample just happened to include only members with certain characteristics—but for large samples, this chance is extremely small.) However, truly random sampling can be impractical for large populations. For small populations, one could, for instance, put a slip of paper representing each member of the population in a bowl and draw the desired number of slips, but this clearly wouldn't be feasible for populations with thousands of members.

Systematic Sample

A **systematic sample** is a sample chosen from the population by arranging the members of the population in some order and then choosing at fixed intervals from a random starting place—choosing every 10th member, for example, or every 100th member, or some other interval depending on the desired size of the sample. For instance, the sample could consist of every 100th student chosen from an alphabetical list by name of students at a particular school, or every 20th house on a long street. Systematic samples are often simpler to carry out than random samples, though they still may not be practical for large populations that cannot be ordered in any straightforward way. As with a random sample, each member of the population has an equal chance of being chosen. However, unlike with a random sample, the probabilities of choosing different members are not independent, and if there is some correlation between the ordering of the members and the characteristics being studied then the systematic sample may cause some unforeseen biases—although in most cases this is unlikely and a systematic sample may be as representative of the population as a random sample would be.

Convenience Sample

A **convenience sample** is a sample chosen simply from those members of the population that are readily available or easily reached. One common type of convenience sample for human subjects is a **voluntary response sample**—a sample consisting of those people who volunteered to participate in a particular study or who voluntarily answered a survey.

The main advantage of a convenience sample is that, as the name implies, it is convenient; it is in general much easier to put together a convenience sample than a random sample or a systematic sample. In some cases, it may not be possible to get a truly random sample and a convenience sample may be the only practical option. However, because of the nature of the convenience sample, it may not be well representative of the population as a whole. Although scientists may have methods of trying to account for possible bias in a convenience sample, those methods are imperfect, and conclusions drawn from a convenience sample are considered less reliable than those from a random sample or a systematic sample.

Fundamental Counting Principle

If an event has N equally likely (and mutually exclusive) possible outcomes, then the probability that any one outcome will occur is $1/N$. For instance, suppose you roll a fair six-sided die. (Fair in this context just means that any side of the die is equally likely to come up.) There are six possible outcomes, so the probability of rolling any particular number is $1/6$.

The **fundamental counting principle** comes into play when you have two or more independent events, each with its own set of outcomes. The principle states that the total number of possible outcomes is the product of the numbers of outcomes of each event. For instance, suppose that you simultaneously roll a six-sided die, flip a coin, and draw a tile representing a letter of the alphabet. (Assume that there is one tile for each letter, so each letter is equally likely to be drawn.) There are six possible outcomes of the die roll, 2 for the coin, and 26 for the letters, so the total number of possible outcomes is $6 \times 2 \times 26 = 312$, and the probability of obtaining any one outcome—such as 3-tails-Q—is $1/312$.

Permutations and Combinations

Permutations and combinations refer to the number of ways of choosing a number of objects from a larger set. In a **permutation**, the order matters: *A, B, C* is considered distinct from *B, C, A*. In a **combination**, only which objects are chosen matters; the order is ignored.

The number of distinct ways of choosing k objects from a set of n, when the order of the objects matters, is written ${}_nP_k$ (P for permutation), and it is equal to:

$$\frac{n!}{(n-k)!} \text{ where } n! = n \times (n-1) \times (n-2) \times \ldots \times 3 \times 2 \times 1$$

So, for example, the number of ways of choosing 4 out of 7objects in order is:

$${}_7P_4 = \frac{7!}{(7-4)!} = \frac{7 \cdot 6 \cdot 5 \cdot 4 \cdot 3 \cdot 2 \cdot 1}{3 \cdot 2 \cdot 1} = \frac{5{,}040}{6} = 840$$

The probability of choosing any particular ordered set of four is 1/840.

The number of distinct ways of choosing k objects from a set of n and order of the objects *doesn't* matter is written as ${}_nC_k$ (C for combination), and it is equal to:

$$\frac{n!}{k!\,(n-k)!}$$

Therefore, the number of ways of choosing 4 out of 7 objects ignoring order is:

$${}_7C_4 = \frac{7!}{4!\,3!} = \frac{5{,}040}{(24)(6)} = 35$$

The probability of choosing any particular unordered set of four is 1/35.

Review Video: Probability: Permutation and Combination
Visit mometrix.com/academy and enter code: 907664

Presenting Science Information Using Numbers, Symbols, and Graphics

Using Graphics

Graphics can often hold a reader's interest better than long text passages, and they can convey information more compactly. One obvious use of a graphic is to display what something *looks* like, either the object under study or the apparatus used to study it. This is common even in technical papers: a paper about a newly discovered fossil would be incomplete without a photograph or drawing of the fossil in question. More abstract schematic diagrams are also useful to show how things fit together, such as a circuit diagram showing the makeup of an electrical circuit. A map is another example of a useful graphic, to show where phenomena were found or where discoveries were made.

These uses of graphics show information that arguably could not be adequately conveyed in any other way; however, visually pleasing graphics are also sometimes used as a more eye-catching alternative to a graph or table. These graphics are often known as infographics, and they involve creative use of images that relate to the data being displayed. Instead of a simple bar graph of the amount of oil produced by different countries, for example, an infographic could use scaled images of oil derricks.

Using Symbols

A symbol is a figure that represents some other object or concept. Symbols allow information to be conveyed much more concisely than they could be in words (although technically words are a kind of symbol themselves). For example, chemists use a one- or two-letter symbol for each element; carbon is C, sodium is Na, and so on. This makes chemical equations much more compact and readable than if the full name of the element were written out each time it appears.

Different fields of science have established symbols that are known to everyone working in the field and can be used without explanation, such as the aforementioned chemical symbols, or the use in physics of c for the speed of light and G for the gravitational constant. Sometimes in a particular study, however, it may be necessary to modify a symbol to specify what it applies to: v is an accepted symbol for velocity, but you may want to use the symbols v_A and v_B to refer to the velocities of two specific objects in your study. Sometimes it may be necessary to define brand-new symbols. It's important to clearly and unambiguously define what each new symbol represents.

Using Numbers

Uncertainty

Scientific papers and presentations are often full of numbers, showing the sizes of objects, the duration of events, and many other measurable quantities. However, any measurement or calculation has some uncertainty, and the presentation should reflect that as well. The uncertainty can be given explicitly, either as a range of values (the result is between 0.32 and 0.52 ms) or with a plus-or-minus sign (0.42 ± 0.10 ms). Such explicit uncertainties are the norm in technical papers, but even in more informal contexts, the uncertainty is implied by the place value of the last digit of the number. For instance, if you are measuring a length with a tape measure that has markings to the nearest millimeter, and the length is right on the 2 m mark, you would write the length as 2.000 m—not just 2 m, because this implies that you don't know the length any more precisely than that, and not 2.0000 m, because that implies that you know the length down to the nearest tenth of a millimeter, which you don't. The digits of a number that carry meaning—excluding any leading zeros, but including following zeros after a decimal point—are called **significant figures**.

Units

Most quantitative values in a scientific report are incomplete if they do not include units. If you write that something has a duration of 3.0, that's meaningless—is it 3.0 seconds? 3.0 minutes? 3.0 years? There are some exceptions—ratios of quantities, for example, where the units cancel, and the final value is unitless—but in general each quantity should be accompanied by appropriate units. In science, it's most common to use metric units—meters, kilograms, and so on. Although in everyday life in the United States other units such as pounds and feet are common, these are seldom used in scientific contexts.

Units should be chosen that are appropriate to the scale of the measurement. If you're discussing the distances between stars, kilometers may be an appropriate unit, or even light-years. If you're discussing the width of an atom, it may be more appropriate to use nanometers. Each unit has a standard abbreviation that should be used: m for meters, s for seconds, and so on. Some measurements have a **compound unit** that combines different basic quantities: velocities, for example, can be measured in meters per second, or m/s.

Comparing Different Methods of Presenting Scientific Information

There are many ways of presenting scientific data that each have their advantages and disadvantages, any of which may be more suitable than others in specific contexts. The most obvious method of presentation is just text: simple statements of data or results. This is particularly appropriate for qualitative explanations or for simple data sets that only involve one or two quantities. For more complicated data sets, however, other methods of presentation may make it easier for the reader to visualize data.

Tables are useful if the data consist of multiple sets that can be compared but each set is relatively simple on its own. Each data set would make up a row of the table. Tables can also be used for data sets with two variables, as long as those data sets are relatively small; one can be the rows of the table, and one can be the columns. However, for large data sets or data sets in which it's important to visually convey the relationship between the variables, it may be more appropriate to use a graph, which can depict large data sets in a compact way at a cost of not including the exact numerical values.

Science Knowledge Overview

Chemical Properties

Structure of Matter

Matter is a substance that has mass and takes up space (i.e., volume). Solid, liquid, and gas are the three states of matter. These states come from the differences in the distances and angles between molecules or atoms. This causes differences in the energy that keeps them together.

> **Review Video: Chemical and Physical Properties of Matter**
> Visit mometrix.com/academy and enter code: 717349

States of Matter

In the past, there were three states of matter. **Solid** states are rigid or nearly rigid and have strong bonds. The molecules or atoms in **liquids** move around and have weak bonds. However, these bonds are not weak enough to break. Molecules or atoms of **gases** move almost independently of each other. They are far apart and do not make bonds.

Today, matter has four states. The fourth is **plasma**. This is an ionized gas that has some electrons. These electrons are described as free because they are not tied to an atom or molecule.

> **Review Video: Properties of Liquids**
> Visit mometrix.com/academy and enter code: 802024
>
> **Review Video: States of Matter [Advanced]**
> Visit mometrix.com/academy and enter code: 298130

The Atom

All matter is made of **atoms**. These atoms are made of a nucleus and electrons. The **nucleus** has **protons** and **neutrons**. They have mass and an electrical charge. The nucleus has a positive charge because of protons. Neutrons are the uncharged atomic particles that are in the nucleus. **Electrons** have a negative charge, and they orbit the nucleus. The nucleus has much more mass than the surrounding electrons.

The number of protons in the nucleus is the atomic number of an element. Carbon atoms have six protons. So, the atomic number of carbon is 6. The nucleon is the combination of neutrons and protons.

> **Review Video: Structure of Atoms**
> Visit mometrix.com/academy and enter code: 905932

Atoms can bond together to make molecules. Atoms that have an equal number of protons and electrons are electrically neutral. The number of protons and electrons in an atom may not be equal. In this case, the atom has a positive or negative charge and is an ion. The number of protons minus the number of electrons gives the charge of an atom.

Atoms are very small. A hydrogen atom is about 5×10^{-8} mm in diameter. Some estimates say that five trillion hydrogen atoms could fit on the head of a pin. Atomic radius is the average distance between the nucleus and the outermost electron.

There are many ways to picture the model of an atom. Remember that these models are not to scale. In other words, this is only a helpful picture, not an actual model. Some models of atoms show the electrons to be very close to the nucleus and circling around it. However, there are better ways to think about the model of an atom. One model is the earth as an electron that moves around the Sun as the nucleus. Another model has the earth as the nucleus. So, its atmosphere has electrons. This is the source for the "electron cloud" idea. Finally, think of a nucleus with a diameter of about 2 cm in a football stadium. Now, think of the electrons as in the bleachers. This model is like the solar system model.

Atomic Number and Atomic Mass

The **atomic number** of an element is the number of protons in the nucleus of an atom. Atoms with a neutral charge have an atomic number that is equal to the number of electrons.

Atomic mass is also known as the mass number. The **atomic mass** (A) is equal to the number of protons (Z) plus the number of neutrons (N). This can be seen in the equation $A = Z + N$. The mass of electrons in an atom is not counted because it is so small.

Atomic mass unit (amu) is the smallest unit of mass. This is equal to 1/12 of the mass of the carbon isotope carbon-12. A mole (mol) is a measurement of molecular weight. This measurement is equal to the molecule's amu in grams. As an example, carbon has an amu of 12. So, a mole of carbon weighs 12 grams. One mole is equal to about 6.02×10^{23} atoms or molecules. This amount is also known as the Avogadro constant or Avogadro's number (N_A). Another way to say this is that one mole of a substance is the same as one Avogadro's number of that substance. As an example, one mole of chlorine is 6.02×10^{23} chlorine atoms.

Review Video: What is the Mole Concept?
Visit mometrix.com/academy and enter code: 593205

Electrons

Electrons orbit the nucleus at different levels. These levels are known as layers, shells, or clouds. An electron will move to the lowest energy level that it can. An atom has a stable layout of electrons when an atom has all its electrons in the lowest available positions.

The outermost electron shell of an atom in its uncombined state is known as the **valence shell**. The electrons there are called valence electrons. Their number decides their bonding behavior. Atoms will act to fill or to empty their valence shells. Electrons can absorb or release energy. This can change the location of their orbit. Also, this can allow them to break free from the atom. The valence layer can have or share eight electrons.

Chemical bonds have a negative-positive attraction between an electron or electrons and the nucleus of an atom or nuclei of more than one atom. The attraction keeps the atom connected. Also, it helps to make bonds with other atoms and molecules.

The attractive force between the electrons and the nucleus is called the electric force. A positive (+) charge or a negative (-) charge creates a field of sorts in the empty space around it, which is known as an electric field. An electron within the force of the field is pulled towards a positive charge because an electron has a negative charge. A particle with a positive charge is pushed away, or repelled, by another positive charge. Like charges repel each other and opposite charges attract. Lines of force show the paths of charges. The electric force between two objects is directly proportional to the product of the charge magnitudes and inversely proportional to the square of the distance between the two objects. Electric charge is measured with the unit Coulomb (C). It is the amount of charge moved in one second by a steady current of one ampere ($1C = 1A \times 1s$).

Ions

Most atoms are neutral. The reason is that the positive charge of the protons is balanced by the negative charge of the nearby electrons. Electrons are transferred between atoms when they come into contact with each other. This makes a molecule or atom where the number of electrons does not equal the number of protons. So, this gives it a positive or negative charge.

A negative ion is created when an atom gains electrons. A positive ion is created when an atom loses electrons. An ionic bond is made between ions with opposite charges. However, since the charges are balanced, the resulting compound is neutral. Ionization is the term for changing the number of electrons around a neutral atom or compound, thus giving it a charge and making it an ion.

Bonding

Atoms interact by transferring or sharing the electrons furthest from the nucleus. Outer or valence electrons are responsible for the chemical properties of an element. Bonds between atoms are created when electrons are paired up by being transferred or shared. If electrons are transferred from one atom to another, the bond is ionic. If electrons are shared, the bond is covalent.

Molecules are made by a chemical bond between atoms. This bond happens at the valence level. Two basic types of bonds are covalent and ionic. A covalent bond is made when atoms share electrons. An ionic bond is made when an atom transfers an electron to another atom. A hydrogen bond is a weak bond, neither ionic nor covalent, between a hydrogen atom of one molecule and an electronegative atom (like nitrogen, oxygen, or fluorine) of another molecule. The Van der Waals force is a weak force between molecules. This type of force is much weaker than actual chemical bonds between atoms.

Review Video: What is an Ionic Bond?
Visit mometrix.com/academy and enter code: 116546

Elements

An element is matter with one type of atom. It can be known by its atomic number. Today, there are about 117 known elements. There are 94 that are not made by humans. Some well-known elements on the periodic table are hydrogen, carbon, iron, helium, mercury, and oxygen. Atoms can come together to make molecules. As an example, take two atoms of hydrogen (H) and one atom of oxygen (O). These atoms will come together to make water (H_2O).

Isotopes

The number of protons in an atom determines the element of an atom. For example, all atoms that have exactly two protons are helium atoms and all atoms that have exactly eight protons are oxygen atoms. If two atoms have the same number of protons, then they are the same element. However, the number of neutrons in two atoms can be different from each other without the atoms being different elements.

The term isotope is used to show the difference between atoms that have the same number of protons but a different number of neutrons. The name of an isotope is the element name with the mass number. Remember that the mass number is the number of protons plus the number of neutrons.

For example, carbon-12 is an atom that has six protons and six neutrons. This means that it is carbon. You can add 6 protons + 6 neutrons = 12. Now, carbon-13 has six protons and seven neutrons. Carbon-14 has six protons and eight neutrons. Isotopes can also be written with the mass number in superscript before the element symbol. For example, carbon-12 can be written as ^{12}C.

Periodic Table

1	2	3	4	5	6	7	8	9	10	11	12	13	14	15	16	17	18
1 **H**																	2 **He**
3 **Li**	4 **Be**											5 **B**	6 **C**	7 **N**	8 **O**	9 **F**	10 **Ne**
11 **Na**	12 **Mg**											13 **Al**	14 **Si**	15 **P**	16 **S**	17 **Cl**	18 **Ar**
19 **K**	20 **Ca**	21 **Sc**	22 **Ti**	23 **V**	24 **Cr**	25 **Mn**	26 **Fe**	27 **Co**	28 **Ni**	29 **Cu**	30 **Zn**	31 **Ga**	32 **Ge**	33 **As**	34 **Se**	35 **Br**	36 **Kr**
37 **Rb**	38 **Sr**	39 **Y**	40 **Zr**	41 **Nb**	42 **Mo**	43 **Tc**	44 **Ru**	45 **Rh**	46 **Pd**	47 **Ag**	48 **Cd**	49 **In**	50 **Sn**	51 **Sb**	52 **Te**	53 **I**	54 **Xe**
55 **Cs**	56 **Ba**	57 - 71	72 **Hf**	73 **Ta**	74 **W**	75 **Re**	76 **Os**	77 **Ir**	78 **Pt**	79 **Au**	80 **Hg**	81 **Tl**	82 **Pb**	83 **Bi**	84 **Po**	85 **At**	86 **Rn**
87 **Fr**	88 **Ra**	89 - 103	104 **Rf**	105 **Db**	106 **Sg**	107 **Bh**	108 **Hs**	109 **Mt**	110 **Ds**	111 **Rg**	112 **Cn**	113 **Nh**	114 **Fl**	115 **Mc**	116 **Lv**	117 **Ts**	118 **Og**

← Atomic Number
← Symbol

Lanthanides	57 **La**	58 **Ce**	59 **Pr**	60 **Nd**	61 **Pm**	62 **Sm**	63 **Eu**	64 **Gd**	65 **Tb**	66 **Dy**	67 **Ho**	68 **Er**	69 **Tm**	70 **Yb**	71 **Lu**
Actinides	89 **Ac**	90 **Th**	91 **Pa**	92 **U**	93 **Np**	94 **Pu**	95 **Am**	96 **Cm**	97 **Bk**	98 **Cf**	99 **Es**	100 **Fm**	101 **Md**	102 **No**	103 **Lr**

The periodic table groups elements with similar chemical properties. The groups are based on atomic structure. This table can show families of elements that have properties. Also, this is a common model for organizing and understanding the elements.

In the periodic table, each element has its own cell. In this cell, there is information about the properties of the element. Cells in the table are placed in rows (i.e., periods) and columns (i.e., groups or families).

Elements are placed on the table by their atomic number from left to right and top to bottom. There are many different types of information that may be included in a periodic table, but at the least, a cell has the symbol for the element and its atomic number. For example, the cell for hydrogen is first in the upper left corner. This has an *H* and a *1* above the *H*.

Review Video: Periodic Table
Visit mometrix.com/academy and enter code: 154828

In the periodic table, the groups are numbered columns from 1 to 18. These columns group elements that have similar outer electron shell forms. Elements in the same group have similar chemical properties. The reason is that the form of the outer electron shell affects an element's chemical properties.

Today, the periodic table groups are:

- Group 1: alkali metals
- Group 2: alkaline earth metals
- Groups 3-12: transition metals
- Group 13: boron family

- Group 14: carbon family
- Group 15: pnictogens
- Group 16: chalcogens
- Group 17: halogens
- Group 18: noble gases

In the periodic table, there are seven periods (i.e., rows). In each period, there are blocks that group elements with the same outer electron subshell. The number of electrons in that outer shell decides the group of an element. Each row's number matches with the highest number for an electron shell that is in use. For example, row 2 uses only electron shells: 1 and 2. Then, row 7 uses all shells from 1-7.

From left to right, electronegativity increases. **Electronegativity** is an atom's likeliness of taking another atom's electrons. In a group, electronegativity decreases from top to bottom. **Ionization energy** is the amount of energy that is needed to get rid of an atom's outermost electron. This increases across a period and decreases down a group. Electron affinity will be more negative across a period. However, this will not change much in a group. The melting point decreases from top to bottom in the metal groups. This increases from top to bottom in the non-metal groups.

Review Video: Electronegativity
Visit mometrix.com/academy and enter code: 823348

PHYSICAL AND CHEMICAL PROPERTIES

Chemical properties cannot be seen or measured without chemical reactions. Physical properties can be seen or measured without chemical reactions. These properties are color, elasticity, mass, volume, and temperature.

Mass measures how much of a substance is in an object.

Weight measures the gravitational pull of the earth on an object.

Density is a measure of the amount of mass per unit volume. The formula to find density is mass divided by volume (D = m/V). It is expressed in terms of mass per cubic unit (e.g., grams per cubic centimeter $\frac{g}{cm^3}$).

Volume measures the amount of space taken up. The volume of an irregular shape can be known by finding out how much water it displaces.

Specific gravity measures the ratio of a substance's density to the density of water.

Review Video: Mass, Weight, Volume, Density, and Specific Gravity
Visit mometrix.com/academy and enter code: 920570

Physical changes and chemical reactions are everyday events. **Physical changes** do not bring about different substances. An example is when water becomes ice. It has gone through a physical change, not a chemical change. It has changed its state, not what it is made of. In other words, it is still H_2O.

Chemical properties deal with the particles that make up the structure of a substance. Chemical properties can be seen when chemical changes happen. The chemical properties of a substance are influenced by its electron configuration. This is decided somewhat by the number of protons in the nucleus (i.e., the atomic number). An example is carbon that has 6 protons and 6 electrons. The outermost valence electrons of an element mainly determine its chemical properties. Chemical reactions may give or take energy.

Nuclear Reactions and Radioactivity

The protons and neutrons are tied together by nuclear force. This is also known as residual strong force. Chemical reactions involve electrons. Nuclear reactions happen when two nuclei or nuclear particles collide. This reaction releases or absorbs energy. Also, products are different from the particles at the beginning. The energy released in a nuclear reaction can take many forms. This includes the release of kinetic energy from the particles of the product. Another form of the released energy is the release of very high energy photons known as gamma rays. Some energy may also stay in the nucleus.

Radioactivity is the particles that come out of nuclei. This comes from nuclear instability. There are many nuclear isotopes that are unstable. They can send out some kind of radiation without notice. There are many types of radioactive decay. The most common types of radiation are alpha, beta, and gamma radiation.

Conductors and Insulators

Conductor: a material that has little resistance to heat transferred between its particles.

Insulator: a material that has resistance to heat transferred between its particles.

When studying atoms at a microscopic level, some materials (e.g., metals) have properties that allow electrons to flow easily. Metals are good conductors of electricity because their valence electrons are loosely held in a network of atoms. The reason is that the valence shells of metal atoms have weak attractions to their nuclei. This results in a "sea of electrons," and electrons can flow between atoms with little resistance.

In insulating materials (e.g., glass), electrons hardly flow at all. In between materials can be called semiconducting materials. They have intermediate conducting behavior. At low temperatures, some materials become superconductors. So, they have no resistance to the flow of electrons. Thermal conductivity is a material's capacity to conduct heat.

Conservation of Mass Number and Charge

Mass number, A, is the sum of the number of neutrons, N, and protons, Z, in the nucleus ($A = N + Z$). The conservation of mass number is an idea connected with nuclear reactions. Two conditions are needed to balance a nuclear reaction. They are **conservation of mass number** and **conservation of nuclear charge**.

In a **nuclear equation**, the mass numbers should be equal on each side of the arrow. In this type of equation, the mass number is in superscript in front of the element and the atomic number is in subscript. The total number of nucleons is the same even though the product elements are different.

An example is a specific isotope of uranium that decays into thorium and helium. The original mass number of uranium is 238. After the reaction, the mass number of thorium is 234. The mass number of helium is 4. This relationship can be shown as $238 = 234 + 4$, where the mass number is the same on both sides of the equation.

Inorganic Compounds

The main trait of **inorganic compounds** is that they lack carbon. Inorganic compounds include mineral salts, alloys, non-metallic compounds such as phosphate, and metal complexes. A metal complex has a central atom (or ion) bonded to surrounding ligands (molecules or anions). The ligands sacrifice the donor atoms (in the form of at least one pair of electrons) to the central atom. Many inorganic compounds are ionic, meaning they form ionic bonds rather than share electrons. They may have high melting points because of this. They may also be colorful, but this is not an absolute identifier of an inorganic compound. Salts, which are inorganic compounds, are an example of inorganic bonding of cations (positive ions) and anions (negative ions). Some examples of salts are magnesium chloride ($MgCl_2$) and sodium oxide (Na_2O). Oxides, carbonates, sulfates, and halides are classes of inorganic compounds. They are typically poor conductors, are very water soluble, and crystallize easily. Minerals and silicates are also inorganic compounds.

ORGANIC COMPOUNDS

Two of the main characteristics of **organic compounds** are that they include carbon and are formed by covalent bonds. Carbon can form long chains, double and triple bonds, and rings. While inorganic compounds tend to have high melting points, organic compounds tend to melt at temperatures below 300° C. They also tend to boil, sublimate, and decompose below this temperature. Unlike inorganic compounds, they are not very water soluble. Organic molecules are organized into functional groups based on their specific atoms, which helps determine how they will react chemically. A few groups are alkanes, nitro, alkenes, sulfides, amines, and carbolic acids. The hydroxyl group (-OH) consists of alcohols. These molecules are polar, which increases their solubility. By some estimates, there are more than 16 million organic compounds.

Review Video: Organic Compounds
Visit mometrix.com/academy and enter code: 264922

NOMENCLATURE FOR ORGANIC COMPOUNDS

Nomenclature refers to the manner in which a compound is named. First, it must be determined whether the compound is ionic (formed through electron transfer between cations and anions) or molecular (formed through electron sharing between molecules). When dealing with an ionic compound, the name is determined using the standard naming conventions for ionic compounds. This involves indicating the positive element first (the charge must be defined when there is more than one option for the valency) followed by the negative element plus the appropriate suffix. The rules for naming a molecular compound are as follows: write elements in order of increasing group number and determine the prefix by determining the number of atoms. Exclude mono for the first atom. The name for CO2, for example, is carbon dioxide. The end of oxygen is dropped and "ide" is added to make oxide, and the prefix "di" is used to indicate there are two atoms of oxygen.

BALANCING CHEMICAL EQUATIONS

Chemical equations describe chemical reactions. The reactants are on the left side before the arrow. The products are on the right side after the arrow. The arrow is the mark that points to the reaction or change. The coefficient is the number before the element. This gives the ratio of reactants to products in terms of moles.

The equation for making water from hydrogen and oxygen is $2H_{2(g)} + O_{2(g)} \rightarrow 2H_2O_{(l)}$. The number 2 before hydrogen and water is the coefficient. This means that there are 2 moles of hydrogen and 2 of water. There is 1 mole of oxygen. This does not need to have the number 1 before the symbol for the element. For additional information, the following subscripts are often included to indicate the state of the substance: (g) stands for gas, (l) stands for liquid, (s) stands for solid, and (aq) stands for aqueous. Aqueous means the substance is dissolved in water. Charges are shown by superscript for individual ions, not for ionic compounds. Polyatomic ions are separated by parentheses. This is done so the kind of ion will not be confused with the number of ions.

An unbalanced equation does not follow the law of conservation of mass. This law says that matter can only be changed, not created. If an equation is unbalanced, the numbers of atoms shown by the coefficients on each side of the arrow will not be equal.

To balance a chemical equation, you start by writing the formulas for each element or compound in the reaction. Next, count the atoms on each side and decide if the number is equal. Coefficients must be whole numbers. Fractional amounts (e.g., half a molecule) are not possible. Equations can be balanced by multiplying the coefficients by a constant that will make the smallest possible whole number coefficient. $H_2 + O_2 \rightarrow H_2O$ is an example of an unbalanced equation. The balanced equation is $2H_2 + O_2 \rightarrow 2H_2O$. This equation shows that it takes two moles of hydrogen and one of oxygen to make two moles of water.

Review Video: How Do You Balance Chemical Equations?
Visit mometrix.com/academy and enter code: 341228

Reactions

Some types of reactions give off energy in the form of heat and light. Some types of reactions involve the transfer of either electrons or hydrogen ions between reacting ions, molecules, or atoms. In other reactions, chemical bonds are broken down by heat or light. This forms reactive radicals with electrons that will make new bonds. Processes like the formation of ozone and greenhouse gases in the atmosphere are controlled by radical reactions. Also, the burning and processing of fossil fuels are controlled by radical reactions.

Chemical Reactions

Chemical reactions can take fractions of a second or billions of years. The rates of chemical reactions are decided by how often reacting atoms and molecules make contact with each other. Rates are also affected by the temperature and different properties (e.g., shape) of the reacting materials. Catalysts speed up chemical reactions. Inhibitors slow down reaction rates.

One way to organize chemical reactions is to put them into two categories. One category is oxidation/reduction reactions. These are also called redox reactions. The second category is metathesis reactions. These have acid/base reactions.

Redox reactions can involve the transfer of one or more electrons. Also, they can happen from the transfer of oxygen, hydrogen, or halogen atoms. The element or compound that loses electrons is oxidized. So, this is known as the **reducing agent**. The element or compound that gains electrons is reduced. So, this is known as the **oxidizing agent**.

The element going through oxidation experiences an increase in its oxidation number. The element going through reduction experiences a decrease in its oxidation number. Single replacement reactions are types of redox reactions. In a single replacement reaction, electrons are transferred from one chemical compound or element to another. The transfer of electrons changes the nature and charge of the chemical compound or element.

Review Video: Understanding Chemical Reactions
Visit mometrix.com/academy and enter code: 579876

One reactant can be displaced by another to make the final product. This kind of reaction can be seen in single substitution, displacement, or replacement reactions. The equation for this reaction is: $(A + BC \rightarrow B + AC)$.

SINGLE SUBSTITUTION REACTION

Single substitution reactions can be cationic or anionic. When a piece of copper (Cu) is placed in a solution of silver nitrate ($AgNO_3$), the solution turns blue. The copper looks to be replaced with a silvery-white material. The equation is $2AgNO_3 + Cu \rightarrow Cu(NO_3)_2 + 2Ag$. With this reaction, the copper dissolves. Also, the silver in the silver nitrate solution precipitates (i.e., becomes a solid). So, this makes copper nitrate and silver. The copper and silver have changed places in the nitrate.

Review Video: What is a Single-Replacement Reaction?
Visit mometrix.com/academy and enter code: 442975

COMBINATION REACTION

In a **combination reaction**, two or more reactants combine to make one product. This can be seen in the equation $A + B \rightarrow AB$. These reactions are also known as synthesis or addition reactions. An example is burning hydrogen in air to make water. The equation is $2H_{2(g)} + O_{2(g)} \rightarrow 2H_2O_{(l)}$. Another example is when water and sulfur trioxide react to make sulfuric acid. The equation is $H_2O + SO_3 \rightarrow H_2SO_4$.

Ions or bonds can be exchanged by two compounds to make different compounds. This reaction can be seen in double displacement, double replacement, substitution, metathesis, or ion exchange reactions. An example of an equation is ($AC + BD \rightarrow AD + BC$). An example of this is when silver nitrate and sodium chloride make two different products. These products are silver chloride and sodium nitrate when they react. So, this reaction can be written as $AgNO_3 + NaCl \rightarrow AgCl + NaNO_3$.

DOUBLE REPLACEMENT REACTIONS

Double replacement reactions are metathesis reactions. In a **double replacement reaction**, the chemical reactants exchange ions. However, the oxidation state stays the same. One of the signs of this is the building of a solid precipitate. In acid/base reactions, an acid is a compound that can donate a proton. A base is a compound that can accept a proton. In these types of reactions, the acid and base react to make salt and water. When the proton is donated, the base becomes water. So, the remaining ions make a salt. One way to know if a reaction is a redox or a metathesis reaction is to note the oxidation number of atoms in the reaction. It does not change during a metathesis reaction.

When one compound takes H^+ from another, this is known as a neutralization, acid-base, or proton transfer reaction. Usually, these types of reactions are double displacement reactions. The acid has an H^+ that is transferred to the base and neutralized to make a salt.

DECOMPOSITION REACTIONS

Decomposition reactions are also known as desynthesis, decombination, or deconstruction reactions. In a **decomposition reaction**, a reactant is broken down into two or more products. This can be seen in the equation $AB \rightarrow A + B$. These reactions are also called analysis reactions. Basically, decomposition breaks down one compound into two or more compounds or substances. The two or more compounds or substances are different from the original. The separation sorts the substances from the original mixture into like substances.

Thermal decomposition is caused by heat. Electrolytic decomposition is due to electricity. An example of this type of reaction is the decomposition of water into hydrogen and oxygen gas. This can be seen in the equation: $2H_2O \rightarrow 2H_2 + O_2$.

Decomposition is a chemical reaction where a single compound breaks down into component parts or simpler compounds. A compound or substance can break down into these simpler substances.

So, the byproducts are often substances that are different from the original. You can think of decomposition as the opposite of combination reactions.

Most decomposition reactions are endothermic. Heat needs to be added for the chemical reaction to happen. Separation processes can be mechanical or chemical. Usually, this involves re-organizing a mixture of substances without changing their chemical nature. The separated products may be different from the original mixture in terms of chemical or physical properties. Types of separation processes are filtration, crystallization, distillation, and chromatography.

Catalysts

Catalysts are substances that help change the rate of reaction. This happens without changing the substance's form. Catalysts can increase reaction rate by decreasing the number of steps that it takes to make products. The mass of the catalyst should be the same from the beginning of the reaction to the end.

Activation energy is the smallest amount of energy needed to get a reaction started. Activation energy causes particles to collide with enough energy to start the reaction. A catalyst allows more particles to react. So, this lowers the activation energy.

Review Video: What is a Catalyst?
Visit mometrix.com/academy and enter code: 288189

Combustion

Combustion (i.e., burning) is a series of chemical reactions. This involves fuel and an oxidant that makes heat and sometimes makes light. There are many types of combustion. Some types are rapid, slow, complete, turbulent, microgravity, and incomplete. Fuels and oxidants decide the compounds that are made by a combustion reaction.

For example, rocket fuel is made of hydrogen and oxygen. So, when rocket fuel combusts, water vapor comes out of the reaction. After air and wood burn, nitrogen, unburned carbon, and carbon compounds come from the reaction. Combustion is an exothermic process. This means that it releases energy. Exothermic energy is commonly released as heat. However, it can take other forms. These forms are light, electricity, or sound.

Review Video: Combustion
Visit mometrix.com/academy and enter code: 592219

Solutions and Mixtures

A solution is a homogeneous mixture. A mixture is two or more substances that are mixed together, but not combined chemically. A homogeneous mixture has the same structure in the whole mixture. An example of a homogeneous mixture is air. There are many gases, but we are not aware of the differences without special tools.

Solutions have a solute and a solvent. A **solute** is the substance that is dissolved. A **solvent** is the substance that does the dissolving. An example is sugar water. The solvent is the water, and the solute is the sugar. Solvation is the interaction between the solvent and the solute.

A solute is dissolved when its internal molecular bonds are overcome by the strength of the bonds between the atoms in the solvent and the solute. An example is when salt (NaCl) dissolves in water to make a solution. The Na^+ and the Cl^- ions in salt interact with the molecules of water and vice versa to overcome the intramolecular forces of the solute. Hydration is the name for solutions where water is the solvent.

The term **dilute** is used when there is less solute. Adding more solvent is known as diluting a solution. Also, removing a part of the solute is known as diluting a solution. A concentrated solution is when there is more solute. Adding more solute makes a solution more **concentrated**. Removing a part of the solvent makes a solution more concentrated.

For solvation to happen, bonds of similar strength must be broken and made. Usually, nonpolar substances are soluble in nonpolar solvents. Ionic and polar matter is usually soluble in polar solvents. Water is a polar solvent. Oil is nonpolar.

NH_3 (ammonia), SO_2 (sulfur dioxide), and H_2S (hydrogen sulfide) are polar molecules. They are known as **hydrophilic**. This means that they easily combine with water. Noble gases and other gases like CO_2 (carbon dioxide) are some nonpolar molecules. They are known as **hydrophobic**. This means that they repel or do not easily combine with water. You can remember this with the statement that "like dissolves like." Polar solvents dissolve polar solutes. Nonpolar solvents dissolve nonpolar solutes.

Solids will dissolve faster when the temperature is increased. Higher temperatures help break bonds through an increase in kinetic energy. Solubility can increase for solids being dissolved in water as the temperature approaches 100°C. However, at higher temperatures ionic solutes will become less soluble. Gases can be less soluble at higher temperatures.

When solutions are saturated at high temperatures, no more solute will dissolve in the solution. Then, as the solution cools, the solute will "fall out" of the solution. Melting points can be lowered by using a solvent. An example is using salt on icy roads which lowers the freezing point of ice. A solution's melting point is usually lower than the melting point of the solvent by itself. Pressure has little effect on the solubility of liquid solutions. For gas solutions, an increase in pressure increases solubility. Also, a decrease in the pressure leads to a decrease in solubility.

Review Video: Solutions
Visit mometrix.com/academy and enter code: 995937

Molarity

The concentration of a solution is measured in terms of molarity. One molar (M) is equal to the number of moles of solute per liter of solution. Adding one mole of a substance to one liter of solution would likely cause a molarity greater than one. The amount of substance should be measured into a small amount of solution. Then, more solution should be added to reach a volume of one liter to have accuracy.

Properties of Water

The important properties of water (H_2O) are high polarity, hydrogen bonding, cohesiveness, adhesiveness, high specific heat, high latent heat, and high heat of vaporization. Water is vital to life as we know it. The reason is that water is one of the main parts of many living things.

Water is a liquid at room temperature. The high specific heat of water means that it does not easily break its hydrogen bonds. Also, it resists heat and motion. This is why it has a high boiling point and high vaporization point.

Most substances are denser in their solid forms. However, water is different because its solid-state floats in its liquid state. Water is cohesive. This means that it is drawn to itself. It is also adhesive.

This means that it draws in other molecules. If water will attach to another substance, the substance is said to be hydrophilic. Because of its cohesive and adhesive properties, water makes a good solvent. Substances with polar ions and molecules easily dissolve in water.

Review Video: Properties of Water
Visit mometrix.com/academy and enter code: 279526

Potential of Hydrogen (pH)

The potential of hydrogen (pH) is a measurement of the concentration of hydrogen ions in a substance in terms of the number of moles of H+ per liter of solution. A lower pH indicates a higher H+ concentration, while a higher pH indicates a lower H+ concentration. Pure water has a neutral pH, which is 7. Anything with a pH lower than water (less than 7) is considered acidic. Anything with a pH higher than water (greater than 7) is a base. Drain cleaner, soap, baking soda, ammonia, egg whites, and sea water are common bases. Urine, stomach acid, citric acid, vinegar, hydrochloric acid, and battery acid are acids. A pH indicator is a substance that acts as a detector of hydrogen or hydronium ions. It is halochromic, meaning it changes color to indicate that hydrogen or hydronium ions have been detected.

Review Video: Overview of pH Levels
Visit mometrix.com/academy and enter code: 187395

Vocabulary

Elements: These are substances that are made of only one type of atom.

Compounds: These are substances that have two or more elements. Compounds are made from chemical reactions. Often, they have different properties than the original elements. Compounds are broken down by a chemical reaction. They are not separated by a physical reaction.

Solutions: These are homogeneous mixtures. They are made of two or more substances that have become one.

Mixtures: Two or more substances that are combined. However, they have not reacted chemically with each other. Mixtures can be separated with physical methods and compounds cannot.

Heat: This is the transfer of energy from a body or system from thermal contact. Heat is made of random motion and the vibration of atoms, molecules, and ions. Higher temperatures cause more motion with atoms or molecules.

Energy: The capacity to do work.

Work: the amount of energy that must be transferred to overcome a force. An example of work is lifting an object in the air. The opposing force that must be overcome is gravity. Work is measured in joules (J). The rate that work is done is known as power.

Physical Science

Thermodynamics Concepts and Terminology

Thermodynamics: This refers to a branch of physics that studies the conversion of energy into work and heat. It is especially concerned with variables such as temperature, volume, and pressure.

Thermodynamic equilibrium: This refers to objects that have the same temperature because heat is transferred between them to reach equilibrium.

Open, **isolated**, and **closed systems**: Open systems are capable of interacting with a surrounding environment and can exchange heat, work (energy), and matter outside their system boundaries. A closed system can exchange heat and work, but not matter. An isolated system cannot exchange heat, work, or matter with its surroundings. Its total energy and mass stay the same.

Surrounding environment: In physics, this term refers to everything outside a thermodynamic system (system). The terms "surroundings" and "environment" are also used. The term "boundary" refers to the division between the system and its surroundings.

Conservation, Transformation, and Flow of Energy

Heat is energy that is transferred or moved from one body or system to another from thermal contact. Everything tries to become less organized over time. This is known as **entropy**. In all energy transfers, the end result is that the energy is spread out in a balanced way. This transfer of heat energy from hotter to cooler objects is done by conduction, radiation, or convection.

Temperature measures an object's stored heat energy. In other words, temperature is the average kinetic energy of an object's particles. When the temperature of an object increases and its atoms move faster, then the kinetic energy also rises. Temperature is not energy since it changes and is not conserved. Thermometers measure temperature.

Review Video: What is the Difference between Heat and Temperature?
Visit mometrix.com/academy and enter code: 879095

There are three main ways to measure temperature. **Celsius** uses the points of water for freezing at 0 degrees and for boiling at 100 degrees. **Fahrenheit** uses the points of water for freezing at 32 degrees and for boiling at 212 degrees. Celsius and Fahrenheit are both relative temperature scales. The reason is that they use water as their reference point. The **Kelvin** temperature scale is an absolute temperature scale. Water's freezing point is 273.15 Kelvin and boiling point is 373.15 Kelvin. Celsius and Fahrenheit are measured in degrees. Kelvin does not use degree terminology. Converting between the scales can be done with the following relationships:

		To		
		Kelvin	**Celsius**	**Fahrenheit**
From	**Fahrenheit**	$\frac{5}{9}(°F - 32) + 273.15$	$\frac{5}{9}(°F - 32)$	1
	Celsius	$°C + 273.15$	1	$\frac{9}{5}°C + 32$
	Kelvin	1	$K - 273.15$	$\frac{9}{5}(K - 273.15) + 32$

Conduction is a form of heat transfer that happens at the molecular level. This happens because molecules are stirred or agitated. This can happen in an object, body, or material while the material stays motionless.

An example of this is when a frying pan is placed on a hot burner. At first, the handle is not hot. The pan becomes warmer because of conduction. Over time, the handle becomes hot as well. In this example, energy is moved farther down the handle to the colder end. The reason is that the higher speed particles collide with the slower ones and give energy to the slower ones. When this happens, the original material becomes cooler. So, the second material becomes hotter until equilibrium (i.e., balance) is reached.

Thermal conduction can also happen between two substances. Examples are a cup of hot coffee and the colder surface that it is placed on. Heat is moved, but matter is not.

Convection is the movement of heat that happens with the movement or circulation of fluids (i.e., liquids or gases). Some of the fluid becomes or is hotter than the surrounding fluid and is less dense. Heat is moved away from the source of the heat to a cooler, denser area.

An example of convection is boiling water. Another example is the movement of warm and cold air currents in the atmosphere and the ocean. Forced convection happens in convection ovens where a fan helps to circulate hot air.

Radiation is heat transfer that occurs through the emission of electromagnetic waves, which carry energy away from the emitting object. All objects with temperatures above absolute zero radiate heat.

Latent heat refers to the amount of heat required for a substance to undergo a phase (state) change (from a liquid to a solid, for example).

Endothermic and Exothermic Reactions

Endothermic reactions are chemical reactions that take in heat. **Exothermic** reactions are chemical reactions that release heat. Reactants are the substances that are consumed during a reaction. Products are the substances that are made.

A balanced equation is when the number of each type of atom and the total charge stays the same. The reactants are on the left side of the arrow, and the products on the right are balanced.

The heat difference between endothermic and exothermic reactions is generated by bonds that are made and broken.

Let's say that reactant bonds are made. So, more energy is needed to break those bonds than what is released. In this case, the reaction is endothermic. Heat is taken in, and the environmental temperature decreases.

Let's say that energy is released when product bonds are made. The amount of energy is more than what is needed to break the reactant bonds. So, the reaction is exothermic. Heat is released, and the environmental temperature increases.

Heat Capacity and Specific Heat Capacity

Heat capacity, also known as thermal mass, refers to the amount of heat energy required to raise the temperature of an object, and is measured in Joules per Kelvin or Joules per degree Celsius. The equation for relating heat energy to heat capacity is $Q = C\Delta T$, where Q is the heat energy transferred, C is the heat capacity of the body, and ΔT is the change in the object's temperature. **Specific heat capacity**, also known as specific heat, is the heat capacity per unit mass. Every element and compound has its own specific heat. For example, it takes different amounts of heat energy to raise the temperature of the same amounts of magnesium and lead by one degree. The equation for relating heat energy to specific heat capacity is $Q = mc\Delta T$, where m represents the mass of the object, and c represents its specific heat capacity.

Review Video: Specific Heat Capacity
Visit mometrix.com/academy and enter code: 736791

Molar Mass, Charles's Law, and Boyle's Law.

Molar mass: This refers to the mass of one mole of a substance (element or compound), usually measured in grams per mole ($\frac{g}{mol}$). This differs from molecular mass in that molecular mass is the mass of one molecule of a substance relative to the atomic mass unit (amu).

Charles's law: This states that gases expand when they are heated. It is also known as the law of volumes.

Boyle's law: This states that gases contract when pressure is applied to them. It also states that if temperature remains constant, the relationship between absolute pressure and volume is inversely proportional. When one increases, the other decreases. Considered a specialized case of the ideal gas law, Boyle's law is sometimes known as the Boyle-Mariotte law.

Energy

The two types of energy that are important in mechanics are potential and kinetic energy. **Potential energy** is the amount of energy that an object has stored inside itself because of its position or orientation.

There are many types of potential energy. The most common is gravitational potential energy. It is the energy that an object has because of its height (h) above the ground. It can be calculated as $PE = mgh$. In this formula, m is the object's mass, and g is the acceleration of gravity.

Kinetic energy is the energy of an object in motion. It is calculated as $KE = \frac{mv^2}{2}$. In this formula, v is the magnitude of its velocity. To better understand this, think of an object that is dropped. The potential energy of the object becomes kinetic energy as it falls. The kinetic and potential energy equations can be used to find the velocity of an object at any point in its fall.

Electromagnetic waves are a type of energy contained by a field.

Electrical energy is a type of potential energy. This is the energy that it takes to pull apart positive and negative electrical charges.

Chemical energy is the way that atoms turn into molecules. This energy can be released or taken in when molecules regroup.

Solar energy is in the form of visible light and non-visible light (e.g., infrared and ultraviolet rays).

Sound energy is the energy in sound waves.

Energy is always changing forms and moving back and forth. An example of a heat to mechanical energy transformation is a steam engine. Coal can be a source of heat that is used to boil water. The steam that is made turns a shaft. This turning shaft will turn the wheels of a train.

A pendulum swinging is an example of a kinetic to potential and a potential to kinetic energy transformation. A pendulum can be moved from its center point (i.e., where it is closest to the ground) to a higher point before it returns to the center. This is an example of a kinetic to potential transformation.

Stretching a rubber band gives it potential energy. That potential energy becomes kinetic energy when the rubber band is released.

Review Video: Potential and Kinetic Energy
Visit mometrix.com/academy and enter code: 491502

WAVES

Waves are divided into types. These types are based on the direction of particle motion in a medium and the direction of wave creation. A medium can be air, water, or other matter. Some common examples of waves are sound, seismic, water, light, micro, and radio waves.

WAVE TYPES

Longitudinal waves are waves that travel in the same direction as the particle movement. They are also known as pressure, compressional, or density waves. Longitudinal sound waves are the easiest to make. Also, they have the highest speed. A longitudinal wave has compressions and rarefactions. This is like the extending and collapsing in a Slinky toy. A compression is a point where particles are forced together. A rarefaction is a point where particles move farther apart and their density decreases.

Shear or transverse waves move perpendicular to the direction of the particle movement. As an example, the particles in a medium move up and down. So, a transverse wave will move forward. Transverse waves only happen in solids. They are slower than longitudinal waves.

Surface or circular waves travel at the surface of a material. These waves move in elliptical orbits. They are a little slower than shear waves.

Plate waves move in elliptical orbits. They only happen in very thin pieces of material.

WAVE INTERACTION

Waves can be in phase or out of phase. An example is two separate waves that start from the same point. Their peaks (i.e., crests) and valleys (i.e., troughs) are in line with each other. So, they are said to be in phase. If the peak of a wave is in line with the valley of another wave, then they are out of phase. When waves are in phase, their displacement is doubled. If they are out of phase, they cancel each other out.

If they are between being completely in phase and completely out of phase, the wave interaction is a wave that is the sum of the amplitudes of all points along the wave. If waves start from different points, the amplitude of particle displacement is the combined sum of the particle displacement amplitude of each individual wave.

A wave can travel in the same medium and have contact with other waves. This is known as wave interference. A single wave generally stays the same in terms of waveform, frequency, amplitude, and wavelength. Several waves traveling through particles in a medium will change after they have contact with other waves.

The final properties of a wave depend on many factors. These factors are the point where the wave begins and if the waves are in phase, out of phase, or somewhere in between.

Constructive interference is what happens when two crests or two troughs of a wave meet. So, the amplitude of the crest or trough that comes from this meeting is doubled. Destructive interference is when the crest of one wave and the trough of another that are the same shape meet. When this happens, the two waves cancel each other out. An example of destructive interference is when two unlike sound waves reduce the volume of the sound.

ENERGY IN A WAVE

Waves have energy and can transfer energy when they come into contact with matter. Though waves transfer energy, they do not move matter. Waves are a disturbance of matter that transfers energy from one particle to a nearby particle.

TRAITS OF WAVES

The two basic categories of waves are mechanical and electromagnetic. **Mechanical waves** send energy through matter. **Electromagnetic waves** send energy through a vacuum. A transverse wave gives a good picture of the features of a wave. These features are crests, troughs, amplitude, and wavelength.

There are many important traits of waves. Frequency measures how often particles in a medium vibrate when a wave passes through the medium with a certain point (i.e., node) in mind. Usually measured in Hertz (Hz), frequency can be given in cycles per second, vibrations per second, or waves per second. One Hz is equal to one cycle per second.

Period measures how long it takes to complete a cycle. It is the opposite of frequency. While frequency can be measured in cycles per second, period can be thought of as seconds per cycle. However, period can be measured only in units of time.

Speed is how fast or how slow a wave travels. It is measured in terms of distance divided by time. Frequency is measured in terms of cycles per second. Speed can be measured in terms of meters per second.

Amplitude is the maximum amount of displacement of a particle from its rest position. In other words, this is a measure of a wave's strength. This shows the amount of energy carried by the wave. High-energy waves have greater amplitudes. Low energy waves have lesser amplitudes.

Rest position is also known as equilibrium. This is the point where there is neither positive nor negative displacement.

Crest (i.e., the peak) is the point where a wave's positive (i.e., upward) displacement from the rest position is at its maximum.

Trough (i.e., valley) is the point where a wave's negative (i.e., downward) displacement from the rest position is at its maximum.

A **wavelength** is one complete wave cycle. This can be measured from any point of a wave to a matching point on the next wave. Examples are crest to crest, trough to trough, rest position to rest position.

SOUND WAVES

Sound is a vibrating pressure disturbance that moves through a medium in the form of mechanical waves. This vibration transfers kinetic energy from a source to the surrounding particles and then those particles transfer energy to the particles surrounding them and so on in a chain reaction. Waves of sound energy spread out in all directions from the source, distributing the kinetic energy over an ever-increasing area. This is why sounds are perceived as quieter over longer distances. Sound waves are made of compressions (sections of high density) and rarefactions (sections of low density). A wavelength of sound has one compression and one rarefaction; the equivalent of a crest and a trough, respectively. Different sounds have different wavelengths.

Review Video: Sound
Visit mometrix.com/academy and enter code: 562378

The **Doppler effect** refers to the effect the relative motion of the source of the wave and the location of the observer has on waves. The Doppler effect is easily observable in sound waves. What a person hears when a train approaches or a car honking its horn passes by are examples of the Doppler effect. The pitch of the sound is different not because the *emitted frequency* has changed, but because the *received frequency* has changed. The frequency is higher (as is the pitch) as the train approaches, the same as emitted just as it passes, and lower as the train moves away. This is because the wavelength changes.

Electromagnetic Waves

Electromagnetic waves are also affected in the same way. The motion of the medium can also affect the wave. Some waves do not travel in a medium (e.g., light waves). In this case, it is the difference in velocity that decides the outcome.

The **electromagnetic spectrum** is known by frequency (f) and wavelength (λ). **Frequency** is usually measured in hertz. **Wavelength** is usually measured in meters. Now, light travels at a fairly constant speed. So, the frequency is inversely proportional to wavelength. This can be seen in the formula $f = \frac{c}{\lambda}$. In this equation, c is the speed of light (about 300 million meters per second).

Review Video: Electromagnetic Spectrum
Visit mometrix.com/academy and enter code: 771761

Frequency multiplied by wavelength equals the speed of the wave. For electromagnetic waves, this is the speed of light. There is some difference for the medium that it is traveling through. Electromagnetic waves from largest to smallest wavelength are radio waves, microwaves, infrared radiation (i.e., radiant heat), visible light, ultraviolet radiation, x-rays, and gamma rays.

The energy of electromagnetic waves is carried in packets that have a magnitude inversely proportional to the wavelength. Radio waves have a range of wavelengths from about 10^{-3} to 10^{5} meters. Their frequencies go from 10^{3} to about 10^{11} Hz.

Atoms and molecules can gain or lose energy only in specific amounts. So, they can take in and send out light at wavelengths that match with those amounts.

Light Waves

Light is the part of the electromagnetic spectrum that can be seen. The reason is that it can excite the retina of your eye. The light wave is absorbed and sent out by electrons, atoms, and molecules. These particles move from one energy level to another. Visible light also has contact with matter through moving plasma. This happens in metals. Visible light is between ultraviolet and infrared light on the spectrum. The wavelengths of visible light go from 380 nm (violet) to 760 nm (red). Different wavelengths go with different colors.

Review Video: What is Light?
Visit mometrix.com/academy and enter code: 900556

The human brain understands visible light from the Sun and other stars as color. When the entire wavelength of light reaches the retina, the brain understands the color as white. When no part of the wavelength reaches the retina, the brain understands the color as black.

The **color** of an object depends on what is taken in and what is sent out or reflected. An example is the leaves on plants. The leaves have chlorophyll molecules. In those molecules, the atoms take in almost all wavelengths of the visible light spectrum except for green. This is why a leaf looks green. Certain wavelengths of visible light can be absorbed when they have contact with matter. Wavelengths that are not absorbed can be transmitted by clear materials. Another option is that they are reflected by materials that are not clear.

When light waves make contact with an object, they are reflected, transmitted, or absorbed. Let's say that the light is **reflected** from the surface of the object. So, the angle that makes contacts with the surface will be the same as the angle on leaving the surface. If the ray of light is perpendicular to the surface, it will be reflected back in the direction from which it came.

When light passes through the object, its direction may be changed after entering the object. This is called **refraction**. When light waves are refracted (i.e., bent), an image can look deformed. The degree of the refracted light depends on the speed of the light that travels in the object.

Light that is not reflected or transmitted will be **absorbed** by the surface. So, this light will be stored as heat energy. Every time that light hits an object it will either be absorbed, reflected, refracted, or some combination of these three.

Review Video: Reflection, Transmission, and Absorption of Light
Visit mometrix.com/academy and enter code: 109410

Diffraction is the bending of waves around small objects. This includes the spreading out of waves past small openings. With narrower openings, there will be greater levels of diffraction. Larger wavelengths also increase diffraction. A diffraction grating can be created by placing a number of slits close together. This is used more often than a prism to separate light. Different wavelengths are diffracted at different angles.

The different properties of light have many uses in real life. For example, polarized sunglasses have lenses that help to reduce glare. Non-polarized sunglasses reduce the total amount of light that reaches the eyes. Polarized lenses have a chemical film of molecules that are lined up in parallel. This allows the lenses to block wavelengths of light that are intense and horizontal. So, they can be reflected from smooth, flat surfaces. The "fiber" in fiber optics is the tube or pipe that channels light. The materials in the fiber allow light to be sent over greater distances before losing the signal.

Review Video: Diffraction of Light Waves
Visit mometrix.com/academy and enter code: 785494

Motion, Force, and Work

Mechanics is the study of matter and motion. This includes topics like force, energy, and work. Examples of concepts in mechanics are vectors and scalars. Vectors are quantities with both magnitude and direction. Scalars have only magnitude. Scalar quantities include length, area, volume, mass, density, energy, work, and power. Vector quantities include displacement, velocity, acceleration, momentum, and force.

Motion is simply a change in the location of an object. This change could arise from an unbalanced net force acting on the object, or the object could simple already be moving. To understand motion, you need to understand three basic quantities: displacement, velocity, and acceleration.

Displacement

When something moves from one place to another, this is known as **displacement**. Displacement on a straight line is a very simple example of a vector quantity. If an object travels from position $x = -5$ cm to $x = 5$ cm, it has been displaced 10 cm. If it takes the same path in the opposite direction, its displacement is -10 cm. A vector that stretches from an object's starting point to its ending point is known as a displacement vector.

Review Video: Displacement in Physics
Visit mometrix.com/academy and enter code: 236197

Velocity

Two main types of velocity are average velocity and instantaneous velocity. To find the **instantaneous velocity**, the object needs a constant velocity. Another way is to have an equation for the velocity. Without a constant velocity or equation, you will need calculus to find the instantaneous velocity.

To find the **average velocity** of an object, you need to know two things. The first thing is the displacement (i.e., the distance it has covered). The second thing is the time that it took the object to cover this distance.

So, the formula for average velocity is the distance traveled divided by the time required. In other words, the average velocity is equal to the change in position divided by the change in time. Average velocity is a vector and will always point in the same direction as the displacement vector because time is a scalar and always positive.

Acceleration

Acceleration is the change in the velocity of an object. Normally, the acceleration will be a constant value. Like position and velocity, acceleration is a vector quantity. So, it will have magnitude and direction.

Review Video: Velocity and Acceleration
Visit mometrix.com/academy and enter code: 671849

Momentum

Linear momentum can be found by multiplying the mass and velocity of a particle: $P = mv$. Momentum has units of $\frac{\text{kg m}}{\text{s}}$. Like velocity, momentum is a vector quantity. So, it will always have the same direction as the velocity. Newton's second law describes momentum. The law says that the rate of change of momentum is proportional to the force exerted. Also, this is done in the direction of the force. **Impulse** is the force put on an object over a period of time.

A constant net force of 10 N is put on an object for 5 seconds. So, this gives the object an impulse of 50 N s. An impulse of 50 N s is a change in momentum of 50 $\frac{\text{kg m}}{\text{s}}$ in the direction of the force. In equation form, $Ft = \Delta mv$, where F is a constant net force. If the force is changing, it will be necessary to combine the force over time.

For example, a 2 kg block starts at rest on a frictionless surface. Then, a constant net force of 8 N is put on the block for 5 seconds. You need to know how fast the block is moving. So, we need to find the impulse that was given to it, $Ft = 40$ N s. This means that the change in momentum of the block was $40\,\frac{\text{kg m}}{\text{s}}$. The block has a mass of 2 kg. Now, this gives you an increase in velocity of $20\,\frac{\text{m}}{\text{s}}$. So, the block will be traveling at $20\,\frac{\text{m}}{\text{s}}$ after 5 seconds.

Collisions

All examples assume a frictionless surface.

Example 1

A 0.01 kg bullet travels at $400\,\frac{\text{m}}{\text{s}}$ and hits a still 10-kg block of wood. The bullet stays inside in the wood. Find the final velocity of the block and the bullet.

The bullet starts with $4\,\frac{\text{kg m}}{\text{s}}$ of momentum and the block of wood—sitting still—has no momentum, so the total momentum is $4\,\frac{\text{kg m}}{\text{s}}$. Since the combined mass of the wood and the bullet is 10.01 kg, the final velocity is about $0.4\,\frac{\text{m}}{\text{s}}$.

Example 2

Block one has a mass of 10 kg. Block two has a mass of 40 kg. The blocks are traveling toward each other. The velocity of block one is $-20\,\frac{\text{m}}{\text{s}}$. The velocity of block two is $10\,\frac{\text{m}}{\text{s}}$. If the collision was perfectly elastic, find the final velocities of each body. If it was perfectly inelastic, find the final velocity of the resulting single body.

For elastic collisions, two conditions hold: $KE_i = KE_f$ and $P_i = P_f$. Calculating the beginning conditions gives $KE_i = 4000$ J and $P_i = 200\,\frac{\text{kg m}}{\text{s}}$ total for both blocks. Place those numbers in the equation. So, you have $5v_{1f}^2 + 20v_{2f}^2 = 4000$ and $10v_{1f} + 40v_{2f} = 200$. Then, solve both equations to have your final answers: $v_{1f} = 28\,\frac{\text{m}}{\text{s}}$ and $v_{2f} = -2\,\frac{\text{m}}{\text{s}}$.

The inelastic case is much simpler. The two blocks came together to make one block. So, the final momentum, $200\,\frac{\text{kg m}}{\text{s}}$, is divided by the combined mass. This gives you a final velocity of $4\,\frac{\text{m}}{\text{s}}$.

Newton's Laws

First Law: An object at rest or in motion will stay at rest or in motion. This will continue until an outside force acts on the object. When a body stays in its present state of motion, the object is in a state known as inertia.

Review Video: Newton's First Law of Motion
Visit mometrix.com/academy and enter code: 590367

Second Law: An object's acceleration depends on two things. One is the net force that acts on the object. The other is the mass of the object. This can be seen with the formula: $F = ma$. F is the net force acting on a body, m is the mass of the body, and a is its acceleration. Note that the mass is always a positive quantity. So, the acceleration is always in the same direction as the force.

Review Video: Newton's Second Law of Motion
Visit mometrix.com/academy and enter code: 737975

Third Law: This law says that for every action, there is an equal and opposite reaction. An example is a hammer that strikes a nail. In this event, the nail hits the hammer just as hard as the hammer hits the nail. For two objects A and B you can show the contact between them with the equation $F_{AB} = -F_{BA}$. In the equation, the order of the subscripts shows which object is applying the force.

At first glance, you may think that this law does not allow any movement. Every force is being countered with an equal and opposite force. However, these equal and opposite forces are acting on different objects with different masses. So, they will not cancel out each other.

Review Video: Newton's Third Law of Motion
Visit mometrix.com/academy and enter code: 838401

Gravitational Force

Gravitational force is a universal force. This causes every object to apply a force on every other object. The **gravitational force** between two objects can be seen with the formula, $F = \frac{Gm_1m_2}{r^2}$. In this example, $m_1$and m_2 are the masses of two objects, r is the distance between them, and G is the gravitational constant, $G = 6.672 \times 10^{-11}\frac{\text{N m}^2}{\text{kg}^2}$.

For this force to have an effect that can be noticed, one or both of the objects must be extremely large. So, the equation is used only in problems that deal with objects in space. Problems that deal with objects on Earth are affected by Earth's gravitational pull. So, the force of gravity is calculated as $F = mg$. In this formula, g is $9.81\frac{\text{m}}{\text{s}^2}$ toward the ground.

Work

Work is the amount of energy that comes from finishing a set goal. A basic equation for mechanical work (W) is $W = Fd$. In the equation, F is the force put on the object, and d is the displacement of the object. This equation needs the force to be applied in the same direction as the displacement. If force and displacement have the same direction, then work is positive. If they are in opposite directions, then work is negative. If they are perpendicular, the work done is zero.

An example is a man who pushes a block horizontally across a surface. He uses a constant force of 10 N for a distance of 20 m. So, the work done by the man is 200 N m or 200 J.

Another example is that the block is sliding, and the man tries to slow it down by pushing against it. So, his work done is -200 J. The reason is that he is pushing in the opposite direction of the block.

Now, let's say that the man pushes down on the block while it slides. In this example, his work done is zero. The reason is that his force vector is perpendicular to the displacement vector of the block.

Review Video: Work
Visit mometrix.com/academy and enter code: 681834

Machines

Simple machines are the inclined plane, lever, wheel and axle, and pulley. These simple machines have no source of energy inside them. More complex or compound machines can be made from simple machines. Simple machines give a force that is known as a mechanical advantage. This advantage makes it easier to finish a task.

SIMPLE MACHINES

Inclined plane: helps a force that is less than the object's weight to push an object to a greater height.

Lever: helps to multiply a force.

Wheel and axle: allow for movement with less resistance.

Single or double pulley: allow for easier direction of force.

Wedge: turns a small force that is working over a greater distance into a larger force.

Screw: this is an inclined plane that is wrapped around a shaft.

A certain amount of work is needed to move an object. The amount cannot be reduced. However, you can change the way the work is done. So, a mechanical advantage can be gained. A certain amount of work can be done to raise an object to a given height. By getting to the given height at an angle, the effort needed is reduced. However, the distance that is needed to reach a given height is increased. An example of this is walking up a hill.

A lever has a bar (i.e., plank) and a pivot point (i.e., fulcrum). Work is done with the bar. This bar moves at the pivot point to change the direction of the force. There are three types of levers: first, second, and third class. Examples of a first-class lever are balances, see-saws, and nail removers.

In a second-class lever, the fulcrum is placed at one end of the bar. So, the work is done at the other end. The weight or load to be moved is in between. When the weight is closer to the fulcrum, then the weight is easier to move. Force can be increased, but the distance that it is moved is decreased. Examples are pry bars, bottle openers, nutcrackers, and wheelbarrows.

In a third-class lever, the fulcrum is at one end. So, the positions of the weight and the location where the work is done are reversed. Examples are fishing rods, hammers, and tweezers.

The center of a wheel and axle can be compared to a fulcrum on a rotating lever. As it turns, the wheel moves a greater distance than the axle but with less force. However, this type of simple machine can be used to apply a greater force. An example is a person who can turn the handles of a winch. They can apply a greater force at the turning axle to move an object.

A clear example of the wheel and axle is the wheels of a car. Other examples are steering wheels, wrenches, faucets, waterwheels, windmills, gears, and belts. The four basic types of gears are spur, rack and pinion, bevel, and worm gears. Gears work together to change a force. The larger gear turns slower than the smaller. However, this larger gear applies a greater force. Gears at angles can be used to change the direction of forces.

A single pulley has a rope or line that is placed around a wheel. This allows force to go in a downward motion to lift an object. The force that is needed is not decreased. Instead, the force just changes its direction. The load is moved the same distance as the rope pulling it.

A combination pulley (e.g., a double pulley) moves the weight half the distance of the rope. In this way, the work effort is doubled. Pulleys are never 100% efficient because of friction. Examples of pulleys are cranes, chain hoists, block and tackles, and elevators.

Review Video: Simple Machines
Visit mometrix.com/academy and enter code: 950789

Common Energy Measurements

A **calorie** is the amount of energy that it takes to raise the temperature of a gram of water by one degree Celsius. One calorie is equal to 4.184 joules. Similarly, a kilocalorie is equal to the amount of energy that it takes to raise the temperature of a kilogram of water by one degree Celsius and is therefore equal to 4,184 joules or 4.184 kilojoules. BTU, British thermal unit, is the amount of energy that it takes to raise the temperature of a pound of water by one-degree Fahrenheit. A BTU is equal to 252 calories or 1.054 kilojoules.

A **calorimeter** is a measurement device with a thermometer and an insulated container used to determine thermodynamic properties of chemical or physical processes. This is done using specific equations that combine the change in temperature with known properties of the calorimeter.

Review Video: What is a Calorimeter Used For?
Visit mometrix.com/academy and enter code: 703935

Enthalpy is a measure of heat content in a system. In most cases, it is assumed that the system is closed, and the pressure is constant. The symbol H stands for enthalpy. The heat of a reaction is the difference between the heat stored in the reactants and in the products. This is shown by the symbol ΔH. In this symbol, the triangle means "change in."

Human Body and Health

Organ Systems

The 11 major organ systems are: skeletal, muscular, nervous, digestive, respiratory, circulatory, skin, excretory, immune, endocrine, and reproductive.

Skeletal: This system is about the bones and joints. The human body has an endoskeleton. This means that bones are inside the body. The purpose of the skeleton is to give a structure for the muscles and organs to connect and to protect the organs. Examples are the skull and the ribs. The skull protects the brain. The ribs protect the organs from impact.

The skeletal system is connected to the muscular system. These systems work together to help the body move. The skeletal system is connected with the circulatory system as well. The marrow inside the bones helps to make both white and red blood cells.

Review Video: Skeletal System
Visit mometrix.com/academy and enter code: 256447

Muscular: This system is about the muscles. The muscular system helps the body to move and to respond to surroundings. Skeletal muscle is strong, quick, and able to contract when you think about the action. Smooth muscle is weak, slow, and usually contracts on its own. Examples in humans are blood vessels, bladder, uterus, hair follicles, and parts of the eye. Cardiac (i.e., heart) muscle is strong, quick, and always contracts on its own.

Review Video: Muscular System
Visit mometrix.com/academy and enter code: 967216

Nervous: This system is about the brain, spinal cord, and nerves. The nervous system is a signaling system. These signals help with communication among systems, responses to stimuli, and interaction inside an environment. Thoughts, memories, and senses happen in the nervous system. This system controls involuntary muscles and functions. Some examples are breathing and heart beats.

Review Video: The Nervous System
Visit mometrix.com/academy and enter code: 708428

Digestive: This system is about the mouth, pharynx, esophagus, stomach, intestines, rectum, anal canal, teeth, salivary glands, tongue, liver, gallbladder, pancreas, and appendix. Those parts help to change food into a different form. The reason is that the body needs to process food for energy and nutrients. Eventually, food is taken out of the body as waste.

Digestive actions can be mechanical. Examples are chewing food and mixing it in the stomach. Also, they can be chemical. Examples are producing hydrochloric acid to kill bacteria and converting protein to amino acids. Overall, the digestive system changes large food particles into molecules so the body can use them. The small intestine moves the molecules to the circulatory system. The large intestine absorbs nutrients. Then the unused parts of food are removed from the body.

Review Video: Gastrointestinal System
Visit mometrix.com/academy and enter code: 378740

Respiratory: This system is about the nose, pharynx, larynx, trachea, bronchi, and lungs. The respiratory system trades gases with the environment. The purpose of the respiratory system is to bring oxygen into the body and remove carbon dioxide.

The respiratory system can take in viruses, bacteria, and dangerous chemicals. So, it is open to toxins and diseases. An example is pneumonia which causes the lungs to fill with fluid until they cannot take in enough oxygen to help the body. Emphysema can be caused by smoking tobacco. This disease can destroy the tissues in the lungs. Once the tissues are destroyed, they cannot come back.

The respiratory system works with the digestive system. The mouth and pharynx are used to swallow food and to breathe. The respiratory system also works with the circulatory system. The blood vessels that pass through the lungs are given fresh oxygen. Then, this oxygen is carried by the circulatory system throughout the body.

Review Video: Respiratory System
Visit mometrix.com/academy and enter code: 783075

Circulatory: This system is about the heart, the blood vessels, and the blood. This system moves the blood throughout the body. So, this gives nutrients and other important materials to the body cells. Also, some waste products (e.g., carbon dioxide and ammonia) are removed with this system. Arteries bring blood away from the heart. Veins bring blood back to the heart. Inside the body tissues, tiny capillaries spread out blood to the different body cells.

The heart takes blood that has oxygen from the lungs. Then this blood is spread out through the body. When blood comes back and carries carbon dioxide, the heart sends it to the lungs to be removed. Some organs are not thought of as working with this system. Examples are the kidneys and the spleen. These systems help to remove some waste from the blood.

Review Video: Cardiovascular System
Visit mometrix.com/academy and enter code: 376581

Skin (i.e., integumentary): This system is about the skin, hair, nails, sense receptors, sweat glands, and oil glands. This system helps to protect the body against disease, helps to maintain body temperature with perspiration, and produces chemicals and hormones. Also, this system gives a place for nerves from the nervous system and parts of the circulation system to travel through.

Skin has three layers: epidermis, dermis, and subcutaneous. The epidermis is the thin, outermost, waterproof layer. The dermis has the sweat glands, oil glands, and hair follicles. The subcutaneous layer has connective tissue. Also, this layer has adipose (i.e., fat) tissue, nerves, arteries, and veins.

Review Video: Integumentary System
Visit mometrix.com/academy and enter code: 655980

Excretory: This system is about the kidneys, ureters, bladder, and urethra. The excretory system helps to keep the right amount of fluids in the body. Wastes from the blood and extra water are removed in urine. The system also helps to remove solid waste.

Review Video: Urinary System
Visit mometrix.com/academy and enter code: 601053

Immune: This system is about the lymphatic system, lymph nodes, lymph vessels, thymus, and spleen. The body uses many weapons to try to defeat infections. The skin helps to hold off most things that would cause infection. Many things made by the body (e.g., mucus, saliva, and tears) also fight against infection. Now, these parts cannot stop all infections. So, this is the need for the immune system. The spleen is where antibodies are made. The thymus gland strengthens white blood cells that will find and work to defeat infections. The lymph nodes filter bacteria and other pathogens.

Review Video: Immune System
Visit mometrix.com/academy and enter code: 622899

Endocrine: This system is about the pituitary gland, pineal gland, hypothalamus, thyroid gland, parathyroid glands, thymus, adrenal glands, pancreas, ovaries, and testes. The endocrine system controls systems and processes by sending hormones into the blood system. Endocrine glands send hormones straight into the blood stream without the use of ducts. Adrenal glands are located above each kidney. The four parathyroid glands at the rear of the thyroid send out parathyroid hormone.

Review Video: Endocrine System
Visit mometrix.com/academy and enter code: 678939

Reproductive: In the male, this system has the testes, vas deferens, urethra, prostate, penis, and scrotum. In the female, this system has the ovaries, fallopian tubes (i.e., oviduct and uterine tubes), cervix, uterus, vagina, vulva, and mammary glands.

Sexual reproduction helps with genetic diversity. The reason is that gametes from each parent give half of their DNA to the zygote offspring. This system gives a way to move the male gametes to the female. Also, this system allows for the growth of the embryo. Hormones in this system are testosterone, interstitial cell stimulating hormone (ICSH), luteinizing hormone (LH), follicle stimulating hormone (FSH), and estrogen. Estrogens sent out from the ovaries are estradiol, estrone, and estriol. They help with growth. Progesterone helps to prepare the endometrium for pregnancy.

HOMEOSTASIS AND FEEDBACK LOOPS

Homeostasis is when an organism, cell, or body makes changes to stay balanced. A human body can maintain homeostasis with the release of hormones. Some hormones work in pairs. When a condition reaches an upper limit, a hormone is released to correct the condition. When a condition reaches the lower limit, another hormone is released. Hormones that work in this way are known as antagonistic. Insulin and glucagon are a pair of antagonistic hormones that help to manage the level of glucagon in the blood. Positive feedback loops can unbalance systems by increasing changes. A negative feedback loop acts to make a system more stable by handling changes.

HUMAN NUTRITION

Energy from food gives the body the necessary fuel to work. Food energy is measured in the thousands of calories (i.e., kilocalories). The number of calories that you have (i.e., caloric intake) needs to be balanced with how much you work or exercise (i.e., caloric output). This will help you to have good health and an ideal weight. There are many ideas on what should be an ideal weight. It is accepted that serious disorders can happen when your weight is at one of the extremes of a weight range.

The amount of work or exercise is different for everyone. These differences are age, activity, genetic structure, metabolism, gender, and social and emotional environment. For most people, caloric intake and output can balance over long periods of time. Weight can stay constant in these settings. **Obesity** is high levels of fat in the body's adipose tissues. This comes from not having a balance in caloric intake and output.

NUTRITIONAL REQUIREMENTS

Carbohydrates are an important source of energy. The reason is that they can be easily changed to glucose.

Fats (i.e., oils or lipids) are usually not very water soluble. Vitamins A, D, E, and K are fat soluble. Fats are needed to help process these vitamins. They can also store energy. Fats have the highest calorie value per gram (9,000 calories).

Dietary fiber helps the excretory system. In humans, fiber can help manage blood sugar levels, reduce heart disease, help food pass through the digestive system, and add bulk.

Proteins are made of amino acids. Proteins are broken down in the body into amino acids. Then, these are used for protein biosynthesis or fuel.

Vitamins are compounds that are not made by the body. They come from what we eat and drink. Water is needed to prevent dehydration. The reason is that water is lost through the excretory system and perspiration.

VITAMINS

Humans need dietary vitamins. These can be known as water soluble or fat soluble. Vitamins A, D, E, and K are fat soluble. Vitamins C and B are water soluble. Vitamin A can be found in milk, eggs, liver, and some vegetables and fruits. It helps with the immune system, cell growth, and eyes.

Vitamin C is in berries, peppers, and citrus fruits. It helps with bringing cells together. It also helps with healthy bones, teeth, and gums. Better brain performance and absorbing some minerals are benefits from this vitamin.

Other vitamins are: vitamin D which strengthens bones; B_{12} which is important for red blood cell and nerve function; and B_1 (thiamine), which is needed to change carbohydrates. It is also important for the heart, muscle, and nervous system.

MINERALS

Dietary minerals are important for humans. These minerals are:

- Potassium: helps with ATP synthesis. This can be found in beans, bananas, and potatoes.
- Chloride: helps to make hydrochloric acid in the stomach. This can be found in salt.
- Sodium: helps to manage levels of water in the body and helps to digest food. This can be found in many processed foods. However, a healthy diet without processed foods gives the needed amount of sodium.
- Calcium: helps the muscles, heart, digestive system, and bones. This can be found in dairy, nuts, and green leafy vegetables.
- Phosphorus: helps with bone growth and building cells. This can be found in meat, dairy, nuts, and eggs.
- Magnesium: helps with ATP synthesis. This can be found in nuts and soy beans.
- Zinc: helps enzymes to work correctly and helps to strengthen the immune system. This can be found in beef, eggs, oysters, and whole grains.
- Iron: Used by proteins and enzymes. This can be found in green leafy vegetables, fish, eggs, beans, whole and enriched grains, and red meat.
- Manganese: helps with bone growth and managing blood sugar. This can be found in whole grains, nuts, and green leafy vegetables.
- Selenium: helps to strengthen immune system. Also, this can lower the chance of some cancers. This can be found in nuts and seafood.
- Copper: helps to make red blood cells and prevent defects in bones. This can be found in sesame seeds, cashews, whole grains, and leafy greens.
- Iodine: the thyroid gland uses iodine to make hormones that will manage the making of blood cells. Also, these hormones will manage the workings of nerves and muscles. This can be found in iodized salt, dairy, and seafood.
- Molybdenum: acts as a catalyst for enzymes and helps to breakdown some amino acids in the body. This can be found in beans, peas, leafy greens, and cereals.

DISEASES

Communicable diseases are caused by microorganisms. Examples of communicable diseases are measles, smallpox, influenza, and scarlet fever. They can be moved from one infected person or animal to an uninfected person or animal. Some diseases are passed on by direct contact with an infected individual. However, many can be spread by being close to an infected person or animal. Airborne bacteria or viruses are responsible for many diseases. Some communicable diseases need certain settings to move. An example is tetanus which is spread by infected soil or dirt. Any disease that cannot be spread from one person or animal to another is non-communicable.

Infectious diseases are caused by a virus, bacterium, or parasite. Infectious diseases are different from non-infectious diseases. The difference is that they come from biological causes, not physical (e.g., burns) or chemical causes (e.g., poisoning). An infectious disease will always have an agent. An agent is something that has the disease and spreads it to others. Also, an infectious disease will always have a vector. A vector is a way of moving the disease. An example can be malaria. A mosquito that carries the disease can put it into a bloodstream. The vector of an infectious disease does not need to be biological. For example, many diseases are moved through water.

Bacteria

Bacteria are simple, one-celled organisms. They are the most common microorganism and pathogen. Most bacteria do not cause disease. In fact, many bacteria are important to the human body. Bacteria can harm the body when they release enzymes that digest other body cells. They can also cause harm when they make toxins.

Bacteria are different from the normal body cell. So, they can usually be treated with antibiotics. However, not just any antibiotic can be used to treat every bacterial infection. A doctor must know the strain of bacteria that is causing the problem. Then, a doctor can write a prescription. Over time, bacteria can fight off antibiotics. So, different antibiotics have to be made.

Viruses

The number of virus types is thought to be in the millions. Viruses are microbes that utilize host cells to reproduce. Generally, they are smaller than and not as complex as living cells. Viruses can move to other organisms in many ways. This includes by insects, by air, and through direct contact. Viruses reproduce by taking control of a host cell. Then, they force the cell to make a copy of the viral DNA instead of its own. Viruses do not have nuclei. Also, they do not have membrane-bound organelles, ribosomes, and cytoplasm.

All viruses have a head. The head of a virus is also known as a protein capsid. This has genetic material in the form of DNA, RNA, or enzymes. Some have a tail that is made of protein. The tail is used to attach to a host cell and enter it. This is one way for viruses to bring their genetic material to the host.

Review Video: Viruses
Visit mometrix.com/academy and enter code: 984455

Disease Prevention

Immunizations

A **vaccination** is a shot that brings a small amount of an antigen into the body. This stirs up the immune system to learn how to fight that antigen. There is much evidence that shows how the use of immunizations can prevent life-threatening diseases. However, many Americans do not get the basic immunizations. Today, the American Academy of Pediatrics recommends that every child be immunized against measles, mumps, smallpox, rubella, diphtheria, tetanus, and hepatitis B. Some vaccinations need to be repeated on a set schedule.

First-Aid

When an emergency happens, you need to act fast. So, it is a good idea to think ahead and have a plan. If you are in a public place, you may need to begin by shouting for help. You need to let everyone know that a doctor is needed. Someone should call 911. Do not try to do CPR unless you are trained. If you have a car and it is necessary, you should take the person to the closest hospital.

Also, every home needs some basic first-aid supplies. A good first-aid kit will have bandages, sterile gauze pads, scissors, adhesive tape, calamine lotion, cotton balls, thermometer, a sharp needle, and safety pins.

Functions for Life and Energy

Cellular Respiration

Cellular respiration is a set of metabolic reactions. These reactions change chemical bonds into energy that is stored in the form of ATP. Respiration has many oxidation and reduction reactions. This happens with the electron transport system inside the cell.

Oxidation is a loss of electrons. Reduction is a gain of electrons. Electrons in C-H (carbon/hydrogen) and C-C (carbon/carbon) bonds are given to oxygen atoms. Some systems in cellular respiration are glycolysis, the Krebs cycle, and the electron transport chain.

The two forms of respiration are aerobic and anaerobic. Aerobic respiration is very common. With aerobic respiration, oxygen is the final electron acceptor. In anaerobic respiration, the final electron acceptor is not oxygen. Aerobic respiration causes more ATP than anaerobic respiration.

Photosynthesis

Photosynthesis changes sunlight into energy in plant cells. This can also happen in some types of bacteria and protists. Carbon dioxide and water are changed into glucose during photosynthesis. Light is needed in this process. Cyanobacteria are thought to come from the first organisms to use photosynthesis about 3.5 billion years ago.

Photosynthesis is a form of cellular respiration. It happens in chloroplasts that use thylakoids. These thylakoids are structures in the membrane that have light reaction chemicals. Chlorophyll is a pigment that takes in light. During the process, water is used, and oxygen is released.

The equation for the chemical reaction that happens during photosynthesis:

$$6H_2O + 6CO_2 \rightarrow C_6H_{12}O_6 + 6O_2$$

During photosynthesis, six molecules of water and six molecules of carbon dioxide react. So, one molecule of sugar and six molecules of oxygen are the products.

Review Video: Photosynthesis
Visit mometrix.com/academy and enter code: 227035

Fermentation

Fermentation is an anaerobic reaction. In this event, glucose is only partly broken down. Sugars or other types of organic molecules go through oxidation. So, energy is given off in this reaction. Sometimes oxygen has a part. However, this does not always happen. Fermentation is different from respiration. A reason is that it does not use the Krebs cycle. Other reasons are that it does not use the electron transport chain, and the last electron acceptor is an organic molecule.

It uses substrate-level phosphorylation to make ATP. NAD^+ is reduced to NADH. Then, NADH reduces pyruvic acid to other end products. Fermentation can lead to more waste products. Also, this event is less efficient than aerobic respiration. Homolactic fermentation is lactic acid fermentation when sugars are converted to lactic acid only. In other words, there is one end product. In heterolactic fermentation, the sugars are converted to many products.

An example of fermentation is lactic acid fermentation. This happens when streptococcus and lactobacillus bacteria make an end product of lactic acid. The lactic acid can be broken down into propionic acid and carbon dioxide. This process is used to make Swiss cheese.

Organization of Life

Important Events for Life

Metabolism is all of the chemical reactions that happen in a living organism. These chemical changes turn nutrients to energy and macromolecules.

Macromolecules are large and complex. They have an important role in cell structure and function.

Metabolic pathways are a series of reactions where the product of one reaction is the substrate for the next. These pathways depend on enzymes that act as catalysts.

An **anabolic reaction** builds larger and more complex molecules (i.e., macromolecules) from smaller ones. The four basic organic macromolecules made by anabolic reactions are carbohydrates (i.e., polysaccharides), nucleic acids, proteins, and lipids.

Catabolic reactions are the opposite. Larger molecules are broken down into smaller, simpler molecules. Catabolic reactions give off energy. Anabolic reactions need energy. The four basic building blocks in catabolic reactions are monosaccharides (e.g., glucose), amino acids, fatty acids (e.g., glycerol), and nucleotides.

Cells in Living Organisms

There are many differences between how a plant and animal cell work. Also, how different cells work in one organism can be very different. Animal and plant cells are similar in structure because they are eukaryotic. This means that they have a nucleus. The nucleus is a round structure that controls the actions of the cell and has chromosomes.

Both types of cells have cell membranes, cytoplasm, vacuoles, and other structures. The main difference between the two cells is that plant cells have a cell wall made of cellulose. This cell wall can handle high levels of pressure within the cell.

These high levels of pressure can happen when liquid enters a plant cell. Plant cells also have chloroplasts. These are used during the event of photosynthesis. This event turns sunlight into food for plants. Usually, plant cells have one large vacuole. Animal cells can have many smaller ones. Plant cells have a regular shape. The shapes of animal cells can be different.

Water and Gas in Cells

Water molecules are important for many reasons:

- Most cells are mainly made of water
- Water is a great solvent for ionic compounds (e.g., salts)
- Water acts as a transport medium for polar solutes
- Metabolic reactions happen in solutions that have water
- Water can act as a temperature buffer for enzyme-catalyzed reactions
- Photosynthesis needs water to work
- Water molecules are used or made in oxidation and reduction reactions

Gas molecules are also important for many reasons

- Carbon dioxide is used by plants in photosynthesis which makes oxygen.
- Oxygen is used by organisms during respiration.

- Nitrogen is also used by organisms because it is a nutrient for plants. It is also used to make amino and nucleic acids after it is reduced (e.g., nitrogen fixation). This is important for cell growth and reproduction.

Gases are also used to make and break down important molecules. These molecules are proteins, nucleic acids, carbohydrates, and lipids. For example, carbohydrates are made of carbon, hydrogen, and oxygen.

CELL STRUCTURE

NUCLEAR PARTS OF A CELL

All eukaryotic cells have a **nucleus**. The nucleus is a small structure that holds the chromosomes. Also, the nucleus manages the DNA of a cell. The nucleus is the defining structure of eukaryotic cells. The nucleus is responsible for passing on genetic traits between generations. The nucleus has a nuclear envelope, nucleoplasm, a nucleolus, nuclear pores, chromatin, and ribosomes.

Review Video: Cell Structure
Visit mometrix.com/academy and enter code: 591293

Chromosomes: These are tight, threadlike rods of DNA (deoxyribonucleic acid). DNA is the genetic material that stores information about the plant or animal.

Review Video: Chromosomes
Visit mometrix.com/academy and enter code: 132083

Chromatin: This is a combination of DNA and protein that makes up chromosomes.

Nucleolus: This structure inside the nucleus is made of protein. The nucleolus is small and round. It does not have a membrane. This piece works in protein synthesis. Also, it combines and stores RNA (ribonucleic acid).

Nuclear envelope: This surrounds the structures of the nucleus. It has inner and outer membranes that are made of lipids.

Nuclear pores: These help in the trade of material between the nucleus and the cytoplasm.

Nucleoplasm: This is the liquid inside the nucleus. It is similar to cytoplasm.

OTHER PARTS OF A CELL

Ribosomes: Ribosomes help to put together proteins from amino acids. There are many in one cell. They make up about one fourth of the cell. Some cells have thousands of ribosomes. Some are free to move. Others are tied down in the rough endoplasmic reticulum.

Golgi complex (i.e., Golgi apparatus): This helps to put together materials. An example is proteins that are moved out of the cell. It is near the nucleus and has layers of membranes.

Vacuoles: These are sacs used for storage, digestion, and waste removal. There is one large vacuole in plant cells. Animal cells have small vacuoles. Sometimes animal cells have many vacuoles.

Vesicle: This is a small organelle inside a cell. It has a membrane and has many roles. One role is moving materials inside a cell.

Cytoskeleton: This has microtubules that help to shape and to support the cell.

Microtubules: These are part of the cytoskeleton and help support the cell. They are made of protein.

Cytosol: This is the liquid material in the cell. The liquid is mostly water. However, it also has some floating molecules.

Cytoplasm: This is a general term for the cytosol and the substructures (i.e., organelles) inside the plasma membrane. This is not for the parts in the nucleus.

Cell membrane (or plasma membrane): This is a barrier for the cell. It keeps cytoplasm in and keeps substances not inside the cell out of the cell. It decides what can enter and exit the cell.

Endoplasmic reticulum: There are two types of endoplasmic reticulum. One is rough that has ribosomes on the surface. The other is smooth and does not have ribosomes on the surface. It is a network of tubes that is the transport system of a cell. It is tied to the nuclear membrane. Also, it goes through the cytoplasm to the cell membrane.

Mitochondrion (plural: mitochondria): These cell structures can be different in their size and how many are in a cell. Some cells may have one mitochondrion. Other cells may have thousands. The mitochondrion has many roles. One important role is to make ATP. The mitochondrion also helps with cell growth and death. Mitochondria have their own DNA. This DNA is separate from what is in the nucleus.

Mitochondria Functions

Four functions of mitochondria are:

1. the making of cell energy
2. cell signaling: the communications that are carried out in a cell
3. cellular differentiation: this is how a cell becomes a cell with a more specialized purpose
4. cell cycle and growth regulation: the part where the cell gets ready to make copies. Then, it makes copies of itself.

There are many mitochondria in eukaryotic cells. There may be hundreds or thousands of mitochondria in one cell. Mitochondria can take part in many roles. Their main one is to supply the cell with energy. Mitochondria have an inner and outer membrane. The inner membrane encloses the matrix. This has the mitochondrial DNA (mtDNA) and ribosomes. Between the inner and outer membranes are folds. The folds are known as cristae. The chemical reactions that happen here release energy and control water levels in cells. They also recycle and make proteins and fats. Aerobic respiration is another event in the mitochondria.

Review Video: Mitochondria
Visit mometrix.com/academy and enter code: 444287

Eukaryotic and Prokaryotic Cells

Eukaryotic cells have a nucleus. Prokaryotic cells do not have a nucleus. Eukaryotic cells are more complex. Prokaryotic cells are smaller and simpler.

Eukaryotic cells have membrane-bound organelles that have many roles. So, these add to the complexity of these types of cells. Prokaryotic cells do not have membrane-bound organelles.

In prokaryotic cells, the genetic material (DNA) is not inside a membrane-bound nucleus. Instead, it comes together in the cytoplasm in a nucleoid. In eukaryotic cells, DNA is mostly inside chromosomes in the nucleus. However, there is some DNA in mitochondria and chloroplasts.

Usually, prokaryotic cells divide by binary fission and are haploid meaning they have only a single full set of chromosomes. Eukaryotic cells divide by mitosis and are diploid meaning they have two full sets of chromosomes. Prokaryotic structures have plasmids, ribosomes, cytoplasm, a cytoskeleton, granules of nutritional substances, a plasma membrane, flagella, and a few others. They are single-celled organisms. Bacteria are prokaryotic cells.

Review Video: Prokaryotic and Eukaryotic Cells
Visit mometrix.com/academy and enter code: 231438

Plant and Animal Cell Structure

Plant Cells

Cell wall: This piece is made of cellulose and has many layers. The cell wall gives plants a strong barrier that can hold fluid inside the cell. The cell wall surrounds the cell membrane.

Chloroplast: This is a special organelle that plant cells use for photosynthesis. Chloroplasts have chlorophyll which has a green color.

Plastid: This is a membrane-bound organelle. It is found in plant cells and is used to make chemical compounds and store food. It can also have pigments that are used in photosynthesis. Plastids can become structures, such as chloroplasts, chromoplasts, amyloplasts, and leucoplasts. Chromoplasts make and hold yellow and orange pigments. Amyloplasts store starch. Leucoplasts do not have pigments. However, they can change.

Plasmodesmata (singular: plasmodesma): These are channels between the cell walls of plant cells. They allow transport between cells.

Animal Cells

Centrosome: This is made of the pair of centrioles that are located at right angles to each other. They are surrounded by protein. The centrosome helps in mitosis and the cell cycle.

Centriole: These are cylinder-shaped structures close to the nucleus. They help with cellular division. Each cylinder has nine groups of three microtubules. Centrioles come in pairs.

Lysosome: This digests proteins, lipids, and carbohydrates. Also, the lysosome transports undigested substances to the cell membrane. The reason is that they need to be removed. The shape of a lysosome depends on the material being moved.

Cilia (singular: cilium): These are members on the surface of the cell. When they move, the cell can move. They can also help with fluid being moved by the cell.

Flagella: These are tail-like structures on cells. They use whip-like movements to help the cell move. They are similar to cilia. However, they are usually longer, and the cell does not have as many. Usually, a cell only has one or a few flagella.

Differences in Plant and Animal Cells

Plant cells can be much larger than animal cells. Plant cells can be from 10 to 100 micrometers. Animal cells are 10 to 30 micrometers in size. Plant cells can have much larger vacuoles that take up a large part of the cell. They also have cell walls. These walls are thick barriers of protein and sugars. Animal cells do not have cell walls.

Chloroplasts in plants absorb sunlight and change it into energy. Mitochondria make energy from food in animal cells. Plant and animal cells are eukaryotic. This means that they have a nucleus. Plant and animal cells make copies of genetic material and separate it.

Then, they divide it in half to make copies. Plant cells build a cell plate between the two new cells. Animal cells make a cleavage furrow. Then, they divide in half. Microtubules are parts of the cytoskeleton in plant and animal cells. Microtubule organizing centers (MTOCs) make microtubules in plant cells. Centrioles make microtubules in animal cells.

Review Video: Difference Between Plant and Animal Cells
Visit mometrix.com/academy and enter code: 115568

Vertebrates and Invertebrates

Invertebrates do not have a backbone, whereas vertebrates do. The great majority of animal species (an estimated 98 percent) are invertebrates, including worms, jellyfish, mollusks, slugs, insects, and spiders. They comprise 30 phyla in all. Vertebrates belong to the phylum Chordata. The vertebrate body has two cavities. The thoracic cavity holds the heart and lungs and the abdominal cavity holds the digestive organs. Animals with exoskeletons have skeletons on the outside. Examples are crabs and turtles. Animals with endoskeletons have skeletons on the inside. Examples are humans, tigers, birds, and reptiles.

Cell Theory

The basic ideas of cell theory are that all living things are made up of cells and that cells are the basic units of life. Cell theory has changed over time and can be understood in many ways. The beginnings of cell theory are credited to Matthias Schleiden and Theodor Schwann who shared the idea in the early 1800s. Early cell theory had four main statements:

1. All organisms (i.e., living things) are made of cells.
2. New cells are made from cells that already exist.
3. All cells are similar.
4. Cells are the most basic units of life.

Other ideas of classic and modern cell theory have statements like:

1. Cells give the basic units of performance and structure in living things.
2. Cells are stand-alone units and basic building blocks.
3. Energy flow happens inside cells.
4. Cells have genetic information in the form of DNA.
5. All cells are mostly made of the same chemicals.

Cell Cycle

A **cell cycle** is when a cell reproduces. This includes cell growth, the copy of genetic material, and cell division. Complex organisms with many cells use the cell cycle. The cell cycle replaces cells as they wear out. The entire cell cycle in animal cells can take 24 hours. The time needed is different for different cell types. An example is human skin cells. They are always reproducing. Other cells rarely divide.

When neurons are mature, they do not grow or divide. The two ways that cells can make more cells are through meiosis and mitosis. When cells make copies through mitosis, the "daughter cell" is an exact copy of the parent cell. When cells divide through meiosis, the daughter cells have different genetic coding than the parent cell. Meiosis only happens in special reproductive cells called gametes.

Cell Division

Cell division happens in organisms so they can grow and replace cells that are old, worn out, or damaged.

Review Video: Cellular Division: Mitosis and Meiosis
Visit mometrix.com/academy and enter code: 109813

Chromatids: During cell division, the DNA is copied. So, the chromatids are the two exact copies of chromosomes that are joined at the centromere to make an "X."

Gametes: These are cells used by organisms to reproduce sexually. Gametes in humans are haploid. This means that they have 23 chromosomes. This is half of the organism's genetic information. Other human cells have all 46 chromosomes.

Haploid/diploid: Haploid means there is one set of chromosomes. Diploid means there are two sets of chromosomes. There is one set from each parent.

Mitosis

The following are the stages of **mitosis**:

Interphase: The cell gets ready for division by making copies of its genetic and cytoplasmic material. This step can be further divided into G_1, S, and G_2.

Prophase: The chromatin thickens into chromosomes. Then, the nuclear membrane begins to break down. Pairs of centrioles move to opposite sides of the cell. Then, spindle fibers are made. The mitotic spindle is made from cytoskeleton parts. This spindle moves chromosomes inside the cell.

Metaphase: The spindle moves to the center of the cell. Then, chromosome pairs line up along the center of the spindle structure.

Anaphase: The pairs of chromosomes are called sisters. In this stage, these pairs begin to pull apart and can bend. When they are pulled apart, they are called daughter chromosomes. In the cell membrane, grooves can be seen.

Telophase: In this stage, the spindle breaks down, the nuclear membranes are made again, and the chromosomes return to chromatin. In animal cells, the membrane is divided. In plant cells, a new cell wall is made.

Cytokinesis: This is the physical splitting of the cell into two cells. Some think that this happens after telophase. Others say that it happens from anaphase through telophase.

Review Video: Mitosis
Visit mometrix.com/academy and enter code: 849894

MEIOSIS

Meiosis has the same phases as mitosis. However, these stages happen twice. Also, different events happen during some phases of meiosis than mitosis. The events that happen in the first phase of meiosis are interphase (I), prophase (I), metaphase (I), anaphase (I), telophase (I), and cytokinesis (I).

In this first phase of meiosis, chromosomes cross over and genetic material is traded. Also, tetrads (i.e., four) of four chromatids are made. The nuclear membrane dissolves. Homologous pairs of chromatids are separated. Then, they move to different poles. At this point, one cell has been divided to make two cells.

Next, each cell goes through a second cell division. The stages are prophase (II), metaphase (II), anaphase (II), telophase (II), and cytokinesis (II). This makes four daughter cells with different sets of chromosomes. The daughter cells are haploid. This means that they have half the genetic material of the parent cell.

> **Review Video: Meiosis**
> Visit mometrix.com/academy and enter code: 247334

ENZYMES

Enzymes can be divided into six classes: oxidoreductase, transferase, hydrolase, lyase, isomerase, and ligase. Most enzymes end with the suffix "-ase." Each enzyme catalyzes (i.e., starts up) a chemical reaction.

Enzymes act as catalysts by lowering the activation energy needed for a reaction. They are proteins with certain roles. An enzyme has an active site where a substrate attaches and products are made and released. Most enzymes need a non-protein coenzyme that attaches to the enzyme to make the active site.

Oxidoreductase enzymes catalyze oxidation reduction (redox) reactions. In this reaction, hydrogen and oxygen are gained or lost. Examples are cytochrome oxidase, lactate, and dehydrogenase.

Transferase enzymes catalyze the transfer of functional groups (e.g., amino or phosphate group). Examples are acetate kinase and adenine deaminase.

Hydrolase enzymes break chemical bonds by using water. Examples are lipase and sucrase.

Lyase enzymes break chemical bonds or remove groups of atoms without using water. Examples are oxalate decarboxylase and isocitrate lyase.

Isomerase enzymes catalyze the reordering of atoms in a molecule. Examples are glucose-phosphate isomerase and adenine racemase.

Ligase enzymes join two molecules by making a bond between atoms. Examples of ligases are acetyl-CoA synthetase and DNA ligase.

> **Review Video: Enzymes**
> Visit mometrix.com/academy and enter code: 656995

Organic Molecules

Nucleic Acids

Nucleic acids are macromolecules that are made of nucleotides. Hydrolysis is a reaction where water is broken down into hydrogen cations (H or H^+) and hydroxide anions (OH or OH^-). This is part of the event where nucleic acids are broken down by enzymes. This event makes shorter strings of RNA and DNA (oligonucleotides).

Oligonucleotides are broken down into smaller sugar nitrogenous units called nucleosides. These can be digested by cells since the sugar is divided from the nitrogenous base. Then, this leads to the five types of nitrogenous bases, sugars, and the preliminary substances. These pieces are part of the building of new RNA and DNA.

Macromolecular nucleic acid polymers (e.g., RNA and DNA) are made from nucleotides. Cells need energy in the form of ATP to put together proteins from amino acids and make copies of DNA.

Nitrogen fixation is used to put together nucleotides for DNA and amino acids for proteins. Nitrogen fixation uses the enzyme nitrogenase in the reduction of dinitrogen gas (N_2) to ammonia (NH_3). Nucleic acids store information and energy. They are also important catalysts. RNA catalyzes the transfer of DNA genetic information into protein coded information.

ATP is an RNA nucleotide. Nucleotides are used to make the nucleic acids. Nucleotides are made of a five-carbon sugar (e.g., ribose or deoxyribose) a nitrogenous base and one or more phosphates. Nucleotides have more than one phosphate. They can also store energy in their bonds.

Review Video: Nucleic Acids
Visit mometrix.com/academy and enter code: 503931

Lipids

Carbohydrates, proteins, and nucleic acids are groups of macromolecules that are polymers. **Lipids** are short polymers with high molecular weights. They are hydrophobic. This means that they do not bond well with water or mix well with water solutions.

Lipids can have many forms and different roles. These roles are storing energy and acting as a building block of cell membranes. Lipids are made by anabolysis.

Lipids have many C-H bonds. So, they are like hydrocarbons. A hydrocarbon is a substance that is made of only carbon and hydrogen. The major roles of lipids are energy storage and structural functions. Examples of lipids are fats, phospholipids, steroids, and waxes.

Fats are made of long chains of fatty acids. Fatty acids are chains with reduced carbon at one end and a carboxylic acid group at the other. An example is soap that has the sodium salts of free fatty acids.

Phospholipids are lipids that have a phosphate group rather than a fatty acid. **Glycerides** are another type of lipid. Examples of glycerides are fat and oil. Glycerides are made from fatty acids and glycerol (i.e., a type of alcohol).

Review Video: Lipids
Visit mometrix.com/academy and enter code: 269746

Glycolysis

In **glycolysis**, glucose is turned into pyruvate. Also, energy stored in ATP bonds is released. Glycolysis can have many series of steps. Different agents are made that are used in other events. Then, the pyruvic acid made by glycolysis can be used for respiration by the Krebs cycle or in fermentation.

Review Video: Glycolysis
Visit mometrix.com/academy and enter code: 466815

Glycolysis happens in aerobic and anaerobic organisms. Oxidation of molecules makes reduced coenzymes (e.g., NADH). The coenzymes move hydrogens to the electron transport chain. Then, the proton is moved through the cell membrane. So, the electron is moved down the chain by proteins.

At the end of the chain, water is made when the final acceptor gives up two electrons that combine with oxygen. The protons are put back into the cell or organelle by the ATP synthase enzyme. This enzyme uses energy to add a phosphate to ADP to make ATP. The proton motive force is made by the protons being moved across the membrane.

Monosaccharides, Disaccharides, Starches

The simple sugars can be grouped into monosaccharides (e.g., glucose, fructose, and sucrose) and disaccharides. Both are types of carbohydrates. Monosaccharides have one monomer of sugar and disaccharides have two.

Monosaccharides (CH_2O) have one carbon for every water molecule. Aldose and ketose are monosaccharides with a carbonyl (i.e., C=O, double bonded oxygen to carbon) functional group. There is a difference between aldose and ketose. The difference is that the carbonyl group in aldose is connected at an end carbon. The carbonyl group in ketose is connected at a middle carbon. Glucose is a monosaccharide that has six carbons. This makes it a hexose and an aldose.

A **disaccharide** is made from two monosaccharides with a glycosidic link. Examples are:

- two glucoses making a maltose
- a glucose and a galactose making a lactose
- a glucose and a fructose making a sucrose

A **starch** is a polysaccharide made only of glucose monomers. Examples are amylose, amylopectin, and glycogen.

Important Vocabulary

Organelle: A general term for an organ or smaller structure inside a cell. Membrane-bound organelles are in eukaryotic cells.

RNA: Ribonucleic acid is a type of molecule that has a long chain (i.e., polymer) of nucleotide units.

Polymer: This is a compound of large molecules made by repeating monomers.

Monomer: A monomer is a small molecule. It is a single compound that makes chemical bonds with other monomers to make a polymer.

Nucleotides: These are molecules that combine to make DNA and RNA.

Nucleoid: This is the nucleus-like mass of DNA that has the chromatin in a prokaryotic cell.

Gene expression: This is the use of information in a gene. Usually, this is done in the processes of transcription and translation and ends in a protein product.

Transcription: This is the putting together of RNA. The information for this event comes from DNA.

Translation: This is the decoding of mRNA (i.e., messenger RNA) that is used in the building of protein. It happens after transcription.

Cellular differentiation: This is the event where a less specialized cell becomes a more specialized cell.

GENETICS

DNA

Chromosomes are made of genes. A gene is a single unit of genetic information. Genes are made of deoxyribonucleic acid. **DNA** is a nucleic acid in the cell nucleus. DNA is also in the mitochondria. DNA makes copies of itself to pass on genetic information. The DNA in almost all cells is the same. It is also part of the biosynthesis of proteins.

Review Video: What is DNA? Visit mometrix.com/academy and enter code: 639552

The model of DNA is known as a double helix. A helix is a curve. So, a double helix is two congruent curves that are connected by horizontal pieces. The model can be compared to a spiral staircase.

The British scientist Rosalind Elsie Franklin is the one who took the x-ray diffraction image in 1952. This image was used by Francis Crick and James Watson to put together the double-helix model of DNA. With this information, they were able to think about its important role in carrying and moving genetic information.

DNA STRUCTURE

DNA has the shape of a **double helix**. This shape looks like a twisted ladder. It is made of nucleotides. Nucleotides have a five-carbon sugar (i.e., pentose), a phosphate group, and a nitrogenous base. Two bases pair up to make the bars of the ladder. The "side rails" or backbone is made of the covalently bonded sugar and phosphate. The bases are connected to each other with hydrogen bonds. These bonds can be easily separated for replication to happen.

There are four types of nitrogenous bases: adenine (A), guanine (G), cytosine (C), and thymine (T). Adenine (A) pairs with thymine (T). Cytosine (C) pairs with guanine (G). There are about 3 billion bases in human DNA. The bases are almost the same in everybody. However, their order is different. The order of these bases makes diversity in people.

DNA REPLICATION

Pairs of chromosomes are made of DNA. This DNA is tightly wound to save space. When replication starts, the DNA unwinds. The steps in DNA replication are controlled by enzymes. The enzyme helicase starts the breaking of hydrogen bonds between the bases. This is done to split the two strands.

The splitting starts at the A-T bases. The reason is that there are only two hydrogen bonds. The cytosine-guanine base pair has three bonds. The term "origin of replication" is used to point to where the splitting starts. The part of the DNA that is unwound to be replicated is called the replication fork. Each strand of DNA is transcribed by an mRNA. The mRNA copies the DNA onto itself base by base in a similar way. The exception is that uracil replaces thymine.

Types of DNA Replication

Semiconservative: This type of DNA replication is where the two replicated copies of DNA have one strand of the original parent DNA. This is half of the original genetic material.

Antiparallel replication: In this DNA replication, the nucleotides (A, C, G, T, and U) on leading and lagging strands run in opposite directions. RNA synthesis is said to happen in a $5' \rightarrow 3'$ (five prime to three prime) direction. This means that the phosphate group of the nucleotide that is being added to the chain (5′) is attached to the end of the chain at the end of a hydroxyl group (3′).

Base pairing: This explains how RNA transcribes DNA in a reverse way. C on DNA is put in as a G on RNA. Also, A on DNA becomes U on RNA.

Functions of Proteins in DNA Replication

Many proteins help in the replication of DNA. Each protein has a specific role. Helicase is a protein that helps the unwinding of DNA. Single strand binding (SSB) proteins attach to each strand to prevent the DNA strands from joining back together.

After DNA is unwound, there are leading and lagging strands. The leading strand is synthesized continuously. The lagging strand is put together in Okazaki fragments. Primase is an RNA polymerase (i.e., catalyzing enzyme). It acts as a starting point for replication by making short strands (i.e., primers) of RNA.

The DNA clamp (i.e., sliding clamp) helps to keep DNA polymerase from coming apart from the strand. DNA polymerase helps to make the DNA strand by linking nucleotides. As the event continues, RNase H removes the primers. Then, DNA ligase links the existing shorter strands into a longer strand.

Types of RNA

RNA is a helper to DNA and has many other roles. Types of RNA are **ribosomal** RNA (rRNA), **transfer** RNA (tRNA), and **messenger** RNA (mRNA). Viruses can use RNA to carry their genetic material to DNA. Many scientists think that ribosomal RNA has not changed much over time. So, it can be used to study relationships in organisms. Messenger RNA carries a copy of a strand of DNA. Also, it moves this copy from the nucleus to the cytoplasm.

Transcription is the process by which DNA is copied onto RNA. DNA unwinds itself and then serves as the blueprint for enzymes to put the RNA together.

Translation is when ribosomes use transcribed RNA to put together the needed protein. Transfer RNA is a molecule that helps in the translation process. It is in the cytoplasm. Ribosomal RNA is in the ribosomes.

Differences in RNA and DNA

RNA and DNA are different in structure and role. RNA has a different sugar than DNA. This is a ribose sugar, not a deoxyribose sugar. The RNA nitrogenous bases are adenine (A), guanine (G), cytosine (C), and uracil (U). Uracil is found only in RNA. Thymine is found only in DNA. RNA has a single strand. DNA has two strands. If straightened out from its spiral shape, DNA has two side rails.

Review Video: DNA vs. RNA
Visit mometrix.com/academy and enter code: 184871

RNA only has one "backbone," or strand of sugar and phosphate group parts. RNA uses the fully hydroxylated sugar pentose which has extra oxygen compared to deoxyribose. RNA helps in the roles that are carried out by DNA. RNA helps with gene expression, replication, and transportation.

Mendelian Genetics

Mendel's Laws

Mendel's laws are the law of segregation (the first law), the law of independent assortment (the second law), and the law of dominance (the third law). The **law of segregation** states that there are two **alleles** and that half of the total number of alleles are contributed by each parent organism. The **law of independent assortment** states that traits are passed on randomly and are not influenced by other traits. The exception to this is linked traits. A **Punnett square** can illustrate how alleles combine from the contributing genes to form various **phenotypes**. One set of a parent's genes are put in columns, while the genes from the other parent are placed in rows. The allele combinations are shown in each cell. The **law of dominance** states that when two different alleles are present in a pair, the **dominant** one is expressed. A Punnett square can be used to predict the outcome of crosses.

Review Video: What is a Punnett Square?
Visit mometrix.com/academy and enter code: 853855

Gene, Genotype, Phenotype, and Allele

A **gene** is a part of DNA. It shows how traits are expressed and passed on for an organism. A gene is part of the genetic code. Together, all genes make the **genotype** of an individual. The genotype has genes that may not be expressed (e.g., recessive genes).

The **phenotype** is what we can see about a person (e.g., eye color or height). It is decided by the basic genetic information and how genes have been affected by their environment. An allele is a variation of a gene. This is also known as a trait. An allele decides what traits will be for a person (e.g., eye color or height). The genetic information for eye color is a gene. Locus (plural: loci) is the location of a gene or allele.

Review Video: Genotype vs Phenotype
Visit mometrix.com/academy and enter code: 922853

Dominant and Recessive Genes

Gene traits come in pairs with an upper-case letter for the dominant trait (A) and a lower-case letter for the recessive trait (a). There is one gene on each chromosome. Each parent gives a chromosome to the organism. A **dominant** trait only needs one gene of a gene pair to be expressed in a phenotype. A **recessive** trait needs both genes to be manifested.

For example, the mother's genotype is Dd. The father's is dd. So, the possible combinations are Dd and dd. The dominant trait will be seen if the genotype is DD or Dd. The recessive trait will be seen if the genotype is dd. The gene pairs DD and dd are homozygous pairs. Dd is heterozygous.

Monohybrid and Hybrid Crosses

Genetic crosses are the possible combinations of alleles. They can be shown with Punnett squares. A monohybrid cross is a cross that has only one trait. Usually, the ratio is 3:1 (DD, Dd, Dd, dd). This is the ratio of dominant genes being seen to recessive genes being seen. This ratio happens when both parents have a pair of dominant and recessive genes.

Let's say that one parent has a pair of dominant genes (DD). The other has a pair of recessive (dd) genes. Now, the recessive trait cannot be expressed in the next generation. The reason is that the crosses all have the Dd genotype.

A dihybrid cross is one that has more than one trait. This means that more combinations are possible. The ratio of genotypes for a dihybrid cross is 9:3:3:1 when the traits are not linked. The ratio for incomplete dominance is 1:3:1. This goes with dominant, mixed, and recessive phenotypes.

Co-Dominance and Incomplete Dominance

Co-dominance is the expression of both alleles so that both traits are shown. For example, cows can have hair colors of red, white, or red and white. For the red and white color, both traits are fully expressed. Incomplete dominance is when the dominant and recessive genes are expressed.

This causes a phenotype that is a mixture of the two. A good example is snapdragons. They can be red, white, or pink. The dominant red gene (RR) causes a red flower because of large amounts of red pigment. White (rr) happens because both genes call for no pigment. Pink (Rr) happens because one gene is for red and one is for no pigment. In other words, the colors mix to make pink flowers. A cross of pink flowers (Rr) can cause red (RR), white (rr), or pink (Rr) flowers.

Crossing Over, Pedigree Analysis, and Probability Analysis

Crossing over: The trading of genetic material between homologous chromosomes. This leads to different combinations of genes showing up in a phenotype. This is part of gene recombination, which is when DNA breaks down and is put back together.

Pedigree analysis: This is when a trait in an organism is separated. Then, someone works to find out how it is shown. Often, pedigree charts are used for this type of analysis. A family pedigree shows how a trait can be seen over generations.

Probability analysis: This calculates the chances of a trait or combination of traits being expressed in an organism.

Mutations

Gene disorders come from DNA mutations. DNA mutations can cause some unwanted gene disorders. Also, they can create more differences in the gene pool. This diversity can lead to better chances of a species not becoming extinct.

Mutations can be neutral, beneficial, or harmful. Mutations can be hereditary. This means that they are passed from parent to child. Polymorphism refers to the differences in humans (e.g., eye and hair color) that may have a gene mutation in the past. However, they are now part of the normal differences of the species.

Mutations can be *de novo*. This means that they happen either only in sex cells or shortly after fertilization. They can also be acquired (or somatic). This happens from DNA changes because of environmental factors or replication errors. Mosaicism is when a mutation happens in a cell during an early embryonic stage. The result is that some cells will have the mutation and some will not.

Review Video: Types of Gene Mutation
Visit mometrix.com/academy and enter code: 955485

DNA Level Mutation

A **DNA mutation** happens when the normal gene sequence is changed. Mutations can happen when DNA is damaged by environmental factors (e.g., chemicals, radiation, or ultraviolet rays from the sun). It can also happen when errors are made in DNA replication. The bonds between oxygen and phosphate groups can be disconnected. If this happens, the phosphate-sugar side rail of DNA can be damaged. Translocation happens when the broken bonds try to bond with other DNA. This repair can cause a mutation. The nucleotide itself can be changed.

An example is a C that may look like a T. During replication, that damaged C is replicated as a T and paired with a G., which is the wrong base pairing. This happens about once for every 100,000,000 bases. When the DNA polymerase replicates a base, this type of error could lead to a mutation, so a repair protein reviews the code to identify mistakes that may be fixed.

Translocation

Translocation is a genetic mutation where one piece of a chromosome is transferred to another chromosome. Burkitt's lymphoma, chronic myelogenous leukemia, and Down syndrome are examples. Trisomy 21 (Down syndrome) happens when a copy of chromosome 21 connects to chromosome 14. Most Down syndrome cases happen because a pair of chromosomes (the 21st) does not split in meiosis. Both divided cells will have a number of chromosomes that is not normal. One will have 22. The other will have 24. When this egg is fertilized, it will have three copies of chromosome 21 instead of two.

Down syndrome can also be caused by translocation between the 14th and 21st chromosomes. In this event, genetic material is traded. There are 200 to 250 genes on the 21st chromosome. The overexpression of the gene causes the following Down syndrome traits: premature aging, decreased immune system function, heart defects, skeletal abnormalities, disruption of DNA synthesis and repair, intellectual disabilities, and cataracts.

Random Mutations, Nonrandom Mating, and Gene Migration

Random mutations: These are genetic changes from DNA errors or environmental factors (e.g., chemicals and radiation). Mutations can be helpful or harmful.

Nonrandom mating: The probability of two organisms mating in a population is not the same for all pairs. Nonrandom mating can come from isolation, small populations, and other factors. Nonrandom mating can cause inbreeding which is mating with a relative. Nonrandom mating can lead to a decline in physical fitness as seen in a phenotype. It can also lead to lower allele frequency and occurrence.

Gene migration (i.e., gene flow): This is the movement of alleles to another population. It can happen with immigration. This is when members of a species move into an area. Or, it can happen with emigration, when individuals of a species move out of an area.

Linkage

Linkage is about the traits that are on the same chromosome. This leads to two different traits that come together more often than not. Linkage is the exception to independent assortment. Sex-linked traits are found on a sex chromosome. Autosomal is the non-sex chromosomes.

In humans, there are 22 autosomal pairs of chromosomes and a pair of sex chromosomes. Depending on the sex, pairs are XX (female) or XY (male). So, alleles on the Y chromosome are only seen in males. Males can only pass on sex-linked traits on the X chromosome to their daughters.

Hemizygous means that there is only one copy of a gene. Color blindness happens more in males than females. The reason is that it is a sex-linked trait on the X chromosome. This trait is recessive. So, females have a better chance of expressing the dominant property of non-color blindness.

Allele Frequency

The gene pool is all the alleles of a gene and their combinations. The Hardy-Weinberg principle says that the allele frequency for dominant and recessive alleles will stay the same in a population for following generations if certain conditions happen. These conditions are: no mutations, large populations, random mating, no migration, and equal genotypes. This is not how most populations work. Changes in the frequency and types of alleles in a gene pool can come from gene flow, random mutation, nonrandom mating, and genetic drift.

Reproduction isolation is something that acts as a barrier to two species reproducing. These barriers are labeled as prezygotic and postzygotic.

Evolution

Types of Evolution

The three types of evolution are divergent, convergent, and parallel.

Divergent evolution is when two species become different over time. This can be caused by one of the species changing to a different environment.

Convergent evolution is when two species start out fairly different. However, they evolve to share many similar traits.

Parallel evolution is when species do not become more or less similar over time. Also, this is for species that are not similar.

Mechanisms of evolution are descent (i.e., the passing on of genetic information), mutation, migration, natural selection, and genetic variation and drift. The biological definition of **species** is a group of individuals that can mate and reproduce. **Speciation** is the evolution of a new biological species. The biological species concept (BSC) says that a species is a community of individuals that can reproduce and have a clear role in nature.

Evidence for the Theory of Evolution

Scientific evidence for the theory of evolution can be found in biogeography, comparative anatomy and embryology, the fossil record, and molecular evidence. **Biogeography** studies how animals and plants have spread out over areas. Evidence of evolution in the area of biogeography shows species that are well fitted for extreme areas.

The fossil record shows that species lived only for a small amount of time before becoming extinct. The fossil record can also show the line of plants and animals. Living fossils are existing species that have not changed much in form. Also, they are very similar to ancient examples in the fossil record. Examples are the horseshoe crab and the gingko.

Comparative embryology studies how species are similar in the embryonic stage. However, they become more specialized and diverse as they age. Vestigial organs are organs that still exist but do not have a role. Examples are the appendix in humans and the wings of birds that do not fly (e.g., ostriches).

Theories of Evolution

Natural selection: This theory says that the traits that give a species a better chance of survival are passed on to future generations. Members of a species that do not have the trait die before they reproduce. Charles Darwin's four principles are:

- From generation to generation, there are different members in a species
- Genes decide differences
- More members are born than will survive to a mature stage
- Certain genes help an organism to survive

Gradualism: This is the idea that evolution goes at a steady pace. Also, it does not have sudden additions of new species or features from one generation to the next. This can be contrasted with punctuated equilibrium.

Punctuated equilibrium: This idea says that evolution has very long stretches of time with no change (i.e., stasis). Then, this stasis is followed by smaller amounts of time (e.g., hundreds of thousands of years) of fast change. This can be contrasted with gradualism.

Macroevolution and Microevolution

Macroevolution can be known as the major phenotypic changes that happen over long periods of time. These changes bring about a new taxonomic level above species. Effects of macroevolution are major changes in anatomy and physiology and basic changes in body design. An example of this change is the evolution of stomata and cell guards in plants. These pieces allow them to manage gas exchange. Let's think about an example for animals. The foreleg of a reptile evolving into the wing of a bird is one example. In general, macroevolution causes major changes in the appearance and roles of plants and animals. This leads to new taxonomic levels of a high order.

By contrast, microevolution works on a much smaller scale. **Microevolution** is the small-scale changes in gene frequencies that make new species, not a higher taxonomic order. Microevolution is the different characteristics within the same family of organisms. An example is the Galápagos tortoises that Darwin studied. On the Galápagos Islands, the same species of tortoise became multiple sub-species that were split up among the islands. Macroevolution is the changing from one organism to a completely different organism.

Adaptation

In the **biosphere**, there are many environments in which organisms can live. However, temperature, light, climatic conditions, and many other factors are always changing. This forces an organism to adapt in order to survive. Any form of life must maintain a reasonably constant internal environment in a range of conditions to continue living. This range is the limit of tolerance for the organism. The population and distribution of organisms depends on these tolerances and environmental variation.

An organism lives in a **habitat** and that defines its niche. In this way, niche is all of the biological and environmental factors at work in the habitat. Organisms in large niches are called **generalists**. Organisms in small niches are called **specialists**. Generalists have a wider range of tolerance than specialists. Also, they can change with more ease to more conditions than specialists. These specialists need specific conditions to survive.

Mimicry is an adaptation that is a response to predation. It is when an organism has a similar appearance to another species. This similar appearance is meant to fool the predator into thinking that the organism is dangerous.

Two examples of mimicry are the drone fly and the Io moth. The fly looks like a bee but cannot sting. The Io moth has markings on its wings that make it look like an owl. The moth can scare predators and gain time to escape. Predators can also use mimicry to bring their prey closer to them.

Ecosystems

Community

A **community** is any number of species that have contact in an area. A niche is the role of a species in a community. Species diversity is the number of species in a community.

A **biome** is an area where species have changed to fit with their setting. The six major biomes in North America are desert, tropical rain forest, grassland, coniferous forest, deciduous forest, and tundra.

Biotic factors are the living factors (e.g., organisms) that affect a community or population. Abiotic factors are nonliving factors (e.g., rocks and rain) that affect a community or population.

Ecology is the study of plants, animals, their environments, and how they interact. An ecosystem is a community of species and all of the environmental factors that affect them.

Social Behaviors

Territoriality: This is when members of a species protect areas from others and claim the area as their own.

Dominance: This is the species in a community that has the most members.

Altruism: This is when a species or individual in a community acts to help another individual. The species or individual has to give up something to help. In biology, altruism does not have to be a planned action.

Threat display: This is an action by an organism that is meant to frighten another organism.

Gause's Law is the idea of competitive exclusion. Basically, this law says that if there are not enough resources in an area, and species are fighting for them, then the species will not be able to co-exist. The outcome is that one of the species will become extinct or be forced into a behavioral or evolutionary change.

Interspecific Relationships

Predation, parasitism, commensalism, and mutualism are all types of contacts between species. These interactions affect the populations of species. Intraspecific relationships are relationships among members of the same species. Interspecific relationships are relationships between members of different species.

Predation: A relationship where one individual (i.e., predator) feeds on another (i.e., the prey).

Symbiotic Relationships: A relationship where at least one of the organisms benefits. Mutualism, competition, commensalism, and parasitism are all types of symbiotic relationships.

- **Mutualism**: A relationship where both organisms benefit from having contact.
- **Competition**: A relationship where both organisms are harmed.
- **Commensalism**: A relationship where one organism is benefitted while the other organism is not affected.
- **Parasitism**: A relationship where one organism benefits and the other is harmed.

Review Video: Mutualism, Commensalism, and Parasitism
Visit mometrix.com/academy and enter code: 757249

Biomass: In ecology, biomass is the mass of one or all of the species (i.e., species biomass) in an ecosystem or area.

Predation

Predator-prey relationships are studied easily when there is one predator and one prey. They become complicated with many predators and preys. Predator-prey activity causes several adaptation events. This can be seen with the evolution of escape behavior. This can also be seen with protective coloring in animals. Predation is a major event in organizing communities.

Energy in a Community

Primary Production

Primary production is the amount of energy made by green plants over a fixed amount of time. It is highest in tropical rainforests and lower in temperate climes. It is very low in arctic and desert environments. Total primary production is evenly spread out over land and sea. Production on land and sea is limited mainly by the supply of usable nutrients in each community.

Communities turn solar energy into chemical energy to live. Therefore, photosynthesis is the foundation for all levels of life in a community. A small amount of the solar energy reaches the earth. This amount is about one percent or less and is used by plants to support life.

Secondary Production

Secondary production is the total amount of energy made by green plants that is used by the other organisms in the biosphere. Energy made by green plants is eaten, burned in respiration, or lost as waste.

Much of the energy is lost at each stage of the food chain. So, this means that large amounts of green plant material are needed to support a small number of animals. Only a small percentage of energy goes from one level of the food chain to the next. Animals have a small role in the food chain. Plants and organic matter are the main parts to the support of ecosystems. Secondary production is limited by interacting pieces in the ecosystem. Nutrients, climate, environmental changes, and disturbances all upset the secondary production of an ecosystem.

Food Chains and Biomagnifications

A **food chain** links organisms in a community. These links are based on how organisms use each other as food sources. A food chain begins with a producer (e.g., plants). Herbivores are organisms that eat plants. So, they are the next link in the food chain. The top of the food chain has levels of consumers. These consumers can eat herbivores or producers.

Biomagnification (or bioamplification) is an increase in the amount of a substance in a food chain. Examples are pesticides or mercury. Mercury comes out of coal-fired power plants. So, the mercury gets into the water supply and is taken in by fish. Larger fish eat smaller fish, and humans eat fish. Now, the amount of mercury in humans has risen. Biomagnification is affected by the staying power of a chemical and whether it can be broken down or negated.

FOOD WEBS

A **food web** is made of connected food chains in a community. The organisms can be linked to show the direction of energy flow. Energy flow in this sense is the flow of calories through a system from trophic level to trophic level. A trophic level is a link in a food chain or a level of nutrition. The 10% rule is that from trophic level to level about 90% of the energy is lost. As an example, the energy can be lost in the form of heat.

The lowest trophic level has primary producers which is usually plants. Then, there are primary consumers. The next in line is secondary consumers. Then, the next in line is tertiary consumers which are large carnivores (e.g., bears and sharks). The final link is decomposers. A decomposer breaks down the consumers at the top. Usually, food chains do not have more than six links. These links can also be called ecological pyramids.

Review Video: Food Webs
Visit mometrix.com/academy and enter code: 853254

ECOSYSTEM STABILITY AND ECOLOGIC SUCCESSION

Ecosystem stability: This concept says that a stable ecosystem is perfectly efficient. Seasonal changes or expected climate changes are balanced by homeostasis. It also says that interspecies interactions are part of the balance of the system. There are four principles of ecosystem stability:

- waste disposal and nutrient replenishment by recycling is complete
- the system uses sunlight as an energy source
- biodiversity remains
- populations are stable when they do not over consume resources.

Ecologic succession: This is the idea that says that there is an orderly progression of change in a community. Let's think about an example of primary succession. One example could be that over hundreds of years, bare rock decomposes (i.e., breaks down) to sand. This would lead to soil formation. Then, this would lead to the growth of grass and trees.

Review Video: What is Ecological Succession?
Visit mometrix.com/academy and enter code: 466994

Secondary succession happens after a major event that affects a community. Examples are a wild fire or building of a dam.

POPULATION

With increases in human population, humans have more influence on the environment. The number of humans on the planet today is pushing the limits of the biosphere that supports them. The earth cannot support the current population if developed countries continue to consume as much as they do now.

The greenhouse effect and global warming have important effects on the earth's ecosystems. The burning of fossil fuels for energy and the clearing of natural habitats raises the atmospheric levels of carbon dioxide. This can change the global cycles of ecosystems. So, this leads to climate change and other disorders. If this does not change, there could be great changes to the pattern of life on Earth. Animal communities will be affected when the plants that they need for energy are affected.

Distribution of Species

There are common patterns for how species spread out in their environments. Most species have small geographic ranges, and a few have very wide ranges. There is a strong tie between the amount of resources and how a population is spread out in an environment. This pattern is called **Hanski's Rule**.

This rule says that widespread species have more members than species that are not widespread. This rule is subject to considerable variation. Much is still unknown about geographic ranges.

One guideline is **Rapoport's rule**. This rule says that polar species spread out more than tropical species. Climate, glacial development, and competition are reasons for their spreading out. Geographical ranges for many species are not known because of lack of data. Usually, ranges for larger plants and animals in modern countries are just estimates.

Extinction

Extinction is the permanent loss of a species. Extinction has been the eventual end for almost all species. About 4 billion species have lived on Earth. Only 30 million or less are still alive today. Extinction can be mass extinction, where multiple species are lost, or it can be an individual extinction, where only a single species is lost.

Scientists believe that there have been five mass extinctions in history. Two have caused huge species loss. In the past 600 million years, an average of about one species has become extinct each year. Today's rate of extinction is at least 1,000 species a year. One of history's great mass extinctions is happening right now. This is the loss from destroying the species-rich tropics and rainforests. The best remedy for extinction is preserving habitats.

Earth's Structure and Systems

Latitude and Longitude

For the purposes of tracking time and location, the earth is divided into sections with imaginary lines. Lines that run vertically around the globe through the poles are **lines of longitude**, sometimes called meridians. The Prime Meridian is the longitudinal reference point of 0. Longitude is measured in 15-degree increments toward the east or west. Degrees are further divided into 60 minutes, and each minute is divided into 60 seconds. **Lines of latitude** run horizontally around the earth parallel to the equator, which is the 0 reference point and the widest point of the earth. Latitude is the distance north or south from the equator, and is also measured in degrees, minutes, and seconds.

Tropic of Cancer, Tropic of Capricorn, and Antarctic and Arctic Circles

Tropic of Cancer: This is located at 23.5 degrees north. The Sun is directly overhead at noon on June 21st in the Tropic of Cancer, which marks the beginning of summer in the Northern Hemisphere.

Tropic of Capricorn: This is located at 23.5 degrees south. The Sun is directly overhead at noon on December 21st in the Tropic of Capricorn, which marks the beginning of winter in the Northern Hemisphere.

Arctic Circle: This is located at 66.5 degrees north, and marks the start of when the Sun is not visible above the horizon. This occurs on December 21st, the same day the Sun is directly over the Tropic of Capricorn.

Antarctic Circle: This is located at 66.5 degrees south, and marks the start of when the Sun is not visible above the horizon. This occurs on June 21st, which marks the beginning of winter in the Southern Hemisphere and is when the Sun is directly over the Tropic of Cancer.

Cycles of Matter

The **water cycle** is the movement of water on the earth. Water can be in any of its three states for different parts of the cycle. The three states of water are liquid water, frozen ice, and water vapor. The parts of the water cycle are precipitation, canopy interception, snow melt, runoff, infiltration, subsurface flow, evaporation, sublimation, advection, condensation, and transpiration.

Precipitation is the condensed water vapor that falls to the ground. Examples are rain, hail, fog drip, snow, and sleet.

Canopy interception is when precipitation lands on plants instead of falling to the ground and evaporating.

Snow melt is runoff made by melting snow.

Runoff is the precipitation that moves across the surface and reaches the streams.

Infiltration happens when water goes from the surface to the ground.

Subsurface flow is the water that goes underground.

Evaporation is when water goes from a liquid to a gas.

Sublimation is when water goes from a solid state (e.g., snow or ice) to water vapor (i.e., a gas state). So, it does not change to a liquid state.

Advection is the movement of water through the atmosphere.

Condensation is when water vapor becomes liquid water.

Transpiration is when water vapor is released from plants to go into the air.

Review Video: Hydrologic Cycle
Visit mometrix.com/academy and enter code: 426578

The **rock cycle** is when the materials that make up the earth go through the three types of rock: igneous, sedimentary, and metamorphic. Rocks cannot be created or destroyed. Instead, they go through a series of changes. Also, they take on different forms through the stages of the rock cycle. Plate tectonics and the water cycle are the driving forces behind the rock cycle. These events force rocks and minerals out of balance and make them change to different external conditions.

The rock cycle works as follows: rocks beneath Earth's surface melt into magma. This magma either erupts through volcanoes or stays inside the earth. Then, this magma cools and makes igneous rocks. On the surface, these rocks go through weathering and erosion. These events break them down and spread the pieces across the surface. These fragments make layers and later become sedimentary rocks. Then, sedimentary rocks are transformed to metamorphic rocks which will become magma inside the earth. Or, the sedimentary rocks will melt down into magma.

Natural Hazards

Cyclones are large air masses that rotate in the same direction as the earth. They are made in low pressure areas. Cyclones come in many sizes. Some are mesoscale systems that can be 5 to hundreds of kilometers wide. Some are synoptic scale systems that can be about 1,000 km wide. The size of subtropical cyclones is in between mesoscale and synoptic scale.

Cold-core polar and extratropical cyclones are synoptic scale systems. Warm-core tropical, polar low and mesocyclones are mesoscale systems. Extratropical cyclones, mid-latitude or wave cyclones are seen in the middle latitudes. They do not have tropical or polar traits.

Extratropical cyclones are everyday events that move the weather over much of the earth. They can bring clouds, light showers, heavy gales, and thunderstorms. Anticyclones also help move weather over the earth. They happen in areas of high atmospheric pressure when the air is closer to the earth's surface. Anticyclones are connected with clearing skies and drier, cooler air.

A **hurricane** is one of the three weather events that can come from a tropical cyclone. A **tropical cyclone** is a warm-core, low-pressure condition that rotates counterclockwise in the northern hemisphere and clockwise in the southern hemisphere. A **tropical depression** has constant winds of up to 30 miles per hour. Also, there are rotational winds around a center. A **tropical storm** is more circular than a depression, with more rotation and higher wind speeds from 39mph to 73 mph.

Some hurricanes are well-organized. Sometimes, you can find the eye (i.e., center) with strong rotation. The wind speed is more than 73 mph. Hurricanes are put into categories with the Saffir-Simpson Scale. This scale labels hurricanes from category 1 to category 5. A category 5 hurricane has wind speeds of more than 155 mph. Every season, a list of names is made for hurricanes. The first storm has a name that begins with *A*. So, each storm has a name that follows in alphabetical order (e.g., Aaron, Blake, Cameron...). The letters *Q*, *U*, and *Z* are not used. There are six lists of names that are used from year to year. The names of hurricanes that caused great destruction are not used again.

Most **earthquakes** are caused by tectonic plate movement. They happen on fractures called faults or fault zones. Friction in the faults does not allow smooth movement. Tension builds up over time, and the release of that tension causes earthquakes. Faults have labels that are based on the type of slippage. The types of faults are dip-slip, strike-slip, and oblique-slip.

A **dip-slip fault** is an up or down movement on the fault plane. In a normal dip-slip fault, the wall that is above the fault plane moves down. In a reverse dip-slip fault, the wall that is above the fault plane moves up.

A **strike-slip fault** is a left or right movement on the fault plane.

Oblique-slip faults have up/down and left/right movement.

The Richter magnitude scale measures how much energy was given off by an earthquake.

A deformation is a change in the earth's surface. There are two types of deformations made by an earthquake fault rupture: static and dynamic. **Static deformation** leaves a lasting change to the ground. Examples are when a road or railroad track is split by an earthquake. Plate tectonics puts stress on the fault by putting tension on slow plate movements. An earthquake releases the tension.

Plate tectonics also cause another type of deformation. **Dynamic deformation** has intense motions that come in the form of sound waves. These sound waves can be compressional waves (i.e., primary or P waves) or shear waves (i.e., secondary or S waves). P waves travel faster with speeds between 1.5 and 8 kilometers per second.

Shear waves are slower. P waves shake the ground in the direction that they are spreading. S waves have a perpendicular shake to their spreading direction. A seismograph is a tool that measures the motion in the ground. Seismographs use a simple pendulum to track earthquake movement in a record called a seismogram. A seismogram can help scientists predict the distance, direction, Richter magnitude, and type of faulting of an earthquake.

Review Video: What is Plate Tectonics?
Visit mometrix.com/academy and enter code: 535013

Review Video: What Causes Earthquakes? | Overview
Visit mometrix.com/academy and enter code: 252531

A **thunderstorm** comes from the constant process of heat moving through the earth's atmosphere. Thunderstorms are made when there is moisture to make rain clouds, unstable air, and lift.

Unstable air is made from warm air that rises quickly through cold air. Lift can be caused by fronts, sea breezes, and high terrain (e.g., mountains). Single cell thunderstorms have one main draft. Multicell clusters have groups of storms. Multicell lines have severe thunderstorms along a squall line. A squall line is a line of thunderstorms that travel with a cold front.

Supercell thunderstorms are large and harsh. They have the strength to make damaging tornadoes. Thunder is a sonic shock wave made by the fast movement of air around lightning. Lightning is the discharge of electricity in a thunderstorm.

During a **tornado**, wind speeds can reach 300 mph. Tornados are funnel-like clouds that spin. They have a very high energy density. This means that they are very damaging to a small area. Also, tornados last for a short time. About 75% of the world's tornados happen in the United States.

Most are seen in an area of the Great Plains that is known as Tornado Alley. Two or more columns of air are known as a multiple vortex tornado. A satellite tornado is a weak tornado that is made close to a larger tornado. The two tornados are made in the same mesocyclone.

Review Video: What Makes up a Tornado?
Visit mometrix.com/academy and enter code: 540439

A **waterspout** is a tornado over water. The power of tornadoes is measured with the Enhanced Fujita Scale. An EF-0 rating is to a 3-second wind gust that is between 65 and 85 mph. An EF-5 is for wind speeds that are more given than 200 mph.

Seismic sea waves or **tsunamis** happen with seismic activity. In other words, tsunamis are caused by earthquakes, submarine landslides, and volcanic eruptions. A tsunami is a series of waves with long wavelengths and long periods. Far out at sea, the heights of these waves are less than one meter. The wavelength may be 100 km. The wave period may range from five minutes to one hour.

This will change as seismic sea waves come to the shoreline. The bottom of the wave is slowed down by the shallow sea floor. The top is not slowed as much. Also, the wave height rises to as much as 20 meters. These waves can hit the shore at speeds of 30 miles per hour.

Volcanoes can happen on any type of tectonic plate boundary. At a divergent boundary, as plates move apart, magma rises to the surface. This magma cools and makes a ridge. An example of this is the mid-Atlantic ridge.

Often, convergent boundaries (i.e., one plate slides under another) are areas with a lot of volcanic activity. The subduction process makes magma. When the magma rises to the surface, volcanoes can be made.

Volcanoes can be created in the middle of a plate over hot spots. Hot spots are places where narrow plumes of magma rise through the mantle in a fixed place. This continues for a long stretch of time. The Hawaiian Islands and Midway are examples. The plate shifts, and the island moves. Magma continues to rise through the mantle. So, this makes another island. Volcanoes can be active, dormant, or extinct. Active volcanoes are those that are erupting or will erupt soon. Dormant volcanoes may erupt in the future. Also, they still have volcanic activity on the inside. Extinct volcanoes will not erupt again.

The three types of volcanoes are shield, cinder cone, and composite. A **shield volcano** is made by a long-term, gentle eruption. This type of volcanic mountain is made by each progressive lava flow that comes over time. A **cinder cone volcano** is made by explosive eruptions. Lava shoots out of a vent into the air. As it falls to the ground, the lava cools into cinders and ash. This builds up around the volcano in a cone shape. A **composite volcano** is a combination of the other two types of volcanoes. In this type, there are layers of lava flows. Also, there are layers of ash and cinder.

Human Affairs and the Environment

With the industrial revolution, science and technology have made a great influence on humans. There have been more discoveries in many fields. Many discoveries have led to better things for many people. These discoveries have led to longer life because of better nutrition, better medical care, and better workplaces. These changes have helped the lives of many humans. However, they have brought changes to the environment. Not every problem has been solved. Many still exist in one way or another. For example, there are ways to recycle, yet not everyone recycles because of the cost.

Ecosystems

Human influences on ecosystems have many forms and causes. These changes have an influence on plants and animals in many biomes and ecosystems. So, the changes can be seen in widespread areas and small areas. Humans take many natural resources to have food or to make energy. This changes their environment to make food, energy, and shelter.

Changes come from:

- use or overuse of pesticides
- the invasion of a habitat
- over hunting and over fishing
- bringing plant and animal species into non-native ecosystems
- people refusing to recycle
- people bringing dangerous wastes into the environment

These actions have many effects. Some are acid rain, decrease of ozone, destruction of forests, and loss of more species. Other effects are genetic flaws and harm to animals.

Greenhouse Effect

The greenhouse effect is a natural and important event. Greenhouse gases (e.g., ozone, carbon dioxide, water vapor, and methane) trap infrared radiation that is reflected to the atmosphere. So, warm air is trapped as well. Without the greenhouse effect, temperatures on Earth would be 30 degrees less on average. Some human activity puts out more greenhouse gas than necessary. These events put more greenhouse gases into the air:

- burning natural gas and oil
- farming actions that release methane and nitrous oxide
- factory actions that make gases
- destroying forests put more greenhouse gases into the air

So, those events decrease the amount of oxygen available to balance out greenhouse gases. Now, too many greenhouse gases trap infrared radiation. So, this increases the temperature at the earth's surface.

Global Warming

Rising temperatures may lead to:

- higher sea levels as polar ice melts
- lower amounts of fresh water as coastal areas flood
- species extinction from changes in habitat
- increases in certain diseases
- lower standard of living for humans

Less fresh water and loss of habitat can lead to less agricultural production and food supply. Global warming brings drier and warmer weather. When dry areas become very arid, this upsets habitats for humans and other species. Increases in damaging weather (e.g., hurricanes or snowstorms) may be seen at unlikely latitudes. There may be more moisture in the atmosphere from evaporation. Global warming may cause the loss of glaciers and permafrost. Also, there is a greater chance for air pollution and acid rain.

Price of Consumerism

There is a connection between growth in an economy or higher standards of living and a wasteful cycle of production. Goods are made as cheap as possible with little or no thought for the environment. Some steps in the production process can be wasteful. So, this can have dangerous effects on the environment. After a product has been used, it may be sent to a landfill. Landfills can be a dump for illegal substances, business and government waste, construction industry waste, and medical waste. When consumer products are dumped in landfills, they can pollute the groundwater.

Removing Waste

Landfills: Methane is a greenhouse gas that is used to generate electricity. Sometimes this gets into the atmosphere. Carbon dioxide, nitrogen, oxygen, water vapor, sulfur, and mercury are common gases in landfills. Radioactive contaminants (e.g., tritium) can be found in landfills as well. Landfill leachate is the water that is contaminated by solid waste.

This leachate may have:

- acids from car batteries
- solvents
- heavy metals
- pesticides
- motor oil
- paint
- household cleaning supplies
- plastics

Some of these are dangerous when they get into the ecosystem.

Incinerators: These add to air pollution because they can put out nitric and sulfuric oxides. These can cause acid rain.

Sewage: When dumped into oceans, sewage can have human waste and disease-causing organisms. So, this can harm ocean life and cause sickness in humans.

Types of Energy Production

Coal-fired power plants: These generate electricity. They are the largest source of greenhouse gases: sulfur oxides, carbon dioxide, mercury, and nitrogen oxides.

Nuclear power plants: Nuclear waste is very toxic to humans. This waste can cause burns, sickness, and hair loss at low levels. Higher levels can cause death. Mining for uranium and precious metals brings chemicals into close areas. So, the natural balance and beauty of an area is damaged. Some nuclear waste can stay harmful for billions of years.

Gasoline: The burning of gas and other fossil fuels puts carbon dioxide into the atmosphere.

Earth's Atmosphere

The atmosphere is made of 78% nitrogen, 21% oxygen, and 1% argon. Other pieces are water vapor, carbon dioxide, dust particles, and chemicals from Earth. The air in the atmosphere becomes thinner at higher levels above the earth's surface. At about 3 km above sea level, you will have difficulty breathing. As you go higher, the atmosphere begins to fade into space.

Review Video: Earth's Atmosphere
Visit mometrix.com/academy and enter code: 417614

Atmospheric Layers

Earth's atmosphere has five main layers. From lowest to highest, these are the troposphere, the stratosphere, the mesosphere, the thermosphere, and the exosphere. A transition layer is between each pair of layers. This layer is known as a pause.

The lowest layer of the atmosphere is called the **troposphere**. Its thickness is different at the poles and the equator. The thickness at the poles is about 7 km. The thickness at the equator is about 17 km. Most weather events happen at this layer. As you go higher in this layer, the temperature decreases. The troposphere has the tropopause which is the transitional layer of the stratosphere.

The **stratosphere** is the next level. This layer goes to a height of about 51 km. In the stratosphere, the temperature is reversed. In other words, the temperature increases as you go higher in this layer. The stratosphere includes the ozone layer. The ozone layer helps to block ultraviolet light from the Sun. The stratopause is the transitional layer to the mesosphere.

The **mesosphere** goes from the stratosphere to a height of about 81 km. In this layer, meteors are likely to burn. This is the coldest layer. So, as you go higher in this layer, the temperature drops. This layer is thought of as the coldest place on Earth. The average temperature is -85 degrees Celsius.

The next layer is the **thermosphere**. This is where the International Space Station orbits. Temperature increases as you go higher in the thermosphere. The transitional layer to the exosphere is known as the thermopause.

Just past the thermosphere is the exobase. This is the base layer of the **exosphere**. The exosphere is the outermost layer that goes to 10,000 km. This layer is mostly made of hydrogen and helium.

Beyond the five main layers are the ionosphere, homosphere, heterosphere, and magnetosphere.

Tropospheric Circulation

Air near the equator is warmed by the Sun and rises. Then, cool air rushes under the warm air. So, the high and warm air is moved toward Earth's poles. At the poles, the warm air cools and lowers to the surface. Now, the cool air moves under the warm air. So, the air flows back to the equator. Air currents combined with ocean currents move heat around the planet. This creates winds, weather, and climate. As the seasons change, the winds can change direction.

For example, in Southeast Asia and India, summer monsoons are caused by air being heated by the Sun. This air rises, draws moisture from the ocean, and causes daily rains. Then, in winter, the air cools, sinks, pushes the moist air away, and creates dry weather.

Ocean

The ocean is the body of salt water around the earth. This body is divided into three large oceans: the Pacific Ocean, the Atlantic Ocean, and the Indian Ocean. Other divisions are gulfs, bays, and seas. The ocean covers 70.8 percent of the surface of the earth and has about 97 percent of the planet's water. The deepest point in the ocean is at Challenger Deep in the Mariana Trench. The ocean floor at Challenger Deep is 10,924 meters below sea level. The depths of the ocean are mapped by echo sounders and satellite altimeter systems. Echo sounders give a sound pulse from the surface. Then, the time it takes for the sound to return is recorded. Satellite altimeters give better maps of the ocean floor.

Ocean's Importance

The ocean is an important part of the biosphere, the water cycle, and tropospheric circulation. So, it is a key part to Earth's weather and climate. Humans use the ocean and coastal areas for food, transport, oil, gas, and pleasure. The ocean gives some kind of help for almost 50 percent of all species on Earth.

Seawater

Salinity measures the amount of dissolved salts in ocean water. Dryer areas with higher rates of evaporation have more salt. Areas that are mixed with fresh water and ocean water have less salt. Hydrogen and oxygen make up about 96.5% of sea water. The major parts of the dissolved solids of sea water are chlorine (55.3%), sodium (30.8%), magnesium (3.7%), sulfur (2.6%), calcium (1.2%), and potassium (1.1%). The salinity of ocean water is mostly constant.

Shoreline

The area where the land meets the sea is called the **shoreline**. This marks the average position of the ocean. Longshore currents create longshore drift or transport (i.e., beach drift). This is when ocean waves move toward a beach at an angle and moves water along the coast. Sediment is eroded (i.e., broken down) from some areas and deposited (i.e., left behind) in other areas. In this way, it is moved along the beach.

Rip currents are strong, fast currents. These happen when a part of a longshore current moves away from the beach. Man-made structures built perpendicular to the beach can trap sand on the up-current side. Erosion happens on the down-current side. Features made by the deposited sediment are spits, bay-mouth bars, tombolos, barrier islands, and buildups. Sand is made of granular materials (e.g., quartz and orthoclase). In some areas, sand is made of rock and basalt.

Beaches

Weathering erodes the rock and soil of beaches into sand. Other parts of the soil (e.g., clay and silt) are deposited in areas of the continental shelf. The larger sand grains get deposited in the form of a beach. This includes:

- a near shore which is underwater
- a fore shore which is thought of as the beach
- a back shore

The offshore starts about 5 meters from the shoreline and goes to about 20 meters. The beach has wet and dry parts and a fore dune and rear dune. Waves move sand from the sea to the beach. Then, gravity and waves move it back again. Slowly, the wind pushes sand grains uphill in a jumping motion called saltation. Sand that stays deposited in one place is a dune. Storms can erode a beach and bring more deposition.

Ocean Currents

Surface currents are caused by winds. Subsurface currents happen deep beneath the ocean's surface. They are caused by land masses and the earth's rotation. The density of ocean water can also affect currents. Sea water with a higher salinity is denser than sea water with a lower salinity. Water flows from areas of high density to areas of low density. Currents are labeled by their temperature. Cold polar sea water flows to warmer water, which makes cold currents. Warm water currents swirl around the basins and equator. Then, that heat is lost and gained by the ocean to make winds. Ocean currents play an important part in moving this heat to the poles. This process helps to create many types of weather events.

Deep Sea Currents

Deep sea currents can be compared to a conveyor belt because they move across the entire ocean. The currents are weak. So, they slowly mix deep and shallow water. In the winter, deep circulation brings cold water from high latitudes to lower latitudes across the world. This takes place in areas where most water is at a depth of 4 and 5 km. Water in these areas can be colder than 4°C. Surface ocean temperatures average about 17°C. However, they can range from -2°C to 36°C. Much of the cold sea water is dense and has a high salinity. This high salinity forces the cold water to sink at high latitudes. So, the water spreads out, forms into layers, and fills the ocean basins. Then, deep mixing happens, and the water moves up. The movement of deep-sea currents is known as abyssal circulation.

Ocean Floor

The ocean floor has features that are also on land (e.g., mountains, ridges, plains, and canyons). The oceanic crust is a thin, dense layer that is about 10 km thick. The greatest volume of water is in the basins. Smaller volumes are in the low-lying areas of the continents. These low-lying areas are known as the continental shelves.

The **continental slope** connects the shelf to the ocean floor of the basin. The **continental rise** is a sloping area between the slope and the basin. A **seamount** is an undersea volcanic peak that rises to a height of at least 1,000 meters. A **guyot** is a seamount with a flat top. A **mid-ocean ridge** is an undersea mountain chain. **Sills** are low parts of ridges that separate ocean basins or other seas. **Trenches** are long, narrow troughs.

Ocean Waves

Most waves in the ocean are made by winds. Stronger winds bring larger waves. The highest point of a wave is the crest. The lowest point of a wave is the trough. The wavelength is measured from crest to crest. The wave height is measured from the bottom of the trough to the top of the crest. The wave frequency is the number of wave crests that pass a point every second. A wave period is the time that it takes for a wave crest of a second wave to reach the point of the wave crest of the first wave.

The energy in a wave runs into the shallow sea floor. This causes the wave to become taller. Then, the wave will fall over or break. Waves that reach the shore are not all the same size. They can be larger or smaller than average. About once an hour, there is usually a wave that is twice the size of others. There are even larger--but rare--rogue waves. The waves often travel alone and in a direction that is different than other waves.

Swells are waves that have traveled a long distance. These waves are usually large waves with flat crests. They are very regular in shape and size.

The sea level slowly rises and falls over the period of a day. These types of waves on the sea surface are known as tides. Tides have wavelengths of thousands of kilometers. They are different from other waves. The reason is that they are created by slow and very small changes in gravity. These changes in gravity come from the motion of the Sun and the Moon in connection with the earth.

Rift Valley

Rift valleys are seen on land and in the ocean. They happen because of plate tectonics. When plates spread apart, rift valleys are made. In the ocean, this is part of the crust development cycle. In this cycle, new crust is created at mid-ocean ridges and old crust is lost at the trenches. The Mid-Atlantic Ridge is an example. The cycle happens at divergent Eurasian and North American plates. Other places are the South Atlantic, African, and South American plates. The East Pacific Rise is also a mid-oceanic ridge. The longest rift valley is located on the crest of the mid-ocean ridge system. It happens from the spreading of the sea floor.

Erosion

Erosion is the wearing away (i.e., breaking down) of rock materials from the earth's surface. Two main forms of erosion are natural geologic erosion and erosion from human action. Natural geologic erosion happens from weathering and gravity. The steps in natural geologic erosion are filled with long term forces. Human activity (e.g., building, farming, and clearing forests) happens in less time.

Soil is the topmost layer of organic material. This is the part that helps plants grow. One type of erosion is **sheet erosion**. This is the slow and somewhat steady removal of surface soil. Rills are small rivulets that cut into soil. Gullies are rills that have become larger from more water run-off. Sand blows are made by wind blowing away sand grains.

A damaging effect of erosion is sedimentation in rivers. This can pollute water and damage ecosystems. When erosion removes topsoil, crops are destroyed and other plants cannot grow. So, ecosystems are changed. Also, less food is available for people.

Deposition

Eroded material can be moved or added to a land form or land mass. This is known as deposition or sedimentation. Erosion and sedimentation are actions that happen together. Running water brings materials in fresh water and coastal areas.

Examples of deposition are:

- gravity moving material down a mountain and depositing it at the base
- sandstorms that deposit sand grains in other locations
- glaciers melting and retreating that deposit sediments

Evaporation can cause deposition because dissolved materials are left behind when water evaporates. Deposition can be the buildup of organic materials. An example is chalk that is made of the small calcium carbonate skeletons of marine plankton.

Weathering

There are two basic types of weathering: mechanical and chemical. Weathering is a very important process on the earth's surface. Materials weather (i.e., break down or fade) at different speeds. This is known as differential weathering. Mechanical and chemical weathering work together. For example, **chemical weathering** can loosen the bonds between molecules. So, this allows mechanical weathering to take place. **Mechanical weathering** can expose the surfaces of land masses which allows chemical weathering to take place.

Impact, abrasion, frost wedging, root wedging, salt wedging, and uploading are types of mechanical weathering. Types of chemical weathering are dissolution, hydration, hydrolysis, oxidation, biological, and carbonation. A common type of chemical weathering is done by water dissolving a mineral. Water that is very acidic is better at weathering. Carbonic and sulfuric acids can enter rain when they are in the atmosphere. This lowers the pH value of rain and makes it more acidic. Normal rain water has a pH value of 5.5. Acid rain has a pH value of 4 or less.

Tilt of the Earth

The tilt of the earth on its axis is 23.5°. This tilt causes the seasons and affects the temperature. The reason is that this tilt affects the amount of Sun that covers an area. The hemisphere that is tilted toward the Sun has summer. So, the other hemisphere has winter. This reverses as the earth revolves around the Sun. Fall and spring happen between the two extremes.

Review Video: Earth's Tilt and Seasons
Visit mometrix.com/academy and enter code: 602892

The equator gets the same amount of sunlight every day of the year (e.g., 12 hours). So, this area does not experience seasons. Both poles have days during the winter when they are tilted away from the Sun and have no daylight. During the summer, the poles experience 24 hours of daylight and no night.

Layers of Earth

The earth has many layers. Each has its own traits:

- Crust is the outermost layer of the earth. It has the continents and the ocean basins. There are different thicknesses in different areas. For example, it is 35-70 km in the continents. Ocean basins can be about 5-10 km in thickness. Also, it is made of aluminosilicates.
- Mantle is about 2900 km thick. It is made of ferro-magnesium silicates. The mantle is divided into an upper and lower mantle. Most of the internal heat of the earth is in the mantle. Large convective cells circulate heat. So, this may cause plate tectonic movement.
- Core is separated into the liquid outer core and the solid inner core. The outer core is 2300 km thick. This is made of nickel-iron alloy. The inner core is almost entirely iron. It is 12 km thick. The earth's magnetic field is thought to be controlled by the liquid outer core.

Review Video: Earth's Structure
Visit mometrix.com/academy and enter code: 713016

Organization of Outer Space

Beginnings of the Universe

The universe is the source of everything that we know about space, matter, energy, and time. It is likely that there are still events that have yet to be discovered. The Big Bang theory is a widely accepted idea that explains how the universe began.

The Steady-State theory and the Creationist theory are other ideas on the start of the universe. The **Big Bang theory** says that a long time ago all the matter in the universe was in one place. Then, this matter exploded and spread across space. So, galaxies came from this material, and the universe is still increasing in size.

The size of the universe is thought to be at least 93 billion light years across. To understand this, the Milky Way galaxy is about 100,000 light years across. Matter in space is organized into stars, galaxies, clusters (i.e. groups of galaxies), and superclusters (i.e. groups of clusters). Galaxies typically consist of billions of stars.

Some estimates say that the universe is about 13 billion years old. Space is thought to have 73 percent dark energy, 23 percent cold dark matter, and 4 percent regular matter.

After dark energy and dark matter, the two most common elements in the universe are hydrogen (H) and helium (He). After hydrogen and helium, the most common elements are oxygen, neon, nitrogen, carbon, silicon, and magnesium.

Review Video: Dark Matter
Visit mometrix.com/academy and enter code: 251909

Development of the Earth

Scientists think that about 4.5 billion years ago, Earth was a rock with a cloud of gas. Many think that this rock did not have water or even the type of atmosphere that we have today. Over time, heat from radioactive materials in the rock and pressure in the interior of the earth melted the interior. This caused the heavier materials (e.g., iron) to sink. Lighter silicate-type rocks rose to the earth's surface. These rocks made the earth's first crust. Other chemicals rose to the earth's surface. These chemicals helped to make the water and atmosphere.

Radioactive Dating

Radioactive dating is a way to know the age of rocks and the earth. The process compares the amount of radioactive material in a rock to the amount of material that has "decayed." **Decay** is when the nucleus of an element loses subatomic particles over time. The process has a parent element that changes to make a daughter element (i.e., the decay product). The daughter element can be unstable and lose particles. So, this makes another daughter element. This is known as a **decay chain**. Decay continues until all of the elements are stable.

Three types of dating methods are radiocarbon dating, potassium-argon dating, and uranium-lead dating. These methods can be used to date different kinds of natural and manmade materials.

Fossils

Fossils are preserved plants, animals, their remains, or their traces. Some fossils date back to about 10,000 years ago. Fossils and their place in rock layers make up the fossil record. Fossils are made with a very specific set of conditions. The fossil must not be damaged by predators or scavengers after death. Also, the fossil must not break down. Usually, this happens when the organism is quickly covered with sediment. This sediment builds up, and the molecules in the organism's body are replaced by minerals. Fossils come in many sizes. They can be anywhere from single-celled organisms to large dinosaurs.

Fossils have much information about the past. There is information about the geologic history of our planet and how the earth and organisms began. Some fossilized remains in the geohistorical record show patterns in the earth's environment that continue today (e.g., weathering, glaciation, and volcanism). These have all led to evolutionary changes in plants and animals. Some fossils support the theory that powerful events caused many changes in the earth and its living creatures. One example of this type of theory is that a meteor hit the earth and caused dinosaurs to become extinct. Both types of fossils give scientists a way to predict if these types of events will happen again.

Astronomy

Astronomy studies the positions, movements, and structures of celestial objects. Celestial is something that is in the sky or outer space. These objects are the Sun, the Moon, planets, asteroids, meteors, comets, stars, galaxies, the universe, and other space objects. The term astronomy has its roots in the Greek words "astro" and "nomos," which means "laws of the stars."

Review Video: Astronomy
Visit mometrix.com/academy and enter code: 640556

Galaxies

Galaxies are made of stars and dark matter. Dwarf galaxies can have as few as 10 million stars. Giant galaxies can have as many as 1 trillion stars. Galaxies are gravitationally bound. This means that the stars, star systems, gases, and dust spin around the galaxy's center. The earth is in the Milky Way galaxy. The nearest galaxy to the Milky Way is the Andromeda galaxy.

Galaxies can be labeled by their visual shape. Examples are the elliptical, spiral, irregular, and starburst galaxies. It is estimated that there are more than 100 billion galaxies in the universe. The space between two galaxies is a gas that has an average density of less than one atom per cubic meter. Galaxies are organized into clusters which make superclusters. Up to 90% of the mass of galaxies may be dark mark. Today, dark matter is not understood very well.

Stars

There are different life cycles for stars after they begin and enter into the main sequence stage. Small, somewhat cold red dwarfs with low masses burn hydrogen slowly. They will remain in the main sequence for hundreds of billions of years. Large, hot supergiants will leave the main sequence after just a few million years. Hydrogen--in its plasma state--is the most common chemical element in stars' main sequences.

A **nuclear fusion reaction** is when multiple atomic nuclei collide to make a new nucleus. If nuclear fusion of hydrogen into helium begins, a star is born. The "main sequence" of a star's life has nuclear fusion reactions. During this time, the star shrinks over billions of years to make up for the lost heat and light energy. As the star shrinks, the temperature, density, and pressure rise at the star's core. So, the cycle continues.

The Sun is a mid-sized star that may be in the main sequence for 10 billion years. After the main sequence, the star will grow to become a red giant. Depending on the original mass of the star, it can become a black dwarf. Then, it will become a small, cooling white dwarf. Massive stars become red supergiants and sometimes blue supergiants. Then, they explode in a supernova and become neutron stars. The largest stars can become black holes.

A **nebula** is a cloud of dust and gas that is mostly made of hydrogen (97%) and helium (3%). Gravity causes parts of the nebula to group together. This grouping continues to add atoms to the center of an unstable **protostar**. A protostar needs to balance between gravity that pulls atoms and gas pressure that pushes heat and light away from the center. A star dies when it is no longer able to keep this balance. A protostar may never become a star if it does not reach an important core temperature. Instead, the protostar may become a brown dwarf or a gas giant.

Black hole: A black hole is a space where the gravitational field is very powerful. So, everything--even light--is pulled into it. When objects enter the surface (i.e., the event horizon), they cannot escape.

Quasar: A quasi-stellar radio source is an energetic galaxy with an active galactic nucleus that has a focused beam of electromagnetic radiation directed somewhat toward an observer. Quasars were first spotted by their shedding of large amounts of electromagnetic radiation (e.g., radio waves and visible light).

Blazar: A quasar with a beam that is directed exactly at an observer, such that they get the full blast of the radiation.

Dark matter: The existence of this matter has not yet been proven. Much of the universe's mass may be dark matter. This matter cannot be observed because it does not put out any radiation. However, some think that it does exist because of gravitational forces put on visible objects.

Meteors, Meteoroids, and Meteorites

A **meteoroid** is the name for a rock from space before it enters the earth's atmosphere. Most meteoroids burn up in Earth's atmosphere. This happens before they reach altitudes of 80 km.

A **meteor** is a meteoroid that burns in Earth's atmosphere. The streak of light is known as a shooting star. Meteor showers happen when the earth passes through the debris of a comet. Pieces of this debris are about the size of a grain of sand.

Meteorites are rocks that reach Earth's surface from space. There are many types of meteorites, and they are made of many materials:

- Iron meteorites: made of iron and nickel
- Stony iron meteorites: made of iron, nickel, and silicate materials
- Stony meteorites: mainly made of silicate. They also have iron and nickel

Comets

A **comet** is made of frozen gases and rocky and metallic materials. Usually, comets are small and have long tails. A comet's tail is made of ionized gases. Their orbits are elliptical, not round. There may be as many as 100 billion comets in our solar system.

About 12 new comets are discovered each year. Some scientists think that short-period comets start in the Kuiper Belt. Long-period comets start in the Oort Cloud. Comets orbit the Sun in time periods. Some comets are seen every few years. Other comets are not seen for hundreds of thousands of years.

A well-known comet is Halley's Comet. Every 76 years, this comet can be seen from Earth. The comet is made of frozen water, carbon dioxide, ammonia, and methane.

Solar System

A solar system has a star and other objects that move in or around it. The start to the solar system began with the collapse of a cloud of interstellar gas and dust. This collapse made the solar nebula. The reason for the collapse is that the cloud was disturbed. As it collapsed, it heated up and compressed at the center. This made a flat protoplanetary disk with a protostar at the center. A protoplanetary disk is spinning disk of gas that is around a new star. Planets were made from the growth of the disk.

Then, gas cooled and condensed into small pieces of rock, metal, and ice. These pieces collided and made larger pieces. Then, the pieces became the size of small asteroids. Eventually, some became large enough to have enough gravity to affect objects around it.

Objects move around and are tied by gravity to a star called the Sun. These objects include: planets, dwarf planets, moons, asteroids, meteoroids, cosmic dust, and comets. The definition of planets has changed. At one time, there were nine planets in the solar system. There are now eight. Planetary objects in the solar system include four inner planets: Mercury, Venus, Earth, and Mars. These planets are small, dense, and rocky. They do not have rings, and they have few or no moons.

The four outer planets are Jupiter, Saturn, Uranus, and Neptune. These planets are large and have low densities, and they have rings and moons. They are also known as gas giants. The asteroid belt comes between the inner and outer planets. Beyond Neptune is the Kuiper belt. Inside this belt are five dwarf planets: Ceres, Pluto, Haumea, Makemake, and Eris.

Review Video: The Solar System
Visit mometrix.com/academy and enter code: 273231

Review Video: Terrestrial Planets
Visit mometrix.com/academy and enter code: 100346

Sun

The **Sun** is at the center of the solar system. This star is more than 99.8% of the total mass of the solar system. It is made of 70% hydrogen (H) and 28% helium (He). The other 2% is made up of metals. The Sun is one of 100 billion stars in the Milky Way galaxy.

- Diameter: 1,390,000 km
- Mass: 1.989 x 10^{30} kg
- Surface temperature: 5,800 K
- Core temperature: 15,600,000 K

The surface is called the photosphere. The chromosphere lies above this. The corona is next and goes millions of kilometers into space. Temperatures in the corona are over 1,000,000 K. Sunspots are cooler parts on the surface with a temperature of 3,800 K. The magnetosphere (i.e., heliosphere) goes far beyond Pluto.

Review Video: The Sun
Visit mometrix.com/academy and enter code: 699233

The Sun's energy is made by nuclear fusion reactions. Each second about 700,000,000 tons of hydrogen are converted (i.e., fused) to about 695,000,000 tons of helium. The other 5,000,000 tons of energy is converted in the form of gamma rays. In nuclear fusion, four hydrogen nuclei are fused into one helium nucleus. So, this gives off energy.

In the Sun, the energy goes to the surface and is absorbed. Then, it is released again at lower temperatures. Most energy is in the form of visible light when it comes to the surface. It is estimated that the Sun has used about half of the hydrogen at its core since its birth. It is expected to radiate (i.e., give off energy) in this way for another 5 billion years.

Eventually, the Sun will finish off its hydrogen fuel. Then, it will become brighter and grow to about 260 times its diameter. So, it will be known as a red giant. Over time, the outer layers will be destroyed and the Sun will become a dense white dwarf about the size of the earth.

Inner Planets

Mercury is the closest to the Sun. It is the smallest planet. Mercury moves around the Sun every 88 days. The planet has no atmosphere. Mercury is bright and has a surface with craters. The planet is dense and rocky with a large iron core.

Venus is the second planet from the Sun. It moves around the Sun every 225 days. The planet is like the earth in size, gravity, and overall structure. It has a dense atmosphere made of carbon dioxide and some sulfur. The planet is covered with reflective clouds that are made of sulfuric acid. Venus shows signs of volcanism. Also, lightning and thunder have been recorded on the surface.

Earth is the third planet from the Sun. It comes around the Sun every 365 days. About 71% of its surface is salt-water oceans. The earth is rocky and has an atmosphere made mainly of oxygen and nitrogen. The planet has one moon and millions of species. Earth has the only known life in the solar system. Oxygen (O), silicon (Si), and aluminum (Al) are the most abundant elements in the earth's crust.

Mars is the fourth planet from the Sun. The surface looks red because of iron oxide, and there is a thin atmosphere. The planet moves around the Sun at a rate like the earth and has cycles of seasons.

Mars has volcanoes, valleys, deserts, and polar ice caps. The planet has the tallest mountain, the largest canyon, and the largest impact crater discovered in our solar system.

Oort Cloud, Asteroid Belt, and Kuiper Belt

The **asteroid belt** is between Mars and Jupiter. The many objects in this belt are made of rock and metal like those on the inner planets.

The **Kuiper Belt** is past Neptune's orbit. However, the influence of the gas giants may bring these objects from the Kuiper Belt to pass Neptune's orbit. Objects in the Kuiper Belt are still being discovered. Scientists think that they are made of frozen water, ammonia, and methane. These may be the source of short-period comets. It is estimated that there are 35,000 Kuiper Belt objects that are greater than 100 km in diameter. There may be 100 million objects about 20 km in diameter.

There is a possible **Oort Cloud** that may exist far past the Kuiper Belt. This could be another source for long-period comets.

Outer Planets

Jupiter is the fifth planet from the Sun. This is the largest planet in the solar system. It is made mainly of hydrogen, and about 25% of its mass is helium. In the tropopause, there are clouds made of ammonia crystals. The clouds bring storms and violent winds. Jupiter is known for its Great Red Spot. This spot is an anticyclonic storm. The planet has a planetary ring and 63 moons. On the surface, Jupiter has wind speeds of 100 m/s.

Saturn is the sixth planet from the Sun. This is the second largest planet in the solar system. It is made of hydrogen, some helium, and methane and ammonia. Saturn has a small core of rock and ice and a thick layer of metallic hydrogen. Also, there is a gas-filled outer layer. On the surface, there are wind speeds of up to 1,800 km/h. The planet has a system of rings and 61 moons.

Uranus is the seventh planet from the Sun. Its atmosphere is made mainly of hydrogen and helium. Also, there is water, ammonia, methane, and traces of hydrocarbons in the atmosphere. With a low temperature of 49 K, Uranus has the coldest atmosphere. Uranus has a ring system, a magnetosphere, and 13 moons.

Neptune is the eighth planet from the Sun and has the third largest mass. It has an atmosphere similar to Uranus. The planet has a Great Dark Spot. Uranus has the strongest winds of any planet. These winds can be as high as 2,100 km/h. Neptune is cold (about 55 K) and has a ring system. The planet has 12 moons.

Moon

The **Moon** is the fifth largest satellite in the solar system. It moves around the earth about every 27.3 days. Its diameter is about 3,474 km. There are many impact craters on the Moon. There were more impact craters on Earth at one time. However, they have eroded over time. So, very few can still be seen.

The position changes of the earth, Sun, and Moon cause the phases of the Moon. These phases repeat every 29.5 days. Waxing is the two weeks where the Moon goes from a new moon to a full moon. Then, waning is the two weeks where the Moon goes from a full moon to a new moon.

The phases of waxing are:

- **New Moon**: The Moon is not lit and rises and sets with the Sun
- **Crescent Moon**: A small slice of the Moon is lit

- **First quarter**: Half the Moon is lit
- **Gibbous**: More than half of the Moon is lit. It looks like the shape of a football
- **Full Moon**: The Moon is fully lit. It rises at sunset and sets at sunrise

After a full moon, the Moon is waning. The phases of waning are:

- **Gibbous**: The left side is lit. The Moon rises after sunset and sets after sunrise.
- **Third quarter**: Half the Moon is lit. It rises at midnight and sets at noon.
- **Crescent Moon**: A small slice of the Moon is lit
- **New Moon**: The Moon is not lit. It rises and sets with the Sun.

Earth-Moon-Sun System

The Earth-Moon-Sun system is responsible for eclipses. An eclipse of the Sun happens during a new Moon. This is when the side of the Moon facing the earth is not lit by the Sun. The Moon passes in front of the Sun. So, the Sun cannot be seen on Earth. Eclipses do not happen every month. An eclipse of the Moon happens during the full Moon phase. The Moon passes through the shadow of the earth and blocks sunlight from reaching it. So, this causes darkness for a short amount of time. In a lunar eclipse, there are two parts to the shadow. The umbra is the dark, inner region. The Sun is completely blocked in this area. The penumbra is the somewhat lighted area around the umbra.

Review Video: Eclipses
Visit mometrix.com/academy and enter code: 691598

Tides

The gravitational pull of the Sun and Moon causes the oceans to rise and fall each day. This creates high and low tides. Most areas have two high tides and two low tides per day. The gravitational pull is much greater. The reason is that the Moon is closer to the earth than the Sun. So, its gravitational pull is much greater.

The water on the side of the earth that is closest to the Moon along with the water on the opposite side has high tide. The two low tides happen on the other sides. This can change as the Moon moves around the earth.

Tidal range is the height difference between low and high tide. Tidal range also changes with the location of the Sun and Moon throughout the year. So, this makes spring and neap tides. When all these bodies are in a line, the combined gravitational pull is greater and the tidal range is also greater. This is what creates the **spring tide**. The **neap tide** is when the tidal range is at its lowest. This happens when the Sun and Moon are at right angles.

Chapter Quiz

Ready to see how well you retained what you just read? Scan the QR code to go directly to the chapter quiz interface for this study guide. If you're using a computer, simply visit the bonus page at **mometrix.com/bonus948/ged** and click the Chapter Quizzes link.

Social Studies

Transform passive reading into active learning! After immersing yourself in this chapter, put your comprehension to the test by taking a quiz. The insights you gained will stay with you longer this way. Scan the QR code to go directly to the chapter quiz interface for this study guide. If you're using a computer, simply visit the bonus page at **mometrix.com/bonus948/ged** and click the Chapter Quizzes link.

Reading for Meaning in Social Studies

Main Ideas and Details in Social Studies Readings

When reading a complex text, it's easy to get bogged down in details and minutiae and miss the main idea that the text is trying to convey. If the source in question is a textbook or other reference work with clear sections and headings, those headings generally state the main ideas of the text. It may be helpful to read the headings first, to know the ideas that the text is intended to present. Otherwise, if the main idea of a text is unclear at first read, it may help to break it down a piece at a time.

Look at each paragraph: What is the paragraph about? Is there a topic sentence at the beginning or end or a question raised at the beginning? Is there a particular subject that comes up in nearly every sentence? Is there a detail that's given especial emphasis? Any of those factors points to the main idea of the paragraph. When you know the main topic that each paragraph is meant to convey, put them together and look for a common thread or a repeated idea that keeps coming up. That idea is likely related to the main idea of the text as a whole.

Often, information can be inferred from a text that is not explicitly stated. A text may suggest connections that the writer doesn't call out. If a text relates that a settlement had poor sanitation and later mentions a high prevalence of disease there, it's a reasonable inference that the former caused the latter. A writer's word choice can often allow the reader to make inferences about the writer's attitude toward the subject. If a writer refers to one side in a conflict as brave, the writer probably sympathizes with that side; if the writer refers to that side as reckless, the opposite may be true.

Sometimes inferences can be drawn from what the writer *doesn't* include. If a detailed description of a war between two ancient civilizations only mentions the use of soldiers on horseback by one side, it may be a reasonable inference that the other side didn't have access to horses. Sometimes outside information helps with inferences. A description of a merchant's household by itself may not be illuminating, but by comparison with what the reader knows of the usual standard of living at the time, the reader may infer that the merchant was especially well off.

How Authors Use Language in Social Studies

As with other academic disciplines, social studies has its own form of language that may not be exactly the same as the language used in everyday life outside of the field. Most notably, social studies has its own vocabulary, comprising words that are more or less unique to the discipline (such as oligarchy and populism) and words that have a different meaning than in most other contexts (such as capital and nation). It also has a different emphasis, often focusing more on abstract principles and connections than on concrete details. Even the grammar structures are different: Most social studies texts use a more formal tone and more complicated sentences than are typically found in conversational language.

Social studies, more so than other academic fields such as science and mathematics, makes heavy use of sentence structures referring to sequences of events, to causality, and to other connections between events and ideas. Social studies is heavily concerned with histories and with how concepts and events relate to each other, and the language reflects that. Readers of social studies texts should watch for words, phrases, and sentence structures indicating such temporal and causal relationships, such as "in the following years" or "as a consequence."

Fact Versus Opinion

When reading a historical document or other source, it's important to separate fact from opinion. A **fact** is a relation of an event that happened, or a statement of a condition, without judgment as to whether the event or condition was good or bad, or speculation about its causes and consequences. These judgments and speculations reflect the writer's **opinion**—the writer's own subjective feelings and thoughts about the topic in question.

It's important to separate fact from opinion: The facts about a historical happening may not be in dispute (if the writer is reliable and not lying or stretching the truth), but opinions may differ, and they cannot be taken as truth. That doesn't mean, however, that opinions don't have their place. Although a writer's opinion may not change the facts—and the reader may even disagree with it—it still has value. It helps show the writer's attitudes and thought processes, which help the reader judge the writer's reliability. It may reflect or illuminate common attitudes of the time. And it may possibly provoke further thought on a subject or help the reader to see a different perspective on it.

Claims and Evidence in Social Studies

Not everything you read or hear can be taken at face value. Before believing a claim in a passage, it's important to check whether it's supported by evidence. This is especially important when the passage comes from a highly biased source or if it goes strongly against conventional wisdom—that doesn't necessarily mean that the claim is false, but it definitely suggests that it should be checked.

Is the claim based on facts, rather than just on opinion and emotion? Can those facts be verified? Does the passage cite its sources, and, if so, do those sources really say what the passage says they do? (That's important to check, too; just because a passage cites a source doesn't mean that source really supports its argument.) Look for some other sources about topics related to the claim—do they agree with the facts stated in the passage? Do they provide any important details that the passage omits? Does the passage follow a valid chain of reasoning from the facts to the claim, or does it leap to conclusions or contain an important fallacy?

It may not always be simple to check the evidence behind a claim, but you shouldn't believe every claim without doing so.

Common Fallacies in Arguments

A **fallacy** is a method of argument that might seem superficially convincing but doesn't really lead reliably to the conclusion. There are many different fallacies that are common in arguments in social studies and in other contexts; the following are just a few of the most frequent.

- **Post hoc fallacy**: The assumption that because one event occurred after another, it must have been caused by it.
- **Circular reasoning** (begging the question): An argument that starts by assuming the conclusion must be true.

- **False dichotomy** (excluded middle): An argument based on the assumption that one of two options must be true, ignoring other possibilities.
- **Appeal to ignorance**: An argument that the conclusion must be true just because it hasn't been proven to be false.
- **Argument from authority**: An argument that the conclusion must be true just because some respected person said so.
- **Hasty generalization**: The assumption that something true of a small sample must be true of an entire population.
- **False analogy**: Drawing an analogy between two subjects based on some point of similarity and then assuming that they must be similar in other ways as well.
- **Slippery slope**: The argument that a small allowance must inevitably lead to an extreme consequence.

Sources with Conflicting Information

Historical documents and secondary sources such as textbooks and encyclopedias may contradict each other about social studies topics—or, even if there is no direct contradiction, one source may contain some important details not contained in the other. These differences may be due to bias; one source may be distorting the facts, intentionally or subconsciously, in the interests of pushing a point of view. However, one source may also have an error due to an honest mistake or a misunderstanding. The difference in sources may only be due to their purpose or target audience: A source may omit some facts simply because they weren't relevant to its purpose.

In any case, this possible difference in information between sources is one reason why it's important, where possible, to draw on multiple sources. If two secondary sources contradict each other, it may help to check the primary sources that they draw from. If this isn't possible, or if the primary sources themselves contradict each other, then you can examine the sources for possible bias and check many sources to see which might be outliers. Even when no one source gives full information, with multiple sources it may be possible to arrive at the truth.

Analyzing Historical Events and Arguments in Social Studies

Making Inferences

Inference refers to drawing conclusions based on data—putting together what you know and using logic and analysis to figure out details that aren't explicitly given. Available primary sources may not explicitly state all the facts, and some things may need to be inferred—or sometimes the primary sources actually *mis*state facts due to bias or limited knowledge but there's enough information to infer the truth. Things that are commonly inferred include cause-and-effect relationships, motivations and attitudes of historical individuals, or details about everyday life or environments in ancient civilizations that the people of the time didn't bother to explicitly write down. For instance, if there are a lot of similarities between two civilizations in different places, one might infer that the second civilization was founded by people who emigrated from the first.

Review Video: Inference
Visit mometrix.com/academy and enter code: 379203

Because they go beyond the available facts and rely on some supposition and probability, inferences may be mistaken. For instance, in the example above, the similarities between the two civilizations could be coincidental or they could both have been borrowed from a third civilization.

It's useful to look for more evidence to support an inference or to make predictions based on the inference that can be verified.

Connections Between Different Social Studies Elements (People, Events, Places, Processes)

Not only can events be directly caused by prior events, but they can also be influenced by events and ideas. For instance, the founding fathers of the American government did not come up with their revolutionary ideas in a vacuum. They were heavily influenced by the philosophy of the Enlightenment that had recently developed in Europe. Had this philosophy not developed, the Revolution might not have occurred, or at least it may not have proceeded exactly as it did. This goes both ways: Just as events can be influenced by ideas, ideas can form because of or in reaction to events. The Enlightenment itself might not have happened as it did were it not for the Thirty Years' War, which broke the power of the Holy Roman Empire and raised doubts in many writers' minds about nationalism and dogmatism.

Of course, it's rarely correct to say that one event or idea was the *only* cause of another event or idea. Events have many causes, and it's often difficult to determine the main influences leading to a particular event or process. Nevertheless, finding patterns and possible cause-and-effect relationships can lead to a better understanding of the processes involved.

Cause-and-Effect Relationships

History is not a series of disconnected events. Prior events have an influence on future events, and events can be said to be **caused** by events in the past. These relationships are said to be cause-and-effect relationships because the first event is a cause of the second event, which is an **effect** of the first.

The fact that one event comes after another does *not* necessarily mean that the first event caused the second. For example, in the years 735 to 737, an epidemic of smallpox killed about a quarter of the population of Japan. In 739, there was a major rebellion against the oppressive government of northwestern Africa. Did the smallpox epidemic cause the rebellion? It seems very unlikely that there's any connection; they happened in different parts of the world that were not in direct communication. To establish cause and effect, it's important to come up with a plausible explanation as to *how* the first event could have affected the second. The idea can be tested by looking for similar events to the first, and checking whether they led to similar effects. Deciding whether a cause-and-effect relationship exists is not always straightforward, and historians often debate particular examples.

Role of Individuals in History

On a large scale, history may seem like it's mostly about the clashes and relationships of nations and cultures. But those nations and cultures are made up of individual people, and some of those people may have especially large influences. There has been some controversy about to what extent history should be seen as directed by a few exceptional individuals, or to what extent those people were themselves products of their environment and culture, meaning that if they hadn't come around then someone else would inevitably have taken their place. The truth may be somewhere in between; certainly, people are influenced by their cultures, but there are still particular individuals without whom the course of history would not have gone exactly as it did.

The most obvious people of significance are political leaders: kings, emperors, and presidents. But they are not the only people who change the course of history, nor are they even necessarily the most important ones. Writers and philosophers who bring about important changes in ideas, scientists and inventors who pioneer new technologies, revolutionaries who overthrow established orders, and traders and explorers who bring cultures together—all of these and more may have important impacts on world events.

Role of Places in History

Historical events are influenced not only by the people involved in them and the prior events that led up to them, but by the places in which they occur. Different countries and communities have different cultures and traditions that may impact the events that happen there, and different geographical areas may have different environments that likewise have their importance for events.

To understand historical processes, it may be important to know not just where they initially occurred, but also the layout of the surrounding area and the locations and nature of other places nearby. The particular path that an idea took to spread, the route taken by an army, or the course of a trade route that led to important cultural cross-fertilization may all have been constrained by geographical and cultural considerations. To understand why the idea, army, or trade route took the track it did, it may be necessary to know the lay of the land and the characteristics of the places that it passed through—and of the places it did *not* pass through. These routes may have enormous impacts on the course of history.

Role of Available Resources in the Development of a Culture

The availability of resources places important constraints on the development of a culture or a civilization. A place rich with fertile soil ripe for farmland may lead to rapid development and prosperous civilizations, whereas one in which agriculture is difficult will force its people to find other means of acquiring food and is likely to be more sparsely settled. It's no coincidence that the ancient Egyptian civilization was concentrated along the Nile River and not in the open desert. A civilization with considerable mineral wealth that it can exploit will develop differently from one in a forested area that relies instead on wood; each will develop its own types of tools and structures that make the best use of the resources available.

Of course, local limitations in resources can be ameliorated by trade: A settlement rich in one resource but poor in another can trade with another settlement to get the resources it needs. But this itself has a significant impact on the civilizations that are involved in the trade: The necessity of opening and maintaining trade routes may lead to further innovations, and the two civilizations in contact for trade will also engage in cultural exchange and share ideas with each other.

Role of Climate in the Development of a Culture

Climate refers to the prevailing weather and temperature patterns in a particular region. Its effects on the development of cultures and settlements in that region can be profound. Most obviously, it affects the possible agriculture there: Depending on the temperature and rainfall, different crops can be grown, and cultures may develop around the available crops; in extreme climates, agriculture might not be possible at all, and people must find other ways to subsist. Other resources, too, may be affected by climate: For example, wood is only available in climates that permit trees to grow and clay is only available in wet climates.

Extreme climates require special cultural developments to adapt to them. The Inuit of northern Canada must deal with extreme cold, the Bedouins of the Sahara must deal with heat and aridity, and both of these cultures are heavily and clearly shaped by these climate conditions very differently from people of temperate climes. Even today, in our industrial societies, our construction practices are constrained to some degree by climate conditions. In places where hurricanes and tornadoes are frequent, for instance, houses are constructed with storm cellars and reinforced windows to protect against these climatic disasters.

Physical and Cultural Geography

Physical geography refers to the natural characteristics of a region—landforms, climate, water sources, and so on. **Cultural geography** refers to the variation in human customs and cultures in different places. The physical geography of a region can have many important effects on the development of settlements and cultures there. The terrain may affect the available resources: A well-watered lowland may have plenty of wood and clay available, whereas a mountainous highland might have useful stone and ore.

The physical geography, too, constrains the extent of trade and the routes it can take. One reason that major world cities have usually been on seacoasts or on large rivers is because they enable efficient trade by ship. On the other hand, a civilization that arises in a mountainous area is likely to be more isolated due to the difficulty of reaching and trading with other settlements.

But it goes both ways: People can affect the physical geography as well. To create more arable land, people might fill bogs, dig canals for irrigation, and create terraces on slopes. But sometimes the changes can be counterproductive: Careless deforestation, overexploitation, and pollution can devastate the landscape and make it less useful in the future.

Order of Events in a Historical Process

In a complicated process, it may not always be easy to determine the order of events or to remember that order. But most processes in social studies, or in any other endeavor, are not just series of separate events in arbitrary order. There is a reason for the order: one event leads to another. Recognizing that makes it easier to understand the order of events. If you find one event that seems likely to be the cause of another because, for instance, it set up the conditions that the second event required, then the cause must come before the effect. For instance, in 13th-century England, King Henry III called the first parliament and King John signed the Magna Carta. Which came first? Before the Magna Carta, the king's power was more or less absolute, and there would have been no need for a parliament, so King John must have come before King Henry III.

One useful tool in social studies for visualizing the order of events is a **timeline**. In a timeline, events are ordered along a line, with a mark for each event labeled with the event and date. Below is a sample time line of some significant events in 13th-century England.

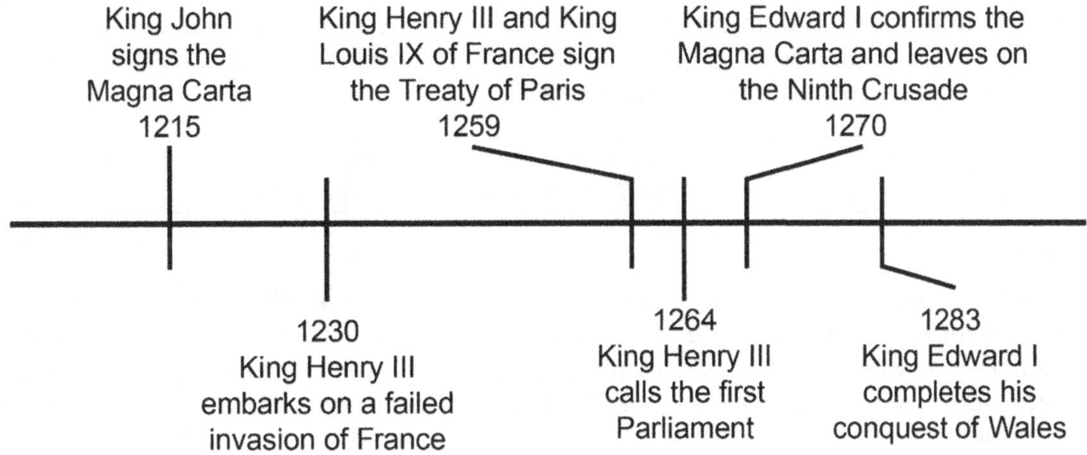

Understanding the Steps in a Social or Governmental Process

Like the order of historical events, the order of steps in a process is not arbitrary; it relies on cause and effect and on one step setting up the necessary preconditions for the next. Understanding the relationships between the steps, and the reasons for each step, makes it easier to understand their order.

For example, here are some of the main steps in the process of a bill becoming a law in the United States:

- The bill is drafted (written).
- The bill is introduced in the Senate or the House of Representatives.
- The bill goes to a committee.
- The committee votes to accept the bill.
- The entire house debates the bill.
- The members vote to confirm the bill.
- The bill goes to the other house (House or Senate), and the process repeats.
- The bill goes to the president, who has a chance to veto it.

These steps wouldn't really make sense in another order. Clearly, the bill has to be written before anything else can be done. It wouldn't make sense for legislators to debate the bill *after* they've voted on it, and they can't do either until it's been introduced.

The Effect of Different Social Studies Concepts on an Argument or Point-Of-View

Author's Point of View

Primary and secondary sources are written by human beings who have their own points of view that affect their writing. Every author has a point of view, an opinion on the topics that the author writes about, shaped by the author's experiences and environment.

Many authors may be biased toward their own nations and civilizations and may tend to present them in a positive light and rationalize away any shortcomings. Along similar lines, events that negatively affected the authors' civilizations, or the authors themselves, may color their opinion of ideas associated with those events.

An author always has a purpose for writing a passage and an audience in mind for it. Looking into the context of the passage, the situation the author was in when it was written, and events that may have recently affected the author can help give clues as to what the purpose and the audience were. Understanding the author's point of view, the purpose of the passage, and its intended audience helps the reader more reliably interpret the passage.

Review Video: Point of View
Visit mometrix.com/academy and enter code: 383336

Evidence

For primary sources to give compelling evidence toward a conclusion, the evidence must be factual, relevant, and sufficient. **Factual** evidence is evidence that is based on objective and verifiable facts, rather than relying solely or primarily on opinions and emotions. Many persuasive essays may be very light on facts, instead just appealing to the prejudices and feelings of the intended audience, making speculative predictions as to what the author thinks will happen if the author's advice is not followed, and so on. Such passages may show the author's point of view and perhaps give some illumination about common attitudes at the time, but they are not otherwise useful as evidence for actual events and situations.

Some sources may go beyond omitting factual material and may actually invent or distort facts and give misinformation. In the absence of other contemporary sources that provide the correct information, such distortion of facts may be hard to recognize, but it can help to examine sources for possible bias. Highly biased sources are much more likely to misrepresent the facts.

Evidence supporting a particular conclusion is **relevant** if it can be used as part of a reasonable logical argument for or against the conclusion. A passage may present evidence for a point of view that is *factual*, in the sense that it gives correct and verifiable information, but it may not be *relevant*, in the sense that it doesn't actually support the desired conclusion. This doesn't mean that the irrelevant information is out of left field and completely unrelated to the conclusion, but it may be irrelevant because the author assumes a connection that may not be supported. For example, an author may argue that a civilization is in decline and soon to fall by relating an account of an older civilization that shared with the modern civilization certain characteristics of which the author disapproves, and that was destroyed soon after adopting these characteristics. But it may be that there's no reason to believe that those characteristics were a contributing factor to the fall and that there are other features of the older civilization *not* shared by the modern civilization that can be shown to be responsible for its decline. In this case, the account of the older civilization may be *factual*, but not *relevant*.

Evidence supporting a particular conclusion is **sufficient** if it can be used to prove the conclusion beyond a reasonable doubt. It is possible for a passage to supply evidence that is *factual*, in the sense that it gives correct and verifiable information, and *relevant*, in that it does support the conclusion, but not *sufficient*, in that it leaves open the possibility that the conclusion is incorrect. For example, suppose an author wants to argue that a past writer's account of a certain conflict was fabricated. To support this, the author gives evidence that the writer was biased toward one side of the conflict—perhaps the writer had given financial support to the favored side. This may be *factual*; the writer may really have had that bias. It is certainly *relevant*; the writer's bias makes it more likely that the writer distorted the facts. But it is not *sufficient*: Just because the writer was biased toward one side of the conflict, that doesn't necessarily *prove* that the writer lied about it. If, however, other, less-biased contemporary accounts can be found that contradict the writer's account, then that may come closer to being sufficient evidence.

Assessing an Author's Argument

An author's point of view is affected not only directly by events that occurred to or around the author, but by ideas as well, by philosophies and principles that the author came into contact with. Understanding an author's point of view, and so better comprehending the author's argument, may be facilitated by knowing about some of the prevailing ideas that were current in the author's time and place and that may have affected the author's writing. Even the most independent-minded, free-thinking author must be to some extent a product of his or her environment and is not completely unaffected by the ideas of others.

For example, suppose you read a passage from a Chinese writer in the first century BC. This was a time when Confucianism was at its height in China, and had recently become officially adopted by the Chinese government. Certainly, the philosophy of Confucianism would have had some influence on the writer—even if the writer personally disagreed with the philosophy, the passage may represent the writer's reaction *against* this way of thinking that dominated the writer's society. A knowledge of Confucianist thought will therefore be helpful in fully understanding the writer's point of view.

IDENTIFYING BIAS AND PROPAGANDA IN SOCIAL STUDIES READINGS

Bias refers to the presentation of events in a way that is disproportionately favorable to a person, group, or idea that the presenter favors, or in a way that is disproportionately unfavorable to one that the presenter does not favor. It is not necessarily intentional; writers may let bias creep into their work without realizing it.

Sometimes a writer's bias may be obvious from the language used, with one side always referred to with positive language (heroic, just) and the other with negative language, or even by slurs. But bias isn't always that obvious or easy to identify. Sometimes it can be recognized by comparing different accounts. Do the accounts disagree? Did one writer omit an important fact that changes the impression of a particular group? (Bias can be by omission; a writer may *leave out* a detail that portrays a group in a different light—or may not mention at all a person or group that he or she doesn't like.) It may also be useful to consider the source: a study funded by a company with a financial interest in the result may not *necessarily* be biased, but it is certainly more likely to be. Readers should always be sensitive to the possible presence of bias in a text.

Propaganda is communication designed to manipulate or sway people toward the presenter's point of view. Often it relies more on emotion than on fact, playing on the target's own possible prejudices and beliefs. Propaganda differs from bias in that it is always conscious and intentional; indeed, it is generally the primary purpose of the work in question. Because it is done purposefully, however, propaganda can be carefully planned and worked out to maximize its effectiveness.

Propaganda often uses more obviously charged and inflammatory language than unconsciously biased writing, even using strong symbols and metaphors to demonize or dehumanize the opponent. Nazi propaganda, for instance, often referred to Jews as rats. Other specific propaganda techniques to look out for include bandwagon appeals (trying to convince the targets that *everyone else* already shares the propagandist's point of view), the similar common man or plain folks approach (suggesting that the propagandist's point of view is just what the average person believes anyway and that those who disagree are arrogant elitists), and cults of personality (holding up a charismatic individual who others may be drawn to follow as the face of the propagandist's movement).

SOCIAL STUDIES IN VISUAL MEDIA

PHOTOGRAPHS

Photographs are invaluable tools in social studies, showing real records of historical places and events. Like any other primary sources, however, they require skill and care to analyze effectively. Analyzing a photo involves more than just glancing at it and making a snap judgment of what's going on in it. First, spend some time to take a close look at the photograph. Pay attention not just to the foreground elements, but to the background elements as well—including signs and landmarks that may give an indication as to the location, people in the background who may be reacting to foreground events, and so on. Take careful note of all the people and objects in the photograph and all the activities that are going on. Based on what you see in the photograph, including people's clothing, background elements, etc., try to make a guess as to where and when the photograph was likely taken, who the people in it were, and what they were doing. Try to think of a question raised by what you've determined so far, and then look for evidence in the photograph that might point to a possible answer to that question.

POLITICAL CARTOONS

Political cartoons, or editorial cartoons, have been used since the 18th century as a way for artists to comment on contemporary events and prominent figures. Their purpose is not to objectively show what was going on at the time, but rather to express the cartoonist's opinions. They are useful as reflections of prevailing attitudes at the time they were drawn, as well as occasionally providing provocative points of view or hinting at other sides of issues.

Often, political cartoonists explicitly label the elements of their cartoons to clarify what they represent. At other times, they rely on common symbols and on recognizable faces. Symbols and faces that were well known in the past, however, may not be so well known today; we may still recognize elephants and donkeys as representing the Republican and Democratic Parties, and we can identify a drawing of Barack Obama, but we may not recognize John Bull (an old personification of England) or Boss Tweed (a notoriously corrupt 19th-century politician). Therefore, some historical knowledge may be necessary to interpret an old cartoon. Once you know what each symbol or figure represents, look at their relations and interactions to determine what point the cartoonist is trying to make.

Using Numbers and Graphics in Social Studies

USING DATA PRESENTED IN VISUAL FORM, INCLUDING MAPS, CHARTS, GRAPHS, AND TABLES

UNDERSTANDING GRAPHICS

There are many ways that qualitative data may be presented: in words, in graphs, in tables, or in charts. It's straightforward to compare two graphs with each other or two tables. But when two data sets are presented in different ways—when, for instance, one is presented in a table and the other in a graph—then it may not be easy to compare them at a glance.

If you only need to compare a few specific data points, it's relatively straightforward to just pick out those data points from each set and then consider them independently of the rest of the data. However, you may want to compare the data sets as a whole, looking for similarities in trends or behavior and picking out a handful of points isn't enough. In that case, the simplest approach may be to take one of the data sets and represent it in the form of the other. If you want to compare a graph and a table, for instance, take the data from the table and draw it as a graph, or vice versa. That way, you're left with two tables or two graphs that can easily be compared.

ANALYZING INFORMATION FROM A MAP

Maps are a very common and valuable tool in social studies, showing spatial expanses and relationships at a glance. However, effective use of a map requires understanding some key features. First of all, the title of the map may give important indications of what it's supposed to represent, and the main idea it's intended to get across. It's always important to check the **scale** of a map to get an idea of the distances involved. (There are exceptions—special maps that resize states or countries proportional to their populations or other factors do not have consistent scales—but they are unusual.) If there are symbols, patterns, or colors involved, the meanings of which aren't clear, the map should also have a **key** explaining them. A map may also have a **compass rose** showing which way is north; usually the top of the map is north, but not always.

Curved surfaces such as the surface of the earth can't be fit exactly onto flat maps, so be aware of the distortions of shapes and distances in maps, especially maps of large areas. The Mercator projection, long popular for school world maps, is notorious for drastically exaggerating the sizes of landmasses near the poles.

Dependent and Independent Variables

As in science, when you compare two variables in social studies, generally you can consider one as the independent variable and the other as the dependent variable. In a graph, the dependent variable goes on the *x* axis, and the dependent variable goes on the *y* axis.

To see which one is the dependent variable and which one is the independent variable, consider which one can better be said to cause or influence the other. For instance, if one compares the average population of settlements at different elevations, it makes more sense to choose the elevation as the independent variable and the population as the dependent. The elevation may well affect the population, but the population does not affect the elevation—the land will not rise or fall depending on the number of people living in a settlement.

Sometimes two variables may be interdependent, each affecting the other in a feedback loop. Suppose you're comparing families' wealth to their education levels. Wealthier families are better able to send their children to good universities, but more highly educated people may have a better opportunity to accrue wealth. So, which is the cause and which is the effect? In cases such as these, the choice may be arbitrary and may depend on the specific relationship you're looking for.

Analyzing Information from a Table

Tables are simple, compact, and widely used methods of conveying information that falls into different categories. They're especially common and useful when there are two sets of categories according to which the data can be arranged—one set of categories then makes up the rows of the table, and the other makes up the columns—or when there are discrete data sets with multiple values that can be arranged in rows.

To make effective use of a table, first check the title of the table, if one is provided, to get a big picture of the table's purpose and then look at the labels of the rows and columns. Each cell of the table gives a quantity or quality associated with the categories in the corresponding row and column. Consider the following sample table:

Crop Yields in Provinces of Tabolia (in hundreds of tons)

Province / Season	Ablia	Betal	Catabel	Datia	Elbatia
Spring	23	33	55	29	20
Summer	35	46	60	40	33
Autumn	65	87	93	66	59
Winter	11	15	22	13	12

The title tells what the table is about: crop yields in the provinces of the (fictitious) nation of Tabolia. Each cell represents the yields in a particular province and season; thus, for instance, the intersection of the first row and third column gives the yield in Catabel during the spring, which is 55 (i.e., according to the units given in the title, 5,500 tons).

Analyzing a Pie Chart

A **pie chart** is one common kind of chart often used in social studies in which different categories are represented as sectors of a circle. As with other charts and graphs, it's important to first read the title of the chart to see an overview of what it is about. The sectors may be labeled directly with the corresponding categories, or they may be given different colors or patterns, in which case you should look for a key to see what each represents. The percentage of the circle occupied by each sector also may or may not be explicitly labeled. If it is not, it can be estimated visually: Half the circle is 50%, a quarter is 25%, and so on.

Consider the following sample pie chart:

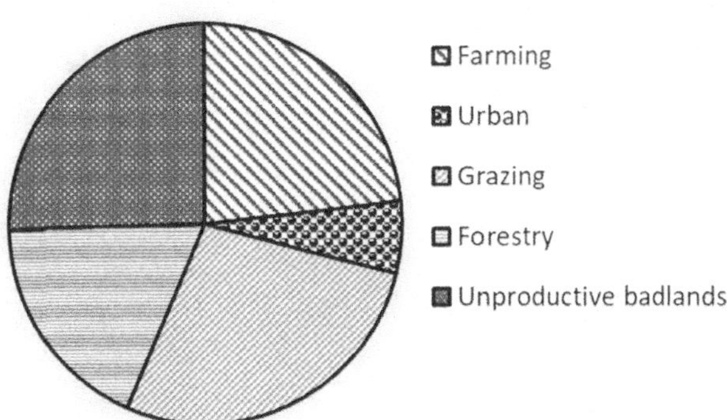

According to the title, this chart shows land use in the (fictitious) country of Picharat. The key to the right shows what each sector represents: The blue striped sector in the upper right, for instance, represents the percentage of the land used for farming. Although the percentages are not explicitly given in the chart, we can estimate them: The farming sector takes up a little less than a quarter of the circle, so it looks like around 23%.

INTERPRETING A LINE GRAPH

A **line graph** is a type of graph that shows a relationship between two variables, the dependent variable on the *y* axis and the independent variable on the *x*. In interpreting a line graph, it's useful to first look at the title to observe the overall relationship that it is intended to convey and then look at the labels of the axes to see what two variables are involved. The overall shape of the graph shows the general relationship between the variables. For instance, if the graph slopes upward, the variables are positively correlated: As one increases, so does the other. If the graph slopes downward, they are negatively correlated: An increase in one accompanies a decrease in the other.

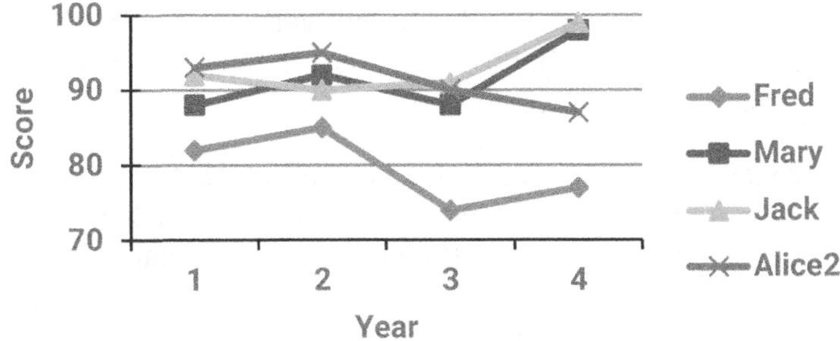

To find the value of the dependent variable for a specific value of the independent variable, find the appropriate value of the independent variable on the *x* axis, interpolating between labels if necessary. Trace a line straight upward until you hit the graph, and then trace a line from there left to the *y* axis; the position on which gives the value of the dependent variable. The reverse process can provide the value of the independent variable for a specific value of the dependent variable.

Interpreting a Bar Graph

A **bar graph** is a graph showing the relationship between two variables in which the height of a bar for each value of the independent variable indicates the corresponding value of the dependent variable. Unlike for a line graph, the independent variable need not be quantitative, but it may represent qualitative values such as countries or types of terrain.

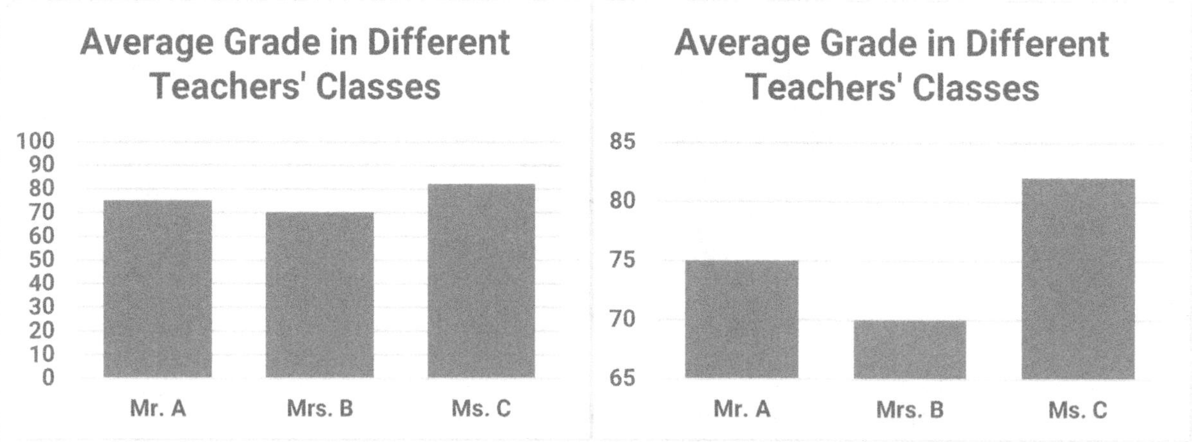

Interpreting a bar graph is relatively straightforward. To find the value of the dependent variable corresponding to a particular value of the independent variable, first find the appropriate value on the x axis and then look at the height of the corresponding bar, checking it against the scale of the y axis. One pitfall to look out for, however, is that if the scale of the y axis does not start at 0, the difference between values may be exaggerated. Compare the following two graphs, which show the same data, but with the y axis starting at 0 on the left graph and starting at 65 on the right. If you don't look carefully, you could get the mistaken impression from the graph on the right that the average grade of students in Ms. C's class is more than three times that in Mrs. B's!

Utilizing Graphics

Making a Table

A table is a convenient way to concisely display data that depend on two different variables or that depend on one variable but include several different quantities. In the former case, the independent variable usually goes in the columns and the dependent variable goes in the rows, although this rule isn't as hard and fast as it is for graphs. In the latter case, the independent variable goes in the first column and each other quantity in its own column.

For instance, suppose that you want to record the population, elevation, and area of several different cities. Each city would get its own row in the table, and the first column would be the name of the city because the city is effectively the independent variable. Then the second column could hold the population of each city, the third could hold the elevation, and the fourth could hold the area, with each going in the appropriate row.

As with any other form of data presentation, it's important that a table be clearly labeled so the reader can easily see what each value represents. For instance, the table described above might look as follows:

City	Population (thousands)	Elevation (feet)	Area (square miles)
A-Ville	39	1,200	1.2
B-Town	220	30	5.0

City	Population (thousands)	Elevation (feet)	Area (square miles)
C-Burg	45	-200	2.5
D-Grad	23	330	0.8
...	...	...	...

Creating a Pie Chart

A pie chart is a circular chart showing the relative quantity of various categories, each category being represented by a sector or wedge of the circle with its size proportional to its value. Many utilities such as Microsoft Excel can generate pie charts automatically, but it's useful to know how to create them yourself. To draw a pie chart, the first step is to represent each of the values as a percentage of the whole; these percentages must add to 100%. The simplest way to do this is to total all the values and then divide each value by the total; these quotients give the fraction or percentage of the whole that each value represents. For instance, if your values are 40, 20, 15, and 5, then the percentages are $\frac{40}{80} = 100\%$, $\frac{20}{8} = 25\%$, $\frac{15}{80} \approx 19\%$, and $\frac{5}{80} \approx 6\%$. Then draw a circle where each category is allotted a fraction of the circle equal to its fraction of the whole. Either label the values directly on the chart, or assign a color or pattern to each value and fill in the appropriate sectors accordingly, making sure you also include a key so the reader knows which is which.

Drawing a Line Graph

To create a line graph to show the relationship between two variables, first decide on your axes. The dependent variable goes on the y axis, and the independent variable goes on the x axis. Be sure to label the axes with the appropriate quantities. Now, decide on the scale for the axes. In general, you want to avoid leaving too much blank space on any side of the graph, so the scale should start shortly before to the minimum value of the variable and end shortly after the maximum. Grid lines and labels should be evenly spaced at round intervals, such as 5 or 10, not at arbitrary intervals such as 2.4 or 7.

Once you have set up and labeled the axes and the scale, you're ready to plot points. For each point on the graph, trace a vertical line up from the value of the independent variable on the x axis and a horizontal line right from the value of the dependent variable on the y axis and plot the point where those two lines cross. Once you've plotted all the points, you can connect them to produce the line graph.

Making a Bar Graph

Bar graphs are useful when you want to show how a quantitative variable differs for various values of a qualitative variable—they can also be used to show the relationship between two quantitative variables, but generally a line graph is better for that. The qualitative variable (or the independent variable, if they're both quantitative) goes on the x axis, and the other goes on the y axis. The value at the top of the y axis should be not much more than the maximum value of the dependent variable, but for the bottom you have a decision to make. Starting the scale at zero may wash out small differences between values, but starting the scale just below the minimum value may exaggerate the differences. The latter is usually preferable; the onus is on the reader to interpret the graph correctly.

Above each value of the independent variable, draw a bar with its top at the appropriate value of the dependent variable. You can extend a horizontal line to the right from the value on the y axis to find where to put the top of the bar. The bars should be evenly spaced and of uniform width; only their heights should differ.

Using a Graph to Predict Trends

Bar graphs and especially line graphs can be used to predict possible trends in data—that is, to make predictions of how the dependent variable will behave past the range of the independent variable that is represented in the graph. In the simplest form, you can look at whether the line seems to be going up or down—that is, whether the variable is increasing or decreasing—and predict that it will continue to do the same. If the value of the dependent variable consistently increases as the independent variable increases, then that represents a probable trend, and you can predict that it will continue to do so.

However, you can also predict more complex trends than that. What if the graph doesn't consistently increase or decrease, but has a more complex shape, such as a sine wave? Or, if it is increasing or decreasing, *how fast* is it increasing or decreasing? Linearly? Quadratically? Exponentially? Again, you can roughly predict the trend just by observing what the graph is doing during its range and assuming that it will continue to do the same. There are mathematical methods to find patterns in data more precisely, but they may not be necessary.

Correlation Versus Causation

Correlation refers to how closely the changes in two quantities tend to be connected. If the changes in one quantity closely mirror changes in the other—as one quantity rises, the other always rises as well, or as one rises the other always falls—then the two quantities are said to be highly correlated. (Correlation can be quantified by statistical techniques.) **Causation** refers to one event directly causing another or to the change in one quantity causing a change in another.

There is a common saying in statistics that correlation is not causation. What this means is that just because two quantities are correlated, it is not necessarily the case that one causes the other. Even if the correlation is a real phenomenon and not a coincidence, there could be some third factor behind both changes. For example, suppose that a survey of students at a K–12 school shows that taller students have larger vocabularies. Does a large vocabulary cause students to grow taller? Or does height make it easier to learn words? Neither: Older students tend to be taller, and older students tend to have larger vocabularies. The two quantities are correlated, but neither one causes the other.

Using Statistics in Social Studies

Mean, Median, Mode, and Range of a Set of Data

The **mean** of a set of data is what is usually meant by the average. To find the mean, add all the elements of the set together and divide by the number of elements. For example, consider the data set {48, 50, 55, 56, 60, 63, 68, 72, 77}. The sum of the elements is 549. There are nine elements, so the mean is $\frac{549}{9} = 61$. Note that, as in this example, the mean is not necessarily one of the elements itself.

The **median** of a set of data is the value in the middle of the set, when its elements are put in order. To find the median, you first order the elements of the set and then count them and find the element in the middle. For example, consider the data set {56, 22, 42, 99, 14, 22, 45, 40, 12}. Put in order, these elements are {12, 14, 22, 22, 40, 42, 45, 56, 99}. There are nine elements, so the middle element is the fifth, 40. Therefore, the median of this data set is 40.

In the case of a data set with an even number of elements, the median is the average of the two middle elements. For example, consider the data set {200, 150, 209, 222, 180, 184, 210, 190}. Put in order, this data set becomes {150, 180, 184, 190, 200, 209, 210, 222}. There are eight elements, so the middle elements are the fourth and fifth, 190 and 200, and the median is their average, 195.

The mean and median are both **measures of central tendency**: They both measure in some sense the center of a collection of data, or an average value—in fact, usually when people speak of the average, they're referring to the mean. For symmetrically distributed data sets such as classic bell curves, the mean and median are the same, but for other data sets, this may not be true. The mean has the advantage of accounting for all the data: A change in any element will change the mean. However, the median is less affected by **outliers**—unusual data points far from the other values—and may be more representative of a typical value for highly skewed data sets.

For example, suppose in a small village of 100 people, 33 people have a monthly income of $1,500, 33 people have a monthly income of $2,000, and 33 people have a monthly income of $2,500, and 1 very wealthy resident has a monthly income of $1,000,000. The *mean* income of the residents is:

$$\frac{33 \times 1{,}500 + 33 \times 2{,}000 + 33 \times 2{,}500 + 1{,}000{,}000}{100} = \$11{,}980$$

All but one of the residents earn much less than this. In this case, the *median* of $2,000 better represents the income of a typical resident.

The **mode** of a set of data is the value that appears most often. For instance, in the data set {2, 4, 5, 5, 6, 6, 7, 9, 9, 9, 10, 11, 11, 12, 14, 16, 18}, the value 9 appears three times; 5, 6, and 11 each appear twice; and each of the other values in the data set only appears once. The mode of the data set is 9.

It is possible for a data set not to have a mode. For instance, in the data set {22, 24, 26, 27, 31, 33, 36, 38, 41, 49}, each value appears exactly once; no value appears more than any other. It is also possible for a data set to have multiple modes; in the data set {5, 6, 6, 7, 10, 13, 15, 16, 16, 18, 20}, the values 6 and 16 each appear twice, while each other value appears once, so 6 and 16 are both modes. A data set with two modes is said to be **bimodal**.

The **range** of a set of data is the difference between the largest and the smallest values. To find the range, just subtract the smallest value in the data set from the largest. For example, for the data set {5, 7, 8, 8, 10, 12, 15, 17, 19, 30, 45}, the range is $45 - 5 = 40$.

The range is a rough measurement of the spread, or **dispersion**, of a set of data. It has the disadvantage, however, that it's very sensitive to **outliers**—individual data points far from the rest. For instance, in the data set {3, 5, 6, 7, 8, 11, 13, 13, 20,003}, the range is $20{,}003 - 3 = 20{,}000$—but most of that range is just due to the last data point, 20,003. Take out that single point, and the range shrinks to $13 - 3 = 10$. There are other measurements of dispersion that are less affected by outliers, but they can be more complicated to calculate.

Qualitative and Quantitative Data Sets

A **quantitative** data set is a data set of numerical values. These values may or may not have units; what is important is that they can be compared and mathematically manipulated. A **qualitative** data set is a data set of properties or objects that cannot be meaningfully ranked or added. For instance, {1950, 1952, 1977, 2002, 2005} is a set of quantitative data. So is {30 km, 35 km, 44 km, 62 km}. {Red, red, blue, white, green, white, red} is a set of qualitative data. The values—red, blue, white, and green—are not numerical, cannot be ranked (it doesn't make sense to say that red is greater than white, or vice versa), and cannot be added or otherwise combined mathematically.

Qualitative data sets do not have means, medians, or ranges; all of these properties depend on comparisons or arithmetical operations that cannot be carried out on unranked, nonnumeric values. Qualitative data sets *can*, however, have modes; the mode depends only on which values appear the most often, and it does not depend on any comparison or operation between values.

Social Studies Knowledge Overview

Civics and Government

Relevant Vocabulary

An **alliance** is an agreement between two or more countries to work together toward a common goal or against a common enemy.

An **amendment** is a change or addition to a document or agreement, while leaving most of it intact. In the United States, the term is especially commonly used to refer to the 27 amendments to the United States Constitution.

Amnesty refers to a government's forgiveness of some crime or offense, especially granted on a large scale.

Anarchy is the state of being without a strong central political authority, often because of a weak or failed government.

Apartheid refers to legally enforced separation of races, especially (but not exclusively) to the system that existed in 20th-century South Africa.

A **colony** is a territory settled by people from a distant country who are still subject to that country's government.

Migration in general refers to the movement of people from one country to another; emigration and immigration are special cases. **Emigration** refers to movement *out* of a country; **immigration** refers to movement *into* it. If a woman moves from Iran to the United States, she is emigrating from Iran and immigrating to the United States. (The relationship between the words is similar to that between **export** and **import** of goods—a good is exported *from* one country, and imported *into* another.)

Consensus refers to agreement of all or most of the people involved in a vote or deliberation.

Culture refers to the shared beliefs, values, and traditions of a community of people.

A **referendum** is a direct vote by the general population on a particular political matter, as opposed to a vote by elected representatives.

A **reform**, in the political sense, is a measure specifically intended to improve an undesirable state of affairs, often but not always involving some kind of corruption or abuse of a system.

A **treaty** is a formal written agreement between two countries.

Forms of Government

There are the four main ideas about the beginnings of government.

- Evolutionary—the state evolved from the family. The head of the state is like the family's male ruler or female ruler.
- Force—one person or group brought everyone in an area under their control. In this area, they formed the first government.
- Divine Right—certain people were chosen by a ruling god or goddess to be the rulers of the nation. The nation itself is created by the deity or deities.

- Social Contract—the idea that no natural order exists. People allow themselves to be ruled to keep order and avoid disorder. In turn, the state promises to protect the people they govern. If the government fails to protect the people, the people have the right to bring in new leaders.

Since ancient days, many types of government have organized society. Most forms of governments have worked in different ways from each other. These governments differ on many things. They differ on how the citizens are involved in selecting the leaders and the amount of power given to the government. Also, they differ on how often leadership changes occur and how the change in leadership will happen.

Monarchy

Monarchy was the major form of government for Europe for hundreds of years. A monarchy is led by a king or a queen. This ruling position is passed down to the children of the king and queen. In other words, the rulers are not elected. In modern times, constitutional monarchy has developed. A king or queen still exists in a constitutional monarchy. However, most of the decisions for the country are made by democratic institutions (e.g., British parliament).

Parliamentary Democracy

In a parliamentary system, the government has a legislature and many political parties. The head of the government, usually a Prime Minister, is typically the head of the party with the most members in parliament. A head of state can be elected, or this position can be taken by a monarch. An example would be Great Britain's constitutional monarchy system.

Direct and Indirect Democracy

In a democratic system of government, the people elect others to represent them in government. The word *democracy* is a Greek word that means "for the rule of the people." There are two forms of democracy: direct and indirect.

In a direct democracy, each issue or election is decided by voters who each have one vote. An indirect democracy, also known as representative democracy, uses a legislature (e.g., Congress) to vote on issues. In other words, the people are elected to the legislature. Those elected people vote for the people that they represent. Democracy can exist as a parliamentary system or a presidential system. The United States has a mix of a presidential system and an indirect democracy.

Presidential Democracy

A presidential system is like a parliamentary system. In a presidential system, there is a legislature and political parties. However, there is no difference between the head of state and the head of government. Instead of separating these roles, an elected president works in both areas. Election of the president can be direct or indirect. Also, the president may not belong to the largest political party.

Development of American Government

In the U.S. Constitution, there are many important ideas on government:

- **Individual rights**—there is no total freedom in a democracy. A person in a democracy cannot do whatever he or she wants. So, there are powers set up to protect people's rights. In addition, those powers do not become controlling and break people's rights.
- **Natural rights**— John Locke thought a person had rights at birth of "life, liberty, and private property." Thomas Jefferson agreed with Locke. In the Declaration of Independence, he wrote that people have the right to "life, liberty, and the pursuit of happiness."

- **Popular sovereignty**—the government is decided by the people. So, the government gains its rule and power from the people.
- **Separation of powers**—the government is divided into three branches: executive (e.g., President), legislative (e.g., Congress), and judicial (e.g., Supreme Court). Each branch has its own set of powers.
- **Constitutionalism**—the government must follow the ideas and rules in the constitution.
- **Checks and balances**—there is not one branch that can rule on its own. Each branch has the power to review the decisions of another
- **Limited government**—the powers of the government are limited. There are rights (e.g., Bill of Rights) for the people that cannot be broken by the government.
- **Federalism**—the power of the government does not belong only to the national government. Instead, power is divided between national and state governments.
- **Majority rule and minority rights**—the idea in a democracy that a greater number of people will make the right choice over a small group. However, the small group has rights that the majority cannot break.
- **Rule of law**—a government or rulers are not outside the boundaries of the law. They must follow the same laws as the people that they serve.

FEDERALISM

Disagreements on how federalism should be practiced have existed since the writing of the Constitution. There were—and still are—two main groups on this issue:

- **States' rights**—People who want the state governments to take the lead in managing problems.
- **Nationalist**—People who want the national government to take the lead in managing problems.

STRUCTURE AND DESIGN OF U.S. GOVERNMENT

In general political theory, there are the four major purposes of any government.

- **Ensuring national security**—the government protects against international, domestic, and terrorist attacks. The government makes sure that security continues by negotiating and having good relationships with other governments.
- **Providing public services**—the government should "promote the general welfare…to ourselves and [future generations]," as stated in the Preamble to the U.S. Constitution. This is done by providing what is needed to its citizens. This may be roads, libraries, or schools.
- **Ensure social order**—the government takes care of conflicts among citizens and writes laws to protect the nation, state, and city.
- **Make decisions about the economy**—there are laws that shape the economic policy of the country. These policies concern domestic and international trade (e.g., the transfer of goods and services). Also, these policies concern the issues that are linked to domestic and international trade.

The structure of the U.S. government divides powers between national and state governments. There are powers that are assigned to the national government by the Constitution:

- **Expressed powers**—the powers that can be found in the Constitution. Some of these are the power to raise and maintain an army, to declare war, to manage commerce (i.e., exchange of goods), to print money, and to gather taxes.

- **Implied powers**—the powers that are not written in the Constitution. However, they are understood powers of the national government. In Article 1, Section 18 of the U.S. Constitution, the Necessary and Proper Clause allows these powers. So, Congress can do things that are not directly stated. Some of these powers are to draft people for war, to punish people who don't pay taxes, to set a minimum wage, and to limit immigration.

There are three branches of the U.S. Federal government.

- **Legislative Branch**—this is the two Houses of Congress: the House of Representatives and the Senate. All members of the U.S. Congress are elected officials.
- **Executive Branch**—this branch is for the President, the Vice President, the presidential advisors, and cabinet members (e.g., Secretary of State and Secretary of Defense). These advisors are suggested by the President, and Congress must approve each member.
- **Judicial Branch**—this branch is made of the federal court system. The system is headed by the Supreme Court.

LEGISLATIVE BRANCH

The Legislative Branch is concerned with making laws. All laws are bills before they are passed by Congress. Every bill must be approved by Congress before it is passed into law. The Legislative Branch manages money and trade, approves appointments from the president, and establishes organizations like the postal service and federal courts. Congress can suggest amendments to the Constitution. Congress can impeach (i.e., bring charges against the president). Congress is the only branch that can declare war.

House of Representatives: There are 435 members in this side of Congress. That number can change as the population of a state changes. Every state is guaranteed at least one representative. States with higher populations have more representatives. The members face elections every two years. Most of their work is done in committees.

Senate: There are 100 members in this side of Congress. That number can change if more states join the United States of America. So, each state has two senators. The members face elections every six years. However, a third of the senators must face election every two years. So, the Senate is a stable group of members. Also, the senators do their work in committees and on the Senate floor.

Officers in Congress:

- **Speaker of the House**: The elected leader of the House and the leader of the majority party. The Speaker signs all bills passed by the House and puts motions to a vote. In addition, the Speaker chooses members of committees and allows members to speak on the House floor.
- **President of the Senate**: This position is given to the Vice President of the United States. However, the Vice President is not a member of the Senate. So, the Vice President has similar powers to the Speaker, but the Vice President cannot speak on the Senate floor. Also, the Vice President can vote when there is a tie.
- **President Pro Tempore**: When the Vice President is absent, the President Pro Tempore takes the Vice President's place in the Senate. The President Pro Tempore is elected by the Senate and is a member of the majority party.

Review Video: What Does the Legislative Branch Do?
Visit mometrix.com/academy and enter code: 405303

Executive Branch

The Executive Branch carries out the laws, treaties, and war declarations from Congress. The President may veto (i.e., refuse to accept) bills that are approved by Congress. Also, the president serves as commander-in-chief of the U.S. military. The president suggests cabinet members, ambassadors to foreign countries, and federal judges. Every year, the President delivers a State of the Union address to Congress. Also, the President sends a budget to Congress that they will review and debate to approve.

Review Video: What Does the Executive Branch Do?
Visit mometrix.com/academy and enter code: 210629

Judicial Branch

The Judicial Branch reviews the challenges on laws that are passed by Congress. This branch reviews these challenged laws to make sure that they agree with the U.S. Constitution. The Supreme Court may choose to review decisions made by lower courts. These lower courts include the U.S. Courts of Appeals and the U.S. District Courts.

Review Video: Three Branches of Government
Visit mometrix.com/academy and enter code: 718704

Individual Rights and Civic Responsibilities

The Amendment Process

The United States Constitution has been amended 27 times. The first ten are the Bill of Rights. Over two hundred years, many amendments have been suggested. However, only 17 have been accepted and added to the Constitution since the Bill of Rights. There are two ways to propose an amendment to the Constitution. One way is for the House and the Senate to pass the amendment with two-thirds accepting the amendment. The other way is for two-thirds of state legislatures to petition for an amendment. Then, Congress would call a national convention to pass the amendment.

If a proposed amendment passes, then the amendment must be ratified. Congress decides which way will be used. There are two ways for an amendment to be ratified. One way is for three-fourths of the state legislatures to approve the amendment. The other is for a convention to be called in every state. Three-fourths of these state conventions must approve the amendment. If the proposed amendment is accepted, then the proposed amendment becomes a part of the Constitution.

Bill of Rights

The first ten amendments of the U.S. Constitution are known as the **Bill of Rights**. These amendments keep the government from breaking the basic freedoms. The founding fathers argued that these amendments were natural rights that belong to everyone. These rights include freedom of speech, freedom of religion, and the right to bear arms. Many of the rights were written with the mistreatment of the British government in mind.

Review Video: What is the Bill of Rights?
Visit mometrix.com/academy and enter code: 585149

The first ten amendments were passed by Congress in 1789. Three fourths of the original thirteen states had approved them by December of 1791.

- **First Amendment**—the freedom of religion, freedom of speech, freedom of the press, freedom to assemble, and freedom to petition.
- **Second Amendment**—protects the right to bear arms.
- **Third Amendment**—Congress cannot force individuals to house troops.
- **Fourth Amendment**—Protection from unreasonable search and seizure.
- **Fifth Amendment**—no one is forced to testify against oneself, and no person may be tried twice for the same crime.
- **Sixth Amendment**—in a criminal trial, one has the right to a speedy and public trial with a fair jury. One has the right to know their criminal charges. One has the right to meet witnesses and to have witnesses come to the trial. One has the right to legal counsel.
- **Seventh Amendment**—right to civil trial by jury for cases that deal with claims of more than twenty dollars.
- **Eighth Amendment**—no extreme amount for bail. No cruel and unusual punishment.
- **Ninth Amendment**—the Bill of Rights is not a complete list of every individual freedom. So, the ninth amendment was added to guarantee other freedoms that are not written in the Bill of Rights.
- **Tenth Amendment**—any rights that are not given directly to the national government belong to the states or to the people

Sometimes, the government may hold back on some pieces of First Amendment rights. For example:

- **Freedom of religion**—when a religion does something that is illegal, the government does not allow the practice. Examples are animal sacrifice and use of illegal drugs or illegal substances.
- **Freedom of speech**—can be restricted if exercise of free speech endangers other people. Examples are lying about a fire in a crowded place or lying about a bomb on an airplane.
- **Freedom of the press**—in the United States, there is no prior restraint on the press. Prior restraint is when a government does not allow material to be published. The material may damage someone's reputation or be offensive. When the country is at war, some material may not be given to the public. This material could fall into the wrong hands and lead to violence.

In **emergency situations** (e.g. war or terrorist attack), there are more restrictions on these rights. The rights to free speech and assembly and freedom of the press are restricted in order to maintain national security.

Equality means that every man, woman, and child has the same rights and should be treated the same by the government. Amendments to the U.S. Constitution have given citizenship and voting rights to every American. The Supreme Court reviews laws and court decisions to decide if they agree with the idea of equality. An example is the Supreme Court case of Brown v. Board of Education. In 1954, the court said that "separate-but-equal" did not agree with the U.S. Constitution.

Who is a **citizen** of the United States? Anyone born in the U.S. is considered a citizen of the United States. Anyone born in another country to parents with U.S. citizenship status is considered a citizen of the United States. Also, anyone who has gone through a process of naturalization to become a citizen is considered a citizen of the United States.

Citizens of the United States have rights and responsibilities under the U.S. government. Duties of a U.S. citizen are:

- Paying taxes
- Serving on juries when summoned
- Loyalty to the government. The U.S. does not prosecute those who criticize or want to change the government.
- Support and defend the U.S. Constitution
- Serve in the Armed Forces as needed by law
- Obeying laws that are made by each level of government (e.g., city, state, and national laws).

Responsibilities of a U.S. citizen are:

- Voting in elections
- Staying informed about political and national issues
- Respecting one another's beliefs
- Respecting one another's rights

The terms civil liberties and civil rights are used synonymously, but there is a difference between the two terms. The terms are used to define the basics of a free state.

Civil liberty is the role of a government to have equal rights and opportunities for citizens. An example is non-discrimination policies when someone wants to become a citizen.

Civil rights are the limits on state rights. These rights are guaranteed to citizens and cannot be broken by the government. Examples of these rights include freedom of religion, political freedom, and overall freedom to live how we choose.

Suffrage and **franchise** are terms for the right to vote. In the early years of America, white male landowners were able to vote. By the 1800s, most states had given the right to vote to all adult white males. The Fifteenth Amendment of 1870 gave the right to vote to men without thought to their race. The Nineteenth Amendment gave women the right to vote. In 1971, the twenty-sixth amendment gave voting rights to any U.S. citizen over the age of eighteen. However, people who do not have full U.S. citizenship do not have voting rights. Also, citizens who have committed certain crimes do not have voting rights.

Campaigns, Elections, and Political Parties

Political Parties

Different types and numbers of political parties can have an important effect on a government. If there is a **single party** (i.e., a one-party system), the government is defined by that one party. All policy that comes from the government is based on that party's beliefs. In a **two-party system**, there are different viewpoints that compete for power and influence. There are checks and balances to make it difficult for one party to gain complete power over the other. In some governments, there are **multi-party systems** (i.e., three or more parties). In multiparty systems, two or more parties will come to agreements in order to form a majority and change the balance of power.

While other parties enter the picture in U.S. politics, the government is basically a two-party system. Today, the system is influenced by the Democrats and the Republicans.

Currently, there are four main political positions:

- **Liberal**—a position that thinks that government should work to increase equality. This may come at the expense of some freedoms. Also, the government should care for those in need of help. With this position, there is a need for social justice and free education for everyone.
- **Conservative**—a position that upholds that government should be limited in most cases. Government should allow its citizens to help one another and solve their own problems. The government should not bring about solutions. For example, rules for businesses should be loose and not limiting. A conservative person wants a free market.
- **Moderate**—a position that brings in some values from two sides. Generally, a moderate person shares some values from liberals and conservatives.
- **Libertarian**—a position that wants the responsibility of government to be limited to protecting the life and freedom of citizens. Also, the government should not trouble its citizens. The reason that the government would become involved is when a citizen interferes with the rights of another citizen.

Campaigns and Elections

In the history of the U.S., there have been a few ways to nominate someone to run for public office. At first, caucuses were used to select candidates. A **caucus** is a meeting for members of a political party. The members come together to nominate candidates for offices. Currently, some states still use caucuses.

Today, the common way to choose candidates for office is through primaries. A **primary** is a publicly held election to choose candidates. There are two kinds of primaries: closed and open. A **closed primary** is for members of one party. An **open primary** is for any voter who is willing and able to vote. Voters choose the ballot of the party that they want to use.

Presidential Elections

After the campaigns and primaries, the members of a party will nominate a candidate for the upcoming elections. The Democratic National Convention and the Republican National Convention choose the candidate that they want to run in the presidential election. On the first Tuesday that comes after the first Monday in November, registered voters choose the candidate that they want to be president.

As the votes are gathered for a state, the candidate with the most votes wins that state. Each state has a number of votes that go to the candidate. This number of votes is decided by the population of a state. So, a state like California has a high population, and they have 55 electoral votes. A state like Alaska with a smaller population has 3 electoral votes.

These electoral votes are a part of the voting system known as the **Electoral College**. The candidate does not need the most votes from the people (i.e., the **popular vote**). Instead, the candidate with 270 electoral votes wins the election.

United States History

European Settlement and Population of the Americas

The Age of Exploration, or Age of Discovery, is thought to have started in the early fifteenth century. This age continued into the seventeenth century. Major advances of the Age of Exploration are the growth of technology with navigation, mapmaking, and shipbuilding. These advances led to more European exploration through the rest of the world. These European countries included Portugal, Spain, France, and England. The goal of these countries was to find new routes to Asia. In Asia, many items (e.g., herbs, spices, and silk) could be sold to people in Europe. This travel led to the discovery of new lands. So, areas in Asia, Africa, North America, and Oceania were colonized by European settlers.

Review Video: Age of Exploration
Visit mometrix.com/academy and enter code: 612972

In 1492, King Ferdinand and Queen Isabella of Spain gave Christopher Columbus money to find a sea route to Asia. At the time, sailors needed to go around Africa to reach Asia. However, Columbus wanted to try sailing to Asia by going west. With three ships, the *Niña*, the *Pinta*, and the *Santa Maria*, he came to what is now the Bahamas. Columbus did not find a western route to Asia. However, he is known as the man who discovered the Americas. This discovery created more interest in exploration, conquest, and colonization.

Review Video: Christopher Columbus
Visit mometrix.com/academy and enter code: 496598

American Colonies

The **New England colonies** were New Hampshire, Connecticut, Rhode Island, and Massachusetts. The colonies in New England were started by people who wanted to escape religious persecution. Most people of the New England colonies were from England and Scotland. The beliefs of the Puritans, who went to America in the 1600s, had an important influence on these colonies. In the northeast coastal areas of America, the New England colonies had many harbors and thick forests. These colonists had trouble with planting in this area. The soil is rocky and the growing season is short.

Review Video: The Massachusetts Bay Colony
Visit mometrix.com/academy and enter code: 407058

The **Middle or Middle Atlantic colonies** were New York, New Jersey, Pennsylvania, and Delaware. Some people of the Middle colonies were from the Netherlands, Holland, and Sweden. These people came to the Middle colonies for many reasons. The Middle colonies had better soil than New England. So, they grew many crops like rye, oats, potatoes, wheat, and barley. Some wealthy people owned large farms and/or businesses.

The **Southern colonies** were Maryland, Virginia, North Carolina, South Carolina, and Georgia. Virginia was the first permanent English colony and Georgia was the last. The warm climate and good soil of the South helped with planting. Also, the growing season was long. As a result, the Southern economy was centered on plantations. Crops included tobacco, rice, and indigo.

Review Video: The Southern Colonies
Visit mometrix.com/academy and enter code: 703830

Review Video: The English Colony of Virginia
Visit mometrix.com/academy and enter code: 537399

Triangular Trade

Triangular trade began in the Colonies with ships that carried rum. These ships sailed to Africa. In Africa, gold and slaves were traded for the rum. The gold and slaves were brought to the West Indies (i.e., what is now the Caribbean). In the West Indies, slaves were traded for sugar, molasses, or money.

To complete the triangle, the ships returned to the colonies with sugar or molasses and gold or silver. The sugar and molasses were used to make more rum. This trade triangle broke the Molasses Act of 1733. The Molasses Act called for the colonists to pay taxes to Britain on molasses that came from French, Dutch, and Spanish colonies. The colonists ignored these taxes. So, the British government used a plan of salutary neglect. In other words, Britain did not force the colonies to follow the Molasses Act.

Review Video: Triangular Trade
Visit mometrix.com/academy and enter code: 415470

CHANGE OF POWER IN EUROPE AND THE FRENCH AND INDIAN WAR

The British defeated the Spanish Armada (i.e., groups of battleships) in 1588. This defeat led to the drop of Spanish power in Europe. The drop in Spanish power led the British and French into battle for several wars between 1689 and 1748. These wars were:

- King William's War, or the Nine Years War, 1689-1697.
- The War of Spanish Succession, or Queen Anne's War, 1702-1713
- War of Austrian Succession, or King George's War, 1740-1748

The fourth and final war was the French and Indian War (1754-1763). Most of the battles were fought in the North American territory. The French had many advantages. They had more help from the colonists and many Native Americans. However, the strong leadership of William Pitt led the British to victory. At the end of the French and Indian War, France lost colonial power in much of North America. The cost of the four wars was felt by the colonies and was a spark to the American Revolution.

Review Video: French and Indian War
Visit mometrix.com/academy and enter code: 502183

The French and Indian War put the British in a situation of needing more money. These needs included:

- The need to pay off the war debt.
- The need for money to defend the growing empire
- The need for money to govern Britain's thirty-three colonies, including the American colonies

These needs led the British to pass more laws that increased payment from the colonies. The British thought that they had spent a great deal of money to defend the American colonies. So, the British thought that it was right to collect higher taxes from the colonies. The people in the thirteen colonies disagreed and thought that higher taxes were unfair. Many protested the higher taxes, and those protests led to violence.

AMERICAN REVOLUTION

New towns and other legislative districts started in America. So, the colonists began to practice direct representative government. These legislative groups were made up of elected representatives chosen by male property owners in the districts. These men represented the concerns of the people in their district. The colonists argued that they had no such representatives in British Parliament.

By contrast, the British Parliament represented the entire country. Parliament was not elected to represent individual districts. Instead, they represented specific classes. So, the British disagreed with the colonists. They said that the American colonies did have representation in parliament.

Important Moments Leading to the American Revolution

In the mid-1760s, the British government passed a series of unpopular laws that were directed at the American colonies:

The Sugar Act, 1764: This act not only required taxes to be collected on molasses brought into the colonies but also gave British officials the right to search the homes of anyone suspected of not paying the tax.

The Quartering Act, 1765: This act forced colonists to give supplies to British troops. Also, the colonists were forced to give the British troops a place to live. In addition, colonists were not allowed to settle west of the Appalachians until given permission by Britain.

The Stamp Act, 1765: The Stamp Act taxed printed materials such as newspapers and legal documents. Protests led the Stamp Act to be repealed in 1766. However, the repeal brought about the Declaratory Act. This act said that parliament had full power to make laws for the colonies.

The Townshend Acts, 1767: These acts taxed paper, paint, lead, and tea that came into the colonies. Colonists led boycotts in protest. In Massachusetts, leaders like Samuel and John Adams began to organize resistance to British rule.

One piece of the Townshend Acts that Britain did not remove was the tax on tea. In 1773, the Tea Act was passed. This allowed the East India Company (i.e., an English company that traded in Asia) to sell tea for much lower prices.

The Tea Act also allowed the East India Company to avoid American distributors. A distributor is a person or company that gives shopkeepers their needed supplies. Instead, they could sell directly to shopkeepers. Colonial tea distributors saw this as a direct attack on their business. In December of 1773, 150 distributors climbed on to ships in the Boston Harbor. Then, they dumped over 300 chests of tea into the sea in protest of the new laws. This protest was known as the **Boston Tea Party**.

The Coercive Acts of 1774 punished Massachusetts for not obeying British authority. The four **Coercive Acts**:

- Shut down ports in Boston until the city paid for the tea that was destroyed during the Boston Tea Party.
- Required local government officials in Massachusetts to be chosen by the governor rather than being elected by the people.
- Allowed trials of British soldiers to be moved to Britain rather than have them in Massachusetts.
- Required locals to give British soldiers a place to stay any time there was a disturbance. Private homes were forced to open their doors if no other place was available.

These acts led to the **First Continental Congress** in Philadelphia on September 5, 1774. Fifty-five men were chosen by the people of their colony. These men came from twelve of the American colonies. They wanted an agreement with England about the harsh treatment of the colonies. The Congress maintained that they were loyal to Britain. They agreed that Parliament had the power to rule the colonies. However, they demanded that the Intolerable Acts be removed. So, they started a trade embargo (i.e., refusal to trade) with Britain until the acts were removed.

In response to the embargo, George III of Britain said that the American colonies must obey or face military action. The British tried to end assemblies that opposed British policies. These assemblies came together to collect weapons and form militias. A militia is a group of citizens who come together for military force. On April 19, 1775, the British military was ordered to break up a meeting of the Massachusetts Assembly. A battle started on Lexington Common as the armed colonists fought back. The battles were known as the Battles of Lexington and Concord: the first battles of the American Revolution.

DECLARATION OF INDEPENDENCE

The **Second Continental Congress** met in Philadelphia on May 10, 1775. The Congress talked about the defense of the American colonies. They talked about what to do with the growing war. Also, they talked about what to do with local government. A serious idea for the Congress was being independent from Britain. So, they established an army. On June 15, they named George Washington as commander in chief of the army. By 1776, there was no turning back from war with Britain. The delegates of the Continental Congress drafted the Declaration of Independence on July 4, 1776.

> **Review Video: The First and Second Continental Congress**
> Visit mometrix.com/academy and enter code: 835211

Drafted by Thomas Jefferson, the **Declaration of Independence** was signed on July 4, 1776. The Declaration of Independence said that King George III had ignored the rights of the colonists. Also, the paper said that King George III had set an oppressive rule over them. Many of the ideas in the Declaration of Independence can be found in an earlier document known as the Magna Carta.

Many of Jefferson's ideas on natural rights and property rights came from John Locke. Jefferson focused on natural rights. He wrote of people's rights to "life, liberty and the pursuit of happiness." Locke's similar idea said "life, liberty, and private property." Both felt that the purpose of government was to protect the rights of the people. Also, they thought that individual rights were more important than someone's duties to their country.

> **Review Video: Declaration of Independence**
> Visit mometrix.com/academy and enter code: 256838

MAJOR EVENTS DURING THE AMERICAN REVOLUTION

The **Battles of Lexington and Concord** (April, 1775) is known as the first fight of the Revolutionary War.

The **Battle of Bunker Hill**, in June 1775, was one of the bloodiest of the entire war. American troops withdrew, but almost half of the British forces were lost in the battle. The colonists proved that they could fight against professional British soldiers. In August 1775, Britain said that the American colonies were officially in rebellion.

The **Battle of Saratoga** ended a plan to separate the New England colonies from the Southern colonies. France came to help the Americans when British general John Burgoyne surrendered to American troops. Generally, this is thought to be a turning point of the war.

On October 19, 1781, General Cornwallis surrendered after a defeat in the Battle of Yorktown, Virginia. This battle ended the Revolutionary War.

The **Treaty of Paris** was signed on September 3, 1783. This treaty brought an official end to the Revolutionary War. In the treaty, Britain officially recognized the United States of America as an independent nation. At the meeting, the Mississippi River was set as the country's western border. The treaty also gave Florida back to Spain. Also, France reclaimed African and Caribbean colonies taken by the British in 1763. On November 24, 1783, the last British troops left the newly formed United States of America.

Review Video: The American Revolutionary War
Visit mometrix.com/academy and enter code: 935282

U.S. Constitution

Articles of Confederation

The **Articles of Confederation** was the first attempt by the independent colonies to write out the basics of their independent government. The Continental Congress passed the Articles on November 15, 1777. They went into effect on March 1, 1781, following ratification (i.e. approval) by the thirteen states.

The Articles kept a central government from gaining too much power. Instead, power went to a Congressional body made up of delegates from all thirteen states. However, the individual states had final rule. Without a strong central executive (e.g., a president), this weak alliance was not effective in settling conflicts or keeping laws. These weaknesses led to the drafting of a new document: The Constitution.

Review Video: Articles of Confederation
Visit mometrix.com/academy and enter code: 927401

Development of Bicameral Legislature

Delegates from twelve of the thirteen states (Rhode Island was not represented) met in Philadelphia in May of 1787. At first, the men wanted to revise the Articles of Confederation. However, they realized that a simple revision would not help the newly formed country.

The delegates agreed that the new nation needed a strong central government. However, they knew that its overall power should be limited. They made sure that the branches of the government would have balanced power, so no one group could control the others. They gave final power to the citizens. These citizens could vote officials into office that they knew would represent them best. In other words, this one person would speak and make decisions for the group.

Disagreement came between delegates from large states and those from smaller states. Edmond Randolph, the governor of Virginia, wanted a **bicameral legislature** (i.e., two houses for legislators). An example of a bicameral legislature is the Senate and House of Representatives in the United States.

Drafting the U.S. Constitution

During debate on the U.S. Constitution, a disagreement came between the Northern and Southern states. The disagreement was about how slaves should be counted when deciding a state's number of representatives. In the South, slaves were used to work on plantations. Delegates from the South wanted slaves to be counted to decide the number of representatives. However, they did not want the number of slaves in their state to decide the amount of taxes that the states would pay. The

Northern states wanted the opposite plan. So, the final decision was to count a slave as three-fifths of a person. This plan was used for tax purposes and to decide representation. This plan was called the **Three-Fifths Compromise**.

Another disagreement came between the representatives of Northern and Southern States. This disagreement set up the **Commerce Compromise**. In the North, the economy was centered on industry and trade. The Southern economy was centered on agriculture (i.e., planting crops and herding animals). The Northern states wanted the new government to manage exports with other countries and trade between the states. The South disagreed with this plan.

In the end, Congress gained power to manage all trade. Also, Congress gained power to collect tariffs on exported goods. A **tariff** is a tax that is paid on an import or export. In the South, this raised another red flag about the slave trade. The South was concerned about their economy if tariffs were put on slaves. The final agreement allowed importing slaves to continue for twenty years without government involvement. Import taxes on slaves were limited. After 1808, Congress could decide on whether to allow continued imports of slaves.

Once the Constitution was drafted, it was shown to the states for acceptance. Nine states needed to accept the document for it to become official. However, debate and disagreement continued among the representatives. Major concerns included:

- The lack of a bill of rights to protect individual freedoms.
- States felt that too much power was being handed over to the central government.
- Voters wanted more control over their elected representatives.
- Talks about needed changes to the Constitution divided into two camps: Federalists and Anti-Federalists. Federalists wanted a strong central government. Anti-Federalists did not want the central government to have too much power.

Major Federalist leaders were Alexander Hamilton, John Jay, and James Madison. They wrote letters called the **Federalist Papers**. These papers were meant to persuade the states to approve the Constitution. Anti-Federalists included Thomas Jefferson and Patrick Henry. They argued against the Constitution as it was originally drafted. Their arguments were called the Anti-Federalist Papers.

The final compromise made a strong central government controlled by checks and balances. A Bill of Rights was added. Those rights became the first ten amendments to the Constitution. These amendments protect rights such as freedom of speech, freedom of religion, and other basic rights. Since the first draft, twenty-seven amendments have been added to the Constitution.

Review Video: Drafting the Constitution
Visit mometrix.com/academy and enter code: 662451

Federalists and Jeffersonian Republicans

George Washington was elected as the first President of the United States in 1789. John Adams, who finished second in the election, became the first Vice President. Thomas Jefferson was named by Washington as Secretary of State. Alexander Hamilton was named Secretary of the Treasury.

Many in the U.S. were against political parties. People remembered the way parties, or factions, worked in Britain. The factions in Britain were more interested in personal gain than the good of the country. However, the different opinions between Thomas Jefferson and Alexander Hamilton led to political parties. Hamilton wanted a stronger central government and Jefferson thought that more power should stay with the states.

Specifically, Jefferson was in favor of a strict constitutional interpretation (i.e. limited to the expressed powers in the Constitution) and Hamilton was in favor of a flexible approach (i.e. expressed *and implied* powers). Others began to join these two groups; those who supported Hamilton called themselves Federalists and those who supported Jefferson called themselves Democratic-Republicans (also known as Jeffersonian Republicans).

Moving into Native American Lands

In the Treaty of Paris, large areas of land were given to the U.S. However, Native Americans lived on these lands. So, the new government tried to claim the land and treat the natives as conquered people. This approach was not supported.

Next, the government tried to buy the land from the Indians. The government used a series of treaties as the country grew westward. In practice, however, these treaties were not honored. The Native Americans were simply dislocated. So, they were forced to move farther from their homes as Americans moved to the West. Sometimes military action was used to move the Native Americans.

Economic Overview of Parts of U.S. in Late 18th Century

In the Northeast, the economy mostly depended on manufacturing, industry, and industrial development. This led to a division between rich business owners and their poor workers. The South continued to depend on agriculture. Slaves and indentured servants continued to work large-scale farms or plantations. In the West, where new settlement had started, the area was wild. The areas in the West mostly depended on agriculture. They grew crops and raised livestock. The differences between regions led each to support different political and economic interests.

The Louisiana Purchase

During this time, conflict remained between France and Britain. Napoleon, the ruler of France, needed money to support his battles. So, Napoleon decided to sell the Louisiana Territory to the U.S. to bring in money. At the same time, President Thomas Jefferson wanted to buy New Orleans. President Jefferson thought that U.S. trade was not well protected from Spain and France at that port.

So, Napoleon sold the entire territory for the bargain of fifteen million dollars to the U.S. The Louisiana Territory was larger than all of the United States put together. From that territory, fifteen states were added to America. Federalists in Congress did not want to purchase the land. They feared that the Louisiana Purchase would increase slavery. Also, they feared that more growth in the West would weaken the power of the northern states.

President Jefferson wanted the new area mapped and explored. So, he chose Meriwether Lewis and William Clark to take charge of exploring the Louisiana Territory.

After two years, Lewis and Clark returned from their exploration. They had traveled all the way to the Pacific Ocean. From their journey, they brought maps, detailed journals, and other items from the new land. The Lewis and Clark Expedition helped to open up the area for more exploration and settlement.

Review Video: What Was the Purpose of the Lewis and Clark Expedition?
Visit mometrix.com/academy and enter code: 570657

Three major ideas supported the early growth of the United States:

- **Isolationism** – The early U.S. government did not try to set up colonies. However, they did plan increase in size within North America.
- **No permanent alliances** – George Washington and Thomas Jefferson were opposed to making any permanent alliances with other countries. Also, they did not become involved in other countries' internal issues.
- **Nationalism** – a positive patriotic feeling about the United States grew among its citizens. This feeling grew stronger after the War of 1812 when the U.S. defeated Britain. The Industrial Revolution also sparked more nationalism. The Industrial Revolution allowed the most distant areas of the U.S. to communicate by telegraph and the growing railroad.

Review Video: Overview of the War of 1812
Visit mometrix.com/academy and enter code: 507716

Review Video: What is Nationalism?
Visit mometrix.com/academy and enter code: 865693

The American System

Henry Clay, a politician from Kentucky, and others wanted to protect American interests. The concern for protecting American interests came after the trade conflicts that led to the War of 1812. So, they created an economic plan called the **American System**. With the American System, tariffs were put on imported items. This made items made in the U.S. cheaper than other items. Removing some competition led to growth in employment and an increase in American industry.

The higher tariffs also brought in money for the government to pay for improvements. Congress passed high tariffs in 1816 and chartered a federal bank. The Second Bank of the United States was given the job of managing America's money supply.

Monroe Doctrine

On December 2, 1823, President Monroe delivered a message to Congress. In his message, Monroe introduced the **Monroe Doctrine**. Monroe talked about European powers making new colonies on the North American continent. He said that these efforts would be seen as interference in American politics. So, he said that the U.S. would stay out of European matters, and he wanted Europe to stay out of American matters. This plan of foreign policy said that America would not allow any new European colonies in the New World. Also, the events that happened in Europe would no longer influence the plans and ideas of the U.S.

Review Video: The Monroe Doctrine
Visit mometrix.com/academy and enter code: 953021

Industrial Revolution

The Industrial Revolution began in Great Britain. This revolution brought more coal and steam-powered machines into use. In the past, goods were made in small workshops or homes. With industry, more goods were made in factories. In the past, society was centered on the farm. Now, society centered on industry. Electricity and internal combustion engines replaced coal and steam as energy sources.

Review Video: The Industrial Revolution
Visit mometrix.com/academy and enter code: 372796

To guarantee access to raw materials, Europe took control of parts of Africa and Asia. Expert workers were in high demand. Also, many businesses grew in this time. These businesses started monopolies and increased world trade and city populations. During the revolution, agriculture saw important changes. This led to a second Agricultural Revolution as new technologies improved agriculture.

The first part of the Industrial Revolution came in 1750 and ended in 1830. The textile industry saw many changes as more work was done by machine. The invention of the steam engine was important to mining. Waterways were improved and more railroads were built. So, transportation became easier and opened to more people.

The second part of the revolution came in 1830 and ended in 1910. In this time, industries continued to improve. The improvements made work faster and better. In addition, new industries included photography, chemical processes, and electricity. These industries opened the chance to make new goods or to improve old goods. Oil and hydroelectric became major sources of power. During this time, the Industrial Revolution spread into the United States.

Review Video: Second Industrial Revolution: The American Railroad System
Visit mometrix.com/academy and enter code: 843913

The revolution led to more education and mass communication. Companies and their employees had conflict over fair treatment and fair wages. Unions gained power and became more active. Industries came under more government management. At the same time, new businesses fought for the right to less government management. Many industries were found in cities. So, these areas had larger populations. Changes in science led to better agriculture and more supply of goods. Also, more knowledge of medicine led to better health.

Jacksonian Era

The Federalist Party began to decline after Thomas Jefferson was re-elected. Alexander Hamilton, the major figure of the Federalist Party, died in 1804 in a duel with Aaron Burr. By 1816, the Federalist Party had few members. So, new parties were made to replace the Federalist Party. After 1824, the Democratic-Republican Party had a divide. So, the Whigs Party arose and supported John Quincy Adams and industrial growth. In opposition to the Whigs, the new Democratic Party was created. The candidate for the Democratic Party was Andrew Jackson.

In 1828, Jackson was elected as president. By the 1850s, the issues about slavery led to the creation of the Republican Party. The new Republican Party did not approve of slavery. The Democratic Party had more interests in the South. So, the Democratic Party approved of slavery. This Republican and Democrat division started the two-party system that we have today.

Review Video: Andrew Jackson's Presidency
Visit mometrix.com/academy and enter code: 667792

Review Video: Andrew Jackson – Key Events and Major Issues
Visit mometrix.com/academy and enter code: 739251

Jacksonian-Democracy is seen as a shift in politics. This shift favored the common man over the wealthy. All free white males were given the right to vote, not just property owners. Jackson's plan favored the patronage system. The patronage system is when a political party gives jobs or positions to people who supported the winning candidate. Jackson approved of laissez faire economics. This economic plan said that the government should leave the marketplace alone. In other words, the government should not become overinvolved with the marketplace. Another part of Jackson's plan included moving the Native American tribes from the Southeast United States.

Jackson did not want a federal bank. So, he vetoed a bill that would renew the charter of the Second Band of the United States. During Jackson's presidency, South Carolina claimed that it could ignore any federal law that it thought was unconstitutional. South Carolina said that the tariffs that followed the War of 1812 did not agree with the constitution. So, the state said that the tariffs were "null and void" within South Carolina. Jackson sent troops to the state to enforce the protested tariff laws. However, an agreement was made by Henry Clay in 1833 and settled the matter.

INDIAN REMOVAL ACT

The Indian Removal Act of 1830 gave the new American government power to make treaties with Native Americans. As an idea, America would claim land east of the Mississippi. So, land west of the Mississippi would be set apart for the Native Americans to volunteer to move west. In reality, many tribal leaders were forced to sign the treaties. Then, many Native Americans were forced to move.

Review Video: Indian Removal Act
Visit mometrix.com/academy and enter code: 666738

The Treaty of New Echota is an example. The treaty was supposed to be an agreement between the U.S. government and Cherokee tribes in Georgia. However, the treaty was not signed by tribal leaders. Instead, the treaty was signed by a small portion of the people of the tribe. So, the tribal leaders refused to be removed. However, President Martin Van Buren used the treaty to send soldiers to the area. During the Native American's forced relocation, more than 4,000 Cherokee Indians died on what is known as the Trail of Tears.

MANIFEST DESTINY

Nationalism is a strong belief in and commitment to a nation or people. This belief unified many people into one group. Sometimes this led people to care more for their own country. As nationalism grew, nations tried to grow by bringing in smaller areas. Many of these areas shared similar traits (e.g., language and cultural beliefs). At times, conflict or war was a side effect of these growing nationalistic beliefs. In the U.S., Manifest Destiny became the rallying cry as people moved to the West.

In the 1800s, many believed that God had destined America to grow west. This belief was given the name Manifest Destiny. The U.S. government worked to bring more of the North American continent under control. With the Northwest Ordinance and the Louisiana Purchase, more of the continent became American. The Northwest Ordinance was an act of Congress that created the Northwest Territory (e.g., the area that is now Ohio, Indiana, Illinois, and Michigan).

Review Video: Manifest Destiny
Visit mometrix.com/academy and enter code: 957409

19TH CENTURY DEVELOPMENTS

As America increased its size, new technology was made to travel the growing country. Roads and railroads crossed the nation. The **Transcontinental Railroad** eventually allowed travel from one coast to the other. Canals and steamboats made traveling and shipping by water easier and less expensive.

The Erie Canal (1825) connected the Great Lakes with the Hudson River. Other canals connected major water ways. This helped with the progress of transportation and the shipment of goods. With growing numbers of settlers moving into the West, wagon trails were made for travel. Three well-known trails are the Oregon Trail, the California Trail, and the Santa Fe Trail. The most common vehicles seen on these westbound trails were covered wagons (also known as prairie schooners).

Second Great Awakening

Led by Protestant evangelical leaders, the **Second Great Awakening** happened between 1800 and 1830. The ideas behind the Second Great Awakening centered on personal responsibility. This focus on responsibility was in response to injustice and suffering. The American Bible Society and the American Tract Society provided passages for traveling preachers to share their message.

New denominations were made from this Awakening. These included the Latter-Day Saints and Seventh-Day Adventists. Another movement that is linked with the Second Great Awakening was the temperance movement. This movement focused on ending the production and use of alcohol. One major organization behind the temperance movement was the Society for the Promotion of Temperance. Several missionary groups came out of the movement. One group was the American Home Missionary Society which formed in 1826.

Women's Rights Movement

The women's rights movement began in the 1840s. The leaders of this movement were Elizabeth Cady Stanton, Ernestine Rose, and Lucretia Mott. Later, in 1869, the National Woman Suffrage Association was created. This group fought for women's suffrage (i.e., right to vote). It was led by Susan B. Anthony, Ernestine Rose, and Elizabeth Cady Stanton.

Review Video: What was the Women's Rights Movement in America?
Visit mometrix.com/academy and enter code: 987734

In 1848 in Seneca Falls, the first women's rights convention (i.e., meeting) was held. About three hundred people went to the meeting. The Seneca Falls Convention talked about the issue that women could not vote or run for office. The convention made a "Declaration of Sentiments" which outlined a plan for women to gain the rights that they deserved. Frederick Douglass supported the women's rights movement and the abolition (i.e., put an end to) movement. In fact, women's rights and abolition movements often went hand-in-hand at this time.

Sectional Crisis and Civil War

During the 1800s, there were very different ideas and values in the North and South. The different viewpoints of this time are known as sectionalism. The North was industrial, and life centered on cities. The South was agricultural, and life centered on farms. The conflict between North and South was centered on the issue of slavery. However, other things added to the growing disagreement.

Review Video: American Civil War: North vs. South Overview
Visit mometrix.com/academy and enter code: 370788

Most farmers in the South worked small farms with few or no slaves. However, the huge Southern plantations run by the wealthy used slaves or indentured servants to make money. The plantations depended more on cotton. So, slave populations grew with the quick increase in cotton production. In the North, workers were free men who went to work at factories and shipyards. People in the North argued that free workers led to more growth. They pointed to their factories and schools as examples of a better society. However, people in the South disagreed and wanted to hold on to tradition.

THE ABOLITIONIST MOVEMENT

The abolitionist movement grew regularly. Harriet Beecher Stowe's *Uncle Tom's Cabin* gave many people an idea of the pains of slavery. A growing number of anti-slavery organizations formed during this time. Many worked to free slaves in the South and bring them to the North.

By 1819, the United States had a delicate balance between slave and free states. There were twenty-two senators in Congress from each group. Then, Missouri wanted to join the United States. As a slave or free state, the balance would change in Congress. To avoid this change, Congress passed the Missouri Compromise.

At this time, Massachusetts was separated into two areas. The northern area (i.e., the part that is now Maine) was brought into the United States as a free state. So, Maine's entrance to the U.S. balanced the entrance of Missouri as a slave state. In addition, the remaining part of the Louisiana Purchase remained free north of latitude 36° 30′. Since cotton did not grow well this far north, congressmen of slave states accepted this latitude line.

However, there was a problem in Missouri. The draft of the Missouri constitution outlawed immigration of free blacks into the state. Another compromise was needed. This time Henry Clay came forward to talk about the agreement. Clay earned his title as the Great Compromiser by arguing that the U.S. Constitution overruled Missouri's.

In addition to the pro-slavery and anti-slavery groups, a third group gathered with another idea. They thought that each state should decide whether to allow slavery within its borders. This idea was known as popular sovereignty.

DRED SCOTT DECISION

Abolitionist groups united around the case of Dred Scott. They used Scott's case to test the country's laws about slavery. Dred Scott, a slave, had been taken by his owner to Missouri which was a slave state. Later, Scott was sold in Missouri to another man. Then, Scott traveled to Illinois, a free state with his owner. Then, Scott and his owner left for the Minnesota Territory which was a free territory based on the Missouri Compromise. Then, Scott and his owner returned to Missouri. Scott's master died, and the master's wife continued to own Scott. When Scott tried to purchase his freedom, his owner refused.

Abolitionists helped Scott take his case to court. Scott and the abolitionists said that he was no longer a slave since he had lived in free territory. The case went to the Supreme Court. The Supreme Court denied Scott's request. The Court made this decision because Scott was sold as a slave, not a U.S. citizen. The time that Scott was in free states did not change his status. Also, he did not have the right to sue. In addition, the Court decided that the Missouri Compromise did not agree with the Constitution. The Court said that Congress had gone outside its power by outlawing slavery in the territories.

CIVIL WAR AND THE EMANCIPATION PROCLAMATION

The Northern states (i.e., **the Union**) had a few distinct advantages:

- Larger population: The North had 24 states to the South's 11.
- Better transportation and finances: With railroads mostly in the North, the flow of supplies was more dependable.
- More raw materials: The North held most of America's gold, iron, copper, and other minerals that are important in war.

The South's (i.e., **the Confederacy**) advantages included:

- Better-trained military officers: Many of the Southern officers were from West Point (i.e., the United States Military Academy). Also, many had commanded in the Mexican and Indian wars.
- More familiar with weapons: The lifestyle of the South meant that most of the people knew their guns and horses. The industrial North had less experience with weapons.
- Defensive position: The South was protecting their lands. The North would be invading.
- Well-defined goals: The South was fighting a war so they could govern themselves and to maintain their way of life.

The **First Battle of Bull Run**, July 21, 1861, was the first major land battle of the war. Some people thought that would enjoy watching a small fight. So, they set up picnics near the battlefield. However, they realized that they were watching a bloodbath. The Union forces were defeated, and the battle set the course of the Civil War as long, bloody, and costly. The **Capture of Fort Henry** by Ulysses S. Grant in February of 1862 was the Union's first major victory.

In 1862, President Lincoln issued the **Emancipation Proclamation** after the Battle of Antietam. This proclamation freed all slaves in Confederate States that did not return to the Union by the beginning of the year. The original proclamation did not free any slaves that were under Union control. However, the proclamation did set an example for the emancipation (i.e., being set free) of slaves as the war continued.

The Emancipation Proclamation worked for the Union because many freed slaves and other black troops joined the Union Army. Almost 200,000 blacks fought in the Union Army. Over 10,000 served in the Union Navy. By the end of the war, over 4 million slaves had been freed. By 1865, slavery was banned by the thirteenth amendment.

Review Video: Emancipation Proclamation
Visit mometrix.com/academy and enter code: 181778

The **Battle of Gettysburg**, July 1-3, 1863, is seen as the turning point of the war. Gettysburg saw the most casualties (i.e., deaths) of the war. Over 50,000 men died at the battle. Robert E. Lee was defeated, and the Confederate army withdrew. During May and June of 1864, General Ulysses S. Grant started the Overland Campaign. The campaign was a series of battles in Virginia. Now, Grant commanded all of the Union armies. Grant led this high casualty campaign that put the Union in position for victory.

The Civil War ended with the surrender of the South on April 9, 1865. Five days later, Lincoln and his wife, Mary, went to the play *Our American Cousin* at the Ford Theater. John Wilkes Booth, who did not know that the war was over, did his part in a plot to help the Confederacy by shooting Lincoln. Booth was tracked down and killed by Union soldiers twelve days later. Lincoln was carried from the theater to a nearby house, where he died the next morning.

Review Video: Overview of the Civil War
Visit mometrix.com/academy and enter code: 239557

Reconstruction Era

The Civil War left the South in great disorder. From 1865 to 1877, government on all levels worked to help bring back order to the South. This time was used to guarantee rights and freedom to slaves. Also, the government worked to bring the Confederate states back into the Union.

In 1866, Congress passed the **Reconstruction Acts**. The acts put previous Confederate states under military rule. The Freedmen's Bureau was made to help previous slaves and poor whites in the South who needed basic things like food and clothing. Also, the bureau wanted to keep people from abusing previous slaves.

In the years after the Civil War, three new amendments were added to the US Constitution. The **thirteenth amendment** was passed on December 18, 1865. This amendment made slavery illegal in the United States. The **fourteenth amendment** was approved on July 9, 1868. This amendment guaranteed citizens the right to file a lawsuit or serve on a jury. The **fifteenth amendment** was approved on February 3, 1870. The amendment says that no citizen of the United States can be refused the right to vote. A person's race, color, or past position as a slave does not decide their chance to vote.

Scalawags and Carpetbaggers

The disorder in the South brought in many people who wanted to take positions of power. **Scalawags** were southern whites who came to work in local governments. Many in the South who could have taken political offices did not because they did not approve of Reconstruction. So, many opportunities for Scalawags and others became available to work in local governments.

Carpetbaggers were northerners who traveled to the South for various reasons. Many joined with the Freedmen's Bureau and came to help freed slaves. Some came to make money or to gain power in politics during this time of disorder.

Black Codes

Southern states passed the **Black Codes** in 1865 and 1866. These laws suggested controlling freed slaves. So, freed slaves would not be allowed to have weapons, assemble, serve on juries, or testify against whites. Also, schools would be segregated (i.e., separated or divided). An unemployed black person could be arrested and forced to work.

The 1866 the **Civil Rights Act** opposed these Black Codes. The act gave more rights to the freed slaves. Andrew Johnson, who became president after Lincoln's death, supported the Black Codes. So, he vetoed the Civil Rights bill. However, Congress overrode his veto. Later, Congress impeached (i.e., accuse of wrong actions) Johnson. This impeachment was the top of tensions between Congress and President Johnson. A single vote kept Johnson from being convicted and removed from office.

By 1877, many people felt that Reconstruction was not working. In addition, the country had economic troubles, and the Democratic Party was gaining influence. In the 1890s, some states in the South had passed new Black Codes that were known as **Jim Crow laws**. These laws did not allow for white people and black people to share public areas. Schools, restaurants, and bathrooms were made for whites and blacks.

Review Video: Reconstruction Era
Visit mometrix.com/academy and enter code: 790561

Plessy v. Ferguson

In 1896, the Supreme Court ruled on the **Plessy v. Ferguson** case. The Supreme Court said that "separate but equal" did agree with the Constitution. So, blacks and whites had access to equal transportation, restaurants, and education. In reality, these separate places were not equal. In many places, white people had better conditions. By the 1960s, the Jim Crow laws were removed by the Civil Rights Acts.

Second Industrial Revolution

The time from the end of the Civil War to the start of the First World War is called the Gilded Age. The Gilded Age is also called the **Second Industrial Revolution**. The U.S. was changing from an economy that was centered on agricultural to an industrial economy. This change came with a great deal of growth. In addition, the country itself was spreading across the West. This time saw the beginning of banks, department stores, chain stores, and trusts. Many citizens and immigrants began to move out of the country and into the city.

Review Video: Second Industrial Revolution
Visit mometrix.com/academy and enter code: 608455

Progressive Era

From the 1890s to the end of the First World War, Progressives grew in number with ideas that drove many levels of society and politics. The Progressives favored workers' rights and safety. Also, they wanted actions taken against waste and corruption. Progressives thought that science could help make society better. In addition, this group thought that the government could—and should—give answers to some social problems. Progressives came from many different backgrounds. However, they were united in their desire to make society better.

Populist Party

The Knights of Labor, formed in 1869 by Uriah Stephens, was an important workers organization in the 1880s. At this time, the organization was able to bring workers into a union to protect their rights. The Farmers Alliance and the Knights of Labor were unhappy with the ideas of industrialists. So, these two groups joined to make the **Populist Party**. The Populist Party wanted elitism to decrease. **Elitism** is the idea that a person or group deserves special treatment because of their wealth or education. The Populist Party wanted to make the voice of the common man heard in the political process. Some important things to the Populist Party included:

- Income tax. As one had increases in income, the percent of taxes that they owed would increase.
- More money being circulated through the country
- Government ownership of railroads, telegraphs, and telephone systems
- Secret ballot for voting
- Immigration restriction
- Term limits for President and Vice-President

Amendments to the U.S. Constitution

The early twentieth century saw many amendments made to the U.S. Constitution. These amendments largely came from the Progressive Era. In this time, many citizens worked to make American society better. These included:

- **Sixteenth Amendment** (1913): set a graduated income tax.
- **Seventeenth Amendment** (1913): allowed direct election of Senators.
- **Eighteenth Amendment** (1919): banned the sale, production, and importation of alcohol. This amendment was later removed by the Twenty-First Amendment.
- **Nineteenth Amendment** (1920): gave women the right to vote.

EXPOSING POOR WORK CONDITIONS

"**Muckrakers**" was a term used to point out bold investigative journalists. These journalists wrote on scandals, corruption, and many other wrongs of late nineteenth century society. The work of these journalists made many new rules and plans. These rules and plans included workmen's compensation, child labor laws, and trust-busting. Among these bold writers were:

- Ida Tarbell—she exposed John D. Rockefeller's monopoly of the oil trade.
- Jacob Riis—a photographer, he helped improve the environment of the poor in New York.
- Lincoln Steffens—he worked to show political corruption.
- Upton Sinclair—his book *The Jungle* brought changes to the meat packing industry.

Ida Tarbell and Lincoln Steffens showed how trusts were damaging. A trust was a huge corporation that worked to have monopolies on products. A monopoly is a business that has full control of a supply or trade. With full control, a corporation-controlled prices and delivery. The Sherman Act and the Clayton Antitrust Act made rules for competition among corporations. Also, these acts worked to remove these trusts. The Federal Trade Commission was created to enforce antitrust efforts. In addition, the commission confirms that companies are operated fairly and do not create monopolies.

Review Video: The Progressive Era
Visit mometrix.com/academy and enter code: 722394

AMERICAN IMPERIALISM

THEODORE ROOSEVELT'S PRESIDENCY

According to Theodore Roosevelt, his famous quote, "Speak softly and carry a big stick," has African origins. He used this quote to defend more involvement in foreign concerns during his time as president. The U.S. military was used to protect American interests in Latin America. As a result, the U.S. Navy grew larger, and the U.S. became more involved in international concerns. Roosevelt thought that if any country was left open to control, then the U.S. should help. This led to U.S. involvement in Cuba, Nicaragua, Haiti, and the Dominican Republic over several decades.

WILLIAM HOWARD TAFT'S PRESIDENCY

After Roosevelt, William Howard Taft was elected president. During Taft's presidency, he started **Dollar Diplomacy**. This plan described American efforts to influence Latin America and East Asia through economic ways, not military force. Taft saw previous work in these areas to be political and warlike. So, his work centered on peaceful economic goals.

Taft's reason for this policy was to protect the Panama Canal which was important to U.S. trade. Taft was confident that the Dollar Diplomacy was a peaceful plan. However, the involvements did not bring peace. During Latin American rebellions, such as those in Nicaragua, the U.S. sent troops to settle the rebellion. After the rebellion, bankers moved in to help support the new leaders with loans. Dollar Diplomacy continued until 1913. Then, Woodrow Wilson was elected president.

WOODROW WILSON'S PRESIDENCY

Turning away from Taft's Dollar Diplomacy, Wilson started a foreign policy that he called **Moral Diplomacy**. This plan still influences American foreign policy today. Wilson thought that representative government and democracy in every country would lead to worldwide security. According to Wilson, democratic governments would be less likely to threaten American interests. Wilson thought of the U.S. and Britain as champions of world peace and self-government. With free trade and international business, the U.S. would be able to speak on world events.

Main parts of Wilson's ideas included:

- Maintaining a strong military
- Promoting democracy throughout the world
- Increasing international trade to strengthen the American economy

World War I

The First World War, also known as the Great War (1914-1918) was fought mainly in Europe. After the killing of Austrian Archduke Francis Ferdinand, the war quickly broke out. There were two sides in the Great War. The main Allied Powers were France, Great Britain, Russia, Italy, and Japan. The main Central Powers were Germany, Austria-Hungary, and the Ottomans.

At the beginning, Woodrow Wilson said that the U.S. would not enter the war. Also, the U.S. would not favor a side. However, the U.S. entered the Great War in 1917.

During the war, American railroads came under government control in December 1917. The widespread system was collected into a single system and put into regions. Each region had a director. This control of the railroads increased the performance of the railroad system. In 1920, the railroads returned to private control. In 1918, the telegraph, telephone, and cable services came under Federal control. In the next year, they were returned to private management. The American Red Cross helped the war effort by making clothes for Army and Navy troops. In addition, they helped supply hospital and refugee clothing and surgical dressings.

The war left Europe in much debt and ruined the German economy. The Great Depression made the situation worse. The ruined economy opened the door for Communist, Fascist, and Socialist governments to gain power.

Wilson's Fourteen Points

President Woodrow Wilson offered his **Fourteen Points** as the basis for a peace settlement to end the war. Presented to the U.S. Congress in January 1918, the Fourteen Points included:

- Five points on general ideals
- Eight points to solve immediate problems of political and territorial nature
- One point on creating an organization of nations with the purpose of maintaining world peace. This organization would be known as the League of Nations.

In November of that same year, Germany agreed to an armistice (i.e., truce or ceasefire). Germany assumed that the final treaty would be based on Wilson's Fourteen Points. However, during the Treaty at Versailles, the peace conference in Paris in 1919, there was much disagreement. The final agreement at the conference seriously punished Germany and the other Central Powers.

Review Video: WWI Overview
Visit mometrix.com/academy and enter code: 659767

1920s

The 1920s saw many Americans move from the farm to the city. The United States continued to experience success in this time. The 1920s are known as the **Roaring Twenties**, or the Jazz Age. The success of this time came from growth in the automobile and entertainment industries.

Many people added to the American admiration of individual accomplishment. One example is Charles Lindbergh who was the first person to make a solo flight across the Atlantic Ocean.

Telephone lines, widespread use of electricity, highways, radio, and other inventions brought great changes to everyday life.

World War I created many jobs for many people around the world. However, after the war ended these jobs came to an end. So, many people were unemployed (i.e., without a job). From these changes in employment, new organizations and parties were created.

Examples are the International Workers of the World and the Socialist Party headed by Eugene Debs. Workers started strikes to bring back the better working conditions that had been put into place before the war. Unfortunately, many of these strikes became violent. "Reds," or Communists were blamed for trying to spread their ideas into America. The Bolshevik Revolution was recent news in Russia. So, many Americans feared a similar revolution. The Red Scare began with many people put in jail for supposedly holding communist, anarchist, or socialist beliefs.

Review Video: 1920's
Visit mometrix.com/academy and enter code: 124996

Great Depression and New Deal

The **Great Depression**, which began in 1929 with the **Stock Market Crash**, grew out of several factors in the past years:

- Growing economic differences between the rich and middle-class. The rich gained wealth much more quickly than the lower classes
- Differences in economic distribution in industries. In other words, some industries have more land and resources than others.
- Growing use of credit. This led to an inflated demand for some goods
- Government support of new industries rather than providing more support for agriculture
- Risky stock market investments

Review Video: What Caused the Great Depression?
Visit mometrix.com/academy and enter code: 635912

Franklin D. Roosevelt's Presidency

Franklin D. Roosevelt was elected president in 1932. During his campaign, he promised a "**New Deal**" for Americans. This New Deal contained many goals. One goal was to start government work programs to provide jobs. The jobs provided wages and relief to many workers throughout the nation. During this time, the U.S. Congress gave Roosevelt almost free control to create relief legislation. The goals of this legislation were:

- Relief: Accomplished by creating jobs
- Recovery: Motivate the economy through the National Recovery Administration
- Reform: Pass legislation to prevent future economic crashes

The Roosevelt administration passed several laws and established several institutions to start the "reform" part of the New Deal:

- Glass-Steagall Act—separated investment from the business of banking
- Securities Exchange Commission (SEC)—helped manage Wall Street investment practices. So, the investment efforts became less dangerous to the overall economy.

- Wagner Act—provided worker and union rights to improve the relationship between employees and employers. Later, this act was amended by the Taft-Hartley Act of 1947 and the Landrum Griffin Act of 1959 which further clarified and codified employee and employer rights.
- Social Security Act of 1935—provided benefits after retirement and unemployment insurance
- Davis-Bacon Act (1931)—provided fair payment to workers on public work projects.
- Walsh-Healey Act (1936)—set a minimum wage, child labor laws, safety standards, and overtime pay.

World War II

The Great Depression was terrible to the German economy. The U.S. gave reconstruction loans to Germany to help the country rebuild. However, Germany suffered again when the U.S. had to stop providing loans. Unemployment and frustration with the government grew in Germany. At this time, fascist and communist parties promised change and improvements.

Led by Adolf Hitler, the Nazi Party gained power in parliament. The votes of hopeless German workers went to this party that promised change. Hitler became Chancellor of Germany in 1933. With this power, Hitler started plans to spread out German influence. These plans broke the peace treaties that had ended WW I. Under Hitler, military power increased. So, the military started to take control of countries. This led to conflict which brought about WW II.

The Holocaust

The Holocaust was an event of genocide, which is the mass murder of one ethnic group. This great loss of human life included the loss of many traditions, histories, and ideas. After World War II, the United Nations called genocide a crime against humanity. The UN passed the Universal Declaration of Human Rights to state the rights that the organization protected. Nazi war criminals faced justice in the Nuremberg Trials. At the trials, these criminals were held responsible for war crimes.

Review Video: The Holocaust
Visit mometrix.com/academy and enter code: 350695

The Second Great War

The two sides were the Allied Powers and the Axis Powers. The main **Allied Powers** were the United Kingdom, the Soviet Union, China, and the United States. The main **Axis Powers** were Nazi Germany, Japan, and Italy.

In the 1930s, the U.S. Congress passed the Neutrality Acts. During this time, tension increased in Europe and Asia. So, the U.S. passed these laws to avoid entering any conflicts outside the United States. When war broke out in Europe in 1939, President Roosevelt said that the U.S. would not enter the war, and the U.S. would not favor a side. However, his overall plan was thought of as "interventionist." Roosevelt was willing to give any necessary help to the Allies without officially entering the fight. So, the U.S. gave many war materials to the Allied nations.

Isolationists thought that the U.S. should not give any help to the Allies. They thought that Roosevelt's help to the Allies would bring the U.S. into a war. Led by Charles A. Lindbergh, the Isolationists thought that any involvement in the European conflict would weaken the United States' national defense.

However, in 1937, Japan invaded China which motivated the US to stop all exports to Japan. In 1941, General Tojo came to power as the Japanese Premier. General Tojo recognized America's ability to bring a stop to Japan's growth, so he ordered the bombing of Pearl Harbor on December 7, 1941. The U.S. responded by declaring war on Japan. With the Tipartite Pact among the Axis Powers, Germany and Italy declared war on the U.S. Also in 1941, German submarines attacked U.S. ships so, in response, Congress removed the Neutrality Acts and decided to enter World War II.

Atomic Bomb

The atomic bomb was developed during WWII. The bomb was carried by one plane and held enough power to destroy an entire city. This devastating effect was shown with the bombing of Hiroshima and Nagasaki in 1945. The bombings immediately killed about 200,000 people. Many deaths followed as time passed after the bombings. These deaths were due to radiation poisoning. The post WWII era saw many countries develop similar weapons to match the new military power of the U.S. The impact of those developments and use of nuclear weapons continues into international relations today.

The End of World War II

In February 1945, Joseph Stalin (USSR), Franklin D. Roosevelt (USA), and Winston Churchill (UK) met in Yalta to talk about the post-war treatment of Europe, particularly Germany. Though Germany had not yet surrendered, the defeat of Germany was understood to be near. After Germany's official surrender, Clement Attlee (UK), Harry Truman (USA), and Joseph Stalin (USSR) met to determine the treatment of Europe. This meeting was called the Potsdam Conference. Basic pieces of these agreements included:

- Dividing Germany and Berlin into four zones of occupation
- Demilitarization (i.e., removing weapons) of Germany
- Poland remaining under Soviet control
- Outlawing the Nazi Party
- Trials for Nazi leaders
- Relocation of numerous German citizens
- The USSR joined the United Nations in 1945
- Establishment of the United Nations Security Council. The council had the US, the UK, the USSR, China, and France

Following WWII, the U.S. became one of the strongest political powers in the world. Also, the U.S. became a major player in world affairs and foreign policies. The U.S. decided to stop the spread of Communism. In addition, America came out of the war with a greater sense of itself as an integrated nation. Many regional and economic differences decreased during this time. The government worked for greater equality. Also, the growth of communications increased contact among different areas of the country.

The aftermath of the Great Depression and the needs of WWII had given the government more control over different areas. This meant that the American government took on greater responsibility for the wellbeing of its citizens. In domestic areas, this included basic needs. In international areas, this meant protecting citizens from foreign threats.

Review Video: World War II
Visit mometrix.com/academy and enter code: 759402

The Cold War and the 1960s through the 1980s

After World War II, major nations (e.g., the US and USSR) worked on developing the atomic bomb. Later, the hydrogen bomb and other advanced weapons became important. These countries worked to outpace each other with the development of many deadly weapons. These weapons were expensive and very dangerous. It is possible that the war between the U.S. and the Soviets remained "cold" from fear that one side or the other would use these powerful weapons.

Harry S. Truman's Presidency

Harry S. Truman took over the presidency from Franklin D. Roosevelt near the end of WW II. Truman made the final decision to drop atomic bombs on Japan. Also, he had a major role in the final decisions about treatment of post-war Germany.

On the domestic front, Truman started a 21-point plan known as the Fair Deal. This plan developed Social Security, provided public housing, and made the Fair Employment Practices Act permanent. Truman helped support Greece and Turkey under threat from the USSR. He supported South Korea against communist North Korea. Also, he helped with recovery in Western Europe.

Events Leading to the Cold War

The U.S. made many decisions on international concerns after World War II:

- **Marshall Plan**—this plan supported an economic recovery plan with financial aid from the United States. This work was centered on preventing the spread of communism.
- **Containment**—proposed by George F. Kennan. Containment was the effort on preventing the spread of Soviet communism.
- **Truman Doctrine**—Harry S. Truman stated that the U.S. would give both economic and military support to any country threatened by Soviet takeover.
- **National Security Act**—passed in 1947, this act created the Department of Defense, the Central Intelligence Agency, and the National Security Council.

The combination of these works led to the Cold War. The Soviet communists wanted to spread their influence. The U.S. and other countries worked to contain or stop this spread.

The relationship between East (Soviets) and West (USA) became worse with military alliances and border restrictions:

- **NATO**, the North Atlantic Treaty Organization, came into being in 1949. An agreement between the U.S. and Western European countries. This agreement said that an attack on any one of these countries was to be thought of as an attack against the entire group.
- Under the influence of the Soviet Union, the Eastern European countries of USSR (e.g., Bulgaria, East Germany, Poland, Romania, Albania, Poland, and Czechoslovakia) responded with the **Warsaw Pact**. This created a similar agreement among those nations.
- In 1961, a wall was built to separate Communist East Berlin from democratic West Berlin. A similar wall came between East and West as well. This wall was a metaphor that was known as the **Iron Curtain**.

Review Video: How Did the Cold War End?
Visit mometrix.com/academy and enter code: 278032

Korean War

The Korean War began in 1950 and ended in 1953. For the first time, a world organization—the United Nations—played a military role in a war. North Korea sent Communist troops into South Korea. The North wanted to bring the entire country under Communist control. The UN sent out a call to member nations. The UN asked them to support South Korea. Truman and many other UN member nations sent troops to fight North Korea. The war ended three years later with a truce, not a peace treaty. Today, Korea remains divided at 38 degrees north latitude. Communist rule remains in the North. A democratic government rules in the South.

Dwight Eisenhower's Presidency

Eisenhower used a moderate plan with international concerns. Also, he brought much needed attention to equal rights. He worked to reduce strain during the Cold War. He worked out a peace treaty with Russia after the death of Stalin. Also, he required desegregation by sending troops to Little Rock, Arkansas. In addition, he ordered the desegregation of the military. Organizations created during his time as president included the Department of Health and the Department Education and Welfare. He also worked to create the National Aeronautics and Space Administration (NASA).

Civil Rights Movement

Almost a century had passed since the Emancipation Proclamation and Reconstruction, and African-Americans still faced poor treatment. Throughout the 1950s and '60s, African Americans worked to demand equal rights. Important people in this time included:

- Rosa Parks—often called the mother of the Civil Rights Movement. In 1955, she refused to give up her seat on the bus to a white man.
- Dr. Martin Luther King, Jr.—the best-known leader of the movement. King drew on Mahatma Gandhi's beliefs and encouraged non-violent opposition. He led a march on Washington D.C. in 1963. In 1964, he received the Nobel Peace Prize. In 1968, he was assassinated.
- Malcolm X— an African-American Muslim who supported less peaceful ways of change. Also, he supported Black Nationalism.
- Stokely Carmichael—Carmichael invented the term "Black Power." He served as head of the Student Nonviolent Coordinating Committee. He believed in black pride and black culture. Also, he wanted separate political and social institutions for blacks.
- Adam Clayton Powell—chairman of the Coordinating Committee for Employment. He led rent strikes and boycotts of buses. The efforts were an effort to increase the hiring of blacks.
- Jesse Jackson—Jackson was selected by Martin Luther King Jr. to head the Chicago Operation Breadbasket in 1966. He went on to organize boycotts and other actions. He also had an unsuccessful run for President of the United States.

Major events from the Civil Rights Movement include:

- **Montgomery Bus Boycott**—in 1955 Rosa Parks refused to give away her seat on a bus to a white man. As a result, she was tried and convicted of disorderly conduct and of violating local laws. A 381-day boycott came after the ruling on Parks.
- **Desegregation of Little Rock**—in 1954 the Supreme Court ruled on Brown vs. Board of Education. The case said that "separate but equal" was unconstitutional. So, in 1957 the Arkansas school board voted to desegregate their schools. So, the governor brought in the National Guard to keep nine black students from entering Central High School in Little Rock. President Eisenhower responded by making the National Guard a federal organization. So, he ordered the National Guard to assist in helping the black students walk into the school.
- **Birmingham Campaign**—Protestors that wanted to raise national attention to the integration work in Birmingham. The protestors organized sit-ins and a march to launch a voting campaign. Then, the City of Birmingham banned the protests. The protestors did not stop and were arrested and jailed.

Dr. Martin Luther King, Jr. and others were arrested and put into jails at Birmingham. While Dr. King was in jail, he received a newspaper which had "A Call for Unity." This statement argued that Dr. King and his followers should fight for their rights in courts, not the streets. So, Dr. King wrote a response on the newspaper. His response is known as "Letter from Birmingham Jail." The letter responds to concerns in "A Call for Unity" and calls for rights to come soon.

These events led to major pieces of legislation:

- **Civil Rights Act** of 1964—said that discrimination is illegal in employment, education, or public assistance.
- **Voting Rights Act** of 1965—this law ended practices that kept blacks from voting. These practices included poll taxes and literacy tests.

Warren's Supreme Court

From 1953 to 1969, Chief Justice Earl Warren led the Supreme Court. The court cases of the Warren Court included some that changed American society:

- **Brown vs. Board of Education** (1954)—the Supreme Court said that "separate but equal" did not agree with the U.S. Constitution.
- **Mapp v. Ohio** (1961) —the decision said that any evidence that is found in an illegal search and seizure cannot be used in a trial.
- **Gideon v. Wainwright** (1963) —the Supreme Court said that the Constitution requires states to provide a lawyer to a defendant who cannot afford a lawyer.
- **Miranda v. Arizona** (1966) —the decision said that arrested people must be told their rights (e.g., right to an attorney and right to remain silent). This is known as the Miranda Rights.

John F. Kennedy's Presidency

During his term as president (1961-1963), John F. Kennedy created economic programs that led to a time of great growth in the U.S. This level growth had not been seen since before WW II. Kennedy created the Alliance for Progress and the Peace Corps.

The **Cuban Missile Crisis** happened in 1962. Russian Premier Nikita Khrushchev decided to place nuclear missiles in Cuba to protect the island from American invasion. U-2 planes from the U.S. flew over the island and photographed the missile bases as they were being built. The U.S. became very concerned about nuclear missiles being close to its shores.

The USSR was concerned about American missiles that had been placed in Turkey. Over time, the missile sites were removed. In addition, a U.S. naval blockade turned back Soviet ships carrying missiles to Cuba. During negotiations, the U.S. agreed to remove their missiles from Turkey. Also, they agreed to sell surplus wheat to the USSR. A telephone hot line between Moscow and Washington was set up for instant communication between the two heads of state to prevent similar incidents in the future.

Lyndon B. Johnson's Presidency

After Kennedy's assassination, Lyndon Johnson, Kennedy's Vice President, became president. Johnson supported civil rights bills, tax cuts, and other ideas that Kennedy had supported. Johnson worked with bills that centered on fighting disease and poverty. Also, he wanted to renew urban areas, support education, and protect the environment. Johnson continued to support space exploration. Also, he is remembered for how he handled the Vietnam War.

From 1964 to 1965, Lyndon Johnson started a series of programs to improve America. This series of programs was known as the Great Society. These programs improved connections between races. Also, the programs worked to remove poverty from American society. Education and medical care were improved as well. Medicare and Medicaid were important pieces. Congress passed many laws on the environment during this time. These laws protected the environment and improved air and water quality. Later, some programs received less money or were removed. However, many of the Great Society programs help Americans today.

Vietnam War

After World War II, the U.S. promised to come to help any country threatened by Communism. Between 1954 and 1975, Vietnam was divided into a Communist North and a democratic South. Over time, the North tried to unify the country under Communist rule. These efforts led to the U.S. fighting in Vietnam for the South. In America, the Vietnam War became very unpopular. Many Americans became unhappy with the U.S. not accomplishing the goals that they set for Vietnam.

Richard Nixon's Presidency

In 1969, Richard Nixon became president, and he promised to send American troops home. Nixon increased the use of American troops in Vietnam in May of 1970. This action led to protests at Kent State in Ohio. At this protest, four students were killed by National Guard troops. After this protest, the compulsory (i.e., forced) draft ended in 1973. In that same year, U.S. troops left Vietnam. In 1975, the South surrendered. So, Vietnam became a unified country under Communist rule.

Richard Nixon is known for illegal activities during his presidency. However, other important events marked his time as president:

- America leaves the Vietnam War
- Improved diplomatic relations between the U.S. and China, and the U.S. and the USSR
- National Environmental Policy Act passed
- Compulsory draft ended
- Supreme Court legalizes abortion in Roe v Wade
- Watergate

Watergate

In 1972, a group broke in at the Democratic National Committee office in Washington, D.C. The group was caught trying to tap phone lines and steal secret documents. After two years, many people began to think that President Nixon was involved in the crime. Later, Nixon was forced to give up recording tapes that he set up in his office. The audio tapes connected Nixon to the scandal. **The Watergate scandal** of 1972 ended Nixon's presidency. He resigned from office instead of facing impeachment and removal from office. In September 1974, President Ford pardoned Nixon from any wrongs during his time in office.

Gerald Ford's Presidency

With Nixon's resignation, Gerald Ford became president. Ford's presidency saw negotiations with Russia to limit nuclear arms. In addition, he wanted to prevent more conflicts in the Middle East. Also, Ford worked to deal with inflation, economic downturn, and energy shortages. Ford worked to reduce governmental control of various businesses and reduce the role of government overall.

Jimmy Carter's Presidency

Jimmy Carter was elected president in 1976. Carter faced many difficulties: a budget deficit, high unemployment, and continued inflation. Also, Carter faced many concerns with international diplomacy:

- Panama Canal Treaties
- **Camp David Accords**—negotiations between Anwar el-Sadat, the president of Egypt, and Menachem Begin, the Israeli Prime Minister. These talks led to a peace treaty between the two nations.
- Strategic Arms Limitation Talks (SALT) and the resulting agreements and treaties
- **Iran Hostage Crisis**—when the Shah of Iran was removed from power, an Islamic cleric, the Ayatollah Ruholla Khomeini, came into power. Fifty-three American hostages were taken and held for 444 days in the U.S. Embassy.

Ronald Reagan's Presidency

Ronald Reagan, at 69, became the oldest American president. The two terms of his presidency included important events such as:

- **Reaganomics**, also known as supply-side or trickle-down economics. This gave major tax cuts to those in the higher income brackets
- Economic Recovery Tax Act of 1981
- First female justice appointed to the Supreme Court: Sandra Day O'Connor
- Massive increase in the national debt—increased from $600 billion to $3 trillion
- Reduction of nuclear weapons from negotiations with Mikhail Gorbachev
- Loss of the space shuttle Challenger
- Iran-Contra scandal—cover-up of U.S. involvement in revolutions in El Salvador and Nicaragua
- Deregulation of savings and loan industry

End of the Cold War

In the late 1980s, Mikhail Gorbachev ruled the Soviet Union. He started a series of reform programs. During this time, the Berlin Wall came down. This event ended the separation of East and West Berlin. The Soviet Union gave up control of the various republics in Eastern Europe. These republics became independent nations with their own individual governments. With the end of the USSR, the Cold War came to an end.

Recent History

George H.W. Bush's Presidency

George H. W. Bush became president after Ronald Reagan. Bush's run for president included the famous "thousand points of light" speech. This speech was important in increasing his positions in the election polls. An **election poll** is a survey that predicts which candidate is favored by the people.

During Bush's presidency, many major international events took place:

- Fall of the Berlin wall and Germany's unification
- Panamanian dictator Manuel Noriega captured and tried on drug and racketeering charges
- Breaking up of the Soviet Union
- Gulf War, or Operation Desert Storm, started by Iraq's invasion of Kuwait

- Tiananmen Square Massacre in Beijing, China
- The arrival of the World Wide Web

William Clinton's Presidency

William Jefferson Clinton was the second president in U.S. history to be impeached. However, he was not found guilty. Even with the impeachment, he maintained high approval ratings.

Major events during Clinton's presidency included:

- Family and Medical Leave Act
- Don't Ask Don't Tell: a compromise position for homosexuals serving in the military
- North American Free Trade Agreement, or NAFTA
- Defense of Marriage Act
- Oslo Accords
- Siege at Waco, Texas, involving the Branch Davidians led by David Koresh
- Bombing of the Murrah Federal Building in Oklahoma City, Oklahoma
- Troops sent to Haiti, Bosnia, and Somalia to help with domestic problems in those areas

George W. Bush's Presidency

On September 11, 2001, during his first year in office, Bush's presidency was challenged by the first terrorist attack on American soil. This attack came from al-Qaeda terrorists who flew planes into the World Trade Center, into the Pentagon, and into a field in Pennsylvania. These attacks led to major changes in security in the United States. After the attack, U.S. troops were sent to Afghanistan. Later, the U.S. thought that Iraq held weapons of mass destruction. So, on March 20, 2003, U.S. troops and other troops from more than 20 other countries invaded Iraq.

The last months of Bush's administration saw a serious economic meltdown in the U.S. and worldwide. Dramatic increases in oil price increased gasoline prices. This, along with the meltdown of the mortgage industry, created serious and overwhelming economic issues for the Bush administration.

Barack Obama's Presidency

In 2008, Barack Obama, a U.S. Senator from Illinois, became the first African-American president of the United States. He ran an emotional and energizing campaign. Obama presented himself as the exact opposite of his predecessor. He was a candidate of change who would work on the economy. Also, he wanted to bring in a new era of accountability and responsibility in government.

After his election, Obama chose to continue many of the same plans started by Bush. These actions included reinforcement of the wars in Iraq and Afghanistan. Other actions included use of drones, the use of the Guantanamo Bay prison, and the use of stimulus and bailout packages. During his first term, Obama and his congressional allies passed his signature piece of legislation: the Affordable Care Act, also known as Obamacare. Obama was reelected to a second term in 2012.

Donald Trump's Presidency

In 2016, Donald Trump, previously a real estate developer and television personality, was elected 45th president after a tumultuous election in which he won the electoral college but lost the popular vote. Marked by tension between the administration and domestic media, Trump's initiatives included:

- Appointing two Supreme Court Justices: Neil Gorsuch and Brett Kavanaugh
- Passing a major tax reform bill

- Enacting travel and emigration restrictions on eight nations: Iran, Libya, Syria, Yemen, Somalia, Chad, North Korea, and Venezuela
- Recognizing Jerusalem, rather than Tel Aviv, as the capital of Israel
- Responding to the novel coronavirus (SARS-CoV-2) outbreak

Almost completely along party lines, Donald Trump was impeached by the House on charges of abuse of power and obstruction of Congress; he was acquitted by the Senate.

GLOBALISM

Today, globalism is a popular political idea. **Globalism** is the idea that all people and nations depend on each other. One country depends on one or more countries to produce certain goods and markets for goods. The ease of international travel and communication has increased this sense of depending on others. Globalism and the global economy have shaped many economic and political choices since the start of the 20th century. Problems with the environment, economy, and warfare need the help of many countries if they are to be solved.

FOREIGN POLICY

Foreign policy is the ideas and plans that decide how one nation will communicate with other countries. These plans change for actions or events that happen in other countries. Often, a nation's foreign policy is based on a set of ideals and national needs.

Examples of U.S. foreign policy include isolationism and internationalism. In the 1800s, isolationism was the practice of the United States. Isolationism is the unwillingness to become involved in another nation's concerns. However, the World Wars brought about internationalism.

Internationalism is the willingness of a nation to become involved in the concerns of other nations. When the U.S. entered these wars, the U.S. supported other countries and joined the United Nations. The foreign policy of the United States today can be called interdependent or globalist. Interdependence and globalism are plans that address issues like economic health and growth of technology.

DIPLOMATS

A **diplomat** is someone who lives in another country in order to keep communication between one country and their home country. They help negotiate trade agreements, environmental policies, and share official information to foreign governments. A diplomat also helps to resolve conflicts between countries. Diplomats take care to sort out issues without making the conflicts worse. Diplomats, or ambassadors, are appointed in the U.S. by the president. The appointments by the president must be approved by Congress.

IGOS AND NGOS

Intergovernmental organizations (IGOs) are organizations that are made of members from governments of other countries. The United Nations is an example of an intergovernmental organization. Treaties among the member nations decide the use and powers of these groups.

Nongovernmental organizations (NGOs) are outside the scope of any government. Usually, they are supported through private donations. The International Red Cross is an example of an NGO. The International Red Cross works with governments all over the world when their countries are in crisis. However, the organization has no formal connections with a particular country or government.

Foreign Policy after 9/11

After the attacks on September 11, President Bush declared a war on terrorism. American troops went to war in Afghanistan from 2001 to 2014. The goal of the war was to break up al-Qaeda forces and remove the Taliban from power. In 2011, American troops left Iraq. In addition to the battlefront, American forces have trained foreign armies to defend their countries. Also, the United States helps other countries with defense supplies that they need with the Foreign Military Financing program.

Economics

Relevant Vocabulary

Barter refers to the direct trade of goods or services without the use of an intermediate medium of exchange.

Aside from its meaning as a seat of government, **capital** refers to any money and goods used to produce income. A related word is **capitalism**, an economic system in which goods are privately produced and owned.

Currency refers to a medium of exchange agreed on by a community, which may not have any intrinsic value—i.e., money.

Goods in general in economics are tangible objects that satisfy people's needs and wants, such as food, clothing, and electronic devices. **Public goods** are goods or services not owned by individuals, but that are provided by the government, such as public libraries and police services.

An **opportunity cost** is what a person must give up, not necessarily financially, when a particular alternative is chosen. For example, when you spend a day studying for an important exam, you're giving up the opportunity to play a video game instead, which you might have preferred to do—but doing well on the exam may be worth that cost in the long run.

A **surplus** is a supply of a good or service that exceeds the demand; there is more of something available than people want or need.

Basics of Economics

Economics is the study of how a society divides their resources (i.e., a service or other asset). These resources can be divided among the groups and people in the society. Also, the choices that a society makes on what efforts are funded and which are not are important. Resources in any society are limited. So, the way they get used can show what is important to the society. In general, the economic system that drives an individual society is based on:

- What goods are made
- How those goods are made
- Who gets the goods or benefits from them

Economics has two main groups. **Macroeconomics** looks at larger systems. **Microeconomics** looks at smaller systems.

A market economy is based on supply and demand. **Demand** is what customers want and need. Also, demand is about the amount that those customers are able to buy. **Supply** is how much can be made to meet demand. The amount suppliers are willing and able to sell is also a concern for supply. Where the needs of customers meet the needs of suppliers is known as the **market**

equilibrium (i.e., a balance between two things) price. This price can change for many reasons. These reasons may be the health of a society's economy, their beliefs, or other reasons.

Elasticity—how the supply/demand of a product reacts to a price change. If the quantity reacts quickly to changes in price, the supply/demand is said to be elastic. If they do not react quickly, then it is inelastic.

Market efficiency—when a market is able to make more to meet customer demand, that market is efficient.

Comparative advantage—in the field of international trade, this means a country focuses more on a certain product. Usually, this happens because they can make it faster and cheaper than another country. This gives them an advantage in making that product.

In a **market economy**, supply and demand are determined by customers. In a planned economy, a public body makes the decisions about what resources will be made. They also decide how they will be made and who can benefit from them.

In addition, the means of production (e.g., factories) are owned by a public body rather than by private interests. In **market socialism**, the economic structure falls somewhere between the market economy and the planned economy. Planning groups determine how resources at higher economic levels are given out. Consumer goods are driven by a market economy.

Microeconomics

Economics studies how resources are divided up. So, microeconomics looks at economic factors. An example is the way that customers behave. Also, microeconomics looks at how income is distributed and output and input markets. Studies are limited to the industry or company level rather than a whole country or society. Some of the things studied in microeconomics are factors of production, costs of production, and factors of income. These factors decide how much a business will make based on resources and costs.

The current conditions in a given market are used to classify markets. Conditions considered include:

- Existence of competition
- Number and size of suppliers
- Influence of suppliers over price
- Variety of available products
- Ease of entering the market

An economist should first think about these conditions. Then, they can label a certain market according to its structure and the type of competition within the market.

There are four kinds of market structures in an output market.

1. **Perfect competition**—all current firms sell an identical product. The firms are not able to control the final price. Also, it is not hard to enter or leave the industry. Anything that would stop entering or leaving an industry is called a barrier to entry. An example of this market structure is agriculture.
2. **Monopoly**—a single seller controls the product and its price. Barriers to entry (e.g., high fixed cost structures) keep other sellers from entering the market.

3. **Monopolistic competition**—a number of firms sell similar products, but they are not the same. Examples are different brands of clothes or food. Barriers to entry are low.
4. **Oligopoly**—only a few firms control the production and distribution of products. An example is cars. Barriers to entry are high. This stops large numbers of firms from entering the market.

There are four types of monopolies.

- **Natural monopoly**—happens when a single supplier has an advantage over the others
- **Geographic monopoly**—only one business offers the product in a certain area
- **Technological monopoly**—a single company controls the technology needed to supply the product
- **Government monopoly**—a government agency is the only provider of a certain good or service

The US government has passed several acts to control businesses:

- Sherman Antitrust Act (1890) — banned trusts, monopolies, and any other situations that eliminated competition.
- Clayton Antitrust Act (1914) — banned price discrimination.
- Robinson-Patman Act (1936) — strengthened plans in the Clayton Antitrust Act.

The government has taken other actions to protect competition and requirements for public disclosure. The Securities and Exchange Commission (SEC) makes companies that provide public stock also provide financial reports on a regular basis. Banks have more rules and requirements because of their kind of business. So, banks have to provide other types of information to the government.

Marketing is made up of all of the things that are needed to get customers to buy goods. One way to get a customer to buy a good is to tell them that the good will satisfy a need. How well a good or service satisfies the need of a customer is called **utility**.

There are four types of utility:

- **Form utility**—a good's appeal is in its physical characteristics.
- **Place utility**—a good's appeal is linked to its location and convenience.
- **Time utility**—a good's appeal is decided by its availability at a certain time.
- **Ownership utility**—a good's appeal is greater when ownership of the good is passed to the customer.

Marketing behavior will put importance on any or all of the types of utility to the customer to sell the product.

Successful marketing depends on several things. One is making the customer believe that they need the product. Another is to focus the marketing on those who have a need or desire for the good. Before releasing a product into the general marketplace, many producers (i.e., makers of the product) will test markets. They are trying to decide which market will be the most willing to accept the product.

There are three steps taken to check a product's market:

- **Market research**—researching a market to decide if the market will be receptive to the product.
- **Market surveys**—a part of market research. Market surveys ask certain questions of customers to help decide the marketability of a product to a certain group. Marketability is how easy it is to market a product.
- **Test marketing**—releasing the product into a small area to see how it sells. Often, test marketing is followed by wider marketing if the product does well.

There are four major factors to any marketing plan.

- **Product**—any factors related directly to the product. This includes packaging, presentation, or services that come with the product.
- **Price**—finds the cost of production, distribution, advertising, etc. Also, this factor finds the desired profit which decides the final price.
- **Place**—what outlets will be used to sell the product. They can be traditional outlets (e.g., brick and mortar stores). Also, they can be through direct mail or Internet marketing.
- **Promotion**—ways to let customers know the product is available. This can be through advertising and other means.

Once these factors have been decided, the producer can start production and distribution of their product.

Distribution channels decide the route a product takes on its journey from producer to consumer. It can also influence the final price and availability of the product. There are two major types of distributions: wholesale and retail. A **wholesale distributor** buys in large amounts and then resells smaller amounts to other businesses. **Retailers** sell directly to the consumers.

In the modern marketplace, additional distribution channels have shown up. These include club warehouse stores and buying through catalogs or over the Internet. Most of these newer distribution channels bring products straight to the consumer. This helps cut out the need for middlemen.

Macroeconomics

Macroeconomics looks at economies on a much larger level than microeconomics. Macroeconomics looks at economic trends and structures on a national level. Variables studied in macroeconomics include:

- Output
- Consumption (i.e., the use of a resource)
- Investment
- Government spending
- Net exports (i.e., goods sent to another country)

The overall economic condition of a nation is defined as the **Gross Domestic Product**, or GDP. GDP measures a nation's economic output over a limited amount of time, such as a year.

There are two major ways to measure the Gross Domestic Product (GDP) of a country.

- The expenditures approach calculates the GDP based on how much money is spent in each individual sector.
- The income approach calculates based on how much money is earned in each sector.

Both methods give the same results. Also, they are based on four economic sectors that make up a country's macroeconomy: consumer, business, government, and foreign sectors.

Aggregate supply is the amount of national output. **Aggregate demand** is the amount of the output that is purchased. Ideally, an economy operates well with the aggregate supply equal to the aggregate demand. In these cases, the economy is stable and well-off. In reality, economies go through phases. These phases happen often. They happen in cycles that are not very predictable or regular. These phases are:

- **Boom**—GDP is high and the economy is well-off
- **Recession**—GDP falls and unemployment rises
- **Trough**—the recession reaches its lowest point
- **Recovery**—Unemployment lessens, prices rise, and the economy begins to recover

When demand exceeds supply, prices are driven artificially high or inflated. This happens when too much spending causes the economy to not be balanced. In general, inflation happens because an economy is growing too quickly.

When there is too little spending and supply has moved far beyond demand, there is a surplus of product. Companies cut back on production and reduce the number of workers they employ. So, unemployment rises as people lose their jobs. This imbalance happens when an economy becomes too slow.

In general, both of these economic situations are caused by supply and demand not being balanced. Often, the government has to get involved to stabilize an economy when inflation or unemployment becomes too serious.

There are five different forms of unemployment. Any of these factors can increase unemployment in certain sectors.

- **Frictional**—when workers change jobs and are unemployed while waiting for a new job.
- **Structural**—when economical shifts reduce the need for workers.
- **Cyclical**—when natural business cycles bring about loss of jobs.
- **Seasonal**—when seasonal cycles reduce the need for certain jobs.
- **Technological**—when advances in technology reduce the need for workers.

Inflation is categorized by the overall rate at which it occurs.

- **Creeping inflation**—an inflation rate of about one to three percent annually.
- **Galloping inflation**—a high inflation rate of 100 to 300 percent annually.
- **Hyperinflation**—an inflation rate over 500 percent annually. Hyperinflation usually leads to complete monetary collapse in a society. Individuals are unable to have enough income to purchase their needed goods.

An economy may have too much spending or not enough spending. In these imbalances, government intervention may be needed to put the economy back on track. Government Fiscal Policy can take several forms:

- Monetary policy
- Contractionary policies
- Expansionary policies

Contractionary policies help correct inflation. These include increasing taxes and decreasing government spending to slow spending in the overall economy. **Expansionary policies** increase government spending and lower taxes to reduce unemployment and increase the level of spending in the economy overall. **Monetary policy** can take several forms and affects the amount of money available to banks for making loans.

Money is used in three major ways:

- As an accounting unit
- As a store of value
- As a form of exchange

In general, money must be acceptable throughout a society. This money is used for debts or to purchase goods and services. Money should be fairly limited. Its value should remain stable, and it should be easily carried. Also, it should be durable and easy to divide up.

There are three basic types of money: commodity, representative, and fiat. **Commodity money** includes gems or precious metals. **Representative money** can be exchanged for items such as gold or silver which have built-in value. **Fiat money**, or legal tender, has no inherent value. However, the government has stated that this should act as money. Often, fiat money is backed by gold or silver. However, this is not in a one-to-one ratio.

The Federal Reserve System, the Fed, works on all monetary policy in the US. Monetary policy controls the amount of money available in the American banking system. The Fed can decrease or increase the amount of available money for loans. This helps to control the national economy.

Monetary policies put into action by the Fed are part of expansionary or contractionary monetary policies. They help correct inflation or unemployment. The Discount Rate is an interest rate charged by the Fed when banks borrow money from them. A lower discount rate leads banks to borrow more money. This leads to increased spending. A higher discount rate has the opposite effect.

Banks earn their income by loaning out money and charging interest on those loans. If less money is available, fewer loans can be made. This affects the amount of spending in the overall economy.

While banks operate by making loans, they are not allowed to loan out all the money that they hold in deposit. The amount of money they must keep in reserve is known as the **reserve ratio**. If the reserve ratio is raised, less money is available for loans and spending decreases. A lower reserve ratio increases available funds and increases spending. This ratio is determined by the Federal Reserve System.

The Federal Reserve System can increase or decrease the overall money supply through **Open Market Operations**. In this case, the Fed can buy or sell bonds that it has purchased from banks or from individuals. A bond is a type of debt investment. When the Fed buys bonds, more money is put into circulation. This creates an expansionary situation to help the economy.

When the Fed sells bonds, money is taken out of the system. This creates a contractionary situation to slow an economy that is suffering from inflation. American banks often borrow and lend money in markets outside the US. Sometimes, domestic markets and other businesses move their attention to international markets. This allows them to get around the Fed's contractionary policies.

There are five major characteristics of a **developing nation**.

- Low GDP
- Fast growth of population
- Economy that relies on subsistence agriculture (i.e., farming to feed themselves)
- Poor conditions: high infant death rates, high disease rates, poor sanitation, and not enough housing
- Low literacy rate (i.e., portion of population able to read)

Often, developing nations have harsh governments. They do not give private property rights. In addition, they hold back on education and rights for women. They may have a great difference between upper and lower classes. In many cases, lower classes have little chance to improve their position.

Economic development happens in three stages that are divided up by the ways they drive the economy:

- Agricultural stage
- Manufacturing stage
- Service sector stage

Many developing countries have difficulty with gaining money to provide equipment and training for higher stages of economic development. Some can get help from developed countries. This happens through foreign aid and investment from international organizations. Examples of these organizations are the International Monetary Fund or the World Bank. Also, developed countries can give monetary, technical, or military assistance. This can help countries move on to the next step in their development.

Developing nations have a hard time getting past difficulties that prevent or slow economic development. Major difficulties can include:

- Fast or uncontrolled population growth
- Limits on trade
- Misused resources
- Traditional beliefs that can slow or refuse change

Fast growth across the world leaves some nations behind. This makes some governments move forward too soon into industrialization. So, they experience quick artificial economic growth. Slow or absent economic growth causes problems in a country. However, fast industrialization has its own problems. Four major problems of fast industrialization are:

- Use of technology not meant for the products or services being supplied
- Poor investment of capital
- Lack of time for the population to adapt to changes
- Lack of time to experience all stages of development and welcome each stage

The **knowledge economy** is a growing part of the economy of developed countries. It includes the trade and development of:

- Data
- Intellectual property
- Technology: Especially communications

Knowledge as a resource is becoming more important. The Information Age has brought many changes in life and culture, changes that have proven to be as important as those from Agricultural and Industrial Revolutions.

The growth of the Internet has brought many changes to society. This is true for business as well. E-commerce makes it possible for nearly any individual to set up a direct market. Also, they can have direct contact with suppliers. Competition is strong. In many cases, e-commerce can give quick satisfaction with many products.

Whoever makes the best product in the shortest amount of time can reach the top of a marketplace. The influence of e-commerce on the economy in the future remains to be seen. Today, many industries are trying to find the best ways to make fast changes.

Related to the knowledge economy is what has been called "**cybernomics**." This is economics driven by e-commerce and other computer-based markets and products. Marketing has changed a lot with the growth of cyber communication. This allows suppliers to connect with an individual customer. Other issues for cybernomics are:

- Secure online trade
- Intellectual property rights
- Rights to privacy
- Including developing nations

Today, these issues are going through debate. In addition, new laws are being made and many industries are changing. Many of the old ways of doing business no longer work. So, this leaves industries looking for new ways to make money within this changing system.

Review Video: Microeconomics and Macroeconomics
Visit mometrix.com/academy and enter code: 538837

Ancient World History

Development of Classical Civilizations

Prehistory is the time of human history before humans started writing. The four major periods of prehistory are:

- **Lower Paleolithic** or Old Stone Age, about one million years ago—early humans used tools like needles, hatchets, awls, and other cutting tools.
- Upper Paleolithic (Neolithic) or New Stone Age, 6,000-8,000 BC—There was growth in the ideas of family, religion, and government. Humans learned to train animals. In addition, humans started to grow crops, build houses, and made fires with friction tools. Also, textiles and pottery were developed.

- Bronze Age, 3,000 BC—metals were discovered, and the first civilizations began with advanced technology.
- Iron Age, 1,200-1,000 BC—iron tools replaced bronze tools as humans developed tools for work, art, and war.

Early Civilizations

The earliest civilizations are known as fluvial, meaning they were started near rivers. The water that came from the rivers was very important to early civilizations. Irrigation methods moved water where it was most needed.

The water was used to keep herds of domestic animals alive. Another need of the water was to grow crops of increasing size and quality. The flooding of the rivers made the surrounding soil very rich. **Civilizations** are defined as having the following traits:

- Use of metals to make weapons and tools
- Written language
- A specific territorial area
- A calendar

The earliest civilizations came from river valleys where stable, fertile (i.e., soil that produces many crops) land was easily found:

- Nile River valley in Egypt and northeast Africa
- Tigris-Euphrates valley in Mesopotamia
- Indus River valley in Pakistan, formerly India
- Hwang Ho valley in China

The earliest civilizations came out of the Tigris-Euphrates valley in Mesopotamia and in Egypt's Nile valley. These civilizations started between 4,000 and 3,000 BC (i.e., Before Christ). The area where these civilizations started is known as the Fertile Crescent. In the Fertile Crescent, the geography and the availability of water allowed many people to live in the area.

The major civilizations of **Mesopotamia** (i.e., the Fertile Crescent) were:

- Sumerians
- Amorites
- Hittites
- Assyrians
- Chaldeans
- Persians

These groups controlled different areas of Mesopotamia at different times. Each group's control was autocratic. In other words, one ruler served as the head of the government. This ruler may have served as the main religious ruler as well. Often, these leaders took over all parts of life. These parts were law, trade, and religious activity. Some parts of these civilizations' mythologies and religions remain in cultures today. Also, remnants of the advances the Mesopotamians made in mathematics and as well as influences in written alphabets can still be seen throughout modern life across the globe.

Sumer, located in the southern part of Mesopotamia, had a dozen city-states. A **city-state** is an area that has its own government and a city in the area (e.g. Athens and Sparta). Each city-state had its own gods. The leader of each city-state also served as the high priest. Important parts of Sumer include:

- Invention of writing
- Invention of the wheel
- The first library—built in Assyria by Ashurbanipal
- The Hanging Gardens of Babylon—one of the Seven Wonders of the Ancient World
- First written laws—Ur-Nammu's Codes and the Codes of Hammurabi
- The *Epic of Gilgamesh*—the first epic story in history

The Sumerians were the first to invent the wheel. Also, they brought irrigation systems into use. Their cuneiform writing was simpler than Egyptian hieroglyphs. The timekeeping system they developed is essentially the same as what we use today. The Babylonians established the Code of Hammurabi, an advanced law code that influenced many subsequent codes of law. The Assyrians had an extremely organized military that was bolstered by horse-drawn chariots.

Review Video: The Sumerians
Visit mometrix.com/academy and enter code: 939880

The **Egyptians** were one of the most advanced ancient cultures. They had construction methods to build the great pyramids. In addition, they made their own form of writing known as hieroglyphics. Their religion was very developed. Also, they had advanced ways for preserving bodies after death. They made paper by working with papyrus, a plant commonly found along the Nile. The Egyptians invented the decimal system. Also, they made a solar calendar and made discoveries in arithmetic and geometry.

Review Video: Ancient Egypt
Visit mometrix.com/academy and enter code: 398041

The **Hittites** were centered in what is now Turkey. However, their empire reached into what is now Palestine and Syria. They conquered the Babylonian civilization, but they took their religion and their system of laws. Overall, the Hittites put up with other religions. In addition, they absorbed gods from other cultures into their own belief systems. The Hittite Empire reached its peak in 1600-1200 BC. After a war with Egypt, they were weakened. The Assyrians took over the Hittites in 700 BC.

Many religions were practiced throughout the area and time period. The Hebrew or ancient Israelite culture developed a monotheistic (i.e., belief in one god) religion. Modern Judaism and Christianity would come from this religion. The Persians were conquerors. However, the people that they conquered got to keep their laws, customs, and religious traditions. The Persians are well-known for their alphabet. Zoroastrianism, Mithraism, and Gnosticism are religions from this area that have influenced modern religions.

The **Minoans** are known for their syllabic writing system and their large, colorful palaces. These palaces included sewage systems, running water, bathtubs, and flush toilets. Their writing system known as Linear Script A has yet to be deciphered (i.e., understood). The Mycenaeans practiced a religion that grew into the Greek pantheon. In Greece, they worshiped Zeus and other Olympian gods. The Mycenaeans developed Linear Script B. This is the earliest form of Greek writing.

The Minoans lived on the island of Crete just off the coast of Greece. This civilization had control from 2700 to 1450 BC. Minoans is not the name that they used for themselves. The name is a variation on the name of King Minos, a king in Greek mythology. King Minos is believed by some to have been a native of Crete. The Minoan civilization lived on trade. Often, their way of life was disrupted by earthquakes and volcanoes. Much is still unknown about the Minoans. The Minoan culture was taken over by the Mycenaean civilization.

The **Mycenaean** civilization was the first major civilization in Europe. The Mycenaeans relied more on conquest than on trade. Mycenaean states included Sparta, Metropolis, and Corinth. Homer, a Greek poet, recorded the history of this civilization and the Trojan War. Homer's work was thought to be mythical. However, archeologists discovered evidence of the city of Troy in Hisarlik, Turkey. No one knows for sure who attacked the Mycenaeans. Some scholars think that a Dorian invasion or an attack by Greek invaders from the north destroyed the Mycenaeans around 1200 BC.

The **Phoenicians** are known as great sailors and navigators. At night, they used the stars to navigate their ships. In the ancient world, some thought of purple as a color of royalty. The Phoenicians were able to make a purple dye for clothing. Then, they could sell the highly demanded material to the wealthy. In addition to clothing, the Phoenicians worked with glass and metals. Also, they are known for their phonetic alphabet. This alphabet used symbols to represent individual sounds rather than whole words or syllables.

In **ancient China**, civilization developed along the Yangtze River. The Chinese people produced silk, grew millet, and made pottery. Many historians think that the Chinese civilization is the oldest uninterrupted civilization in the world. In other words, the Chinese civilization is one that was not attacked or disturbed by invasions.

The Neolithic age in China goes back to about 9000 BC. Agriculture in China starts near 7000 BC. Then, their system of writing dates to 1500 BC. Other early Chinese settlements started by the Yellow River. In Ningxia, a region in northwest China, there are carvings on cliffs that date back at least 6,000 years ago. Literature from ancient China includes Confucius' *Analects*, the *Tao Te Ching*, and poetry.

In **the Indus Valley**, an urban (i.e., city) civilization arose in what is now India and Pakistan. These ancient people worked on the idea of zero in mathematics. They were known for practicing an early form of the Hindu religion. Also, they set up a caste (i.e., social class) system which still exists in India. Archeologists are still uncovering information about this ancient civilization. Hinduism and Buddhism, two major world religions, started with these ancient people. Yoga, a popular practice in the West, has roots in the earliest Indian civilizations. Major epics in ancient India include the *Ramayana* and the *Mahabharata*. Important stories in the *Mahabharata* are the *Bhagavad Gita* and the *Rishyasringa*. The *Vedas* is an important collection of Hindu scriptures.

Indo-European languages (e.g., English, Spanish, French, and Hindi) find their start in these ancient cultures. Ancient Indo-Aryan languages such as Sanskrit are still used in some formal Hindu practices. Yoga poses are still known by Sanskrit names.

Kush, or Cush, was located south of ancient Egypt. The earliest existing records of this civilization were found in Egyptian texts. At one time, Kush was the largest empire on the Nile River. In Neolithic times, Kushites lived in villages with buildings made of mud bricks. They were settled people, not nomadic. So, they practiced hunting and fishing. On their land, they cultivated grain and herded cattle. Kerma, the capitol, was a major center of trade.

The leadership in Kush was decided through the line of ancestry of the mother. Their heads of state, the Kandake, or Kentake, were female. Their polytheistic religion included the primary Egyptian gods as well as regional gods. These regional gods included a lion god which is commonly found in

African cultures. Archeological evidence shows that the Kushites were a mix of Mediterranean and Negroid peoples. Kush was taken over by Nubia in 800 BC.

There are few things known about ancient **American civilizations**:

- The **Norte Chico** civilization lived in Peru over 5,000 years ago. This group was an agricultural society of 20 communities. This is the oldest known civilization in the Americas.
- The Anasazi, or Ancient Pueblo People, lived in what is now the southwestern United States in 1200 BC. During this time, the Anasazi built complex adobe dwellings. They were the forerunners of later Pueblo Indian cultures.
- The Mayans came from southern Mexico and northern Central America as early as 2,600 BC. They developed a written language and a complex calendar.

Hellenistic Age

Ancient Greece made many major additions to cultural development:

- Theater—Aristophanes and other Greek playwrights set the foundations for modern theatrical performance.
- Alphabet—the Greek alphabet was pulled from the Phoenician alphabet. This became the Roman alphabet and the modern-day alphabet for English.
- Geometry—Pythagoras and Euclid worked on much of the concerns of geometry still taught today. Archimedes made mathematical discoveries such as the value of pi.
- Historical writing—much of ancient history doubles as mythology or religious texts. Herodotus and Thucydides used research and interpretation to record events.
- Philosophy—Socrates, Plato, and Aristotle served as the fathers of Western philosophy. Today, their work is required reading for many students.

The Spartans and the Athenians, two Greek city-states, developed different cultures.

- The Spartans, located in Peloponnesus, were ruled by an oligarchic military state. In addition to their military, they worked at farming. The military arts and strict discipline were important to Spartans. So, they became the strongest military force in the area. At one time, a small group of Spartans held off a huge army of Persians at Thermopylae.
- The Athenians were centered in Attica where there was little land for farming. Like the Spartans, the Athenians came from invaders who spoke Greek. Their government was very different from Sparta's. In Athens, democracy was set up by Cleisthenes of Athens in 510 BC. Athenians are known for their art, theater, architecture, and philosophy.

Athens and Sparta fought each other in the Peloponnesian War from 431-404 BC.

Cyrus the Great ruled the **Persian Empire**. The empire covered an area from the Black Sea and beyond into Central Asia. After the death of Cyrus, Darius became king in 522 BC. The empire reached its peak during his reign. From 499-448 BC, the Greeks and Persians fought in the Persian Wars. Battles of the Persian Wars included:

- The Battle of Marathon: outnumbered Greek forces won against Persian forces.
- The Battle of Thermopylae: a small group of Spartans held off many Persian troops for several days.
- The Battle of Salamis: a naval battle where outnumbered Greeks won against Persian forces.
- The Battle of Plataea: another Greek victory. However, Greeks outnumbered the Persians.

The Persian Wars were not the end of the Persian Empire. However, these wars did discourage other attempts to invade Greece.

Born to Philip II of Macedon and tutored by Aristotle, **Alexander the Great** is thought to be one of the greatest conquerors in history. He conquered Egypt and the Persian Empire and spread his empire as far as India and the Iberian Peninsula. Alexander died at the age of 32. In his lifetime, his efforts spread Greek culture into the East. This spread of culture left a greater mark on history than Alexander's empire.

Review Video: Ancient Greece Timeline
Visit mometrix.com/academy and enter code: 800829

The **Maurya Empire** was a large, powerful empire set up in India. The empire was one of the largest ever to rule in the Indian subcontinent and lasted from 322 to 185 BC. After Alexander the Great withdrew from the area, Chandragupta Maurya took over the area and started an empire. The Maurya Empire was very developed. The people had a standardized economic system, waterworks, and private corporations. The Maurya Empire made trade with the Greeks and others a common practice. This trade included goods like silk, exotic foods, and spices. Religious development included the rise of Buddhism and Jainism.

In China, history was divided into a series of dynasties. The Han Dynasty, one of the most famous dynasties, lasted from 206 BC to 220 AD. The Chinese accomplished the following:

- Building the Great Wall of China
- Many inventions: paper, paper money, printing, and gunpowder
- High level of artistic development
- Silk production

Roman Empire

Rome was set up as a town that came from Etruscan settlements and traditions. According to legend, Rome started with twin brothers Romulus and Remus. The twins were raised by wolves. At one point, Romulus killed Remus. From Romulus' legacy, Rome continued to grow. A thousand years later, the Roman Empire covered many parts of the known world. This area is now much of Europe and the Middle East.

Review Video: The Roman Republic: Part One
Visit mometrix.com/academy and enter code: 360192

Review Video: The Roman Republic: Part Two
Visit mometrix.com/academy and enter code: 881514

Hellenization (i.e., the spread of Greek culture throughout the world) served as a model for the spread of Roman culture. Rome used beliefs from people that they had conquered. Improvements in technology and science were brought to Rome. These different parts gave Rome a strong core.

Rome's overall government was autocratic. However, local officials came from the provinces where they lived. This limited administrative system was an important piece to the long life of the empire.

In the early fourth century, the Roman Empire split. The eastern part became the Eastern Empire, also known as the **Byzantine Empire**. In 330 AD, Constantine founded the city of Constantinople. This became the center of the Byzantine Empire. Major influences on the Eastern Empire came from

Mesopotamia and Persia. For the Western Empire, traditions were linked closely to Greece and Carthage.

Byzantium's position gave it an advantage over invaders from the West and the East. Also, this position gave control over trade from both regions. The Eastern Empire protected the Western empire from invasion from the Persians and the Ottomans. The Eastern Empire practiced a more centralized rule than the West. The Byzantines were famous for grand art and architecture. In addition, the Byzantines are known for the Code of Justinian. This code put Roman law into a clear system.

At this time, Germanic tribes, Visigoths, Ostrogoths, Vandals, Saxons, and Franks controlled most of Europe. The Roman Empire faced major opposition from these tribes. The increasing size of the empire also made it harder to manage. This led to disappointment throughout the empire as the Roman government became less efficient. The Franks proved their strength by defeating Muslims in 732. In 768, Charlemagne became king of the Franks. These tribes fought several wars against Rome. These wars included the invasion of Britannia (i.e., Great Britain) by the Angles and Saxons. Later, Rome lost control over this area. Eventually, Rome was invaded and fell.

GEOGRAPHY

BASICS OF GEOGRAPHY

Geography is the study of physical characteristics of the earth as it is, as it was, and as it may be in the future. A significant aspect of geography is the human factor: both how humans have been shaped by it and how humans have shaped it. Some specific topics in the study of geography include: locations, regional characteristics, spatial relations, and natural or manmade forces that change elements of the earth. The tools used to study geography include mapping, field studies, statistics, interviews, and various scientific instruments. These tools can be applied to studying geography from different perspectives including:

- **Topical**—the study of one quality of the earth. Also, this can be one specific human activity that happens around the world.
- **Physical**—the different physical qualities of the earth. This topic centers on how these qualities are created and the forces that change them. Also, an important part is how these qualities relate to each other and to different human activities.
- **Regional**—certain characteristics of a place and region.
- **Human**—how human activity affects the environment. This includes looking at how politics, history, society, and culture work in an area.
- **Cultural**—the study of how the different parts of physical geography affect cultures.

CARTOGRAPHY

A **cartographer** is a person who makes maps. Mapmakers create detailed illustrations of an area to show where different things are located within that area. There are five main parts to any map:

- **Title**—tells basic information about the map
- **Legend**—also known as the key. The legend explains the use of certain symbols on a particular map.
- **Grid**—most commonly shows the Geographic Grid System. This system uses latitude and longitude marks to show specific locations.

- **Directions**—a compass rose or other symbol used to show the cardinal directions (i.e., North, East, South, and West).
- **Scale**—shows the relation between a certain distance on the map and the actual distance. For example, one inch may represent a number of miles or kilometers.

Cartographers must be aware of distortion or bends in their maps. Because the earth is round, a flat map of a very large area does not correctly show the surface of the area. Maps must be designed in a way that minimizes this distortion and maximizes accuracy. Displaying the earth's features on a flat surface is achieved through projection.

Review Video: 5 Elements of any Map
Visit mometrix.com/academy and enter code: 437727

Types of commonly used map projections:

- **Cylindrical projection**—this map is created by wrapping a piece of paper around a globe to form a cylinder. Then a light is used to project the globe onto the paper. The largest distortion happens at the polar regions. For example, the size of Greenland is very large on a cylindrical projected map. In reality, Greenland is closer to the size of Mexico.
- **Conical projection**—a piece of paper in the shape of a cone is wrapped around a globe. This type of projection is best for middle latitudes. An example of an area in the middle latitudes is the continental United States.
- **Flat-Plane projections**—also known as a Gnomonic projection. This type of map is projected onto a flat piece of paper that only touches the globe at a single point. Flat-plane projections are good for showing the shortest route between points.
- **Winkel tripel projection**—a common projection for world maps. In 1998, the National Geographic Society accepted this projection as a standard. The Winkel tripel projection balances size and shape and greatly reduces distortion.
- **Robinson projection**—the east and west sections of the map do not have much distortion. However, the polar regions of the map are stretched into long lines.
- **Goode's interrupted equal-area projection**—Sizes and shapes are accurate, but distances are not accurate. This projection shows a globe that has been cut in a way that allows it to lie flat.
- **Mercator projection**—distortion is high in areas farther from the equator. This cylindrical projection is used by sailors.

Review Video: Map Projections
Visit mometrix.com/academy and enter code: 327303

Geographical Features

There are many different ways to group geographical features. One way to classify these features is by elevation above sea level. **Mountains** are elevated areas that measure 2,000 feet or more above sea level. Often steep and rugged, they are found in groups called chains or ranges. Six of the seven continents on Earth contain at least one range. **Hills** measure at about 500-2,000 feet above sea level. Usually, hills are more rounded than mountains. Also, they can be found everywhere on Earth. **Foothills** are the areas that change from the plains to the mountains. This feature has hills that increase in size as they come up to the mountain range.

Mesas are flat, steep-sided mountains or hills. The term is sometimes used to refer to plateaus. **Plateaus** are elevated but flat on top. Some plateaus are very dry (e.g., the Kenya Plateau) because surrounding mountains keep back rainfall. **Valleys** come between hills and mountains. Different valleys have different features depending on their location. One valley may be fertile and habitable. Another valley may be rugged and inhospitable. **Plains** are large, flat areas and can be very fertile. The majority of Earth's population is supported by crops grown on large plains. **Basins** are areas of low elevation where rivers drain.

Another way to classify features is by how much water is in the area. **Deserts** receive less than ten inches of rain each year. Usually, deserts are large areas: the Sahara Desert in Africa or the Australian Outback. **Marshes** and **swamps** are lowlands. However, they are very wet and covered in vegetation (e.g., reeds and rushes). **Deltas** happen at river mouths (e.g., Nile River Delta). Because the rivers carry sediment to the deltas, these areas can be very fertile.

There are different classifications for bodies of water. **Oceans** are the largest bodies of water on Earth. They are salt water and cover about two-thirds of the earth's surface. The five major oceans are the Atlantic, Pacific, Indian, and Arctic. Generally, seas are salt water. However, they are smaller than oceans. Some examples are the Mediterranean Sea, the Caribbean Sea, and the Caspian Sea.

Lakes are bodies of freshwater that are found inland. Over 110 million lakes can be found across the world. **Rivers** are moving bodies of water that flow from high to low elevations. Usually, they start as rivulets (i.e., a small stream) or streams. Then, they grow until they empty into a sea or an ocean. **Canals** (e.g., Panama Canal and Suez Canal) are manmade waterways that connect two large bodies of water.

Natural Processes

According to the geological theory of **plate tectonics**, the earth's crust is made up of ten major and several minor tectonic plates. These plates are the solid areas of the crust. They float on top of the earth's mantle which is made up of molten rock. Because the plates float on this liquid component of the earth's crust, they move. This movement makes major changes in the earth's surface.

These changes can happen very slowly (e.g., continental drift). However, changes can happen quickly (e.g., earthquakes). When two plates come in contact with each other, they can be constructive or destructive. Constructive changes would be mountain ranges or deep rifts. Destructive changes would be volcanic activity and earthquakes.

Plate tectonics defines three types of plate boundaries. A type is decided by how the edges of the plates contact other places. These plate boundaries are:

- **Convergent boundaries**—the bordering plates move toward one another. A direct collision of the plates is known as continental collision. This event can create very large, high mountain ranges (e.g., the Himalayas and the Andes). If one plate slides under the other, this is called subduction. Subduction can lead to intense volcanic activity (e.g., the Ring of Fire along the northern Pacific coastlines).
- **Divergent boundaries**—at this boundary, plates move away from each other. This movement leads to rifts (e.g., Mid-Atlantic Ridge and Africa's Great Rift Valley).
- **Transform boundaries**—plate boundaries slide in opposite directions against each other. High pressure builds up along transform boundaries as the plates grind along each other's edges. This movement leads to earthquakes. Many major fault lines (e.g., the San Andreas Fault) lie along transform boundaries.

Plate tectonics is not the only natural process that changes geographical features:

- **Erosion**: the movement of any loose material on the earth's surface. This can include soil, sand, or pieces of rocks. This material can be moved by natural forces: wind, water, ice, plant cover, and human factors. Mechanical erosion happens from natural forces. Chemical erosion happens with human activities.
- **Weathering**: the effect of atmospheric elements on the earth's surface. Water, heat, ice, and pressure can change the form of an object.
- **Transportation**: the movement of loose material by wind, water, or ice. For example, glacial movement can carry everything from pebbles to boulders over long distances.
- **Deposition**: material that is left behind after transportation. As material is moved around, some of it builds up to make moraines and sand dunes.

Review Video: What is Plate Tectonics?
Visit mometrix.com/academy and enter code: 535013

CLIMATES

Weather and climate are physical systems that affect geography. They center on similar information. However, this information is measured and gathered in different ways. **Weather** involves daily conditions in the atmosphere that affect temperature, precipitation (rain, snow, hail, or sleet), wind speed, air pressure, and other factors. Weather looks at the short-term.

The short-term includes what the conditions will be today, tomorrow, or over the next few days. By contrast, **climate** collects information about daily and seasonal weather conditions in a region over a long period of time. Climate includes looking at average temperatures and precipitation for each month and year. Another important area of climate is the growing season of an area.

Because the earth is tilted, its rotation brings about the changes in seasons. Areas that are close to the equator and the poles see very little change in seasonal temperatures. Mid-range latitudes are most likely to see specific seasons. Large bodies of water also affect climate.

Ocean currents and wind patterns can change the climate for an area. An area that lies in a cold latitude (e.g., England) can have a different climate from being surrounded by water. Mountains can affect both short-term weather and long-term climates. Some deserts exist because precipitation is stopped by the wall of a mountain range. Over time, one climate pattern can change to another pattern. While the issue is debated, some think that human activity has led to climate change.

Climates are classified by their latitude (i.e., how close they lie to the earth's equator). The three major divisions are:

- **Low Latitudes**: lying from 0 to 23.5 degrees latitude (e.g., from the equator to Central America)*
- **Middle Latitudes**: found from 23.5 to 66.5 degrees (e.g., from Central America to Canada)*
- **High Latitudes**: found from 66.5 degrees to the poles (e.g., from Canada to North Pole)*

*These examples are for the Northern Hemisphere.

Desert, savanna, and rainforest climates happen in low latitudes. **Rainforest** climates have high average temperatures, humidity, and rainfall. **Savannas** are grasslands that see dry winters and wet summers. **Desert** regions have hot, dry climates. They see little rainfall (less than ten inches per year on average). Also, temperatures can change up to fifty degrees from day into night. The climate regions found in the middle latitudes are:

- Mediterranean
- Humid-subtropical
- Humid-continental
- Marine
- Steppe
- Desert

The **Mediterranean** climate happens between 30- and 40-degrees latitude north and south. Characteristics include a year-long growing season with hot, dry summers. The summer is followed by mild winters and little rainfall. Most of the rainfall comes during the winter months.

Humid-subtropical regions are in southeastern coastal areas. Winds that blow in over warm ocean currents make long summers, mild winters, and a long growing season. These areas support more of the earth's population than any other climate. The **humid continental** climate produces the familiar four seasons. Some of the most productive farmlands in the world are in these climates. Winters are cold and summers are hot and humid.

Marine climates are found near water or on islands. Ocean winds help make these areas mild and rainy. Summers are cooler than humid-subtropical summers. Winters bring milder temperatures than humid-subtropical winters because of the warmth of the ocean winds.

Steppe climates, or prairie climates, are found far inland in large continents. Summers are hot and winters are cold. There is less rainfall than continental climates. **Desert** climates happen where steppe climates receive even less rainfall. Examples include the Gobi Desert in Asia as well as desert areas of Australia and the southwestern US.

The high latitudes have two major climate areas: the tundra and the taiga. **Tundra** means frozen ground. In the long, cold winters, there is little snowfall. During the short summers, the land becomes wet and marshy. Tundras are not open to crops, but many plants and animals have adapted to the conditions.

Taigas lie south of tundra regions. They include the largest forest areas in the world with swamps and marshes. Large mineral deposits are in these areas. Also, many animals with valuable fur live in these areas. In the winter, taiga regions can be colder than the tundra and summers are hotter. The growing season is very short.

A vertical climate exists in high mountain ranges. Often, these areas have parts of other climate regions. Increasing elevation leads to changing temperatures and difficult growing conditions. This decreases the amount of plant and animal life in these areas. Also, fewer humans live in these climates.

Review Video: Climates
Visit mometrix.com/academy and enter code: 991320

Environmental Geography

Ecology is the study of the relationship between organisms and their environment. Biogeography explores how physical features of the earth affect organisms. Ecology has three levels for study of the environment:

- **Ecosystem**—a specific physical environment and all the organisms that live there.
- **Biomes**—a group of ecosystems. Usually, these have a large area with similar flora and fauna. Also, they have a similar climate and soil. Examples of biomes are deserts, tropical rain forests, taigas, and tundra.
- **Habitat**—an area where a specific species usually lives. The habitat includes the necessary soil, water, and resources for that particular species. Also, the habitat includes predators and other species that fight for the same resources.

Biodiversity is the different habitats and organisms that exist on the planet. More biodiversity increases the chances that one habitat will flourish with the species that depend upon the habitat. Changes in habitat (e.g., climate change, human influence, or other factors) can reduce biodiversity by causing the extinction of a species.

Within one habitat, there are different relationships among the species and members of single species. These relationships fall into three categories:

- Competition
- Predation
- Symbiosis

Competition happens when animals of the same species or of different species fight for the same resources. For example, robins can fight with other robins for food (e.g., insects). However, other animals that eat insects also fight for these resources. **Predation** happens when one species depends on the other species for food. An example is a fox that hunts for small mammals. **Symbiosis** happens when two different species live in the same environment without affecting the other. Some symbiotic relationships are helpful to one or both organisms. In other words, the species do not harm the other.

Sometimes one species is forced to move from one habitat to another. In the new habitat, the species must **adapt** (i.e., change) in order to survive. Some species are better at adapting than others. Those that cannot adapt will not survive. There are different ways that a creature can adapt such as behavior modification and structural or physiological changes. Adaptation is important if an organism's environment changes around it. Humans' ability to adapt is a major reason why they are able to survive in almost any habitat.

The agricultural revolution led people to start changing their surroundings. These changes were made to manage their needs for shelter, food, and their domesticated animals. They cleared ground for crops, and they changed the direction of waterways for irrigation. In addition, they made permanent settlements. Increased agriculture can lead to loose topsoil and damaging erosion. Building large cities leads to poor air quality and water pollution. Recently, many countries have worked on their environmental policies. In other words, they have passed laws to reduce the human impact on the environment and the likely damaging side effects.

Human Geography

The **agricultural revolution** began six thousand years ago when the plow was invented in Mesopotamia. Using a plow drawn by animals, people were able to cultivate (i.e. grow) more crops.

This still required a lot of work and many people for that work. More people working on farms led to the growth of stable communities. Stable farming communities replaced groups of nomadic hunter-gatherers. So, societies became dependent on limited numbers of crops. In addition, they suffered from sudden changes in weather. Trading livestock and extra crops led to trade routes and wide-spread exchange of goods by way of bartering. This trade enabled small communities to grow into larger settlements.

Communities are groups of people who settle together in a specific area. Normally, they gather where certain conditions exist. These conditions are:

- Easy access to resources (e.g., food, water, and raw materials)
- Ability to move raw materials and goods. An example is a waterway.
- Room to house enough workers

People are likely to form groups with others who are similar to them. In a typical community, people share a common language and cultural characteristics. They may share values and have similar religious beliefs. Settlements and communities that continued to grow became the first cities. Such large groups required infrastructure (i.e. roads and sewers), governance (i.e. leaders and laws), and protection (i.e. walls and soldiers), which often attracted even more people to cities. As they continued to grow, cities required more goods and people with specialized skills to sustain life, which offered additional ways for people to survive besides farming or roaming.

Modern statistics show that over half of the world's people live in cities. Currently, cities are growing faster in developing areas. Established cities continue to see growth throughout the world. In developing or developed areas, cities are surrounded by a **metropolitan area**. These areas are made up of **urban** (i.e. inner city) and **suburban** (i.e. near the edge of the city) sections. In some places, cities have joined to become a megalopolis (i.e., one huge city).

Cities develop differently in the various parts of the world depending on the area available as well as cultural and economic forces. For example, North American cities can cover wide areas and are far apart since there was (and, in some regions, still is) an excess of open land. This is one factor that contributed to North America not having much public transportation. In contrast, European cities often cover a small area, since a significant amount of Europe is mountainous and the parts that aren't have many cities close together. As such, they are likely to have more developed public transportation systems, to maximize the use of the limited space.

In other parts of the world, transportation and communication between cities is less developed. Recent inventions in technology (e.g., the cell phone) have increased communication. Urban areas must stay in contact with rural areas to have things that cannot be produced within the city.

Relationships with other human societies have made divisions of areas into countries and other territories. These divisions are important to geographers as they study the relationships of different populations. Often, conflict happens with differences in religion, politics, language, or race. Natural resources are limited. These limitations create conflict over how they are spread out among people, specifically conflict over:

- Control of resources
- Control of important trade routes
- Control of populations

State sovereignty is the division of areas into parts. These parts are controlled by different groups of people. These groups manage the territory, the natural resources, and the people of the area. Earth, except Antarctica, is divided into political areas that are controlled by a government. Alliances are made between countries with similar interests, political goals, cultural values, or military issues. Some international alliances include:

- North Atlantic Treaty Organization (NATO)
- Common Market
- European Union (EU)
- United Nations (UN)
- Caribbean Community
- Council of Arab Economic Unity

Human Systems

Geography studies how people use and change their environment. Geographers study the results, reasons, and consequences of these changes. Also, they study how the environment limits or influences human behavior. These studies can find the best action when a nation or a group of people are thinking about making changes to the environment. A change may be building a dam or removing natural landscapes to build or change roads. Each change to the environment has a consequence. A study of the consequences can decide if these actions are manageable. In addition, these studies may show ways to work on long-term damage.

Human systems show how people settle and gather into large habitations. In addition, the systems show how permanent changes are made to the landscape. Geographers study the movements of people and how they spread goods among each other and to other settlements or cultures.

Migrations, wars, forced relocations, and trade can spread cultural ideas, language, and goods to other areas. Some major migrations or the conquering of one people by another have changed cultures throughout history. In addition, human systems can lead to conflicts or alliances to control the availability and the use of natural resources.

Regional Geography

North America has a variety of geographical features. There are mountain ranges in the eastern and western parts of the continent as well as stretches of fertile plains, lakes, and waterways. The region was shaped by glaciers which left behind very fertile soil. Because the continent is so large and covers a range of latitudes, there are several different climates present. These climates include continental climates with four seasons in median areas, tropical climates in the southern part, and arctic climates in the far north. The influence of humans on an area has changed the productivity of agricultural regions. Many areas have changed to make transportation easier and better for the economy.

South America has high mountains (e.g., the Andes), wide plains, and high-altitude plateaus. The region has many different natural resources. Many of the areas have not been used because of political issues, geographic barriers, and lack of enough economic power. Most climate zones in Latin America are tropical with rainforests and savannahs. The continent does have vertical climate zones and grasslands as well.

Europe spans a wide area with many climate zones. There are mountain ranges in the East and South. The north has a large plains region. The long coastline and the island of some countries (e.g., Britain) make the climate warmer than other lands at similar latitudes. This is because the area is warmed by ocean currents. Many areas of Western Europe have a moderate climate. Areas in the

South have the classic Mediterranean climate. Europe has a high level of natural resources. Many waterways connect the inner areas with the coastal areas. Much of Europe is industrialized, and agriculture has existed in the area for thousands of years.

Russia's area reaches into parts of Asia and Europe. In square feet, Russia is the largest country in the world. So, Russia has many different climates and geographical features. These features include plains, plateaus, mountains, and tundra. Russia's climate can be very rough. Rivers are frozen for most of the year that are used to move the country's natural resources. Siberia, in the north of Russia, has widespread permafrost (i.e., frozen soil). Native peoples in this area still hunt and gather like their ancestors. North central Russia has taigas with widespread woods in north central Russia. In the Southwest, there are steppes with cool weather and grasslands.

The geography of North Africa, Southwest Asia, and Central Asia is complex. The area has many climates and geographical features including seas, peninsulas, rivers, and mountains. Tectonic plates in the area are active; as such, earthquakes are common. Additionally, much of the world's oil lies in this area.

In North Africa, large rivers (e.g., the Nile) had a pattern of drought and flooding. This made the land near the river very fertile, which led people to settle there in ancient times. With better technology, people have tamed the Nile. In other words, people have made the river more predictable and the land around it more productive. The dry nature of this area has led humans to set up irrigation and to increase agricultural production.

South of the Sahara Desert, the high elevations and other geographical characteristics have made it very difficult for human travel or settlement to occur. The geography of the area is dominated by a series of plateaus. There are mountain ranges and a large rift valley in the eastern part of the area. In contrast to the desert areas, Sub-Saharan Africa has many lakes, rivers, and waterfalls. In addition, there are savannas, steppes, and desert areas. Much of the area has a tropical climate. The main natural resources are water, minerals, and gems.

A **floodplain** is an area that is known to flood. An **alluvial plain** is a plain that comes from changing floodplains of major rivers over time. The longest alluvial plain is in South Asia. The Ganges, Indus, and Brahmaputra are major river systems in South Asia. There are large deposits of minerals including iron ore, which is in great demand around the world. Mountains, plains, plateaus, and numerous islands are spread out in South Asia. Three common climates are tropical, highlands, and desert. In some parts of South Asia, there are monsoon winds that cause a long rainy season. Agricultural production is influenced by climate, elevation, and humans.

East Asia includes North and South Korea, Mongolia, China, Japan, and Taiwan. There are many mineral resources in this area. However, the resources are not spread out equally in each country. While many people live in this area, many regions are not suitable for agriculture. As a result, the surrounding oceans are important to the people. East Asia has many climate regions. In the coastal areas, ocean currents provide mild climates. Monsoons provide most of the rainfall for the region. Typhoons, earthquakes, volcanoes, and tsunamis are somewhat common.

Southeast Asia lies largely on the equator, and roughly half of the countries of the region are island nations. Some countries include Thailand, Vietnam, Laos, Myanmar (Burma), the Philippines, Malaysia, and Indonesia. The island nations of Southeast Asia have mountains that are part of the Ring of Fire. Southeast Asia has many rivers. In addition, this area has many natural resources. These resources include gems, fossil fuels, and minerals. Basically, there are two seasons: wet and dry. The wet season comes with the monsoons. In general, Southeast Asia has tropical rainforest climates. However, there are some mountain areas and tropical savannas.

Oceania is the thousands of islands in the Pacific Ocean. Some of these islands include Australia, New Zealand, New Guinea, and Fiji. Many of these islands were made from volcanic activity. Most of the islands have tropical climates with wet and dry seasons. New Zealand has many forests and mountain ranges. In addition, New Zealand experiences moderate temperatures with rainfall throughout the year.

Australia is a country and a continent with widespread deserts with mountains and lowlands. The economy is driven by agriculture (e.g., ranches and farms) and minerals. In Australia, the steppes that border very dry inland areas are good for livestock. In addition, the coastal areas receive enough rainfall for crops without using irrigation. Antarctica is covered with ice. Its major resources are reviewed for scientific information. The continent has some wildlife (e.g., whales and penguins) and little vegetation (i.e., mosses or lichens).

Review Video: Regional Geography
Visit mometrix.com/academy and enter code: 350378

Chapter Quiz

Ready to see how well you retained what you just read? Scan the QR code to go directly to the chapter quiz interface for this study guide. If you're using a computer, simply visit the bonus page at **mometrix.com/bonus948/ged** and click the Chapter Quizzes link.

GED Practice Test #1

Want to take this practice test in an online interactive format?
Check out the bonus page, which includes interactive practice questions and much more: **mometrix.com/bonus948/ged**

Reasoning Through Language Arts

Reading

Questions 1-6 refer to the following passage:

History of England

by Charles Dickens

If you look at a Map of the World, you will see, in the left-hand upper corner of the Eastern Hemisphere, two Islands lying in the sea. They are England and Scotland, and Ireland. England and Scotland form the greater part of these Islands. Ireland is the next in size. The little neighbouring islands, which are so small upon the Map as to be mere dots, are chiefly little bits of Scotland,—broken off, I dare say, in the course of a great length of time, by the power of the restless water.

In the old days, a long, long while ago..., these Islands were in the same place, and the stormy sea roared round them, just as it roars now. But the sea was not alive, then, with great ships and brave sailors, sailing to and from all parts of the world. It was very lonely. The Islands lay solitary, in the great expanse of water. The foaming waves dashed against their cliffs, and the bleak winds blew over their forests; but the winds and waves brought no adventurers to land upon the Islands, and the savage Islanders knew nothing of the rest of the world, and the rest of the world knew nothing of them.

It is supposed that the Phoenicians, who were an ancient people, famous for carrying on trade, came in ships to these Islands, and found that they produced tin and lead; both very useful things, as you know, and both produced to this very hour upon the sea-coast. The most celebrated tin mines in Cornwall are, still, close to the sea. One of them, which I have seen, is so close to it that it is hollowed out underneath the ocean; and the miners say, that in stormy weather, when they are at work down in that deep place, they can hear the noise of the waves thundering above their heads. So, the Phœnicians, coasting about the Islands, would come, without much difficulty, to where the tin and lead were.

The Phœnicians traded with the Islanders for these metals, and gave the Islanders some other useful things in exchange. The Islanders were, at first, poor savages, going almost naked, or only dressed in the rough skins of beasts, and staining their bodies, as other savages do, with coloured earths and the juices of plants. But the Phœnicians, sailing over to the opposite coasts of France and Belgium, and saying to the people there, 'We have been to those white cliffs across the water, which you can see in fine weather, and from that country, which is called Britain, we bring this tin and lead,' tempted some of the French and Belgians to come over also. These people settled themselves on the south coast of England, which is now called Kent; and, although they were a rough people too, they taught the savage Britons some useful arts, and improved that part of the Islands. It is probable that other people came over from Spain to Ireland, and settled there.

Thus, by little and little, strangers became mixed with the Islanders, and the savage Britons grew into a wild, bold people; almost savage, still, especially in the interior of the country away from the sea where the foreign settlers seldom went; but hardy, brave, and strong.

The whole country was covered with forests, and swamps. The greater part of it was very misty and cold. There were no roads, no bridges, no streets, no houses that you would think deserving of the name. A town was nothing but a collection of straw-covered huts, hidden in a thick wood, with a ditch all round, and a low wall, made of mud, or the trunks of trees placed one upon another. The people planted little or no corn, but lived upon the flesh of their flocks and cattle. They made no coins, but used metal rings for money. They were clever in basket-work, as savage people often are; and they could make a coarse kind of cloth, and some very bad earthenware. But in building fortresses they were much more clever.

They made boats of basket-work, covered with the skins of animals, but seldom, if ever, ventured far from the shore. They made swords, of copper mixed with tin; but, these swords were of an awkward shape, and so soft that a heavy blow would bend one. They made light shields, short pointed daggers, and spears—which they jerked back after they had thrown them at an enemy, by a long strip of leather fastened to the stem. The butt-end was a rattle, to frighten an enemy's horse. The ancient Britons, being divided into as many as thirty or forty tribes, each commanded by its own little king, were constantly fighting with one another, as savage people usually do; and they always fought with these weapons.

1. According to the author, why did the ancient Britons regularly fight with each other?

a. They had many weapons.
b. They disliked the Phoenicians.
c. There were no roads or bridges.
d. They were divided into many tribes.

2. Which phrase best shows the change Dickens believes the Phœnicians caused in the ancient Britons?

a. "The Phoenicians traded with the Islanders..."
b. "They were clever in basket-work..."
c. "These people settled themselves on the south coast of England..."
d. "...the savage Britons grew into a wild, bold people..."

3. Which sentence or phrase best expresses the isolation of the islands of England and Scotland and Ireland?

a. "...which are so small upon the Map as to be mere dots"
b. "The Islands lay solitary, in the great expanse of water."
c. "they can hear the noise of the waves thundering above their heads."
d. "Thus, by little and little, strangers became mixed with the Islanders..."

4. Read this phrase from paragraph 7:

But seldom, if ever, ventured far from the shore.

Why does the author include this phrase?

a. To show the ways in which the people used boats
b. To highlight the irony of making boats
c. To show where the people used weapons
d. To explain why the people built fortresses

5. Why does the author begin the passage by describing a map?

a. To explain the location of the islands
b. To show the roads that run through England, Scotland, and Ireland
c. To show how the little bits of Scotland broke away from the main island
d. To show the size of the islands in relation to France and Belgium

6. What sentence or phrase best describes the lands in the interior of the islands? In other words, these lands are the parts away from the coast.

a. "These people settled themselves on the south coast of England, which is now called Kent..."
b. "Especially in the interior of the country away from the sea where the foreign settlers seldom went..."
c. The whole country was covered with forests and swamps.
d. "The ancient Britons, being divided into as many as thirty or forty tribes, each commanded by its own little king..."

Questions 7–12 are for the following passage:

"The Gift of the Magi"

by O. Henry

[Jim and Della are a young husband and wife. They are very poor, and it is Christmas Eve. Della has been able to save $1.87 for a Christmas present. To buy a better gift for her husband, she decides to sell her beautiful hair to buy a fob for Jim. The fob will be for Jim's watch which is his most prized possession.]

When Della reached home her intoxication gave way a little to prudence and reason. She got out her curling irons and lighted the gas and went to work repairing the ravages made by generosity added to love. Which is always a tremendous task, dear friends--a mammoth task.

Within forty minutes her head was covered with tiny, close-lying curls that made her look wonderfully like a truant schoolboy. She looked at her reflection in the mirror long, carefully, and critically.

"If Jim doesn't kill me," she said to herself, "before he takes a second look at me, he'll say I look like a Coney Island chorus girl. But what could I do—oh! What could I do with a dollar and eighty-seven cents?"

At seven o'clock the coffee was made and the frying pan was on the back of the stove hot and ready to cook the chops.

Jim was never late. Della doubled the fob chain in her hand and sat on the corner of the table near the door that he always entered. Then she heard his step on the stairway down on the first flight, and she turned white for just a moment. She had a habit of saying little silent prayers about the simplest everyday things and now she whispered: "Please God, make him think I am still pretty."

* * *

Jim stopped inside the door, as immovable as a setter at the scent of quail. His eyes were fixed upon Della, and there was an expression in them that she could not read, and it terrified her. It was not anger, nor surprise, nor disapproval, nor horror, nor any of the sentiments that she had been prepared for. He simply stared at her fixedly with that peculiar expression on his face.

Della wriggled off the table and went for him.

"Jim, darling," she cried, "don't look at me that way. I had my hair cut off and sold it because I couldn't have lived through Christmas without giving you a present. It'll grow out again—you won't mind, will you? I just had to do it. My hair grows awfully fast. Say 'Merry Christmas!' Jim, and let's be happy. You don't know what a nice—what a beautiful, nice gift I've got for you."

"You've cut off your hair?" asked Jim, laboriously, as if he had not arrived at that patent fact yet even after the hardest mental labor.

"Cut it off and sold it," said Della. "Don't you like me just as well, anyhow? I'm me without my hair, ain't I?"

Jim looked about the room curiously.

"You say your hair is gone?" he said, with an air almost of idiocy.

"You needn't look for it," said Della. "It's sold, I tell you—sold and gone, too. It's Christmas Eve, boy. Be good to me, for it went for you. Maybe the hairs of my head were numbered," she went on with a sudden serious sweetness, "but nobody could ever count my love for you. Shall I put the chops on, Jim?"

Out of his trance Jim seemed quickly to wake. He enfolded his Della.

* * *

Jim drew a package from his overcoat pocket and threw it upon the table.

"Don't make any mistake, Dell," he said, "about me. I don't think there's anything in the way of a haircut or a shave or a shampoo that could make me like my girl any less. But if you'll unwrap that package you may see why you had me going a while at first." White fingers and nimble tore at the string and paper. And then an ecstatic scream of joy; and then, alas! a quick, feminine change to hysterical tears and wails, necessitating the immediate employment of all the comforting powers of the lord of the flat.

For there lay the Combs—the set of combs, side and back, that Della had worshipped for long in a Broadway window. Beautiful combs, pure tortoise shell, with jeweled rims—just the shade to wear in the beautiful vanished hair. They were expensive combs, she knew, and her heart had simply craved and yearned over them without the least hope of possession. And now, they were hers, but the tresses that should have adorned the coveted adornments were gone. But she hugged them to her bosom, and at length she was able to look up with dim eyes and a smile and say: "My hair grows so fast, Jim!"

And then Della leaped up like a little singed cat and cried, "Oh, oh!"

Jim had not yet seen his beautiful present. She held it out to him eagerly upon her open palm. The dull precious metal seemed to flash with a reflection of her bright and ardent spirit.

"Isn't it a dandy, Jim? I hunted all over town to find it. You'll have to look at the time a hundred times a day now. Give me your watch. I want to see how it looks on it."

Instead of obeying, Jim tumbled down on the couch and put his hands under the back of his head and smiled.

"Della," said he, "let's put our Christmas presents away and keep 'em a while. They're too nice to use just at present. I sold the watch to get the money to buy your combs. And now suppose you put the chops on."

7. What is the meaning of the word *ardent*?

a. procrastinate
b. passionate
c. lukewarm
d. uncaring

8. What is the chronological order of these events: ?

(1) Jim gives Della's present to her | (2) Della prepares dinner | (3) Jim assures Della that he is not upset | (4) Della prepares her hair | (5) Della prays for Jim's reaction | (6) Jim receives his present from Della

a. 4, 3, 2, 1, 5, 6
b. 6, 1, 4, 3, 2, 5
c. 4, 2, 1, 5, 3, 6
d. 4, 2, 5, 3, 1, 6

9. In the passage, O. Henry uses several similes. Which of the following is not an example of a simile?

a. "her head was covered with tiny, close-lying curls that made her look wonderfully like a truant schoolboy."
b. "Jim stopped inside the door, as immovable as a setter at the scent of quail."
c. "'I hunted all over town to find it.'"
d. "And then Della leaped up like a little singed cat and cried, 'Oh, oh!'."

10. Which of the following best shows how O. Henry builds tension in the story?

a. "It was even worthy of The Watch. As soon as she saw it she knew that it must be Jim's."
b. "The door opened and Jim stepped in and closed it. He looked very thin and very serious."
c. "Jim looked about the room curiously. 'You say your hair is gone?' he said, with an air almost of idiocy."
d. "Jim was never late. Della doubled the fob chain in her hand and sat on the corner of the table near the door that he always entered."

11. What is the theme of this passage?

a. True love leads to the sacrifice of one's most precious possessions.
b. Christmas is the representation of the love and sacrifice needed by all.
c. The love between two people eventually leads to frustration.
d. People should not try to surprise each other gifts.

12. Who is the narrator of this passage?

a. Della
b. Jim
c. O. Henry
d. None of the above

Questions 13-23 refer to the following passage:

The Story of My Life

by Helen Keller

Have you ever been at sea in a dense fog, when it seemed as if a tangible white darkness shut you in, and the great ship, tense and anxious, groped her way toward the shore with plummet and sounding-line, and you waited with beating heart for something to happen? I was like that ship before my education began...

I felt approaching footsteps. I stretched out my hand as I supposed to my mother. Someone took it, and I was caught up and held close in the arms of her who had come to reveal all things to me, and, more than all things else, to love me.

[One afternoon] we walked down the path to the well-house, attracted by the fragrance of the honeysuckle with which it was covered. Someone was drawing water and my teacher placed my hand under the spout. As the cool stream gushed over one hand she spelled into the other the word water, first slowly, then rapidly. I stood still, my whole attention fixed upon the motions of her fingers. Suddenly I felt a misty consciousness as of something forgotten–a thrill of returning thought; and somehow the mystery of language was revealed to me. I knew then that "w-a-t-e-r" meant the wonderful cool something that was flowing over my hand. That living word awakened my soul, gave it light, hope, joy, set it free! There were barriers still, it is true, but barriers that could in time be swept away. I left the well-house eager to learn. Everything had a name, and each name gave birth to a new thought.

I recall many incidents of the summer of 1887 that followed my soul's sudden awakening. I did nothing but explore with my hands and learn the name of every object that I touched; and the more I handled things and learned their names and uses, the more joyous and confident grew my sense of kinship with the rest of the world.

I had my first lessons in the beneficence of nature. I learned how the sun and the rain make to grow out of the ground every tree that is pleasant to the sight and good for food, how birds build their nests and live and thrive from land to land, how the squirrel, the deer, the lion and every other creature finds food and shelter. As my knowledge of things grew I felt more and more the delight of the world I was in. Long before I learned to do a sum in arithmetic or describe the shape of the earth, Miss Sullivan had taught me to find beauty in the fragrant woods, in every blade of grass, and in the curves and dimples of my baby sister's hand. She linked my earliest thoughts with nature, and made me feel that "birds and flowers and I were happy peers."

But about this time I had an experience which taught me that nature is not always kind. One day my teacher and I were returning from a long ramble. The morning had been fine, but it was growing warm and sultry when at last we turned our faces homeward. Two or three times we stopped to rest under a tree by the wayside. Our last halt was under a wild cherry tree a short distance from the house. The shade was grateful, and the tree was so easy to climb that with my teacher's assistance I was able to scramble to a seat in the branches. It was so cool up in the tree that Miss Sullivan proposed that we have our luncheon there. I promised to keep still while she went to the house to fetch it.

Suddenly a change passed over the tree. All the sun's warmth left the air. I knew the sky was black, because all the heat, which meant light to me, had died out of the atmosphere. A strange odour came up from the earth. I knew it, it was the odour that always precedes a thunderstorm, and a nameless fear clutched at my heart. I felt absolutely alone, cut off from my friends and the firm earth. The immense, the unknown, enfolded me. I remained still and expectant; a chilling terror crept over me. I longed for my teacher's return; but above all things I wanted to get down from that tree.

There was a moment of sinister silence, then a multitudinous stirring of the leaves. A shiver ran through the tree, and the wind sent forth a blast that would have knocked me off had I not clung to the branch with might and main. The tree swayed and strained. The small twigs snapped and fell about me in showers. A wild impulse to jump seized me, but terror held me fast. I crouched down in the fork of the tree. The branches lashed about me. I felt the intermittent jarring that came now and then, as if something heavy had fallen and the shock had traveled up till it reached the limb I sat on. It worked my suspense up to the highest point, and just as I was thinking the tree and I should fall together, my teacher seized my hand and helped me down. I clung to her, trembling with joy to feel the earth under my feet once more. I had learned a new lesson–that nature "wages open war against her children, and under softest touch hides treacherous claws."

13. What is the meaning of the word *beneficence*?

a. Duties
b. Generosity
c. Stinginess
d. Danger

14. Paragraph 3 is mainly about the narrator...

a. Learning to write words with a pencil
b. Learning the difference between cold and hot water
c. Learning the location of the well-house
d. Learning that words have meaning

15. Why did Helen hold out her hand in paragraph 2?

a. She thought the visitor was her mother
b. She wanted to greet the visitor
c. She wanted to please her mother
d. She loved the approaching person

16. In paragraphs 7 and 8, Helen felt nervous because...

a. She was lost
b. She was alone
c. It was raining
d. It was windy

17. Which sentence best explains what Helen learned from Miss Sullivan?

a. "I learned how the sun and the rain make to grow out of the ground every tree that is pleasant to the sight..."
b. "There were barriers still, it is true, but barriers that could in time be swept away."
c. "Everything had a name, and each name gave birth to a new thought."
d. "...nature 'wages open war against her children, and under softest touch hides treacherous claws.'"

18. Which aspect of the selection best shows the close bond between Helen and Miss Sullivan?

a. The moment when Miss Sullivan spelled "w-a-t-e-r" into Helen's hand
b. When Helen learned to find beauty in nature
c. When Miss Sullivan proposed eating lunch by the cherry tree
d. The moment when Miss Sullivan pulled Helen from the tree

19. What is a major theme of the passage?

a. Family ties
b. Discovery
c. Disappointment
d. Youth

20. In paragraph 8, the narrator uses the phrase "hides treacherous claws" to explain that...

a. Miss Sullivan, beneath her kind exterior, is very mean
b. Helen continues to have violent temper tantrums
c. Climbing trees can be very dangerous.
d. Nature can be cruel.

21. By telling the story in the order that events occur, the author helps you understand...

a. The change that Helen went through after meeting Miss Sullivan
b. The way in which Helen learned to be brave
c. The strategies Miss Sullivan used to teach Helen
d. The confusion that Helen felt when she was with Miss Sullivan

22. Based on the passage, you can conclude that Helen...

a. Disliked Miss Sullivan
b. Is scared of nature
c. Didn't understand words before Miss Sullivan arrived
d. Never learned how to read or write

23. What tool of figurative language is used in the sentence: "...each name gave birth to a new thought."?

a. metaphor
b. hyperbole
c. simile
d. personification

Questions 24–29 are for the following letter:

[In 1906, Elinore Pruitt Stewart moved to Denver for housework to support her daughter, Jerrine. Her employer in Denver was Mrs. Juliet Coney. A few years later, she moved to Wyoming to be a housekeeper for a rancher. The following passage is one of many letters that Stewart wrote to Mrs. Coney on life as a homesteader in Wyoming.]

A Letter of Elinore Pruitt Stewart

January 23, 1913

When I read of the hard times among the Denver poor, I feel like urging them every one to get out and file on land. I am very enthusiastic about women homesteading. It really requires less strength and labor to raise plenty to satisfy a large family than it does to go out to wash, with the added satisfaction of knowing that their job will not be lost to them if they care to keep it. Even if improving the place does go slowly, it is that much done to stay done. Whatever is raised is the homesteader's own, and there is no house-rent to pay. This year Jerrine cut and dropped enough potatoes to raise a ton of fine potatoes. She wanted to try, so we let her, and you will remember that she is but six years old.... Any woman strong enough to go out by the day could have done every bit of the work and put in two or three times that much, and it would have been so much more pleasant than to work so hard in the city and be on starvation rations all winter.

To me, homesteading is the solution of all poverty's problems, but I realize that temperament has much to do with success in any undertaking, and persons afraid of coyotes and work and loneliness had better let ranching alone. At the same time, any woman who can stand her own company, can see the beauty of the sunset, loves growing things, and is willing to put in as much time at careful labor as she does over the washtub, will certainly succeed; will have independence, plenty to eat all the time, and a home of her own in the end.

Experimenting need cost the homesteader no more than the work, because by applying to the Department of Agriculture at Washington he can get enough of any seed and as many kinds as he wants to make a thorough trial, and it doesn't even cost postage. Also one can always get bulletins from there and from the Experiment Station of one's own State concerning any problem or as many problems as may come up. I would not, for anything, allow Mr. Stewart to do anything toward improving my place, for I want the fun and the experience myself. And I want to be able to speak from experience when I tell others what they can do. Theories are very beautiful, but facts are what must be had, and what I intend to give some time.

24. The writer of this letter is suggesting that women should own land and farm rather than

a. cook in a restaurant.
b. open a bed and breakfast.
c. do laundry for others.
d. teach in a one-room schoolhouse.

25. Stewart mentions her daughter's potato crop. She does this to show

a. that child labor is acceptable.
b. that there are no schools in the area.
c. that women work just as hard as men do.
d. how easy it is to raise crops.

26. What do you think Mrs. Coney's reaction to the letter might have been?

a. She was probably glad to be rid of such a lazy worker.
b. She may be glad to know that Mrs. Stewart is enjoying her time with homesteading.
c. She may have been sorry that she too did not homestead.
d. She was likely angry that Mrs. Stewart had written.

27. Which of the following does Stewart NOT give as an advantage of homesteading?

a. It takes less strength and work than doing laundry for others
b. The worker cannot lose her job if she wants to keep it.
c. No one has to pay rent.
d. One can always find good company.

28. Which of the following is a risk for the poor in Denver?

a. the possibility of losing their jobs
b. the likelihood of a strike
c. the probability of a landslide
d. their shacks and apartments will burn

29. The tone of the letter is

a. complaining and bitter.
b. sad and lonely.
c. positive and encouraging.
d. hopeless and despairing.

Questions 30 – 35 come from the debate below.

<u>Forest Manager:</u> Salvage logging is removing dead or dying forest stands that are left behind by a fire or disease. This practice has been used for several decades. These dead or dying trees become fuel that feeds future fires. The best way to lower the risk of forest fires is to remove the dead timber from the forest floor. Salvage logging followed by replanting ensures the reestablishment of desirable tree species.

For example, planting conifers accelerates the return of fire resistant forests. Harvesting timber helps forests by reducing fuel load, thinning the forest stands, and relieving competition between trees. Burned landscapes leave black surfaces and ash layers that have very high soil temperatures. These high soil temperatures can kill many plant species. Logging mixes the soil. So, this lowers surface temperatures to more normal levels. The shade from material that is left behind by logging also helps to lower surface temperatures. After an area has been salvage logged, seedlings in the area start to grow almost immediately. However, this regrowth can take several years in areas that are not managed well.

<u>Ecology professor:</u> Salvage logging moves material like small, broken branches to the forest floor. These pieces can become fuel for more fires. The removal of larger, less flammable trees leaves behind small limbs and increases the risk of forest fires. In unmanaged areas, these pieces are found more commonly on the tops of trees where they are unavailable to fires. Logging destroys old forests that are more resistant to wildfires. So, this creates younger forests that are more open to fires. In old forests, branches of bigger trees are higher above the floor where fires may not reach.

Replanting after wildfires creates monoculture plantations where only a single crop is planted. This monoculture allows less biological diversity. Also, it allows plants to be less resistant to disease. So, this increases the chance of fire. Salvage logging also upsets natural forest regrowth by killing most of the seedlings that grow after a wildfire. It breaks up the soil and increases erosion. Also, it removes most of the shade that is needed for young seedlings to grow.

30. According to the professor, why are the broken branches in unmanaged forests preferable to those in logged areas for wildfire resistance?

a. They are left on the forest floor and bring nutrients to the soil.
b. They are left on the forest floor and serve as fuel for fires.
c. They are left on the tops of trees where fires cannot reach.
d. They are spread more evenly across the forest floor.

31. Which of the following is NOT a supporting detail for the forest manager's argument?

a. "This practice has been used for decades."
b. "Logging mixes the soil. So, this lowers surface temperatures to more normal levels."
c. "After an area has been salvage logged, seedlings in the area start to grow almost immediately."
d. "Salvage logging is removing dead or dying forest stands that are left behind by a fire or disease."

32. A study compared two plots of land that were managed differently after a fire. Plot A was salvage logged. Plot B was left unmanaged. After a second fire, they compared two plant groups between Plots A and B. They found that both plant groups burned worse in Plot A than in Plot B. Whose viewpoint do these results support?

a. only the manager
b. only the professor
c. both the manager and professor
d. neither the manager nor the professor

33. What is the main idea of the forest manager's argument?

a. Salvage logging is helpful because it removes dead or dying timber from the forest floor. So, this lowers the risk of future fires.
b. Salvage logging is helpful because it has been practiced for many decades.
c. Salvage logging is harmful because it raises soil temperatures above normal levels. So, this threatens the health of plant species.
d. Salvage logging is helpful because it gives shade for seedlings to grow after a wildfire.

34. Which of the following statements does NOT agree with the professor?

a. In younger forests, small branches are closer to the forest floor and more available for fires.
b. Old growth forests have taller trees, so branches are high up and fires cannot reach them.
c. Monoculture forests have less biological diversity and fewer disease-resistant trees.
d. Larger trees are common in old growth forests and serve as the main fuel source for fires.

35. Whose viewpoints would be proven by a future study looking at the spreading out and regrowth of seedlings for many years after a wildfire in managed and unmanaged forests?

a. only the manager
b. only the professor
c. both the manager and professor
d. neither the manager nor professor

Questions 36-40 refer to the following passage:

Section 1: Improving Diets

A healthier diet is something that many people want for themselves. However, this can be a struggle to put into practice for many people. This does not mean that just because it's hard and frustrating doesn't mean that people should stop trying.

A powerful and easy approach to improving diets is to know that some foods are so good for us that we can almost think of them as medicine. Some foods help to fight heart disease, cancer, or depression. Other foods help to lower cholesterol or blood pressure. Broccoli is high in vitamin K and vitamin C which help build strong bones and fight off cancers. Avocadoes can lower cholesterol and help reduce the risk of heart disease. Sweet potatoes are full of cancer-fighting and immune system-boosting vitamin A. Garlic can slow down the growth of bacteria and has been shown to lower cholesterol and blood pressure. Spinach is a great cancer fighter and has immune-boosting antioxidants important for eye health. Beans help lower risk of heart disease and breast cancer.

At some point, people want to give themselves the full treatment: diet, exercise, and general health overhaul. In the meantime, they can take the baby step of adding in one or more healthy food a week. This step is quick, easy, and painless. It couldn't be simpler to implement. Also, it will make their switch to healthy eating much easier to accomplish when they finally get there.

Section 2: Dietary Guidelines for Americans

The Dietary Guidelines for Americans is put together by the U.S. Department of Health and Human Services and the U.S. Department of Agriculture. The guidelines offer advice to people about food choices that advance good health and lower the risk of certain diseases (e.g., hypertension, anemia, and osteoporosis). In addition, this form offers a detailed outline on the kinds of foods that people should have in their diets. The outline is given so that additional supplements or vitamins may not be necessary. The form also has information on the types of exercise that are necessary for someone to stay healthy. Also, there is information on to handle and prepare certain foods to lower the risk of foodborne illness.

The Food Pyramid gave recommendations for the number of daily servings from each group. The USDA's Food Pyramid was heavily criticized for being unclear and confusing. In 2011, MyPlate replaced the Food Pyramid. MyPlate is much easier to understand because it has a picture of a dinner plate that is divided into four sections. So, this shows how our daily diet should be spread out among the different food groups. Vegetables and grains each take up 30% of the plate. Fruits and proteins each make up 20% of the plate. In the corner of the image is a cup that is marked as Dairy.

Most experts consider MyPlate to be a great improvement over the Food Pyramid. However, some it has still come under criticism from some quarters. Many believe too much emphasis is placed on protein, and some say the dairy recommendation should be eliminated altogether. The Harvard School of Public Health created its own Healthy Eating Plate to address what it sees as shortcomings in MyPlate. Harvard's guide adds healthy plant-based oils to the mix, stresses whole grains instead of merely grains, recommends drinking water or unsweetened coffee or tea instead of milk, and adds a reminder that physical activity is important.

Section 3: Preparing Better Meals in the Food Industry

People in the food industry that want to prepare a healthy meal for their customers should first decide on the nutritional goals of their menu. Once these goals have been set up, you should continue to plan by researching foods. These foods need to meet your goals without going beyond the available time and resource limits. Then, you can put together a meal plan that list several details. These details should have what foods will be included, the average time it takes to prepare and cook each of these meals, and the cost of preparing these meals. The next step is to decide on the best way of preparing the food for these meals. Think about which foods should be prepared first and the best ways to handle or prepare your food to lower the risk of illness. Also, think about methods that can be used to lower the cooking time. Finally, you can prepare the meal according to your plans.

When you need to decide on what foods to prepare, you need to think about several things. You should consider the food's nutritional value, the time it takes to prepare each food, the number of people to be served, and the cost of preparing each food. Each food has its own cooking time and has different nutrients. So, it is important to prepare foods that meet people's nutritional goals without using too much time for cooking the meal. Since you will likely have a budget for the meal, you need to review the number of people to be served and the cost of preparing each food. If the cost is too high, some meals may not be good choices to serve to large groups. For example, you are interested in serving a good source of protein for a meal. So, steak may be a good option for a small group of people. However, that would probably be too expensive for a larger group.

36. What is the main idea of Section 1?

a. Preparing a menu requires thorough research.
b. Some foods are healthier than others.
c. Positive diet changes can be simple.
d. Some people can make dietary changes and some cannot.

37. What is the purpose of including Section 2 in this passage?

a. To explain how the Food Pyramid was poorly designed
b. To cover the government's influence on the dietary recommendations for Americans
c. To show that there is no perfect system for coming up with dietary recommendations
d. To share information on generally accepted nutrition guidelines

38. What is the purpose of including Harvard's Healthy Eating Plate in Section 2?

a. To support the assertion MyPlate has received criticism
b. To suggest Healthy Eating Plate may replace current USDA dietary guidelines
c. It shows another option as a dietary guideline
d. To highlight the influence of an Ivy League school

39. According to the text, when preparing food for customers, all of the following are important EXCEPT which?

a. Foodborne illness
b. Calories in a meal
c. Layering the flavors in a dish
d. Preparation time

40. What is the tone of the three sections?

a. Condemning
b. Informative
c. Serious
d. Pretentious

Writing

Questions 1–9 refer to the following passage:

How Do You Prepare Your Vehicle for Winter?

A

(1) Anyone who live in a climate which brings snow during the winter knows how important it is to have a working vehicle. (2) Before winter begins, get the car or truck serviced. (3) Consider the following tips. (4) Few things are worst than being unable to see in snow or sleet. (5) Most wiper blades do not last no longer than a year. (6) Be sure that while you are at it, the windshield washer reservoir has fluid. (7) First of all, do the windshield wipers work properly? (8) Do not fill it with water because plain water won't work in the winter since it freezes.

B

(9) Now, you need to check a few things under the hood. (10) Are belts and hoses in good shape is the battery in good working order? (11) When was the last oil change? (12) Make sure you have the right blend of antifreeze and water in the radiator. (13) Add to your vehicle's emergency kit extra food water and warm clothes or a blanket. (14) In winter, carry an ice scraper and a small shovel. (15) Consider tire chains and salt, sand, or non-clumping kitty litter to give your vehicle traction if needed.

C

(16) Have a plan if you are stranded. (17) You leave only the car because you know exactly where you are and how far you are from help. (18) Following these precautions will help to keep you and your loved ones safe in winter driving.

1. Sentence (1): ***"Anyone who live in a climate which brings snow during the winter knows how important it is to have a working vehicle."***

What correction should be made to sentence (1)?

a. make live singular
b. place commas around which brings snow
c. set during the winter off in dashes
d. change which to that

2. Sentence (4): ***"Few things are worst than being unable to see in snow or sleet."***

What correction should be made to this sentence?

a. change are to is
b. change Few to Fewer
c. change worst to worse
d. no correction is necessary

3. Sentence (5): ***"Most wiper blades do not last no longer than a year."***

Which of the following is the best way to write the underlined portion of the sentence? If you think the original is the best way to write the sentence, choose answer A.

a. do not last no longer
b. do not last longer
c. do not lasted no longer
d. have not last no longer

4. Sentence (6): ***"Be sure that while you are at it the windshield washer reservoir has fluid."***

What correction should be made to this sentence?

a. move while you are at it to the front of the sentence and place a comma after it
b. move Be sure to the end of the sentence
c. place a question mark at the end of the sentence
d. no correction is necessary

5. Sentence (7): ***"First of all, do the windshield wipers work properly?"***

Which revision should be made to sentence (7) to improve the organization of the paragraph?

a. move sentence (7) to the beginning of paragraph A
b. move sentence (7) after sentence (3).
c. move sentence (7) to the end of paragraph A
d. move sentence (7) to the beginning of paragraph B

6. Sentence (9): ***"Now, you need to check a few things under the hood."***

What correction should be made to sentence (9)?

a. place have between to and note
b. delete under the hood from the sentence
c. change a few to one
d. no change is necessary

7. Sentence (10): ***"Are belts and hoses in good shape is the battery in good working order?"***

Which of the following is the best way to write the underlined portion of the sentence? If you think that the original is the best way to write the sentence, choose answer A.

a. good shape is the
b. good shape, is the
c. good shape and is the
d. good shape; is the

8. Sentence (13): ***"Add to your vehicle's emergency kit extra food water and warm clothes or a blanket."***

What correction should be made to this sentence?

a. remove the apostrophe from vehicle's
b. change the spelling of emergency to emergancy
c. place commas after the words food and water
d. no correction is necessary

9. Sentence (17): ***"You leave only the car because you know exactly where you are and how far you are from help."***

What correction should be made to this sentence?

a. move only to come between You and leave
b. delete exactly
c. put a comma before and
d. no correction is necessary

Questions 10–18 refer to the following passage:

How Slow Is Your Food?

A

(1) A growing grassroots movement is taking place around the world. (2) Developed nations have spent the past half-century creating fast food products, which are designed more for ease and availability than for taste. (3) Today, people worry more over genetically modified crops, food safety, and the cost of shipping food across the nation. (4) So, slow foods is making a comeback.

B

(5) Slow food puts the emphasize on community and sharing. (6) A major concern is to support local farmers and artisans. (7) Examples are those who are trying to save endangered species of animals, grains, the fruits, and the vegetables. (8) A new interest in heirloom varieties has reawakened palates that were used to food which had lost nutritional appeal and flavor. (9) Slow food also seeks to fully use sustainable agriculture. (10) This way soils can be replenished without the use of chemicals.

C

(11) Slow food usa has taken the program to students in elementary and secondary schools through its Garden to Table program. (12) Focusing on pleasure, tradition, and sustainability, the projects offer young people a chance to be involved in hands-on gardening and cooking. (13) I once had a garden in my backyard. (14) Students learn where their food comes from and they find out who grows it and how to cook it and the need to share with others. (15) A similar program, Slow Food on Campus, is conducted by the college and university students. (16) All programs adhere to the basic ideas of slow food: a good, clean, and fair food system.

10. Sentence (2): ***"Developed nations have spent the past half-century creating fast food products, which are designed more for ease and availability than for taste."***

Which of the following is the best way to write the underlined portion of the sentence? If you think that the original is the best way to write the sentence, choose answer A.

a. food products, which are
b. food products which are
c. food product, which are
d. food products, which is

11. Sentence (4): ***"So, slow foods is making a comeback."***

What correction should be made to this sentence?

a. remove the extra comma
b. change is to are
c. capitalize slow foods
d. put a hyphen between *come* and *back*

12. Sentence (5): ***"Slow food puts the emphasize on community and sharing."***

Which of the following is the best way to write the underlined portion of the sentence? If you think the original is the best way to write the sentence, choose answer A.

a. puts the emphasize
b. places the emphasize
c. put the emphasize
d. puts the emphasis

13. Sentence (7): ***"Examples are those who are trying to save endangered species of animals, grains, the fruits and the vegetables."***

Which of the following is the best way to write the underlined portion of the sentence? If you think that the original is the best way to write the sentence, choose answer A.

a. endangered species of animals, grains, the fruits and the vegetables
b. endangered specie of animals, grains, the fruits and the vegetables
c. endangered species of animal, grain, the fruit and the vegetable
d. endangered species of animals, grains, fruits and vegetables

14. Sentence (9): ***"Slow food also seeks to fully use sustainable agriculture."***

What correction should be made to this sentence?

a. change seeks to plural
b. put a dash between replenished and without
c. delete fully
d. no correction is needed

15. Sentence (11): ***"Slow food usa has taken the program to students in elementary and secondary schools through its Garden to Table program."***

What correction should be made to this sentence?

a. remove capital letters from Garden and Table
b. capitalize food usa
c. change the spelling of through to thru
d. no correction is needed

16. Sentence (13): ***"I once had a garden in my backyard."***

Which revision should be made to sentence (13) to improve the organization of this paragraph?

a. move the sentence to the beginning of the paragraph
b. use the sentence as the concluding statement of the article
c. delete sentence (13)
d. move the sentence to the previous paragraph

17. Sentence (14): ***"Students learn where their food comes from and they find out who grows it and how to cook it and the need to share with others."***

What correction should be made to this sentence?

a. add commas
b. make the terms parallel
c. change their to they're
d. make two sentences

18. Sentence (15): ***"A similar program, Slow Food on Campus, is conducted by the college and university students."***

What correction should be made to this sentence?

a. make college and university students the subject
b. remove the commas
c. remove the capital letters on Slow, Food, and Campus
d. change the spelling of similar to simular

Questions 19–28 refer to the following passage:

Are You SAD?

A

(1) For many healthy people, the coming of winter gets them down. (2) Some hibernation tendencies are common. (3) If you notice true depression a sense of hopelessness less energy, or anxiety, you may be suffering from seasonal affective disorder or SAD. (4) Some people experience SAD during spring and summer for most people, however, winter is the season to be SAD.

B

(5) Researchers are not certainly what causes SAD. (6) One suggestion is that having our regular body rhythms disrupted when less sunlight is available is the culprit. (7) Another study blames increased production of melatonin: a hormone related to sleep. (8) During the dark winter months, the body makes more melatonin. (9) At the same time, it makes less serotonin: the brain chemical that effects our moods. (10) Fewer sunlight means less serotonin. (11) So far, risk factors has not been identified.

C

(12) Most people with SAD just tough it out and waiting for spring. (14) If you have symptoms that last more than two weeks, it is time to see a doctor. (15) People with mild cases of SAD need to spend time outside, exercise regularly, and go to social events or travel. (16) The good news is that spring always comes?

19. Sentence (1): ***"For many healthy people, the coming of winter gets them down."***

What correction should be made to this sentence?

a. delete the comma
b. change gets to plural form
c. change healthy to healthly
d. no correction is needed

20. Sentence (3): ***"If you notice true depression a sense of hopelessness less energy, or anxiety, you may be suffering from seasonal affective disorder or SAD."***

What correction should be made to this sentence?

a. remove the comma after disorder
b. place a comma after hopelessness
c. capitalize seasonal affective disorder
d. no correction is needed

21. Sentence (4): ***"Some people experience SAD during spring and summer for most people, however, winter is the season to be SAD."***

Which of the following is the best way to write the underlined portion of the sentence? If you think the original is the best way to write the sentence, choose answer A.

a. and summer for most
b. and summer, for most
c. and summer: for most
d. and summer. For most

22. Sentence (5): ***"Researchers are not certainly what causes SAD."***

What correction should be made to this sentence?

a. change certainly to certain
b. do not use capital letters for SAD
c. end the sentence with a question mark
d. no correction is necessary

23. Sentence (8): ***"During the dark winter months, the body makes more melatonin."***

What correction should be made to this sentence?

a. put a comma between dark and winter
b. change more to much
c. capitalize melatonin
d. no correction is needed

24. Sentence (9): ***"At the same time, it makes less serotonin: the brain chemical that effects our moods."***

What correction should be made to this sentence?

a. change effects to affects
b. move the first phrase to after serotonin
c. change less to fewer
d. no correction is needed

25. Sentence (10): ***"Fewer sunlight means less serotonin."***

What correction should be made to this sentence?

a. change means to mean
b. capitalize serotonin
c. change less to fewer
d. change Fewer to Less

26. Sentence (11): ***"So far, risk factors has not been identified."***

What is the best way to write the underlined portion of the sentence? If you think the original is the best way to write the sentence, choose answer A.

a. So far, risk factors has not
b. so far, risk factors has not
c. So far, risk factor have not
d. So far, risk factors have not

27. Sentence (12): ***"Most people with SAD just tough it out and waiting for spring."***

What correction should be made to this sentence?

a. write SAD as sad
b. change tough to toughing
c. change waiting to wait
d. no correction is necessary

28. Sentence (16): ***"The good news is that spring always comes?"***

What correction should be made to this sentence?

a. change good to well
b. change the question mark to a period
c. capitalize spring
d. no correction is necessary

Questions 29–37 refer to the following article:

Only Temporary

A

(1) Many businesses in the United States regularly hire "temps" or temporary workers. (2) Now known as the staffing industry, temp work employs nearly 3 million people and generating more than $40 billion annually. (3) Because jobs are no longer secure, many people find that moving from job to job is a good way to

improve they're skills. (4) They sometimes find the perfect job and are hired as a full-time employee. (5) Businesses love temps, they save the company money because temps do not receive benefits.

B

(6) Would temp work be a good move for you? (7) If you are the kind of worker who bores quickly and needs new challenges, temping may be the way to go. (8) Temp work may offer a more flexible schedule and it gives a changing work environment. (9) On the down side, you will not get benefits like paid vacations or health insurance. (10) You may not always be treated very well because temp workers come and go.

C

(11) If you're looking for a job, temp work can add valuable experience to your résumé. (12) It also allows you time to look for and interviewing for a new and permanent job. (13) In addition, temp work is a great way to explore different careers. (14) Many temp jobs are temp-to-hire because the company needs to fill a position and is looking among temp workers for a permanant hire. (15) You may be just the employee they are seeking!

29. Sentence (1): ***"Many businesses in the United States regularly hire "temps" or temporary workers."***

What correction should be made to this sentence?

a. remove the quotation marks from temps
b. remove or temporary workers from the sentence
c. change the spelling of temporary to temparary
d. place a comma after temps

30. Sentence (2): ***"Now known as the staffing industry, temp work employs nearly 3 million people and generating more than $40 billion annually."***

What correction should be made to this sentence?

a. change industry to industries
b. change work to works
c. change employs to employing
d. change generating to generates

31. Sentence (3): ***"Because jobs are no longer secure, many people find that moving from job to job is a good way to improve they're skills."***

What correction should be made to this sentence?

a. change Because to Since
b. remove the comma after secure
c. change skills to skill
d. change they're to their

32. Sentence (4): ***"They sometimes find the perfect job and <u>are hired as a full-time employee</u>."***

Which of the following is the best way to write the underlined portion of this sentence? If you think the original is the best way to write the sentence, choose answer A.

a. are hired as a full-time employee.
b. are hired as full-time employees.
c. is hired as a full-time employee.
d. is hired as a fulltime employee.

33. Sentence (5): ***"<u>Businesses love temps, they save</u> the company money, because temps do not receive benefits."***

Which of the following is the best way to write the underlined portion of this sentence? If you think the original is the best way to write the sentence, choose answer A.

a. Businesses love temps, they save
b. Businesses love temps, it saves
c. Businesses love temps; they save
d. Businesses love temps, they saves

34. Sentence (8): ***"Temp work may offer a more <u>flexible schedule and it gives</u> a changing work environment."***

Which of the following is the best way to write the underlined portion of this sentence? If you think the original is the best way to write the sentence, choose answer A.

a. flexible schedule and it gives
b. flexible schedule and it give
c. flexible schedules and it gives
d. flexible schedule, and it gives

35. Sentence (11): ***"If you're looking for a job, temp work can add valueable experience to your résumé."***

What correction should be made to this sentence?

a. put a hyphen between <u>temp</u> and <u>work</u>
b. change <u>you're</u> to <u>your</u>
c. change <u>valueable</u> to <u>valuable</u>
d. no correction is necessary

36. Sentence (12): ***"It also allows you time to look for and interviewing for a new and permanent job."***

What correction should be made to this sentence?

a. change <u>permanent</u> to <u>permanant</u>
b. change <u>look</u> to <u>looking</u>
c. change <u>interviewing</u> to <u>interview</u>
d. no correction is necessary

37. Sentence (14): ***"Many temp jobs are temp-to-hire because the company needs to fill a position and is looking among temp workers for a permanant hire."***

Which of the following is the best way to write the underlined portion of this sentence? If you think the original is the best way to write the sentence, choose answer A.

a. workers for a permanant hire
b. workers for a permanent hire
c. a worker for a permanant hire
d. workers for permanant hires

Questions 38–43 refer to the following passage:

Picking the Perfect Pet

A

(1) Today's choices for pets go beyond the question of whether to get a cat or a dog? (2) Gerbils, rabbits, and amphibians is all popular options. (3) Before heading to an animal shelter, you need to know what pet makes sense for your home or classroom. (4) An obvious question to answer if you rent is if pets are permitted. (5) Some apartment complex places weight and size limits on pets or charge fees. (6) After gaining permission from the manager, your pet needs to be considered for other issues.

B

(7) If allergies effect someone in your home, be sure to select a pet that will not aggravate the condition. (8) Some dog breeds like the schnauzer and the poodle are acceptable pets for those who are sensitive to fur and dander.

C

(9) Irregardless of the pet you choose, think about other costs such as veterinary care and vaccinations, food costs, licensing, and equipment. (10) Does the pet need a special kind of home? (11) Who will be responsible for feeding and cleaning up after the animal? (12) Taking time to do a little research can save you a lot of heartache and expense later.

38. Sentence (1): ***"Today's choices for pets go beyond the question of whether to get a cat or a dog?"***

What correction should be made to this sentence?

a. change the question mark to a period
b. change Today's to Todays
c. change question to questions
d. no correction is necessary

39. Sentence (2): *"Gerbils, rabbits, and amphibians is all popular options."*

What correction should be made to this sentence?

a. remove the comma after Gerbils
b. change amphibians to amfibians
c. change is to are
d. no correction is necessary

40. Sentence (5): *"Some apartment complex places weight and size limits on pets or charge fees."*

Which of the following is the best way to write the underlined portion of this sentence? If you think the original is the best way to write the sentence, choose answer A.

a. Some apartment complex places weight
b. Some apartment complex places wait
c. Some apartment complexes places weight
d. Some apartment complexes place weight

41. Sentence (6): *"After gaining permission from the manager, your pet needs to be considered for other issues."*

What correction should be made to this sentence?

a. delete the comma
b. change permission to permision
c. rewrite the independent clause
d. No correction is needed

42. Sentence (7): *"If allergies effect someone in your home, be sure to select a pet that will not aggravate the condition."*

Which of the following is the best way to write the underlined part of this sentence? If you think the original is the best way to write the sentence, choose answer A.

a. If allergies effect someone
b. If allergies affect someone
c. If allergies affects someone
d. If allergies effects someone

43. Sentence (9): *"Irregardless of the pet you choose, think about other costs such as veterinary care and vaccinations, food costs, licensing and equipment."*

What correction should be made to this sentence?

a. change Irregardless to Regardless
b. change licensing to lisencing
c. remove the extra commas
d. no correction is needed

Questions 44–50 refer to the following passage:

Madame President

A

(1) Before they had the right to vote, women have attempted to gain the nations highest executive office. (2) Victoria Woodhull ran as a third party candidate in 1872. (3) Although she did not win, she became the first woman who owned an investment firm on wall street. (4) In 1884 and 1888, the lawyer Belva Lockwood also ran as a third party candidate. (5) Margaret Chase Smith (who served in both houses of Congress) was the first woman nominated by a major party: the Republicans.

B

(6) Nine other women have seeked for the presidency since the 1970s. (7) Five of them were Democrats and one was a Republican and three represented third parties. (8) I think it's about time this country had a woman as president. (9) Only two women have been nominated as vice president: Democrat Geraldine Ferraro in 1984 and Republican Sarah Palin in 2008. (10) Many people believe that soon the United States will join countries such as Britain, India, Germany, Chile, and Liberia, that have women heads of state.

44. Sentence (1): ***"Before they had the right to vote, women have attempted to gain the nations highest executive office."***

What correction should be made to this sentence?

a. capitalize executive office
b. change nations to nation's
c. put *finally* between to and gain
d. no correction is needed

45. Sentence (3): ***"Although she did not win, she became the first woman who owned an investment firm on wall street."***

What correction should be made to this sentence?

a. change became to become
b. capitalize wall street
c. change Although to Though
d. capitalize investment firm

46. Sentence (5): ***"Margaret Chase Smith (who served in both houses of Congress) was the first woman nominated by a major part: the Republicans."***

What correction should be made to this sentence?

a. change the parentheses to commas
b. do not capitalize Republicans
c. change woman to women
d. no correction is necessary

47. Sentence (6): ***"Nine other <u>women have seeked for</u> the presidency since the 1970s."***

Which of the following is the best way to write the underlined portion of this sentence? If you think the original is the best way to write the sentence, choose answer A.

a. women have seeked for
b. woman have seeked for
c. women have seek for
d. women have sought

48. Sentence (7): ***"Five of them were Democrats and one was a Republican, and three represented third parties."***

What correction should be made to this sentence?

a. add a comma after <u>Democrats</u> and delete the <u>and</u> after <u>Democrats</u>
b. change <u>them</u> to <u>those</u>
c. change <u>were</u> to <u>was</u>
d. no correction is necessary

49. Which revision would improve the overall organization of this article?

a. switch paragraphs A and B
b. place the final sentence at the beginning of paragraph B
c. delete sentence (8)
d. place sentence (2) at the end of paragraph A

50. Sentence (10): ***"Many people believe that the United States will soon join countries such as Britain, India, Germany, Chile, and Liberia, that have women heads of state."***

What correction should be made to this sentence?

a. remove the comma after <u>Liberia</u>
b. remove the unnecessary commas
c. change the spelling of <u>believe</u> to <u>beleive</u>
d. no correction is necessary

Extended Response

The study summary below outlines a problem that has been in America for decades. The next article gives one possible solution to the problem. Analyze the arguments made by the author of the article. Then, decide if his reasoning is sound. Be sure to give evidence from the passage. Also, give evidence from your own knowledge and experience. Explain why you would predict that his idea would succeed or fail.

Study Summary from the Education Resources Information Center

Student scores on standardized tests have steadily declined since 1965. Researchers conducted a literature review and completed data analysis to determine the reasons for this decrease, assessing trends for the period from 1965 to 1983. The reasons for the declining student scores include changes in the composition of test-takers, decreases in the quantity of schooling which students experience, curriculum changes, declines in student motivation, and deterioration of the family system and social environment. These factors, in combination, have contributed to the test score decline for more than fifteen years. Efforts to end the decreases must address the curricular and school climate factors identified.

Excerpt from an article by Roger Sipher

"So That Nobody Has To Go To School If They Don't Want To"

A decline in standardized test scores is but the most recent indicator that American education is in trouble. One reason for the crisis is that present mandatory-attendance laws force many to attend school who have no wish to be there. Such children have little desire to learn and are so antagonistic to school that neither they nor more highly motivated students receive the quality education that is the birthright of every American. The solution to this problem is simple: Abolish compulsory-attendance laws and allow only those who are committed to getting an education to attend.

Most parents want a high school education for their children. Unfortunately, compulsory attendance hampers the ability of public school officials to enforce legitimate educational and disciplinary policies and thereby make the education a good one. Private schools have no such problem. They can fail or dismiss students, knowing such students can attend public school. Without compulsory attendance, public schools would be freer to oust students whose academic or personal behavior undermines the educational mission of the institution.

Abolition of archaic attendance laws would produce enormous dividends:

- First, it would alert everyone that school is a serious place where one goes to learn. Schools are neither day-care centers nor indoor street corners. Young people who resist learning should stay away; indeed, an end to compulsory schooling would require them to stay away.
- Second, students opposed to learning would not be able to pollute the educational atmosphere for those who want to learn. Teachers could stop policing recalcitrant students and start educating.
- Third, grades would show what they are supposed to: how well a student is learning. Parents could again read report cards and know if their children were making progress.

- Fourth, public esteem for schools would increase. People would stop regarding them as way stations for adolescents and start thinking of them as institutions for educating America's youth.
- Fifth, elementary schools would change because students would find out early they had better learn something or risk flunking out later. Elementary teachers would no longer have to pass their failures on to junior high and high school.
- Sixth, the cost of enforcing compulsory education would be eliminated. Despite enforcement efforts, nearly 15 percent of the school-age children in our largest cities are almost permanently absent from school.

Communities could use these savings to support institutions to deal with young people not in school. If, in the long run, these institutions prove more costly, at least we would not confuse their mission with that of schools. Schools should be for education. At present, they are only tangentially so. They have attempted to serve an all-encompassing social function, trying to be all things to all people. In the process they have failed miserably at what they were originally formed to accomplish.

Mathematics

NON-CALCULATOR SECTION

Question 1 is based on the following figure:

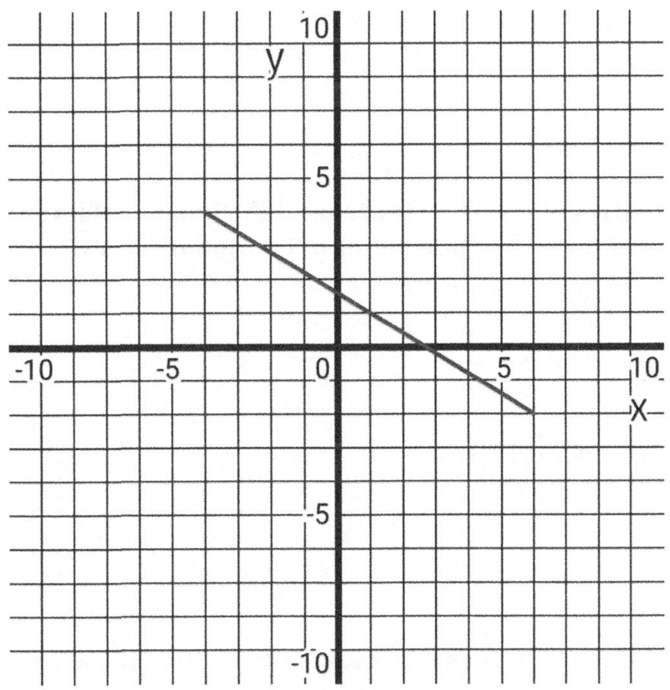

1. For each coordinate pair listed below, consider a line connecting the two coordinates. Which coordinate pairs represent a line that will intersect the line segment in the above figure? (Select all that apply.)

a. (-8, 5) and (5,5)
b. (-3, 2) and (1, -1)
c. (-1, 1) and (3, 5)
d. (0,-4) and (5, -6)
e. (7,3) and (-1,5)
f. (4,2) and (0,-2)

Question 2 is based on the following figure:

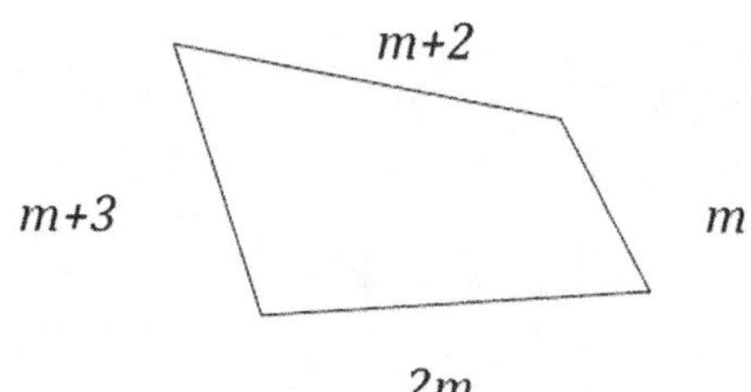

2. The figure shows an irregular quadrilateral and the lengths of its sides. Which of the following equations best shows the perimeter of the quadrilateral?

a. $m^4 + 5$
b. $2m^4 + 5$
c. $4m + 5$
d. $5m + 5$

3. If $a = -6$ and $b = 7$, then $4a(3b + 5) + 2b$ =?

a. 638
b. -610
c. 624
d. 610

4. Which of the following expressions represents the ratio of the area of a circle to its circumference?

a. πr^2
b. $\frac{\pi r^2}{2\pi}$
c. $\frac{2\pi r}{r^2}$
d. $\frac{r}{2}$

5. Mrs. Patterson's classroom has sixteen empty chairs. All the chairs are filled when every student is present. If 2/5 of the students are absent, how many students make up her entire class?

a. 40
b. 32
c. 24
d. 16

CALCULATOR SECTION

6. Jamie had $6.50 in his wallet when he left home. He spent $4.25 on drinks and $2.00 on a magazine. Later, his friend repaid him $2.50 that he had borrowed the previous day. How much money does Jamie have in his wallet now?

a. $12.25
b. $14.25
c. $3.25
d. $2.75

Question 7 is based on the following table:

Metric - English Equivalents

1 meter	1.094 yard
2.54 centimeter	1 inch
1 kilogram	2.205 pound
1 liter	1.06 quart

7. A building is 19 meters tall. What is its height in inches?

a. 254
b. 1094
c. 4826
d. 748

8. Rachel needs to buy extra items for her restaurant. She went to the store and spent $24.15 on vegetables. She bought 2 lbs of onions, 3 lbs of carrots, and $1\frac{1}{2}$ lbs of mushrooms. The onions cost $3.69 per lb, and the carrots cost $ 4.29 per lb. So, what is the price per pound of mushrooms?

a. $2.60
b. $2.25
c. $2.80
d. $3.10

Question 9 is based on the following figure:

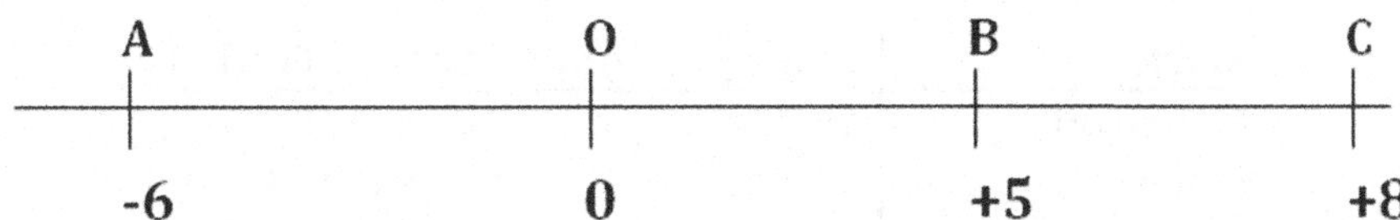

9. In the figure, A, B, and C are points on the number line. Also, O is the origin. What is the ratio of the distance *BC* to distance *AB*?

a. 3:5
b. 8:5
c. 8:11
d. 3:11

10. Jesse invests $7,000 in a certificate of deposit that pays interest at the rate of 7.5% annually. How much interest (in dollars) does Jesse gain from this investment during the first year that he holds the certificate?

11. In an election in Kimball County, Candidate A gained 36,800 votes. His opponent, Candidate B, had 32,100 votes. 2,100 votes went to write-in candidates. What percentage of the vote went to Candidate A?

a. 51.8%
b. 53.4%
c. 45.2%
d. 46.8%

12. Francine can ride 16 miles on her bicycle in 45 minutes. At this speed, how many minutes would it take Francine to ride 60 miles?

Question 13 is based upon the following figure:

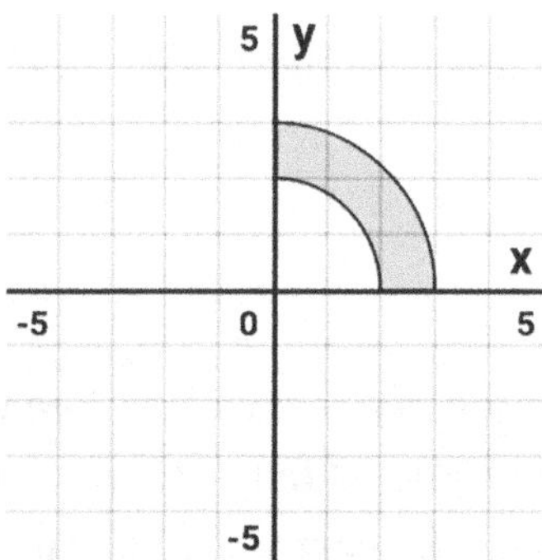

13. Marcus draws a plan for a hot tub in his backyard. He wants to put a concrete path around the tub. So, he starts with one area of the pool to find out how much material he needs. Now, the inner circle has a radius of two units. The outer circle has a radius of three units. What is the area of the shaded part?

Questions 14– 16 are based on the following table. This gives the closing prices of a number of stocks traded on the New York Stock Exchange:

Stock	Price per Share	Shares Traded
Microsoft	$45.14	89,440,000
Oracle	$19.11	12,415,000
Apple Computer	$16.90	17,953,000
Cisco Systems	$3.50	73,019,000
Garmin	$29.30	53,225,000

14. David bought 200 shares of Oracle stock yesterday and sold it today. His profit was $22.00. At what price did he buy the stock yesterday?

a. $18.89
b. $18.96
c. $19.00
d. $19.06

15. Lynn buys a package of stocks that has 100 shares each of Microsoft and Apple. Also, the package has 200 shares of Garmin at the closing prices from the table. What is the average price per share that she pays for these stocks?

16. James decides to invest $4500 in Cisco Systems stock and buys it at the price shown in the table. At what price should he sell it to have a profit of 10%?

17. Erica started work today at 7:00AM and worked until 4:30 PM. She earns $12 per hour for her regular shift which is 8 hours. Also, she works 50% more per hour for overtime. How much did Erica make today?

18. A company is building a track for a local high school. There are two straight sections and two semi-circular turns. Given the dimensions, which of the following most closely measures the perimeter of the entire track?

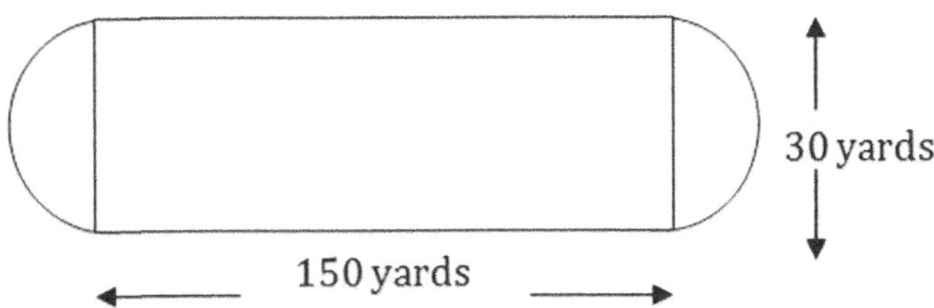

a. 120 yards
b. 180 yards
c. 300 yards
d. 395 yards

19. Elijah drove 45 miles to his job in an hour and ten minutes in the morning. On the way home, however, traffic was much heavier, and the same trip took an hour and a half. What was his average speed in miles per hour for the round trip?

a. 30 mph
b. 32.5 mph
c. 33.75 mph
d. 35 mph

20. The distance traveled by a moving object is found with the formula: $d = rt$, where r is the rate of travel (speed) and t is the time of travel. A major league pitcher throws a fastball at a speed of 125 ft/sec. The distance from the pitching rubber to home plate is 60.5 feet. How long, in seconds, does it take a fastball to travel this distance? Write your answer to the nearest hundredth of a second.

21. Lauren had $80 in her savings account. When she received her paycheck, she put some money in her savings account. This brought the balance up to $120. By what percentage did the total amount in her account increase by putting this amount in her savings account?

a. 50%
b. 40%
c. 35%
d. 80%

Question 22 is based on the following diagram:

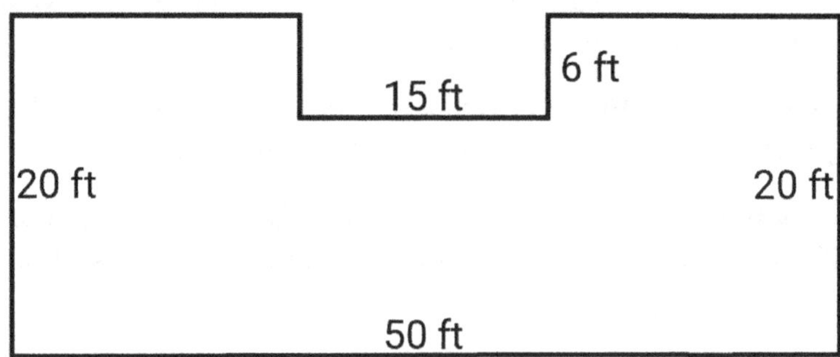

22. What is the area of the figure shown above? Give your answer in square feet.

23. Which of the following is a solution to the inequality $4x - 12 < 4$?

a. 7
b. 6
c. 5
d. 3

24. Mark is leaving a job site and moving equipment to Phoenix which is located 210 miles north. He drives the first ten miles in 12 minutes. If he continues at the same rate, how long will it take him to reach his destination?

a. 3 hours 15 minutes
b. 4 hours 12 minutes
c. 3 hours 45 minutes
d. 4 hours 20 minutes

25. An airplane leaves Atlanta at 2 PM and flies north at 250 miles per hour. A second airplane leaves Atlanta 30 minutes later and flies north at 280 miles per hour. At what time will the second airplane overtake the first?

a. 6:00 PM
b. 6:20 PM
c. 6:40 PM
d. 6:50 PM

Question 26 is based on the following diagram:

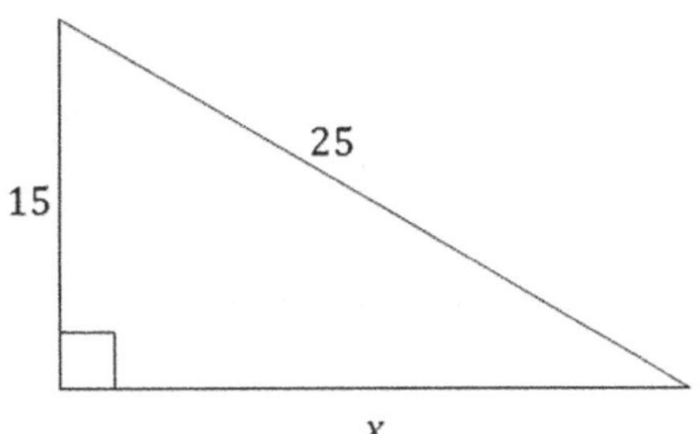

26. Find the length of the side labeled *x*. The triangle is a right triangle.

a. 18
b. 20
c. 22
d. 24

27. A company has been asked to design a building for an athletic event. The building is in the shape of a square pyramid. The pyramid has a height of 481 ft, and the length of each side of the base is 756 ft. What is the volume of the pyramid?

a. $1.21 \times 10^5 \text{ft}^3$
b. $4.85 \times 10^5 \text{ft.}^3$
c. $9.16 \times 10^7 \text{ft.}^3$
d. $2.75 \times 10^8 \text{ft.}^3$

28. If $x + y > 0$ when $x > y$, which of the following cannot be true?

a. $x = 3$ and $y = 0$
b. $x = 6$ and $y = -1$
c. $x = -3$ and $y = 0$
d. $x = 3$ and $y = -3$

29. Which of the following expressions is equal to x^3x^5?

a. $2x^8$
b. x^{15}
c. x^2
d. x^8

30. If $\frac{12}{x} = \frac{30}{6}$, what is the value of x?

a. 3.6
b. 2.4
c. 3.0
d. 2.0

31. Which of the following could be a graph of the function $y = \frac{1}{x}$?

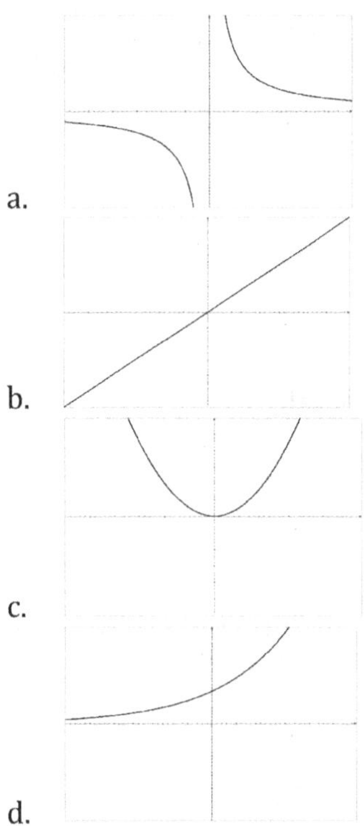

a.

b.

c.

d.

Question 32 is based on the following figure:

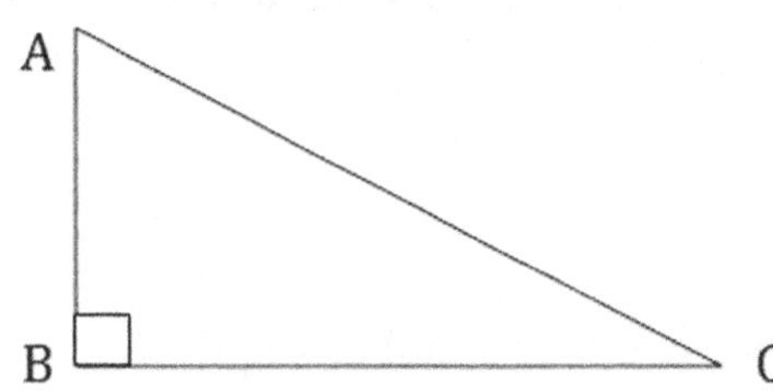

32. ΔABC is a right triangle, and $\angle ACB$=30°. What is the measure of $\angle BAC$?

a. 40°
b. 50°
c. 60°
d. 45°

Question 33 is based on the following table:

Hours	1	2	3
Cost	\$3.60	\$7.20	\$10.80

33. The table shows the cost of renting a bicycle for 1, 2, or 3 hours. Which of the following equations best represents the data? Let C stand for the cost and h stand for the time of the rental.

a. $C = 3.60h$
b. $C = h + 3.60$
c. $C = 3.60h + 10.80$
d. $C = \frac{10.80}{h}$

34. Which of the following statements is true?

a. Perpendicular lines have opposite slopes
b. Perpendicular lines have the same slopes
c. Perpendicular lines have reciprocal slopes
d. Perpendicular lines have opposite reciprocal slopes

35. There are 64 squares on a checkerboard. Bobby puts one penny on the first square, two on the second square, four on the third, eight on the fourth. He continues to double the number of coins at each square until he has covered all 64 squares. How many coins must he place on the last square?

a. 2^{64}
b. $2^{64} - 1$
c. 2^{63}
d. $2^{63} + 1$

36. Carrie wants to decorate her party with bundles of balloons containing three balloons each. Balloons are available in 4 different colors. There must be three different colors in each bundle. How many different kinds of bundles can she make?

a. 18
b. 12
c. 4
d. 6

Question 37 is based on the following figure:

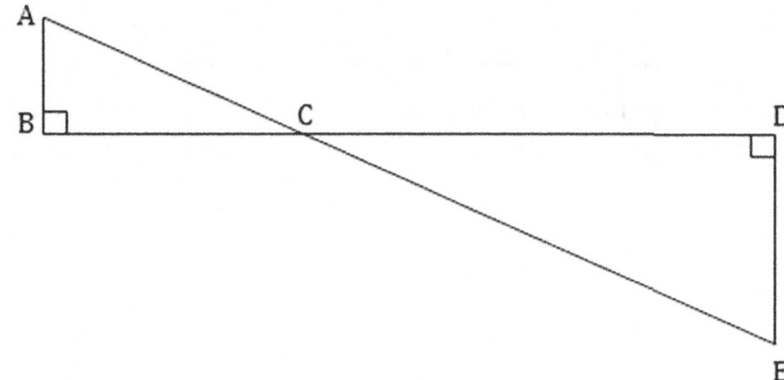

37. In the figure above, segment BC is 4 units long. Segment CD is 8 units long. Segment DE is 6 units long. What is the length of segment AC?

a. 7 units
b. 5 units
c. 3 units
d. 2.5 units

38. The expressions $y = -3x + 6$ and $y = 2x - 4$ represent straight lines. Find the coordinates of the point at which they intersect.

39. In a game of chance, 3 dice are thrown at the same time. What is the probability that all three will land with a 6?

a. 1 in 6
b. 1 in 18
c. 1 in 216
d. 1 in 30

40. Rafael has a business selling computers. He buys computers from the manufacturer for $450 each and sells them for $800. Each month, he must also pay fixed costs of $3000 for rent and utilities for his store. If he sells *n* computers in a month, which of the following equations can be used to find his profit?

a. $P = n(800 - 450)$
b. $P = n(800 - 450 - 3000)$
c. $P = 3000\,n(800 - 450)$
d. $P = n(800 - 450) - 3000$

41. Put the following numbers in order from the least to greatest $2^3, 4^2, 6^0, 9, 10^1$.

a. $2^3, 4^2, 6^0, 9, 10^1$
b. $6^0, 9, 10^1, 2^3, 4^2$
c. $10^1, 2^3, 6^0, 9, 4^2$
d. $6^0, 2^3, 9, 10^1, 4^2$

Questions 42-43 are based on the following chart:

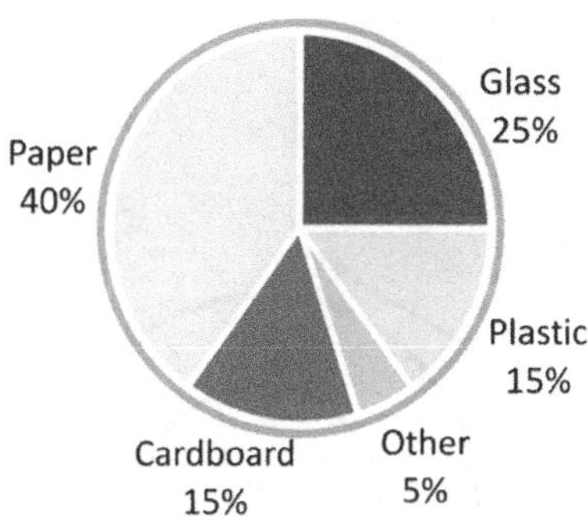

42. The Charleston Recycling Company collects 50,000 tons of recyclable material every month. The chart shows the kinds of materials that are collected by the company's five trucks. What is the second most common material that is recycled?

a. Cardboard
b. Glass
c. Paper
d. Plastic

43. About how much paper is recycled every month?

a. 40,000 tons
b. 50,000 tons
c. 15,000 tons
d. 20,000 tons

44. Dorothy is half of her sister's age. In 20 years, she will be three-fourths of her sister's age. What is Dorothy's current age?

a. 10 years
b. 15 years
c. 20 years
d. 25 years

45. Chan receives a bonus from his job. He pays 30% in taxes, gives 30% to charity, and uses another 25% to pay off an old debt. He has $600 remaining from his bonus. What was the total amount of Chan's bonus?

Question 46 is based on the following diagram:

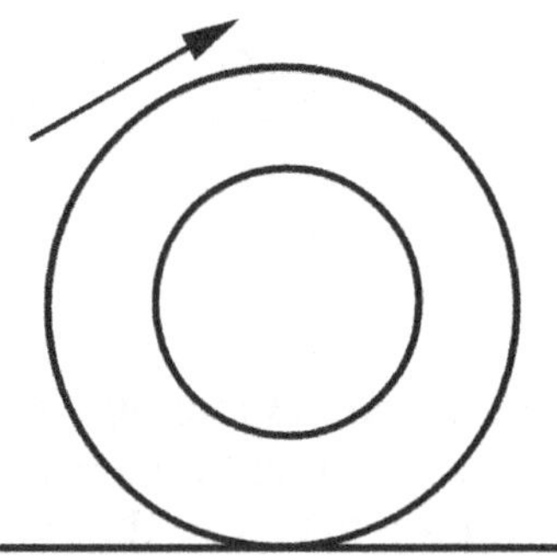

46. A tire on a car rotates at 500 RPM (revolutions per minute) when the car is traveling at 50 km/hr (kilometers per hour). What is the circumference of the tire? Give your answer in meters.

a. $\frac{50,000}{2\pi}$
b. $\frac{50,000}{60\times2\pi}$
c. $\frac{50,000}{60}$
d. $\frac{10}{6}$

47. A farmer installed a new grain silo on his property for the fall harvest. The silo is in the shape of a cylinder with a diameter of 8 m and a height of 24 m. How much grain will the farmer be able to store in the silo, in cubic meters, rounded to the nearest integer multiple of pi?

a. $192\pi\ m^3$
b. $384\pi\ m^3$
c. $512\pi\ m^3$
d. $768\pi\ m^3$

48. Which of the following expressions is equivalent to $(a+b)(a-b)$?

a. $a^2 - b^2$
b. $(a+b)^2$
c. $(a-b)^2$
d. $ab(a-b)$

Questions 49 and 50 are based upon the following table:

Kyle bats third in the batting order for the Badgers baseball team. The table shows the number of hits that Kyle had in the 7 consecutive games played during one week in July.

Day of Week	Number of Hits
Monday	1
Tuesday	2
Wednesday	3
Thursday	1
Friday	1
Saturday	4
Sunday	2

49. What is the mode of the numbers in the distribution shown in the table?

a. 1
b. 2
c. 3
d. 4

50. What is the mean of the numbers in the distribution shown in the table?

a. 1
b. 2
c. 3
d. 4

Science

1. A normal human sperm must have:

a. An X chromosome
b. A Y chromosome
c. 23 chromosomes
d. B and C

Questions 2 and 3 are based upon the following figures and text:

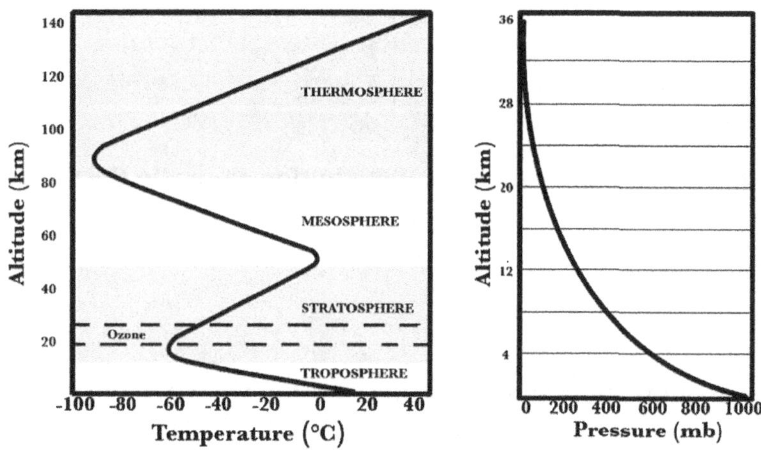

The Earth's atmosphere is comprised of multiple layers with very different temperature characteristics. Closest to the surface, the *troposphere* contains approximately 75 percent of the atmosphere's mass and 99 percent of its water vapor and aerosols. Temperature fluctuations cause constant mixing of air in the troposphere through convection, but it generally becomes cooler as altitude increases.

The *stratosphere* is heated by the absorption of ultraviolet radiation from the sun. Since its lower layers are composed of cooler, heavier air, there is no convective mixing in the stratosphere, and it is quite stable.

The *mesosphere* is the atmospheric layer directly above the stratosphere. Here, temperature decreases as altitude increases due to decreased solar heating and--to a degree--CO_2. In the lower atmosphere, CO_2 acts as a greenhouse gas by absorbing infrared radiation from the Earth's surface. In the mesosphere, CO_2 cools the atmosphere by radiating heat into space.

Above this layer lies the thermosphere. At these altitudes, atmospheric gases form layers according to their molecular masses. Temperatures increase with altitude due to absorption of solar radiation by the small amount of residual oxygen. Temperatures are highly dependent on solar activity and can rise to 1,500°C.

2. Commercial jetliners normally cruise at altitudes of 9-12 km which are the lower parts of the stratosphere. Which of the following might be the reason for this choice of cruising altitude?

a. Jet engines run more efficiently at colder temperatures.
b. There is less air resistance than at lower altitudes.
c. There is less turbulence than at lower altitudes.
d. All of the above are possible reasons.

3. The lowest temperatures in the Earth's atmosphere are recorded within the:

a. Troposphere
b. Stratosphere
c. Mesosphere
d. Thermosphere

Questions 4 and 5 are based on the following figure and paragraph:

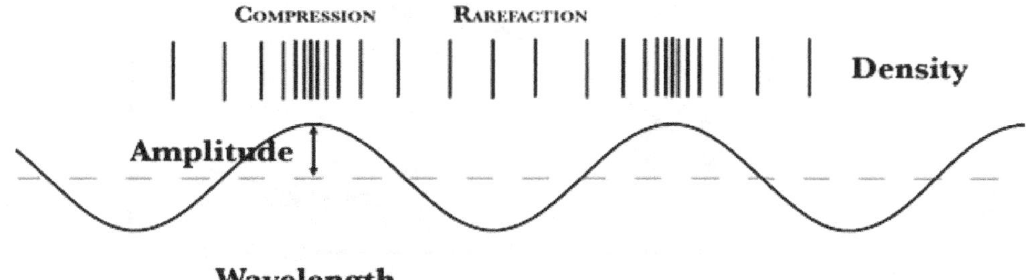

A vibrating source will produce sound by alternately forcing the air molecules in front of it closer together as it moves towards them, and then further apart as it draws away from them. In this way, alternating regions of high and low pressure, called compressions and rarefactions, are produced. The figure shows a typical sound wave. The volume of the sound corresponds to the magnitude of the compression, represented by the amplitude of the wave. The sound's pitch corresponds to the wave's frequency, the distance between successive compressions. Humans can hear sounds with frequencies between 20 and 20,000 Hertz. Sound waves propagate in all directions from their source. The speeds at which sound waves travel depend upon the medium they are traveling through. In dry air, sound travels at 330 m/sec at 0 °C. It travels 4 times faster through water, and 15 times faster through a steel rod.

4. The sound made by a drum is much louder and lower pitched than that made by a bell. What is true about the sound wave made by a drum compared to that made by a bell?

5. Two sound waves of exactly the same frequency and amplitude are made by sources that are in the same position. If the sound waves are out of phase by half a wavelength, what will an observer hear by standing a short distance away?

a. A sound twice as loud as either individual signal
b. A sound at twice the frequency of either individual signal
c. A sound at twice the wavelength as either individual signal
d. No sound at all

Questions 6 and 7 are based on the following figure and text:

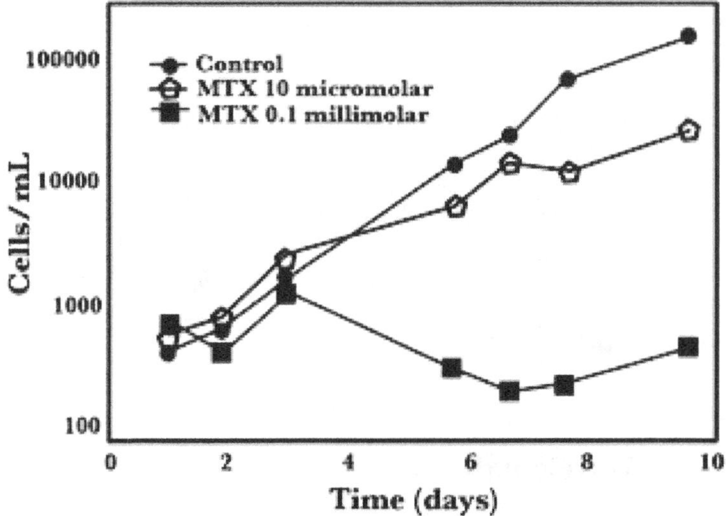

Cancer cells of the murine erythroleukemia (MEL) cell line were cultured in normal growth medium (control) and in two different concentrations of the anti-cancer drug methotrexate (MTX) for a period of ten days. Samples were removed periodically, and the number of cells per milliliter of culture was determined. Each point in the figure represents the mean of five determinations.

6. The growth of cells in the absence of drugs in this experiment can best be described as:

a. Linear
b. Exponential
c. Derivative
d. Inhibited

7. Which of the following statements is supported by the data?

a. Methotrexate does not prevent cell growth.
b. 0.1 millimolar methotrexate prevents the growth of bacteria.
c. 10 micromolar methotrexate effectively holds back cell growth.
d. 100 micromolar methotrexate effectively holds back cell growth.

8. The major advantage of sexual reproduction over asexual forms is that:

a. It requires two individuals.
b. It promotes diversity.
c. It produces more offspring.
d. It can be undertaken at any time of year.

Questions 9 and 10 are based on the following text:

Isotopes

The nucleus of an atom contains both protons and neutrons. Protons have a single positive electric charge, while neutrons have a charge of zero. The number of protons that a nucleus contains, called the atomic number and abbreviated as Z, determines the identity of an atom of matter. For example, hydrogen contains a single proton ($Z = 1$), whereas helium contains two ($Z = 2$). Atoms of a single element may differ in terms of the number of neutrons in their atomic nuclei, however. The total number of protons and neutrons in an atom is referred to as the atomic mass, or M. Helium typically has an atomic mass equal to 4, but there is another helium isotope for which $M = 3$. This form of helium has the same number of protons but only one neutron.

In an atomic fusion reaction, nuclei collide with one another with enough force to break them apart. The resulting nuclei may have a lower atomic mass than the reactants, with the difference being released as energy. Electric charge, however, is always conserved.

9. Two atoms of helium-3 (atomic mass = 3) collide in a fusion reaction to make a single atom of helium-4 (atomic mass = 4). What might be another product of this reaction?

a. A neutron
b. A proton
c. Two electrons
d. Two protons

10. Hydrogen atoms usually have a single nucleon (nucleon refers to either a neutron or a proton). Deuterium is an isotope of hydrogen that has two nucleons. Also, tritium is an isotope of hydrogen that has two and three nucleons. How many electrons orbit the tritium nucleus if the atom is electrically neutral?

a. 0
b. 1
c. 2
d. 3

Questions 11 and 12 are based on the following figure and text:

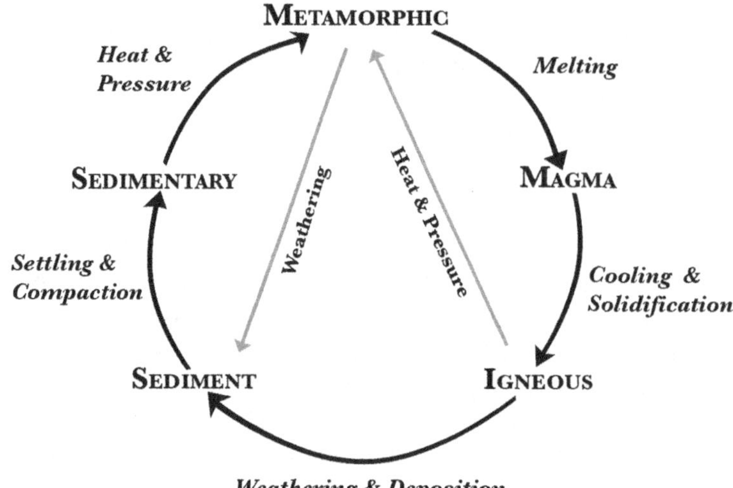

Rock Cycle

Rocks are created and destroyed in a recurrent process known as the rock cycle. Rocks are made from minerals, which are naturally occurring, crystalline solids of characteristic chemical composition. The actions of heat, pressure, and erosion can change the form of these minerals drastically. *Igneous* rocks form when molten magma flows out from the Earth's molten core, and then cools and solidifies near the surface. *Sedimentary* rocks are made of fragments of other rocks that are worn by weathering or erosion. Sand particles form sediments as they settle to the bottom, and are eventually compacted into stone by the weight above them. This is a process known as *lithification*. Heat and pressure can change the crystal structure of these minerals. This step alters them into denser *metamorphic* rocks. As these sink deeper into the hot core, they melt again into magma.

11. A process that can lead to igneous rock formation is:

a. Weathering
b. Sedimentation
c. Erosion
d. Volcanic activity

12. Which of the following rock types is made at the greatest distances below the Earth's surface?

a. Igneous
b. Metamorphic
c. Sedimentary
d. Slate

13. Which of the following animals displays the greatest fitness?

a. A male wolf that dies young but has 4 cubs that are raised by an unrelated female
b. A female wolf that has 3 cubs and lives to be quite old
c. A male wolf that lives to old age and has 1 cub
d. A female wolf that dies young after raising 3 cubs

Questions 14-19 are based upon the following figure, table, and text:

Protein Synthesis

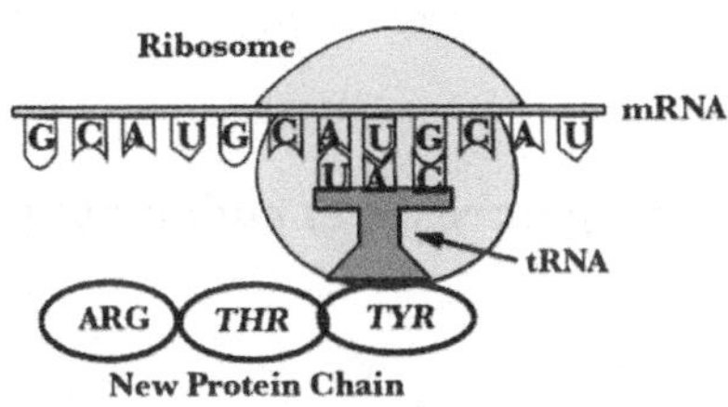

THE GENETIC CODE

First	Codon	AA	Codon	AA	Codon	AA	Codon	AA
T	TTT	Phenylalanine	TCT	Serine	TAT	Tyrosine	TGT	Cysteine
	TTC	Phenylalanine	TCC	Serine	TAC	Tyrosine	TGC	Cysteine
	TTA	Leucine	TCA	Serine	TAA	STOP	TGA	STOP
	TTG	Leucine	TCG	Serine	TAG	STOP	TGG	Tryptophane
C	CTT	Leucine	CCT	Proline	CAT	Histidine	CGT	Arginine
	CTC	Leucine	CCC	Proline	CAC	Histidine	CGC	Arginine
	CTA	Leucine	CCA	Proline	CAA	Glycine	CGA	Arginine
	CTG	Leucine	CCG	Proline	CAG	Glycine	CGG	Arginine
A	ATT	Isoleucine	ACT	Threonine	AAT	Asparagine	AGT	Serine
	ATC	Isoleucine	ACC	Threonine	AAC	Asparagine	AGC	Serine
	ATA	Isoleucine	ACA	Threonine	AAA	Lysine	AGA	Arginine
	ATG	Methionine (START)	ACG	Threonine	AAG	Lysine	AGG	Arginine
G	GTT	Valine	GCT	Alanine	GAT	Aspartate	GGT	Glycine
	GTC	Valine	GCC	Alanine	GAC	Aspartate	GGC	Glycine
	GTA	Valine	GCA	Alanine	GAA	Glutamate	GGA	Glycine
	GTG	Valine	GCG	Alanine	GAG	Glutamate	GGG	Glycine

The genetic information for making different kinds of proteins is stored in segments of DNA molecules called genes. DNA is a chain of phosphoribose molecules containing the bases guanine (G), cytosine (C), adenine (A), and thymine (T). Each amino acid component of the protein chain is represented in the DNA by a trio of bases called a codon. This provides a code which the cell can use to translate DNA into protein. The code, which is shown in the table, contains special codons for starting a protein chain (these chains always begin with the amino acid methionine) or for stopping it. To make a protein, an RNA intermediary called a messenger RNA (mRNA) is first made from the DNA by a protein called a polymerase. In the mRNA, the thymine bases are replaced by uracil (U). The mRNA then moves from the nucleus to the cytoplasm, where it locks onto a piece of protein-RNA machinery called a ribosome. The ribosome moves along the RNA molecule, reading the code. It interacts with molecules of transfer RNA, each of which is bound to a specific amino acid, and strings the amino acids together to form a protein.

14. Gene variants are called:

a. Codons
b. Alleles
c. Methionine
d. Amino acids

15. Which of the following protein sequences is encoded by the DNA base sequence GTTACAAAAAGA?

a. Valine-threonine-lysine-arginine
b. Valine-leucine-glycine-histidine
c. Valine-aspartate-proline-serine
d. Valine-serine-tyrosine-STOP

16. A polymerase begins reading the following DNA sequences with the first base shown. Which sequence specifies the end of a protein chain?

a. GTACCCCTA
b. GTACCCACA
c. GTTAAAAGA
d. GTTTAAGAC

17. The part of a DNA molecule that encodes a single amino acid is a(n):

a. Codon
b. Allele
c. Methionine
d. Phosphoribose

18. Proteins are made by:

a. Polymerases
b. Transfer RNAs
c. Ribosomes
d. DNA molecules

19. Which of the following is NOT part of a gene?

a. Codon
b. Cytosine
c. Ribosome
d. Phosphoribose

20. The pilot of an eastbound plane finds his wind speed in relation to his aircraft. He measures a wind velocity of 320 km/h with the wind coming from the east. A woman on the ground sees the plane pass overhead, and she measures its velocity as 290 km/h. What is the wind velocity in relation to the observer?

a. 30 km/h east-to-west
b. 30 km/h west-to-east
c. 320 km/h east-to-west
d. 290 km/h east-to-west

21. What causes a spring tide?

a. The Moon being so close to the Earth
b. The Sun and Moon are at right angles
c. The Sun, Moon, and Earth are in a line
d. The spin of the Earth

Question 22 is based on the following figure:

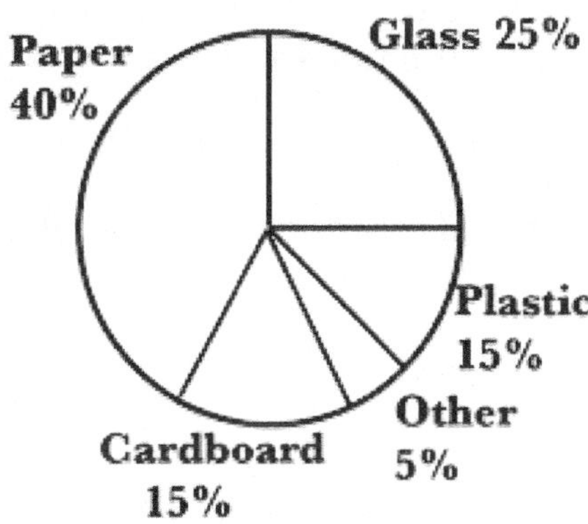

22. A recycling company collects sorted materials from its clients. The materials are weighed and processed for re-use. The chart shows the weights of different classes of materials that were collected by the company in one month. Which of the following statements is NOT supported by the data in the chart?

a. Paper products and cardboard make up a majority of the collected materials.
b. One quarter of the materials collected are made of glass.
c. More plastic is collected than cardboard.
d. The largest category of collected materials includes newspapers.

Questions 23-25 are based upon the following figure and passage:

Electrochemical Battery

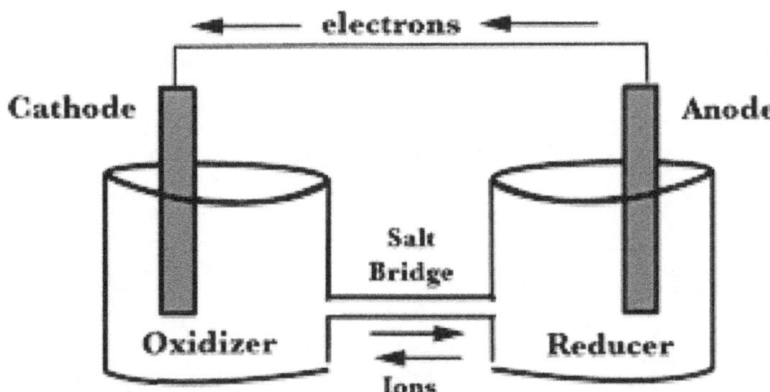

An electrochemical battery is a device powered by oxidation and reduction reactions that are physically separated so that the electrons must travel through a wire from the reducing agent to the oxidizing agent. The reducing agent loses electrons, and is oxidized in a reaction that takes place at an electrode called the anode. The electrons flow through a wire to the other electrode: the cathode. At the cathode, an oxidizing agent gains electrons and is reduced. To maintain a net zero charge in each compartment, there is a limited flow of ions through a salt bridge. In a car battery, for example, the reducing agent is oxidized by the following reaction that involves a lead (Pb) anode and sulfuric acid (H_2SO_4). Lead sulfate ($PbSO_4$), protons (H^+), and electrons (e^-) are produced:

$$Pb + H_2SO_4 \Rightarrow PbSO_4 + 2H^+ + 2e^-$$

The cathode is made of lead oxide (PbO_2). At the cathode, the following reaction occurs. During this reaction, the electrons produced at the anode are used:

$$PbO_2 + H_2SO_4 + 2e^- + 2H^+ \Rightarrow PbSO_4 + 2H_2O$$

23. Electrons are made by a chemical reaction that takes place at the:

a. Anode
b. Cathode
c. Lead oxide electrode
d. Oxidizer

24. In an oxidation reaction:

a. An oxidizing agent gains electrons.
b. An oxidizing agent loses electrons.
c. A reducing agent gains electrons.
d. A reducing agent loses electrons.

25. In a car battery, a product of the oxidation reaction that happens at the cathode is:

a. Lead oxide
b. Lead
c. Electrons
d. Water

Questions 26-27 are based upon the following figure:

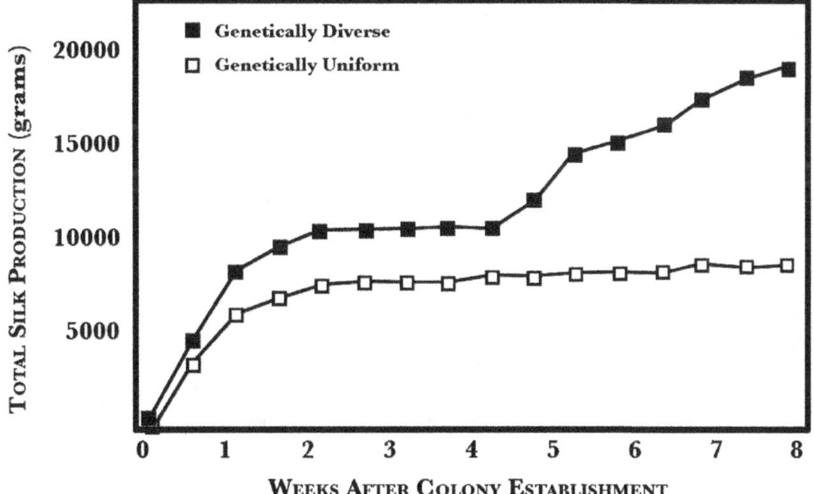

Colonies of silkworms that had the same number of genetically identical or genetically different animals were established. For several weeks after the colonies were created, silk production was estimated by removing small samples of silk from the colonies and weighing them. The results are shown in the graph. The open symbols are for the production of silk by genetically uniform worms. The closed symbols are for the production of silk by genetically diverse worms.

26. Which of the following conclusions can be drawn from the data?

a. Genetically diverse worms produce more silk than genetically uniform worms.
b. Genetically uniform worms produce more silk than genetically diverse worms.
c. Genetically diverse silkworm colonies produce more silk than genetically uniform colonies.
d. Genetically uniform silkworm colonies produce more silk than genetically diverse colonies.

27. If the generation time of a silkworm is about four weeks, what is a hypothesis that best explains the difference in silk productivity between the two colonies?

____

____

____

28. The digestion of starch begins:

a. In the mouth
b. In the stomach
c. In the pylorus
d. In the duodenum

Questions 29-32 are based upon the following figure and passage:

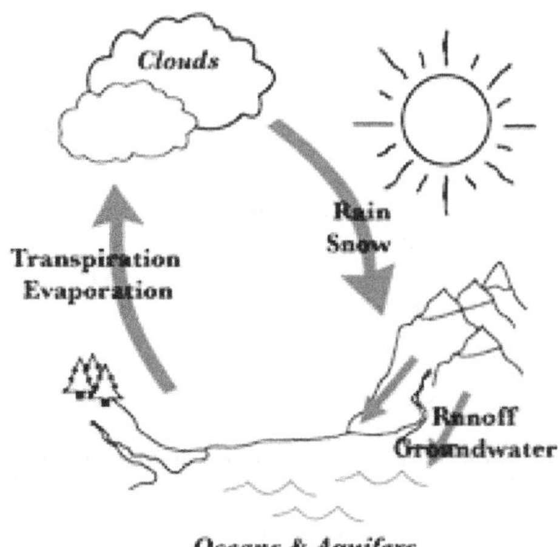

Energy from the sun heats the water in the oceans and causes it to evaporate. This makes water vapor that rises through the atmosphere. Cooler temperatures at high altitudes cause this vapor to condense and form clouds. Water droplets in the clouds condense and grow, eventually falling to the ground as precipitation. This continuous movement of water above and below ground is called the hydrologic cycle, or water cycle, and it is essential for life on our planet. All the Earth's stores of water, including that found in clouds, oceans, underground, etc., are known as the *hydrosphere*.

Water can be stored in several locations as part of the water cycle. The largest reservoirs are the oceans, which hold about 95% of the world's water, more than 300,000,000 cubic miles. Water is also stored in polar ice caps, mountain snowcaps, lakes and streams, plants, and aquifers below ground. Each of these reservoirs has a characteristic *residence time*, which is the average amount of time a water molecule will spend there before moving on. Some typical residence times are shown in the table.

Average Reservoir Residence Times of Water

Reservoir	**Residence Time**
Atmosphere	9 days
Oceans	3000 years
Glaciers and ice caps	100 years
Soil moisture	2 months
Underground aquifers	10,000 years

The water cycle can change over time. During cold climatic periods, more water is stored as ice and snow, and the rate of evaporation is lower. This affects the level of the Earth's oceans. During the last ice age, for instance, oceans were 400 feet lower than today. Human activities that affect the water cycle are agriculture, dam construction, deforestation, and industrial activities.

29. Which of the following is another name for the water cycle?:

a. The hydrosphere
b. The atmosphere
c. The reservoir
d. The hydrologic cycle

30. Water is stored underground. It is also stored in oceans and ice caps. These underground storage reservoirs are called:

a. Storage tanks
b. Aquifers
c. Evaporators
d. Runoff

31. Other than atmospheric water, where do water molecules spend the least time?:

a. Aquifers
b. Oceans
c. Glaciers
d. Soil

32. Which of the following statements is NOT true?

a. Cutting down trees affects the water cycle.
b. Ocean levels rise in an ice age.
c. Oceans hold most of the world's water.
d. Clouds are formed because of cold temperatures.

Questions 33-37 are based on the following figure and passage:

Heat and the States of Matter

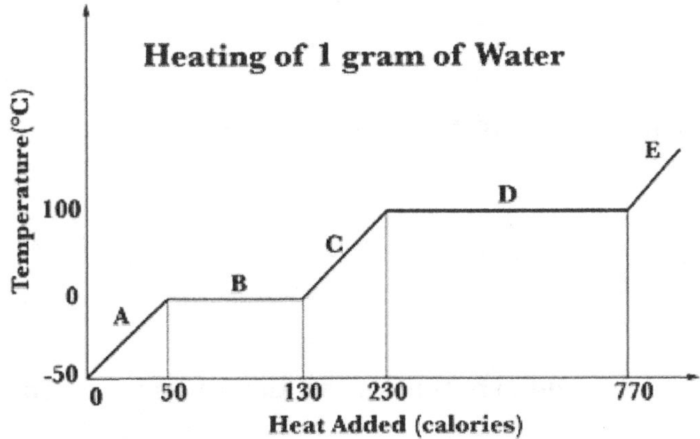

When the molecules of a substance absorb energy in the form of heat, they begin to move more rapidly. This increase in kinetic energy may be a more rapid vibration of molecules held in place in a solid, or it may be motion through molecular space in a liquid or a gas. Either way, it will be observed as either a change in temperature or a change in state. Heat has traditionally been measured in terms of calories. One calorie is equal to 4.186 Joules.

The specific heat capacity of a substance is the energy required to raise the temperature of 1 kg of the substance by 1°C. For water, this is 1000 calories. If heat continues to be applied to ice that is already at its melting point of 0°C, it remains at that temperature and melts into liquid water. The amount of energy required to produce this change in state is called the heat of fusion. For water it is equal to 80 calories per gram. Similarly, the amount of energy required to change a gram of liquid water at 100°C into steam is called the heat of vaporization which equals 540 calories.

The graph shows an experiment in calorimetry: 1 gram of water at -50°C is heated slowly from a solid state until it has all turned to gas. The temperature is monitored and reported as a function of the heat added to the system.

33. Heat is a form of:

a. Potential energy
b. Chemical energy
c. Kinetic energy
d. Temperature

34. Which of the following statements is true?

a. Adding heat to a system always increases its temperature.
b. The average speed of a gas molecule is slower than the average speed of a liquid molecule of the same substance.
c. Adding heat to a system always increases the average speed of the molecules of which it is made of.
d. Heat must be added to liquid water to make ice.

35. In which region(s) of the diagram is liquid water present? (Select all that apply.)

a. Region A
b. Region B
c. Region C
d. Region D
e. Region E

36. How much heat must be added to 1 gram of water at 1°C to raise its temperature to 101°C?

a. 100 calories
b. 540 calories
c. 770 calories
d. 640 calories

37. In the diagram, as heat is added to the system, the water in region B can be said to be:

a. Condensing
b. Melting
c. Freezing
d. Evaporating

Questions 38-40 are based on the following figure and passage:

Neurons

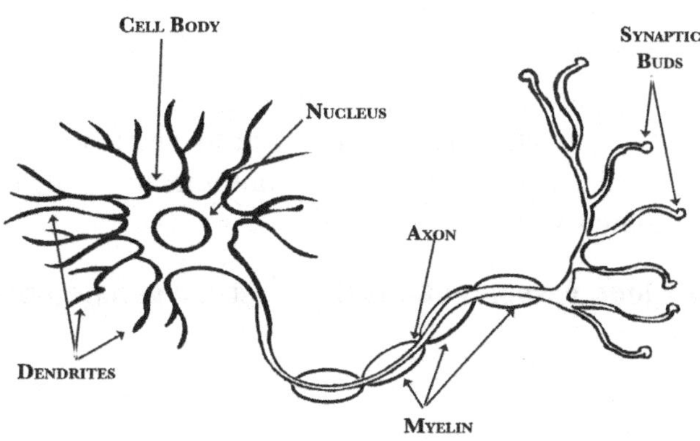

Messages travel between the brain and other parts of the body in the form of electrical impulses. A specialized cell, the neuron, produces these impulses. Neurons make up the brain and the nervous system. They number more than 100 billion in the human body.

Neurons have their own characteristic cellular anatomy consisting of three main parts. A cell body, containing a nucleus, is the center of metabolism. Dendrites project from the cell body and receive messages from neighboring neurons. At the other end, messages are sent through the *axon*, a long fiber extending from the cell body to the dendrites of other neurons, or to *effectors*, such as muscles, that perform actions based on neuronal input. Axons are sheathed in a material called myelin that helps nerve signals travel faster and farther.

At the end of the axon, messages must cross a narrow gap, the *synapse*, to reach effectors or the next neuron. Electrical impulses cannot cross this gap. The transfer of information from cell to cell occurs as a result of the release of chemical *neurotransmitters* into the space between the axon and the dendrites. The electrical impulse triggers the release of neurotransmitters into the synapse from swellings called *synaptic buds* at the axon terminal. They cross the synapse and bind to special *receptor* molecules on the dendrites of the next cell. Each neurotransmitter can bind only to a specific matching receptor, which triggers an appropriate response to the signal. This may be another electrical impulse, carrying the message along further, the contraction of a muscle, or some other effect.

38. A neuron is made of three main parts. These are: (Select all that apply.)

a. effector
b. cell body
c. axon
d. synapse
e. receptor
f. dendrite

39. Chromosomes are located within the:

a. Cell body
b. Dendrites
c. Axon
d. Synapse

40. Which of the following statements is true?

a. Information in neurons flows in one direction: from dendrites to axon.
b. Information in the nervous system is carried by both electrical and chemical means.
c. Myelin assists in the transmission of electrical, but not chemical, information.
d. All of the above statements are true.

41. Of the following, the blood vessel that has the least-oxygenated blood is:

a. The aorta
b. The vena cava
c. The pulmonary artery
d. The capillaries

42. A tsunami may be caused by:

a. Earthquakes
b. Volcanoes
c. Landslides
d. A, B, and C

Question 43 is based on the following figure:

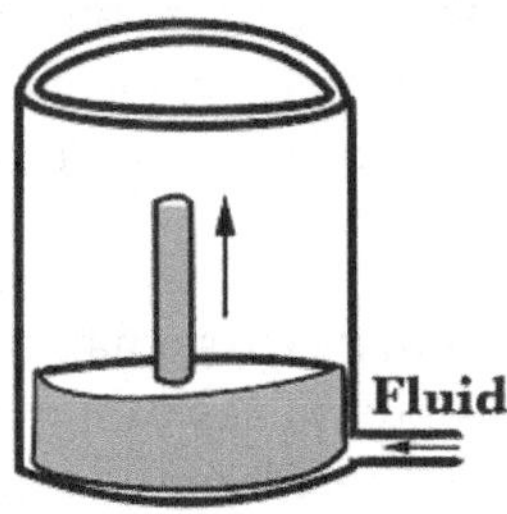

The figure shows an airtight cylinder where fluid may be injected from the bottom. In addition, the cylinder has a heavy piston. The injected fluid raises the piston until the rod on top of the piston touches the top of the cylinder container. Fluids of different densities are injected. Then, an observer records the volume needed to make the rod reach the top.

43. Which of the following fluids will need the least injected volume?

a. Water
b. Oil
c. Grease
d. The same volume will be required for all fluids.

44. Mark and Nancy both take three measurements of the length of a pencil that is 15.1 cm. Mark records 15.0, 15.0, and 15.1 cm. Nancy records 15.1, 15.2, and 15.2 cm. Which of the following statements is true about Mark and Nancy's measurements?

a. Mark's measurement is more precise.
b. Nancy's measurement is more accurate.
c. Mark's measurement is more accurate.
d. Both sets of measurements are equally accurate and precise.

45. All living organisms on Earth use:

a. Oxygen
b. Light
c. Neurotransmitters
d. A triplet genetic code

Questions 46-47 are based upon the following figure:

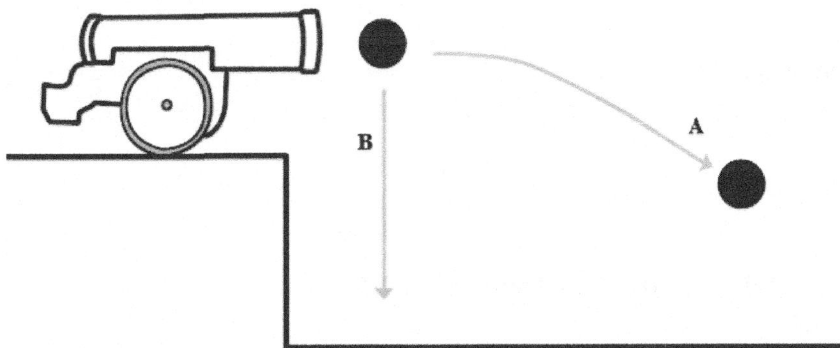

46. A cannon sits on top of a cliff that is 20 meters above an area of level ground. It fires a 5 kg cannonball horizontally (cannonball A) at 5 meters/second. At the same time, a second cannonball (cannonball B) is dropped from the same height. If air resistance is ignored, which cannonball will hit the ground first?

Note: The gravitational acceleration due to the Earth is 9.8 m/s^2.

a. Cannonball A
b. Cannonball B
c. Both will hit the ground at the same time.
d. It cannot be found from the given information.

47. The cannon weighs 500 kg and is on wheels. It will recoil when firing cannonball A. If friction is ignored, what will be the recoil speed of the cannon? Note: Momentum is the product of mass and velocity.

a. 5 meters/second
b. 5000 cm/second
c. 5 cm/second
d. It cannot be found from the given information.

Questions 48-50 are based on the following figure:

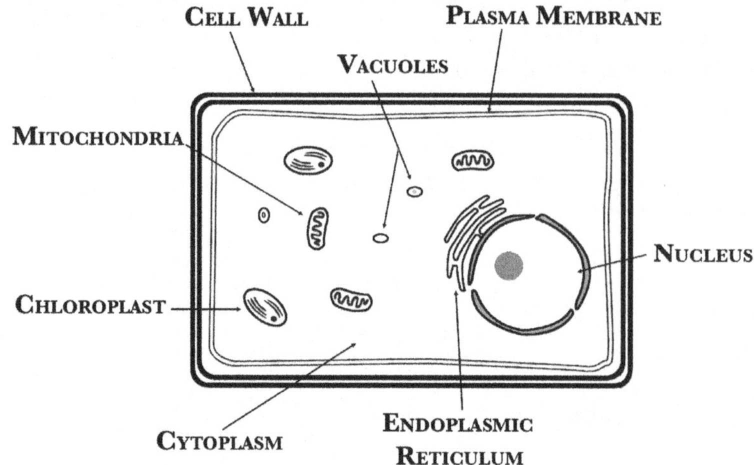

48. The cell above is a(n):

a. Animal cell
b. Plant cell
c. Bacterial cell
d. Virus

49. Which of the following structures contains DNA?

a. Cytoplasm
b. Vacuole
c. Mitochondrion
d. Nucleus

50. The mitochondria:

a. Produce energy for the cell in the form of ATP.
b. Are responsible for digesting starch.
c. Are the sites of protein synthesis.
d. Are not present in muscle cells.

Social Studies

Questions 1–3 refer to the following information:

Important Dates in the International Slave Trade

Date	Country	Event
1517	Spain	Begins regular slave trading
1592	Britain	Begins regular slave trading
1792	Denmark	Abolishes slave trade
1794	France	Abolishes slave trade
1807	Britain	Abolishes slave trade
1834	Britain	Abolishes slavery in all colonies
1865	United States	Abolishes slavery
1888	Brazil	Abolishes slavery

1. Which nation was the first to abolish slavery?

a. Spain
b. Britain
c. Denmark
d. France

2. If the United States had lost the Revolutionary War, when would slavery have been outlawed?

a. 1792
b. 1794
c. 1807
d. 1834

3. Which of the following conclusions is true? Use your prior knowledge and the information above.

a. More slaves worked in Brazil than in any other nation.
b. France realized its ideals of independence sooner than the United States.
c. Denmark was the largest slave-holding country in Europe.
d. Britain freed enslaved peoples only after losing the Asian nations of the British Empire.

Questions 4 and 5 refer to the following map:

NOTE: The year listed with each country is when the nation gained independence.

4. Which South American nations were the *last* to have independence? (Select all that apply.)

a. Argentina
b. Paraguay
c. Ecuador
d. Bolivia
e. Venezuela
f. Uruguay

5. Which of the following conclusions is true?

a. The nations of North America were also fighting for independence at the same time as nations in South America.
b. France lost most of its control in the New World because of these revolutions.
c. Nations on the west coast gained independence first.
d. South America had many revolutions in the first three decades of the 19th century.

Questions 6 and 7 refer to the following information:

Native Civilizations in Central and South America

Civilization	Location	Conquered by	Date Empires Ended
Maya	Central America	Internal collapse	950
Aztec	Mexico	Spanish under Hernán Cortés	1519
Inca	Peru	Spanish under Francisco Pizarro	1533

6. Mayan civilization is unlike the Aztec and Incan civilizations because

a. it collapsed without an outside conqueror.
b. it was the last empire to end.
c. it was located in North America.
d. it was taken over by the Spanish.

7. Which of the following conclusions is supported by the information above?

a. Several nations in South America were taken over by Portugal.
b. The Aztec civilization is the oldest of the three given in the table.
c. Spain had a demanding plan of taking over new lands in the 16th century.
d. Incan warriors tried to help the Aztec fight against the Spanish.

Question 8 refers to the following passage:

Islam spread to Europe during the medieval period, bringing scientific and technological insights. The Muslim emphasis on knowledge and learning can be traced to an emphasis on both in the Qur'an [Koran], the holy book of Islam. Because of this emphasis, scholars preserved some of the Greek and Roman texts that were lost to the rest of Europe. The writings of Aristotle, among others, were saved by Muslim translators. Islam scholars modified a Hindu number system. Their modification became the more commonly used Arabic system, which replaced Roman numerals. They also developed algebra. Muslim contributions also include inventing the astrolabe, a device for telling time that also helped sailors to navigate. In medicine, Muslim doctors cleaned wounds with antiseptics. They closed the wounds with gut and silk sutures. They also used sedatives.

8. Based on the information above, which of the following conclusions is likely true?

a. Muslims were braver than others when facing surgery.
b. Fewer Muslim patients died of wound infections than Europeans.
c. The silk market expanded because of the Muslim use of silk sutures.
d. Math classes would be easier without Muslim influence.

Question 9 refers to the following passage:

In July 1862, President Abraham Lincoln told his cabinet that he wanted to issue an emancipation proclamation. However, the Northern Army was not winning many battles of the Civil War that summer. Lincoln agreed with his cabinet advisers that it was a bad time to announce the plan. The following month, Horace Greeley, a respected journalist, printed an open letter criticizing Lincoln for waiting to announce the plan for the emancipation proclamation. The following is part of Lincoln's response.

" ... My paramount object in this struggle is to save the Union, and it is not either to slave or destroy Slavery. If I could save the Union without freeing any slave, I would do it; and if I could save it by freeing all the slaves, I would do it; and if I could do it by freeing some and leaving others alone, I would also do that. What I do about Slavery and the colored race, I do because I believe it helps to save this Union; and what I forbear, I forbear because I do not believe it would help to save the Union...."

9. Lincoln's primary goal was to

a. free the slaves.
b. repay slave owners for their losses.
c. save the Union.
d. win the war.

Questions 10 and 11 refer to the following information:

Westward Migration

Year	Estimated Number of People Headed West
1844	2,000
1849	30,000
1854	10,000
1859	30,000
1864	20,000

10. What event caused the increase of westward movement between 1844 and 1848? Use your general knowledge to answer the question.

a. Silver was discovered in Nevada.
b. The Transcontinental Railroad was completed.
c. Roman Catholics developed missions along the California coast.
d. Gold was discovered at Sutter's Mill in California.

11. Given the increase of population, which of the following statements is most likely to be true?

a. More children were being born in 1849 and 1858.
b. Most of the new migrants were women who wanted to open businesses.
c. The Civil War increased the westward migration.
d. Cities and towns in the West grew and supported many businesses.

Questions 12 and 13 refer to the following information:

Time Needed to Ship Freight from Cincinnati, Ohio, to New York City

Date	Route	Average Amount of Time
1817	Ohio River keelboat to Pittsburgh, wagon to Philadelphia, wagon or wagon and river to New York	52 days
1843–1851	Ohio River steamboat to Pittsburgh, canal to Philadelphia, railroad to New York	18–20 days
1852	Canal across Ohio, Lake Erie, Erie Canal, and Hudson River	18 days
1852	All rail via Erie Railroad and connecting lines	6–8 days
1850s	Steamboat to New Orleans and packet ship to New York	28 days

12. Think about a business owner in Cincinnati during the 1850s. Which kind of transportation would you be most likely to choose?

a. steamboat
b. railroad
c. canal
d. keelboat

13. Which change in transportation caused the *most* time saved over its predecessor?

a. railroad over steamboat and packet
b. railroad over canals
c. canal over steamboat and packet
d. steamboat, canal, and railroad over keelboat and wagon

Question 14 refers to the following information:

Group	Arrived in New World	Settled in
British Catholics	1632	Maryland
British Pilgrims	1620	Plymouth Colony, Massachusetts
British Puritans	1607	Virginia
British Quakers	1681	Pennsylvania
Dutch traders	1625	Manhattan Island
French traders	1608	Quebec

14. Which of the following conclusions can you draw from the information above?

a. Religious influences strongly affected the growth of the North American colonies.
b. The French had large settlements in what became the eastern United States.
c. The Dutch did not get a fair deal for the land they purchased.
d. The Spanish were the first to settle in North America.

Question 15 refers to the following passage:

In 1917, Orville Wright wrote of the invention of the airplane: "When my brother and I built and flew the first man-carrying flying machine, we thought that we were introducing into the world an invention which would make further wars practically impossible. That we were not alone in this thought is evidenced by the fact that the French Peace Society presented us with medals on account of our invention. We thought governments would realize the impossibility of winning by surprise attacks, and that no country would enter into war with another when it knew it would have to win by simply wearing out the enemy."

15. Which of the following statements do you think best expresses what the Wright brothers thought of World War I?

a. "Ah, that splendid little war!"
b. "How exciting to see airplanes extending fighting into the air!"
c. "Using airplanes in war is unacceptable."
d. "We can't wait to join the fight."

Question 16 refers to the following passage:

In 1988, the federal government, as part of the Clean Air Act, began to monitor visibility in national parks and wilderness areas. Eleven years later, the Environmental Protection Agency set forth an attempt to improve the air quality in wilderness areas and national parks.

16. Who of the following historical persons would NOT have agreed with this effort?

a. President Richard M. Nixon, who signed the act in 1970.
b. Rachel Carson: environmentalist and author of Silent Spring.
c. President Theodore Roosevelt, who set aside land for public parks.
d. the senator who campaigned in the early 1900s on the promise "Not one penny for scenery!"

Question 17 refers to the following passage:

Mother Jones, who was a labor activist, wrote the following about children working in cotton mills in Alabama: "Little girls and boys, barefooted, walked up and down between the endless rows of spindles, reaching thin little hands into the machinery to repair snapped threads. They crawled under machinery to oil it. They replaced spindles all day long; all night through...six-year-olds with faces of sixty did an eight-hour shift for ten cents a day; the machines, built in the North, were built low for the hands of little children."

17. Which of the following do you think happened after this was published?

a. More children signed up to work in the factories.
b. Cotton factories in the South closed.
c. Laws were passed to prevent child labor.
d. The pay scale for these children was increased.

18. Why was the city of Antwerp in Belgium building so many forts in 1914?

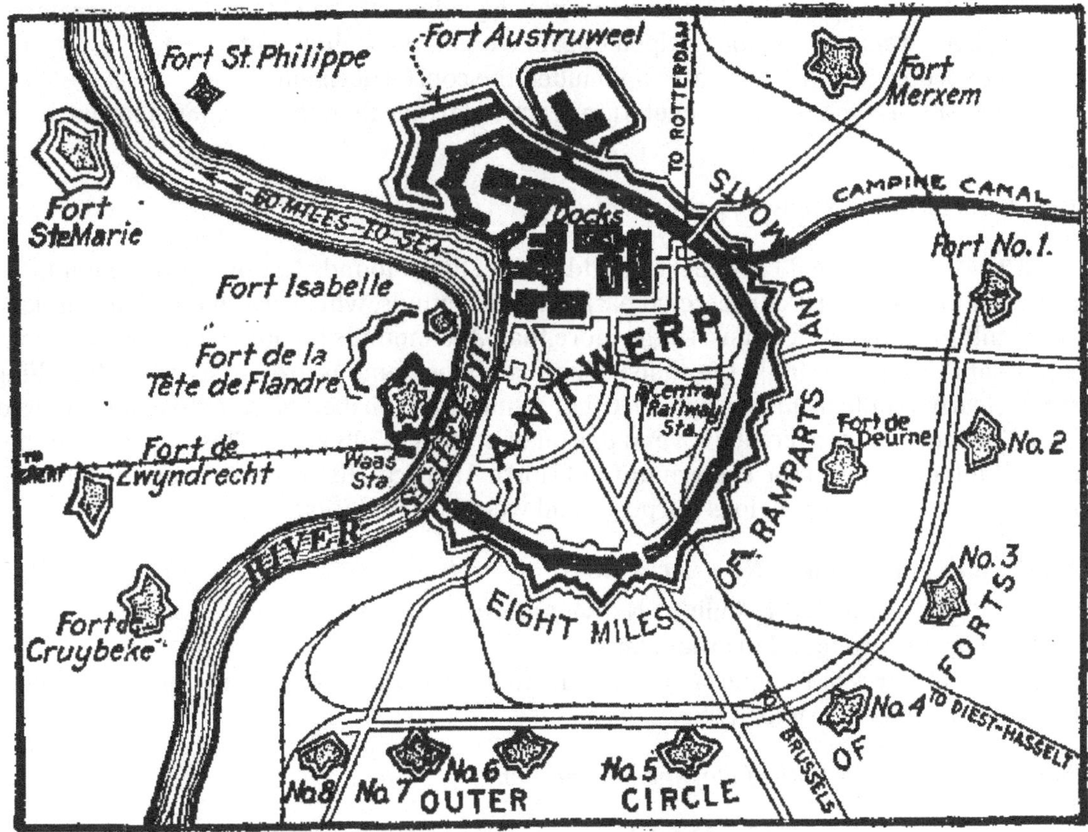

ANTWERP AND ITS FORTIFICATIONS

a. World War I had started. Germany had invaded other Belgian cities and was moving to invade Antwerp.
b. World War I had started. Italy had invaded other Belgian cities and was moving to invade Antwerp.
c. Antwerp was fortifying against possible British air attacks in World War I.
d. Antwerp feared a Russian invasion after the start of World War I.

Question 19 refers to the following passage:

In 1781, a county court in Massachusetts heard the case Brom & Bett v. Ashley. What was unusual about the case was that the plaintiffs were both enslaved by John Ashley's family. They had walked out and appealed to a lawyer for help after Mrs. Ashley tried to hit Mum Bett's sister. Mum Bett, whose real name was Elizabeth Freeman, claimed that if all people were free and equal, as she had heard while serving at the Ashley table, slaves too were equal. The court agreed by basing their decision on the Massachusetts constitution of the previous year. The decision, affirmed in subsequent cases, led to the abolishing of slavery in that state.

19. Which of the following statements is most accurate?

a. Mrs. Ashley was probably just having a bad day when she tried to strike another person.
b. Elizabeth Freeman's actions helped to gain women the right to vote.
c. White people in Southern states applauded the court's decision.
d. The ideals of the American Revolution reached farther than the founders may have intended.

Question 20 refers to the following passage:

In 1949, the National Parks Service added the Effigy Mounds National Monument in northeast Iowa to its list of protected parks. Effigy mounds, which are shaped like animals, were built by Native Americans. Of the more than 200 mounds created by the Mississippian Culture at the park, 31 are in the shape of animals. Most famous are the so-called Marching Bears, clearly visible from an airplane. Other mounds are bird effigies or shaped in cones or lines. The mounds were created over a period of at least 1,500 years. This is just one of the moundbuilders' sites in the eastern third of North America. Historians speculate that the mounds were used for religious purposes and were burial places.

20. Which of the following is NOT accurate?

a. The Effigy Mounds were built by Native Americans in 1949.
b. Mounds are also found in other states.
c. President Harry S. Truman signed the law that made the mounds a national monument.
d. Effigy mounds are shaped like animals.

Questions 21 and 22 refer to the following information:

United States Foreign Trade 1960–1970

(by Category Percentages)

Category	1960		1970	
	Exports	Imports	Exports	Imports
Chemicals	8.7	5.3	9.0	3.6
Crude materials (except fuel)	13.7	18.3	10.8	8.3
Food and beverages, including tobacco	15.6	22.5	11.8	15.6
Machinery and transport	34.3	9.7	42.0	28.0
Mineral fuels and related materials	4.1	10.5	3.7	7.7

21. From 1960 to 1970, which of the following categories had the greatest difference between percentage of exports and imports?

a. chemicals
b. crude materials
c. food and beverages
d. machinery and transport

22. Which category saw the greatest percentage decrease in imports between 1960 and 1970?

a. chemicals
b. crude materials
c. food and beverages
d. machinery and transport

Questions 23 and 24 refer to the following information:

Per Capita National Debt

Year	Historical Context	Amount
1790	Following American Revolution at the beginning of the national government	$19
1816	After the War of 1812	$15
1866	Following the Civil War	$78
1919	After World War I	$240
1948	Three years after World War II ended	$1,720
1975	After the Vietnam War	$2,475
1989	Near the close of Reagan's administration	$11,545

23. Which of the following armed conflicts increased the per capita national debt by the largest *percentage* over the previous conflict listed?

a. War of 1812
b. Civil War
c. World War I
d. World War II

24. Which of the following is a possible explanation for the change of per capita national debt between 1790 and 1816?

a. The United States borrowed more money to pay for the War of 1812.
b. The new nation enacted fiscal policies that focused on paying off debts owed from the Revolutionary War.
c. People did not spend very much money between those wars.
d. More citizens bought Treasury bonds in those days.

Questions 25 and 26 refer to the following information:

Women in the Labor Force, Selected Years

Year	Women in Labor Force (thousands)	Percentage of Total Labor Force
1900	5,114	18.1
1920	8,430	20.4
1940	12,845	24.3
1950	18,412	28.8
1970	31,560	36.7

25. In what year did women first make up more than 25 percent of the total labor force?

a. 1900
b. 1920
c. 1940
d. 1950

26. How could you express the change in percentage of women as part of the total labor force from 1900 to 1970?

a. The percentage rate declined by half.
b. The percentage rate stayed constant.
c. The percentage rate doubled.
d. The percentage rate fluctuated up and down over the years.

27. When the euro was introduced in January 2002, a single euro was valued at 88 cents in United States currency. In the summer of 2008, at one point it required $1.60 U.S. to buy 1 euro. In late October 2008, the euro fell to its lowest level against the dollar in two years. Which of the following statements is a correct conclusion?

a. The global economy in 2008 was headed for another Great Depression.
b. The dollar regained strength after much devaluing against the euro.
c. The euro is the world's strongest currency.
d. Investors need to keep buying stocks.

Questions 28 and 29 refer to the following information:

Revenue Sources: 2004

Source	Amount in Millions	Percentage of Budget
Corporation income taxes	$189.3	10.1
Excise [sales] taxes	$69.9	3.7
Individual income taxes	$809.0	43.0
Social insurance and retirement receipts	$733.4	39.0
Other	$78.4	4.2

28. If the government ended the use of offshore tax havens for corporations, how would the above information change?

a. Corporate income taxes would decrease.
b. Retirement receipts would increase.
c. Individuals would pay less in income taxes.
d. The share of corporate income taxes would increase.

29. Which category of taxpayer gives the most to the federal budget?

a. individuals
b. corporations
c. businesses paying Social Security tax
d. federal government agencies

Question 30 refers to the following information:

Number of Small Business Administration Loans

to Minority-Owned Small Businesses in 2000 and 2005

Minority Group	2000	2005
African American	2,120	6,635
Asian American	5,838	3,456
Hispanic American	3,500	8,796
Native American	541	835

30. Which of the following statements is accurate?

a. The number of loans increased in every ethnic group category.
b. The number of loans to African Americans doubled in five years.
c. Native Americans represent the smallest number of loans.
d. The greatest number of loans in 2000 was to Hispanic Americans.

Question 31 refers to the following voter issue from 2008:

ISSUE 3: PROPOSED CONSTITUTIONAL AMENDMENT TO AMEND THE CONSTITUTION TO PROTECT PRIVATE PROPERTY RIGHTS IN GROUND WATER, LAKES AND OTHER WATERCOURSES (Proposed by Joint Resolution of the General Assembly of Ohio) To adopt Section 19b of Article I of the Constitution of the State of Ohio A YES vote means approval of the amendment. A NO vote means disapproval of the amendment. A majority YES vote is required for the amendment to be adopted. If approved, this amendment shall take effect December 1, 2008.

League Explanation of Issue 3: This proposed amendment resulted from the Ohio legislature's passage of the Great Lakes Water Compact this past spring. Some lawmakers feared final approval of the Compact might limit private water rights. The constitutional amendment is intended to recognize that:

- Property owners have a protected right to the "reasonable use" of the ground water flowing under their property, and of the water in a lake or watercourse that is on or flows through their property.
- An owner has the right to give or sell these interests to a governmental body.
- The public welfare supersedes individual property owners' rights. The state and political subdivisions may regulate such waters to the extent state law allows.
- The proposed amendment would not affect public use of Lake Erie and the state's other navigable waters.
- The rights confirmed by this amendment may not be limited by sections of the Ohio Constitution addressing home rule, public debt and public works, conservation of natural resources, and the prohibition of the use of "initiative" and "referendum" on property taxes.

31. Which of the following conclusions is correct?

a. The state of Ohio will give up rights to the control of Lake Erie in favor of public rights.
b. People who own property with water on it cannot sell that land to the state.
c. The state considers the public's welfare to be more important than an individual property owner's rights.
d. This issue was created without input from any lawmakers or organization.

32. The United States Congress funds Amtrak, a national railroad system. Railroads did not exist when the framers wrote the Constitution. However, this use of money is legal and is covered in Article 1 of the Constitution as

a. a delegated power.
b. a denied power.
c. an expressed power.
d. an implied power.

33. In 1957, President Dwight Eisenhower sent federal troops to Little Rock, Arkansas. They were to enforce integration at Little Rock Central High School. The reason was that the governor of the state had tried to prevent integration. Eisenhower's action is an example that shows how

a. acting like a dictator with power he did not legally have.
b. trying to keep federal troops out of Vietnam.
c. states' rights being more important than federal law.
d. upholding federal law if state or local officials will not.

34. In two referendums, citizens of New York City voted to limit key office holders (e.g., the mayor, the City Council members, and the comptroller) to two consecutive four-year terms. In November 2008, however, Mayor Michael Bloomberg signed into law a proposal that removed these limits. Which of the following conclusions might you draw?

a. The referendum votes were improperly counted.
b. Mayor Bloomberg was nearing the completion of his two terms in office.
c. People petitioned to have the earlier referendums revoked.
d. City Council members pressured the mayor.

35. Increasing border patrols at the U.S.-Canada border was part of which legislation?

a. USA PATRIOT Act of 2001
b. Trade Act of 2002
c. Protection of Lawful Commerce in Arms Act of 2005
d. Secure Fence Act of 2006

36. In 1983, Dianne Feinstein was mayor of San Francisco. She called for a women-mayors' caucus to be part of the U.S. Conference of Mayors. The organization exists to encourage women to run for mayor and to be more involved in the larger organization. This goal is an example of:

a. cronyism
b. networking
c. lobbying
d. patronage

Questions 37–39 refer to the following information:

Issues and Compromises in the United States Constitution

Issue	New Jersey Plan	Virginia Plan	Constitution
Legislative branch	A single house with members appointed by state legislatures	Two houses: Upper House with members elected by the people; Lower House elected by Upper House	Two houses: originally Senate members were elected by state legislatures, and representatives were and are still elected by the people.
Executive branch	Congress to choose an executive committee	Congress to choose a single president	President chosen by Electoral College, with electors selected by each of the states.
Judicial branch	Executive committee to appoint national judges	Congress chooses national judges	President appoints and Senate confirms Supreme Court judges.
Representation	Each state receives equal number of representatives	Representation to be based on wealth or population	Two houses created: House of Representatives based on population; Senate has two delegates from each state.

37. Which of the following conclusions can you draw on the issue of representation?

a. Virginia's people were very poor.
b. New Jersey started using the phrase "Liberty, Equality, and Fraternity."
c. Virginia was probably a state with many people.
d. Many wealthy citizens lived in New Jersey.

38. The Virginia Plan for the legislative branch closely mirrors

a. the Mayflower Compact.
b. Britain's Parliament.
c. the government of the Sioux.
d. France's monarchial system.

39. The Electoral College was created to resolve the issue of

a. how the wealthiest people would be represented.
b. who would appoint the Supreme Court members.
c. how to elect senators.
d. who would elect the chief executive.

Questions 40 and 41 refer to the following passage:

In 1969, 13 African American members of the House of Representatives gathered to form the Congressional Black Caucus (CBC). They felt that a unified voice for minorities was needed. President Richard Nixon met with the group two years later; his weak response to their list of 60 recommendations increased their efforts. These efforts included ending apartheid in South Africa, reforming welfare, expanding educational opportunities, and developing of businesses by minorities. For nearly 20 years, the CBC has proposed an alternative annual budget; it generally varies widely from the budget that the president submits. In 2008, the organization has 43 members from urban and rural areas. The CBC is sometimes called the conscience of Congress.

40. Which of the following statements is true?

a. The Congressional Black Caucus was started right after the Civil War.
b. The major goal of the CBC is to elect an African American president.
c. Since its beginning, the organization has grown by about 30 members.
d. The president usually implements the budget recommendations of the CBC.

41. Which of the following statements is an opinion?

a. The Congressional Black Caucus began in 1969.
b. Every year for two decades, the CBC has proposed a national budget.
c. In 2008, there were 43 members of the Congressional Black Caucus.
d. Apartheid was the worst political system of the twentieth century.

Question 42 refers to the following passage:

ARTICLE XXVII (Ratified July 1, 1971)

Section 1. The right of citizens of the United States, who are eighteen years of age or older, to vote shall not be denied or abridged by the United States or by any State on account of age.

42. This amendment to the Constitution was ratified in part because of what historic moment?

a. Women gained the right to vote.
b. Suffrage was extended to all African Americans.
c. Young men were being drafted to serve in the Vietnam War.
d. The number of people under 21 years of age increased.

Questions 43–45 refer to the following information:

Ethnic Groups in Selected Central American Countries

	Honduras	Nicaragua	El Salvador	Costa Rica	Belize
Mestizo [European and Native American]	90%	69%	90%		49%
Amerindian	7%	5%	1%	1%	
Black	2%	9%		3%	
White	1%	17%	9%	94% [includes Mestizo]	
Chinese				1%	
Creole [African and European]					25%
Mayans					11%

43. To which nation would you go to study the living traditions of the Mayans?

a. Honduras
b. Costa Rica
c. Belize
d. Nicaragua

44. Which of the following conclusions is correct?

a. The Creole population is the largest ethnic group in Latin America.
b. The Mayans have completely died out.
c. Costa Rica used Chinese labor to build the canal.
d. The Amerindian population of many Central American countries was destroyed by war and disease.

45. How do you explain the large Creole population of Belize? Use your own general knowledge.

a. Belize is near the Caribbean, where many Africans were once enslaved.
b. Belize has long been a trading partner with West African nations.
c. Many Creole who once lived in New Orleans left after Hurricane Katrina.
d. The Creole came to Belize to start new restaurants.

Question 46 is for the following map:

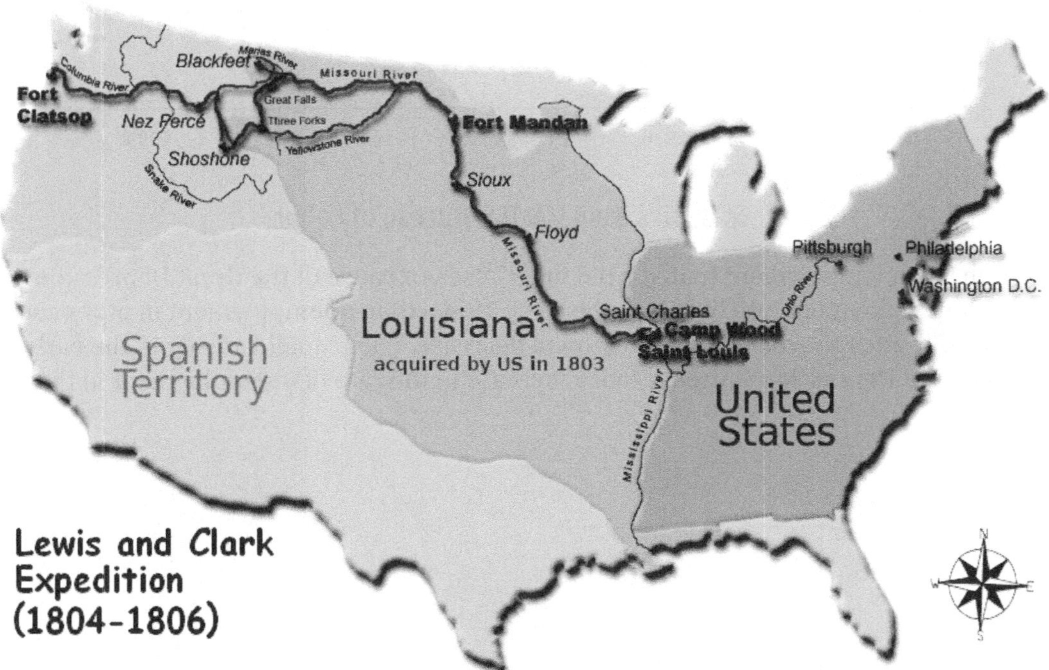

46. The Lewis and Clark expedition of 1803 set out from

a. Washington, D.C.
b. the Rocky Mountains.
c. Fort Mandan.
d. the Mississippi River.

47. What is one conclusion that can be made from this chart?

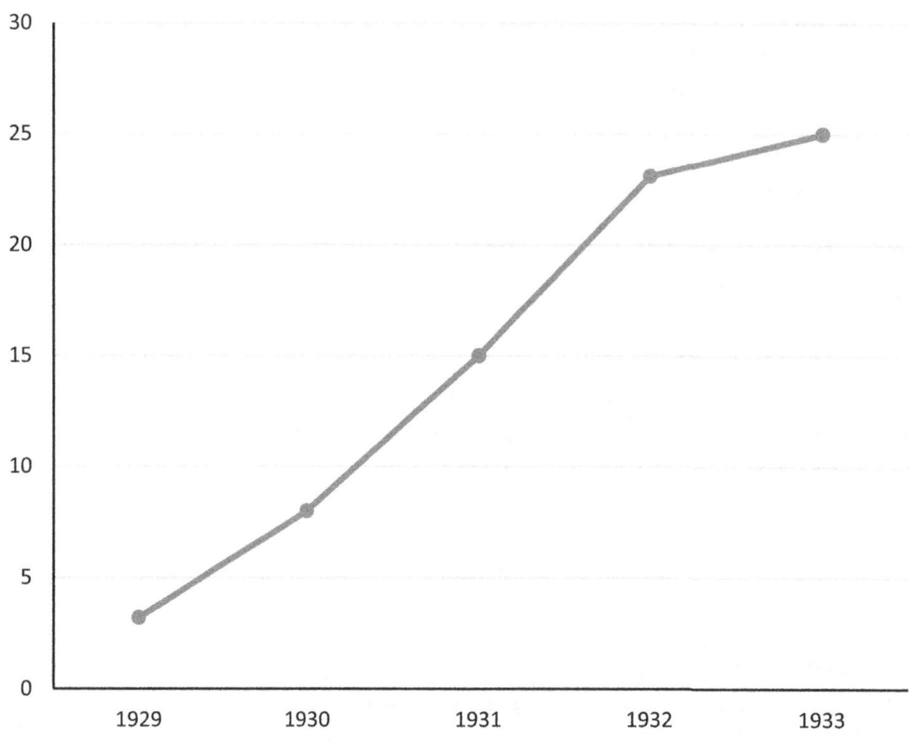

Statistics from the U.S. Bureau of Labor

a. High U.S. unemployment that started in 1929 was a cause of the Great Depression
b. U.S. unemployment was higher in the early 1930s than unemployment in other countries
c. High U.S. unemployment showed a small decrease. Then, it held steady in the early 1930s
d. The Great Depression caused a sharp increase in the rate of unemployment in the U.S.

Questions 48–50 refer to the following map:

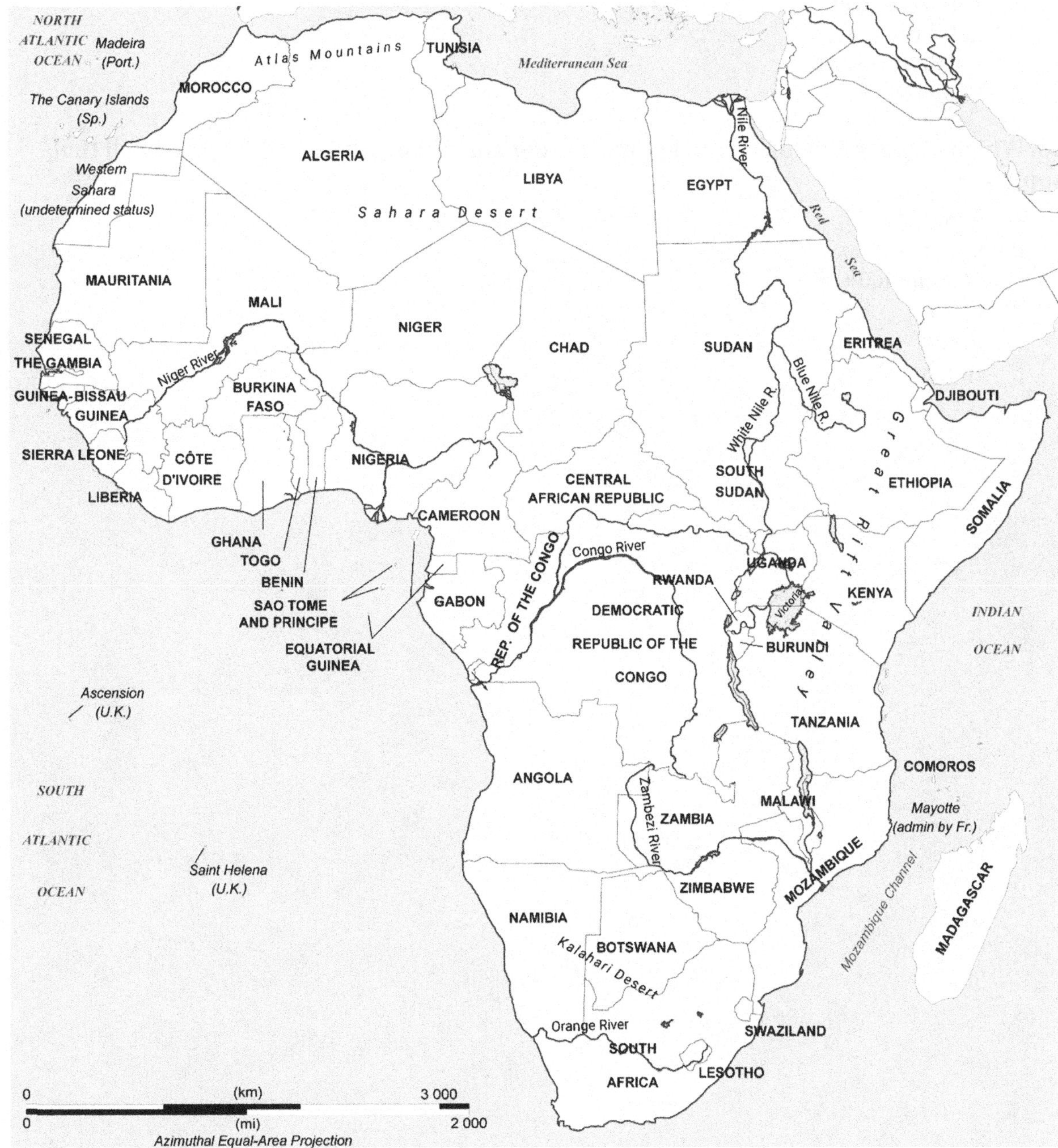

48. In Sudan, the Nile River splits into which bodies of water?

a. Gulf of Aden and Red Sea
b. Congo River and Lake Chad
c. Lake Victoria and the White Nile
d. The Blue Nile and the White Nile

49. What major geographical feature is located in Botswana?

a. Zambezi River
b. Lake Tanganyika
c. Kalahari Desert
d. Congo River

50. Which of the following countries are located along the Indian Ocean? (Select all that apply.)

a. Somalia
b. Cameroon
c. Mozambique
d. Chad
e. Kenya
f. Angola

Answer Key and Explanations for Test #1

Reasoning Through Language Arts

Reading

1. D: The correct answer is D because the author says that the ancient Britons were divided into many tribes and each had a king. The passage does say Choice A is incorrect because the passage says the ancient Britons had weapons, however, it doesn't say the weapons were the reason they fought. Choice B is incorrect because the text says the ancient Britons fought each other. It does not mention them fighting the Phoenicians. Choice C is incorrect because paragraph 6 says that there were no roads or bridges. The author gives this detail in order to describe the land. This detail does not support paragraph 7 which says that the ancient Britons regularly fought.

2. D: The correct answer is D because the word *grew* shows that the ancient Britons changed after the Phoenicians arrived. Choice A is incorrect because the answer choice only shows something that the Phoenicians did with the Britons; however, it does not describe how the Britons changed. Choice B is incorrect because basket-work is something the ancient Britons did before the Phœnicians interacted with them. Choice C is incorrect because it refers to the French and Belgians who moved to England.

3. B: The word *solitary* refers to isolation or being alone. Also, the sentence says that the islands are alone in a great expanse of water. So, this shows that other lands do not surround the islands. Choice A is incorrect because the sentence only talks about the size of the small islands around Scotland. It does not talk about where the islands are in relation to larger lands. Choice C is incorrect because it refers to people on the island, not the island in relation to the rest of the world. Choice D is incorrect because it shows the opposite of isolation; the sentence shows how the people who came to the islands (e.g., the French, Belgians, and Spanish) mixed with the ancient Britons.

4. B: The phrase "But seldom, if ever, ventured far from the shore" means that the boats didn't go far from shore. This implies that the boats may not have had much use in spite of the effort to build them. Choice A is incorrect because the text does not explain specifically how the boats were used. The author does describe weapons in the same paragraph. However, the phrase in the question focuses on the boats that the people made. The paragraph only moves onto weapons in the second sentence. Choice D is incorrect because the author does not connect the boats (discussed in paragraph 7) to the fortresses (discussed at the end of paragraph 6).

5. A: Choice A is the best answer because the first paragraph describes the location of the islands on the map. Choice B is incorrect because there were no roads that ran through England, Scotland, or Ireland during the time period that the passage is describing. Choice C is incorrect because the details about the small islands are only a small part of the first paragraph. Most of the paragraph describes how the islands appear on the map. Choice D is incorrect because the paragraph does not mention the size of the main islands. Also, the paragraph does not mention France or Belgium. Those countries are first mentioned in paragraph 4.

6. C: Choice C is the correct answer because this answer choice describes the lands by mentioning swamps and forests. Choice A is incorrect because it describes the coast, not the interior land of the island. Choice B is incorrect. It is about the interior of the island, but does not describe the land. Choice D is incorrect because it discusses the tribes and the people rather than the features of the lands (e.g., the swamps and forests).

7. B: The word *ardent* means passionate or devoted. Look at the word in the context of the sentence: "The dull precious metal seemed to flash with a reflection of her bright and ardent spirit," and think about Della's actions. Choice A is not correct because Della has planned and saved to buy her husband a Christmas present. So, she has not procrastinated (i.e., waited too long to start on something). Choices C and D are synonyms. They are wrong because Della shows over and over again that she cares very much for her husband.

8. D: The first event in the story is Della preparing her hair (4). The next event in the story is Della preparing a meal for the night (2). Then, Della prays about the reaction that Jim will have to her hair (5). The next event is Jim assuring Della that he is not upset about her decision to cut her hair (3). Then, Jim gives the combs to Della (1). Finally, Della gives the fob chain to Jim (6).

9. C: The sentence "'I hunted all over town to find it.'" is an exaggeration or hyperbole. The other answer choices have similes.

10. C: In the beginning of the story, Della has her hair cut off. She does this so she can get money for Jim's gift. However, she is worried about how she will appear to her husband and is concerned that he will be very angry or worse. When Jim keeps asking about Della's hair, it almost seems as if he is angry about it.

11. A: The entire story is about how Della and Jim are deeply in love. They sell a prized possession to buy a present for the other. Choice B is wrong because the overall meaning of this passage is not about a holiday. Choice C is wrong because it fails to recognize how Della and Jim overcome difficulty and have a deeper love for each other after giving their gifts. Choice D is wrong because the focus of the passage is not on buying the right gift for a loved one. Instead, the focus is on giving up a thing that you care about to show how much you love someone.

12. D: The narrator of the passage is not named. Della and Jim are simply characters in the story. O. Henry is the author of the story, not the narrator.

13. B: The word *beneficence* is used to show how nature helps the plants and animals on Earth. For example, nature provides sunlight and rain to help trees grow. Choice A is incorrect because duties and beneficence are not synonymous. Choice C is incorrect because nature gives the sunlight and the rain. This makes it the opposite of stingy. Later, Keller experiences the dangers of nature. However, choice D is incorrect because paragraph 5 is about the generosity of nature.

14. D: The paragraph shows the narrator's discovery that words have meaning. Choice A is incorrect because the narrator and Miss Sullivan do not use a pencil. Instead, Miss Sullivan uses her fingers to spell words into the narrator's hand. Choice B is incorrect because the narrator does not focus on the distinction between hot and cold water. Choice C is incorrect because the focus of the paragraph is not on learning the locations of places.

15. A: Helen says in the second sentence that she stretches out her hand to who she thinks is her mother. Choice B is incorrect because Helen is not aware that a visitor is coming. Choice C is incorrect because there is no mention that she wants to please her mother. Choice D is incorrect. Helen assumes the person approaching is her mother, but she does not mention loving her mother in the passage.

16. B: Helen is alone and defenseless as the storm approaches. Choice A is incorrect because Helen is not lost. She knows where she is, but she is unable to get out of the tree to go home. The wind and approaching rain make Helen uncomfortable, however, choices C and D are incorrect. We know

Helen is upset about being alone because of the relief she expresses in Miss Sullivan's presence later.

17. C: Miss Sullivan opens up Helen's world by showing her that words have meaning and every object has a name. Choice A is incorrect because Helen is only able to learn about nature through the words taught by Miss Sullivan. Choice B is incorrect because the observation about barriers is not what she learned from Miss Sullivan. Choice D is incorrect because the sentence is not about what Helen learned. Instead, it is about the idea of learning.

18. D: Helen describes "[longing]" for Miss Sullivan's return and clings to her upon being rescued. Choice A is incorrect because Miss Sullivan teaches Helen water early in their relationship before they had developed a bond. Choice B is incorrect because that is a personal growth in Helen, not a growth in the relationship of Helen and Miss Sullivan. Choice C is incorrect because it does not show the bond between Helen and Miss Sullivan. Instead, this moment simply shows something Helen and Miss Sullivan are doing together.

19. B: The passage shows Helen's discoveries about language and nature. While Helen develops a close tie with Miss Sullivan, Miss Sullivan is not Helen's family. So, choice A is incorrect. Choice C is incorrect because the passage never mentions or implies disappointment. Choice D is incorrect because the text does not emphasize Helen's youth.

20. D: This phrase is used to explain how nature, although generous and peaceful, can be violent and dangerous. Choice A is incorrect because Miss Sullivan does not show any cruelty towards Helen. Choice B is incorrect because this paragraph shows Helen feeling nervous but does not show her having a temper tantrum. Choice C is incorrect because Helen was in danger from being alone in the tree as the storm approached. The phrase "treacherous claws" is about the danger of being alone in the tree rather than the danger of climbing the tree.

21. A: The narrator describes her life before the arrival of Miss Sullivan, then she explains her life after and all the changes she experiences. Helen may have become braver with Miss Sullivan, but this is not the focal point of the story. This makes choice B incorrect. Choice C is incorrect because only part of the passage shows the strategies that Miss Sullivan uses to teach Helen. Choice D is incorrect because Helen feels security rather than confusion when she is with Miss Sullivan.

22. C: The passage is about how Miss Sullivan teaches Helen words have meaning. Choice A is incorrect because Helen expresses a clear fondness for Miss Sullivan. Choice B is incorrect because Helen is not scared of nature; rather, she realizes that nature can be generous and dangerous. The passage does not clearly say that Helen learns to read or write. Instead, it shows the beginning of her relationship with words and implies that Helen will continue to learn.

23. D: A non-human thing (e.g., a name) is described with a human quality or action (e.g., birth). Choice A is not correct because there is not a comparison being made. Choice B is not correct because there is no exaggeration in the sentence. Choice C is not correct because there is not a comparison being made with the words *like* or *as*.

24. C: The question asks which job is less desirable than homesteading according to the writer. Choice C is correct because Stewart speaks of going out to wash as less preferable than homesteading. Choice A is incorrect because the letter does not mention cooking or restaurants. Choice B is also incorrect. The reason is that there is no mention of opening a bed and breakfast in the letter. Choice D is also wrong because the letter shares nothing about teaching.

25. D: Growing potatoes is so simple that her six-year-old can do so with little help. The issue is not child labor. So, choice A is incorrect. Stewart does not mention schooling. So, this makes choice B incorrect. Stewart's point has nothing to do with whether women work as hard as men. So, choice C is not the correct response.

26. B: Stewart mentions the hard work of laundry, but she does not speak of any enjoyment of it as she does about homesteading. Choice A cannot be correct because Stewart does not seem to be lazy. Choice C is possible, but there is no evidence to support that idea. Choice D cannot be correct because no reason for anger is given.

27. D: Stewart says that homesteading is a lonely task. For example, she mentions that "persons afraid of ...loneliness had better let ranching alone." Stewart explains in the letter that her work uses less strength than washing. So, choice A is wrong. Choice B is also incorrect because it is addressed in the first paragraph of the letter. Choice C is incorrect because it is mentioned as an advantage in the first paragraph.

28. A: Stewart directly states that women would have "the added satisfaction of knowing that their job will not be lost to them if they care to keep it." Although going on strike was common at the time, Stewart does not mention it. So, choice B is incorrect. Denver is in the Rocky Mountains, but landslides are not mentioned as a risk. So, choice C cannot be the correct answer. Fire is always a risk, but Stewart does not bring it up in the letter. So, choice D is not the correct answer.

29. C: The letter is very positive and full of reasons on why homesteading is a good choice. Choice A is incorrect. The reason is that there is no complaint of hard work, weather, or loneliness. Choice B is also not correct because the letter does not speak of sadness or loneliness. Instead, Stewart rejoices in the good success of the homestead. Also, choice D is not correct because there is no hopelessness expressed in the letter.

30. C: The professor argues that small, woody material is left on the tops of trees and is less likely to be reached by fire.

31. D: Choice D is not a supporting detail because it is a definition of salvage logging. The other choices are supporting details of the Forest Manager's argument.

32. B: Plot A was salvage logged and burned worse than the unmanaged plot (Plot B). This study supports the professor's view that salvage logging increases the risk and severity of fire.

33. A: The question asks which option is the chief argument regarding fire prevention. Choices B and D are not helpful for fire prevention. Choice C is incorrect because logging decreases soil temperature.

34. D: The professor says the larger trees in old growth forests are more resistant to fire than smaller, younger trees. Answers A, B, and C all agree with the professor.

35. C: A study looking at the regrowth of seedlings in logged and unmanaged forests would help to explain and/or prove both arguments. The reason is that the manager and the professor talk on the importance of seedling growth after a fire.

36. C: The first section covers how people want to change and the options that are available to them. As people move towards a healthier lifestyle, they can work at small steps on their way to better health. Choice A is incorrect because the first section does not mention menus. Choice B is incorrect because the paragraph lists benefits of certain foods but does not suggest any are better than others. Choice D is incorrect because the passage mentions that the process is a struggle for many, not an impossible task.

37. D: The overall passage is information for someone who is interested in the food industry. So, choice A is not correct. The reason is that there is not much of a comparison or contrast between the Food Pyramid and MyPlate. Choice B is incorrect because the focus of the passage is not on government involvement. Choice C is incorrect because the text says some groups disagree about certain dietary suggestions but does not make recommendations.

38. A: Choice B is wrong because there is no mention of Harvard's guidelines replacing MyPlate. Choice C is also incorrect. It is another approach to dietary guidelines, but it was included to support a claim, not provide diet options. Choice D is wrong because Harvard is included for their material, not their Ivy League status.

39. C: This passage was written for people who have an interest in the food industry. So, choice A is wrong because the passage is not meant for those who are new to dieting. Choice B is wrong because experienced professionals don't need introductory-level material on preparing food. Choice D is incorrect because there is no mention of parents or children in the passage.

40. B: Each section of the passage has the tone of educating readers. So, choice A is wrong because the tone is not blaming readers. Choice C is close, but it is not the best answer choice. Choice D is wrong because the tone of the material is not snobbish or cocky.

Writing

1. A: The problem in this sentence is subject-verb agreement. Remember that the indefinite pronouns are always singular. Choice B is incorrect because the clause is essential to the sentence. So, commas are not needed. Choice C is wrong because the prepositional phrase does not need punctuation. Choice D is incorrect because there is no need to change *which* to *that*.

2. C: The question tests you on the correct word for comparison with adjectives. The correct adjective is the comparative form of the adjective *bad* which is *worse*, not the superlative form *worst*. Choice A will create a problem with subject-verb agreement. So, it is incorrect. Choice B is wrong as well. The reason is that it creates an adjective comparison problem, and this is the problem you want to correct. Choice D is incorrect because there is a problem that needs to be corrected.

3. B: The sentence is written as a double negative. Choice B is the only choice that corrects the problem. So, choice A is incorrect because the sentence needs to be changed. Choice C is incorrect because it does not solve the problem of the double negative and makes another problem with verb tense. Also, choice D does not solve the problem of the double negative. So, it can be eliminated.

4. A: The sentence has a clarity problem. The dependent clause should come at the beginning of the sentence rather than interrupting the independent clause. Choice B does not make a correction to the sentence. Choice C makes the sentence into a question which is not necessary. Choice D is incorrect because the sentence needs to be reworded to have clarity.

5. B: This sentence should come after the third sentence because it is the first "tip" to consider. Choice A is incorrect because this sentence is only one part to a working vehicle. Choice C is not correct because a sentence that begins with *First of all* should not be the concluding sentence. Choice D is wrong because the sentence belongs with paragraph A. In paragraph B, the focus is on working under the hood and the inside of the vehicle.

6. D: The sentence is written correctly. Choice A is incorrect because splitting the infinitive will be a mistake, not a correction. Choice B is not correct because you need to know which area of the car needs to be checked. Choice C is incorrect because that would only create a problem in agreement.

7. D: Sentence (10) is a run-on sentence and needs correct punctuation. The use of a semicolon between two sentences that are connected in thought is the only acceptable answer choice. You cannot leave the sentence alone. So, choice A is not the correct choice. Choice C places a conjunction between the two sentences. However, it does not include the necessary comma before the conjunction. So, it is an incorrect choice.

8. C: These words are three items in a series. So, commas are needed to separate them. Choice A is not correct because the apostrophe shows possession, and it is used correctly. Choice B is also wrong because the word *emergency* is spelled correctly in the sentence. Choice D is incorrect because the sentence needs commas.

9. A: This sentence has a misplaced modifier. Currently, you can read the sentence and think that you should take everything with you except the car. When you move the word, you understand the reason that you are leaving the car is that you know where you are going and what you are doing. Choice B is not correct because the word is important to the sentence. Choice C is wrong because there is no need for a comma. Choice D is not correct as well. The reason is that there is an error in the sentence.

10. A: There is nothing wrong with the sentence. So, choice A is the correct choice. Everything after the comma could be removed without harming the independent clause at the beginning of the sentence. So, the nonessential adjective clause needs a comma. Choice B is incorrect because it suggests removing the comma. Choice C makes *products* singular. This is incorrect because it creates a problem with subject-verb agreement. The same problem is in choice D; however, the verb is singular.

11. B: This question is about subject-verb agreement. *Slow foods* is plural and needs the plural form of *to be* which is *are*. When you change *is* to *are*, the sentence is corrected. Choice A is not correct because there is not an extra comma in the sentence. Choice C is also wrong because *slow foods* is not a proper noun. So, it does not need capitalization. Choice D is incorrect because *comeback* is one word.

12. D: The question reviews correct spelling. *Emphasize* is the verb, and *emphasis* is the noun which is needed here. Choice A is incorrect because it does not address the problem. Choice B changes the verb from *puts* to *places*, yet there is no problem with the verb choice. Choice C makes the verb plural, but this only adds to the problem.

13. D: This question is about parallel structure. Placing the definite article *the* in front of the final two terms in the series hurts the structure. Removing *the* makes all the items parallel. So, choice A is incorrect. Choice B is also wrong. By making *species* singular, another problem is introduced. Choice C is incorrect because making all nouns singular does not correct the problem.

14. C: The error in this sentence is a split infinitive. The adverb *fully* comes between the words *to* and *use*, and this is not correct grammar. Choice A is incorrect because the change would cause a subject-verb disagreement. Choice B is wrong because the prepositional phrase is not an aside. Also, choice D is wrong because there is an error in the sentence.

15. B: *Slow Food USA* is the name of an organization. So, this makes it a proper noun that needs capitalization. Choice A is not correct because this is the proper name of a specific program. So, the capital letters are correct. Choice C is also wrong because *thru* is a shortcut spelling, but *through* is Standard English. Choice D is incorrect because the sentence has an error.

16. C: Sentence (13) is not important to the article. The writer's garden is not a concern. Choice A is wrong. The reason is that placing the sentence at the beginning of the paragraph makes readers think that the paragraph will be a narrative about the writer's garden. Choice B is incorrect because the last sentence of an essay should be related to the rest of the essay. Choice D is not correct because the sentence should be removed from this passage.

17. D: The sentence is a run-on. So, the best answer choice is to make two sentences of the run-on sentence. Choice A is incorrect because adding commas does not correct the run-on. For choice C, the original word is the correct word. So, this is not correct. Choice B is incorrect because it suggests that the terms are not parallel.

18. B: The proper noun *Slow Food on Campus* is an essential appositive. So, the commas can be removed. Now, the sentence is in passive voice. Choice A would help move the sentence to active voice which is preferred over passive voice. However, this is not the error of the sentence. So, choice A is incorrect. Choice C is wrong because *Slow Food on Campus* is a proper noun that needs capital letters. Choice D is also wrong because *similar* is the correct spelling.

19. D: This sentence is written correctly. Choice A is wrong because the introductory prepositional phrase needs a comma. Choice B is not correct because the verb needs to stay in singular form. Choice C is incorrect because *healthy* is spelled correctly.

20. B: Items in a series need commas between each item. Choice A is wrong because there are no commas for this series. There is no need to capitalize the name of a disease. So, choice C is incorrect. There is an error in the sentence. So, choice D cannot be correct.

21. D: This sentence is a run-on. The sentence has two independent clauses. So, you can place a period between them and capitalize the word *for*. Choice A is wrong because the original sentence is not correct. Choice B is wrong as well. The reason is that a comma between two independent clauses does not correct the problem. Choice C is wrong because a colon cannot be used to separate independent clauses.

22. A: The sentence does not need an adverb. Instead, it needs a predicate adjective to modify the subject *researchers*. Choice B is incorrect because SAD is an acronym that should have capital letters. The sentence is not a question. So, choice C is wrong because it does not need a question mark. Choice D is not correct because there is a mistake in the sentence.

23. D: The sentence is written correctly. So, choice A is not correct because the adjectives are not coordinate. Choice B is not correct because the sentence is making a comparison to months that are not during the winter. In other words, the body makes less melatonin in the summer months. Choice C is wrong because *melatonin* does not need to be capitalized.

24. A: The question tests on the use of *effect* and *affect*. In this sentence, you are looking for the verb that means *influence*. So, affect is the correct word in this sentence. Choice B is wrong because the prepositional phrase should not come after *serotonin*. Choice C is incorrect because *Less* is for amounts which is true for this sentence. *Fewer* is for numbers and applies to things that can be counted. So, the correct adverb is being used in this sentence. Choice D is wrong because the sentence has an error.

25. D: Again, *fewer* is for numbers and applies to things that can be counted. Sunlight cannot be counted. *Less* is for an amount which is true for this sentence. Also, making the change brings back the intended parallelism of the sentence. Choice A is incorrect because the subject and verb agree as they are written. Choice B is also incorrect because the word is not a proper noun and does not need capitalization. Choice C is incorrect. The reason is given in the explanation above for choice D.

26. D: *Factors* is plural and needs a plural verb. The verb *has* is singular. So, this makes a disagreement between subject and verb. *Have* is the plural form of *has* and needs to be used here. Choice A is incorrect because the sentence has an error with subject-verb agreement. Choice B is wrong because removing the capital letter causes another error. Choice C is incorrect. The change simply switches the problem in agreement rather than eliminating it.

27. C: The sentence has a problem with parallel structure. The verbs *tough* and *wait* need to be parallel. Choice A is incorrect because SAD is an acronym and needs capital letters. Choice B is also incorrect. There is an attempt to correct the problem of parallelism. However, *toughing* needs an auxiliary verb. Choice D is wrong because there is an error that needs to be corrected.

28. B: The sentence is not interrogative; it is declarative. In other words, it needs a period at the end, not a question mark. Choice A is incorrect because *well* is an adverb, and the noun *news* needs an adjective modifier. Choice C is incorrect because the seasons are not capitalized. Choice D is wrong because there is an error that needs to be corrected.

29. A: Choice A is correct because the word is not being used in a different way from a dictionary definition. Choice B is not correct because readers need an explanation of the word *temp*. Choice C is wrong because *temporary* is spelled correctly. Choice D is incorrect because a comma is not needed.

30. D: This question is about parallel structure. *Employs* and *generating* are verbs that need to be changed to be parallel. The best way to make them parallel is by putting both in the present tense. Choice A is incorrect because *the staffing industry* is a single unit. So, it does not need the plural form. Choice B is incorrect because the noun is singular and needs a singular verb. Choice C cannot be done without adding more words.

31. D: The problem in the sentence is the wrong homonym. The word *their* is possessive and is needed in this sentence. *They're* is a contraction of *they are*. So, this is the wrong word. In this sentence, *because* is used correctly. So, this makes choice A incorrect. Choice C makes *skills* singular; however, this is not the correct choice. After all, an employer wants a worker who has more than one skill.

32. B: The problem in this question is with antecedent agreement. The pronoun *they* needs a plural noun: *employees*. Choice A is incorrect because of the problem with antecedent agreement. Choice C is incorrect because it has disagreement between subject and verb. Choice D is also wrong. The hyphen in *full-time* does not need to be removed. Also, choice D has disagreement between subject and verb. So, choice D is not correct.

33. C: The problem with the sentence is a comma splice. A semicolon shows that the thoughts of both sentences are related. So, the problem is corrected with the semicolon. Choice A cannot be correct because the original has a comma splice. Choice B is also wrong. The reason is that it has a pronoun-antecedent agreement problem. Choice D is incorrect because it creates a subject-verb agreement problem.

34. D: Adding a comma eliminates the problem of the run-on sentence. Choice A is wrong because there is an error in the sentence. Choice B is also incorrect because it creates a problem with subject-verb agreement. Choice C is incorrect because it creates a subject-verb disagreement in a different part of the sentence.

35. C: The problem in this sentence is a misspelling of valuable. Choice A is wrong because a hyphen is not needed to connect the two words. Choice B cannot be correct because *you're* is the right homonym. Choice D is not correct because there is an error in the sentence.

36. C: This sentence has no parallelism. *To look for* and *interviewing* can be made parallel by making this change. Choice A is not correct because the word *permanent* is spelled correctly. Choice B is not correct. The reason is that it tries to correct the problem, but it fails. Choice D cannot be correct because of the error with parallel structure in the sentence.

37. B: The problem is a misspelled word. Choice B corrects the problem. So, choice A cannot be correct because of the spelling error. Choice C is incorrect because the preposition *among* suggests that there is more than one worker who is being considered for a position. Choice D corrects the spelling error. However, it changes *workers* from plural to singular. So, it is incorrect.

38. A: The sentence is declarative, not interrogative. So, the sentence needs a period as the end mark. Choice B is not correct because the apostrophe is needed to show possession. Choice C is incorrect because it does not solve the problem, and it creates a problem of agreement. Choice D is incorrect as well. The reason is that the sentence has an error that needs to be corrected.

39. C: The sentence has disagreement between the compound subject and the singular verb. Changing *is* to *are* solves the problem. Choice A is incorrect because the comma is needed for items in a series. Choice B is not correct because the word is spelled correctly. Choice D is incorrect because the sentence has an error that should be corrected.

40. D: The problem in the sentence is subject-verb agreement. *Some* suggests that more than one apartment complex is being discussed. So, it is necessary to change the subject and verb to plural. Choice A is incorrect because the sentence has an error that needs to be fixed. Choice B is not correct because the correct homonym is being used in this sentence. Choice C is incorrect because it creates a different subject-verb agreement problem.

41. C: The problem in this sentence is a dangling modifier. To correct the problem, you can write the independent clause as *"you need to consider the other issues about keeping your pet at your apartment."* Choice A is wrong because the comma needs to come after the introductory prepositional phrase. Choice B is not correct because the word is spelled correctly. Choice D cannot be correct because there is an error in the sentence.

42. B: This question is on the use of *affect* and *effect. Affect* is the verb that means to influence, and it is needed here. *Effect* is the noun that points to the influence. Choice A is incorrect because there is a problem in the sentence. Choice C is also incorrect because it creates a subject-verb agreement problem. Choice D is not correct because it does not address the word choice and creates a subject-verb agreement problem.

43. A: *Irregardless* is used very often in informal communication. However, it is not an acceptable word in Standard English. The correct word is *regardless.* Choice B is not correct because the word *licensing* is spelled correctly. Choice C is not correct because the sentence does not have extra commas. The first comma separates the dependent clause. The other commas are needed for the items in a series. Choice D is incorrect as well because the sentence does have an error.

44. B: The apostrophe is needed in *nations* to show possession of the *highest executive office*. Choice A is not correct because executive office is not a proper noun that needs capitalization. Choice C is wrong because you do not want to separate an infinitive. Also, choice D is wrong because there is an error in the sentence.

45. B: *Wall Street* is the name of a street in New York. So, it needs capitalization. Choice A is wrong because this would make an error in verb tense. Choice C is incorrect because the words *although* and *though* are nearly synonyms. So, choosing *although* is not an error. Choice D is incorrect as well because *investment firm* is a common noun. It is not the name of a certain investment firm. So, no capitalization is needed.

46. A: The information in the parentheses is not necessary information. However, the information is closely connected to the sentence. So, commas should be used instead of parentheses. Choice B is wrong because *Republicans* is the name of a certain political party and needs capitalization. Choice C is incorrect because the sentence needs a singular noun for *Margaret Chase Smith*. Choice D is not correct because there is a mistake in the sentence.

47. D: The question tests on irregular verb forms. The sentence needs the past participle of *seek* which is *sought*. So, choice A is incorrect. Choice B is also wrong because the singular subject causes a problem with subject-verb agreement. Choice C is incorrect because the problem is not with the verb tense.

48. A: This is a run-on sentence that can be corrected with a comma between the short independent clauses. Choice B is not correct because the pronoun *them* is correct. Choice C is incorrect. If you made the change, then you would have an error in subject-verb agreement. Choice D is wrong because there is an error in the sentence.

49. C: Sentence (8) is a personal opinion that does not help this passage. Choice A is incorrect. Changing the order of the paragraphs only hurts the chronological order of the passage. Choices B and D are incorrect. The reason is that moving these sentences upsets the unity and coherence of the piece.

50. A: The sentence places a comma after each country correctly because they are items in a series. However, a comma is not needed after Liberia because it is the last item in the series. Choice B is incorrect because the commas are necessary for the items in the series. The exception is the comma after Liberia. Choice D is incorrect because believe is spelled correctly and there is an error in the sentence.

Mathematics

1. C and F: The other coordinates make lines that do not intersect the line in the figure.

2. D: The perimeter (P) of the quadrilateral is simply the sum of its sides:

$$P = m + (m + 2) + (m + 3) + 2m$$

Put together like terms by adding the variables (m terms) together. Then, add the constants. This gives you: $P = 5m + 5$.

3. B: Substitute the given values for the variables into the expression:

$$4 \times -6\,(3 \times 7 + 5) + 2 \times 7$$

Using order of operations, find the expression in the parentheses first. Remember that first you must multiply 3 by 7. Then, add 5 to follow the order of operations

$= 4 \times -6(21 + 5) + 2 \times 7$	Next add the values in the parenthesis
$= 4 \times -6(26) + 2 \times 7$	Simplify by multiplying the numbers outside the parenthesis
$= -24(26) + 14$	Multiply -24 by 26
$= -624 + 14$	Add
$= -610$	Final answer

4. D: The area of the circle is πr^2. The circumference is $2\pi r$. First, take the ratio of these two expressions: Ratio=$\frac{\pi r^2}{2\pi r}$. Then, reduce it to: $\frac{r}{2}$.

5. A: There are 16 empty chairs. This gives 2/5 of the total enrollment. So, the full class must be:

$$\text{Class} = 5/2 \times 16 = 40 \text{ students}$$

Another option is to use proportions:

$$\frac{2}{5} = \frac{16}{x}$$

First, cross multiply to get: $2x = 80$. Then, divide each side by 2 to solve for x. So, $x = 40$ students

6. D: Jamie had $2.75 in his wallet. To solve this problem, you subtract $4.25 and $2.00 from the first sum of $6.50. So, you are left with $0.25. Then, you add $2.50. So, you come to the final answer of $2.75.

7. D: There are two ways to solve this problem. First, you can convert meters to centimeters. Then, use the conversion factor in the table to convert centimeters to inches. Second, use the table to convert meters to yards. Then, convert to inches.

For the first way, remember that there are 100 centimeters in a meter (*centi* means "hundredth"). So, $19 \text{ m} = 1900 \text{ cm} = \left(\frac{1900}{2.54}\right) = 748$ inches.

In the second way to solve the problem, remember that there are 36 inches in a yard.

So, $19 \text{ m} \times 1.094 \frac{\text{yd}}{\text{m}} = 20.786 \text{ yd} \times 36 \frac{\text{inches}}{\text{yd}} = 748$ inches.

Often, proportions are used for conversions. After converting meters to centimeters, you set up proportions to solve for an unknown variable, x.

$$\frac{1900\text{ cm}}{x\text{ in}} = \frac{2.54\text{ cm}}{1\text{ in}}$$

Cross multiply to get: $1900 = 2.54x$. Then, divide each side by 2.54 to solve for x. So, $x = 748$

8. A: You know the price for each pound of onions and carrots. So, start by finding the total cost of the onions and carrots. This will equal $(2 \times \$3.69) + (3 \times \$4.29) = \$20.25$. Next, this sum is subtracted from the total cost of the vegetables. This is done to find the cost of the mushrooms: $\$24.15 - \$20.25 = \$3.90$. Finally, the cost of the mushrooms is divided by the quantity (lbs) to find the cost per pound:

$$\text{Cost per pound lb} = \frac{\$3.90}{1.5} = \$2.60$$

9. D: The figure is a number line. So, the distance from point A to point B will be the difference of B − A. This is $5 - (-6) = 11$. Also, the distance from point B to point C will be the difference of C − B. This is $8 - 5 = 3$. So, the ratio BC:AB will be 3:11.

10. The correct answer is $525. In the first year that he holds the certificate, Jesse's income will be equal to 7.5% of the principal that he has invested which was $7,000. Remember the formula: $I = Prt$ where I is interest, P is principal, r is rate (given as a decimal) and t is time (in years). So, $I = \$7{,}000 \times 0.75 \times 1$. This equals $525.

11. A: Candidate A's vote ratio is the number of votes that he obtained divided by the total number of votes cast. Then, multiply that decimal by 100 to convert the decimal into a percentage. Now, Candidate A's vote is: $\frac{36800}{36800+32100+2100} \times 100$. So, you have a percentage of 51.8%

12. The correct answer is 168.75 minutes. First, find the time that is needed to ride 1 mile.

This is equal to 45 / 16 or 2.8125 minutes. Next, multiply this by the total number of miles to be ridden, or 60, to have the final answer. When you put all of this together, you have:

$$\text{Time} = \frac{45}{16} \times 60 = 168.75\text{ minutes}$$

Another way is to use proportions. To begin set up your proportions:

$$\frac{16\text{ miles}}{45\text{ min}} = \frac{60\text{ miles}}{x\text{ min}}$$

Then, cross multiply to get: $16x = 2700$. Now, divide each side by 16. So, you have $x = 168.75$ minutes

13. The area is 3.93 square units. Note that the shaded area is one fourth of the difference between the areas of the inner and outer circles. The formula for finding the area of a circle is: $A = \pi r^2$. The radius (r) of the outer circle is 3. So, you have $A_{out} = \pi \times 3^2$, or 9π. The radius of the inner circle is $A_{in} = \pi \times 2^2$, or 4π. So, one fourth of the difference between the areas is: $\frac{1}{4}(9\pi - 4\pi)$ Then, factor out π. So, you have: $\frac{1}{4}\pi(9 - 4) = \frac{5\pi}{4} \cong 3.93$

14. C: Divide David's total profit of $22.00 by the number of shares he purchased, 200, to determine David's profit per share.

$$P = \$22.00 \div 200 = \$0.11$$

So, the price he paid was 11¢ lower than the closing price shown in the table. Since the table shows that Oracle closed at $19.11 today, the price David paid was $\$19.11 - \$0.11 = \$19.00$ per share.

15. The correct answer is $30.16 per share. To find this weighted average, you multiply the number of shares purchased per stock by the stock price. Then, add these totals together and divide by the total number of shares. Lynn bought 100 shares of Microsoft at $45.14, 100 shares of Apple Computer at $16.90, and 200 shares of Garmin at $29.30. So, the total amount that she spent was:

$$\text{Total} = (100 \times \$45.14) + (100 \times \$16.90) + (200 \times \$29.30) = \$12064$$

She gained a total of 400 shares of stock. So, the average cost per share is:

$$\text{Avg} = \frac{\text{Total}}{\text{shares}} = \frac{\$12064}{400} = \$30.16$$

16. The correct answer is $3.85. To make a profit of 10%, James must sell the stock at a price that is 10% higher than what he paid for it. So, he must sell it at 110% of the purchase price. He buys the stock at $3.50 per share. So, he must sell it at a price (P) as follows:

$$P = \frac{110 \times \$3.50}{100} = \$3.85$$

17. The correct answer is $123. To calculate this, first find the total number of hours worked. From 7AM until noon is 5 hours. From noon until 4:30 PM is 4.5 hours. So, the total number of hours worked is: $5 + 4.5 = 9.5$ hours. Next, find the number of hours paid at the overtime rate. This is $9.5 - 8 = 1.5$ hours. The overtime pay rate is 50% greater than the regular rate of $12 per hour or $1.5 \times \$12 = \$18$ per hour. Finally, calculate the amount of pay at each rate, regular and overtime. Then, add these together to find the total pay: $\text{Total} = (8 \times \$12) + (1.5 \times \$18) = \$123$

18. D: First, add the two straight 150-yard portions. Also, note that the distance for the two semi-circles put together is the circumference of a circle. Since the circumference of a circle is π times the diameter, the length of the circular portion of the track is simply 30π. Then, add this to the length of the two straight portions of the track.

$$\text{Perimeter} = 30\pi + (2 \times 150) \approx 394.25$$

Therefore, the perimeter of the entire track is approximately 395 yards.

19. C: To determine this, first determine the total distance of the round trip. This is twice the 45 miles of the one-way trip to work in the morning, or 90 miles. Then, to determine the total amount of time Elijah spent on the round trip, first convert his travel times into minutes. One hour and ten minutes is the same as 70 minutes, and an hour and a half is 90 minutes. So, Elijah's total travel time was $70 + 90 = 160$ minutes. Elijah's average speed can now be determined in miles per minute:

$$\text{Average Speed} = \frac{90 \text{ miles}}{160 \text{ min}} = 0.5625 \text{ miles per minute}$$

Finally, to convert this average speed to miles per hour, multiply by 60, since there are 60 minutes in an hour: Average speed (mph) $= 60 \times 0.5625 = 33.75$. Therefore, his average speed for the round trip was 33.75 mph.

20. The correct answer is 0.48 seconds. Modify the relationship given in the question to solve for the time. You know that the distance is the product of the rate and time: $d = rt$. To change the relationship for this problem, you need to put time (t) by itself. So, this will look like: $t = \frac{d}{r} = \frac{60.5\text{ft}}{125\text{ ft/sec}} = 0.484$ sec. When you round to the nearest hundredth of a second, you have the answer of 0.48 seconds.

21. A: The rate of increase equals the change in the account balance divided by the original amount: \$80. Multiply that decimal by 100 to know the percentage of increase. So, to find the change in the balance, subtract the original amount from the new balance: Change $= \$120 - \$80 = \$40$ Now, you can find the percentage of increase: Percent $= \frac{\$40}{\$80} \times 100 = 50\%$

22. The correct answer is 910 square feet. The answer is found by computing the area of the large rectangle and the area of the rectangular cutout. Then, the area of the cutout is subtracted from the larger rectangle. The area of the rectangle is the product of its length and width, $A_{rect} = 20 \times 50 = 1000$ square feet. The cutout is a rectangle as well. So, its area is computed in the same way: $A_{cutout} = 6 \times 15 = 90$ square feet. Then, subtracting gives you the answer: $Area = A_{rect} - A_{cutout} = 1000 - 90 = 910$ square feet.

23. D: Begin as you would with a regular equation: $4x - 12 > 4$.

$4x - 12 + 12 > 4 + 12$	Add 12 to each side
$4x/4 > 16/4$	Divide each side by 4
$x > 4$	Final result

Note that the direction of the inequality does not change. The reason is that the division was by a positive 4. Only choice D follows the condition that it needs to be less than 4.

24. B: The rate, miles per minute, is constant. So, this can be solved by setting up a proportion: $\frac{\text{miles}}{\text{min}} = \frac{10}{12} = \frac{210}{x}$. Now, solve for time: $t = \frac{210 \times 12}{10} = 252$ minutes. Finally, convert to hours by dividing this total by 60. The reason is that there are 60 minutes in an hour:

$$t = 252/60 = 4 \text{ hours and } 12 \text{ minutes}$$

Note: When dividing 252 by 60, you get a decimal answer of 4.2 hours. However, the answers are given in a different unit of measurement. 4.2 hours is not the same as 4 hours and 2 minutes. In order to find the number of minutes, the decimal (0.2) has to be converted into minutes. To convert, multiply 0.2 by 60 which becomes 12 minutes.

25. C: Define the variable t as the passed time (in hours) from the time the first airplane takes off. Then, at any time the distance traveled by the first plane is $d_1 = 250t$. The second plane takes off 30 minutes later. So, at any time the distance that it has traveled is $d_2 = 280(t - 0.5)$. The units used for the half hour should remain in hours, not minutes, and they must be negative since the second plane left after the first plane. This plane will overtake the first when the two distances are equal: $d_1 = d_2$ or $250t = 280(t - 30)$.

Result	Next Step

$250t = 280(t - 0.5)$	Use the distributive property
$250t = (280 \times t) - (280 \times 0.5)$	Simplify the parentheses
$250t = 280t - 140$	Add 140 to each side
$250t + 140 = 280t - 140 + 140$	Subtract $250t$ from each side
$250t - 250t + 140 = 280t - 250t$	Divide both sides by 30
$140/30 = 30t/30$	Final result
$4\frac{2}{3} = t$	

This gives the value of t in hours. So, you have the found an elapsed time of 4 hours and 40 minutes. The first plane left at 2 PM. So, 4 hours and 40 minutes later is 6:40 PM.

26. B: The figure is a right triangle. So, the Pythagorean Theorem can be used. The side that is 25 units long is the hypotenuse. Its square will equal the sum of the squares of the other two sides. That is $25^2 = 15^2 + x^2$. Solve for x^2 by subtracting 15^2 from each side of this equation. Then, take the square root to find x.

$$x = \sqrt{25^2 - 15^2} = \sqrt{625 - 225} = \sqrt{400} = 20$$

27. C: The formula for the volume of a pyramid is $V = \frac{1}{3}BH$, where B is the area of the base and H is the height of the pyramid. The base is a square with a length of 756 ft on each side. So, the area of the base is $A = s^2 = (756\text{ ft})^2 = 571{,}536\text{ ft}^2$. With a base of $571{,}536\text{ ft}^2$ and a height of 481 ft, the volume of the pyramid is $V = \frac{1}{3}(571{,}536\text{ ft}^2)(481\text{ ft}) = 9.16 \times 10^7\text{ft.}^3$

28. D: First, test each expression to see which follows the condition $x > y$. This condition is met for all the answer choices except choice C. Next, test the remaining choices to see which follows the inequality $x + y > 0$. It can be seen that this inequality holds for choice A and choice B. However, this does not hold for choice D. The reason is that $x + y = 3 + (-3) = 3 - 3 = 0$. In this case, the sum $x + y$ is not greater than 0.

29. D: To multiply two powers that have the same base, you need to add their exponents. So, $x^3x^5 = x^{3+5} = x^8$. Also note that $x^3 = x \times x \times x$ and $x^5 = x \times x \times x \times x \times x$. So, the expression equals $(x \times x \times x) \times (x \times x \times x \times x \times x) = x^8$.

30. B: Take the cross product of the numerators and denominators from either side for this proportion.

$$\frac{12}{x} = \frac{30}{6}$$

Cross multiply to get: $30x = 72$. Then, divide each side by 30. So, you are left with $x = 2.4$

31. A: This is a typical plot of an inverse variation where the product of the dependent and independent variables, x and y, is always equal to the same value. In this case, the product is always equal to 1. So, the plot is in the first and third quadrants of the coordinate plane. As x increases and goes to infinity, y decreases and goes to zero while keeping the constant product. In contrast, choice B is a linear plot for an equation of the form $y = x$. Choice C is a quadratic plot for the equation $y = x^2$. Choice D is an exponential plot for the equation $y = 2x$.

32. C: The internal angles of a triangle always add up to 180°. Since ΔABC is a right triangle, then $\angle ABC = 90°$ and $\angle ACB$ is given as 30°. The middle letter is for the vertex. By using the triangle addition theorem, the answer must be: $\angle BAC = 180 - (90 + 30)$. This equals 60°.

33. A: This equation is a linear relationship that has a slope of 3.60 and passes through the origin. The table shows that for each hour of rental, the cost increases by $3.60. This matches with the slope of the equation. Of course, if the bicycle is not rented at all (0 hours), there will be no charge ($0). If plotted on the Cartesian plane, the line would have a y intercept of 0. Choice A is the only one that follows these requirements.

34. D: The slopes of perpendicular lines are reciprocals and have the opposite sign. In the figure below, Line A has a slope of -1/2, and Line B has a slope of 2.

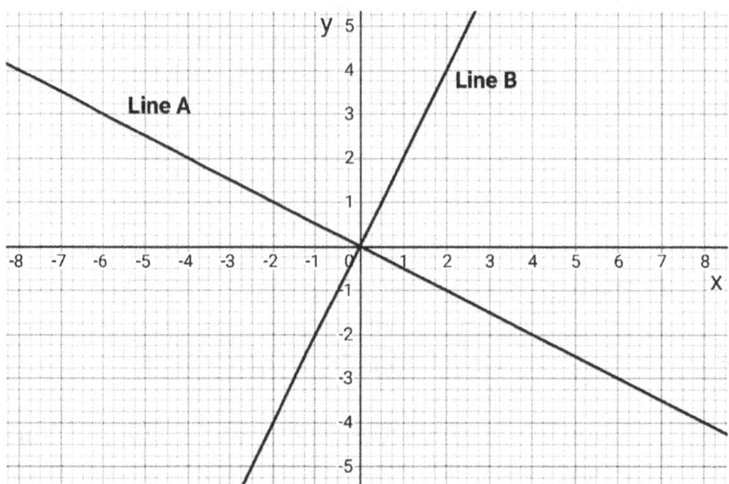

35. C: This table shows the numbers of coins added to the first few squares and the equivalent powers of 2:

Square	1	2	3	4
Coins	1	2	4	8
Power of 2	2^0	2^1	2^2	2^3

In this series, the number of coins on each is the consecutive powers of 2. The reason is that the number doubles with each consecutive square. However, the series of powers begins with 0 for the first square. For the 64th square, the number of coins will be 2^{63}.

36. C: There are four different colors. So, one color must be held back from each balloon bundle. So, there is one color set for each excluded color or four in all.

When the order of the individual parts is not important, this is called a combination. The number of combinations of n objects taken k at a time is given by $C = \frac{n!}{(n-k)!k!}$. The ! notation is for a *factorial* product where $n! = 1 \times 2 \times 3 \times \ldots \times (n-1) \times n$. In this case, $n = 4$ colors, and $k = 3$ balloons per bundle. Then, substitute into the equation above and simplify:

$$C = \frac{4!}{(4-3)! \times 3!} = \frac{1 \times 2 \times 3 \times 4}{(1)(1 \times 2 \times 3)} = 4$$

37. B: The two right triangles are similar because they share a pair of vertical angles. Vertical angles are always congruent (e.g., angle ACB and angle DCE). Obviously, both right angles (e.g., angle B and angle D) are congruent. So, angles A and E are congruent because of the triangular sum theorem.

With similar triangles, corresponding sides will be proportional. Segment BC is $\frac{1}{2}$ the length of segment CD. So, AC will be $\frac{1}{2}$ the length of CE. The length of CE can be computed from the Pythagorean theorem. The reason is that it is the hypotenuse of a right triangle, and the lengths of the other two sides are known: $CE = \sqrt{6^2 + 8^2} = \sqrt{100} = 10$.

The length of segment AC will be $\frac{1}{2}$ of this value or 5 units.

38. The correct answer is (2,0). To come to this answer, set the two expressions to be equal and solve for the variable x. This is the substitution method since we are substituting the expression for y:

$-3x + 6 = 2x - 4$	Gather like terms on each side of the equation and isolate the variable
$10 = 5x$	Divide each side by 5
$2 = x$	x value

Now, substitute this value of x into either of the original equations to find the y coordinate

$$y = -3x + 6 = -6 + 6 = 0$$

39. C: For each die there is a 1 in 6 chance that a 6 will be on top. The reason is that the die has 6 sides. The probability that a 6 will show for each die is not affected by the results from another roll of the die. In other words, these probabilities are independent. So, the overall probability of throwing 3 sixes is the product of the individual probabilities: $P = \frac{1}{6} \times \frac{1}{6} \times \frac{1}{6} = \frac{1}{6^3} = \frac{1}{216}$

40. D: Rafael's profit on each computer is the difference between the price he pays and the price he charges his customer: \$800-\$450. If he sells n computers in a month, his total profit will be n times this difference: $n(800 - 450)$. However, it is necessary to subtract his fixed costs of \$3000 from $n(800 - 450)$ to find his final profit per month.

41. D: When a number is raised to a power, you multiply the number by itself by the number of times of the power. For example, $2^3 = 2 \times 2 \times 2 = 8$. A number raised to the power of 0 is always equal to 1. So, 6^0 is the smallest number shown. Similarly, for the other numbers:

$$9^1 = 9;\ 10^1 = 10;\ 4^2 = 4 \times 4 = 16$$

Since $1 < 8 < 9 < 10 < 16$, we can write the order as $6^0, 2^3, 9, 10^1, 4^2$.

42. B: This pie chart shows the relative amounts of each variable as a slice of the whole circle. The larger variables have larger slices. Also, the percentage of each variable (e.g., recycled material) is shown next to each slice. In this chart, paper is the most common recycled material (i.e., the largest variable). This is 40% of the total. The next largest is glass at 25% of the total. All of the other materials stand for smaller portions of the total.

43. D: The chart indicates that 40% of the total recycled material is paper. Since 50,000 tons of material are recycled every month, the total amount of paper will be 40% of 50,000 tons, or $\frac{40}{100} \times 50{,}000 = 20{,}000$ tons.

44. A: Let D represent Dorothy's age and S represent her sister's age. Since she is half of her sister's age today, we have $D = \frac{S}{2}$, or $S = 2D$. In twenty years, her age will be $D + 20$, and her sister's age will be $S + 20$. At that time, Dorothy will be $\frac{3}{4}$ of her sister's age. Therefore, $D + 20 = \frac{3}{4}(S + 20)$. Substitute $2D$ for S in this equation.

$$D + 20 = \frac{3}{4}(2D + 20)$$

Use the distributive property and reduce.

$$D + 20 = \frac{3}{2}D + 15$$

From here, solve for D.

$$\begin{aligned} 20 - 15 &= \frac{3}{2}D - D \\ 5 &= \frac{1}{2}D \\ 10 &= D \end{aligned}$$

Dorothy is 10 years old today, and her sister is 20 years old. In twenty years, Dorothy will be 30 years old, and her sister will be 40 years old.

45. The correct answer is $4000. Chan has paid out a total of 30% + 30% + 25% = 85% of his bonus for the items in the question. So, the $600 is the remaining 15%. To find out his total bonus, solve $\frac{100}{15} \times 600 = \$4000$.

46. D: It is not necessary to use the circle formula to solve the problem. Note that 50 km/hr matches with 50,000 meters per hour. You have the car's revolutions per minute, and the answer must be given in meters. So, the speed must be converted to meters per minute. This matches with a speed of $\frac{50{,}000}{60}$ meters per minute. The reason is that there are 60 minutes in an hour. In any given minute, the car travels at $\frac{50{,}000}{60}$ meters/min. The tires rotate 500 times around. So, this is 500 times its circumference. This matches with $\frac{50{,}000}{60 \times 500} = \frac{10}{6}$ meters per revolution. This is the circumference of the tire.

47. B: The volume of the cylinder is the amount of grain that the farmer will be able to store in the silo. The formula for the volume of a cylinder is $V = \pi r^2 h$, where r is the radius of the circular base and h is the height of the cylinder. The cylinder has a diameter of 8 m. The radius is half of the diameter, or 4 m. The height is 24 m. So, your equation becomes $V = \pi(4\text{ m})^2(24\text{ m}) = 384\pi\text{ m}^3$.

48. A: Find the product using the FOIL method. As a result, $(a + b)(a - b) = a^2 + ba - ab - b^2$. Since ab is equal to ba, the middle terms cancel each other. This leaves you with $a^2 - b^2$.

49. A: The mode is the number that appears most often in a set of data. If no item appears most often, then the data set has no mode. In this case, Kyle had one hit for a total of three times. There were two times that he had two hits. Also, on one day, he had three hits. Then, on another day, he had four hits. One hit happened the most times. So, the mode of the data set is 1.

50. B: The mean, or average, is the sum of the numbers in a data set. Then, the sum is divided by the total number of items. This data set has seven items (i.e., one for each day of the week). The total number of hits that Kyle had during the week is the sum of the numbers in the right-hand column. The sum is 14. So, to find the average: Mean $= \frac{14}{7} = 2$.

Science

1. C: A normal sperm must have one of each of the human chromosome pairs. There are 23 chromosome pairs in all. Twenty-two of these are *autosomal* chromosomes. They do not play a role in deciding gender. The remaining pair has two X chromosomes in the case of a female. In the case of a male, there is an X and a Y chromosome. So, a normal sperm cell will have 22 autosomal chromosomes and either an X or a Y chromosome, not both.

2. D: The graph shows that temperatures in the lower stratosphere are -50°C or lower. This allows more efficient engine operation. The paragraph explains that 75% of the Earth's atmosphere is in the troposphere which is below the stratosphere. It also says that the convective mixing of air and the effects of weather are characteristic of the troposphere. In the stratosphere, temperature-based layering of air leads to a stable environment. All of these effects combine to allow jets to operate with the best fuel efficiency possible in the lower stratosphere.

3. D: This can be read from the graph. The thermosphere has both the coldest and the highest temperatures in the atmospheric regions beneath outer space. In the thermosphere, atmospheric gases make layers of nearly pure molecular species. In its lower areas, carbon dioxide adds to cooling through radiative emission. An example is the mesosphere. In its upper areas, molecular oxygen absorbs solar radiation and causes much warming.

4. Sample Response: The amplitude is greater and the wavelength is longer.

The pitch of a sound depends on the frequency of the sound wave. As the frequency rises, the sound's pitch will rise as well. Frequency varies inversely with wavelength. So, a higher pitched sound with a higher frequency will have a longer wavelength. The volume of a sound depends on the degree that the molecules of air (or any other medium through which the sound travels) are compressed. This compression is represented by the wave amplitude. As the amplitude becomes greater, the sound becomes louder.

5. D: The two sound waves are added together. This means that the values of the two waves at each point are combined or added together. Since the two waves are out of phase by exactly half a wavelength, this means that when one wave has a positive value, the other has a negative value. Being out of phase by half a wavelength is the same as being perfectly out of phase. Since they are perfectly out of phase, they will cancel one another out. In other words, the amplitude peak of one wave will match in space with the amplitude trough of the other. This event is called cancellation. The opposite is also possible. If the waves were perfectly in phase, their peaks and troughs would match each other. So, instead of canceling out, the sum of the two waves would be twice as strong as each individual wave. This would make a much louder sound.

6. B: The vertical axis of this graph is an exponential scale. Each tick mark for a day matches with an increase in the number of cells per mL. The curve for the control cells (i.e., those grown in the absence of the drug) shows a cell concentration of about 500 cells/mL at the start. Then, there are 5000 cells/mL after 4 days, and 50,000 cells per mL after 8 days. This shows an exponential growth pattern where the number of cells increases by a factor of ten every four days.

7. D: The effects of two concentrations of methotrexate (MTX) on the growth of cancer cells are shown by the open pentagons and solid squares in the figure. These growth curves may be compared to the growth of untreated cells (the control) shown by the solid circles. At a concentration of 10 micromoles per liter (10 micromolar), cell growth is slightly inhibited when compared to the control. At the greater concentration of 100 micromoles per liter (i.e., equivalent to

0.1 millimolar), the cells do not grow at all. Also, the experiment is concerned with cancer cells, not bacteria. So, choice B cannot be correct.

8. B: Sexual reproduction allows the genetic information from two parents to mix. Recombination events between the two parental copies of individual genes can happen. So, this will create new genes. The production of new genes and of new gene combinations leads to an increase in diversity in the population. This is a great advantage for adapting to changes in the environment.

9. D: The charge must be conserved in the reaction. Each reactant (i.e., two helium atoms) has two protons. So, they will have a total electric charge of +4. The reaction product (i.e., helium-4) also has two protons. Thus, it has a total charge of +2. Two positive charges are lacking to balance the reaction. Choice D with two protons has a charge of +2.

10. B: Tritium is an isotope of hydrogen. So, the nucleus has a single proton that has a charge of +1. The extra neutrons do not add to the charge. Electrons have a charge of −1. In order to neutralize the single positive charge of the nuclear proton, one electron is needed.

11. D: Volcanic activity allows molten magma to reach the surface of the Earth. This is where it cools and solidifies into rock. The diagram and paragraph show that these types of rocks are known as *igneous* rocks. Examples of igneous rocks are obsidian and basalt. The type of igneous rock that is made depends on the chemical makeup of the magma.

12. B: A metamorphic rock is a rock with a changed form. These rocks are made at great depths. Usually, they come from previous sedimentary rocks. As more sediment builds above them, there is increased pressure and heat. This forces the relatively open crystal structure of the sedimentary rocks to collapse. Then, they take on a denser structure. Examples of metamorphic rocks are quartz and gneiss.

13. A: Evolutionary fitness measures the ability to pass on genes to future generations. So, it is marked by the ability to have offspring. The male wolf in choice A died young. However, he lived long enough to have 4 offspring. As you can see, this is more than any other wolf described in the other choices. So, his genes have the greatest chance of being passed on. It is important to know that evolutionary fitness simply requires an organism to live long enough to reproduce. This is measured only by reproductive success.

14. B: An allele is a variant of the original DNA sequence for a gene. It may differ from the original by a single base. For example, it may have a C in place of a G. Also, it may differ by a whole region where the sequence of bases is different. It may have extra bases in it (i.e., insertions) or be missing some material (i.e., deletions). Whatever the difference, it will result in RNA and a protein. This RNA sequence differs from the original. Sometimes, these differing proteins are broken. They may result in disease or developmental anomalies. Sometimes they are mild. An example is the difference between blue and brown eyes in humans.

15. A: The sequence can be read directly from the table. It is read three bases at a time. Three bases makeup a codon and give the information needed to specify one amino acid. In the sequence given, the first codon is GTT. The table shows that this matches with the amino acid *valine*. Similarly, the second codon is ACA. So, this matches with threonine. The third codon (i.e., AAA) matches with lysine. The fourth (i.e., AGA) goes with arginine. Each sequence of amino acids makes a specific protein.

16. D: Begin by looking over each sequence from the first base. Then, break it into triplets for each codon. The sequence in choice A is GTA CCC CTA. This is for valine-proline-leucine. Only the sequence in choice D has one of the three STOP codons. The STOP codons are TGA, TAA, and TAG. In choice D, the second codon is TAA. When the polymerase reaches this codon, it will start the process of disengaging from the DNA. This process ends the mRNA copy and ultimately the protein product of the gene.

17. A: The DNA molecule is a long chain of phosphoribose that has attached bases. The sequence of bases defines the individual amino acids that are connected to make a protein. There are 4 different bases and 23 different amino acids. Each amino acid is specified by a three-base "word." This "word" is known as a codon in the language of DNA. The four bases can be put together in 64 different ways to encode the 23 different amino acids and STOP signals. Some amino acids are defined by more than one codon.

18. C: Proteins are *encoded* in the DNA. However, they are *made* by ribosomes that string the proteins together from amino acids in the cell's cytoplasm. The information needed to string proteins into the correct sequence comes from mRNAs that are made by polymerases. These polymerases read the codons in the DNA. Transfer RNAs bring the amino acids to the ribosomes where they are built into proteins.

19. D: Phosphoribose gives the backbone of the DNA chain which makes up genes. In this area, bases like cytosine and guanine are strung together. Then, they are organized into triplets known as codons. These codons encode the protein to be made. The protein itself will be put together far away from the gene that is in the cell's nucleus. The ribosome is in the cytoplasm of the cell and will help to build the protein.

20. A: Vectors can show the velocities of the wind and the aircraft. The length of the vector can be for the speed. The direction of the vector can be for the direction of either the wind or the airplane.

The wind speed is going against the plane. The pilot will measure the sum of the actual wind speed plus the speed of his aircraft:

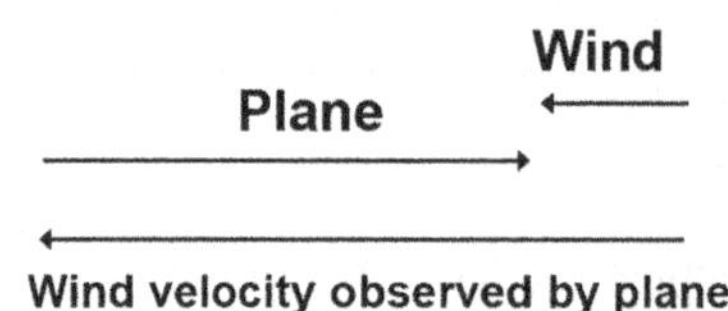

21. C: Spring tides happen when the Sun, Moon, and Earth are in a line. Neap tides happen when the Sun and Moon are at right angles.

22. C: The chart shows that plastic and cardboard materials are made of 15% of the collected materials. So, it is incorrect to say that there is more plastic than cardboard. They are present in equal amounts.

23. A: The reactions described in the paragraph happen when electrons are made by a reaction that reduces the positively-charged lead anode. The reducing agent, in turn, is oxidized by this reaction. These electrons travel through the wire to the negatively-charged cathode where they react with the sulfuric acid oxidizer and reduce it. This makes a lead sulfate. In a car battery, the anode is the positively-charged electrode. Normally, you can find it with the red marking on the battery.

24. A: In an oxidation reaction, an oxidizing agent gains electrons from a reducing agent. By adding electrons, the reducing agent reduces (i.e., makes more negative) the charge on the oxidizer. In the car battery, reduction of the positively-charged anode provides electrons. Then, these electrons flow to the cathode where an oxidation takes place. In an oxidation, an oxidizing agent increases (i.e., makes more positive) the charge on a reducer. In this way, the extra electrons in the negatively charged cathode are neutralized by the surrounding oxidizing agent.

25. D: The reaction described in the paragraph happens when two water molecules (H_2O) are made for each lead oxide (PbO_2) molecule that reacts at the cathode.

26. C: The data shows that up until about 4 weeks, the silk production from both colonies was similar. This suggests that the worms from each colony made the same amount of silk. So, choices A and B are incorrect. Over the long term, the data shows that the silk made by the entire colony of genetically diverse worms was greater than the silk made by the entire colony of genetically uniform worms. This might be because the worms made silk for a longer time. This could be due to some other mechanism. The experiment does not give information on that mechanism.

27. Sample Response: *Genetically diverse silkworms reproduce more than genetically uniform worms.* The increase in productivity from the diverse culture happens at about 4 weeks. This comes at the same time when new worms are hatched and start to make silk.

28. A: The digestion of starch starts with its exposure to the enzyme amylase that is found in the saliva. Amylase attacks the glycosidic bonds in starch. This attack separates them to release sugars. This is the reason why some starchy foods may taste sweet if they are chewed for a long time. Another form of amylase is made by the pancreas. This amylase continues the digestion of starches in the upper intestine. The di- and tri-saccharides are the first products of this digestion. Later, they are converted to glucose. The glucose is a monosaccharide that is easily absorbed through the intestinal wall.

29. D: The term *hydrologic cycle* is defined in the first paragraph. It is described as being equal to the *water cycle*. It comes from the Greek root *hydros* which means "water."

30. B: The second paragraph gives examples of different storage reservoirs for water in the water cycle. An underground aquifer is one example. An *aquifer* is any geologic formation that has ground water. The word comes from the Latin root *aqua* which means "water."

31. D: According to the table, the average residence time of water in soil is only two months. Only its residence time in the atmosphere (9 days) is shorter. *Residence time is the average amount of time a water molecule spends in a reservoir before it moves on to another reservoir in the water cycle.*

32. B: According to the final paragraph, ocean levels actually fall during an ice age. More water is stored in ice caps and glaciers when the temperatures are very cold so less water stays in the oceans as liquid.

33. C: Adding heat causes the molecules of a substance to increase their rate of motion. This is why heat is known as a form of kinetic energy. The temperature of a substance is proportional to the kinetic energy of the molecules that make up the substance. Adding heat to a system usually raises the temperature. However, temperature is not a form of heat. Instead, temperature measures the amount of heat that is in a system.

34. C: Energy in the form of heat is always absorbed by the molecules of a substance to make them move faster. During a change of state, some molecules absorb energy and escape the solid phase to become liquid. Others escape the liquid phase to become gas. Since molecules in a gas move faster than those in a liquid and molecules in a liquid move faster than those in a gas, the average speed increases.

35. B, C, and D: In region B of the graph, the water is at 0°C. Heat is being added to it, and it is slowly changing to a liquid. In region C, the temperature is climbing from 0°C to 100°C, and all of the water is in a liquid phase. In region D, the water is at 100°C. So, it is slowly changing to a gas as more energy is added. Once it has all changed to a gas, the temperature will increase again as more heat is added (region E).

36. D: Water at 1°C is in the liquid phase. Using the definition of the specific heat capacity, it will take 99 calories to raise the temperature of 1 gm of liquid water to 100°C. Using the definition of the heat of vaporization given in the text, it will take an additional 540 calories to turn it into the gaseous phase as it reaches 100°C. Finally, an additional calorie must be added to bring the temperature of the gas up to 101°C. So, the total amount of heat which must be added is 640 calories.

37. B: Region B of the graph is the transition between the solid and liquid phases of water. If heat is added to the system, solid ice melts into liquid. Conversely, if heat is removed from the system, liquid water will freeze in this area of the graph. Similarly, region D is the transition between liquid and gaseous water. In this region, water either evaporates or condenses. This depends on whether heat is added to or removed from water.

38. B, C, and F: The cell body has the nucleus. This is the control center of the cell and the site of its metabolic activity. Dendrites extend from this cell body. The dendrites receive signals from other cells in the form of neurotransmitters. This triggers an electrical impulse that travels down the axon to the next cell on the route of the signal. At the end of the axon, neurotransmitters are released again. Then, they cross the synapse and act on the following cell.

39. A: The cell body has the nucleus as shown in the diagram. *Eukaryotic* cells have a nucleus. The nucleus is where the chromosomes stay. The chromosomes carry the genes and manage the activities of the neuron.

40. D: Information flow is in one direction and moves from dendrite to axon in a neuron. Then, it crosses from axon to dendrite to move from cell to cell at the synapse. The electrical impulse that carries information along the axon is helped by myelin. However, there is no myelin at the synapse. So, it can have no role there. The flow of information across the synapse is done through the medium of neurotransmitters. These neurotransmitters spread out across the synapse to interact with dendritic receptors on the other side.

41. C: The pulmonary artery carries oxygen-drained blood from the heart to the lungs. Then, carbon dioxide is released, and the supply of oxygen is filled again. Next, this blood returns to the heart through the pulmonary artery. Then, it is carried through the aorta and a series of branching arteries to the capillaries. At the capillaries, much of the gas exchange with the tissues happens. Oxygen-drained blood returns to the heart through branching veins into the vena cava. Then, the vena cava carries the blood again to the heart. The pulmonary artery is the last step before replenishment of the blood's oxygen content. So, it has blood with very small amounts of oxygen.

42. D: A tsunami is a large wave or series of waves caused by the displacement of a large volume of water. The most common cause is an earthquake. However, large landslides or explosive volcanic action may also cause a tsunami. Tsunamis look like very high, sustained tides. They can move water very far inland. Large storms (e.g., cyclones or hurricanes) may also move large amounts of water. This can cause a high tide known as a storm surge that looks like a tsunami.

43. D: Since the cylinder is airtight, the piston cannot sink into the injected fluids. So, it will not displace a volume of fluid equal to its weight. Since liquids are not compressible, the density of the injected fluid does not make a difference in this experiment. Equal volumes of any fluid will raise the cylinder by an equal amount.

44. D: The terms accuracy and precision are used in place of each other in informal speech. However, they have specific meanings as scientific terms. Accuracy is how close a measurement is to the actual target. Precision is how many times that you have the same measurement. In this case, both sets of measurements have the same accuracy and the same precision. One measurement in each set is exactly correct and two are off by one millimeter.

45. D: All living organisms on Earth use the same triplet genetic code. This code has a three-nucleotide sequence called a codon. This codon gives information that matches to an amino acid that will be added to a protein. In contrast, many organisms-- especially certain types of bacteria-- do not use oxygen. These organisms live in oxygen-poor environments and may make energy through fermentation. Other organisms may live in dark environments (e.g., caves or deep underground). Only the most evolutionarily-advanced organisms use neurotransmitters in their nervous systems.

46. C: Both cannonballs will be subject to a vertical acceleration due to the force of gravity. There is an additional horizontal component to the velocity of cannonball A. However, its vertical velocity will be the same. In each case, the height of the object at time t seconds will be $h = -\frac{1}{2}t^2 + 20$.

47. C: First, note that 5 meters equals 500 cm. So, the horizontal speed of the cannonball is 500 cm/sec. Momentum must be conserved in the recoiling system. The vertical motion due to gravity can be ignored. The reason is that it involves the conservation of momentum between the cannonball and the Earth rather than the cannon. In the horizontal dimension, conservation of momentum says that $MV = mv$, where M and V are for the mass and the velocity of the cannon. Also, m and v are for the mass and the velocity of the cannonball. Solving for V gives:

$$V = \frac{1}{M} \times mv = \frac{1}{500} \times 5 \times 500 = 5 \text{ cm/s}$$

48. B: This cell has chloroplasts and a cell wall. This is characteristic of plant cells. They are not found in the other cell types listed as answer choices. Chloroplasts have the pigment known as chlorophyll. They are the engines of photosynthesis. Also, they bring energy to the cell from sunlight. The cell wall is made of cellulose and gives a protective covering.

49. D: The nucleus is the home for the chromosomes. These chromosomes are made of DNA and a protein component. The chromosomes have the genetic code in a certain sequence of bases that make up the DNA chain.

50. A: Mitochondria give chemical energy for the cell in the form of ATP (i.e., adenosine triphosphate). They give energy by converting nutritional energy sources (e.g., glucose) through a complex series of chemical reactions. These reactions take place on the extensive membrane system located in the mitochondria's outer membranes.

Social Studies

1. C: Denmark abolished slavery in 1792. France did not abolish slavery for another two years. The chart does not include information on Spain abolishing slavery. Britain was the third European nation to abolish slavery in 1807.

2. D: The United States was a British colony before winning independence. So, they would have been required to end slavery in 1834 with all British colonies. Denmark abolished slavery in 1792, but the American colonies did not have a major relationship with Denmark. In 1794, France banned slavery. However, most of the colonies were not French possessions by the time of the American Revolution. In 1807, Britain ended slavery. However, that rule was not for the colonies.

3. B: France's Revolution began in 1789. Only five years later, the slave trade was abolished. This seems to show an understanding and spreading out of the ideals of independence. The United States Revolution began in 1776. Then, almost a century passed before slavery finally ended in 1865. None of the other conclusions can be supported from the chart. Brazil was a large slave-holding nation, but that information is not given in the chart. It is unlikely that Denmark, a small nation with few colonies, would have been a large slave-holding state. The Asian nations stayed in Britain's empire until the mid-twentieth century.

4. C and E: Ecuador and Venezuela did not have independence from Spain until 1830. Argentina received independence from Spain in 1810, and Paraguay declared independence in 1811. So, choice A and choice B cannot be correct answer choices. Bolivia became independent from Spain in 1825, and Uruguay followed three years later.

5. D: Ten nations received independence in the first thirty years of the nineteenth century. Choice A is incorrect because the American Revolution was fought during the latter 1770s and early 1780s. This was decades before the independence movements in South America. In fact, the American Revolution inspired some of the movements. France did not have many possessions in South America. So, choice B is wrong. Nations on the west coast were among the last to gain independence. So, that makes choice C incorrect.

6. A: The Mayan Empire collapsed from the inside. The other civilizations were taken over by the Spanish. The Incan Empire was the last to fall. So, this makes choice B an incorrect answer. None of the empires was located in North America. The title of the chart makes this clear. So, choice C is not correct. The Mayans were not taken over by Spain like the Aztecs and the Incans. This makes choice D incorrect.

7. C: The Spanish conquistadors were active in Central and South America in the sixteenth century. Choice A is incorrect. The reason is that Portugal was active in Brazil, but that location is not mentioned in the chart. The Mayan empire is older than the Aztec and Incan civilizations. So, this makes choice B incorrect. There is no sign that the Incan warriors in Peru tried to help the Aztec of Mexico.

8. B: Antiseptics kept infections down. By using antiseptics, Muslim doctors prevented infections that often led to loss of limbs or life for Europeans. The other choices are opinions or statements that are not supported by the paragraph. There is no way to compare the bravery of Muslims with the bravery of other faiths when facing surgery. So, choice A can be eliminated. Also, choice C is incorrect. There would not be a noticeable rise in silk use for sutures to explain a larger silk market. Choice D is an opinion, not a fact.

9. C: Lincoln repeats the phrase "save the Union" four times. He explains that slavery is not his primary issue. So, he explains all the ways that he would manipulate that institution to preserve the Union. Lincoln says directly that his object is neither to free the slave nor to destroy slavery. So, this makes choice A incorrect. Choice B is also incorrect. There is no mention of payment to the slave owner in this passage. He does not mention winning the war. So, choice D is not correct.

10. D: In 1848, gold was discovered in California at John Sutter's mill. This event led to the migration of people known as the Forty-Niners. The silver rush in Nevada came later. So, this makes choice A incorrect. The transcontinental railroad was finished in 1869. This date is not included in the chart. So, choice B cannot be correct. Choice C is also incorrect. The reason is that the founding of Spanish missions in California and the Southwest happened several centuries earlier.

11. D: With an increasing population, cities and towns were made. These places became the sites of hotels, brothels, laundries, and saloons. Choice A is not likely. Most of the migration was men coming to seek their fortunes and planning to return to the East. The key term in choice B is *most.* Many of the women who went west set up businesses. However, most of the new migrants were men. The Civil War did not begin until 1860. That is more than a decade after the Gold Rush.

12. B: The railroad required only 6 to 8 days. So, this was a 20-day advantage over all the other ways of moving goods or people. Choice A is an incorrect choice. The reason is that a steamboat to New Orleans that is combined with a packet ship to New York needed 28 days. The route across the Erie Canal needed 18 days. So, this makes choice C incorrect. The keelboat was used in the earliest part of the nineteenth century. This boat was only part of the difficult 52-day route that needed water and overland travel to reach New York.

13. D: Using the keelboat and the wagon called for 52 days of travel. Combining steamboat, canal, and railroad cut the time by more than 30 days. This was a larger amount of time saved than any other new development. Steamboat and packet needed 28 days of travel, and the railroad took 6 to 8 days. This was a savings of 20 to 22 days. So, this makes choice A incorrect. Also, choice B is wrong. The canal took 18 days, and the railroad took 6 to 8 days. So, this was a savings of 10 to 12 days. The canal route took 18 days, and the steamboat and packet needed 28 days. So, this saved 10 days and makes choice C wrong.

14. A: Catholics, Pilgrims, Puritans, and Quakers were important in developing new colonies. So, this shows you the importance of religion to these people. Choice B is incorrect because the French did not hold much territory in the eastern United States. They did have land in areas west of the Appalachians and in what became Canada. Choice C is incorrect because there is nothing on the chart to confirm this information. Choice D is true. However, that information cannot be known from the chart.

15. C: The men had expected their invention to end war. Instead, it became a new weapon. Choice A is often cited as a reference to the Spanish-American War of 1898. So, it is incorrect. The Wright brothers hoped that their invention would put an end to war. So, choice B is the opposite idea. Rickenbacker was a famous World War I ace pilot. Since the Wright brothers wanted peace, they probably would not be interested in fighting. So, choice D is incorrect.

16. D: A politician who did not want to give even a penny for "scenery" would likely not have favored the Clean Air Act. All others would have favored the measures. Choice A is not the right answer because Nixon signed the bill. In 1970, he was still a popular president. So, he did not need to sign it to create goodwill. Rachel Carson sounded an early warning about the effects of DDT. So, she would likely have been excited about the act. Theodore Roosevelt was a strong supporter of environmental causes and would have championed the bill.

17. C: Mother Jones wanted laws to protect child workers. Legislators finally responded to appeals from her and others. None of the other answer choices would logically follow. The words would not have been an encouragement for children to work in factories. So, choice A is incorrect. Choice B is also not right. The South continued to be a major textile region. Increasing pay for child labor was not the solution to the problem. So, choice D is incorrect.

18. A: The other choices are incorrect because Italy, Russia, and England were not invading Belgium.

19. D: Many of the founders were also slaveholders, yet they believed that the practice was wrong. Choice A is an assumption that cannot be supported. Choice B is false. Freeman's actions had no effect on women's suffrage. However, it did have an impact on slavery. Many white Southerners wanted slavery to continue. Thus, they were unlikely to applaud the decision of the court. This makes choice C incorrect.

20. A: The mounds were built much earlier. 1949 is the date that they came under the protection of the National Park Service. Mounds are located in other places in the United States. So, choice B is not the right choice. In 1949, Truman was president, and he would have signed the bill into law. So, choice C is not a correct answer. Effigy mounds are shaped like animals. So, choice D is not correct.

21. D: Machinery and transport jumped from 34.3 to 42.0 percent in exports. Also, they went from 9.7 to 28.0 percent in imports. Chemicals increased exports from 8.7 to 9.0. Imports declined from 5.3 to 3.6. So, choice A is incorrect. Crude material exports declined from 13.7 to 10.8. For imports, they declined from 18.3 to 8.3. So, this makes choice B incorrect. The decline in exports of food and beverages was just under 4 percent, and imports declined 7 percent. So, choice C is not correct.

22. B: Crude material imports declined by 10 percentage points. All other categories saw imports that declined less than 10 points over the decade. Chemicals decreased in that time by only 1.7 percent. So, this makes choice A incorrect. Choice C is also incorrect. Food and beverages decreased during those ten years by just over 7 percent. Imports of machinery and transport nearly tripled, rather than decreased. This means that choice D is incorrect.

23. C: After World War II, the per capita national debt increased by over 600 percent compared to World War I. Choice A is not an accurate choice; the amount of debt per capita actually decreased after the War of 1812 compared to the American Revolution. After the Civil War, the percentage of debt increased by 420 percent. So, choice B is also incorrect. The per capita national debt increased after World War I by just over 200 percent. So, this makes choice C wrong as well.

24. B: The only time that the national debt level fell after a war was after the American Revolution. One conclusion is that the new government felt the need to show fiscal responsibility to the world. Choice A is incorrect. To borrow more money would increase the debt, not lower it. Choice C is not correct. The amount of money that people spent had nothing to do with the per capita national debt. Purchase of Treasury bonds would show a growing debt. This was the opposite of what was actually happening. So, this makes choice D incorrect.

25. D: By 1950, the number of women in the workforce had climbed to 28.8 percent. This was the first time that the percentage was above 25 percent. Choice A is incorrect because women in 1900 made up only 18 percent of the workforce. By 1920, women still made up only 20.4 percent of the workforce. So, choice B is not correct. In 1940, 24.3 percent of women were in the labor force, but the question asks for a percentage higher than 25.

26. C: The percent of women in the workforce steadily increased through seven decades and beyond. By 1970, it reached 36.7 percent. This was double the 18.1 percent of 1900. Choice A is wrong because the rate did not decline. Choice B is also incorrect. The reason is that the rate climbed. Choice D is not correct because the rate did not go up and down. Instead, it increased steadily.

27. B: Although the nation faced recession, the U.S. dollar made a comeback in world currency during the fall of 2008. Choice A cannot be concluded from the information which is about the dollar and the euro, not the whole world. Choice C is incorrect as well; the euro fell in 2008 against the dollar. The wisdom of buying stocks cannot be known from the information given. So, choice D is not correct.

28. D: Corporate taxes would be paid in greater amounts because businesses would no longer be able to use offshore havens. Choice A suggests the opposite situation. So, it is clearly incorrect. The offshore tax havens have nothing to do with retirement receipts. So, choice B is also incorrect. Again, individual income tax is not related to the problem of offshore tax havens. So, choice C is incorrect as well.

29. A: Individuals give the largest part of the total revenue at 43 percent. Choice B is incorrect. The reason is that corporations were adding only 10.1 percent of the revenue in 2004. Social Security is part of the 39 percent of the amount that comes from social insurance and retirement receipts. So, this makes choice C incorrect. Choice D is also wrong. Government agencies do not pay taxes and do not appear on the chart.

30. C: Loans to Native Americans remain fewer than a thousand and are the smallest category represented. Choice A is incorrect; the number of loans to Asian Americans decreased during this five-year period. The number of loans to African Americans more than doubled during this period. So, this makes choice B incorrect. In 2000, the highest number of loans went to Asian Americans, not to Hispanic Americans. So, choice D is incorrect.

31. C: Public welfare overrides private rights. Choice A is incorrect. The reason is that the proposal does not suggest that Ohio will lose rights to the control of the lake. Choice B is also incorrect. The property owners are said to have a protected right to their land and to be able to give or sell those rights. Choice D is wrong. The reason is that the amendment clearly refers to the lawmakers' response to passing the Great Lakes Water Compact.

32. D: Implied powers in Article I, Clause 18, Section 8. This section has the "necessary and proper" clause. An example of this clause being used is when Congress funds a national railroad system. Choice A is incorrect. The reason is that the delegated powers did not include funding for a railroad. Choice B is incorrect because the power to support rail travel was not a denied power. This power is not expressed directly in the Constitution. So, choice C is not correct.

33. D: The president makes sure that laws are carried out. National laws are not subject to state laws or interpretations. Choice A is not correct because Eisenhower had the legal power to send federal troops. The conflict in Vietnam had nothing to do with the event in Arkansas. So, choice B is not correct. Choice C cannot be correct because Eisenhower would not have been able to send troops into the state.

34. B: Bloomberg's term ended in 2009. A majority of City Council members who approved the measure finished their terms as well. Now, choice A is not discussed in the question. So, it is unlikely to have happened twice. There is no mention of a voter initiative to overturn the earlier referendums. So, choice C is not correct. Also, there is no mention of action by the City Council that would be thought of as pressuring him. So, this makes choice D wrong.

35. A: Increasing border controls on the Canada-U.S. border was part of the USA PATRIOT Act of 2001 and affected the private and public sectors of people traveling between those two countries. The other choices sound like they could be related to events between the U.S. and Canada. For example, lawful commerce in arms could relate to guns sold between countries, but it was for guns within the United States. So, choice C is incorrect. Choice B is wrong because a Trade Act might apply to U.S.-Canada trade, but not to border patrols. Choice D is wrong because the "Fence" Act applied to the Mexico-U.S. border, not the Canada-U.S. border.

36. B: Women in the organization have the opportunity to meet others and bring their involvement into the larger organization. Choice A is wrong because cronyism is using power to place your friends and associates in power. Choice C is also incorrect because lobbyists are not mayors. Instead, they are people who try to influence legislators. Patronage is a system of supporting worthy persons or causes. So, this makes choice D incorrect.

37. C: Virginia's plan called for representation based on population. So, that plan would help states with larger populations. Choice A is incorrect because Virginia would not want representation based on wealth if it were a poor state. Choice B uses the motto of the French Revolution. So, this has nothing to do with the U.S. Constitution. Choice D is incorrect because the New Jersey plan did not ask for representation to be based on wealth.

38. B: Britain's Parliament has a two-house system. So, this may have been a model for the Virginia Plan. Choice A is not correct because the Mayflower Compact set up a more theocratic system of government. Choice C is also wrong because some historians believe that the Iroquois system of government influenced the framers' ideas. However, there is no sign that the Sioux system had an influence. Choice D is clearly incorrect because the legislature is not a monarchy.

39. D: The Electoral College was a compromise for a way to elect the president. Choice A is incorrect because wealth has nothing to do with the role of the Electoral College. Choice B is wrong as well. The appointment of Supreme Court justices is not part of the Electoral College. That is a job for the chief executive. Electing senators is also not the responsibility of the Electoral College. So, this makes choice C incorrect.

40. C: In 1969, there were 13 members. In 2008, there were 43. So, this is an increase of 30. Choice A is not correct because the CBC was set up 100 years after the Civil War. Choice B is also incorrect because there is nothing in the passage about a goal of a black president. Choice D is wrong as well. The reason is that the passage clearly says that the alternative budget has many differences from the president's budget.

41. D: When you see a superlative in a sentence, you may have an opinion. Choice D says that apartheid was the worst political system. That sentence is an opinion that can be challenged. The other answer choices can be proven as fact. The passage clearly says that the founding of the CBC was in 1969. So, this makes choice A incorrect. Choice B can also be found in the passage as a fact. Choice C is confirmed in the passage as well.

42. C: Young people protested that they were old enough to fight and die for their country, yet they could not vote. Choice A is incorrect because women had the right to vote after the Nineteenth

Amendment passed in 1920. Choice B is also wrong. African American males were able to vote after the Civil War. African American females gained the right in 1920. The baby boom ended in 1964. So, choice D is not correct.

43. C: The Mayan population of Belize stands at about 10 percent. The other answers do not have much of a Mayan population according to the table.

44. D: Choice A is incorrect because the Creole population is not the largest ethnic group in the entire region. Choice B is also wrong because the Mayans make up about 10 percent of the Belize population. Choice C is incorrect. The reason is that Costa Rica does not have a canal, and the chart does not explain how Chinese people came to Costa Rica.

45. A: Belize is close to Haiti and Jamaica. These countries have many people of African heritage. There is no evidence of trade between Belize and the nations of West Africa. So, choice B is wrong. It is possible that many Creole in New Orleans left after Hurricane Katrina. However, there is no evidence that they went to Belize. So, choice C cannot be correct. Choice D cannot be supported.

46. D: The route began at the Mississippi River. Choice A is incorrect because the order came from President Jefferson in Washington, D.C. However, the journey did not start from that city. Instead, St. Louis was the starting point. Choice B is also incorrect. The reason is that the group had to cross the Rockies, but they did not start their journey from that area. Fort Mandan was one of the forts built farther west. So, choice C cannot be the correct answer.

47. D: The rate was not high in 1929. However, it did steadily increase in the years after 1929. You may think that the graph shows the rate as "steady" at one point. However, it is still going up between 1932 and 1933. The unemployment rate of other countries is not shown on the graph. So, choice B cannot be correct.

48. D: Khartoum is Sudan's capital. At this point, the Nile splits into the White and Blue Nile rivers. Choice A is not correct. The Gulf of Aden and the Red Sea is north of Somalia. Choice B is incorrect because the Congo River and Lake Chad are not in Sudan. Also, they do not come from the Nile. Choice C is not correct because Lake Victoria is not in Sudan at all.

49. C: The Kalahari Desert is located in the middle western part of Botswana. Choice A is not correct because the Zambezi River runs through Zambia and Angola. These are countries that are north of Botswana. Choice B is also wrong. The reason is that Lake Tanganyika is northeast of Botswana which is along Tanzania's western border. Choice D is not correct because the Congo River is in the Democratic Republic of the Congo which is north of Botswana.

50. A, C, and E: Somalia, Mozambique, and Kenya are bordered by the Indian Ocean. The other answer choices are not bordered by the Indian Ocean.

GED Practice Tests #2 and #3

To take these additional GED practice tests, visit our bonus page:
mometrix.com/bonus948/ged

How to Overcome Test Anxiety

Just the thought of taking a test is enough to make most people a little nervous. A test is an important event that can have a long-term impact on your future, so it's important to take it seriously and it's natural to feel anxious about performing well. But just because anxiety is normal, that doesn't mean that it's helpful in test taking, or that you should simply accept it as part of your life. Anxiety can have a variety of effects. These effects can be mild, like making you feel slightly nervous, or severe, like blocking your ability to focus or remember even a simple detail.

If you experience test anxiety—whether severe or mild—it's important to know how to beat it. To discover this, first you need to understand what causes test anxiety.

Causes of Test Anxiety

While we often think of anxiety as an uncontrollable emotional state, it can actually be caused by simple, practical things. One of the most common causes of test anxiety is that a person does not feel adequately prepared for their test. This feeling can be the result of many different issues such as poor study habits or lack of organization, but the most common culprit is time management. Starting to study too late, failing to organize your study time to cover all of the material, or being distracted while you study will mean that you're not well prepared for the test. This may lead to cramming the night before, which will cause you to be physically and mentally exhausted for the test. Poor time management also contributes to feelings of stress, fear, and hopelessness as you realize you are not well prepared but don't know what to do about it.

Other times, test anxiety is not related to your preparation for the test but comes from unresolved fear. This may be a past failure on a test, or poor performance on tests in general. It may come from comparing yourself to others who seem to be performing better or from the stress of living up to expectations. Anxiety may be driven by fears of the future—how failure on this test would affect your educational and career goals. These fears are often completely irrational, but they can still negatively impact your test performance.

Review Video: 3 Reasons You Have Test Anxiety
Visit mometrix.com/academy and enter code: 428468

Elements of Test Anxiety

As mentioned earlier, test anxiety is considered to be an emotional state, but it has physical and mental components as well. Sometimes you may not even realize that you are suffering from test anxiety until you notice the physical symptoms. These can include trembling hands, rapid heartbeat, sweating, nausea, and tense muscles. Extreme anxiety may lead to fainting or vomiting. Obviously, any of these symptoms can have a negative impact on testing. It is important to recognize them as soon as they begin to occur so that you can address the problem before it damages your performance.

Review Video: 3 Ways to Tell You Have Test Anxiety
Visit mometrix.com/academy and enter code: 927847

The mental components of test anxiety include trouble focusing and inability to remember learned information. During a test, your mind is on high alert, which can help you recall information and stay focused for an extended period of time. However, anxiety interferes with your mind's natural processes, causing you to blank out, even on the questions you know well. The strain of testing during anxiety makes it difficult to stay focused, especially on a test that may take several hours. Extreme anxiety can take a huge mental toll, making it difficult not only to recall test information but even to understand the test questions or pull your thoughts together.

Review Video: How Test Anxiety Affects Memory
Visit mometrix.com/academy and enter code: 609003

Effects of Test Anxiety

Test anxiety is like a disease—if left untreated, it will get progressively worse. Anxiety leads to poor performance, and this reinforces the feelings of fear and failure, which in turn lead to poor performances on subsequent tests. It can grow from a mild nervousness to a crippling condition. If allowed to progress, test anxiety can have a big impact on your schooling, and consequently on your future.

Test anxiety can spread to other parts of your life. Anxiety on tests can become anxiety in any stressful situation, and blanking on a test can turn into panicking in a job situation. But fortunately, you don't have to let anxiety rule your testing and determine your grades. There are a number of relatively simple steps you can take to move past anxiety and function normally on a test and in the rest of life.

Review Video: How Test Anxiety Impacts Your Grades
Visit mometrix.com/academy and enter code: 939819

Physical Steps for Beating Test Anxiety

While test anxiety is a serious problem, the good news is that it can be overcome. It doesn't have to control your ability to think and remember information. While it may take time, you can begin taking steps today to beat anxiety.

Just as your first hint that you may be struggling with anxiety comes from the physical symptoms, the first step to treating it is also physical. Rest is crucial for having a clear, strong mind. If you are tired, it is much easier to give in to anxiety. But if you establish good sleep habits, your body and mind will be ready to perform optimally, without the strain of exhaustion. Additionally, sleeping well helps you to retain information better, so you're more likely to recall the answers when you see the test questions.

Getting good sleep means more than going to bed on time. It's important to allow your brain time to relax. Take study breaks from time to time so it doesn't get overworked, and don't study right before bed. Take time to rest your mind before trying to rest your body, or you may find it difficult to fall asleep.

Review Video: The Importance of Sleep for Your Brain
Visit mometrix.com/academy and enter code: 319338

Along with sleep, other aspects of physical health are important in preparing for a test. Good nutrition is vital for good brain function. Sugary foods and drinks may give a burst of energy but this burst is followed by a crash, both physically and emotionally. Instead, fuel your body with protein and vitamin-rich foods.

Also, drink plenty of water. Dehydration can lead to headaches and exhaustion, especially if your brain is already under stress from the rigors of the test. Particularly if your test is a long one, drink water during the breaks. And if possible, take an energy-boosting snack to eat between sections.

Review Video: How Diet Can Affect your Mood
Visit mometrix.com/academy and enter code: 624317

Along with sleep and diet, a third important part of physical health is exercise. Maintaining a steady workout schedule is helpful, but even taking 5-minute study breaks to walk can help get your blood pumping faster and clear your head. Exercise also releases endorphins, which contribute to a positive feeling and can help combat test anxiety.

When you nurture your physical health, you are also contributing to your mental health. If your body is healthy, your mind is much more likely to be healthy as well. So take time to rest, nourish your body with healthy food and water, and get moving as much as possible. Taking these physical steps will make you stronger and more able to take the mental steps necessary to overcome test anxiety.

Mental Steps for Beating Test Anxiety

Working on the mental side of test anxiety can be more challenging, but as with the physical side, there are clear steps you can take to overcome it. As mentioned earlier, test anxiety often stems from lack of preparation, so the obvious solution is to prepare for the test. Effective studying may be the most important weapon you have for beating test anxiety, but you can and should employ several other mental tools to combat fear.

First, boost your confidence by reminding yourself of past success—tests or projects that you aced. If you're putting as much effort into preparing for this test as you did for those, there's no reason you should expect to fail here. Work hard to prepare; then trust your preparation.

Second, surround yourself with encouraging people. It can be helpful to find a study group, but be sure that the people you're around will encourage a positive attitude. If you spend time with others who are anxious or cynical, this will only contribute to your own anxiety. Look for others who are motivated to study hard from a desire to succeed, not from a fear of failure.

Third, reward yourself. A test is physically and mentally tiring, even without anxiety, and it can be helpful to have something to look forward to. Plan an activity following the test, regardless of the outcome, such as going to a movie or getting ice cream.

When you are taking the test, if you find yourself beginning to feel anxious, remind yourself that you know the material. Visualize successfully completing the test. Then take a few deep, relaxing breaths and return to it. Work through the questions carefully but with confidence, knowing that you are capable of succeeding.

Developing a healthy mental approach to test taking will also aid in other areas of life. Test anxiety affects more than just the actual test—it can be damaging to your mental health and even contribute to depression. It's important to beat test anxiety before it becomes a problem for more than testing.

Review Video: Test Anxiety and Depression
Visit mometrix.com/academy and enter code: 904704

Study Strategy

Being prepared for the test is necessary to combat anxiety, but what does being prepared look like? You may study for hours on end and still not feel prepared. What you need is a strategy for test prep. The next few pages outline our recommended steps to help you plan out and conquer the challenge of preparation.

STEP 1: SCOPE OUT THE TEST

Learn everything you can about the format (multiple choice, essay, etc.) and what will be on the test. Gather any study materials, course outlines, or sample exams that may be available. Not only will this help you to prepare, but knowing what to expect can help to alleviate test anxiety.

STEP 2: MAP OUT THE MATERIAL

Look through the textbook or study guide and make note of how many chapters or sections it has. Then divide these over the time you have. For example, if a book has 15 chapters and you have five days to study, you need to cover three chapters each day. Even better, if you have the time, leave an extra day at the end for overall review after you have gone through the material in depth.

If time is limited, you may need to prioritize the material. Look through it and make note of which sections you think you already have a good grasp on, and which need review. While you are studying, skim quickly through the familiar sections and take more time on the challenging parts. Write out your plan so you don't get lost as you go. Having a written plan also helps you feel more in control of the study, so anxiety is less likely to arise from feeling overwhelmed at the amount to cover.

STEP 3: GATHER YOUR TOOLS

Decide what study method works best for you. Do you prefer to highlight in the book as you study and then go back over the highlighted portions? Or do you type out notes of the important information? Or is it helpful to make flashcards that you can carry with you? Assemble the pens, index cards, highlighters, post-it notes, and any other materials you may need so you won't be distracted by getting up to find things while you study.

If you're having a hard time retaining the information or organizing your notes, experiment with different methods. For example, try color-coding by subject with colored pens, highlighters, or post-it notes. If you learn better by hearing, try recording yourself reading your notes so you can listen while in the car, working out, or simply sitting at your desk. Ask a friend to quiz you from your flashcards, or try teaching someone the material to solidify it in your mind.

STEP 4: CREATE YOUR ENVIRONMENT

It's important to avoid distractions while you study. This includes both the obvious distractions like visitors and the subtle distractions like an uncomfortable chair (or a too-comfortable couch that makes you want to fall asleep). Set up the best study environment possible: good lighting and a comfortable work area. If background music helps you focus, you may want to turn it on, but otherwise keep the room quiet. If you are using a computer to take notes, be sure you don't have any other windows open, especially applications like social media, games, or anything else that could distract you. Silence your phone and turn off notifications. Be sure to keep water close by so you stay hydrated while you study (but avoid unhealthy drinks and snacks).

Also, take into account the best time of day to study. Are you freshest first thing in the morning? Try to set aside some time then to work through the material. Is your mind clearer in the afternoon or evening? Schedule your study session then. Another method is to study at the same time of day that you will take the test, so that your brain gets used to working on the material at that time and will be ready to focus at test time.

STEP 5: STUDY!

Once you have done all the study preparation, it's time to settle into the actual studying. Sit down, take a few moments to settle your mind so you can focus, and begin to follow your study plan. Don't give in to distractions or let yourself procrastinate. This is your time to prepare so you'll be ready to fearlessly approach the test. Make the most of the time and stay focused.

Of course, you don't want to burn out. If you study too long you may find that you're not retaining the information very well. Take regular study breaks. For example, taking five minutes out of every hour to walk briskly, breathing deeply and swinging your arms, can help your mind stay fresh.

As you get to the end of each chapter or section, it's a good idea to do a quick review. Remind yourself of what you learned and work on any difficult parts. When you feel that you've mastered the material, move on to the next part. At the end of your study session, briefly skim through your notes again.

But while review is helpful, cramming last minute is NOT. If at all possible, work ahead so that you won't need to fit all your study into the last day. Cramming overloads your brain with more information than it can process and retain, and your tired mind may struggle to recall even previously learned information when it is overwhelmed with last-minute study. Also, the urgent nature of cramming and the stress placed on your brain contribute to anxiety. You'll be more likely to go to the test feeling unprepared and having trouble thinking clearly.

So, don't cram, and don't stay up late before the test, even just to review your notes at a leisurely pace. Your brain needs rest more than it needs to go over the information again. In fact, plan to finish your studies by noon or early afternoon the day before the test. Give your brain the rest of the day to relax or focus on other things, and get a good night's sleep. Then you will be fresh for the test and better able to recall what you've studied.

STEP 6: TAKE A PRACTICE TEST

Many courses offer sample tests, either online or in the study materials. This is an excellent resource to check whether you have mastered the material, as well as to prepare for the test format and environment.

Check the test format ahead of time: the number of questions, the type (multiple choice, free response, etc.), and the time limit. Then create a plan for working through them. For example, if you have 30 minutes to take a 60-question test, your limit is 30 seconds per question. Spend less time on the questions you know well so that you can take more time on the difficult ones.

If you have time to take several practice tests, take the first one open book, with no time limit. Work through the questions at your own pace and make sure you fully understand them. Gradually work up to taking a test under test conditions: sit at a desk with all study materials put away and set a timer. Pace yourself to make sure you finish the test with time to spare and go back to check your answers if you have time.

After each test, check your answers. On the questions you missed, be sure you understand why you missed them. Did you misread the question (tests can use tricky wording)? Did you forget the information? Or was it something you hadn't learned? Go back and study any shaky areas that the practice tests reveal.

Taking these tests not only helps with your grade, but also aids in combating test anxiety. If you're already used to the test conditions, you're less likely to worry about it, and working through tests until you're scoring well gives you a confidence boost. Go through the practice tests until you feel comfortable, and then you can go into the test knowing that you're ready for it.

Test Tips

On test day, you should be confident, knowing that you've prepared well and are ready to answer the questions. But aside from preparation, there are several test day strategies you can employ to maximize your performance.

First, as stated before, get a good night's sleep the night before the test (and for several nights before that, if possible). Go into the test with a fresh, alert mind rather than staying up late to study.

Try not to change too much about your normal routine on the day of the test. It's important to eat a nutritious breakfast, but if you normally don't eat breakfast at all, consider eating just a protein bar. If you're a coffee drinker, go ahead and have your normal coffee. Just make sure you time it so that the caffeine doesn't wear off right in the middle of your test. Avoid sugary beverages, and drink enough water to stay hydrated but not so much that you need a restroom break 10 minutes into the test. If your test isn't first thing in the morning, consider going for a walk or doing a light workout before the test to get your blood flowing.

Allow yourself enough time to get ready, and leave for the test with plenty of time to spare so you won't have the anxiety of scrambling to arrive in time. Another reason to be early is to select a good seat. It's helpful to sit away from doors and windows, which can be distracting. Find a good seat, get out your supplies, and settle your mind before the test begins.

When the test begins, start by going over the instructions carefully, even if you already know what to expect. Make sure you avoid any careless mistakes by following the directions.

Then begin working through the questions, pacing yourself as you've practiced. If you're not sure on an answer, don't spend too much time on it, and don't let it shake your confidence. Either skip it and come back later, or eliminate as many wrong answers as possible and guess among the remaining ones. Don't dwell on these questions as you continue—put them out of your mind and focus on what lies ahead.

Be sure to read all of the answer choices, even if you're sure the first one is the right answer. Sometimes you'll find a better one if you keep reading. But don't second-guess yourself if you do immediately know the answer. Your gut instinct is usually right. Don't let test anxiety rob you of the information you know.

If you have time at the end of the test (and if the test format allows), go back and review your answers. Be cautious about changing any, since your first instinct tends to be correct, but make sure you didn't misread any of the questions or accidentally mark the wrong answer choice. Look over any you skipped and make an educated guess.

At the end, leave the test feeling confident. You've done your best, so don't waste time worrying about your performance or wishing you could change anything. Instead, celebrate the successful completion of this test. And finally, use this test to learn how to deal with anxiety even better next time.

Review Video: 5 Tips to Beat Test Anxiety
Visit mometrix.com/academy and enter code: 570656

Important Qualification

Not all anxiety is created equal. If your test anxiety is causing major issues in your life beyond the classroom or testing center, or if you are experiencing troubling physical symptoms related to your anxiety, it may be a sign of a serious physiological or psychological condition. If this sounds like your situation, we strongly encourage you to seek professional help.

Tell Us Your Story

We at Mometrix would like to extend our heartfelt thanks to you for letting us be a part of your journey. It is an honor to serve people from all walks of life, people like you, who are committed to building the best future they can for themselves.

We know that each person's situation is unique. But we also know that, whether you are a young student or a mother of four, you care about working to make your own life and the lives of those around you better.

That's why we want to hear your story.

We want to know why you're taking this test. We want to know about the trials you've gone through to get here. And we want to know about the successes you've experienced after taking and passing your test.

In addition to your story, which can be an inspiration both to us and to others, we value your feedback. We want to know both what you loved about our book and what you think we can improve on.

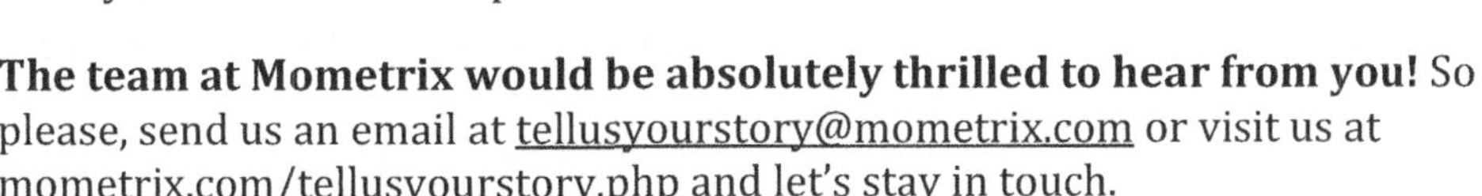

The team at Mometrix would be absolutely thrilled to hear from you! So please, send us an email at tellusyourstory@mometrix.com or visit us at mometrix.com/tellusyourstory.php and let's stay in touch.

Additional Bonus Material

Due to our efforts to try to keep this book to a manageable length, we've created a link that will give you access to all of your additional bonus material:

mometrix.com/bonus948/ged

Made in the USA
Las Vegas, NV
25 October 2023